Schloss Neuschwanstein, Bavaria
© Giovanni Simeone/Sime/Photononstop

THEGREENGUIDE
Germany

How to...

Green Guides - Discover the Destination

Main sections

PLANNING YOUR TRIP
The blue-tabbed section gives you **ideas for your trip** and **practical information.**

INTRODUCTION
The orange-tabbed section explores **Nature, History, Art and Culture** and the **Country Today.**

DISCOVERING
The green-tabbed section features Principal Sights by region, **Sights, Walking Tours, Excursions,** and **Driving Tours.**

Region intros

At the start of each region in the Discovering section is a brief introduction. Accompanied by the region maps, these provide an overview of the main tourism areas and their background.

Region maps

Star ratings

Michelin has given star ratings for more than 100 years. If you're pressed for time, we recommend you visit the three or two star sights first:

★★★ Highly recommended

★★ Recommended

★ Interesting

Tours

We've selected driving and walking tours that show you the best of each town or region. Step by step directions are accompanied by detailed maps with marked routes. If you are short on time, you can follow the star ratings to decide where to stop. Selected addresses give you options for accommodation and dining en route.

Addresses

We've selected the best hotels, restaurants, cafès, shops, nightlife and entertainment to fit all budgets. See the Legend on the cover flap for an explanation of the price categories. See the back of the guide for an index of where to find hotels and restaurants.

Other reading

- ◆ Green Guides Austria and Switzerland
- ◆ Must Sees Prague
- ◆ Michelin Local Maps of Germany
- ◆ Michelin Regional Maps of Germany
- ◆ Michelin German Country Map or Road Atlas

Welcome to Germany

Germany is a rich quilt of dynamic cities, awe-inspiring scenery and spirit-lifting culture. Although the country became a nation only in 1871, its influence on history goes back at least a couple of millennia. No matter what your itinerary, you will inevitably come upon intriguing relics of the past, from Roman ruins to mighty cathedrals and dazzling palaces. Be sure to venture off the main tourist trail for those extra-special personal discoveries.

Dom, Magdeburg, Central Germany © Christina Hanck/iStockphoto.com

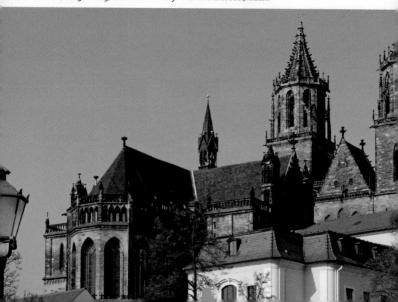

Planning Your Trip

Introducing Germany

Discovering Germany

Museumsinsel (Museum Island), Bode-Museum, Berlin
© visitBerlin / Wolfgang Scholvien

Regions of Germany

Berlin and Brandenburg (pp116-159)

Sassy, confident and irreverent, Berlin is a sly seductress who tempts you with her explosive creativity, vibrant cultural landscape and keen sense of history. Visit major landmarks such as Checkpoint Charlie and the Brandenburg Gate, then soak up the city's idiosyncratic spirit by drifting about its distinct neighbourhoods. For a break from urbanity, hop on a train to Brandenburg, a timelessly beautiful rural area shaped by water and accented by the dreamy palaces and parks of Potsdam.

Port of Hamburg
© www.mediaserver.hamburg.de/C. Spahrbier

BODE-MUSEUM

The Baltic Coast and Inland (pp160-193)

Germany's Baltic Coast once revelled in the wealth of its Hanseatic League towns. The proud red-brick buildings of Lübeck, Wismar, Stralsund and Greifswald still hark back to those medieval glory days. Fringing the coast is a landscape of often startling beauty: a pastiche of bays, islands and cliffs accented by beach-fringed seaside resorts whose dazzling white spa architecture has drawn royalty and the rich for over a century.

The Northwest (pp194-263)

Germany's northwest stretches from the wind-battered beaches of the Frisian Islands to the historic towns of Münster, Goslar and Celle and the fairytale cities of Bremen and Hamelin. Take a day in the slow lane roaming around the Harz Mountains, or opt for an urban jolt in maritime Hamburg, which will charm you with cutting-edge couture, culture and cuisine.

The West (pp264-361)

This region wraps culturally vibrant conurbations and laid-back countryside into one attractive package. Get a dose of world-class art and architecture in Düsseldorf, Cologne and Frankfurt, then make a date with the Romans in Trier and with Charlemagne in Aachen. Whatever you do, do not miss a trip down the Rhine or Moselle rivers to explore a remarkably beautiful mosaic of vine-clad slopes, dreamy half-timbered villages and medieval hilltop fortresses.

The Southwest (pp362-429)

Nowhere does Germany feel more radiantly Old World than in the Black Forest, a rustic landscape of "Hansel-and-Gretel" woods, undulating hills, gushing waterfalls and snow-dusted mountaintops. Along with nearby Lake Constance, it has long been a favourite holiday playground. Key cities include the elegant spa town of Baden-Baden, Freiburg with its vibrant student scene and Stuttgart, which is a must-see not just for those who worship at the altar of the automobile.

Ulm at Danube River, the Southwest

Aerial view of downtown Munich

Munich and Southern Bavaria (pp430-495)

Few cities in Germany exude the contagious energy that you'll find bubbling away in the streets and legendary beer halls of Munich. Outside of the city, natural and manmade beauty is all around. Crane your neck while marvelling at the sky-etching Alps, explore higgledy-piggledy villages where ancient traditions still thrive, or visit Ludwig II's fantasy castles. This is truly a land of superlatives ready to deliver a lifetime of memories.

Northern Bavaria (pp496-533)

One of Germany's most iconic drives is along the Romantic Road, which runs through soul-stirring scenery from Würzburg and its wine country past the cobblestoned perfection of Rothenburg ob der Tauber as far as peaceful Füssen near the Alps. Slow down – this region wants to be savoured. History buffs should point the compass towards Nuremberg, music lovers at Bayreuth and architecture fans at Bamberg.

Central Germany (pp534-575)

Though central Germany cradles the natural splendours of the Thuringian Forest, its appeal is largely in the region's contributions to literature, music, the arts, philosophy and religion. Here you can walk in the footsteps of Luther and Bach, Goethe and Gropius, Herder and Nietzsche, all of whom lived and worked in such towns as Weimar, Erfurt, Dessau-Rosslau, Magdeburg and Wittenberg. Handel was born here, Liszt lived and taught here, and the region spawned architecture's Bauhaus movement. Germany's oldest Gothic cathedral still stands here, holding the remains of the first Holy Roman Emperor.

The East (pp576-607)

Since reunification, the German East has shaken off its Cold War-era brooding and blossomed into a dynamic, prolific and forward-looking region. Endowed with a stunning city skyline, Dresden draws cultural types with its architectural landmarks and exquisite art collections. The mighty Elbe courses right through town, linking it with the fairytale landscape of Saxon Switzerland and the porcelain hub of Meissen. Youthful and progressive Leipzig has shaped German history since the Middle Ages, most recently as the city that sparked the "peaceful revolution" of 1989, precipitating the fall of the East German regime.

Planning
Your Trip

Planning Your Trip

Bremen
überrasccht

Inspiration

WHAT'S HOT

– **Berlin's** Pergamon Museum (see p134), Charlottenburg Palace p141) and Zoo (p145) continue to retain their huge popularity.

– **Potsdam**, Berlin's neighbour, is known for its splendid Sanssouci Palace and Park (see p154).

– **Lübeck**, on the Baltic Coast, pleases visitors with its island-topped Old Town (see p164) as well as its delicious marzipan.

– A drive through the sparkling **Mecklenburg Lake District** (see p192) is a must for scenic beauty.

– The **Rhine Valley's** (see p323) famed legends and castles still warrant a leisurely river cruise.

– **Cologne's** celebrated 13C Cathedral (see p273) and pre-Lenten Carnival (p271) are compelling reasons to visit.

– The **Black Forest's** (see p368) lakes, mountains, pine trees and villages keep the region at the top of Germany's travel destinations.

– **Munich** (see p436), Bavaria's vibrant capital, captivates all who come here with its beer halls, gardens, Baroque churches and world-class art.

Bastei, Saxon Switzerland, the East © Fox497/Dreamstime.com

Michelin Driving Tours

These Driving Tours guide you through Germany, incorporating area highlights. The **Driving Tours** map *(see the inside back cover)* shows via different coloured lines the recommended itineraries decribed below.

GRAND TOURS

1 HAMBURG AND SCHLESWIG-HOLSTEIN

550km/342mi tour leaving from Hamburg.

This tour through the *Länder* (states) of Hamburg and Schleswig-Holstein meanders through the far north of Germany, a region with a glorious Hanseatic past. The country's second largest city, **Hamburg** is a bustling port set on the banks of the Elbe estuary; its central districts are ideal for a stroll and the richly endowed museums will be much appreciated by art lovers. A mere 70km/43mi from Hamburg is **Lübeck**. This delightful town in northern Germany has been on UNESCO's World Heritage list since 1987. Remarkably preserved, it boasts an exceptional collection of houses and monuments from many different periods. Not far from Lübeck, **Travemünde**, on the shores of the Baltic Sea, is renowned for its sandy beaches, extensive seafront promenade and its casino. The tour continues northwards with the next port of call being **Kiel**, the gateway to Scandinavia. Capital of Schleswig-Holstein, Kiel combines a long maritime tradition with a modern atmosphere. The route then takes a northwesterly direction along the Baltic coast to **Schleswig**, an ideal place to relax and explore. Heading westwards, from one sea to the other, takes you to the island of **Sylt** and the other North Frisian islands. Their fragile sandy shores are pitted against the North Sea in a constant battle against marine erosion. Lastly, the peaceful seaside town of **Husum**, birthplace of the writer Theodor Storm, offers all the attractions of a modern tourist resort.

2 BALTIC SEA, MECKLENBURG-VORPOMMERN

650km/380mi tour leaving from Neubrandenburg.

This itinerary will give you a glimpse of a region of Germany that is wild and captivating and little known among foreign visitors. The town of **Neubrandenburg** has a surprise in store with its imposing medieval ramparts, miraculously spared by the Second World War. The journey continues westwards through the **Mecklenburg lake district**, a well-preserved region and one of the least populated in Germany. With countless lakes and a wide range of activities, it is of particular appeal to nature-lovers. **Schwerin** is without a doubt one of the most pleasant towns in northern Germany. Its refined architecture and the majestic charm of its castle set atop an island facing the old town add to the appeal of this city, the state capital of Mecklenburg-Vorpommern. Our itinerary then takes us north to the coast where **Wismar**, with its trove of red-brick buildings, provides an excellent introduction to the Baltic Coast. The town's historic centre was classed a UNESCO World Heritage Site in 2002, along with that of **Stralsund**. Along with **Rostock** and **Bad Doberan**, Stralsund is well worth a visit on your way to the island of **Rügen**. Here, an astonishing variety of landscapes awaits: bands of sandy dunes, land reclaimed from the sea, salt meadows, cultivated fields, endless mudflats (Watt, or Wadden) and prehistoric tumuli. Rügen, like the neighbouring island of **Usedom**, is a very popular vacation destination with delightful seaside, health and spa resorts and unique late 19C spa architecture. Last stop on the itinerary is **Greifswald**, whose very old architecture reveals a Scandinavian influence.

3 BREMEN, HAMBURG AND LOWER SAXONY

550km/342mi tour leaving from Bremen.

The bustling town of **Bremen** is a true delight. A large port and city of artistic interest where the Weser Renaissance style flourished, it has a number of parks and a charming riverside promenade. After a stop in **Hamburg**, 125km/78mi to the northeast (♿*see description in itinerary* 1), the tour next takes you to **Lüneburg**, which owes its longstanding prosperity to salt and marks the gateway to the vast expanse of the **Lüneburg Heath**. In the face of the increasing advances of agriculture, attempts are being made to preserve this wild environment which is characterized by picturesque copses of birch, pine and juniper. From mid-August to mid-September, the purple carpet of heather in bloom will have you burning up the pixels in your digicam. South of the heath awaits the dignified city of **Celle**. There are many reasons to stop here; treasures from the old city, a magnificently restored ducal palace and a folklore and history museum to name but a few. For car fanatics, a detour to Wolfsburg's **Autostadt** – a vast complex set up by Volkswagen – is a must. You can tour the plant, visit a strikingly designed science museum and roam around landscaped areas of park and water. A stop in **Braunschweig** is followed by a leisurely look around the beautiful city of **Wolfenbüttel** with its exceptional collection of Renaissance houses. Further west, after **Hildesheim**, **Hannover** awaits with its famous Herrenhausen gardens.

4 BERLIN AND BRANDENBURG

600km/373mi tour leaving from Neubrandenburg.

After a look around **Neubrandenburg** (♿*see description in itinerary* 2), head south to explore Schloss **Rheinsberg** where Frederick the Great, by his own account, spent the happiest years of his life as a young man. **Berlin**, Germany's vibrant capital, is a mere 90km/56mi further south. The buzzing city offers a wealth of culture and an after-dark scene not only night-owls will love. It is an amazing metropolis that will captivate you with its world-class museums and art galleries, a lively café scene, monumental landmarks, huge parks and gardens and the easy-going attitude of the locals. Another town marked by the personality of Frederick the Great, who held a brilliant and cosmopolitan court here, **Potsdam** is a genuine "Rococo treasure" of universal appeal. Carry on westwards and, after the small town of **Brandenburg** in the heart of the Havelland lake region, stop off at **Tangermünde**, which is still enclosed within its late 14C ramparts. **Stendal**, just a few kilometres away, was until the mid-16C the most important town in the Brandenburg March before the ravages of the Thirty Years' War sent it on a downward spiral. Several

Berliner Dom by the Spree

© René Mattes/hemis.fr

monuments typical of the Gothic brick architecture still attest to this former period of prosperity. Further north you can admire the beautiful cathedral of **Havelberg**, a pretty town set on the banks of the River Havel.

The itinerary ends with a foray into the picturesque **Mecklenburg lake district**.

5 HARZ, THURINGIA, SACHSEN-ANHALT AND LEIPZIG

750km/466mi tour leaving from Leipzig.
This route is tailor-made for culture vultures, taking you into a region where – particularly in the 18C – literature and music flourished. **Leipzig** is a city of artistic interest that can be proud of its exceptional musical heritage; Bach, Wagner and Mendelssohn all lived here at one time and the city remains very much in the foreground of the German music scene. Around 60km/37mi south, **Naumburg** stands among hills cloaked in vineyards and forests. The town is particularly renowned for its cathedral, which is an exceptional blend of Romanesque and Gothic style elements. **Weimar**, **Jena**, **Erfurt** and **Eisenach** are all names with strong connotations in German culture through their association with such key figures as Luther, Goethe and Schiller. Offering a pleasant distraction from the "cultural pilgrimage", the Thuringian Forest and, further north, the Harz mountains take you right to the very heart of nature.

Steeped in legend, the latter offers a limitless menu of year-round outdoor pursuits. Next, steer towards **Magdeburg** for a look at its fantastic Gothic cathedral before heading to **Wittenberg**, where Martin Luther posted his 95 Theses against church corruption. For this reason, the town is considered the cradle of the Reformation. The route continues via **Dessau**, famous for its Bauhaus legacy and a gateway to the Garden Realm,

a 18C wonderland of landscaped gardens with **Wörlitzer Park** as its finest jewel.

6 DRESDEN AND ERZGEBIRGE

650km/380mi tour leaving from Dresden.
Saxony is a region that has played a key role in Germany's history. A city of art and culture, **Dresden** has undergone extensive restorations of its Baroque treasures (most famously the complete rebuilding of the Frauenkirche), making it once again "the Florence of the Elbe". Southeast of here, the **Sächsische Schweiz** charms with its whimsically eroded sandstone formations and winding gorges gouged from the rock – this region is truly one of Germany's most spectacular natural wonders. The towns of **Bautzen** and **Görlitz** provide an opportunity to sample the culture of the Sorbs. An ethnic German minority, their homeland today straddles the *Länder* (states) of Saxony and Brandenburg. Not only do the Sorbs still speak their own language, but they have also kept alive many traditions. These include the decoration of eggs at Easter and the wearing of the Sorbian national costume and tall embroidered headdresses. Heading northwards takes you to **Branitz**, a stone's throw from Cottbus, where Prince Hermann von Pückler-Muskau built a palace and – indulging his passion for garden design – a fabulous park. Heading back to Dresden, make a stop at **Schloss Moritzburg** and **Meissen**, renowned for its porcelain. If you have the time, extend your tour with a trip through the **Erzgebirge**, a wooded region with a long tradition in both mining and toy making. Make **Annaberg-Buchholz** with its impressive Flamboyant Gothic church a key stop before heading back to Dresden.

7 PFALZ, RHINE VALLEY AND MOSELLE VALLEY

950km/570mi tour leaving from Cologne.

Not far from the borders with Belgium, Luxembourg and France, this extensive loop takes in key sights in western Germany. The Rhine valley is full of surprises; with its steeply terraced vineyards and rocky outcrops dominated by lofty castles, the route from **Koblenz** to **Rüdesheim** or **Bingen** affords some magnificent views. Take a stroll around the historic centre of **Mainz** with its maze of alleyways and old houses. After **Darmstadt**, take the **Bergstraße** southwards to historic **Heidelberg**, a symbol of German Romanticism, whose hillside castle leaves a lasting impression. The route continues west to **Speyer**, whose enormous Romanesque cathedral is the burial place of several Holy Roman Emperors. Heading north takes you along the German Wine Route through the **Pfalz**, a region blessed with a mild microclimate conducive to the cultivation of exotic fruits. Next up is **Worms**, which competes with **Trier** for the title of oldest town in Germany; both were founded by the Romans. From Trier to Koblenz, the winding course of the **Moselle** takes you past picturesque villages, castles and vineyards. Cruises, hiking and cycling are among the activities that beckon along here. **Aachen**, on the border with Belgium and Holland, is next on the agenda. The town is indelibly associated with Charlemagne, who made it capital of his Frankish Empire. Nearly three dozen princes were crowned king or emperor in its cathedral between 936 and 1531. From Aachen it won't be long before the famous twin spires of the cathedral of **Cologne** come into view. This delightful city on the Rhine is also known for its Romanesque churches, colourful historic houses, top-notch art museums and raucous beer taverns serving the local brew called Kölsch.

8 NUREMBERG AND FRANKEN

650km/380mi-tour leaving from Nuremberg.

This itinerary provides a chance to explore the age-old sights of northern Bavaria. It begins with **Nuremberg**, an old bronze casters' and goldbeaters' town and one of the most beautiful medieval cities in Germany. Further south, **Eichstätt** is distinguished by a harmonious mix of Rococo and contemporary architecture. West of here join the **Romantische Straße** (Romantic Road), Germany's most popular holiday route, in Nördlingen. It links some fantastic medieval cities, including **Dinkelsbühl** and **Rothenburg ob der Tauber**, before reaching its northern terminus in Würzburg, where the mid-17C grandeur of the powerful prince-bishops of the Schönborn family is reflected in the splendid Residenz Palace. Next up is **Bamberg** with its pretty-as-a-penny historic quarter (a UNESCO World Heritage Site since 1993) and imposing hilltop cathedral. Our route then continues via **Coburg** to the nearby **Wallfahrtskirche Vierzehnheiligen**. This pilgrimage church is a Baroque masterpiece by Balthasar Neumann with a truly captivating wealth of decoration. **Bayreuth**, the last stop on the tour, is a high point for fans of the composer Richard Wagner as well as the Rococo architectural style.

9 BADEN-WÜRTTEMBERG AND BODENSEE

850km/510mi tour leaving from Freiburg.

Southwest Germany has an astonishing number of remarkable tourist attractions. The easy-going atmosphere of the old university town of **Freiburg** is infectious and its paved alleyways beg to be explored. The town is the southern gateway to the **Schwarzwald**, a region steeped in legend and endowed with great variety of scenery. Add to that its picturesque villages, a passion for cuckoo clocks and the possibilities of hiking in summer and skiing in winter, and it is easy to see why this mountainous region is one of Germany's most popular tourist destinations. Passing through towns such as the elegant spa resort of **Baden-Baden**, which attracts a wealthy clientele all year round, and **Karlsruhe**, the route takes you up to **Bruchsal** whose sumptuous 18C palace houses a museum devoted to mechanical musical instruments. A short distance southeast of here looms **Kloster Maulbronn**; built in 1147, it was one of the earliest Cistercian abbeys in Germany. The school established here during the Reformation (1557) has seen the flowering of many scientific, literary and philosophical talents, including Kepler, Hölderlin and Hermann Hesse. The road south leads to **Tübingen** and **Ulm**. Tübingen's maze of narrow sloping streets lined with half-timbered houses, combined with its animated student life, create a relaxed and lighthearted atmosphere. In Ulm, you can stroll between the canals and the Danube and admire the town's extraordinary cathedral.

The Upper Swabian Plateau is dotted with Baroque churches famous for their dazzling decoration and architecture. **Zwiefalten** and **Weingarten** are two superb illustrations of the Baroque style that flourished so extensively in southern Germany. The tour ends with the magnificent **Bodensee**, a vast lake that also borders Switzerland and Austria. It is regarded by Germans as their very own "Riviera".

1 0 MUNICH AND THE BAVARIAN ALPS

650km/380mi tour leaving from Munich.
A tour through this far southern region, with its magnificent alpine scenery and wealth of culture, will undoubtedly be a high point in your exploration of Germany.

The country's second most popular tourist destination after Berlin, **Munich** – Bavaria's vibrant capital – is a prosperous and lively city. Art lovers will delight in its fabulous museums and Baroque churches. A little over 100km/62mi to the east, on the Austrian border, **Burghausen** is crowned with the biggest medieval fortress in Germany. Its defence system, reinforced at the beginning of the 16C in the face of a threatening invasion by the Turks, stretches for around 1km/0.6mi.

The much-travelled **Deutsche Alpenstraße** kicks off in **Berchtesgaden**, where you can explore underground salt mines, hike in the shadow of the mighty Watzmann mountain or take a cruise on the magical Königssee. The Alpenstraße is an intensely scenic route passing dreamy villages, bucolic meadows as well as famous ski resorts such as **Garmisch-Partenkirchen**, which is lorded over by the Zugspitze, Germany's tallest mountain.

When the Alpenstraße reaches Füssen, make a side trip to **Neuschwanstein**, the famous castle of "fairytale king" Ludwig II. Füssen is also the southern terminus of the fabled Romantische Straße, which you follow as far as **Augsburg**, a founded by the Romans.

Fischerviertel, Ulm

© Dirk Homburg/Ulm/ Neu-Ulm Touristik GmbH

REGIONAL TOURS

In the *DISCOVERING GERMANY* section you will find local driving tours (with corresponding maps, or you can find the route plotted on the region map) for the following Principal Sights:

Rügen Island
Mecklenburg Lake District
Goslar
Hann. Müden
Eifel
Trier
Moselle Valley
Rhine Valley
Frankfurt Am Main
Heidelberg
Pfalz
Black Forest
Baden Wine Route
Lake Constance
Bad Wimpfen

Swabian Jura
Upper Swabian Plateau
Munich
German Alpine Road
Berchtesgaden
Passau
Romantic Road
Würzburg
Nuremberg
Bayreuth
Jena
Eisenach
Dresden
Annaberg-Buchholz

TOURIST ROUTES

♿*See pages 27-28*. Germany has designated several thematic tours throughout the country. Each route is marked with signs to help travellers stay on course.

City Breaks

Germany's well-known cities brim with first-class museums, lovely parks and gardens, magnificent palaces and churches, homes of famous historical figures, fine restaurants, lively beer halls and inviting hostelries.

HAMBURG

Germany's second-largest city is also one of its most beautiful, laced by rivers and canals, characterised by great architecture and endowed with a spirit of openness that harks back to its Hanseatic League days. Wherever you go, it's imbued with maritime flair, from its vast container port, which can be toured by boat, to its riverside promenades that invite strolling. Must-sees include the canal-laced Speicherstadt with its elegant red-brick warehouses, and the Hafen City, which is the largest urban construction project in Europe.

COLOGNE

"Why is it so lovely on the Rhine?" asks a popular German song. You'll quickly find the answer in Cologne. With its famous Gothic cathedral, lively beer halls, lovely river promenades, world-class museums and superb shopping, this is a city that's easy to love. If possible, visit in February during Carnival, a raucous pre-Lent celebration, when locals don fancy dress and demonstrate their legendary *joie de vivre* at parties and street parades.

MUNICH

Beer, lederhosen and Oktoberfest – the Bavarian capital certainly conjures plenty of cliches. But what about BMW, high-tech and world-class music and fashion? Revel in Munich's contradictions as you stroll around the vast English Garden, pick up gourmet treats at the Viktualienmarkt and hoist a mug of foamy beer at an atmosphere-charged beer hall. For culture, report to the amazing Pinakothek museums or tour the royal splendour of the Residenz.

Neue Pinakothek – one of many museums on offer in Munich

Jürgen Sauer/Munich City Tourist Office

BERLIN

Germany's most populous city is also its most popular. Keenly aware of its unique past, the country's capital has shed its dour Cold War demeanour and grown into a confident, sassy and modern city with flourishing art, music and fashion scenes. Take the exciting pulse of a city that's forever in the state of "becoming" as you explore landmarks old and new – the Brandenburg Gate and Checkpoint Charlie to the Holocaust Memorial and Potsdamer Platz. Whether you stand in awe of ancient treasures on Museum Island, explore the park and building at Charlottenburg Palace or sample the famed Berlin nightlife, you'll make memories to last a lifetime.

TOURIST ROUTES

Clearly signposted, these "thematic" itineraries provide a handy means of crisscrossing the country and getting to know it better. They include:

- **Badische Weinstraße (Baden Wine Route)**, from Baden-Baden to Lörrach *(170km/105.6mi)*. Breathtaking scenery, superb cuisine, plenty of sunshine and some of the finest wines in the country await in Germany's southwestern corner.
- **Burgenstraße (Castle Road)**, from Mannheim to Bayreuth and then on to Prague *(975km/605mi)*.

Plunge back into medieval times as you skirt the 70 legend-shrouded castles of this meandering route.

- **Bocksbeutelstrasse (Middle Franconian Wine Route)**, southeast of Würzburg *(50km/31mi)*. Sample delicious Franconian wines bottled in their signature flagons called *"Bockbeutel"* at time-honoured wine estates.
- **Deutsche Alleenstraße (German Tree-lined Road)**, from Rügen Island to Lake Constance *(2 900km/1 812mi)*. Let nature embrace you as you travel beneath a shady canopy of mature beeches, chestnuts and oaks arching over Germany's longest holiday route.
- **Deutsche Ferienstraße Ostsee-Alpen (Baltic Sea to the Alps)**, from the Fehmarn Island to Berchtesgaden *(1 738km/1 086mi)*. From dune-fringed beaches to snowy mountains, the entire quilt of Germany's varied landscapes unfolds on this epic north–south journey.
- **Deutsche Weinstraße (German Wine Road)**, from Bockenheim/Palatinate to Wissembourg/Alsace *(91km/56.5mi)*. Spring arrives early along this route dotted with charming villages steeped in history and hemmed in by rambling vineyards.

USEFUL WEBSITES

www.romantischestrasse.de
A popular tourist destination is the *Romantische Straße*, the Romantic Road. Half-timbered houses, medieval fortresses and city walls, Alpine vistas and art-filled churches stretch along the route. The website offers detailed travel information and maps for each of the towns and cities along the way.

www.burgenstrasse.de
Some of Germany's most romantic castles are on the *Burgenstraße*, or Castle Road, that travels from Mannheim to Prague. For maps and details about the route, visit the website.

www.deutsche-weinstrasse.de
The website of the German Wine Institute offers information about each of Germany's wines and wine regions as well as a listing of the nation's wine festivals.

www.naturparke.de
Germany is home to 15 national parks, 16 biosphere reserves and 104 nature parks. The site offers detailed information for each of Germany's nature parks.

www.deutscher-heilbaederverband.de
Spas and wellness centres have long been considered by Germans as part of healthy living. A visit to the German Spa Association's website provides links to spas nationwide, including lists of those with English-speaking therapists.

www.zoo-infos.de
Parents travelling with young children may want to visit the website prior to arrival. This comprehensive site includes information about and links to the country's zoos and animal parks.

www.oktoberfest.de
Oktoberfest is one of the world's most famous festivals. Visitors to Munich interested in up-to-date festival information can visit the site.

- **Deutsche Fachwerkstraße (Route of Half-timbered Buildings)** showcases nine routes through Lower Saxony, Hessen and Baden-Württemberg, with their centuries-old higgledy-piggledy half-timbered houses, decorated with fancy and artistry.
- **Alte Salzstraße (Old Salt Road)**, from Lüneburg to Lübeck *(100km/62mi)*. Horsecarts needed three weeks to transport salt – the "White Gold" – along this historic trading route. You can do it in just a day or two!
- **Straße der Romanik (Romanesque Road)** loops through Sachsen-Anhalt, leaving from Magdeburg *(about 1 000km/625mi)*. European history was made 1 000 years ago in towns along this route of dignified cathedrals, fierce fortresses and rambling abbeys.
- **Romantische Straße (Romantic Road)**, from Würzburg to Füssen *(315km/196mi)*. On this dreamy route you can check off many of Germany's most famous destinations, including Rothenburg ob der Tauber and Neuschwanstein.
- **Silberstraße (Silver Route)**, from Zwickau to Dresden *(115km/71.4mi)*. This enchanting "ribbon of riches" winds through rural, mountainous countryside steeped in ancient traditions.
- **Klassikerstraße Thüringen (Thuringian Classical Route)**, Goethe to Gropius *(300km/186.4mi)*. Germany's legacy as a land of poets, thinkers and innovators is confirmed along this intensely cultural route.
- **Oberschwäbische Barockstraße (Upper Swabian Baroque Route)**, from Ulm to Lake Constance (Bodensee) *(455m/282.7mi)*, links the churches, abbeys and libraries of the southern German Baroque and Rococo styles.
  ⓒ *See www.germany.travel.*

Outdoor Activities

F or nature-lovers and outdoor sports fans alike, Germany's varied landscapes provide an ideal setting for all sorts of activities. Some very useful information in this respect can be found at www.germany.travel.

IDEAS FOR YOUR VISIT
NATIONAL PARKS
Germany's 15 national parks are wonderful playgrounds for nature-lovers and active types. Further information is available from **Europarc Deutschland**, ℰ(030) 28 87 88 20, www.europarc-deutschland.de.

- **Bavaria:** Bavarian Forest (Bayerischer Wald), Berchtesgaden.
- **Baden-Württemberg:** Black Forest (Schwarzwald).
- **Schleswig-Holstein:** Schleswig-Holstein mudflats (Wattenmeer).
- **Lower Saxony:** Lower Saxon mudflats (Niedersächsisches Wattenmeer), Harz.
- **North Rhine-Westphalia:** Eifel.
- **Hamburg:** Hamburg mudflats (Wattenmeer).
- **Hessen:** Kellerwald-Edersee.
- **Saxony-Anhalt:** Harz.
- **Mecklenburg-Western Pomerania:** Jasmund, Müritz, Vorpommersche Boddenlandschaft.
- **Saxony:** Saxon Switzerland (Sächsische Schweiz).
- **Brandenburg:** Lower Oder valley (Unteres Odertal).
- **Thuringia:** Hainich.

LAKES AND MOUNTAINS
If you want to stand on the top of Germany, you have to travel to Garmisch-Partenkirchen, where the Zugspitze soars 2 964m/9 724ft skywards. Though not as high, many other mountains are steeped in legend, such as the Watzmann in Berchtegaden and the Brocken in the Harz National Park.

The largest lake is the Bodensee (Lake Constance), which shares borders with Austria and Switzerland.
Nearby, Lake Chiemsee is popular for swimming and sailing, while the Mecklenburger Seenplatte lake district is best explored by canoe or kayak.

COASTLINE
Relax on sandy beaches, connect with nature on a walk across the mudflats and feel the brisk wind in your face along the 1 000km/625mi of Germany's windswept coastline.
In the west, the North Sea is rougher and punctuated with numerous islands, including glamorous Sylt and the family-friendly East Frisian Islands. The Baltic Sea in the east is shallow and calm; it is home to Rügen, Germany's largest island, with its famous chalk cliffs.

CANOEING AND KAYAKING
For canoeing, kayaking and rafting, contact **Bundesverband Kanu,** Bövemannstraße 1, 48268 Greven, ℰ(02571) 503 53 20, www.kanutouristik.de.

CYCLING
Cycling can be a practical, economical and "green" way to explore the German countryside. There are about 200 long-distance routes as well as dedicated bike paths in many cities. Information is available from the **Allgemeiner Deutscher Fahrrad-Club** (ADFC, ℰ(030) 209 149 80 , www.adfc.de). The ADFC also publishes the Bett & Bike directory of bicycle-friendly lodging (www.bettundbike.de). The German National Tourist Office offers a free route finder with maps and tips at www.germany.travel.

PARK/PLACE	✆/WEBSITE	NEAREST MOTORWAY EXIT
Bavaria Filmstadt/ Geiselgasteig (Bayern)	(089) 64 99 20 00 www.bavaria-filmstadt.de	A 99: Oberhaching (4)
Churpfalzpark Loifling/ Cham (Bayern)	(099 71) 303 40 www.churpfalzpark.de	A 3: Straubing (106)
Erlebnispark Schloß Thurn/ Heroldsbach (Bayern)	(091 90) 92 98 98 www.schloss-thurn.de	A 73: Baiersdorf Nord (10)
Erlebnispark Tripsdrill/ Cleebronn-Tripsdrill (Baden-Württemberg)	(071 35) 99 99 www.tripsdrill.de	A 81: Mundesheim (13)
Erlebnispark Ziegenhagen/ Witzenhausen (Hessen)	(055 45) 246 www.erlebnispark-ziegenhagen.de	A 75: Hann. Münden (75)
Europa-Park/Rust (Baden-Württemberg)	(01805) 77 66 88 www.europapark.de	A 5: Ettenheim (57)
Fränkisches Wunderland/ Plech (Bayern)	(092 44) 98 90 www.wunderland.de	A 9: Plech (46)
Freizeit-Land/Geiselwind (Bayern)	(095 56) 921 192 www.freizeitlandgeiselwind.de	A 3: Geiselwind (76)
Filmpark Babelsberg/ Potsdam (Brandenburg)	(0331) 721 27 50 www.filmpark-babelsberg.de	A 115: Potsdam– Babelsberg (5)
Fort Fun Abenteuerland/ Bestwig-Wasserfall (Nordrhein-Westfalen)	(029 05) 811 23 www.fortfun.de	A 46: Bestwig (71)
Hansa-Park/Sierksdorf (Schleswig-Holstein)	(045 63) 47 40 www.hansapark.de	A 1: Eutin (15)
Heide-Park/Soltau (Niedersachsen)	(01805) 91 91 01 www.heidepark.de	A 7: Soltau-Ost (44)
HolidayPark/Haßloch (Rheinland-Pfalz)	(06324) 5993 0 www.holidaypark.de	A 65: Neustadt-Süd (13)
Phantasialand/Brühl (Nordrhein-Westfalen)	(01805) 366 200 www.phantasialand.de	A 553: Brühl-Süd (2)
Potts Park/Minden-West (Nordrhein-Westfalen)	(0571) 510 88 www.pottspark-minden.de	A 2: Porta Westfalica (33)
Ravensburger Spieleland/ Meckenbeuren	(075 42) 40 00 www.spieleland.de	A 96: Wangen-West (5)
Hollywood-und Safaripark/ Schloß Holte-Stukenbrock (Nordrhein-Westfalen)	(052 07) 95 24 25 www.safaripark.de	A 2, then A 33: Stukenbrock-Senne (23)
Legoland (Günzburg)	(01805) 70 07 57 01 www.legoland.de	A 7, then A 8: exit Günzburg
Serengeti-Park/Hodenhagen (Niedersachsen)	(05164) 979 90 www.serengeti-park.com	A 7: Westenholz (7)
Taunus Wunderland/ Schlangenbad (Hessen)	(061 24) 40 81 www.taunuswunderland.de	A 66: Wiesbaden– Frauenstein (2)
Weltvogelpark Walsrode/ **Walsrode** (Niedersachsen)	(051 61) 60 440 www.weltvogelpark.de	A 27: Walsrode-Süd (28)
Movie Park Germany/ Bottrop-Kirchhellen (Nordrhein-Westfalen)	(01085) 2045 899 www.movieparkgermany.de	A 31: Kirchhellen– Feldhausen (40)

FISHING

A German fishing licence is required. For information contact:

♦ **Deutscher Angelfischerverband**, Weißenseer Weg 110,10369 Berlin, ✆(030) 97 10 43 79, www.anglerverband.com

GOLF

High-quality golf courses are abundant in both metropolitan areas and the German countryside. For information, contact the **Deutscher Golf Verband**, Kreuzberger Ring 64, 65205 Wiesbaden, ✆(0611) 99 02 00, www.golf.de. Greens fees range from 40€ to 90€ for a one-day pass during the week, rising to about 55€ to 110€ on weekends.

HORSE RIDING

Lists of equestrian centres can be obtained from regional and local tourist offices, or contact the **Deutsche Reiterliche Vereinigung**, Freiherr-von-Langen-Straße 13, 48231 Warendorf, ✆(02581) 636 20, www.pferd-aktuell.de.

HUNTING

For information on hunting in Germany, contact **Deutscher Jagdverband**, Friedrichstraße 185-186, 10117 Berlin, ✆(030) 209 139 40, www.jagdnetz.de.

SAILING AND WINDSURFING

Sail sports are popular along the North Sea and Baltic Sea coasts as well as on such lakes as Lake Constance, Lake Müritz and Lake Starnberg, near Munich. Contact the German Sailing Federation, **Deutscher Segler-Verband** in Hamburg, ✆(40) 632 00 90, www.dsv.org.

WALKING

The **Deutscher Wanderverband**, ✆(0561) 93 87 30, www.wanderverband.de can provide details on regional hikes and publishes guides and maps, many of them online at www.wanderbares-deutschland.de. Information on shelters, trails and overnight huts is available from the **Deutscher Alpenverein** (DAV, German Alpine Club) in Munich, ✆(089) 14 00 30, www.alpenverein.de. For refuge opening times, weather reports, trail conditions, etc., contact the DAV's **Alpine Information Centre** (Alpine Auskunft) at ✆(089) 29 49 40. For the Alpine weather forecast, call ✆(089) 29 50 70.

WINTER SPORTS

Although the Alps and the Black Forest remain the most popular skiing areas in Germany, snow sport is also possible in the central upland regions of the Harz mountains, the Thuringian Forest and the Sauerland.

Hiking on the Schluch, Black Forest

© Tourist-Information Schluchsee

Spas

S pa treatments have been around since Roman times, and Germans still consider them an important component of a healthy lifestyle. The frantic pace of modern life is driving an increasing number of visitors to follow suit at one of Germany's many spa resorts. Not only are spas centres for the treatment or prevention of certain illnesses, they are also ideal places to recharge your energy.

Spa resorts have access to mineral water with medicinal properties, and offer proper facilities for applying the necessary treatments. They are usually found in beautiful natural settings and are an interesting alternative for those wishing to have a quiet vacation, enjoy nature and enhance their well-being.

Information on all of the country's spa resorts can be obtained from the German Spa Association, the **Deutscher Heilbäderverband**, Charlottenstraße 13, 10969 Berlin, ℘(030) 24 63 69 20, www.deutscher-heilbaederverband. de. Another useful website is www.baederkalender.de.

Activities For Kids

I n this guide, sights of particular interest to children are indicated with a KIDS symbol ♣♣. Some attractions may offer discount fees for children.

ZOOS AND ANIMAL PARKS

Kids love animals, and Germany has plenty of places to meet cuddly koalas, pet a sheep or marvel at tiger teeth. An online resource with information about more than 800 zoos in the country is www.zoo-infos.de.

DEUTSCHE SPIELZEUGSTRASSE (GERMAN TOY ROAD)

This enchanting tourist route travels for 300km/186mi from Waltershausen in Thuringia to Schwabach in Franconia, passing through 30 towns where toys, dolls, teddy bears and other playthings are being produced, often in traditional fashion.

For the full scoop, contact Deutsche Spielzeugstraße, Lauterer Straße 60, 96450 Coburg, ℘(095 61) 51 43 22, www.spielzeugstrasse.de.

KINDERLAND BAYERN

The Kinderland initiative in Bavaria is a network of more than 350 lodging properties, restaurants and leisure facilities such as theme parks, fun pools, museums, cable-cars and zoos. Members are classified with three, four or five "bears" according to their family-friendliness.

For more information, see Kinderland Bayern, Arabellastraße 17, 81925 Munich, ℘(0 89) 212 39 70, www.kinderland.by.

THEME PARKS

For a list of the best known and most popular amusement parks in Germany, access www.germany.travel and look under Specials, then Family Attractions, then Theme Parks. Some of the parks described in this guide include Berlin's Legoland Discovery Centre, the Hamburg Dungeon, Europa-Park, Playmobil Funpark and Königstuhl's amusement park.

Shopping

Germany is a shopper's paradise with shopping centres, department stores, boutiques and specialist shops often conveniently clustering in pedestrianised city centres. Most towns also have weekly farmers' markets selling fruit and vegetables in season. Flea markets are great for picking up some offbeat souvenirs.

Generally, though, souvenirs are best purchased directly in the region where they hail from. So in the Black Forest you might acquire a cuckoo clock, in Bavaria a beer stein or a pair of lederhosen, in the Rheingau a bottle of excellent Riesling wine, in Meissen handpainted porcelain, in Nuremberg spicy gingerbread, in Lübeck delicious marzipan and in Berlin an authenticated piece of the Wall. Other popular items to bring back home include natural cosmetics by Dr. Hauschka, Birkenstock sandals, stuffed toys made by Steiff, collectible Käthe Kruse dolls and Solingen-made cutlery. Dedicated shoppers might want to visit in December, when you can stock up on enchanting ornaments and beautiful decorations at the **Christmas markets** that light up nearly every town square.

Antique shop in Meissen

© Manfred J. Bail /Westend 61/Photoshot

Sightseeing

The *DISCOVERING GERMANY* section gives the opening times and admission charges for monuments, museums, churches, etc. On account of the ever-increasing cost of living and frequent variations in the opening times of these monuments, this information should be used only as a rough guide. It is intended for tourists who are travelling on their own and are not entitled to any reduction.

With prior agreement, groups can obtain special conditions as regards both times and charges. Enquire at the ticket office before purchasing your tickets; age-related reductions, in particular, are often available.
See also Discounts p53.
The German Rail Pass, Eurolines Pass and other special passes offer cost-savings on transportation, while major cities generally sell a sightseeing card that discounts local transportation fees and admission charges.

It is always a good idea to make enquiries by phone before setting off, since certain monuments may be temporarily closed for restoration. Visiting conditions for churches are specified only if the interior is of particular interest, if there are set opening times or if there is an admission charge. Churches can generally not be visited during services. If a church is open only during services, visitors should behave respectfully.

Festivals & Events

Listed below are some of the major events and festivals held throughout the year in Germany. More details can be obtained from tourist offices and at www.germany.travel. *See also under "Festivals" in some Address Books in the DISCOVERING GERMANY section.*

JANUARY

1 JANUARY
New Year's Day International Ski Jump, part of the Vierschanzentournee (Four Hills Tournament) – **Garmisch-Partenkirchen**

FEBRUARY

TWO WEEKS IN FEBRUARY
International Film Festival (Berlinale): – **Berlin**

MARCH/APRIL

SUNDAY BEFORE SHROVE TUESDAY
"München Narrisch" Carnival – **Munich**

SHROVE MONDAY
Rosenmontagszug: procession and street carnival – **Cologne, Düsseldorf, Mainz, Munich**

SHROVE MONDAY AND TUESDAY
Narrensprung Carnival (Dance of the Fools): elaborate traditional costumes and expressive wooden masks – **Rottweil**

TEN DAYS AFTER ASH WEDNESDAY
Traditional Sorbian Easter Egg Market – **Bautzen**

APRIL/MAY

30 APRIL/1 MAY
Walpurgisnacht: Witches' Sabbath Festival – **Various towns in the Harz region**

LATE APRIL TO MID-JUNE
Festival of Classical Music – **Schwetzingen**

MAY

MAY TO MID-SEPTEMBER EVERY SUNDAY AT NOON
Rattenfängerspiel: pageant retracing the legend of the Pied Piper – **Hameln**

FRIDAY AFTER ASCENSION
Blutritt: equestrian cavalcade in honour of the Holy Blood relic – **Weingarten**

MAY: Hafengeburtstag, Hamburg

© www.mediaserver.hamburg.de / C. Spahrbier

FIVE DAYS FROM MAY 7
Hafengeburtstag: the world's largest harbour festival – **Hamburg**

SECOND HALF OF MAY
International horse racing at Iffezheim – **Baden-Baden**

MAY TO SEPTEMBER
Der Rhein in Flammen (The Rhine in Flames): fireworks and illuminated castles and boats along the Rhine valley between Koblenz and Bingen – **Koblenz-Oberwesel**, **St. Goar**

WHITSUN
Kuchen und Brunnenfest: dance of the salt workers in traditional 16C costume – **Schwäbisch Hall**

Meistertrunk: performance of the legend of the "Long Drink" during the Thirty Years' War by locals in period costume – **Rothenburg ob der Tauber**

Carnival of Cultures: colourful street festival with international music, dancing and parades – **Berlin**

WHIT MONDAY
Pfingstritt: equestrian parade – **Kötzting**

WHIT TUESDAY
Historische Geißbockversteigerung: auctioning of a goat in period costumes with folk dancing and a local fair – **Deidesheim**

CORPUS CHRISTI
Solemn procession through the decorated town – **Munich**
Mülheimer Gottestracht: procession of boats along the Rhine – **Cologne**
Procession through flower-decked street – **Hüfingen**

LAST SATURDAY OF MAY
Wildpferdefang: capture and auction of young stallions – **Merfelder Bruch**

14 DAYS AFTER WHITSUN, FROM FRIDAY TO MONDAY
Salatkirmes (Salad Fair): commemorates the introduction of the potato to the Hessen region; traditional local costumes – **Schwalmstadt**

JUNE

1ST WEEKEND IN JUNE AND SEPTEMBER, 2ND WEEKEND IN JULY
Castle illuminations (firework displays) – **Heidelberg**

MID-JUNE
Luther's Wedding: celebration of the reformer's marriage with historical costume parade – **Lutherstadt Wittenberg**

Leipzig Bach Festival – **Leipzig**

LATE JUNE
Christopher Street Day: gay pride parades – **Berlin, Cologne, Hamburg, Dresden, Munich**

JUNE TO AUGUST
Summer Music Festival: classical music in the Cistercian abbey – **Chorin**

Festival of Drama and Opera in the abbey ruins; theatre, opera – **Bad Hersfeld**

JUNE TO SEPTEMBER (EVERY 5 YEARS, NEXT: 2017)
Documenta: world's largest international exhibition of contemporary art – **Kassel**

LAST WEEK OF JUNE
Kiel Week: international sailing regatta; city-wide festival – **Kiel**

LAST WEEKEND OF JUNE
Bergstadtfest: parade in historical costumes – **Freiberg**

FOUR SUNDAYS FROM END OF JUNE (EVERY 4 YEARS, NEXT: 2017)
Fürstenhochzeit (Landshut Royal Wedding): historical pageant in period costume – **Landshut**

DURING SUMMER MONTHS
Mecklenburg-Vorpommern Summer Music Festival, held in historic mansions, castles and churches – **throughout Mecklenburg-Vorpommern**

JULY

JULY TO AUGUST
Schleswig-Holstein Music Festival – **throughout Schleswig-Holstein**
Festival on the cathedral steps – **Erfurt**

OCTOBER: Bremer Freimarkt

© Ingrid Krause/BTZ Bremer Touristik-Zentrale, www.bremen-tourismus.de

1ST WEEKEND IN JULY
Spreewald Festival: Sorbian folklore and traditions – **Lübbenau**

EARLY JULY
Archers' Festival: procession of archers – **Hannover**

MID-JULY
Fischerstechen (Fishermen's Festival) – **Ulm**

Kinderzeche: commemorating the saving of the town by a deputation of children (historical costumes) – **Dinkelsbühl**

PENULTIMATE MONDAY IN JULY
Schwörmontag: river procession on the Danube – **Ulm**

THROUGHOUT JULY
Tänzelfest: historical procession by school children – **Kaufbeuren**

LAST SATURDAY IN JULY TO 1ST SUNDAY IN AUGUST
Summer music festival – **Hitzacker**

END OF JULY TO END OF AUGUST
Bayreuther Festspiele: Wagner Opera Festival – **Bayreuth**

AUGUST

FIRST TWO WEEKS IN AUGUST
Further Drachenstich (Slaying of the Dragon): pageant of the legend of St. George, in period costume – **Furth im Wald**

2ND SATURDAY IN AUGUST
Seenachtsfest: evening lakeside festival – **Constance**

THIRD WEEKEND IN AUGUST
Schäferlauf: shepherds' race (barefoot over a field of stubble) – **Markgröningen**

LAST WEEK IN AUGUST TO FIRST WEEK IN SEPTEMBER
International horse racing at Iffezheim – **Baden-Baden**

SEPTEMBER

MID-SEPTEMBER TO MID-OCTOBER
Beethoven Fest: International music festival in composer's home town – **Bonn**

END OF SEPTEMBER TO MID-OCTOBER
Cannstatter Volksfest: popular local fair – **Bad Cannstatt**

TWO WEEKS PRECEDING FIRST SUNDAY IN OCTOBER
Oktoberfest: beer festival. The largest popular festival in the world attracts around 6 million people to the Bavarian capital every year – **Munich**

OCTOBER

FIVE DAYS IN EARLY OR MID-OCTOBER
Frankfurt Book Fair: the world's largest book fair with 1 800 exhibitors from 100 countries – **Frankfurt am Main**

CHRISTMAS MARKETS

A stroll through a German Christmas market is a delightful overture to the senses. The aroma of cinnamon-roasted almonds mingles with that of steaming mulled wine and sausage smoke wafting from beechwood fires. Each stall is festively adorned and laden with tempting arrays of wooden toys, shiny ornaments, filigree lace, Christmas pyramids, adorable little smoking men, hand-blown glass, fragrant candles and other seasonal decorations. Stop for a minute to listen to the local choir singing "O Tannenbaum" while standing below a massive fir tree covered in thousands of sparkling lights. Watch the excitement in children's eyes as they wait for their turn on Santa's knee, and the glee as they bite into a candied apple. Pure magic!

Christmas market wares

© Stadt Nürnberg/Christine Dierenbach

Dresden holds the claim for Germany's oldest Christmas market with a tradition going back to 1434. The most famous in the country, though, is the one in Nuremberg, but there are dozens of others in cities, towns and villages. They're almost always held on the central market square with stalls spilling out into surrounding streets. The nicest markets are in historic settings, backed by cathedrals, half-timbered houses and stately town halls. Most start in late November and run through 24 December, with stalls open daily, including Sundays. For a full list, see www.germany-christmas-market.org.uk.

- ◆ **Nuremberg** ◆ **Rothenburg ob der Tauber** ◆ **Munich**
- ◆ **Dresden** ◆ **Hamburg** ◆ **Cologne** ◆ **Berlin**

Nuremberg Christmas market

© Stadt Nürnberg/Christine Dierenbach

1ST AND 2ND WEEKEND IN OCTOBER
Weinlesefest: wine fair and election of the Queen of Wine – **Neustadt an der Weinstraße**

SECOND HALF OF OCTOBER
Bremer Freimarkt: largest popular fair in northern Germany – **Bremen**

SUNDAY NEAREST 6 NOVEMBER
Leonhardifahrt: similar celebration to that at Bad Tölz (🕭see below) – **Benediktbeuern**

NOVEMBER

6 NOVEMBER
Leonhardifahrt: gaily decorated horse-drawn carts process through town to celebrate Mass in honour of St. Leonard – **Bad Tölz**

DECEMBER

ADVENT
Christmas markets – throughout Germany (🕭see p37) but especially in **Nuremberg**, **Munich**, **Dresden**

24 DECEMBER AND NEW YEAR'S EVE
Weihnachtsschießen und Neujahrsschießen: Christmas and New Year shooting matches – **Berchtesgaden**

Books & Films

BOOKS

HISTORY AND BIOGRAPHY

A Concise History of Germany – Mary Fulbrook

A History of Germany 1815-1985 – William Carr

Exploring the Roman World: Roman Gaul and Germany – Anthony King

In the Garden of Beasts: Love, Terror, and an American Family in Hitler's Berlin – Erik Larson

The Reformation – Owen Chadwick

The Thirty Years' War – Veronica Wedgwood

The Rise and Fall of the Third Reich – William Shirer

The Last Days of Hitler – Hugh Trevor-Roper

The Saddled Cow: East Germany's Life and Legacy – Annie McElvoy Hugh Trevor-Roper

The Wall: The People's Story – Christopher Hilton

Stasiland – Anna Funder

THE ARTS

Bauhaus – Frank Whitford

The Expressionists – Wolf Dieter Dube

The Weimar Years: A Culture Cut Short – John Willett

LITERATURE

Nibelungenlied – Anonymous

The Lost Honour of Katharina Blum – Heinrich Böll

Caucasian Chalk Circle; The Threepenny Opera; Mother Courage – Bertolt Brecht

The Tin Drum; The Flounder; From the Diary of a Snail; My Century – Günter Grass

Grimms Fairy Tales – Jakob and Wilhelm Grimm

The Glass Bead Game; Narcissus and Goldmund; Steppenwolf – Hermann Hesse

Runaway Horse – Martin Walser

Wilhelm Tell – Friedrich von Schiller

The Reader – Bernhard Schlink

Buddenbrooks; The Magic Mountain – Thomas Mann

The Wall Jumper – Peter Schneider

All Quiet on the Western Front – Erich Maria Remarque

A Model Childhood – Christa Wolf

Berlin Alexanderplatz – Alfred Döblin

TRAVEL AND MODERN GERMAN SOCIETY

A Time of Gifts – Patrick Leigh Fermor
A Traveller's Wine Guide to Germany – Kerry Brady Stewart et al
A Tramp Abroad – Mark Twain
Deutschland: A Winter's Tale – Heinrich Heine
Germany and the Germans – John Ardagh
Goodbye to Berlin – Christopher Isherwood
The Simon & Schuster Guide to the Wines of Germany – Ian Jamieson
The Germans – Gordon A Craig
The Origins of Modern Germany – Geoffrey Barraclough
Vanishing Borders – Michael Farr

FILMS

Barbara (2012) – A beautifully told story of loyalty and betrayal in the German Democratic Republic by one of Germany's most interesting directors, Christian Petzold.
Baader-Meinhof Complex (2008) – Academy Award-nominated film tells the story of the formation and early years of the Red Army Faction 1970s terrorist gang.
The Lives of Others (2006) – Academy Award-winner zeroes in on the all-pervasiveness of the East German secret police, the Stasi.
Sophie Scholl – The Final Days (2005) A dramatisation of the final days of Sophie Scholl, co-founder of the Nazi resistance group, The White Rose.
Downfall (2004) – A gripping account of Hitler's final days cooped up in a Berlin bunker.
Head-On (2004) – A powerful look at Turkish-German immigrant life told through a love story.
Goodbye, Lenin! (2003) – A son must protect his sick mother from learning that her beloved German Democratic Republic has vanished while she lay in a coma.
Run Lola Run (1998) – Fast-paced movie about a woman who has 20 minutes to find and bring 100 000 Deutschmarks to her boyfriend so he does not rob a supermarket.

Schindler's List (1993) – Based on a true story, a German businessman acts to save Jews from the Nazis in WWII.
Wings of Desire (1987) – An angel in postwar Berlin falls in love with a trapeze artist and decides to become human and thus mortal.
Das Boot (1981) – Blood, sweat, fear, claustrophia and cameraderie experienced by a German World War II submarine crew under attack.
The Enigma of Kaspar Hauser (1974) – True story set in 1820s Nuremberg about a young man who emerges after being held captive in a dungeon since birth.
Ludwig (1973) – The tragic life and mysterious death of King Ludwig II of Bavaria.
Cabaret (1972) – Lisa Minnelli stars as a nightclub singer in Berlin during the Weimar Republic.
The Young Lions (1958) – Marlon Brando and Maximilian Schell undergo personal battles as German soldiers as well as WWII.
Triumph of the Will (1935) – Leni Riefenstahl's infamous propaganda film of the 1934 Nazi Party rally in Nuremberg.
The Blue Angel (1930) – A nerdy professor's life goes on a downward spiral after he marries a sexy lounge singer (Marlene Dietrich).
Metropolis (1927) – Fritz Lang's silent epic about the uprising of a proletarian class working underground.

Practical Info

TOP TIPS

Best time to go: May–June or September–October.
Best way around: Personal vehicle or local trains.
Best for sightseeing: City walking itineraries; regional driving tours.
Most authentic accommodation: Gasthof and guesthouses.
Need to know: Many Germans understand and speak English.
Need to taste: Bratwurst, Black Forest cake, strudel, German beer.

Viktualienmarkt (food market), Munich

© L. Kaster/Munich City Tourist Office

Before You Go

WHEN TO GO
SEASONS

Whatever the season, the weather in Germany is subject to enormous variation. The period when you are most likely to find good weather extends from May to October (✆it can get very hot during high **summer** in Baden-Württemberg and Bavaria). **Spring** and **autumn**, when tourist crowds are thinner, can be the perfect time to discover the country. It is sensible to pack some waterproof clothing whenever you plan to go. Skiers will find snow-covered slopes in **winter**, from the end of November until late February.

FESTIVALS & HOLIDAYS

Before you leave, find out about any holidays, festivals, fairs or other events that may increase the number of visitors in certain towns and make finding a room difficult (✆see Festival & Events).

TOURIST OFFICES

Information on travel arrangements and accommodation and a variety of brochures are available from the **German National Tourist Board**. For online information refer to www.germany.travel, the German National Tourist Office website. Every destination featured in the *DISCOVERING GERMANY* section of this guide has specific tourist office details. Local tourist offices are marked on town maps in this guide with the 🛈 symbol.

CHICAGO
German National Tourist Office Chicago, PO Box 59594, Chicago, IL 60659-9594, ✆(773) 539-6303, info@gntoch.com, www.germany.travel

LONDON
German National Tourist Office, PO Box 70700, London SW1P 9ZX office-britain@germany.travel, www.germany.travel.

NEW YORK
German National Tourist Office, 122 East 42nd Street, New York, NY 10168-0072 germanyinfo@germany.travel, www.germany.travel

INTERNATIONAL VISITORS
GERMAN EMBASSIES AND CONSULATES ABROAD

IN AUSTRALIA
Embassy of the Federal Republic of Germany, Canberra, 119 Empire Circuit, Yarralumla ACT 2600, ✆(02) 6270 1911 info@canberra.diplo.de, www.australien.diplo.de
Consulate General of the Republic of Germany, Sydney, 13 Trelawney Street, Woollahra NSW 2025, ✆(02) 9328 7733, info@sydney.diplo.de, www.australien.diplo.de

IN CANADA
Embassy of the Federal Republic of Germany, 1 Waverley Street, Ottawa, ON, K2P 0T8. ✆(613) 232 1101, info@ottawa.diplo.de www.kanada.diplo.de
Consulate General of the Federal Republic of Germany, 2 Bloor Street East, 25th Floor, Toronto, Ontario, M4W 1A8. ✆(416) 925 28 13, info@toronto.diplo.de, www.kanada.diplo.de

IN SOUTH AFRICA
Embassy of the Federal Republic of Germany, 180 Blackwood Street, Arcadia, Pretoria 0083, ℘(012) 427 89 00, info@pretoria.diplo.de www.southafrica.diplo.de

Consulate-General of the Federal Republic of Germany, 19th Floor, Triangle House, 22 Riebeek Street, Cape Town 8001 ℘(021) 405 30 00, info@ kapstadt.diplo.de. www.southafrica.diplo.de.

IN THE UNITED KINGDOM
Embassy of the Federal Republic of Germany, 23 Belgrave Square, London SW1X 8PZ, ℘(020) 7824 1300, info@london.diplo.de, www.london.diplo.de

Consulate General of the Federal Republic of Germany, 16 Eglinton Crescent, Edinburgh EH12 5DG, Scotland ℘(0131) 337 2323, info@edinburgh.diplo.de, www.edinburgh.diplo.de

IN THE UNITED STATES
Embassy of the Federal Republic of Germany, 645 Reservoir Road NW, Washington, DC 20007 ℘(202) 298 4000, info@washington.diplo.de, www.germany.info.

Consulate General of the Federal Republic of Germany, 871 United Nations Plaza (1st Avenue @ 49th Street), New York, NY 10017 ℘(212) 610 9700, info@newyork.diplo.de, www.germany.info.de

FOREIGN EMBASSIES AND CONSULATES IN GERMANY
American Embassy
American Embassy, Pariser Platz 2, 10117 Berlin, ℘030 830 50, germany.usembassy.gov

American Consulate General
Willi-Becker-Allee 10, 40227 Düsseldorf, ℘0211 7 88 89 27, duesseldorf.usconsulate.gov

Australian Embassy
Wallstraße 76–79, 10179 Berlin, ℘030 88 00 88 0, www.germany.embassy.gov.au

Australian Consulate General
Neue Mainzer Straße 52–58, 60311 Frankfurt am Main, ℘069-90 55 80

British Embassy Berlin
Wilhelmstraße 70-71, 10117 Berlin, ℘030 20 45 7-0, www.gov.uk/government/world/organisations/british-embassy-berlin

British Consulate-General
Oststraße 86, 40210 Düsseldorf, ℘0211 94 48-0, www.gov.uk/government/world/organisations/british-embassy-berlin/office/british-consulate-dusseldorf

Canadian Embassy
Leipziger Platz 17, 10117 Berlin, ℘030 20 31 20, www.canadainternational.gc.ca

Canadian Consulate General
Benrather Straße 8, 40213 Düsseldorf, ℘0211-17 21 70, www.canadainternational.gc.ca

South African Embassy,
Tiergartenstraße 18, 10785 Berlin, ℘030 22 07 30, www.suedafrika.org

South African Consulate-General, Sendlinger-Tor-Platz 5, 80336 München, ℘089 2 31 16 30

CULTURAL ORGANISATIONS
The Goethe-Institut websites for each of the cities below can be accessed via **www.goethe.de**.

Goethe-Institut Johannesburg, 119 Jan Smuts Ave, Parkwood 2193, Johannesburg, ✆(011) 442 3232.
Goethe-Institut London, 50 Princes Gate, Exhibition Road, London SW7 2PH, ✆(020) 7596 4000.
Goethe-Institut New York, 72 Spring St., 11th Floor, New York, NY 10012, ✆(212) 439 8700.
Goethe-Institut Ottawa, Saint Paul University, 223 Main St., Office: GIG 1144B, Ottawa, ON, K1S 1C4, ✆613 2329000.
Goethe-Institut Sydney, 90 Ocean Street, Woollahra, NSW 2025, ✆(02) 8356 8333.

ENTRY REQUIREMENTS
PASSPORTS AND VISAS

Citizens of European Union countries need a national identity card or a passport to visit Germany; there is no limit to the length of their stay. Under the visa-waiver program, citizens of certain nations (including Australia, Canada, New Zealand and the US) require only a passport, but no visa, to enter Germany as tourists for up to three months within a six-month period. Citizens of all other countries need to apply for a Schengen Visa at the German consulate in their home country. Regulations change from time to time. Check www.auswaertiges-amt.de for up-to-the-minute details.

DRIVING LICENCE

A valid national driving licence is required to drive in Germany. Third-party insurance cover is compulsory; it is advisable to carry an International Motor Insurance Certificate (Green Card), which serves as proof of third-party insurance. If you bring your own car into the country, you will need vehicle registration papers as well as proof of insurance.

CUSTOMS REGULATIONS

In order to find out the latest customs allowances when returning to your country from Germany as well as other regulations about what you may bring back home, **UK citizens** should contact the Customs Office or check online at www.gov.uk/uk-border-control. For **US citizens**, the U.S. Customs and Border Protection agency offers a publication called *Know Before You Go*, which is available as a downloadable pdf at http://publications.usa.gov/USAPubs.php?PubID=187.

Most articles that you take to Germany for your personal use don't incur duty and tax.

If you're arriving from a non-European Union country, the following duty-free allowances apply to travellers over 17 years of age, who may import (duty free): 1L of strong liquor or 2L of less than 22 percent alcohol by volume plus 4L of wine plus 16L of beer

DUTY-FREE ALLOWANCES FOR NON-EU	
Spirits (Whisky, gin, vodka, etc.)	1 litre
Fortified Wines (Vermouth, port, etc.)	2 litres
Wine (including sparkling wine)	4 litres
Beer	16 litres
Cigarettes	200
Cigarillos	100
Cigars	50
Smoking tobacco	250g

and ether 200 cigarettes or 100 cigarillos or 50 cigars or 250g of loose tobacco.

HEALTH

Be sure to obtain adequate travel health insurance before going on your trip. European Union citizens are entitled to free or reduced-cost emergency medical treatment while visiting Germany.

You should carry your European Health Insurance Card (EHIC), available free of charge through your national health authority. Applications can usually be made online. Contact your local office or see http://ec.europa.eu for full details.

Citizens from countries outside the EU should check with their health insurance provider if they are covered for medical emergencies while travelling. If not, definitely obtain travel insurance, preferably one that covers emergency repatriation to your home country. Many German doctors and hospitals require visitors to pay at the time of service. Make sure you understand what kind of documentation your insurance requires for reimbursement.

For referrals to an English-speaking doctor, contact your embassy or consulate in Germany. If you take regular medication, bring a sufficient supply and a letter from your doctor stating it's required to treat your medical condition.

ACCESSIBILITY

Germany is generally a well-equipped country for disabled visitors, and many of the sights described in this guide are accessible to people with special needs. Sights marked with the symbol ♿ in this book offer access for wheelchairs. Still, it is always best to call ahead to your destination to discuss your particular needs.

Access ramps and/or lifts can be found in most public buildings as well as train stations, museums, theatres and cinemas. In historic towns, though, cobblestone streets may present a challenge in getting around. Newer hotels have lifts and rooms equipped for wheelchair-users. Trains, trams, underground trains and buses are becoming increasingly accessible. Guide dogs are allowed on all forms of public transport.

An excellent reference source is the annually updated guide *Handicapped-Reisen Deutschland* (16.80€), published by Escales Verlag. It lists specifics about 400 wheelchair-friendly hotels, apartments and youth hostels and is available at bookshops, online (e.g. at www.escales-verlag.de/handicapped-reisen) and directly from the publisher (☏07841 684 11 33; fax 07841 684 11 45; info@escales-verlag.de). Barrier-free travel planning assistance is also provided by NatKo (☏0211-336 8001; www.natko.de).

Disabled motorists need to be aware that a disabled car badge/sticker does not entitle them to unrestricted parking (local disabled residents are granted special parking permits only in exceptional circumstances).

GETTING THERE
BY PLANE

Numerous airlines operate regular services to Germany's airports, the busiest of which are Frankfurt and Munich. Others are in Berlin, Bremen, Dresden, Düsseldorf, Hamburg, Hannover, Cologne/Bonn, Leipzig, Nuremberg, Saarbrücken and Stuttgart.

© Jon Arnold/hemis.fr

The German national carrier **Lufthansa** can be contacted on the following numbers:
Australia: 📞1300 655 727
Canada: 📞1-800 563 5954
South Africa: 📞0861 842538
UK: 📞0871 945 9747
USA: 📞800 645 3880
Information about flights to and within Germany can also be obtained, and reservations made, at www.lufthansa.com.

Several budget airlines, including Ryanair, EasyJet and Germanwings also fly to several German destinations from throughout Europe. **Ryanair** serves Baden-Baden, Berlin, Bremen, Cologne/Bonn, Dortmund, Weeze (near Düsseldorf), Frankfurt, Hamburg, Hamburg-Lübeck, Leipzig/Halle, Memmingen, Münster, and Nuremberg.
For information and reservations, visit www.ryanair.com or contact one of their call centres. Dial 📞0871 246 0000 (£0.10/min) from within the UK, 📞0900 116 0500 (0.62€/min) in Germany and 📞+44 871 246 0002 (0.10€/min) from the rest of the world.

The route network of **EasyJet** includes Berlin, Cologne/Bonn, Dortmund, Dresden, Düsseldorf, Hamburg and Munich from various airports in the UK. For information and reservations, visit www.easyjet.com, or call 📞0843 104 5000 (£0.05/min) in the UK.
Germanwings flies to Berlin, Bremen, Cologne/Bonn, Dortmund, Dresden, Düsseldorf, Frankfurt, Friedrichshafen, Hamburg, Hannover, Karlsruhe/Baden-Baden, Klagenfurt, Leipzig/Halle, Memmingen, Munich, Nuremberg, Rostock, Stuttgart and Usedom. Contact them on www.germanwings.com or 📞0906 294 1918 (£0.25/min) in the UK.

Inland Flights
There are numerous internal flights in Germany, most of them operated by **Lufthansa** (📞0180 583 84 26, www.lufthansa.com). Other carriers with domestic services include **Air Berlin** (📞030 34 34 34 34 in Germany, www.airberlin.com) and **Germanwings** (📞0180 6 320 320 in Germany, www.germanwings.com, 0.20€/min).

BY SHIP

There are no longer any direct ferry services between the UK and Germany. Check www.ferrybooker.com, a single site covering all sea-ferry routes and operators. The principal routes to the continent are:

- Dover to Calais, France (sailing: 1hr 15min);
- Harwich to Hoek van Holland, Netherlands (sailing: 3hrs 45min);
- Hull to Zeebrugge, Belgium (13hrs 30min);
- Newcastle to Amsterdam (15hrs).

On Arrival

GETTING AROUND
BY TRAIN

International high-speed rail links from London St. Pancras to Aachen and Cologne (Eurostar to Brussels, then Thalys) can make the train an attractive alternative to plane, coach or car in terms of time, price and convenience. Visitors leaving London can reach Aachen in just 3hrs 30min and Cologne in just over 4hrs.

Tickets and Fares
Deutsche Bahn (DB), Germany's leading railway, offers quick and comprehensive service around the country. Major cities are served by DB's high-speed InterCityExpress (ICE) trains or InterCity/EuroCity (IC/EC) services; regional centres are connected by a fleet of RegionalExpress (RE), RegionalBahn (RB) and S-Bahn trains.
Special tickets: **German Rail Pass** (www.raileurope.com) – valid for four to ten days of intra-Germany travel within one month (available only to non-European residents); **Bahncards** (www.bahn.de) – 25 percent or 50 percent discount for frequent travellers within Germany; **InterRail One Country Pass** (www.interrailnet.com) which buys unlimited rail travel within Germany for three, four, six or eight days of travel within one month (available only to European but not to German residents).

In addition, various saver tickets, seasonal promotions and discounted fares for children, seniors, students and groups are also available.
For further information and reservations, contact: Deutsche Bahn UK Booking Centre, ☎08718 808 066 *(open Mon–Fri 9am–8pm, Sat–Sun 9am–1pm)*, www.bahn.com. Alternatively, try SNCF, 193 Piccadilly, London W1J 9EU, ☎08448 485 848. For their brochure, go to http://uk.voyages-sncf.com/en.

BY COACH

Eurolines serves many cities in Germany from the UK. Coaches are equipped with air conditioning, WC, TV/video, reclining seats, etc. Journey times can be quite long (from London Victoria it takes around 19hrs to Berlin, 20hrs to Munich and 13hrs to Cologne), but tickets are inexpensive, especially when booked in advance (a 30-day advance return costs around 82€). For information and reservations, call ☎08717 818 177 (£0.10/min) in the UK, or visit the Eurolines website at www.eurolines.co.uk. The **Eurolines Pass**, valid for 15 or 30 days, allows you to travel for a set price between a choice of 43 cities across Europe, with numerous internal connections available within Germany (low/

high season prices for adults £215/355 for a 15-day pass and £320/465 for a 30-day pass). There are discounts for children, youths (under 26) and senior citizens. Children under four travel free. For further details, call ℘08717 818 177 in the UK or visit www. eurolines-pass.com.

BY BUS

Bus can be useful for travel within Germany, especially in areas where train service is sporadic or non-existent. Bus stations tend to be located next to railway stations. For prices and timetables, contact **Deutsche Touring** (℘069-790 35 01; www.eurolines.de).

BY CAR

Coming from the UK, the fastest and easiest way to Germany is via the Eurotunnel. These shuttle trains whisk cars, motorbikes, bicycles and coaches from Folkestone through the Channel Tunnel to Coquelles (near Calais, France) in about 35 minutes.

From there you can be in Germany in about 3hrs. Check fares and details with your travel agent, call ℘08443-353 535 in the UK or visit www.eurotunnel.com.

With no direct ferry services from the UK to Germany, the closest port to the German border is Hoek van Holland in the Netherlands (served from Harwich). *See By Ship, above, for additional routes.* From these ports numerous routes using autobahns and national roads lead into Germany.

Michelin offers drivers and motorcyclists a free online route planning service at www.viamichelin.com. You can determine stopovers between departure point and destination and define your route using various criteria (such as time, distance, use of motorways, road tolls, etc.). You are given information on mileage, journey time and restaurants along the way (selected from the *Michelin Guide Germany*), and map extracts that can be printed out.

Distances

♦ Calais to Frankfurt via Cologne 600km/374mi.
♦ Hoek van Holland to Munich via Bonn, Mainz, Stuttgart and Augsburg 845km/525mi.
♦ Zeebrugge to Munich via Karlsruhe, Stuttgart and Augsburg 853km/530mi.
♦ Calais to Cologne via Aachen 417km/259mi.

Driving Regulations

Traffic in Germany drives on the right. Drivers in cities with trams should be especially careful before crossing tramlines.

The maximum speed in built-up areas is 50kph/31mph.

On the open road the maximum increases to 100kph/62mph. There is no official limit on motorways (signposted "A" for *Autobahn*), but there are many stretches where slower speeds must be observed; watch for signs. In any case, it's safest not to exceed speeds of 130kph/81mph. There is a compulsory speed limit of 80kph/50mph on roads and motorways for vehicles with trailers. Careless or reckless driving is considered a serious offence in Germany and fines can be stiff. The maximum limit for alcohol in the blood is 0.05%.

German motorways are toll-free and well equipped with 24hr service areas providing: petrol, spare parts and accessories, washrooms, toilets, public telephones, refreshments, accommodation and first-aid equipment.

IMPORTANT WARNING SIGNS:	
Anfang	beginning
Ausfahrt	exit
Baustelle	roadworks, building site
Einbahnstraße	one-way street
Einfahrt	entrance
Ende	end
Gefahr	danger
LKW	HGV; truck
PKW	private car
Rechts abbiegen	turn right
Links abbiegen	turn left
Rollsplitt	gravel chippings
Stau	hold-up, traffic jam
Unfall	accident
Umleitung	diversion
Verengte Fahrbahn	road narrows
Vorfahrt	priority
Vorsicht	look out!

In some city centres car traffic is banned, but there are usually plenty of signposted parking garages *(Parkhaus)*.

Seatbelt usage is compulsory in the back as well as the front of the car. Children under age 12, or less than 1.5m/4ft 11in tall, are required by law to be fastened in a suitable child car seat; there are fines for non-compliance. It is a legal requirement to carry the regulation red emergency triangle, for warning other motorists of a breakdown or enforced roadside halt, and a first-aid box (including disposable gloves and rescue blanket).In Germany emergency services are always given priority and drivers should pull over to the side of the road.

Breakdown Service

For 24-hour service on motorways and main roads, call the German motoring association ADAC at ℘0180/2 22 22 22 (or ℘22 22 22 from mobile phones; www.adac.de). If you don't have a mobile phone, use the orange emergency phones spaced about 2km/1.2mi apart. Small arrows on the roadside posts indicate the direction of the nearest one.

On-the-spot repairs are free, as only the cost of replacement parts or towing is charged. Motorists ringing this service should ask specifically for the *"Straßenwacht"* (road patrol assistance). The *Michelin Guide Deutschland* lists the numbers to use to contact the ADAC service in all big towns.

Petrol

The following grades of petrol are generally available in Germany:

♦ *Super Plus Bleifrei*: Super unleaded (98 octane)
♦ *Super Bleifrei*: Standard unleaded (95 octane)
♦ Diesel

Leaded petrol is no longer available. A lead substitute can be added to the fuel tank of those vehicles that require it; the additive can be purchased at petrol stations.

Car Hire

The minimum age for car hire is 25, although some companies may rent to drivers ages 21 to 24 at a surcharge. You also need to have had your driving licence for more than one year. The major car hire firms have offices at airports and main railway stations and in large towns, but it is generally cheaper to arrange car hire before travelling to Germany. Some useful numbers (in Germany) include:

♦ **Avis**: ℘01806 55 77 55, www.avis.com

- **Europcar**: ☎040 520 187 654, www.europcar.com
- **Hertz**: ☎01806 33 35 35, www.hertz.com
- **Budget/Sixt**: ☎01806 21 77 11, www.budget.com

WHERE TO STAY

Hotel recommendations are located in the Address Books throughout the *DISCOVERING GERMANY* section of this guide. For coin ranges and for a description of the symbols used in the Address Books, see the Legend on the cover flap.

ADDRESSES IN THE GUIDE

We have selected accommodations for their value, location or character, trying to cater for all budgets *(for coin ranges and the symbols used in the Address Books, see the Legend on the cover flap)*. However, popular tourist regions, resorts and big cities are more expensive than others. Likewise, there is often a significant price difference between high and low season. During festivals and other cultural events last-minute accommodations are difficult to find. Tourist information offices have lists of local lodging in hotels, inns *(Gasthof* or *Gasthaus)*, guesthouses, farms, castles, hostels and holiday flats. Room rates always include tax and service charges. There may be an extra charge for breakfast. Many tourist office and hotel websites let you check for room availability and make advance reservations or consult www.booking.com, www.venere.com, www.hotels.com, www.expedia.com and www.opodo.de. Hotels catering specifically for families are at www.familotel.de. For last-minute bargains, check HRS (☎0800 328 4328 in the UK, ☎0221 2077 600 in Germany, www.hrs.com).

HOLIDAY FLATS AND HOMES

Furnished holiday flats and homes are widely available in Germany, increasingly so in the cities as well. Local tourist offices normally have information on availability. Also check www.deutschertourismusverband.de.
Bed and Breakfast
Tourist offices keep lists of private room rentals *(Privatzimmer)*, or look for a sign saying *Zimmer frei* outside private houses. For advance reservations try www.bed-and-breakfast.de or www.bedandbreakfast.de.

CAMPING

With around 2 500 campsites, Germany has plenty of scope for camping. Most are closed between November and March, but a few remain open all year. Fees are usually composed of a charge per person (2.50€ to 7€), for your tent (4€ to 8€) and for your car (2€ to 5€).
More information is available from **Bundesverband der Campingwirtschaft in Deutschland (BVCD)**, www.bvcd.de and from **ADAC**, ☎221 47 27 10 14, www.adac.de. The latter publishes an annually updated guide called *ADAC Camping-Caravaning-Führer.* Online sources include www.eurocampings.de and www.alanrogers.com.

HOSTELS

Germany has almost 600 **Hostelling International-affiliated (HI) youth hostels**, which are managed by the Deutsches Jugendherbergswerk (DJH, www.jugendherberge.de) and open to people of all ages. Staying at a hostel requires membership of an HI association. Non-members can obtain cards directly at the hostels. Advance booking is recommended during the holiday season and at city centre youth hostels. Bookings can be made by phone, fax, email and online at www.hihostels.com. There are also a growing number of independent **backpacker hostels** that don't require membership. They are especially prevalent in big cities, Berlin in particular, and generally cater more to individual travellers than groups or families. Standards vary widely.

For more information, go to www.backpacker-network.de. For online reservations, try www.gomio.com, www.hostelworld.com, and www.hostels.com.

ECONOMY CHAIN HOTELS

Both domestic and international budget chains are becoming increasingly prevalent, even in city centres. Rooms are usually small but have a TV and private bathroom; there's often an extra charge for breakfast.

The German National Tourist Board has put together a list of hotels charging 40€ or less at www.germany.travel/en/ebrochures.html.

◆ **Holiday Inn Express**: www.ihg.com/holidayinnexpress/hotels/us/en/hd/germany-hotels
◆ **Meininger**: www.meininger-hotels.com
◆ **MotelOne**:www.motel-one.com
◆ **Novotel**: www.novotel.com

FARMS

Farm stays are popular with families especially in Bavaria and in the wine-growing regions. For details, check www.landtourismus.de or www.landsichten.de.

HISTORIC BUILDINGS

For information about hotels and restaurants in castles and other historic buildings, contact your country's German National Tourist office or try **Histohotels**, ℘030 20 23 90 462, www.histohotels.de.

WHERE TO EAT

Restaurant recommendations are located in the Address Books throughout the *DISCOVERING GERMANY* section of this guide. *For coin ranges and for symbols used in the Address Books, ⌚see the Legend on the cover flap.*

Weisswuerste

© G. Standl/Munich City Tourist Office

Michelin Guide Deutschland

For a more exhaustive list of restaurants, consult the *Michelin Guide Deutschland*.

German Cuisine

German food is more varied and balanced than is generally supposed. Breakfast **(Frühstück)** is usually a generous spread including cold meats, cheese and an assortment of fresh bread and rolls. Lunch **(Mittagessen)** is traditionally a hot meal consisting of soup and a main course revolving around fish or meat. Many modern Germans, though, eat their main meal at dinnertime, preferring a light one at midday. Snack stands are called **Imbisse** and are ubiquitous. Sausages, especially the grilled **Bratwurst** are a staple and often paired with potato salad or sauerkraut. Choices are greater and more international in the big cities, where the Turkish doner kebab is a popular tummy

filler. Many Germans still indulge in an afternoon coffee break in a café. Most offer a large selection of cakes, such as **Schwarzwälder Kirschtorte** (Black Forest gâteau) or **Käsekuchen** (cheesecake) alongside lighter fruit tarts and the famous **strudel** (fruit wrapped in crisp pastry). The evening meal **(Abendessen)** is either a cold supper of meats, cheese and bread or a cooked dinner.

See also Regional Specialities p629.

Practical A–Z

BUSINESS HOURS
BANKS

Banks are open from 8.30am to 4pm Monday to Friday (sometimes to 6pm on Thursday) and are closed on weekends. Branches in rural and suburban areas usually close for lunch between noon and 1pm. Bureaux de change *(Wechselstuben)* tend to keep longer hours.

SHOPPING

German shopkeepers are able to keep any hours they want, but most stick with the traditional pattern of opening around 9am or 10am and closing between 6.30pm and 8pm Monday to Friday and around 2pm or 4pm on Saturday. In major cities, some central supermarkets and shopping centres now stay open until 9pm or 10pm, sometimes daily, sometimes only on Friday and Saturday. Only bakeries and flower shops open for a few hours on normal Sundays.

All stores are allowed to open on up to 10 pre-determined Sundays per year, including throughout December.

Petrol stations and shops at big city train stations are your main options for stocking up on basics after hours.

MUSEUMS

Museums are usually closed on Mondays. Art museums often have a late-night opening one evening per week. Ticket offices usually close between 30 minutes and one hour before closing time.

COMMUNICATIONS

The international dialling code for Germany is **49**, so from the UK, for example, you would dial 00 49 + local dialling code **omitting** the initial 0 + subscriber's number. **International dialling codes from Germany**:

♦ ☏ 00 44 for the UK
♦ ☏ 00 353 for Ireland
♦ ☏ 00 1 for the USA and Canada

- 📞 00 61 for Australia
- 📞 00 27 for South Africa

National directory enquiries:
- 📞 11 833

International directory enquiries:
- 📞 11 834

Public telephones: phonecards *(Telefonkarten)* for the largely card-operated public telephones are sold at post offices and newspaper kiosks. Some phones also take bank cards.

👉 *Note that phone calls from hotel rooms are generally expensive.*

Mobile phones operate on the GSM900/1800 network. If you have an unlocked phone, you can easily obtain a local German number by buying a SIM card at a telecom store or in such supermarkets as Aldi and Lidl. SIMs cost about 15€ and come with pre-paid airtime that can be recharged by buying scratchcards at newsagents or supermarkets. If your phone is not unlocked, you can buy a pre-paid phone for around 30€ at a major electronics stores such as Saturn or Media Markt.

👉 *Please note that it is illegal to use your phone while driving.*

ELECTRICITY
Voltage is 220V and appliances use two-pin plugs. Appliances operating on 110V, such as those from North America, require a transformer. Most electric shavers and laptops run on both 110V and 220V.

EMERGENCIES
Police: 📞 110
Fire brigade: 📞 112
Medical emergencies: 📞 112
Traffic accidents: 📞 110

POST
Yellow is the trademark colour of the Deutsche Post, as the German postal service is called. Most post offices are open Mondays to Fridays from 8am to 6pm and on Saturdays from 8am to noon. Smaller and rural branches may observe a lunch break, while those in city centres may keep slightly longer hours. Postal rates are 0.60€ for standard letters (up to 20g) sent within Germany, 0.75€ for letters sent internationally.

MEDIA
NEWSPAPERS
Regional daily newspapers are widely read in Germany. The conservative *Frankfurter Allgemeine* and Munich's centrist *Süddeutsche Zeitung* enjoy a broad readership throughout Germany. Berlin's most popular daily is the *Tagesspiegel*, but the *Berliner Zeitung* and the *taz* are also popular with readers in the capital. Among the national newspapers, the sensationalist daily *Bild* is the most widely read. *Die Welt* offers better quality news. *Focus* and *Der Spiegel* are respected weekly news magazines, while *Stern* and *Bunte* belong more in the tabloid category.

The main foreign newspapers are available at airports, train stations and many kiosks and newsagents.

TELEVISION
Germany has two national state television channels, **ARD** and **ZDF**. There are also public regional channels such as Cologne's Westdeutscher Rundfunk (WDR) and Munich's Bayerischer Rundfunk (BR) and the Franco-German cultural television channel **Arte**. In addition, many private channels feature a mix of soap operas, sitcoms, game shows and films.

Although most of them target the general public (RTL 2, PRO 7, SAT 1), there are some theme channels, such as the music channel VIVA and the sports channel DSF.

MONEY

The euro has been the unit of currency in Germany since the beginning of 2002. Foreign currency can be exchanged at the airports, in banks, at hotels and at exchange offices such as those operated by Reisebank and usually located in major train stations. To check on the latest currency exchange rates, consult www.xe.com or www.oanda.com.

CREDIT CARDS

Cash is still the dominant method of payment in Germany, especially in rural areas, although credit cards are slowly gaining in popularity. You can usually whip out your plastic at petrol stations, travel agents, international hotels and better restaurants and boutiques, but it is always best to check first. **In the event of loss or theft of your card**, call the following numbers immediately:

- **Visa** ✆(0800) 811 8440,
- **Eurocard-Mastercard** ✆(0800) 819 10 40,
- **American Express** ✆(069) 97 97 20 00.

ATMS

Generally, the easiest and most convenient way to obtain cash is by using your bank card at a local ATM in Germany. Most are linked to such international networks as Cirrus, Maestro and Star. Credit cards may also be used but fees for cash advances can be steep.

PUBLIC HOLIDAYS

1 Jan, **6 Jan** (in Baden-Württemberg, Bavaria and Sachsen-Anhalt only).
Good Friday, **Easter Sunday**, **Easter Monday**, **1 May**, **Ascension**, **Whit Sunday and Monday (Pentecost)**, **Corpus Christi** (in Baden-Württemberg, Bavaria, Hessen, Nordrhein-Westfalen, Rheinland-Pfalz, Saarland, Sachsen, Thüringen and those communities with a predominantly Roman Catholic population only).
15 Aug (in Roman Catholic communities in Saarland and Bavaria only).
3 Oct (Day of German Unity).
31 Oct (Reformation Day, in Brandenburg, Mecklenburg-Vorpommern, Sachsen, Sachsen-Anhalt and Thüringen).
1 Nov (in Baden-Württemberg, Bavaria, Nordrhein-Westfalen, Rheinland-Pfalz and Saarland only).
Buß- und Bettag (Day of Repentance and Prayer, usually **third Wed in Nov**, observed in Sachsen only), **24**, **25**, **26** and **31 Dec**.

DISCOUNTS

Discounts are widely available for seniors, children, families and the disabled, for local attractions, public transport and tours, for example.
Many city and regional tourist offices issue Welcome Cards, which offer discounts or free access to participating local attractions as well as unlimited public transport during the period of their validity. Students should get an International Student Identity Card (ISIC), which is good for a host of discounts, including air fare and travel insurance.

BY TRAIN

See *Getting Around: Tickets and Fares* for information on special ticket offers available through Deutsche Bahn.

BY AIR

For flying between European cities, discount carriers such as EasyJet, Germanwings and Ryanair usually offer the best fares. If you are under 26 or a student, you may qualify for cheaper fares with major carriers. Check with such travel agents as STA Travel or Flight Centre. Children under the age of two usually travel free.

SMOKING

Germany was the last major European country to succumb, but in January 2008 strict anti-smoking laws kicked in even in this final bastion of nicotine. Confusingly, there is no national policy with each of the *Länder* (states) making its own rules. Generally, smoking is no longer allowed in public buildings, hospitals, trains and train stations. It is also not permitted in restaurants, cafés, bars and nightclubs. In some regions, smoking is permitted if an establishment has a separate room designated for smokers or if it's smaller than 75sq m/800sq ft, serves no food and does not allow anyone under 18. Smoking is usually possible at outdoor tables in restaurants and cafés.

TAXES

The national Value Added Tax (*Mehrwertsteuer*) is 19 percent for goods and services and 7 percent for food and books. It is always included in the price.

TIME

German clocks are set to Central European Time, which is Greenwich Mean Time + 1 hour.

WHEN IT IS NOON IN GERMANY, IT IS	
3am	in Los Angeles
6am	in New York
11am	in Dublin
11am	in London
7pm	in Perth
9pm	in Sydney
11pm	in Auckland

In Germany "am" and "pm" are not used but the 24-hour clock is widely applied.

TIPPING

In restaurants, cafés and bars tipping is not compulsory but most people generally add about 10 percent for good service. Don't leave the tip on the table; pay the waiter in person and tell him or her how much you are tipping (for example, if the bill comes to 12.20€ and you are are rounding up to 13€, say to the waiter "13 euros" as you are handing over your cash. Taxi drivers typically receive a 5 percent tip. In better hotels, porters and others assisting with your luggage expect 2€ per bag. Room cleaning staff should be tipped about 1€ or 2€ per person per day. Cleaners at public toilets or in some bars and restaurants get about 0.50€.

CONVERSION TABLES

Weights and Measures

EU	USA	UK	
1 kilogram (kg)	**2.2 pounds (lb)**	**2.2 pounds**	*To convert*
6.35 kilograms	14 pounds	1 stone (st)	*kilograms*
0.45 kilograms	16 ounces (oz)	16 ounces	*to pounds,*
1 metric ton (tn)	**1.1 tons**	**1.1 tons**	*multiply by 2.2*
1 litre (l)	**2.11 pints (pt)**	**1.76 pints**	*To convert litres*
3.79 litres	1 gallon (gal)	0.83 gallon	*to gallons, multiply*
4.55 litres	1.20 gallon	1 gallon	*by 0.26 (US)*
			or 0.22 (UK)
1 hectare (ha)	**2.47 acres**	**2.47 acres**	*To convert*
1 sq kilometre (km²)	**0.38 sq. miles (sq mi)**	**0.38 sq. miles**	*hectares to acres, multiply by 2.4*
1 centimetre (cm)	**0.39 inches (in)**	**0.39 inches**	*To convert metres*
1 metre (m)	**3.28 feet (ft) or 39.37 inches**		*to feet, multiply*
	or 1.09 yards (yd)		*by 3.28; for*
1 kilometre (km)	**0.62 miles (mi)**	**0.62 miles**	*kilometres to miles, multiply by 0.6*

Clothing

Women	EU	USA	UK
	35	4	2½
	36	5	3½
	37	6	4½
Shoes	38	7	5½
	39	8	6½
	40	9	7½
	41	10	8½
	36	6	8
	38	8	10
Dresses	40	10	12
& suits	42	12	14
	44	14	16
	46	16	18
	36	6	30
	38	8	32
Blouses &	40	10	34
sweaters	42	12	36
	44	14	38
	46	16	40

Men	EU	USA	UK
	40	7½	7
	41	8½	8
	42	9½	9
Shoes	43	10½	10
	44	11½	11
	45	12½	12
	46	13½	13
	46	36	36
	48	38	38
Suits	50	40	40
	52	42	42
	54	44	44
	56	46	48
	37	14½	14½
	38	15	15
Shirts	39	15½	15½
	40	15¾	15¾
	41	16	16
	42	16½	16½

Sizes often vary depending on the designer. These equivalents are given for guidance only.

Speed

KPH	10	30	50	70	80	90	100	110	120	130
MPH	6	19	31	43	50	56	62	68	75	81

Temperature

Celsius (°C)	0°	5°	10°	15°	20°	25°	30°	40°	60°	80°	100°
Fahrenheit (°F)	32°	41°	50°	59°	68°	77°	86°	104°	140°	176°	212°

To convert Celsius into Fahrenheit, multiply °C by 9, divide by 5, and add 32.
To convert Fahrenheit into Celsius, subtract 32 from °F, multiply by 5, and divide by 9.
NB: Conversion factors on this page are approximate.

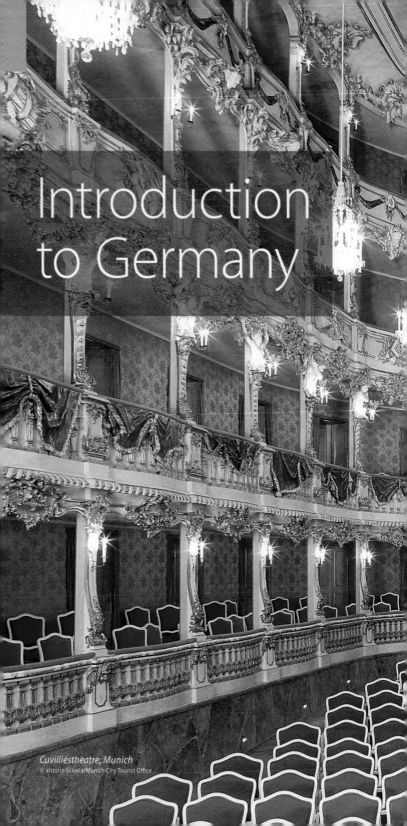

Introduction
to Germany

Cuvilliéstheatre, Munich
© Vittorio Sciosia/Munich City Tourist Office

Features

THE SUNNY
SIDE OF
GERMANY.

BADEN-
WÜRTTEMBERG

WELCOME
TO SUNNY SOUTHWEST GERMANY

With four fabulous seasons, there's always
a right time to visit one of Europe's most
popular holiday destinations. In sunny summer,
explore the romantic Black Forest; in autumn,
watch grapes being picked for award-winning
wines; in winter, shop at Christmas markets
in medieval towns; in spring, photograph
gardens ablaze with flowers and blossom.
And everywhere is so close: tour historic
Heidelberg castle and Stuttgart's glamorous
palace; enjoy Baden-Baden's elegant spas and
casino; watch the sunset on Lake Constance;
ride the rollercoasters at Europa-Park Rust.

We are just a click away: www.tourism-bw.com

THE SUNNY
SIDE OF
GERMANY.

BADEN-
WÜRTTEMBERG

www.tourism-bw.com
info@tourismus-bw.de

Germany Today

A quarter-century after the fall of the Berlin Wall, Germany today is the economic powerhouse of Europe and de facto leader of the European Union. Berlin itself has become a leading avant-garde centre, with art and architecture thriving. Deutschland's citizens are proud of their country's preeminence, welcoming visitors from around the world who come to explore their deep history and modern achievements.

Solar plant in Eberswalde-Finow, Brandenburg © Patrick Pleul/Picture Alliance/Photoshot

A Way of Life

Germany is a highly decentralised federal state whose human, political and administrative facets reflect very individual traits that are rooted in its history. This brief, factual portrait highlights some of the aspects peculiar to the German nation and to life in Germany today.

21C GERMANY

Population

With almost 81 million inhabitants, Germany is the most highly populated country in the European Union and the second-most populous in Europe after Russia. It has been in demographic decline for about 25 years and is experiencing an accelerated ageing of the population (the average age – over 44.3 – is the highest in Europe). By 2030 the population is projected to have dropped to 77 million.

About 7.7 million foreigners live in Germany (more than 9 percent of the population), with the five largest groups being Turks (1.6 million), Poles (610,000), Italians (552,000), Greeks (316,000) and Romanians (267,000).

German society is highly urbanised. The most densely populated areas are Greater Berlin, the Ruhr region, the Frankfurt-am-Main area, Wiesbaden and Mainz, and another region taking in Mannheim and Ludwigshafen.

Lifestyle

Although a thoroughly modern society, many Germans still place a lot of importance on traditions. Having *"Kaffee und Kuchen"* (coffee and cake) on Sunday afternoons is as time-honoured as popping down to a beer garden with friends or screaming your lungs out at football matches. Children and the elderly are well respected, as are dogs and the rights of bicyclists on their dedicated paths. Although the car is a bit of a sacred cow, most Germans use public transport or a bicycle for getting around town. They tend to be culturally curious and regularly patronise museums, theatres, opera, festivals and other such events and institutions. A staggering 70 percent of all Germans older than 14 years are active members of groups, clubs or organisations. Some 36 percent undertake voluntary duties. Even lesser educated or less wealthy individuals tend to be extraordinarily well travelled. German food overall has become lighter and healthier in recent years and many Germans are willing to spend extra for organic products. Recycling is *de rigeur*.

Religion

Germany is predominantly a Christian country, although adherence has dwindled considerably in the past two decades. The main denominations are Roman Catholic (25 million members) and Lutheran (26 million). Both churches levy a church tax, which the state collects, to fund social services. Citizens can opt out of paying this tax. There are also about 4 million Muslims, most of them from among the Turkish immigrant population. The Jewish community has been growing since reunification, replenished mostly by emigrants from the former Soviet Union. It now stands at about 106 000 members in more than 100 congregations.

Sport

Sport is quite popular in Germany. There are around 90 000 sports clubs with 27 million members. In a nation that has hosted the FIFA World Cup twice and won it four times, football is predictably the most popular activity, followed by gymnastics and tennis. Germany has produced such legendary sports figures as Max Schmeling, Michael Schumacher, Boris Becker, Franz Beckenbauer, Dirk Novitzki, Katarina Witt and Steffi Graf.

Fasnacht festival, Black Forest

© Markus Lange/imageBROKER / age fotostock

TRADITIONS AND FESTIVITIES

Germany is a thoroughly modern society but one with strong roots in the past. Some time-honoured festivals have been celebrated for decades or even centuries.

Karneval – Also known as Fasching in Bavaria and Fasnacht in Baden-Württemberg, the pre-Lent season culminates in the week before Ash Wednesday. Street parties and costume parades take over many cities, primarily Düsseldorf, Cologne, Mainz and Munich, as well as the Black Forest villages.

Maifest – Throughout Germany, this end-of-winter celebration on 1 May culminates in dancing and singing around the *Maibaum* (May tree), which is often painted, carved and decorated.

St. Martinstag – This festival, held on 10–11 November, honours a 4C saint known for his humility and generosity with a lantern procession, followed by feasting on stuffed roasted goose.

Bavarian maypole

© ra-photos/iStockphoto.com

Nikolaus – On the eve of 5 December, German children put their shoes outside the door, which St. Nick will fill with sweets and toys by dawn – provided they were well-behaved during the year!

Advent – The four weeks before Christmas are celebrated by counting down the days with an advent calendar, hanging up Christmas decorations and lighting an additional candle every Sunday on the four-candle advent wreath.

Christmas – Celebrations start on Christmas Eve with dinner, presents and a church visit. Christmas Day itself is usually spent with close family; the 26th ("second" Christmas Day) visiting friends and more distant family.

THE WAR ON SMOKING

Change comes slowly in Germany, which in 2008 became one of the last countries in Europe to introduce a smoking ban. Because of the federalised nature of the country it was left to each of the 16 Länder (states) to come up with its own regulations, resulting in confusion. Most states agreed that smoking should be verboten in schools, hospitals, airports, train stations and government buildings. Lighting up in restaurants is also a no-no, but bars, nightclubs and festival tents are a different story. Laws generally allow establishments to build separate, closed-off smoking areas. However, small pub owners, who did not have sufficient space to create such a room, felt discriminated against and brought their case before Germany's highest court. It ruled in their favour: one-room bars or pubs smaller than 75sq m/800sq ft may decide to permit smoking provided they don't serve food and don't admit anyone under 18. Only easy-going Berlin made use of this ruling. Other states, in particular Bavaria, are going the other way. In 2010, the southern state held a referendum in which 61 percent voted in favour of banning smoking in all pubs, restaurants and beer tents. No exceptions, not even at Oktoberfest!

Media

Germany has two public TV consortiums, the Allgemeiner Deutscher Rundfunk (ARD) and the Zweites Deutsches Fernsehen (ZDF). Both are financed largely through public licensing fees. In addition, there are numerous private TV stations, including some specialising in sports or music. The largest-circulation national newspaper is *Bild*, which is known for its sensationalist, gossipy reporting. Well-respected, nationally-read regional papers include Munich-based *Süddeutsche Zeitung* and the *Frankfurter Allgemeine*. *Der Spiegel* and *Focus* are the most widely read weekly news magazines.

Language

The German language has Indo-European origins and is spoken by about 100 million people. Besides "High German" regional dialects are alive and well, especially in Bavaria, Swabia and Hesse. The purest form of German is spoken in the Hannover region in Lower Saxony. *See also Useful Words and Phrases at the back of this guide.*

FOOD AND DRINK

See also PLANNING YOUR TRIP, Where to Stay and Eat, as well as Regional Specialities p629.

Although there is some regional variation, German food is generally rather rich and hearty. Typical dishes pair potatoes with meat (most likely pork, often sausages) and a cooked vegetable (e.g. sauerkraut or red cabbage). A new generation of chefs is modernising traditional menus by using fresh, locally sourced and seasonal ingredients, thus making dishes lighter and healthier. Germany's large immigrant population, especially in the cities, has added pizza, doner kebabs, Thai and Chinese food. Each region has its own specialities, but some dishes are served all over the country, including **Schnitzel** (breaded and pan-fried pork cutlet), **Schweinebraten** (roast pork) **Sauerbraten** (vinegar-marinated braised beef) and **Gulasch** (either in the form of soup or as a stew). Thuringia is the centre for bratwurst, claiming more than 100 varieties.

BEER AND WINE

Germans are justifiably proud of their national beverage, produced by nearly 1 200 breweries throughout the country. Although no longer required by law, most German brewers still adhere to a purity law *(Reinheitsgebot)* decreed in 1516, whereby nothing but barley, hops and plain water may be used in beer (with the addition, today, of yeast). German vineyards cover 102 000ha/252 000 acres, extending from Lake Constance to the Saaletal, and from Trier to Dresden. Growers produce a

THE LÄNDER REGIONS

The Federal Republic comprises 16 *Länder* (states), 11 of which formed the old West Germany and five of which were added in 1990, reconstituted from the 15 districts of the former East German Democratic Republic. Each state organises its constitution within the terms of the Basic Law. The *Länder* have a legislative assembly (**Landtag**) elected by universal suffrage and an executive body consisting of a council of ministers with a President (**Ministerpräsident**). Areas involving the sovereignty of the state, such as foreign affairs, defence or monetary policy, fall under the responsibility of the Federal Government, but the *Länder* possess broad powers; they have exclusive jurisdiction over education and culture, and are actively involved in the areas of justice and the economy.

variety of wines from a wide range of grapes. The most famous German grape is the noble Riesling, which accounts for 22 percent of vineyard area, followed by Müller-Thurgau with 13.1 percent. Wines from the Middle Rhine, Moselle, Saar and Ruwer rivers are aromatic and refreshing, those from the Rheingau delicate and from the Nahe full-bodied and elegant. Also try the potent, dry wines of Franconia and the varied wines of Baden and Württemberg.

Among the **red wines**, choice examples come from Rheinhessen and Württemberg. The Palatinate and the Ahr are known for their well-balanced reds, especially the Spätburgunder, which accounts for 9.5 percent of total output, making it the third-most popular grape varietal in Germany.

Beer garden by the Chinese Tower, Englischer Garten, Munich

© P. Scarlandis/Munich City Tourist Office

ECONOMY

After the Second World War, the economy of West Germany made a spectacular recovery, generally referred to as an **"economic miracle"** *(Wirtschaftswunder)*. The system instituted was the so-called **"social market economy"**, which combined private enterprise with government regulation with the multi-pronged goal of keeping inflation and unemployment in check, setting standards for working conditions, and providing for social welfare.

The **reunification** of the two Germanies in 1990 presented an enormous challenge.

The high cost of the economic integration of the former German Democratic Republic (a total of 2€ trillion) severely impacted the competitiveness of the Federal Republic. To this day, the modernisation of the new *Länder* (states) and social support for employees continues to put a great strain on the federal budget with annual transfers from west to east amounting to about 7.9€ billion in 2012. Unemployment remains high, at 10 percent, compared to 5 percent in the rest of the country.

Today, Germany has the fifth-largest economy in the world based on GDP (2.87€ trillion), after China, the US, Japan and India. Along with the rest of the world, the country was hard hit by the worldwide economic downturn of 2008. Government measures taken to rev up the economic engine included multi-billion euro rescue packages for banks, stimulus packages for business and industry and tax cuts. Although these actions increased the country's budget deficit, they may have had their intended result: in mid-2014 Germany posted a 2.5 percent economic growth rate for the second quarter of the year, its fastest quarterly growth since a brief decline in early 2013.

Industry

Industry remains the cornerstone of Germany's economic strength, representing around one third of Gross Domestic Product (GDP). About 30 major corporations with a global presence (Thyssen-Krupp, Bayer, Hoechst, Siemens, Bosch, BMW, Volkswagen, etc.) are listed on the German share index (DAX).

The true backbone of the economy, though, are the tens of thousands of small and mid-size companies (up to 500 employees) which collectively provide more than 25 million jobs. Key industries are vehicles, mechanical engineering, electrical engineering and chemicals. About 29 million people work in the service sector, especially banking and insurance.

Trade

"Made in Germany" is still considered a seal of quality, and the country is the world's third-largest exporter (mostly cars, machinery, metals). The most important trading partners are France, the Netherlands, the USA and Great Britain. In 2013, Germany's exports totaled 1.2€ trillion.

Of late, demand has been especially great for solar-powered products, where Germany has shown to be especially innovative. In fact, the country is the largest producer of wind turbines and solar power technology.

GOVERNMENT AND ADMINISTRATION

Since 1949, two parties – The centre-right Christian Democratic Union (CDU) with its Bavarian sister party (CSU) and the centre-left Social Democratic Party (SPD) – have dominated political life in the Federal Republic. There are also three minor parties: the liberal Free Democratic Party (FDP); The Left, which is essentially the successor party of the defunct East German Socialist Unity Party, and the environmentalist Alliance '90/The Greens. The federal government usually consists of a coalition between one of the big political parties and one of the smaller ones.

In 1949, the year West Germany was founded, the CDU/CSU joined with the FDP to elect **Adenauer** as chancellor. The party returned to power under the aegis of **Helmut Kohl**, who was elected Chancellor four times (1983, 1987, 1991 and 1994). The SPD came to power for the first time in 1969 led by **Willy Brandt**. In 1974 it allied with the FDP under **Helmut Schmidt**. The SPD also claimed victory in the 1998 elections under the leadership of **Gerhard Schröder** who governed in a coalition with the Alliance'90/The Greens. This marked the first time the environmental party achieved power on national level. The government introduced a variety of social and economic reforms intended to adapt Germany's social market economy to the demands of globalisation. Although the opposition parties made some gains, the Schröder-led coalition government was re-elected in 2002.

Recent Developments

Continued frustration with high unemployment, high taxes and slow economic growth led to an impatience with the SPD/Green coalition and early federal elections in September 2005. When neither SPD and CDU/CSU emerged as a clear winner, the two formed a grand coalition with **Angela Merkel** as Chancellor. Despite hopes that the coalition members would be able to tackle Germany's problems jointly, the liaison ultimately led to stagnation. During the 2009 the CDU/CSU emerged as a strongest party and formed a coalition with the FDP, with Angela Merkel staying on as chancellor and FDP party chief Guido Westerwelle becoming vice-chancellor and foreign minister. In 2013 Merkel won re-election to a third term, this time forming a coalition with the Social Democrats.

A FEDERAL STATE

Germany has a federated governmental structure whose 16 *Länder*, or states, enjoy considerable powers. The **Basic Law** established in 1949 guarantees individual liberties and defines the institutions of a democratic republic. The Federal Parliament is composed of two chambers: the **Bundestag**, a national assembly of approximately 600 members elected by universal suffrage, has legislative powers and chooses the chancellor; and the **Bundesrat**, a federal council with members drawn from the *Länder* governments, which also has some legislative powers, particularly concerning the *Länder*.

The **chancellor** holds executive power and is elected by the Bundestag, to whom he/she is accountable. The chancellor sets the broad lines of government policy, introduces laws (adopted by the Bundestag) and is responsible for their implementation. The role of the federal president (**Bundespräsident**) is essentially representative. He/she concludes foreign treaties, and appoints or removes judges and federal ministers as suggested by the chancellor.

The supreme judicial authority rests with the **Constitutional Court** (Verfassungsgericht), which ensures compliance with the Basic Law, guards constitutional principles and acts as arbitrator in disputes between the Federal Government and the *Länder*.

German History

Germanic peoples have inhabited northern Europe for millennia, but they did not form a nation-state until 1871. After two world wars in the 20C, the country was divided in two in 1945. It did not reunite until 1990, the date on which many would argue Germany finally began to achieve its true national potential.

» Germans and Romans
» The Frankish Empire
» The Holy Roman Empire

» The Late Middle Ages
» The Reformation and the Thirty Years' War
» The Rise of Prussia
» Toward a German National State
» The German Empire
» World War I and the Weimar Republic
» The Nazi dictatorship and World War II
» Germany Postwar-Present
» Reunification

Charlemagne crowned as Emperor on Christmas Day AD 800, in Chroniques de France ou de Saint Denis (14C) ©2008 Hip/Scala, Florence

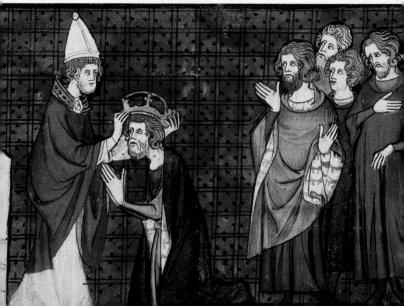

Key Events

Long divided into a number of autonomous states, Germany was slow to achieve unity. This nation of great diversity, which was for a long time marked by feudalism and whose regions still hold considerable powers, is today one of the main spearheads of European unity.

GERMANS AND ROMANS

The earliest evidence of human life on German territory today is the lower jawbone dating back over 500 000 years of the so-called *Homo heidelbergensis*, which was discovered near Heidelberg in 1907. The Middle Paleolithic Age (200 000–40 000 BC) is considered the age of Neanderthal man (*see DÜSSELDORF: Excursions*). The first "modern people", the *Homo sapiens*, who survived on fishing, hunting and gathering, lived during the Late Paleolithic, an epoch of the Stone Age within the last Ice Age. During the Neolithic Era, people began to settle in village-like communities, where they lived for a while, grew plants and began raising animals.

The last prehistoric period, the Iron Age, began around 1 000 BC, following the Bronze Age, thus named because that material was widely used to make implements, weapons and jewellery. The Iron Age is divided up into the La Tène culture and the Hallstatt culture. Economic and political power started becoming more concentrated; evidence from graves suggests a stratified social system.

In the first millennium BC, Germanic tribes began resettling towards Central Europe. The occurrence and extent of this movement was under the auspices of numerous population groups of various origins and cultural levels living in the area between the northern German flatlands and the central mountain ranges. The first written reference to "Germania" is in the works of the Roman author Poseidonius (1C BC). Julius Caesar, too, used this term in his *De Bello Gallico* to describe the non-Gallic regions north of the Alps.

The wars conducted by the Kimbers and the Teutons against the Romans around 100 BC were the first military conflicts between German tribes and the Roman civilisation. The expansion of the western German tribes was stopped by Caesar's conquest of Gaul (58–55 BC). The aims of foreign policy until Emperor Augustus also covered the inclusion of Germania into the Roman Empire all the way to the Elbe, an objective that was never met.

During the 1C AD, the **Limes** was built: A 550km/341.7mi fortified line that sealed the Roman sphere of influence from the Rhine to the Danube. Skirmishes

LA TÈNE CULTURE

The name for this cultural epoch supported by Celtic tribes (5C–1C BC) originated at an excavation site on Switzerland's Neuenburg Lake. Over 2 500 objects were found, including grave furnishings and treasures. The La Tène culture was located primarily in southwestern Germany, along the northern edge of the Alps and in the Main-Moselle area. Fortifications expanded into settlements, the first north of the Alps. The advance of Germanic tribes and the expansion of the Roman Empire brought the La Tène culture to an end.

did break out every now and then, but there were also alliances, trade and cultural exchanges. New towns arose where Roman camps stood and at river crossings (e.g. Cologne, Koblenz, Regensburg).

In the 2C–3C AD, large tribes like the Franks, the Saxons and the Alemanni joined forces. The military kingdoms of the age of mass migration gave way to early medieval states.

AD 9	Three Roman legions under General Varus are annihilated by Germanic troops under prince **Arminius**, resulting in Roman relinquishment of bastions on the Rhine.
314	One year after announcing the Edict of Tolerance, Emperor Constantine establishes the first German bishopric, in Trier.
375	Beginning of the *Völkerwanderung*, the "movement of the peoples": the Huns drive the Goths (eastern Germans) to the west. The former *Imperium Romanum* breaks into partial empires.
800	End of the West Roman Empire brought about by German general Odoaker, who is in turn murdered by the Ostrogoth Theodorich.

THE FRANKISH EMPIRE

The tribal union of the Franks expanded slowly south. Their king, Clovis I, eliminated the remains of the West Roman Empire and adopted Christianity. In the 7C, the Merovingians lost their hegemony to the Carolingians, formerly the highest royal officials under the Merovingians. Since the 8C, the general term *thiutisk* developed from a derivation of the word for "tribe" to describe the peoples speaking Germanic languages. There was still no supra-regional language spoken to the east of the Rhine, the area of the Franks, until the 11C.

In the 10C, the term *Regnum Teutonicorum* appeared for the first time in relation to the Eastern Frankish tribes. During the 11C and 12C it slowly established itself as a term.

751	Pope Zacharias agrees to the deposition of the last of the Merovingian kings, Childeric III, in favour of the palatine Pippin. Three years later the Pope places Rome under the protection of the Frankish kings.

CHARLEMAGNE'S EMPIRE

After being crowned Emperor in St. Peter's Basilica in Rome in 800, Charlemagne followed the lead of the Roman emperors. His empire stretched from Spain to the Elbe, from Rome to the English Channel. Charlemagne's reign introduced the "Carolingian Renaissance" as well as a new administrative structure. The emperor instituted a county constitution, disposing of independent duchies and tribal states. Each administrative district was governed by an officer chosen from the Frankish aristocracy, thus ensuring the coherence of the empire. Vulnerable borders were secured by border marches under authorised margraves. And emissaries with royal powers watched over the imperial administration. The king constantly travelled his empire, visiting the *Pfalzen*, which grew into major economic and cultural centres, and overnighting in Imperial abbeys.

768	Charlemagne becomes ruler. He conquers, among others, the Lombards, divides up Bavaria and defeats the Saxons after a long war.
800	Coronation of Charlemagne in Rome. The emperor legally assumes sovereignty over the former empire.
843	The Treaty of Verdun divides the Carolingian Empire among Charlemagne's grandchildren. The East Frankish Kingdom is given to Ludwig the German. The final division, determined by the treaties of Mersen (870) and Verdun/Ribemont (879–80), would evolve into Germany and France.
911	The East Franks elect the Frankish duke Konrad to become their king, separating themselves from the West Franks.

THE HOLY ROMAN EMPIRE

The Holy Roman Empire consisted of an elective monarchy in which the king was crowned emperor by the pope. From the 11C onwards, the emperor could rely on being king of not only Germany and Italy, but also of Burgundy. An especially "German" Imperial concept gave way to a Roman-universal idea of an emperor, a fact underscored in 1157 by the additional title *sacrum Imperium*.

During the time of the Staufer dynasty, in the mid-13C, the claim to rule in Italy came to an end. In the 15C, the term "Holy Roman Empire of the German Nation" was finally established, implying the politically active community of the German Imperial estates, who acted as a counterweight to the emperor.

Ruling this empire, which during the High Middle Ages stretched from Sicily to the Baltic, was difficult without central administration and technical, financial and military wherewithal. By granting land and privileges (e.g. customs rights), administrative responsibility, security and imperial expansion were domains of the aristocracy.

Beginning in the second half of the 11C, the **Investiture Controversy** pitted the Pope against the Emperor on the issue of the right to invest bishops. This weakened the empire and shook up Christianity. The dispute ended with the Concordat of Worms (1122), declaring that ecclesiastical dignitaries had to be separated from worldly goods. The position of the bishops became similar to that of the princes, since they became vassals of the empire.

THE GOLDEN BULL

Beginning in the 10C, the number of electors for the king began to decline. At the same time the election process became more regulated and formalised. In 1356, the Golden Bull promulgated an Imperial law regulating royal election, defining an institutional framework and limiting the power of the empire. From now on, the king would be elected by three religious electors (the archbishops of Mainz, Cologne and Trier) and four secular ones (the king of Bohemia, the margrave of Brandenburg, the duke of Saxony and the Palatine of the Rhine) and then crowned emperor. The election was set in Frankfurt/Main, and the coronation in Aachen; papal confirmation was no longer necessary. This law, announced by the Luxembourg emperor **Charles IV**, is considered the empire's first constitution and a basis for a federal system of state.

These vassals gradually accumulated more power owing to the heredity laws of the fiefs and regalia. In the long term this weakened the empire, paving the way for the rise of numerous territorial states. The regional princely territorial states replaced the personal union state.

962	In Rome, Otto the Great, having been crowned king in 936, is crowned emperor by the Pope. The Ottonian dynasty rules until the death of Henry II in 1024, and is followed by that of the Salians (Franks).
1073	Pope Gregory VII elected. The reformer disputes the role of secular power in the church. The crux of the conflict was the penitent journey to Canossa (1077) by King Heinrich IV to receive absolution from the Pope, who had excommunicated him.
1152–90	Rule of the Staufer emperor Frederick I Barbarossa, who strengthens Imperial power (*restauratio Imperii*) and captures the duchies of Bavaria and Saxony from the Guelph duke Henry the Lion. He also strives to limit papal power.
1212–50	Frederick II stays in southern Italy and Sicily for much of his reign, holding little interest in the area north of the Alps. Two Imperial edicts (1220–31) confirm the power over the territories of the secular and religious princes.
1254–73	The years between the death of Konrad IV and the election of Rudolf of Habsburg are known as the **Interregnum**. It is a time of lawlessness under "foreign" kings and anti-kings, finally eliminating the empire's power in the High Middle Ages.

THE LATE MIDDLE AGES

After the Interregnum, the power of the Habsburgs grew. Building up and consolidating family power by the 15C though the Luxembourg, Nassau and Wittelsbach families occasionally won the throne. The emperors tried to have a son elected king during their lifetime in order to maintain the ranking of their own dynasties. But during the Renaissance, the Imperial crown surrendered its holiness.

In the Late Middle Ages, the *Hoftage*, or Imperial meetings, became the **Reichstag**, a meeting of 350 secular and religious Imperial estates, foreshadowing a sharp dualism between the emperor and his estates. At the Reichstag in Worms (1495), fundamental reforms created the preconditions for transforming the Reich into a unified legal and pacified territory. The proclamation of the *Ewiger Landfrieden* (eternal peace in the land) prohibited personal feuds, favouring a new legal basis. A permanent Imperial Chamber Court ensured compliance. After a long debate, financial reform was pushed through raising the *Common Penny*, a combination of wealth tax, income tax and poll tax. Later *Reichstage* divided up the empire into administrative units – the *Reichskreise*, or Imperial districts. In 1663, the Permanent Reichstag was set up in Regensburg.

Inspired by the Humanists, the concept of a "German nation" began to arise politically as well as culturally, legitimised by the rediscovery of literary monuments such as "Germania" by Tacitus. Until around 1500, Europeans spoke

THE HANSEATIC LEAGUE

The Hanseatic League existed between the 12C and the 17C. Its basic structure was established by about 1300. Thirty larger and numerous smaller cities joined to safeguard their shipping and trade interests. This union went through its Golden Age in the 14C: over 100 cities, under Lübeck's leadership, formed the most significant economic force in northern Germany. After the Thirty Years' War, the Hanseatic tradition only continued in Hamburg, Lübeck and Bremen.

of the *Deutsche Lande* (German lands); after 1500 the term "Deutschland" in the singular became common.

1273	After a warning from the Pope, electors choose as king Count Rudolf of Habsburg (dynastic power in the Breisgau, Alsace and Aargau).
1346–78	Charles IV of Luxembourg emerges as the most important ruler of the Late Middle Ages.
1386	Founding of the University of Heidelberg, Germany's first.
1414–18	Council of Constance; the largest church meeting of the Middle Ages to date.
1438	After the death of the last Luxembourg emperor, the electors choose the Habsburg duke Albrecht V to become King Albrecht II.
c. 1450	Invention of movable type printing by Johann Gutenberg from Mainz; flourishing and spread of Humanism.
1452	During a military campaign by Frederick III, the last imperial coronation takes place in Rome.
1493	Maximilian I becomes king. As of 1508 he is the "elected Roman Emperor". His successors adopt the Imperial title immediately after the royal coronation in Aachen, avoiding the difficult and dangerous journey to Rome.
1519–56	Emperor Charles V, Maximilian's grandchild, gathers more power during his term than any ruler since the Carolingians.

THE REFORMATION AND THE THIRTY YEARS' WAR

In 1503, **Martin Luther** (1483–1546) entered the Augustinian monastery of Erfurt. A dedicated cleric, he was tormented by the problem of salvation. Appointed Professor of Theology in Wittenberg (1512–17), he found in the Holy Scriptures his answer: "We cannot earn forgiveness for our sins through our deeds, only God's mercy justifies us in our faith in it." Man's salvation, Luther argued, lies entirely within the grace of God. This concept led him to attack the Church's dealing in indulgences. On 31 October 1517, he nailed to the doors of Wittenberg Church his "95 Theses" condemning such practices and reminding the faithful of the importance of Christ's sacrifice and the Grace of God. Luther disagreed with Catholicism's prescribed acts of atonement (confession, monetary contributions) as the only way to achieve salvation. He condemned the priest's role as "mediator" between man and God, advocating instead the "direct line" approach: man and God alone.

PRUSSIAN REFORMS: THE REVOLUTION FROM ABOVE

The reforms already prepared by the General Land Law of 1794 were initially set in motion by Baron von Stein and, after his dismissal, by Baron von Hardenberg. The two men went about installing new structures for government and society virtually by decree and with almost revolutionary energy. Abolition of serfdom by the Edict of 1807 was of particular importance, as was the lifting of guild compulsion and the introduction of a free crafts market. Educational reforms followed, resulting in the founding of the university in Berlin by Wilhelm von Humboldt (1810) and military reform. Other reforms included the emancipation of Jews and the modernisation of the administration.

Luther was denounced in the court of Rome, refused to recant, and in 1520 burned the Papal Bull, threatening him with excommunication. Subsequently he attacked the institutions of the Church. He objected to the primacy of the clergy in spiritual matters, arguing the universal priesthood of Christians conferred by baptism.

Refusing again to recant before the Diet of Worms (1521), where he had been summoned by Charles V, Luther was placed under a ban of the Empire and his works were condemned.

The patronage of Frederick the Wise, Duke of Saxony, enabled the reformer to seek refuge in Wartburg Castle where he translated the Bible from Latin into "everyday" German, making God's Word available to the German-speaking layperson. Indeed, his

©2005 Hip/Scala, Florence

Engraved frontspiece to Luther's Bible (1648)

translation of the Bible is considered the first literary work in modern German. Luther's Bible and 95 Theses were a direct cause of the ensuing split of the Protestants from Roman Catholicism.

The Council of Trent (1545–63) resulted in the renewal of Catholicism and the Counter Reformation, which was resolutely supported by the emperor. The internal struggles of the Protestants and the feud between Rudolf II and his brother Matthias ended the Peace of Augsburg. The Protestant Union led by the Electorate of the Palatinate now faced the Catholic League with the Duchy of Bavaria at its head. The Bohemian Rebellion of 1618 led to the outbreak of the Thirty Years' War, which began as a religious conflict and soon engulfed all of Europe.

The war, which was almost exclusively fought on German territory, devastated the land, caused general havoc, left cities in rubble and ruined economic life in the countryside. By the end of the war, only individual territorial states showed some gain in authority; the empire's significance dwindled.

1530	Invited by Charles V to Augsburg, theologians of the opposing faiths fail to agree. Luther's assistant, Melanchthon, draws up the "Confession of Augsburg", the charter of Protestantism.

THE DEUTSCHER BUND

The Deutscher Bund, or German Confederation, a loose federation with little authority, was founded in 1815. The confederation included 39 politically autonomous states; four free cities; the kings of Holland, Denmark and the Low Countries; and portions of Prussia and Austria. The Bundestag (Parliament) included 11 governmentally-appointed representatives who met in Frankfurt and were led by Austria. Prince Metternich, who came from the Rhineland, played a decisive role in this union after he became Austrian chancellor. In collaboration with Prussia, he mercilessly crushed the libertarian and national movements. The restoration policies of the Bundestag gave rise to a period of extreme calm (Biedermeier period).

1555	The Peace of Augsburg establishes a compromise, and Lutheran Protestantism is recognised as equal to Catholicism. The empire loses its sovereignty over religious matters to the territories.
1618	The Bohemian estates refuse to recognize Archduke Ferdinand, the successor of Emperor Matthias, as the Bohemian king. Instead, they elect the Protestant Elector Frederick V from the Palatinate to be their ruler. After the Defenestration of Prague in May (when the Bohemian king's representatives were thrown out of a window by nobles protesting reduced privileges), the situation intensifies and leads to the Thirty Years' War.
1618–23	The first phase of the war (Bohemian-Palatinate War) is decided by the defeat of Frederick V at the battle of Weißer Berg in 1620 against an army commanded by Tilly.
1625–29	Phase two (the Danish-Dutch War) ends with Denmark's Protestant soldiers defeated by Imperial troops under Wallenstein.
1630–35	Sweden enters the war on the Protestant side (Swedish War). King Gustav Adolph II dies in battle near Lützen.
1635–48	France, under the leadership of Richelieu, participates in the alliance with Bernhard von Weimar (French-Swedish War).
1648	Peace of Westphalia: peace treaty in Münster and Osnabrück after five years of negotiations (◔see MÜNSTER).
1688–97	Palatinate War of Succession. Louis XIV lays claim to the left bank of the Rhine; French troops under Louvois devastate the Palatinate.

THE RISE OF PRUSSIA

In 1415, Burgrave Frederick of Hohenzollern was granted the Electorate of Brandenburg. The Duchy of Prussia, 203 years later, also came under the authority of his dynasty. Frederick William (1640–1688), the Great Elector, turned the small country into the strongest, best-governed northern German state thanks to successful power policies, deprivation of the estates' power,

THE UNIFICATION OF GERMANY
(1866-1871)

0	300 km

The Kingdom of Prussia in 1965
Prussian annexations of 1866
Extent of the German Empire in 1871

K = Kingdom   GD = Grand Duchy
D = Duchy   ● = Free city

a centralised administration and the creation of a standing army. He also expanded the country, adding eastern Pomerania, which he received in the Peace of Westphalia: two peace treaties which ended the Thirty Years' War. After the revocation of the Edict of Nantes in France, thousands of Huguenots fled to Brandenburg and built up the economic basis of Berlin.

His grandson, King Frederick William I continued his efforts by laying the foundations of a Prussian military and official state. Fulfilment of one's duty, industriousness, economy and strict discipline were aspects inspired by the "Soldier King". His son, **Frederick the Great** (1740–1786), took the throne in a country with an exemplary administration, and within a few years it became the second Imperial power. The Silesian War and the Seven Years' War won him Silesia, and the division of Poland extended his power eastwards.

This connoisseur of music and literature, the friend and correspondent of Voltaire, was considered an "enlightened ruler" and had a high reputation among European scholars. The rule of "Old Fritz" left Prussia with a well organised administration and a close relationship between the king and the nobles, all cornerstones of Prussian power.

1701	Elector Frederick III is crowned Frederick I King of Prussia in Königsberg.
1740–48	War of Austrian Succession/Silesian Wars: the legality of the Pragmatic Sanction (1713) pronounced by Charles VI is disputed. The war is triggered by Frederick II's troops marching into Silesia.
1756–63	Prussia joins forces with England against the Emperor during the Seven Years' War. By the end of the war, Prussia is the fifth European power; the system of power will guide Europe until World War I.

TOWARD A GERMAN NATIONAL STATE

Since 1792, war had raged between France and the other powers of Europe. The Peace of Lunéville, signed in 1801, resulted in the loss of German territories on the left bank of the Rhine. The Decision of the Deputation of German Estates (1803) destroyed the political and legal foundations of the old Empire. Bavaria, Prussia, Baden and Württemberg benefited, gaining territory, while the latter two received Elector ranking. Sixteen of the southern and western German states left the Imperial Union and founded the Confederation of the Rhine in 1806 in Paris under the protection of France. At the **Congress of Vienna** (1814–15) leaders discussed the geographical reorganisation, including restoration of the political status quo of 1792, legitimisation of the *Ancien Régime*, and solidarity among the princes in combating revolutionary ideas and movements.

Since the 18C, literature, philosophy, art and music had melded, giving rise to a single German culture that preceded patriotism. The ideals of the French Revolution, the end of the Holy Roman Empire, the experience of French occupation and other reforms led to the growth of a 19C movement towards a free, unified German national state. One important stage on the way to unity was an economic one: the foundation of the German *Zollverein* (Customs Union) at the behest of Prussia.

On 31 March 1848, a pre-Parliament met in Frankfurt and held a National Convention, which opened on 18 May in the Paulskirche in Frankfurt. The aim was to pass a liberal constitution and consideration of the future German state. On the table were the Greater German Solution, with the Habsburg empire under Austrian leadership; and the Smaller German Solution, i.e. without Austria, but with a Hohenzollern emperor at the top. The latter was finally voted in. However, Prussian King Frederick William IV refused the Imperial crown brought to him by a delegate from the Paulskirche Parliament.

Otto von Bismarck, appointed Minister-President of Prussia in 1862, needed only eight years to bring about unification under Prussian rule. With the loyalty of an elite bourgeoisie created by the advances of industry and science, and aided by the neutrality of Napoleon III, he pursued a policy of war aggressively. After joining forces with Austria in defeating Denmark in 1864, Prussia declared war on her German ally and defeated the Imperial troops at the battle of Sadowa, thus ending Austrian-Prussian dualism for good.

A year later, Bismarck created the North German Alliance, including all German states north of the River Main; Hannover, Hessen and Schleswig-Holstein already belonged to Prussia. The Franco-Prussian War of 1870–71 completed the task of unification.

1806	Napoleon marches into Berlin. Emperor Francis II of Austria surrenders the Imperial Crown ending the Holy Roman Empire going back to Charlemagne.
1813	Prussia commands the Coalition in the Wars of Liberation against Napoleon, who is defeated in the Battle of Nations at Leipzig.
1814–15	Congress of Vienna establishes the German Confederation; Holy Alliance between Russia, Prussia and Austria.
1819	The Decisions of Karlsbad include press censorship, prohibitions of fraternities and monitoring of universities.

1833–34	Founding of the German Customs Union *(Zollverein)*, an economic unification of most German states – except Austria – led by Prussia.
1835	First German railway line opens between Nuremberg and Fürth.
1848	Unrest in France in February spreads to Mannheim and then, in March, to all German states. But the "March Revolution" quickly turns into a bourgeois reform movement.

THE GERMAN EMPIRE (1871–1918)

The immediate cause of the Franco-Prussian War of 1870–71 was the claim by the House of Hohenzollern (Leopold von Hohenzollern-Sigmaringen) to the Spanish throne. Bismarck succeeded in kindling national pride on both sides of the border. France then declared war on Prussia.

The southern states united with the states of the North German Union led by Prussia. The German princes all stood against France as they had signed secret alliances with Prussia. After the victory of Sedan (2 September), the southern states opened negotiations with Prussia on the issue of German unification.

The first years following the founding of the German Reich in 1871 were marked by an exceptional economic boom, the **Gründerzeit**, financed in part by the receipt of 5 billion francs in French war reparations. The advantages of the larger boundary-free economic area and efforts to standardise coins, measures and weights combined to create rapid growth in the financial, industrial, construction and traffic sectors.

1871	On 18 January, William I is crowned German Emperor in the Mirror Room of Versailles. Imperial Germany, enlarged by the acquisition of Alsace-Lorraine, remains in theory a federation, but is in fact under Prussian domination. Germany is transformed from an agricultural to an industrial economy.
1888	William II succeeds his father Frederick III's brief reign.
1890	After numerous altercations, the Emperor forces Bismarck's resignation. The Emperor's unabashed expansionary policies and dangerous foreign policy provokes the enmity of England, Russia and France.

WORLD WAR I AND THE WEIMAR REPUBLIC

The assassination of the Austrian Archduke Franz Ferdinand and his wife at Sarajevo on 28 June 1914 unleashed an intense international reaction. Austria-Hungary's declaration of war against Serbia mobilised the great powers of Europe. Germany launched into wars on two fronts: German troops moved into France, halting only once they reached the River Marne; in the east, German troops invaded large sections of Russian territory.

1914	Germany declares war on France and Russia on 3 August.
1917	The armistice agreed with Russia is shattered by revolution. The USA enters the war after Germany declares indiscriminate submarine warfare.
1918	On 28–29 October, the sailors of the German naval fleet at Wilhelmshaven raise up in mutiny.

Revolution erupts in Germany, with workers' and soldiers' councils springing up throughout the land. The revolution is suppressed by the provisional government under Friedrich Ebert with the support of military supreme command. On 9 November, William II abdicates and Philipp Scheidemann proclaims the German Republic in Berlin. Two days later, Matthias Erzberger signs the armistice at Compiègne.

After the November revolution, which dwindled in early 1919 due to the unrest caused by the Spartacists, the model of a liberal democratic state with a strong president was established. On 11 August 1919, Germany adopted a Republican Constitution in Weimar, where the National Convention was meeting. This "republic without republicans" shouldered the burden of the Treaty of Versailles, which took effect in 1920: acceptance of responsibility for the war, diminution of national territory (including important agricultural and industrial areas), loss of colonies, demilitarisation and high reparations.

The only truly republican parties accepting the constitution, the SPD (Social Democrats), the Centre Party and the DDP (German Democratic Party) had a parliamentary majority after 1920. The Weimar Republic had 16 government changes, an average of one every eight-and-a-half months. Galloping inflation erupted, brought about by economic crisis, difficulties in relaunching the industrial sector and by high government debt: the bourgeoisie was ruined, and all financial assets except real estate were worthless.

Germany experienced an economic upswing and relative tranquillity from 1924 to 1929 in spite of major economic burdens and high unemployment. The Dawes Plan can be credited with those successes; it managed German reparations, ended the French occupation of the Ruhr and committed to capital investment. Germany was even accepted into the League of Nations (1926) during the incumbency of Chancellor and Foreign Minister Gustav Stresemann. A year earlier in Locarno, Germany and France signed a pact pledging not to use violent means to revise borders – a corresponding agreement could not be signed for the eastern borders.

However, the world economic crisis hit the Weimar Republic in 1929. High foreign debt, sharp export declines, inflation and dramatic unemployment all led to the rise of radical political parties, especially the German National Socialist Worker's Party, after 1930. They presented a theory that solving social problems would require a people's community, or *Volksgemeinschaft*, based on race.

Nazi storm-troops and Communist groups increasingly fought in the street. Social elites and the business community saw in **Adolf Hitler** a bulwark against Communism: on 30 January 1933, Hitler was named Chancellor of the Reich by President Von Hindenburg; it was the end of the Weimar Republic.

1919	The National Convention meets in Weimar; Friedrich Ebert (SPD) is named its first president (11 February); Versailles Peace Treaty is signed (28 June).
1923	Occupation of the Ruhr region on 11 January by France, because of Germany's failure to make reparation payments. The NSDAP (the National Socialist German Workers' Party) attempts a coup in Munich on 8–9 November led by Adolf Hitler, who had joined the party in 1919. The coup is foiled, Hitler is jailed but released in 1924.

Dresden in ruins, 1945

©UPPA/Photoshot

1925	After the death of Friedrich Ebert, former Field Marshall General Paul von Hindenburg is elected President of the Republic.
1930	An electoral defeat in the Reichstag (Parliament) ushers in several presidial cabinets (Brüning, Von Papen, Von Schleicher), i.e. governments without parliamentary majorities.
1932	At the Reichstag elections in July, the NSDAP assumes leadership with almost 38 percent of the votes. Together with the Communists, the Nazis have an absolute majority, which lets the radical parties block all other parliamentary minorities.

THE NAZI DICTATORSHIP AND WORLD WAR II

No sooner had the NSDAP taken power under Hitler than it began to organise a totalitarian dictatorship and eliminate all democratic rules. In a climate of propaganda, intimidation and terror on the part of the SA, SS and Gestapo, all parties, associations and social organisations were liquidated or dissolved, with the exception of the churches. The NSDAP was declared the sole legal party. Opponents were thrown into concentration camps and murdered. Their power and societal control allowed the party to penetrate every level of state government. Competing authorities and rivalries quietly co-existed, but art and literature were subjected to censorship, forcing numerous artists into exile.

The Nuremberg Laws promulgated at the Reich party rally (September 1935) codified Jewish persecution on racist grounds; prohibitions, loss of civil rights and mass arrests were the instruments of the anti-Semitic ideology. As early as 1 April 1933, the NSDAP had ordered a "boycott of the Jews", initiating the gradual exclusion of Germany's 500 000 Jews from public life. On the night of 9–10 November 1938, the Nazis organised a pogrom *(Reichskristallnacht)* during which synagogues, Jewish homes and shops were damaged or destroyed.

The improved worldwide economic situation helped reduce unemployment as did a program of public works (autobahns, drainage schemes), a policy of rearmament and the recruitment of youth into para-governmental organisations. The National Socialist Reich stood at the zenith of its power: materially speaking and otherwise, many Germans had profited up until that point.

The assault on Poland on 1 September 1939, launched **World War II**. German preparations for an annihilation war had been underway since 1936 in the hopes of eliminating other peoples and creating a European area dominated by Aryan Eurasians. But the war reached German civilians as soon as the British and the Americans began dropping explosive and incendiary bombs on war-related and residential targets. By the end of the war, Germany lay in ruins, the bulk of the inhabitants suffered from under-nourishment and millions had been driven out of the eastern regions. With the liberation of the concentration camps, the world discovered with what cruelty and meticulousness the Nazis had carried out their policy of genocide against the Jews and other groups.

GERMANY FROM POSTWAR 1945 TO THE PRESENT

1945	Germany and Berlin are divided into four zones of occupation. According to the agreement, American and British forces pull out of Saxony, Thuringia and Mecklenburg and redeploy in the western sector of Berlin. At the Potsdam Conference (&see POTSDAM) the victorious powers decide to demilitarise and democratise Germany and administer it jointly.
1946	Amalgamation of the British and American zones.
1948	End of the Four-Power administration of Germany after the Soviet delegate leaves the Allied Control Council (20 March). Soviet blockade of the western sectors of Berlin, the city is supplied by the airlift.
1949	Creation (23 May) of the Federal Republic in the three western zones. The Soviet zone becomes (7 October) the German Democratic Republic.
	Under Konrad Adenauer, chancellor until 1963, and Ludwig Erhard, minister of economic affairs, the Federal Republic enjoys a spectacular economic rebirth and re-establishes normal international relations.
1952	Soviet leadership offers to create a single, neutral, democratic Germany, a reunification initiative which fails.
1961	Construction of the "Berlin Wall" begins (12–13 August).
1972	Signature of a treaty between the two Germanies (East and West), a milestone in Chancellor Willy Brandt's policy of openness towards the East (Ostpolitik).

REUNIFICATION: THE FALL OF THE BERLIN WALL

1989	Citizens of East Germany occupy West German embassies in Prague, Budapest and Warsaw with the aim of travelling to West Germany. The opening of the border between Austria and Hungary launches an East German mass migration. On 4 November the largest demonstration ever brings together

GERMANY IN THE EU

The European Union is the result of a decades-long process of economic and political integration. It began in the 1950s with the goal of putting an end to centuries of bloody wars pitting neighbouring nations against each other and culminating in World War II. Germany was one of the six founding countries, along with Italy, France, Belgium, Holland and Luxembourg.

The EU currently has 28 members, 24 of which share a common currency, the euro. Germany, which held the EU Council Presidency in the first half of 2007, is a strong supporter of the 2007 Treaty of Lisbon that promotes collaboration among EU members on global challenges such as climate change, security and sustainable development.

	over 1 million people in East Berlin. On the night of 9–10 November, the internal German border is opened, the Wall is breached.
1990	Treaty of reunification drawn up; on 3 October the German Democratic Republic (DDR) joins the Federal Republic of Germany (BRD) according to Article 23 of the Basic Law. On 2 December, the first joint German parliamentary elections take place.
2005	Angela Merkel is elected German Chancellor. Bavaria-born Cardinal Joseph Ratzinger is elected Pope Benedikt XVI.
2009	Federal elections result in a coalition government between the centre-right CDU and the liberal FDP. Angela Merkel stays on as Chancellor.
2014	The German team wins the World Cup for the fourth time, joining Brazil as the only two nations to do so.

Keen to achieve rapid reunification, on 28 November 1989, West German Chancellor **Helmut Kohl** put forward a 10-point plan providing for the initial constitution of a confederation. On 3 October 1990 (now one of Germany's national holidays), the parliament sitting in the Reichstag in Berlin ratified the treaty of reunification. Helmut Kohl won the elections in December 1990 and, in 1991, the Bundestag chose Berlin as capital of the reunified country. With the withdrawal of the last Allied troops in 1994, Germany became a sovereign state. It set its sights on the construction of a unified Europe. After the Federal President's move to Berlin, Parliament followed suit in 1999.

Reunification caused considerable economic and social problems, problems that eventually led to the loss of Helmut Kohl's CDU-CSU party in the 1998 elections and the ascendancy of Social Democrat **Gerhard Schröder** in coalition with the Green Party. Germany becomes a leading political and economic force within the European Union, and its military played a peace-keeping role in war-torn Kosovo (1999) and also sent troops to Afghanistan.

But while the country has re-emerged as a positive force internationally, economic stresses continued to take their toll, resulting in Schröder's ousting in the 2005 federal elections. With neither of the big parties able to reach a majority, the two formed a rare Grand Coalition, with the role of Chancellor going to **Angela Merkel**. She became the country's first female chancellor; the first former citizen of East Germany to head a reunified German government; and was the youngest person to be chancellor since World War II. In 2013 she won re-election again.

German Art and Culture

German contributions to world culture range from Beethoven, one of the greatest composers, to Kraftwerk, inventors of industrial rock music; from Friedrich Schiller, author of the words of "Ode to Joy," to Gunter Grass, 1991 Nobel Prize winner; from portraitist Lucas Cranach to Expressionists such as Max Beckmann.

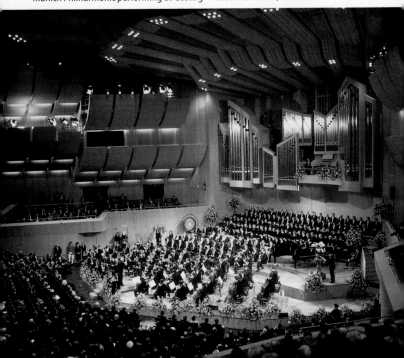

Munich Philharmonic performing at Gasteig © Robert Hertz/Munich City Tourist Office

Architecture

Germany's geographical location and history have left it open to the influence of artistic currents from the rest of Europe – mainly French in the Gothic period and Italian in the Renaissance period. Each style has been interpreted and adapted according to regional tastes. This inventiveness has allowed Germany to develop an originality that is reflected in the sumptuous decoration of the Baroque abbeys in Bavaria and in the Expressionism of the inter-war years.

ROMANESQUE

Carolingian Architecture (9C and early 10C)

Under the impetus of the emperor and the great prelates, a large number of religious buildings were built in Germany on a basilical or central plan (Palatine Chapel at Aachen), both inherited from Antiquity. Carolingian architecture is marked by the building of churches with two chancels: at the west end, a particular form emerged, the **Westwerk**, a tall square structure attached to the nave and often flanked by two towers, like at Corvey, for instance. The Westwerk constitutes almost a church in itself, where the emperor may have worshipped and where a special liturgy developed. It had a long-lasting effect on German Romanesque architecture.

Ottonian Architecture (10C and early 11C)

The restoration of Imperial power by Otto I in 962 was accompanied by a revival of religious architecture in Saxony and in the regions of the Meuse and Lower Rhine. The huge churches of this period, characterised by deeply projecting transepts and wide aisles, feature wooden roofs that were usually painted. The alternation of piers and columns broke up the uniformity of the central portion, and east and west choirs were linked by the nave, with a skilful use of proportion giving a harmonious effect. The churches of St. Michaelis at Hildesheim and St. Cyriacus at Gernrode date back to this period.

Rhineland Romanesque Style

At Cologne and in the surrounding countryside, several churches feature a distinctive ground plan with a triple apse designed in the form of a cloverleaf, a style dating back to the 11C. A fine example can be seen at the church of St. Maria im Kapitol in Cologne. These trefoil extensions are adorned on the outside with blind arcades and a "dwarf gallery" (Zwerggalerie) – a motif of Lombard origin.

In the Middle Rhine region, the style achieves its full splendour in the majestic "Imperial" cathedrals of Speyer (the first church to be entirely vaulted), Mainz and Worms. Typical of these cathedrals are floor plans with a double chancel and no ambulatory, but sometimes a double transept. The exterior features numerous towers, blind arcades and Lombard bands. A characteristic of these Rhineland towers is a pointed roof in the form of a bishop's mitre, the base decorated with a lozenge pattern.

The churches of Limburg and Andernach and the cathedral at Naumburg, which were built early in the 13C, mark the transition between two periods. They are built in a style which combines Romanesque aesthetics and Gothic structures, with pointed rib vaulting and triforia.

GOTHIC
The gradual emergence of the Gothic style (13C)

The French style of Gothic architecture, which attempted to free itself of Romanesque austerity, did not flourish in Germany until the mid-13C. Architecture then reached new heights of refinement, producing such masterpieces as the cathedral in Cologne with its vast interior, two tall slender towers framing the façade in the French style and its soaring pointed vaulting. Also inspired by the French Gothic style are the cathedrals of Regensburg, Freiburg im Breisgau, Magdeburg and Halberstadt. A further manifestation of the predominance of French architecture can be seen in the establishment of Cistercian monasteries between 1150 and 1250. Their churches, usually without towers or belfries and often later modified in the Baroque manner, were habitually designed with squared-off chancels flanked by rectangular chapels. The abbey of Maulbronn is one of very few Cistercian complexes preserved almost in its entirety still extant in Europe.

The originality of German architecture

The German imprint first emerged in the use of brick. In the north of the country the most imposing edifices were brick, complete with buttresses and flying buttresses. Typical of this brick Gothic style (known in German as *Backsteingotik*) are the Nikolaikirche at Stralsund, the Marienkirche in Lübeck, the town halls of those two cities, Schwerin Cathedral and the abbey church at Bad Doberan. Also unique to Gothic German architecture is the adoption of a new layout inspired by Cistercian architecture and manifested in the **hall-churches** *(Hallenkirche)*. In these buildings, the aisles are now the same height as the nave, which therefore has no clerestory windows, and are separated from it only by tall columns. In the Elisabethkirche in Marburg, the three aisles are separated by thin supports, giving an impression of space and homogeneity.

Late Gothic Architecture

The lengthy Late Gothic period (14C, 15C and 16C) witnessed the widespread construction of hall-churches, including Freiburg Cathedral, the Frauenkirche in Munich and the Georgskirche, Dinkelsbühl. The vaulting features purely decorative ribs forming networks in the shape of stars or flowers in stark contrast to the austerity of the walls. St. Annenkirche at Annaberg-Buchholz epitomises this artistic virtuosity, free of all constraints.

Secular Architecture in the Late Middle Ages – Commercial prosperity among merchants and skilled craftsmen in the 14C and 15C led to the construction in town centres of impressive town halls and beautiful gabled and half-timbered private houses, frequently adorned with painting and sculpture. Examples of such architecture are still to be seen in the old town centres of Regensburg, Rothenburg ob der Tauber, Goslar and Tübingen.

THE RENAISSANCE

The Renaissance (1520–1620) is no more than a minor episode in the history of German architecture. Long held at bay by the persistence of the Gothic style, it was finally eclipsed by the troubles of the Reformation. Renaissance-style buildings are therefore rare in German towns. Augsburg is the lone exception. Its beautiful mansions lining Maximilianstraße and its town hall were designed by **Elias Holl** (1573–1646), Germany's most important Renaissance builder.

Southern Germany shows a marked Italian influence: elegant Florentine arcading was used by Jakob Fugger the Rich as decoration for his funerary chapel at Augsburg (1518); the Jesuits, building the Michaelskirche in Munich (1589), were clearly inspired by their own Sanctuary of Jesus (Gesù) in Rome; and in Cologne, the town hall with its two-tier portico reflects Venetian influence.

Northern Germany, on the other hand, was influenced by Flemish and Dutch design. In the rich merchants' quarters, many-storeyed gables, such as those of the Gewandhaus in Brunswick, boast rich ornamentation in the form of obelisks, scrollwork, statues, pilasters, etc. The castles at Güstrow and Heidelberg and the old town of Görlitz are important examples of Renaissance architecture, while the buildings of Wolfenbüttel, Celle, Bückeburg and Hameln are steeped in the particular charm of the so-called "Weser Renaissance" (&see HAMELN).

BAROQUE

After the disruption of the Thirty Years' War (1618–48), the ensuing revival of artistic activity provided an opportunity for the principalities to introduce Baroque architecture by welcoming French and Italian architects. Characterised by an irregularity of contour and a multiplicity of form, the Baroque style seeks, above all, the effect of movement and contrast. Taken to its extreme, it was soon saturated by Rococo decoration, which originated in the French *Rocaille* style; this style was originally secular and courtly but subsequently used in religious buildings.

From the mid-17C, Baroque influence was felt in southern Germany, encouraged by the Counter-Reformation's exaltation of dogmatic belief in Transubstantiation, the cult of the Virgin Mary and the saints, and in general all manifestations of popular piety. The aim was to achieve an emotional response from the spectator. This exuberance did not spread to Protestant Northern Germany.

The Masters of German and Danubian Baroque

There were exceptionally talented individuals in Bavaria who displayed equal skill across a variety of techniques, and who tended to prefer subtle ground plans, such as a round or elliptical focal shape. **Johann Michael Fischer** (Dießen, Zwiefalten and Ottobeuren), the **Asam brothers** (Weltenburg and the Asamkirche in Munich) and **Dominikus Zimmermann** (1685–1766, Steinhausen and Wies) were the virtuosi of this Bavarian School; their vibrant

creations are covered by a profusion of Rococo decoration.

The Baroque movement in Franconia, patronised by the prince-bishops of the Schönborn family, who owned residences in Mainz, Würzburg, Speyer and Bamberg, was closely linked with the spread of similar ideas in Bohemia. The Dientzenhofer brothers decorated the palaces in Prague as well as the one in Bamberg. Perhaps the greatest of all Baroque architects was **Balthasar Neumann** (1687–1753), who worked for the same prelates, and whose breadth of cultural knowledge and creativity, enriched by his contact with French, Viennese and Italian masters, far surpassed that of his contemporaries. One of his finest creations was the Vierzehnheiligen Church near Bamberg, where he managed to combine the basilical plan with the ideal of the central plan. In Saxony, the Zwinger Palace in Dresden—joint masterpiece of the architect **Matthäus Daniel Pöppelmann** (1662–1736) and the sculptor Permoser – is a consummate example of German Baroque with Italian roots. The refinement of the Rococo décor in Schloss Sanssouci at Potsdam is even more astonishing given the reputed Prussian tendency towards austerity, but is explained by the periods of study undertaken in France and Italy by **Georg Wenzeslaus von Knobelsdorff** (1699–1753), official architect and friend of Frederick the Great.

Churches

A sinuous movement, generally convex in line, animates the façades, while the superposition of two pediments, different in design, adds vitality to the whole. They are additionally adorned with twin domed towers. Inside, huge galleries stand above the lateral chapels, at the height of pilaster capitals with jutting abaci. Chapels and galleries stop at the level of the transept, giving it a much greater depth. Clerestory windows at gallery level allow plenty of light to enter. Bohemian and Franconian Baroque is typified by **complex vaulting**, round or oval bays being covered by complicated structures in which the transverse arches bow out in horseshoe shape, only to meet in their keystones.

Illusion is the keyword as regards the often **Rococo** decoration, using the effects of the white stucco, coloured marble and gilding. The numerous paintings and sculptures enhance this celebration of the sacred.

The monumental altarpiece or reredos

Reminiscent of a triumphal arch, in carved wood or stucco, the reredos became the focal point of the church, framing a large painting and/or statuary (Ottobeuren Abbey Church). Columns twisted into spiral form accentuate the sense of movement which characterises Baroque art, and back lighting from a hidden source, with its striking contrasts of brightness and shadow, is equally typical of the style.

Palaces

The one-story construction of these country residences was often lent additional importance by being built on a raised foundation. The focal point was a semi-circular central bloc with the curved façade facing the garden.

Monumental stairways with several flights and considerable theatrical effect are often the centrepieces of the larger German castles and palaces built in the 18C. The staircase, embellished with arcaded galleries and a painted ceiling, leads to the first floor state room which rises majestically to a height of two storeys.

Such elaborate arrangements characterise many of the great abbeys of this period, often complemented by that other ceremonial room, the library.

FROM NEOCLASSICISM TO NEO-GOTHIC

The ideal of an original austerity

From 1750 on, Winckelmann's work on the art of Antiquity, and the excavations taking place at Pompeii, threw a new light on Greco-Roman architecture.

At the same time, the example of Versailles inspired in Germany a new style of court life, particularly in the Rhineland and the Berlin of Frederick II.

Many French architects were employed by the Electors of the Palatinate, of Mainz, of Trier and of Cologne; mainly, they produced plans for country mansions with names such as Monrepos ("my rest") or Solitude. Other German architects, such as **Carl Gotthard Langhans** (1732–1808), were instrumental in the transition from the Baroque to the Neoclassical style (Brandenburg Gate and the Charlottenburg Theatre in Berlin).

Features such as unadorned pediments, balustrades at the base of the roofs and columned porticoes at the main entrance all indicate a desire for unobtrusive elegance. A new fashion arose, in which architects favoured the Doric style coupled with a preference for the colossal – pilasters and columns of a single "order" no longer stood one-storey high but always two. The interior decoration, carried out with a lighter touch, confined itself to cornucopias of flowers mingled with Rococo motifs that were now a little more discreet (garlands, urns, vases and friezes of pearls).

Architecture was now responding to a demand for rationality that had emerged in reaction to the Late Baroque and Rococo styles.

Karl-Friedrich Schinkel (1781–1841)

Appointed state architect by Frederick William III in 1815, he designed many buildings, including the Neue Wache, Altes Museum and Schauspielhaus in Berlin. In a refined approach using elements inspired by Antiquity, this great exponent of Romantic Classicism constantly sought to blend his constructions in with their surroundings. The grandiose style of his buildings with their long Neoclassical colonnades, the dramatic contrasts of light and the use of Gothic elements are typical of the Romantic trend.

The 19C and the Neo-Gothic

19C architecture was characterised by a great diversity of styles. By 1830, the Neoclassical movement had been superseded, except in Munich, by a renewed interest in the Gothic, emblematic for the Romantics of "the old Germany".

At the same time, the **Biedermeier** style – lightweight, cushioned furniture with flowing lines, glass-fronted cabinets for the display of knick-knacks – corresponding perhaps with the later Edwardian style in England, was popular in middle-class homes between 1815 and 1848.

1850 marks the beginning of the **Founders' Period** *(Gründerzeitstil)* with E Ludwig and A Koch pursuing an up-to-date style. But the wealthy industrialists fell for pretentious medieval or Renaissance reproductions, also to be found in public buildings such as the Reichstag in Berlin.

20C Movements

In the late 19C, artists began exploring new avenues in a desire to move away from past styles and into the modern age. **Art Nouveau** or **Jugendstil**, a European movement, became the vogue in Germany. The architects' idea was to create a complete work of art accessible to all, combining structure, decoration and furniture.

This ideal, based on co-operation with industry, its methods of production and the use of its newest building materials (glass, iron, cement), resulted in the fundamental concept of an industrial aesthetic, brought to the fore by such pioneers as Peter Behrens, **Ludwig Mies van der Rohe** and **Walter Gropius**.

This style flourished mainly in Munich, Berlin and Darmstadt (with the Mathildenhöhe artists' colony).

The artists' commitment, expressed within the Secessions (Munich 1892, Berlin 1899), was coupled with a political demand for independence.

The Bauhaus and Beyond

In 1919, Walter Gropius founded the **Bauhaus** (Weimar: 1919–25, Dessau: 1926–32), a school of architecture and applied arts that radicalised the movement for modernisation, displaying an even greater interest in industrial production. The quest for unity between art and technique was a fundamental element *(see DESSAU and WEIMAR)*.

The movement instigated modern reflections on architecture and lent its vocabulary to modern design. The Nazis closed the Bauhaus in 1933 and adopted a pompous and monumental style of architecture intended to reflect their power.

At the end of the war, new concepts, characterised the construction of municipal and cultural enterprises such as Hans Scharoun's Philharmonie in Berlin and the Staatsgalerie in Stuttgart by British architect Sir James Stirling – buildings of an architectural audacity only made possible by the development of entirely new materials and construction techniques.

Richard Meier's dramatic but initially controversial new town hall for the city of Ulm in 1993 introduced the use of white stone, stucco and concrete in curving forms to the cityscape.

21C Expressions

These days, architectural innovation is especially prevalent in Berlin where the world's leading architects – including Daniel Libeskind, Lord Norman Foster and Helmut Jahn – have created such showcases of the avant-garde as the Potdamer Platz quarter or the Jewish Museum. Koblenz boasts the stunning new Forum Confluentes (2013), home to a shopping centre, a museum and other institutions, a tourist information centre, cafés and restaurants.

Cutting-edge buildings can also be seen in such places as Düsseldorf's Medienhafen (Frank Gehry, Renzo Piano) or in Munich, where the new stadium, the BMW World and the Museum Brandhorst made a recent splash.

RELIGIOUS ARCHITECTURE

Plan of a church

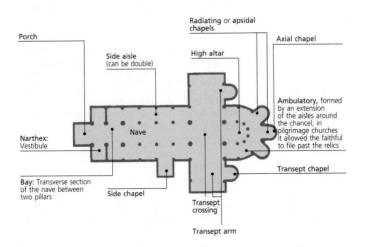

Cross section of a church

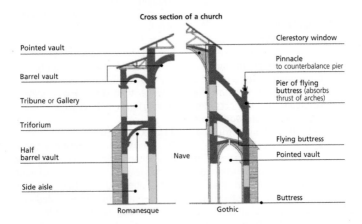

Hall Church

Unlike a basilica, a hall church has aisles the same height as the central nave and covered with one roof their windows let light inside the edifice.

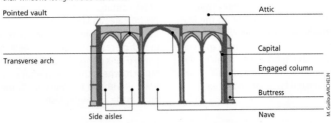

M. Guilbot/MICHELIN

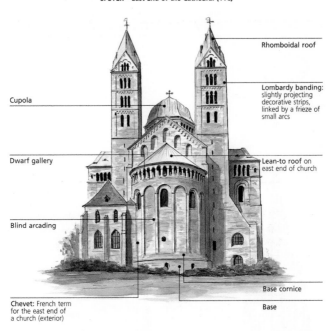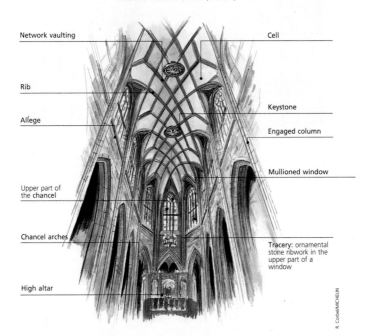

ARCHITECTURE

SPEYER – East End of the Cathedral (11C)

Rhomboidal roof

Lombardy banding: slightly projecting decorative strips, linked by a frieze of small arcs

Cupola

Dwarf gallery

Lean-to roof on east end of church

Blind arcading

Base cornice

Chevet: French term for the east end of a church (exterior)

Base

FREIBURG – Cathedral Altar (14C-16C)

Network vaulting

Cell

Rib

Keystone

Allège

Engaged column

Mullioned window

Upper part of the chancel

Chancel arches

Tracery: ornamental stone ribwork in the upper part of a window

High altar

R. Corbel/MICHELIN

89

COLOGNE CATHEDRAL (1248 to 1880), South façade

The construction of the cathedral began in 1248 and took more than 600 years to complete. It was the first Gothic church in the Rhineland and the original design was based on those in Paris, Amiens and Reims. The twin-towered western façade marks the peak of achievement in the style known as Flamboyant Gothic. Stepped windows, embellished gables, slender buttresses, burst upwards, ever upwards, slimly in line with the tapering spires that reach a height of 157m/515ft.

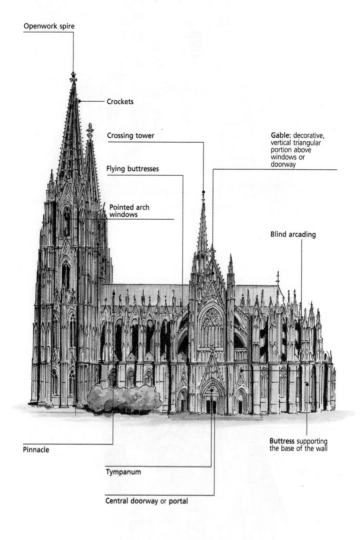

Openwork spire

Crockets

Crossing tower

Gable: decorative, vertical triangular portion above windows or doorway

Flying buttresses

Pointed arch windows

Blind arcading

Pinnacle

Buttress supporting the base of the wall

Tympanum

Central doorway or portal

R. Corbel/MICHELIN

Schloß BRUCHSAL – Garden façade (18C)

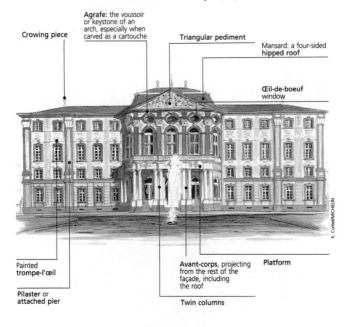

Crowing piece

Agrafe: the voussoir or keystone of an arch, especially when carved as a cartouche

Triangular pediment

Mansard: a four-sided hipped roof

Œil-de-boeuf window

Painted trompe-l'œil

Pilaster or attached pier

Avant-corps, projecting from the rest of the façade, including the roof

Platform

Twin columns

R. Corbel/MICHELIN

POTSDAM – Sanssouci Palace and Park
(Georg Wenzelaus von Knobelsdorff and Friedrich II, 1745-47)

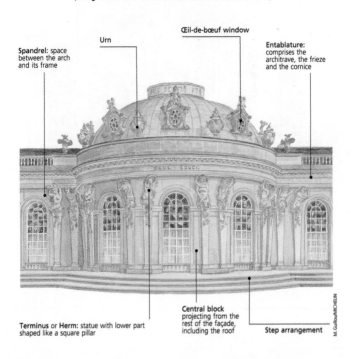

Spandrel: space between the arch and its frame

Urn

Œil-de-bœuf window

Entablature: comprises the architrave, the frieze and the cornice

Terminus or Herm: statue with lower part shaped like a square pillar

Central block projecting from the rest of the façade, including the roof

Step arrangement

M. Guillou/MICHELIN

OTTOBEUREN Abbey Church (18C)

Ottobeuren is characteristic of other Bavarian churches with its dazzling ornamentation and plays of light and symmetry.

Painted vaulting

Spandrel: triangular space between the curve of an arch and the frame in which it is set

Stuccowork

Cornice with projecting ornamental motifs

Retable or **altarpiece**

Tabernacle

Pulpit (or ambo): elevated stand from which sermons were preached

Sounding board

R. Corbel/MICHELIN

"Uncle Tom's Cabin" estate
(Bruno Taut, Hugo Häring, Otto Rudolf Salvisberg, 1926-32)

Designed to house 15 000 people, this estate built under the supervision of Martin Wagner, does not convey an impression of monotony. There is a U-Bahn Station in its centre as well as a shopping centre and a cinema.

Terraced roof

All the buildings are of a moderate size

The simplicity of the façades painted with bright colours, hence the nickname of "parrot estate", is due to a rational building plan and the use of standard, relatively cheap, materials.

The natural surroundings are in keeping with the concept of **garden cities** at the beginning of the century.

Individual houses have re-entrant angles and tall windows characteristic of the style of Salvisberg who designed the buildings along Riemeisterstraße.

Philharmonie (Hans Scharoun, 1960-63) and Chamber Music Hall
(Edgar Wisniewski, from a drawing by Scharoun, 1984-88)

In 1957, during a congress, H Scharoun expressed his wish to build "an adequately shaped hall for music making, where listening to music would be a common experience". The audience sits round the orchestra, which occupies the very heart of the arena.

Aluminium sheeting: perforated, it was only added in 1978-81. Before that time, the concrete roof was painted in an ochre colour.

Philharmonie

The internal structure and the outside appearance are closely related. The place occupied by the orchestra determines the type of structure (three imbricated pentagons in the case of the Philharmonie, a hexagon in the case of the Chamber Music Hall): the tent-shaped roof provides good acoustics and adds a dynamic element to the visual aspect.

Chamber music hall

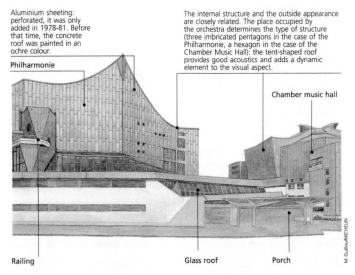

Railing

Glass roof

Porch

M. Guillou/MICHELIN

GLOSSARY OF ARCHITECTURE

Absidiole or **apsidiole chapel**: Small apsidal chapel opening on the ambulatory of a Romanesque or Gothic church.

Aisles: Lateral divisions running parallel with the nave.

Ambulatory: Formed by an extension of the aisles around the chancel; in pilgrimage churches it allowed the faithful to file past the relics.

Apse: Rounded or polygonal end of a church; the outer section is known as the chevet.

Atlantes (or **Telamones**): Male figures used as supporting columns.

Atrium (or **four-sided portico**): Court enclosed by colonnades in front of the entrance to a early Christian or Romanesque church.

Basilica: Rectangular religious building, built on the Roman basilica plan with three or five aisles.

Bossage: Architectural motif or facing made of bosses, uniformly projecting blocks on the outer wall. They are surrounded by deep carving or separating lines. Bossage was in vogue during the Renaissance.

Buttress: External mass of masonry projecting from a wall to counterbalance the thrust of the vaults and arches.

Capital: Crowning feature of a column, consisting of a smooth part, connecting it to the shaft, and a decorated part. There are three orders in classical architecture: Doric, Ionic (with double volute), and Corinthian (decorated with acanthus leaves). The latter is often found in 16C–17C buildings.

Chancel: Part of the church behind the altar set aside for the choir, furnished with variously decorated wooden stalls.

Choir screen or **rood screen**: Partition separating the chancel from the nave.

Ciborium: Canopy over an altar.

Console (or **corbel** or **bracket**): Element of stone or wood projecting from a wall to support beams or cornices.

Corbelling: Projecting course of masonry.

Cornice: In Classical architecture, projecting ornamental moulding along the top of a building. Also designates any projecting decoration around a ceiling.

Cross (church plan): Churches are usually built either in the plan of a Greek cross, with arms of equal length, or a Latin cross, with shorter transept arms.

Crossing: Central area of a cruciform church, where the transept crosses the nave and choir. A tower is often set above this space.

Crypt: Underground chamber beneath a church, where holy relics were placed. Often a chapel or church in its own right.

Diagonal arch: Diagonal arch supporting a vault.

Drum: Circular or polygonal structure supporting a dome.

Embrasure: Recess for a window or door, splayed on the inside.

Entablature: In Classical architecture, the section above the columns consisting of architrave, frieze and cornice.

Gable: Decorative, triangular section above a portal.

Gallery: In early Christian churches, an upper storey opening on the nave. Later used in exterior decoration.

Grotesque: Fanciful ornamental decoration inspired by decorative motifs from Antiquity. The term comes from the old Italian word *grotte*, the name given to the Roman ruins of the *Domus Aurea*, uncovered in the Renaissance period.

Hall-church: Church in which the nave and aisles are of equal height and practically the same width, communicating right to the top.

High relief: Sculpture with very pronounced relief, although not standing out from the background (halfway between low relief and in-the-round figures).

Jamb or **pier**: Pillar flanking an opening (doorway, window, etc.) and supporting the lintel above.

Keystone: Wedge-shaped stone at the crown of an arch.

Lantern: Turret with windows on top of a dome.

Lintel: Horizontal beam connecting pilasters or columns and constituting the lower part of the entablature (in Classical buildings such as temples).

Lombard strips: Romanesque decoration consisting of vertical bands in slight relief or lesenes joined at the top by an arched frieze.

Low relief: Bas-relief, carved figures slightly projecting from their background.

Misericord or **miserere**: Bracket on the underside of a hinged choir stall used for support by canons or monks.

Moulding: ornamental shaped band which projects from the wall.

Mullion window: Window with two arches divided by a central post.

Narthex: Portico preceding the nave of a church.

Nave: Central main body of a church, flanked by aisles.

Oriel window: Window projecting from a wall on corbels.

Ovolo moulding: Egg-shaped ornamentation.

Pediment: Usually triangular ornament above buildings, doors, windows or recesses.

Pendentive: Triangular section of vaulting rising from the angle of two walls enabling the transition from a square space to an octagonal or circular dome.

Polyptych: Painted or carved work consisting of more than three folding leaves or panels.

Predella: Base of a polyptych or altarpiece.

Pulpit (or **ambo**): Elevated stand in various locations from which sermons were preached in a church.

Retable or **altarpiece**: Vertical structure, either painted or carved, above or set back from the altar, often found in Baroque churches.

Rib: Projecting band on the surface of a dome or vault that disperses the weight onto the structures below.

Rococo: Type of decoration in the late Baroque period typified by abstract combinations of shells and volutes.

Rose window: Circular window usually inserted into the front elevation of a church, decorated with delicate fan-shaped stone tracery (small columns, volutes, patterns).

Stalls: Wooden seats reserved for the clergy, grouped together in the chancel.

String course: Ornamental, horizontal band on an exterior wall marking the division between storeys.

Stucco: Form of plaster widely used from the Renaissance period for decoration in relief on walls and ceilings.

Transept: Transverse arms set at right angles to the nave and giving the church a cruciform shape.

Tribune: Upper platform in a church, overlooking the interior.

Triforium: In a Gothic church, a wall-passage above the aisles, opening on the nave, often via a blind arcade.

Triptych: Work comprising three painted or carved panels, whose outer sections can be folded over the central section.

Tympanum: In buildings, doors and windows, the triangular section between the horizontal entablature and the sloping sides of the pediment.

Vault: Arched structure forming a roof or ceiling.

Westwerk or **westwork**: The west end of a church containing a second chancel. A massive structure, often flanked by two stair turrets, typical of Carolingian and Ottonian architecture, sometimes reserved for the emperor.

Art

Germany has a long and illustrious arts pedigree and has produced masters in practically all fields of expression. Religious art dominated until the 19C when Romantic, Realist and Impressionist artists began depicting landscapes, people and scenes from daily life. A key modern movement in German art was Expressionism. After the Second World War, conceptual art and abstract expressionism became the main forms of expression. Since the 1990s, Neo-realism has emerged as a major style, especially as represented by members of the New Leipzig School such as Neo Rauch.

GERMANY'S GREAT PAINTERS AND SCULPTORS
15C

In the fields of painting and architecture, Germany remained for a long time attached to the Late Gothic tradition, which denied the realism so sought after in Italy. The country was divided into a large number of local schools under Dutch influence. Now came the time to seek an outlet for emotional expression and give vent to the religious concerns that marked the end of the Middle Ages.

Stefan Lochner (c. 1410–1451)

This leading master of the Cologne School perpetuated the tradition of international Gothic, giving it a lyrical and refined touch with his sweet expressions and an exquisitely delicate palette. The use of gold backgrounds afforded him a certain amount of leeway as regards the requirements of perspective (*Adoration of the Magi*, Cologne Cathedral; *Virgin and Rose Bush*, Wallraf-Richartz-Museum, Cologne).

Veit Stoß (c. 1445–1533)

Sculptor, painter and engraver with a distinctive, powerful style; one of the greatest woodcarvers of his age. His figures were generally of a pathetic nature (*Annunciation*, Lorenzkirche, Nuremberg; *Reredos of the Nativity*, Bamberg Cathedral).

Tilman Riemenschneider (c. 1460–1531)

Sculptor of alabaster and wood, he was master of an important studio where he created many altarpieces. His intricate works are executed with great finesse and richness of expression (*Tomb of Henry II the Saint*, Bamberg Cathedral; *Adam and Eve*, Mainfränkisches Museum, Würzburg; *Altarpiece to the Virgin*, Herrgottskirche, Creglingen).

The Master of St. Severinus (late 15C)

The intimacy and iridescent colours of his works reflect Netherlandish influence (*Christ before Pilate*, Wallraf-Richartz-Museum, Cologne).

The Master of the Life of the Virgin (late 15C)

Painter of original works, influenced by the Flemish artist Van der Weyden (*Scenes from the Life of the Virgin*, Alte Pinakothek, Munich; *Vision of St. Bernard*, Wallraf-Richartz-Museum, Cologne).

Engraving

First emerging in Germany around 1400, engraving was espoused by the greatest German masters. One pioneer was the unidentified engraver **Master E.S.**, known by the monogram with which he signed his engravings, whose work dates from between 1450 and 1467. Copperplate engraving techniques were later perfected and best demonstrated by virtuosi such as **Mar-**

tin Schongauer (c. 1450–1491), whose designs were later followed by Albrecht Dürer.

16C

The German Renaissance did not emerge until the 16C with Dürer. The observation and idealism of nature resulted in works of increasing refinement. The Danube School showed a new interest in landscape, encouraging its development as a genre, while Holbein breathed new life into the art of portrait painting with his striking realism.

Matthias Grünewald (c. 1480–1528)

An inspired painter of the Late Gothic period, producing works of great emotional intensity capable of expressing the pain of humanity (*Crucifixion*, Staatliche Kunsthalle, Karlsruhe; *Virgin and Child*, Stuppach Parish Church).

Albrecht Dürer (1471–1528)

The greatest artist of the German Renaissance, he was fascinated by the art of Antiquity and the Italian Renaissance, with which he was able to lend Nordic gravity. Based in Nuremberg, Dürer produced woodcuts achieving some magnificent light effects and a broad range of greys (*The Apocalypse*). His religious scenes and portraits are of an extraordinary intensity (*The Four Apostles, Self-Portrait with Cloak*, Alte Pinakothek, Munich; *Charlemagne*, Germanisches Nationalmuseum, Nuremberg).

Lucas Cranach the Elder (1472–1553)

Official painter to the prince-electors of Saxony and master of an important studio, he was the portraitist of the most eminent men of the Reformation, most notably his friend Luther. His works reflect a strong sense of the wonders of nature, allying him with the painters of the Danube School. As court painter in Wittenberg, he produced Lutheran-inspired religious paintings. The more Expressionist works of his youth gave way to paintings full of grace and nobility, typical of the refinement towards which 16C German art was heading. (*The Electors of Saxony*, Kunsthalle, Hamburg; *The Holy Family*, Städel museum, Frankfurt; *Portrait of Martin Luther*, Germanisches Nationalmuseum, Nuremberg).

Albrecht Altdorfer (c. 1480–1538)

Leading member of the Danube School and one of the founders of landscape painting, his use of chiaroscuro creates dramatic and moving works, with the focus on landscapes shrouded in mystery (*Battle of Alexander*, Alte Pinakothek, Munich).

Hans Baldung Grien (c. 1485–1545)

His complex compositions feature dramatic lighting effects, unusual colours and tortured movement (Altarpiece: *The Coronation of the Virgin*, Freiburg Cathedral).

Hans Holbein the Younger (1497–1543)

Painter of German merchants and subjects from court circles and the high aristocracy, he breathed new life into the art of portrait painting. His subjects are depicted with incredible precision in skilfully composed settings that illustrate their office. His compositions, both solemn and realistic, mark a definitive departure from the Gothic tradition (*Portrait of the Merchant Georg Gisze*, Museum Dahlem, Berlin).

17C and 18C

Italian influence remained evident during these two centuries. Court circles played host to many French and Italian artists who introduced an increasingly exuberant Baroque style.

Adam Elsheimer (1578–1610)

Elsheimer's often small-scale mythological and biblical paintings reflect a combination of Italian influence and a concept of landscapes peculiar to Flemish and German painting.

At the same time as Caravaggio, he experimented with the power of light to evoke nature, notably in his dramatic nocturnal landscapes (*The Flight into Egypt*, 1609, Alte Pinakothek, Munich).

Andreas Schlüter (c. 1660–1714)

This master of Baroque sculpture in northern Germany produced powerful works (*Statue of the Great Elector*, Schloss Charlottenburg, Berlin; *Masks of Dying Warriors*, Zeughaus, Berlin).

Balthasar Permoser (1651–1732)

Sculptor to the Court of Dresden, Permoser studied in Rome, Vienna and Venice. His masterful works reflect the exuberant style of the Italian Baroque, particularly at the Zwinger (*Wallpavillon* and *Nymphenbad*, Zwinger, Dresden).

Antoine Pesne (1683–1757)

This French-born painter in the service of the Prussian court became the portraitist of Frederick II. He produced portraits and mythological ceiling paintings and murals (*Portrait of Frederick II and his sister Wilhelmina,* apartments of Schloss Charlottenburg, Berlin).

Joseph Anton Feuchtmayer (1696–1770) and Johann Michael II Feichtmayr (1709–1772)

These family members of German painters and sculptors helped to perpetuate the Rococo style with their fanciful compositions (decoration of the abbey churches of Ottobeuren and St. Gall).

19C

The 19C was first of all dominated by the **Biedermeier style** (1815–48) which glorified middle-class values and way of life, as perfectly illustrated by the genre painting of GF Kersting. Then came the time for rebellion. Romanticism called Classical values into question, launching a dialogue between reason and feeling. Realism and Impressionism, which both originated in France, allowed German artists to express certain budding socialist ideas. These various forms of artistic expression came in response to the moral crisis of modern Europe.

Caspar David Friedrich (1774–1840)

German Romantic painter whose landscapes were represented as manifestations of the divine and places ideal for meditation (*The Monk by the Sea, The Cross on the Mountain*, Alte Nationalgalerie, Berlin; *Wanderer above the Sea of Fog*, Kunsthalle, Hamburg).

Friedrich Overbeck (1789–1869)

Member of the Lucas Brotherhood, he was the most important member of the group of **Nazarenes** who occupied the abandoned monastery of San Isidoro in Rome in 1810. Advocating a form of painting that glorified moral values in a reaction against Neoclassicism, they revived medieval art and sought the purity of the early Italian and Flemish masters of the 15C (*Italia and Germania*, Neue Pinakothek, Munich).

Adolf von Menzel (1815–1905)

Representative of German Realism, initially illustrating anecdotal themes and later producing powerful portrayals of the industrial world, tempered by the influence of Impressionism (*Rolling Mill*, Nationalgalerie in Berlin).

Wilhelm Leibl (1844–1900)

Master of German Realism, he was influenced by Courbet and mostly painted scenes of village life (*Three Women in Church*, Kunsthalle, Hamburg; portrait of *Mina Gedon*, Neue Pinakothek, Munich).

Max Liebermann (1847–1935)

Greatly influenced by French Realism and Naturalism, he painted peasants and workers in all their harsh reality. Later, under the influence of Impressionism, he allowed light to suffuse his already rich palette. He led the Berlin "Sezession" movement in 1899, advocating freedom and realism as opposed to the patriotic insipidness of the court painters (*Jewish Street in Amsterdam*, Wallraf-Richartz-Museum, Cologne).

20C

The Expressionism which marked the beginning of the century gave way to a new form of revolt and glorification of subjective feeling. The shock of World War I and the ensuing social crisis plunged art into a period of darkness and disillusionment. Political and social dissent were embodied in a succession of new avant-garde movements. Art was driven by a desire to change society and expose its failings.

Expressionism

German Expressionism introduced an emotionally charged, often violent or tragic vision of the world to modern painting. The movement owed much to Van Gogh and the Norwegian painter **Edvard Munch** (1863–1944). In Dresden and then in Berlin, the **Brücke (Bridge) Group** united (1905-1913) such painters as Erich Heckel, Ernst Ludwig Kirchner and Karl Schmidt-Rottluff, whose work, with its use of pure colour, recalls that of the Fauves in France. See the works of **Emil Nolde** (1867–1956) at Seebüll and of Expressionism in general at the Brücke Museum in Berlin.

Der Blaue Reiter (The Blue Rider Movement)

Association of artists founded in Munich in 1911 by **Wassily Kandinsky** and **Franz Marc** was later joined by **August Macke** and **Paul Klee**. Although the work of the artists involved differed widely, they were united by a general aim to free art from the constraints of reality, using bold colours and untraditional forms, thus opening the way to abstraction (*Deer in the Forest* by **Franz Marc**, Orangerie Staatliche Kunsthalle, Karlsruhe; *The Dress Shop* by **August Macke**, Folkwang-Museum, Essen). The movement broke up during the war.

The Bauhaus

This movement, which united all art forms, attracted a host of avant-garde painters and sculptors including Klee and Kandinsky, Oskar Schlemmer, Laszlo Moholy-Nagy, **Lyonel Feininger** and **Joseph Albers**.

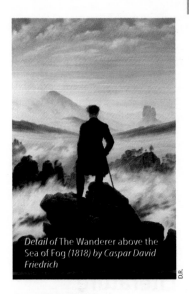

Detail of The Wanderer above the Sea of Fog *(1818) by Caspar David Friedrich*

Neue Sachlichkeit (New Objectivity)

This artistic early-1920s movement aimed to produce a realistic illustration of social facts and phenomena. It corresponds to the harshness of the postwar period. Pioneers of this movement were **Otto Dix** and **George Grosz** (*War* by **Otto Dix**, 1932, Albertinum in Dresden). The Dada movement, present in Cologne and Berlin, and in Hannover with **Kurt Schwitters**, used art for political ends. On the sidelines of these movements, **Max Beckmann** (1884–1950), who was also deeply affected by the war and its consequences, shared his very bleak view of humanity.

Second Half of the 20C

The Nazi regime brought an abrupt end to the artistic experiments labelled as "degenerate art", replacing them with a Neoclassical style glorifying race, war and family. This "Nazi art" died out at the end of the Reich in 1945.

Social Realism, an official art form which served the regime's ideology, was predominant in East German painting until the 1960s–70s. The painters of Leipzig won international acclaim, among them Bernhard Heisig, Wolfgang Mattheuer, Willi Sitte and Werner Tübke. The 1960s saw a turning point in German artistic creativity. **Gruppe Zebra** took up the credo of New Objectivity against German Abstract art, while the members of **Gruppe Zero** (Heinz Mack, Otto Piene, Güntheb Uecker) concentrated on using kinetic art to transform thoughts into material objects. In the 1970s, **Joseph Beuys**, together with the artists of the school of **Constructivist Sculpture** in Düsseldorf, strove to create a direct relationship between the artist and the viewing public in his Happenings and Performances (**Neue Nationalgalerie** in Berlin; **Staatsgalerie** in Stuttgart). From the 1980s, a new generation of German artists broke through onto the international scene with "new Fauves" *(Neue Wilde)* **Georg Baselitz** and **Markus Lüpertz** developing a new form of Expressionism, **Sigmar Polke**, closer to pop art, and **Anselm Kiefer**, focusing on German history.

Since the 1990s, "Young German Artists" have come from Leipzig, Berlin and Dresden. Neo Rauch is the best known representative of the "New Leipzig School". Katarina Sieverding and Andreas Gursky top the photography world. Germany also hosts one of the most influential contemporary art fairs, the Documenta, held in Kassel every five years (next in 2017).

Literature

German literature, from the reign of Charlemagne up to the present day, has demonstrated an enduring vitality, constantly breaking with tradition and inventing new forms of expression. In the wake of Goethe's monumental influence in the 18C, the best authors have been guaranteed international renown.

THE MIDDLE AGES TO THE 17C

German literature in the Middle Ages was written in a great variety of dialects. Largely drawing on the oral tradition, it was characterised by lyrical poetry and genres that can be described – not in any pejorative way – as popular: plays, ballads, songs and epics. One of the earliest works, dating back to Charlemagne's reign, is the **Lay of Hildebrand** (Das Hildebrandslied, 820), of which only a 68-line fragment has survived. The national folk saga of the **Nibelungen**, an anonymous work from the late 12C, draws on the sources of Germanic mythology and celebrates the heroic spirit that faces up to trials and tribulations without ever giving up. One of the big names in courtly epics was **Wolfram von Eschenbach**; his poem *Parzival* (c. 1200), which **recounts the** quest for the Holy Grail, revolves around religious and chivalrous themes. The 14C was an age of mystic literature, with writers such as **Meister Eckhart**. In a departure from the dryness of scholastic teaching, he sometimes forsakes Latin to discuss religious topics in powerful and eloquent German.

Satire took centre stage in the 16C (*The Ship of Fools* by **Sebastian Brant** appeared in 1494) along with folk songs and the poetry of the Meistersänger (master singers). **Hans Sachs** (1494–1576), a poet-cum-cobbler from Nuremberg, was a prominent figure in the latter genre, which provides the theme of Wagner's opera *Tannhäuser*. **Luther**'s contribution during this period also marked a turning point; his hymns and translation of the Bible (1534) paved the way for the writing of literary works in a common, modern German language.

The late 16C witnessed the publication of the *Faust Book* (1587) by **Johann Spies**, a work of remarkable depth, which draws the captivating portrait of a man driven by an unquenchable thirst for knowledge which distances him from God.

The ravages of the Thirty Years' War (1618–48) profoundly marked the collective psyche; 17C literature bears echoes of this traumatic time.

Among the recurrent themes of these often edifying works is the vanity of human things and man's need to find God in order to ensure his salvation. *Adventurous Simplicissimus* (1669) by **Grimmelshausen** (1622–1676) is a picaresque novel whose hero, having experienced the suffering of war, finally chooses a life of retreat and meditation.

AUFKLÄRUNG (AGE OF ENLIGHTENMENT)

The 18C marked the beginning of the golden age of German literature, as its influence began to extend well beyond the German-speaking countries.

The spotlight was now on philosophical and moral themes, the flourishes of language belying a pursuit of the natural. The influence of **Leibniz** (1646–1716), whose *Theodicy* in French and Latin uses rational arguments to justify evil and show that we live in "the best of all possible worlds", still remains strong. **Rationalism**, apparent in the works of **Christian Wolff** (1679–1754), co-existed with the tenacious survival of Pietism, which highlights the emotional experience in any religious phenomenon. This explains how **Lessing** (1729–1781), in his writings on religion (*The Education of the Human Race*, 1780), strives to combine a rationalist deism with a belief in revelation. In the purely literary field, Lessing also set the principles of new German theatre by creating middle-class drama *(Emilia Galotti)*.

His contemporary, **Immanuel Kant** (1724–1804), endeavoured to define the limits of what can be known; only that which is determined by pure forms of understanding can be the subject of rational knowledge. Whatever eludes such determination (the soul, God, etc.) can, of course, be "thought" and give rise to "belief", but cannot be "known".

In the practical field, Kantianism defines the balance between liberty and the "moral law" that governs every rational being: man finds liberty by submitting to the "categorical imperative" and renouncing the influence of his "sensitivity".

STURM UND DRANG AND CLASSICISM

In reaction to the strict rationalism of the Aufklärung, the **Sturm und Drang** (storm and stress) movement, encompassing authors such as **Herder** (1744–1803) and **Hamann** (1730–1788), exalts freedom, emotion and nature. Poetry, "the mother tongue of the human race", takes pride of place and the past is revisited, with particular emphasis placed on folk songs.

The works of the young **Johann Wolfgang von Goethe** (1749–1832), such as *The Sorrows of Young Werther*, bear witness to the influence of *Sturm und Drang*. However, Goethe – poet and universal genius – soon tempered this fashionable enthusiasm with a move towards the **classical humanist** tradition. As the leading light of German literature prior to the emergence of the Romantic trend, in which he never became involved, he penned a great number of works. Classical dramas (*Iphigenie auf Tauris*, *Egmont* and *Torquato Tasso*), novels (*Elective Affinities*, *Wilhelm Meister's Apprenticeship*) and *Faust (Parts I and II*, 1808 and 1832) contain the quintessence of Goethe's philosophy.

After settling in Weimar in 1775, Goethe was joined by Herder, **Wieland** and **Schiller** (1759–1805). The historical dramas of the latter, a poet and dramatist of genius, are undisguised hymns to liberty *(Don Carlos, Wallenstein, Wilhelm Tell)*.

Two major literary figures emerged during the transitional period between Weimarian Classicism and actual Romanticism: **Friedrich Hölderlin** (1770–1843), a tragic, lyric author *(Hyperion, The Death of Empedocles)* with a passion for Ancient Greek civilisation, produced some powerful odes before sinking into madness at the age of 36.

The novelist Johann Paul Friedrich Richter (1763–1825), better known as **Jean Paul**, had a creative imagination, although a somewhat laboured style.

19C: BETWEEN ROMANTICISM AND REALISM

The **Romantic movement** charts the individual soul's quest for the infinite in all its forms. Besides literature, it incorporates the fine arts, philosophy, politics and religion. First Jena, then Heidelberg and Berlin were centres from which the movement blossomed. After initially being theorised by the **Schlegel brothers**, the Romantic doctrine was put into powerful poetic form by **Novalis** (1772–1801); a poet and mystic, Novalis exalts the art and religion of the Middle Ages and his "Blue Flower" symbol comes to represent the Absolute, or object of Romantic longing (*Heinrich von Ofterdingen*). While in the process of theoretical elaboration, budding Romanticism was exposed to the influence of post-Kantian idealist philosophers, in particular **Fichte** (1762–1814), **Schelling** (1775–1854) and **Hegel** (1770–1831). It also reflects a heightened interest in popular literature, often seeking inspiration in the sources of myths and legends, as can be seen in the tales of the **Brothers Grimm** (1812) or the more disturbing tales of **Hoffmann** (1776–1822). On the sidelines of the Romantic movement, the playwright **Heinrich von Kleist**, who tragically, committed suicide in 1811, wrote some remarkable plays, notably *The Prince of Homburg* (1810): A play about a man of action led away by his dreams.

The exuberant idealism of Romanticism was succeeded by a search for greater realism. An outstanding figure and "defrocked Romantic" poet of the *Loreley*, **Heinrich Heine** (1797–1856) treats the naivety of his age with bitter irony and enthuses about St. Simonian ideals. **Hebbel** (1813–1863), a fine psychologist, wrote plays often inspired by biblical or mythical subjects, focusing on conflict between the individual and the existing moral order (*Judith, Herodes und Mariamne, Agnes Bernauer*). Towards the mid-19C, a number of writers sought to bring literature closer to life and everyday experience; novelists such as **Stifter** (1805–1868) and **Keller** (1819–1890) were among the main exponents of this Realist trend. Some of them, such as **Fontane** (1819–1898) and **Raabe** (1831–1910), focus on the social and political conditions of human existence. Social drama is brilliantly illustrated by **Hauptmann** (1862–1946), a prolific author whose Naturalist writing is at times allegorical and symbolic, drawing inspiration from legend and mythology (*The Atrides Cycle*).

In the field of philosophy, **Schopenhauer** (1788–1860), pessimistic theorist of the will to live, describes the will as reality's true inner nature, and this will as suffering (*The World as Will and Idea,* 1819); he had a crucial influence on the thinking of authors such as Nietzsche, Freud and Wittgenstein. Political thought, moreover, took a new direction with **Karl Marx** (*The Communist Manifesto* was published in 1848); rejecting Hegelian idealism, Marx, who was both a philosopher and an economist, developed the theory of "historical materialism", a powerful conceptual tool enabling the analysis of human societies according to their historical development. Together with **Engels**, Marx co-founded "scientific socialism", in opposition to so-called "utopian" socialism, and launched the modern international workers' movement.

THE MODERN PERIOD

Friedrich Nietzsche's (1844–1900) tremendous influence over the history of literature and western thought is still in evidence today. His fundamentally life-affirming philosophy called, with great lyricism, for mankind to surpass itself (*Thus Spake Zarathustra*, 1886).

Focusing on the often irreconcilable duality of the mind and the senses, the irrational and the rational, the works of **Thomas Mann** (*Buddenbrooks, The Magic Mountain*) and **Hermann Hesse**

(Der Steppenwolf) bear the stamp of Nietzscheism; the sanatorium in Davos in *The Magic Mountain* symbolises the "disease" that runs rife in decadent European societies. In this struggle between life and morbid instincts, the shadow of Thanatos hangs over our western civilisations. The Czech-born German-language writer **Franz Kafka** (1883–1924) differs from these authors in both style and thought; his nightmarish novels *(The Trial, The Castle, America)* contain a vision of a dehumanised world dominated by anxiety and the absurd. The works of Vienna-born **Stefan Zweig**, one of Kafka's contemporaries, were of a less tortured nature. This highly cultivated man, citizen of the world, traveller and translator proved in his best short stories *(Amok, Conflicts, The Royal Game)* to be a remarkable storyteller with humanist sympathies. The early 20C also witnessed a revival in poetry. **Stefan George** (1868–1933) published poems which, in their formal perfection, ally him with the French Symbolists, while the Austrians **Rainer Maria Rilke** (1875–1926) and **Hugo von Hoffmannsthal** (1874–1929) reach the peak of lyrical impressionism.

The 1930s and 1940s were marked by an intensified search for the meaning of life; spurred on by Husserlian phenomenology, **Heidegger** and, to a lesser degree, **Jaspers**, put the question of being back at the heart of philosophy. Based on our essential finiteness, Heideggerian existentialism distinguishes between an existence marked by a sense of being and an "inauthentic" existence, led astray into the impersonal self.

The world of theatre was dominated by **Bertolt Brecht** *(The Threepenny Opera, Mother Courage, Galileo)*. A committed socialist, he rejected the "theatre of illusion", advocating *Verfremdungseffekt* ("the alienation effect"): the spectator must observe the action on stage with a critical eye and decipher the methods by which the strong exploit the weak.

National Socialism forced numerous poets and writers into exile (Walter Benjamin, Alfred Döblin, Lion Feuchtwanger, Else Lasker-Schüler, Thomas and Heinrich Mann, Carl Zuckmayer, Stefan Zweig). **Gottfried Benn** (1886–1956) withdrew into silence, while **Ernst Jünger** (1895–1998) courageously published his novel *On the Marble Cliffs* in 1939.

POST-1945 LITERATURE

Twelve years under National Socialist rule had broken the flow of literary creativity in Germany, necessitating repair work in this domain too. The association of authors known as **Gruppe 47** (after the year of its founding), which centred upon **Hans Werner Richter** and **Alfred Andersch**, was instrumental in putting Germany back on the map as far as world literature was concerned. This loosely associated group of writers served as a forum for reading, discussion and criticism, until its last conference in 1967, exerting a lasting and formative influence on the contemporary German literary scene. Authors associated with Gruppe 47 included **Paul Celan**, **Heinrich Böll** (Nobel Prize winner in 1972), **Günter Grass** (Nobel Prize winner in 1999), **Siegfried Lenz**, **Peter Weiss** and **Hans Magnus Enzensberger**. By the end of the 1950s, works of international standing were being published: Günter Grass' masterpiece *The Tin Drum* is an extraordinary novel in the tradition of Celine; **Uwe Johnson**'s *Speculations about Jacob*, **Heinrich Böll**'s *Billiards at Half Past Nine* and **Martin Walser**'s novel *Marriages in Philippsburg*. Increasing politicisation was what finally put an end to Gruppe 47's activities. Authors not associated with Gruppe 47 were hard at work also; **Arno Schmidt** developed a very original and high-quality body of work, while **Wolfgang Koeppen** produced some wickedly satirical novels on contemporary society. The literature of the 1960s was characterised by a wave of criticism but, by the following decade, German literary concerns were withdrawing to a newly discovered "inner contemplation". A particularly prolific amount of good writing was produced by women during the 1970s and 1980s (**Gabriele Wohmann**, **Karin Struck**, **Verena Stefan**).

In the world of theatre, dominated initially by the dramatic theory of Bertolt Brecht, a new band of writers began to emerge, with works by **Tankred Dorst** (*Toller*, 1968), **Peter Weiss** (*Hölderlin*, 1971) and **Heinar Kipphardt**. **Rolf Hochhuth** was particularly successful with his "documentary dramas" in which he examines contemporary moral issues (*The Representative*, 1963), and **Botho Strauß**, the most widely performed modern German dramatist, has won international acclaim with plays such as *The Hypochondriac* (1972), *The Park* (1983) and *Final Chorus* (1991).

The political division of Germany was also reflected in German literature. In the old East German Republic, the leadership viewed literature's *raison d'être* as the contribution it might make to the socialist programme for educating the masses. The Bitterfelder Weg, a combined propaganda exercise and literary experiment launched at the Bitterfeld chemical factory in 1959 as part of the East German Republic's cultural programme under Walter Ulbricht, was intended to unite art and everyday life and break down class barriers.

Factory visits were organised for writers, so they could observe workers and then portray them glowingly in their novels, poems or plays, while the workers themselves were encouraged to write about their lives.

The results of the project were mixed, and although it gave authors a clearer idea of the primitive conditions that most East German workers were obliged to tolerate, those who wrote too honestly about what they saw found their works censored.

Poetry was the literary form least easily subject to Communist censorship, and poets such as **Peter Huchel**, **Johannes Bobrowski** and **Erich Arendt** produced some remarkable work. From the early 1960s the prose work of **Günter de Bruyn**, **Stefan Heym** and **Erwin Strittmatter** was widely appreciated. **Anna Seghers**, who returned from exile in America after the war, was considered the greatest East German writer of the older generation, while rising star **Christa Wolf** won acclaim in both Germanies. Important contributions to the theatre were made by playwrights **Ulrich Plenzdorf**, **Peter Hacks** and above all **Heiner Müller** (*The Hamlet Machine,* 1978).

Any overview of German-language literature since World War II must, of course, acknowledge the enormous contribution made by **Max Frisch** and **Friedrich Dürrenmatt**, of Switzerland, and **Ilse Aichinger**, **Ingeborg Bachmann** and **Thomas Bernhard** of Austria.

Music

G ermany and the German-speaking world have made a considerable contribution to Western music. After reaching an initial high point in the 18C with the Baroque period, German music was propelled back into the limelight by the genius of composers such as Beethoven and Wagner. Modern experimentation since the emergence of the 12-tone system testifies to the continuing vitality of German music.

FROM MINNESÄNGER TO MEISTERSÄNGER

In the 12C and 13C, feudal courts constituted the main forum for musical expression. The **Minnesänger** (essentially troubadours – *minne* meaning "love" in Middle High German), who were often noble knights, such as **Wolfram von Eschenbach** and **Walther von der Vogelweide**, drew inspiration for their songs from French lyric poetry. They would perform their love songs before the nobility, accompanying themselves on the lute.

The *Meistersänger*, or mastersingers, of the 14C–16C preferred a more sedentary lifestyle and organised themselves into guilds. They introduced polyphony to German music and clearly set the musical forms of their art. Anyone wanting to become a *Meistersänger* had to prove himself in a public contest. Among the prominent figures of the time was **Heinrich von Meißen** (1250–1318) who marked the transition from *Minnesang* (courtly love song/lyric) to the poetry of the *Meistersänger*. **Hans Sachs** (1494–1576), a cobbler by trade and an ardent supporter of Luther, was also a prolific poet; many of his compositions were turned into Protestant chorales. Sachs later became the subject of Wagner's opera *The Mastersingers of Nuremberg*.

FROM THE RENAISSANCE TO THE 17C

In the wake of the Reformation, German music began to develop an individual identity with the emergence of the chorale, the fruit of the collaboration between **Luther** and **Johann Walther** (1496–1570). "*Ein' feste Burg ist unser Gott*" (A Mighty Fortress is Our God) composed by the two men in 1529 was reworked by Bach. Originally a hymn with a simple melody, the chorale – sung in the vernacular – soon opened up to the secular repertoire, embracing popular genres of music. It subsequently gave rise to the German cantata and oratorio.

Religious music maestro, **Heinrich Schütz** (1585–1672) managed to produce a skilful combination of German and Italian elements. He composed the first German opera, *Dafne*, a work which was sadly lost. *The Seven Words of Christ* (1645) shows the influence of Monteverdi who, along with Gabrieli, was one of Schütz's masters.

The second half of the 17C witnessed a proliferation of organ schools, one of the most famous of which was in Nuremberg. An inspiration for Bach, who is said to have walked hundreds of miles to hear him play in Lübeck, **Dietrich Buxtehude** (1637–1707) organised the first concerts of sacred music. **Johann Pachelbel** (1653–1706) was the great master of the organ school in southern Germany; the only surviving piece of his work is the *Canon in D Major*.

BACH AND BAROQUE MUSIC

His consummate skill as a composer, his genius for invention and his mastery of counterpoint enabled **Bach** (1685–1750) to excel in every kind of music he wrote. Based in Weimar until 1717, he spent several years at the court of Köthen, during which he composed *The Brandenburg Concertos*. In 1723, he was appointed "Cantor" at St. Thomas' School, Leipzig. Bach's duties included the composition of a cantata for every Sunday service, as well as the supervision of services at four other churches. He also taught Latin and voice and still found time to write his own instrumental and vocal works. His masterpieces include *The Well-Tempered Clavier* (1722 and 1744) and the *St. Matthew Passion* (1727).

A brilliant court composer, influenced by his travels in Italy, **Georg Friedrich Händel** (1665–1759) excelled in both opera and oratorio (*The Messiah*, 1742). Born in Halle, he was organist at the town's cathedral before pursuing his career at the Hamburg opera. Based in England from 1714, he spent most of the last 40 years of his life in London, and even obtained British nationality. Händel's friend, **Georg Philipp Telemann**, (1681–1767) was influenced by French and Italian composers, and was himself a particularly prolific composer. He turned from counterpoint to harmony and composed chamber music and church music as well as operas. Telemann was godfather to Bach's second son, **Carl Philipp Emmanuel** (1714–1788), who popularised the sonata in its classic form.

FROM THE MANNHEIM SCHOOL TO BEETHOVEN

In the mid 18C, the musicians of the **Mannheim School**, under the patronage of Elector Palatine Karl Theodor, helped establish the modern symphonic form, giving a more prominent role to wind instruments. Influenced by the innovations from Mannheim, **Christoph Willibald Gluck** (1714–1787) undertook a "reformation of opera", producing refined works where the lyrics took pride of place; he provoked the enthusiasm of the innovators – and the horror of fans of traditional, Italian-inspired opera – by staging, in Paris, his *Iphigenia in Aulis* and *Orpheus*. This period was also marked by the appearance in Germany of the **Singspiel**, a popular opera in which dialogue is interspersed with songs in the form of Lieder. Mozart's *Magic Flute* (1791) and Beethoven's *Fidelio* (1814) are excellent examples of this genre later identified with operetta.

The contribution of Viennese Classicism during the second half of the 18C proved to be crucial. **Joseph Haydn** (1732–1809) laid down the classical form of the symphony, the string quartet and the piano sonata. **Wolfgang Amadeus Mozart** (1756–1791) perfected these forms and created some truly immortal operas *(The Marriage of Figaro, Don Juan)*.

Born in Bonn, **Ludwig van Beethoven** (1770–1827) went to Vienna to study under Haydn and Antonio Salieri. With his innovative harmonisations, he developed a highly individual style and transformed existing forms of music, heralding the Romantic movement. The depth of his inspiration, ranging from pure introspection to a wider belief in the force and universality of his art, emanates from his work with extraordinary power, perhaps most particularly in his symphonies. It was in 1824, when he had already been suffering from total and incurable deafness for five years, that Beethoven's magnificent *Ninth Symphony* – inspired by one of Schiller's odes – was performed for the first time.

ROMANTIC MUSIC AND WAGNER

Franz Schubert (1797–1826) brought Romantic music to its first high point. He focused much creative energy on the *Lied* (song), blending folk and classical music in a unique style.

Carl Maria von Weber (1786–1826) created Germany's first Romantic opera, *Freischütz* (1821), paving the way for the characters of Wagnerian drama. It was a resounding success when first performed in Berlin, due in part to the use of folk songs. As for the lofty world of **Felix Mendelssohn-Bartholdy** (1809–1879), it was far removed from the forces of evil that inhabit the *Freischütz*. Although espousing classical music forms, Mendelssohn, who was a conductor, pianist and founder of the Leipzig Conservatory, also reveals a Romantic influence.

Robert Schumann (1810–1856), passionate and lyrical in turn, but brought up in the Germanic tradition, strives to reconcile a classical heritage with personal expression. A talented music critic (he founded the *Neue Zeitscrhift für Musik* newspaper in 1834), he initially wrote for piano alone *(Carnival, Scenes from Childhood)*. Then, spurred on by his admiration for Schubert and the advice of his friend Mendelssohn, he began to compose *Lieder (Dichterliebe)*, subsequently turning his attention to symphonies and chamber music. A close friend of Schumann, whose wife Clara he loved with a passion, **Johannes Brahms** (1833–1897) exemplified a more introverted style of German Romanticism. After long being accused of formalism, he was rediscovered in the 20C, notably thanks to the influence of Schönberg *(Brahms the Progressive)*.

Crowning glory of the German Romantic movement, the work of **Wagner** (1813–1883) revolutionised opera. Wagner claimed that music should be subservient to drama, serving as "atmosphere" and a "backdrop of sound" without which the opera's message could not be fully conveyed. Orchestration thus becomes of paramount importance.

Libretto and plot unfold continuously, preserving dramatic reality. Wagner introduces the use of "leitmotifs" – musical phrases used recurrently to denote specific characters, moods or situations – making them essential to the continuity of the action. *Lohengrin* was first performed in 1850 in Weimar, under the supervision of **Franz Liszt**. Designed by Wagner himself as a stage for the performance of the entire work *(Gesamtkunstwerk)*, the Bayreuth Theater was inaugurated in 1876 with *The Ring of the Nibelung (Rheingold, Walküre, Siegfried* and *Götterdämmerung)*. The fruit of 22 years' work, the magnificent first public performance of *The Ring* lasted 18 hours. Although its artistic success was undeniable, the Bayreuth episode ended in financial ruin for the composer. *Parzival*, Wagner's last opera, revolves around the theme of redemption through sacrifice, and was first performed in Bayreuth in 1882.

At the end of the 19C, **Gustav Mahler** (1860–1911), Czech-Austrian composer and creator of the symphonic *Lied*, and **Hugo Wolf** (1850–1903) developed a new musical language which forms a bridge between Romanticism and dodecaphony.

Richard Strauss (1864–1949) excelled in orchestra music *(Thus Spake Zarathustra)*, uniting a certain harmonic audacity with a dazzling and multi-faceted style.

CONTEMPORARY MUSIC

Contemporary musical experimentation is derived principally from the Austrian school of atonal, or serial (especially 12-tone systems) music, represented by **Arnold Schönberg** and his two main disciples **Alban Berg** and **Anton von Webern**. Introducing a new method of composing music, the 12-tone system was first revealed to the public by Schönberg in 1928 in the *Variations for Orchestra*. Berg applied his master's innovation to lyrical drama *(Lulu)*, while Webern, turning his back on Romanticism, focused on the concision of form. The brilliant **Paul Hin-**

demith (1893–1963), initially influenced by Romanticism, remained untouched by Schönberg's innovations; in a break with German tradition, he forged a path of his own between atonality and dodecaphony.

Carl Orff (1895–1982), creator of the Orff Schulwerk, propounded innovative ideas about music education. His highly original theatrical compositions combine drama, speech and song in a fascinating rhythmic framework: his powerful collection of secular songs with infectious rhythms, *Carmina Burana* (1937), soon gained international renown. The compositions – mainly opera and ballet music – of **Werner Egk** (1901–1983), a student of Carl Orff, reveal the influence of Igor Stravinski and Richard Strauss. As for **Kurt Weill** (1900–1950), influenced at the beginning of his career by the atonal composers, he returned under the impact of jazz to tonal music, and composed *The Threepenny Opera* (1928) in collaboration with Brecht.

Although **Wolfgang Fortner** (1907–1987) was influenced initially by Hindemith, he nonetheless later turned to modal 12-tone serial music. His mature works introduce electronic elements into his musical compositions.

Bernd Alois Zimmermann (1918–1970) perceived past, present and future as one, and the multiple layers of reality are reflected in his composition technique. Quotations and collage were particularly important to him. His major work is the opera *The Soldiers*.

From 1950, a younger generation of musicians developed the potential of electronic music under the aegis of **Karlheinz Stockhausen** (1928–2007). **Hans Werner Henze** (1926–2012) created expressive operas, in which modernity and tradition, and atonality and tonality are combined. **Wolfgang Rihm** (b. 1952), a student of Fortner, like Henze, also mixes traditional stylistic elements with new techniques in his extremely complex musical language.

Cinema

After producing a number of masterpieces during the Expressionist period of the 1920s, German cinema fell into a decline from which it did not emerge until the 1960s. Although now struggling to make its mark in the face of the American productions, it has managed to produce some remarkable international award-winning works.

THE GOLDEN AGE OF EXPRESSIONISM

The creation in 1917 of UFA (Universum Film Aktiengesellschaft), a production company of considerable means which, from 1921, was directed by producer **Erich Pommer**, led to some lavish productions. The Expressionism that was apparent in literature, theatre and painting also seeped into film production in the troubled postwar political and social scene. Deliberately turning its back on Realism, it often revelled in angst-ridden atmospheres, cultivating an exaggeration of forms and contrasts; it was typified by the use of chiaroscuro lighting effects and the geometric stylisation of the décor. Very few works could actually be classed as purely Expressionist, but among them is **Robert Wiene**'s masterpiece *The Cabinet of Dr Caligari* (1919), which was well received in the United States and France. Nevertheless, Expressionism was a great source of inspiration for German cinema in the 1920s; this period was dominated by the films of **FW Murnau** (*Nosferatu the Vampire*, 1922; *The Last Laugh*, 1924; *Faust*, 1926) and **Fritz Lang** (*Dr Mabuse*, 1922; *Metropolis*, 1925). Lang's German work reached its high point in 1931 with *M*, the director's first talking picture. Initially entitled *Murderers Among Us* (the title was changed under pressure from the Nazis), *M* paints the picture of a diseased society which, unable to cure its own ills, seeks scapegoat sinners on whom to place the blame. *The Last Will of Dr Mabuse* in 1932 attracted Nazi censure. Soon after being invited by Goebbels to supervise the Reich's film production, Lang went into exile, first moving to Paris and then to California, where he pursued his film-directing career.

The 1920s in Germany also witnessed a shift towards Realism and away from the dominant Expressionist trend. Examples of this new trend include the films of **GW Pabst** (*The Joyless Street*, 1925; *Diary of a Lost Girl*, 1926; *Lulu*, 1929) and **Josef von Sternberg**'s *The Blue Angel* (1930) starring **Marlene Dietrich** and **Emil Jannings**.

AN ABRUPT HALT

The promising surge of German cinema after World War I was sadly stopped in its tracks with the arrival of the Third Reich. Many actors and directors went into exile. The Nazis turned cinema into a tool to serve the regime's ideology. Filmmaker **Leni Riefenstahl** (1902–2003) stands out in the generally disappointing and inartistic genre of propaganda films, with her productions of amazing cinematic beauty, such as *The Gods of the Stadium*, a glorification of the 1936 Berlin Olympics.

The period immediately after World War II was a cultural desert. While "Socialist Realism" prevailed in East Germany, film production in the Federal Republic of the 1950s was of poor quality. Only a few films, such as *The Last Bridge* (1954) and *The Devil's General* (1955) by **Helmut Kaütner**, managed to escape the pervasive mediocrity. The 1962 **Oberhausen Manifesto**, signed by 26 young filmmakers, signalled the birth of a new cinematographic language; the long-awaited revival was here at last.

THE BERLINALE

As one of the pioneers of celluloid history, it's only natural that Germany should be home to one of the world's most prestigious film festivals: The Berlinale (☉ *see BERLIN*), which brings hundreds of international stars to the German capital every February. Founded in 1951 with the encouragement of the Western allies, the festival shows hundreds of flicks from around the world with some of them competing for the coveted Golden and Silver Bear trophies (www.berlinale.de). Munich and Hamburg also host major festivals and there quite literally dozens of other smaller ones, many specialising in particular genres such as documentaries, animated films, short films, children's cinema and gay and lesbian movies.

THE REVIVAL OF THE 1960s AND BEYOND

In the 1960s and 1970s makers of "New German cinema" rose up in the wake of the French *nouvelle vague*, seeking to distance themselves from old-style cinema with its run-of-the-mill commercial superficiality. Films made by **Werner Herzog**, **Volker Schlöndorff** (*Young Törless*, 1966) and **Alexander Kluge** (*Artists at the Top of the Big Top: Disorientated*, 1968) quickly met with success. It was not long – the mid 1970s – before this younger generation had re-established German cinema on an international scale. **Volker Schlöndorff** made *The Lost Honour of Katharina Blum* (in collaboration with **Margarethe von Trotta**, 1975), and *The Tin Drum* (1979). **Werner Herzog** went on to explore a fantastic, often quite exotic world in *Aguirre, Wrath of God* (1972), *Nosferatu the Vampyre* (1979) and *Fitzcarraldo* (1982). Prominent figures in the **Munich School** include **Rainer Werner Fassbinder** (1945–1982), who also worked in television, and who was responsible for a considerable number of excellent films (*Fear eats the Soul (Angst essen Seele auf)*, 1973; *The Marriage of Maria Braun*, 1978; *Berlin Alexanderplatz*, a 14-part television series, 1980), and **Wim Wenders** (*The American Friend*, 1977; *Paris, Texas*, 1984; *Wings of Desire*, 1987; *Buena Vista Social Club*, 1999). Important and innovative women film directors include **Margarethe von Trotta** (*Rosa Luxemburg*, 1986; *Das Versprechen*, 1995). Wolfgang Peterson's fantasy world in *The Neverending Story* (1984) was a resounding commercial success.

Edgar Reitz won international acclaim with his film epic *Heimat* (1984) and its sequel *Heimat 2* (1993).

However, West German cinema has been characterised by a strongly individual narrative feel which perhaps makes it less approachable to outsiders. One refreshing filmmaker worthy of note is **Doris Dörrie** who, with *Men... (Männer)* (1985) and *Bin ich schön?* (1998), reduced the zeitgeist to a humorous point.

CONTEMPORARY CINEMA

Recent successful films include **Tom Tykwer**'s 1999 *Lola rennt (Run Lola Run)* and **Wolfgang Becker**'s *Goodbye Lenin!*, which won the Best European Film award at the 2003 Berlin Film Festival. Another critically acclaimed movie was **Oliver Hirschbiegel**'s *Downfall*, starring Bruno Ganz as Hitler holed up in his bunker during the last days of his life. More controversial was **Dani Levy**'s 2007 satire *Mein Führer*, which ridicules an allegedly depressed Hitler at the end of the war.

The most successful German film of late, however, was *The Lives of Others*, written and directed by **Florian Henckel von Donnersmarck**, which won the Academy Award for Best Foreign Language Film in 2007. A year later, another German movie was nominated in Hollywood: the *Baader-Meinhof Complex*, by **Uli Edel** which tells the story of the early years of the Red Army Faction terrorist group and its impact on German society.

Nature

Germany is largely pastoral land marked by rolling hills and woods, low mountain ranges and in the south, the bulwark of the Alps: the birthplace of Europe's two major rivers, the Rhine and Danube, both of which traverse the country and remain the source of romance and legend.

Red-sandstone cliffs of Helgoland, North Sea © Rainer Jensen/Picture Alliance/Photoshot

Germany's Landscapes

At the heart of Europe, bordered by the Alps to the south and by the Baltic Sea to the north, Germany is virtually without natural frontiers to the east and the west. Such a lack of barriers, and the subsequent accessibility to outside influences, has had a profound effect on the country's history and civilisation.

GEOLOGY

In the **north** is the immense **Germano-Polish Plain**, formed by the glaciation of the Quaternary Era. The resistance of its crystalline bedrock meant that it was scarcely touched by the Hercynian and Alpine mountain-building movements. In the **centre**, during the Primary Era, the formidable Hercynian folding created a complex of minor massifs – now smoothed by erosion and for the most part wooded – separated by geographic depressions.

The most important of these Hercynian massifs are the Black Forest, the Rhenish schist massif and – encircling Bohemia in the Czech Republic – the Bavarian Forest, the Erzgebirge (Ore Mountains) and the Sudeten Mountains. On the edges of this Hercynian zone accumulated the coal-bearing deposits of the Ruhr and Silesia which led to the industrial expansion of the 19C.

The sedimentary basin of Swabia-Franconia, its vast area drained by the Main and the Neckar rivers, offers a less dramatic landscape. Abutting the Black Forest to the west and the Swabian Jura to the south, the limestone plateau is patterned with lines of hills sculpted according to the resistance of the varied strata.

In the **south**, the Alpine portion of Germany is delimited by the **Pre-Alps** (Voralpen) where the debris torn up and crushed during the final exertions of Quaternary glaciation formed the Bavarian plateau – a huge area stretching in a gentle slope as far as the Danube.

NORTHERN GERMANY

Lower Rhine Valley and Westphalia

Lush, green and flat, protected from flooding, the plain of the Lower Rhine brings to mind the landscape of the neighbouring Netherlands. There is similar scenery around Münster, on the Westphalian plain, where farmlands patterned by hedges and trees offer the additional attraction of many moated castles (Wasserburgen).

Great Northern Plain

Despite its apparent monotony, this enormous area (which extends eastwards into Poland) does offer a certain variety of landscapes.

In the south, below the Weser and Harz foothills, the Börde country lies between the Weser and the Elbe – a region covered by an alluvial topsoil whose fertility is legendary. Farms and market gardens flourish in this densely populated zone, which is favoured also with mineral deposits rich in iron and potassium.

Further north, on either side of the Elbe, is the Geest – a region of glacial deposits (sand, gravel, clay) with little to recommend it geographically, since it was covered by the Scandinavian glaciers right up to Paleolithic times. This has resulted in poor drainage and soils that are too sandy; between Berlin and the Baltic, the Mecklenburg plateau is scattered with shallow lakes interspersed with morainic deposits that bear witness to the prolonged glacial presence. The Spree and the Havel, meandering through the flatlands, supply the lakeland regions of the Spreewald and Potsdam. West of the Lower Weser, and in the Worpswede neighbourhood north of Bremen, peat bogs *(Moore)* alternate with very wet pastureland.

Most of the peat moors are now under cultivation, after having been drained using Dutch methods. The nature reserve south of Lüneburg, however, has preserved for all time a typical stretch of the original moorland.

The Baltic Coast

The German section of the Baltic Coast, which stretches from Flensburg all the way to the Stettin Haff, is a murrain landscape which, in addition to very flat parts also has a few elevations that rise above the 100m/320ft mark. Because of the relatively limited tidal differences of the shallow (on average 55m/180ft deep) Baltic Sea, the coastline has been subject to little change. That's why numerous cities with long traditions have evolved here. Between the bays of Lübeck and Kiel lies the Holsteinische Schweiz (Holstein Switzerland), the hilly and lake-dotted remainders of a ground and end moraine from the Ice Age.

The arms of the sea, which are the fjords and bays left over from the glaciers of the last Ice Age, cut deep into the land and form excellent natural harbours. Their banks are lined with beaches, forests and little fishing villages. Further to the east, the Baltic Coast is marked by shallow, water-filled inlets from the post-Ice Age period. Four islands lie offshore; the largest is the water-washed Rügen.

North Sea Coast

Because of the winds and waves, the North Sea Coast between the Netherlands and Denmark is constantly undergoing change. The tides raise and lower the water level by 2m/6.4ft to 3m/9.6ft twice daily. Several island groups lie off shore in the Watt, a 5X30km/3X18mi strip of land that is washed by the sea when the tide is in, but is above sea level at ebb times. The Watt ecosystem is home to nearly 2 000 species, from sea lions to creatures a tenth of a millimetre

in size. A strip of marshland created over centuries lies along the coast.

Once upon a time, the tides used to bring in animal and plant particles together with fine sand, which formed a fertile base for agriculture in the marshlands. Behind this is the less fertile, hilly "Geest". Broad moors have formed in the depressions, some of which have been turned over to farming. Germany's two largest seaports, Hamburg and Bremen, lie at the inner ends of the funnel-shaped Elbe and Weser estuaries.

CENTRAL GERMANY
The Rhenish Schist Massif

This ancient geological mass, cut through by the Rhine – the only continuous natural channel of communication between the north and south of the country – the Lahn and the Moselle, comprises among others the highlands known as the Eifel, the Westerwald, the Taunus and the Hunsrück.

They share the same inhospitable climate and the same evidence of volcanic activity as the crater lakes, known as the *Maare*, of the Eifel plateau.

The Eifel will be familiar to motoring enthusiasts as the home of the Nürburgring Grand Prix race circuit. The Upper Sauerland, a thickly wooded, mountainous region (alt 841m/2 760ft), with its many dams, acts as a water reserve for the Ruhr industrial area.

Mountains of Upper Hessen and the Weser

Between the Rhenish schist massif and the Thuringian Forest *(Thüringer Wald)* lies an amalgam of heights, some of them volcanic (Vogelsberg, Rhön), and depressions which have been used as a highway, linking north and south, by German invaders throughout the ages. Between Westphalia and the north, the Weser Mountains – extended westwards by the Teutoburger Wald – form a barrier that is breached at the Porta Westfalica, near Minden. Further to the east, the Erzgebirge (Ore Mountains) form a natural frontier with the Czech Republic.

Harz Mountains

This relatively high range (alt 1 142m/ 3 747ft at the Brocken) has a typical mountain climate, characterised by heavy snowfalls in winter.

SOUTHERN GERMANY
Plain of the Upper Rhine

Between Basle and the Bingen Gap, a soil of exceptionally fertile loess – accompanied by a climate combining light rainfall, an early spring and a very hot summer – has produced a rich agricultural yield (hops, corn and tobacco) and a terrain highly suitable for the cultivation of vines. The whole of this low-lying, productive tract has become a crossroads for the rest of Europe, which is why certain towns – Frankfurt, for instance – have profited internationally from their development.

Schwarzwald (Black Forest)

This crystalline massif (alt 1 493m/ 4 899ft at the Feldberg), which overlooks the Rhine Gap, is relatively well populated. The region's climate and many thermal springs draw large numbers of tourists every year. The new Black Forest National Park preserves the hillside woods from which the region draws its name.

Swabian-Franconian Basin

Franconia, formed by vast, gently undulating plateaux, is bordered to the southeast by the small limestone massif of the Franconian Jura that produces Germany's building stone, and to the north and northeast by the wooded crystalline ranges flanking Bohemia and Thuringia. Swabia offers a variety of landscapes – barred to the south by the blue line of the Swabian Jura, which rises to 874m/2 867ft. Small valleys, enlivened by orchards and vineyards, alternate here with the gentle slopes of wooded hillsides.

The Alps and the Bavarian Plateau

The Bavarian Alps and the Allgäu Alps offer contrasts between the sombre green of their forests and the shades of grey of their rocks and escarpments, an impressive sight when seen against the backdrop of a blue sky. The Zugspitze, the highest point in Germany, reaches an altitude of 2 962m/9 720ft. Torrents such as Isar, Lech, Iller and Inn, have over time carved out corridors with broad, flat floors suitable for the cultivation of the land and the development of towns (Ulm, Augsburg and Munich).

NATURAL SPACES AND PROTECTION

Although densely populated and highly industrialised, wide open natural spaces still characterise much of the countryside. Germany has 2 389km/1 484mi of coastline, Alpine peaks approaching 3 000m/9 842ft and fertile river valleys. The Zugspitze forms the peak of the country (2 064m/9 724ft). The Black Forest is a *Mittelgebirge* (mid-size mountain range). Other *Mittelgebirge* include the Bavarian Forest, the Harz Mountains and the Sauerland.

Germany has 15 national parks alongside many species of plants and wildlife, thus functioning as natural laboratories for researchers and scientists. Landscapes are hugely varied and include North Sea mudflats, the salt marshes and chalk cliffs on Rügen Island, the evocatively warped basalt and sandstone formations of Saxon Switzerland and the mighty peaks around Berchtesgaden, Germany's oldest national park. Some 104 nature parks have a lower degree of environmental protection and are essentially outdoor playgrounds: these sprawling rural landscapes are crisscrossed by roads and wrapped around villages. Controlled logging and agricultural use is permitted.

As to Germany's fauna, birds include osprey, grouse, owls, passerines and woodpeckers, and protected birds as the black stork, the warbler and the great horned owl. Among the raptors, the rare and endangered sea eagle can still be observed. The Bodden area in western Pomerania has the largest nesting site of cranes in Europe (nearly 30 000 each year).

Discovering
Germany

Pfahlbaumuseum (Stilt Houses Museum), Lake Constance
© Pfahlbaumuseum Unteruhldingen

Berlin and Brandenburg

Brandenburger Tor, Berlin
© visitBerlin / Wolfgang Scholvien

Pariser Platz

Berlin and Brandenburg

Dynamic, intriguing, individualistic, forward-looking – Berlin is Germany's most visited city and the third-most popular in Europe after London and Paris. And for good reason: the wealth and quality of its cultural life is peerless, with world-class museums, opera, theatre, music and a spirited art and gallery scene. Architectural gems also abound, some of them centuries old, others created only during the post-reunification construction maelstrom. By contrast, Brandenburg, the state surrounding it, is imbued with a soothing tranquillity and great natural splendour. This is a region shaped by water – rivers, lakes and canals – wending through a flat, windswept landscape, much of which is protected as a nature preserve. Culturally, Brandenburg's jewel is Potsdam, which packs more palaces and parks into its compact frame than many a small nation.

Highlights

1 Get close-ups of the glass dome atop the **Reichstag** (p129)

2 Meet Nefertiti, Berlin's most beautiful woman, at the **Neues Museum** (p136)

3 Admire the largest collection of 18C paintings outside France at **Schloss Charlottenburg** (p141)

4 Enjoy a picnic in the lovely **Tiergarten** (p144)

5 Explore the "Wild East" on a **Trabi Safari** (p153)

Architecture

It may not feel right to put a positive spin on the destruction brought upon Berlin by war and division, but it did give the German capital the opportunity to redefine itself architecturally, especially since the fall of the Wall. Most of the world's leading architects – Frank Gehry, David Chipperfield, Daniel Libeskind and Lord Norman Foster among them – have created modern masterpieces fit for the 21C. Areas to check out closely are the new government quarter, Potsdamer Platz, Pariser Platz and the Embassy Quarter.

Shopping

The best shopping in Berlin is not done in shopping centres, but in small boutiques and shops lining the streets of its various neighbourhoods. Local designer

Dome of Reichstag

© M. Hertlein/MICHELIN

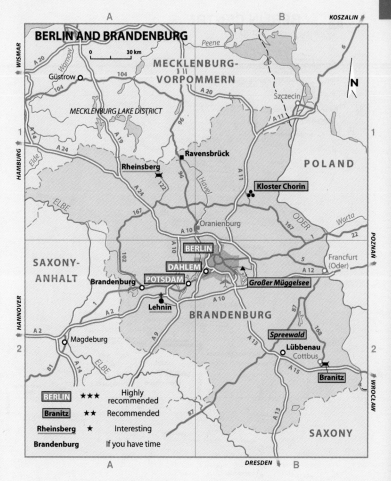

BERLIN AND BRANDENBURG

0 ———— 30 km

BERLIN	★★★	Highly recommended
Branitz	★★	Recommended
Rheinsberg	★	Interesting
Brandenburg		If you have time

---

boutiques cluster in the Scheunenviertel in Mitte, while Friedrichstraße offers upmarket brand names in the glamourous Friedrich-stadtpassagen. In Kreuzberg you can pick up great vintage clothing and the latest in streetwear, while Charlottenburg has an entire street (Kantstraße) devoted to home decorations and furniture. Steps away is the famous Kurfürstendamm boulevard, which is dominated by department stores and chains.

Eating

From snack shacks to gourmet temples, Berlin offers a cornucopia of eating experiences. Traditional local fare includes *Eisbein* (boiled pork knuckle) and *Bouletten* (ground meat patties) but the most famous homegrown dish is the *Currywurst*, a sliv-ered sausage drenched in a spicy tomato sauce and dusted with curry powder. Sophisticated foodies will be happy to hear that Berlin now has a dozen restaurants boasting Michelin stars. And since Berlin is such an international city, you can also dine out on exotic dishes from Austria to Zambia.

Nightlife

When it comes to after-dark diversions, few cities can compete with Berlin. No matter whether your interests run to opera or clubbing, cabaret or comedy, theatre or art-house cinema, you'll be able to sate them in the German capital. Thanks to its legendary tolerance, Berlin also has a happening gay and lesbian scene. The area south of Nollendorf U-Bahn station in Schöneberg has been a traditional hub since the 1920s.

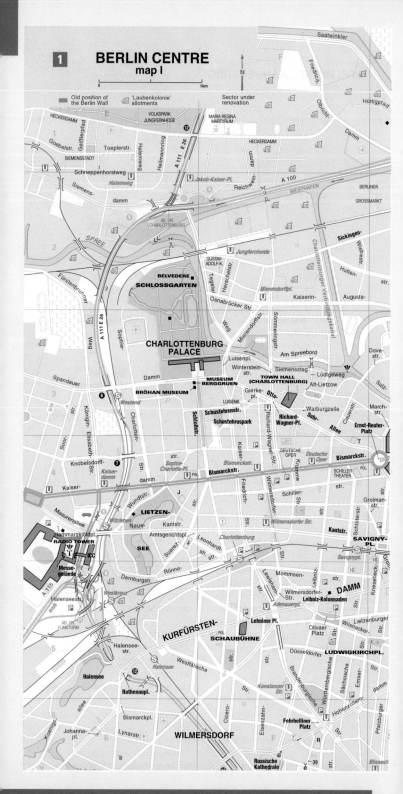

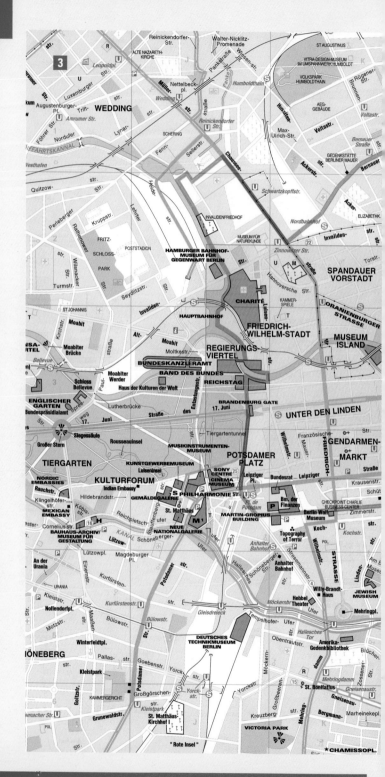

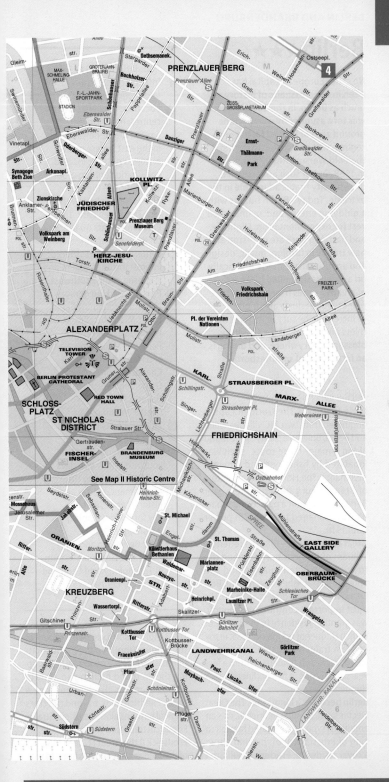

Berlin★★★

No other European capital has been in the crosshairs of history as much as Berlin. In the 20C alone, it was torn asunder by war, became ground zero of Hitler's fascist regime, was split into two during the Cold War and finally reunited in 1989. Out of such adversity has grown a city that is adaptable in the extreme. Today's Berlin buzzes with a giddying energy and an unbridled zest for experimentation. Nightlife and partying here are non-stop and new trends in fashion, music, design and architecture emerge practically on a daily basis fuelled by an influx of creative types from around the planet. But Berlin is also a place of incredible beauty in its forests, rivers and historical sites. Culture blossoms everywhere, and dining is an international smorgasbord.

▶ **Population:** 3 419 623

Info: *see Practical Information, opposite.*

Location: Berlin has two city centres: the Mitte district around Alexanderplatz in the east, where most historic sights are located, and Charlottenburg around Zoo Station in the west. The two are linked by the vast Tiergarten Park. The Potsdamer Platz quarter is off the park's southeastern corner. Outlying districts of interest include Dahlem and Wannsee in the southwest.

P Parking: Parking garages abound throughout Berlin.

Don't Miss: Museum Island (especially the Pergamon Museum and Neues Museum), Charlottenburg Palace, Gemäldegalerie (Picture Gallery), "Historic Centre" Walking Tour.

Timing: You could spend a week in Berlin and not see everything. Prioritise your visit. Allow two days for Mitte, including the government quarter and historic centre, and one day for Charlottenburg, including the palace.

Kids: Berlin Zoo and Aquarium, German Museum of Technology, and Legoland Discovery Centre.

A BIT OF HISTORY

Early history – The German capital originated from two 13C villages: Cölln and Berlin. Built on a sandy Spree island along a major trade route, each was inhabited by fishermen and itinerant merchants. The Hohenzollern Electors of Brandenburg became rulers over Berlin in 1417, built a palace and miraculously managed to remain in power until 1918.

Great Elector (1640–1688) – Frederick-William of Brandenburg fortified the town, constructed quays along the Spree and established laws making Berlin a civilised, well-governed town. His most important contribution, though, was granting residence to thousands of French Huguenot refuges in 1685, many of them trained craftsmen, theologians, doctors and scholars. Within a few years, nearly one in five Berliners was of Huguenot descent.

Berlin becomes a kingdom – The Great Elector's son, Elector Friedrich III, was an ambitious type who elevated himself to king of Prussia in 1701, making Berlin a royal residence. **Frederick-William I** (1713–40), his son (otherwise known as the **Soldier King**), laid the foundations of Prussian military power by introducing the draft and building an army of 80 000 men. He also laid out a new town, Friedrichstadt, beyond the city's original bastions along Leipziger Straße, Friedrichstraße and Wilhelmstraße. **Frederick II the Great** (1740–1786), son of the Soldier King, sent his army to vari-

PRACTICAL INFORMATION

Telephone area code: ✆030

Tourist information

Berlin Tourismus Marketing
(*BTM; info hotline, room and ticket
reservations* ✆*(030) 25 00 23 33;
www.visitberlin.de; Mon–Fri 9am–7pm,
Sat 10am–6pm, Sun 10am–2pm*.
Tourist offices: Brandenburg Gate,
*Pariser Platz, South Wing, daily 9:30am–
7pm (6pm Nov–Mar)*; Hauptbahnhof,
*ground floor near Europaplatz entrance,
daily 8am–10pm*; Neues Kranzlereck,
*Kurfürstendamm 22, Mon–Sat
9:30am–8pm*; Fernsehturm (TV Tower),
daily 10am–6pm (4pm Nov–Mar).

Entertainment

Listings: The bi-weekly city magazines
Zitty and *Tip* and the monthly *Berlin-
Programm* (available at bookshops
and kiosks) are the best sources of
events listings. All are in German.
The monthly English-language
Ex-Berliner magazine also has some
listings and reviews.
Tickets can be booked via www.visit
berlin.de or call the BTM hotline
✆*(030) 25 00 23 33*. Multilingual staff
can also help with room reservations,
a free service with a best-price
guarantee.

Post offices with late hours

The branch at Joachimstaler Straße 41
near Bahnhof Zoo is open Mon–Sat
10am–7pm; near Alexanderplatz, the
branch at Rathausstraße 5 is open
Mon–Fri 9am–7pm, Sat 9am–4pm.
For additional branches, call ✆*(01802)
33 33* or check www.deutschepost.de.

Daily papers

*Berliner Morgenpost, Tagesspiegel,
Berliner Zeitung, Die Tageszeitung.*

Internet

www.berlin.de; www.visitberlin.de;
www.museumsportal-berlin.de;
www.exberliner.com

GETTING THERE AND AROUND

Airport

For general information about Berlin's
two airports, call ✆*(030) 60 91 11 50*.
From **Tegel (TXL)**, northwest of Berlin,
bus nos. 109 and X9 travel through
the western city centre to Zoo Station
(Bahnhof Zoologischer Garten); bus
TXL serves Alexanderplatz in the
eastern city centre. Jakob-Kaiser-Platz
is the closest U-Bahn station. All three
buses stop here as well. **Schönefeld
(SFX)** is southeast of town and linked
by Airport Express train to the city
centre. The opening of the new airport
(**BER**) has been plagued by delays.

Public Transport

Berlin's public transport system
consists of buses, trams, S-Bahn
(light rail) and U-Bahn (underground,
subway). 24hr hotline is✆*19449* or
www.bvg.de. In-person information at
the kiosk on Hardenbergplatz (*outside
Bahnhof Zoo; open 6.30am–9.30pm*)
and at many U-Bahn and S-Bahn
stations. Berlin and its environs are
divided into fare zones A, B and C. For
rides within the city, a Zone AB ticket
suffices. Potsdam and Schönefeld
airport require an ABC ticket. Tickets
are available from vending machines
in all U-Bahn and S-Bahn stations, in
trams and from bus drivers. They must
be stamped prior to your journey.
Single tickets 2.60€ for Zone AB;
day passes (valid until 3am next day)
6.70€.
Berlin Welcome Card (www.visit
berlin.de/welcomecard) is available
for 2, 3 and 5 days and costs
18.50€/25.50€/32.50€
respectively for fare zones AB and
20.50€/27.50€/37.50€ for ABC.
Cards are sold at the tourist offices and
at BVG ticket vending machines.
Useful Tip: Bus no. 100 goes between
Bahnhof Zoo and Alexanderplatz,
passing major sights. Bus no. 200
follows a southerly route via Potsdamer
Platz and the Kulturforum museums.

ous battlefields, but also embraced the ideals of the Age of Enlightenment, surrounding himself with the finest thinkers of the day, including Voltaire. His reign also saw the construction of the Forum Fridericianum (today Bebelplatz) and other buildings along Unter den Linden, many designed by Georg Wenzeslaus von Knobelsdorff (1699–1753). Major monuments completed were the Brandenburg Gate (1789) and the *Neue Wache* (1818).

19C Berlin – Napoleon's defeat of Prussia in 1806 and the three-year occupation by the French of Berlin was a humiliating moment for the fledgling kingdom. However, it also imbued Prussians with a greater sense of patriotism, led to a number of civic reforms and ultimately paved the way for the Industrial Revolution and the formation of the German Empire in 1871 with Berlin as its capital. As the city boomed economically, politically and culturally, its population rose to 1 million around 1870 and twice that by 1900.

Greater Berlin – In 1920 the city united six urban suburbs, seven towns, 59 villages and 27 demesnes under a single administration encompassing 4 million inhabitants. Despite the upheavals following World War I, the 1920s saw immense intellectual and artistic growth. A highlight was the 1928 premiere of Bertolt Brecht and Kurt Weill's *Threepenny Opera*.

The blossoming of this talent was violently interrupted by Hitler's regime, when, along with the persecution of the Jews, a wealth of German artistic and literary heritage was banned or destroyed in the campaign against "degenerate art".

The taking of Berlin – From 21 April to 3 May 1945 the German capital was a battlefield. The Red Army marched against the remnants of the German army, destroying everything above ground, including 120 of Berlin's 248 bridges. On 30 April 1945, the Reichstag was captured and Hitler committed suicide.

Berlin Divided – After the German surrender on 8 May, the four victorious allies – Great Britain, the United States, France and the Soviet Union – took over administration of greater Berlin. But political developments in the Soviet Sector hindered the municipal administration. The Berlin Blockade, triggered by Soviet opposition to currency reform in the western sectors, was undermined by an airlift of supplies from the West (26 June 1948 to 12 May 1949). Although this effort prevented Berlin's absorption into the Soviet state, it did not forestall the division of Germany. In 1949, Berlin's Soviet sector became the capital of the German Democratic Republic (GDR), while West Berlin remained under the control of the western Allies.

At the height of the Cold War, in 1961, the city's division was completed with

"Fall" of the Berlin Wall at the Brandenburg Gate in 1989

© Imagebroker/hemis.fr

Tiergarten in summer

© G. Giuglio/hemis.fr

the construction of a concrete and barbed-wire wall by the East Germans. The goal? To prevent an exodus of its own people seeking freedom and opportunity in West Berlin and the Federal Republic of Germany (West Germany).

The "fall" of the Wall – In November 1989, the GDR government, bowing to increased public pressure, agreed to re-establish free passage between the two Germanies. A night of wild celebration, especially around the Brandenburg Gate, followed the official "opening" of the Berlin Wall on 9 November.

In June 1991, the Bundestag (German parliament) selected Berlin as the capital of a reunited Germany. Since then, Berlin has experienced an extraordinary building boom, and the two city halves have physically grown back together.

An outdoor city – Berlin, the largest city in Germany, covers an area eight times the size of Paris. Devastated by the war, the capital lost much of its historical heritage and is now essentially a modern city shaped by leading architects of the 20C and 21C, including Le Corbusier and Hans Scharoun and, more recently, Daniel Libeskind, Renzo Piano, Helmut Jahn and others. Berlin is also a very green city, with the vast Tiergarten Park at its heart, numerous neighbourhood parks and a greenbelt stretching along its periphery. Waterways, including the Spree River, which cuts through the central city, the Havel River along its western edge and various lakes, including the Wannsee and Grunewaldsee, provide further open spaces and recreational opportunities.

A lively cultural scene – Berlin justly enjoys a reputation for the quality and diversity of its cultural scene. Fashion, art, design and music are all exploding, fuelled by artists and creative spirits from around the world. In February, a galaxy of stars descends for the Berlinale *(see INTRODUCTION: Cinema)*, one of Europe's most prestigious film festivals.

There are venues everywhere, but much of the action centres on the **Scheunenviertel**, the old Jewish Quarter, in the Mitte district, just north of Alexanderplatz. The **Prenzlauer Berg** quarter just north of here also teems with bars, restaurants and cafés. Major hubs are Kollwitzplatz and Helmholtzplatz squares. The **Kreuzberg** district, south of Mitte, has a more alternative, multi-cultural flair, especially along Bergmannstraße, Schlesische Straße and Oranienstraße. The **Potsdamer Platz** and Gendarmenmarkt areas have the most highbrow venues, including the Konzerthaus and the Philharmonie for classical music. Theatres also flank Kurfürstendamm in Charlottenburg and Friedrichstraße in Mitte.

The cosmopolitan sophistication evident throughout Berlin also extends to its cuisine. Restaurants serving traditional local dishes such as pigs' knuckles *(Eisbein)*

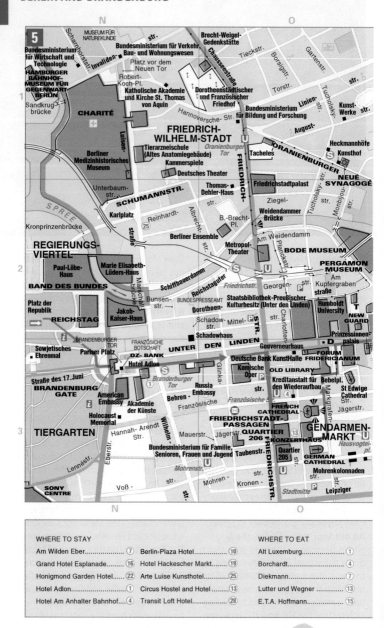

WHERE TO STAY

WHERE TO EAT

with sauerkraut and pease-pudding have become a dying breed while gourmet restaurants catering to a sophisticated, international clientele are on the rise.

WALKING TOUR

HISTORIC CENTRE★★

The itinerary starts at the Reichstag and follows the celebrated Unter den Linden ("Under the Lime Trees") boulevard east from Pariser Platz to Schlossplatz.

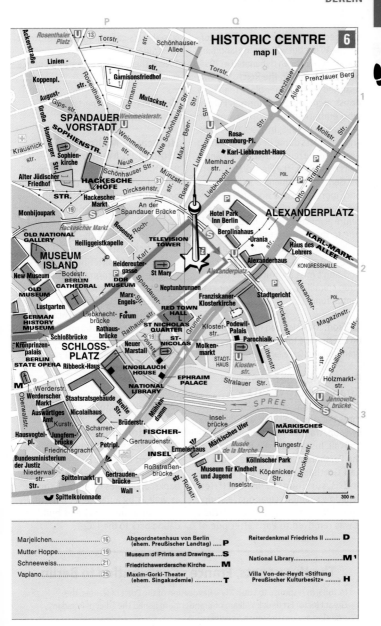

HISTORIC CENTRE
map II
6

Most of the great monuments of the former Prussian capital flank this grand avenue, which originated as a bridle path leading from the city palace to the Tiergarten hunting reserve. A veritable open book of the country's history, Mitte is a kaleidoscope of architecture mixing Baroque with Neoclassical buildings alongside Stalinist behemoths and contemporary designs. It's all best explored on foot.

Reichstag★★

This massive neo-Renaissance government building was inaugurated in 1894, damaged by fire in 1933 and heavily bombed in 1945. It was restored during the 1970s, but without the landmark dome that had been dynamited in 1954. After reunification the Reichstag was returned to its former glory thanks to British architect, **Lord Norman Foster**, who embarked on a top-to-bottom renovation in 1995. In 1999, the sparkling new glass dome became a shining beacon of the reunited city. Poignantly, it sits right above the Plenary Hall where the German parliament (Bundestag) has once more convened since 1999. Register in advance (online or at the service centre across the street) for the free lift ride to the **viewing platform**★★ and take in the fantastic views of the historic centre and vast Tiergarten Park. And don't miss a stroll up the dome's ramp spiralling around its mirror-clad central funnel.

▷ From the Reichstag head south on Ebertstraße towards the Brandenburg Gate.

Brandenburger Tor (Brandenburg Gate)★★

This triumphal arch was for almost three decades the symbol of the city's division, trapped just behind the Berlin Wall. Inspired by the Propylaea of the Parthenon, the gate was built by Carl Gotthard Langhans in 1788–91 and is surmounted by Gottfried Schadow's famous Quadriga, a sculpture of the Goddess of Victory (1793). It was removed to Paris after one of Napoléon's campaigns and returned to Berlin in 1814.

Today, the gate is the emblem of the reunited city.

▷ Head south on Ebertstraße to Behrenstraße.

Holocaust-Mahnmal (Holocaust Memorial)★★

Built to honour the memory of the millions of Jews killed by the Nazis, this powerful memorial was designed by Jewish German-American architect Peter Eisenman. Stretching over 2ha/5 acres just south of the Brandenburg Gate, it consists of some 2 700 concrete pillars of differing heights. The underground information centre *(Ort der Information)* provides historical context on the Holocaust and includes one room where the names of all known victims are read out aloud continuously. The memorial was inaugurated on 10 May 2005, exactly 60 years after the German capitulation.

▷ Return to the Brandenburg Gate and turn right onto Unter den Linden.

Unter den Linden★★

Berlin's most elegant boulevard was conceived by Great Elector Frederick William in 1647. It is lined by embassies, banks, and stores catering to tourists, as well as by a parade of beautifully restored monuments and buildings dating back to the 17C.

The Huguenots, France's Contribution to Berlin

In 1685, in response to Louis XIV's Revocation of the Edict of Nantes, the Great Elector Frederick William of Brandenburg issued the Edict of Potsdam granting asylum to French Calvinists.

These Protestants, or Huguenots, came in droves. In fact, 100 000 passed through Frankfurt-am-Main alone in the space of 20 years. Some 15 000 Huguenots came to Brandenburg, including 6 000 to Berlin, representing one-quarter of the population. Most settled in the Friedrichstadt area around Gendarmenmarkt, developing trades, a textile industry and fruit and vegetable husbandry. They also introduced several popular new dances: the cotillon, the gavotte and the minuet. Until the 19C, Berlin's French community had its own ecclesiastical and legal organisation.

▶ Head south on Friedrichstraße.

Friedrichstadtpassagen★

Friedrichstraße 67–76.

Over the past 20 years, Friedrichstraße, which, until World War II used to be one of Berlin's ritziest boulevards, has definitely returned to its old glamourous self, with chic shops, fancy restaurants and high-end galleries. Some 2.6 billion euros have been invested here, about half of them in three block-size *Quartiere*, a trio of buildings linked by an underground walkway between Mohrenstraße and Französischer Straße. Quartier 207, at the corner of Französische Straße, was designed by architect Jean Nouvel. It houses the Berlin branch of the luxurious French department store Galeries Lafayette, immensely popular with both Berliners and visitors. Its most spectacular feature is the giant central glass cone that playfully catches and reflects light. Next door, Quartier 206 is the brainchild of the American architectural firm Pei Cobb Freed & Partners and is particularly lovely when illuminated at night. The bi-level interior is an Art-Deco inspired kaleidoscope of inlaid coloured marble tented by a glass roof. By comparison, Quartier 205, designed by the late Oswald Mathias Ungers, is more austere. Its most eye-catching element is the *Tower of Clythe*, a three-storey tall sculpture made from crushed cars by the American artist John Chamberlain.

Gendarmenmarkt★★

Berlin's most beautiful square was named after the "Gens d'Armes", a Prussian regiment made up entirely of Huguenots who had settled here after having been forced out of their native France in 1685. The square is bookended by the **Deutscher Dom★** (German cathedral) and the **Französischer Dom★** (French cathedral), both of which contain exhibits. The tower of the latter can be climbed.

Konzerthaus★★ (Concert Hall)

Linking the two Gendarmenmarkt churches is the Konzerthaus, built by Karl Friedrich Schinkel in 1821. Originally a theatre called the Schauspielhaus, it is now a classical concert hall. Schinkel found inspiration in Greek antiquity: note the grand staircase leading to a portico supported by six pillars.

▶ Take Markgrafenstraße north, turn right on Behrensstraße and follow it to Bebelplatz.

Bebelplatz★

This wide open square was once the heart of the **Forum Fridericianum**, a Neoclassical arts and cultural complex conceived by Frederick the Great and designed by Knobelsdorff. Since the king's military exploits diminished his cashflow, only some structures were completed. The most magnificent is the **Staatsoper Unter den Linden** (national opera house) on the east side. The ensemble also encompasses the Baroque Old Royal Library on the western side, the Hotel de Rome in a 19C bank building on the south side and St. Hedwig Cathedral in the southeastern corner.

In 1994, Micha Ullman created the below-ground **Versunkene Bibliothek** (sunken library), a glass-fronted, empty-shelved room in the square's centre. It commemorates the first official book-burning held by the Nazis on Bebelplatz on 10 May 1933.

St. Hedwigs-Kathedrale

Knobelsdorff drafted the plans for this copper-domed Catholic church (1773), which was inspired by the Pantheon in Rome. Since Frederick the Great had been victorious in capturing Silesia, the church was dedicated to St. Hedwig, the patron saint of Silesia. It was badly damaged during World War II and rebuilt with a modern interior.

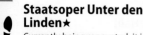

Staatsoper Unter den Linden★

Currently being renovated, it is expected to reopen by 2016.

Built by Knobelsdorff between 1740 and 1743, the national opera house burned down in 1843; Langhans' reconstruction follows the original plans. Destroyed again during World War II, it was rebuilt by Richard Paulick between 1951 and 1955 and is home to one of Germany's most prestigious ensembles.

Alte Königliche Bibliothek★ (Old Royal Library)

Designed by Georg Friedrich Boumann in the Viennese Baroque style for the royal book collection, this library was inaugurated in 1780 and now houses part of the university law school.

Humboldt-Universität

Opposite Bebelplatz.

The palace of Frederick the Great's brother, Prince Heinrich, built in 1753, became a university in 1810 and now enrolls around 37 000 students. Left of the main entrance on Unter den Linden a statue of founder Wilhelm von Humboldt faces that of his brother, the explorer and geographer Alexander von Humboldt. The philosophers Fichte and Hegel and the scientists Einstein and Planck all taught here; Heine and Marx were students.

▷ Continue east on Unter den Linden.

Neue Wache (New Guardhouse)

Designed by Schinkel in 1818, this former guardhouse is now Germany's central memorial "for the victims of war and violence". The austere interior houses the Käthe Kollwitz sculpture called *Mother with Dead Son.*

Deutsches Historisches Museum★★ (German Historical Museum)

Open year-round daily 10am–6pm. Closed Dec 24. ⊚8€. &
℘(030) 20 30 40. www.dhm.de.

Housed in the Baroque former armoury *(Zeughaus)*, this comprehensive exhibit uses multimedia stations and original artefacts to trace some 2 000 years of German history. The upper floor covers the period from the 1C AD to the end of the German Empire in 1918, while the ground floor details events of the Weimar Republic, the Nazi and Cold War years and modern reunification.

Friedrichswerdersche Kirche★ (Friedrichswerder Church)

☛ Closed until further notice. &.
℘(030) 266 42 42 42.
www.smb.museum.

Schinkel, the architect who left his mark on Berlin more than any other, also designed this neo-Gothic brick church just south of Unter den Linden. Completed in 1830, it now houses a collection of **19C sculpture** by Schinkel and his contemporaries.

▷ Cross the Spree canal via the Schloßbrücke adorned with Schinkel sculptures to get to Museum Island (&see below). In front of you looms Berlin Cathedral.

Berliner Dom★ (Berlin Cathedral)

Open Apr–Sept Mon–Sat 9am–8pm, Sun noon–8pm (Oct–Mar daily until 7pm).
⊚7€ (10€ with audioguide). &
℘(030) 20 26 91 36.
www.berlinerdom.de.

This Italian Renaissance cathedral was consecrated in 1905 and features a magnificent **interior★★**. The sarcophagi of Frederick I and his second wife Sophie Charlotte, carved by Andreas Schlüter, are of special artistic merit. More members of the Prussian royal family are buried in the **crypt**. For close-ups of the massive dome and a sweeping panorama of Museum Island and the central city, climb up the 270 stairs to the viewing gallery.

▷ Cross Liebknechtbrücke bridge and take the stairs on your left down to the canal.

DDR Museum Berlin★★

Karl-Liebknecht-Straße 1. Open year-round Sun–Fri 10am–8pm, Sat until 10pm. ✆6€. ♿ ☎(030) 847 123 731. www.ddr-museum.de.

This quirky museum offers a snapshot of what daily life was like for regular people in the former East Germany. In a hands-on fashion it focuses on various aspects that characterised this now extinct society: price controls, product shortages and the Stasi secret service and its ubiquitous surveillance cameras. The holiday photos are especially hilarious. Climb aboard the Trabi, the legendary GDR-made car, and step inside the living room where you can watch some of the most popular shows of the era on a black and white television.

▷ Climb back up the stairs and take a left on Karl-Liebknecht-Straße.

Alexanderplatz★

Named for Tsar Alexander, who visited Berlin in 1805, this square – known as "Alex" – is the commercial and traffic hub of the eastern city centre. It was completely destroyed in World War II and rebuilt in an austere socialist style that is still in evidence today, despite improvements. On your way to Alex, you will pass the 13C **Marienkirche** (St. Mary's Church) with its macabre Dance of Death fresco that recalls the ravages of the Black Plague. The red-brick pile just south of here is the **Rotes Rathaus** (red town hall), where the Berlin mayor makes his home. Above it all looms the 368m/1 207ft-high **Fernsehturm★** (TV tower) with a viewing platform and revolving restaurant at 203m/667ft.

Nikolaiviertel★
(St. Nicholas Quarter)

With its narrow cobbled streets and old taverns, this quarter is home to the **Knoblauch House★** (Poststraße 23; open Tue–Sun 10am–6pm; closed Dec 24 & 31; ☎030 24 00 21 62; www.stadtmuseum.de) as well as **Ephraim Palace★** (Poststraße 16; open Tue and Thu–Sun 10am–6pm, Wed noon–8pm; closed Dec 24 & 31;✆5€; same phone and website as Kno-

blauch House) and other restored period houses. The Nikolaiviertel is dominated by the bell-towers of the Late Gothic 1230 **Nikolaikirche★**, Berlin's oldest church, which is now a history museum.

ADDITIONAL SIGHTS IN THE HISTORIC CENTRE

Hamburger Bahnhof – Museum für Gegenwart Berlin★★
(Hamburg Station – Museum of Contemporary Art)

Invalidenstraße 50–51. Open year-round Tue–Fri 10am–6pm (Thu until 8pm), Sat–Sun 11am–6pm. ✆14€. ♿ ☎(030) 266 42 42 42. www.hamburgerbahnhof.de.

Berlin's key contemporary art museum occupies a former railway station built in the 1840s, closed in 1884 and converted into a transport museum in 1906. Today the main building and an extension in a 300m/984ft-long warehouse present artworks from 1960 to the present. The collection includes such top artists as Anselm Kiefer, Richard Long, Bruce Nauman and Cindy Sherman along with Cy Twombly, Robert Rauschenberg and Andy Warhol. An entire wing is devoted to Joseph Beuys.

Märkisches Museum★
(Berlin Regional History Museum)

Am Köllnischen Park 5. Open year-round Tue–Sun 10am-6pm. Closed Dec 24 & 31. ✆5€. ☎(030) 24 00 21 62. www.stadtmuseum.de.

This rambling red-brick building (1908) tells the history of Berlin and the surrounding region (called the March of Brandenburg) from the Middle Ages onwards. A copy of a 1474 Roland figure – a symbol of civic liberties and privileges – guards the museum entrance.

Madame Tussauds★

Under den Linden 74. Open year-round daily 10am–7pm (Aug until 8pm). ✆21€. ☎(01806) 54 58 00. www.madametussauds.com/berlin.

Meet Elvis, Obama, the Pope, Albert Einstein, George Clooney and dozens of other personalities from entertainment, politics, sports and religion at the Berlin branch of London's famous waxworks. All can be photographed and even touched. The most controversial figure is that of Adolf Hitler, which made headlines when its head was torn off by a local man on opening day. It has since been restored.

Sammlung Boros★★ (Boros Collection)

Reinhardstraße 20. Open year-round Fri–Sun 10am–6pm. ☎12€. ✆(030) 27 59 40 65. www.sammlung-boros.de.

One of the most spectacular contemporary art collections in Germany, the private Sammlung Boros showcases such major players as Olafur Eliasson, Ai Weiwei, Wolfgang Tillmans, Thomas Ruff and Thea Djordjadze in a spectacularly converted bunker from World War II. It can only be seen on hugely popular guided tours, which should be booked online several weeks in advance.

MUSEUMSINSEL★★★ (MUSEUM ISLAND)

The brainchild of Frederick William III, this vast museum complex occupies the northern end of Spree island, where Berlin's settlement first began in the 13C. Its five museums deliver a survey of 6 000 years of the art and cultural history of Europe. Since 1999, they have also been included on UNESCO's list of World Heritage Sites. Under a master plan conceived by British architect David Chipperfield, the compound is undergoing a complete overhaul expected to last until 2025. Restoration of the Bode-Museum and the Alte Nationalgalerie have already been completed. Next up are the Altes Museum and the Pergamon Museum – expect sections to be closed during the process. Open since late 2009, the spectacular Neues Museum is a complete reconstruction of the original that was destroyed in World War II. It houses the famous Egyptian Collection and the Museum of Pre- and Early History. Chipperfield will also design a modern new

entrance building, called the James Simon Gallery. Eventually a walkway called the "Archaeological Promenade" will link all but the Alte Nationalgalerie with each other.

Pergamonmuseum★★★ (Pergamon Museum)

Entry on Kupfergraben. Open year-round daily 10am–6pm (Thu until 8pm). Closed Dec 24; open Dec 31 10am–2pm. ☎12€. ✆(030) 266 42 42 42. www.smb.museum.

The most popular museum on Museum Island was also the last to be completed, in 1930. It harbours three world-class collections. The **Collection of Classical Antiquities★★★** (Antikensammlung) features the **Pergamon Altar★★★**, a masterpiece of Hellenistic art (2C BC); market gate of **Miletus★★** (2C AD); and Greek and Roman sculptures. The **Museum of the Ancient Near East★★** (Vorderasiatisches Museum) includes the **Processional Way and Ishtar Gate★★** from ancient Babylon, 580 BC; the plinth of Asachadon, 7C BC; and the façade of the Temple of Irmin at Uruk. Highlights of the **Museum of Islamic Art★★** (Museum für Islamische Kunst) include the façade of Mshatta Palace (8C) from Jordan; the painted Aleppo room (early 17C); and miniatures (15C–17C).

Alte Nationalgalerie★★ (Old National Gallery)

Entry on Bodestraße. Open year-round Tue–Sun 10am–6pm (Thu until 8pm). Closed Dec 24 and 31. ☎10€. ✆(030) 266 42 42 42. www.smb.museum.

This museum exhibits 19C European paintings and sculptures. Romantic artists take centre stage on the top floor, with outstanding works by **Caspar David Friedrich** and Karl Friedrich Schinkel. Galleries on the middle floor are dedicated to French Impressionists, Realists including Wilhelm Leibl, and German and Flemish historical scenes. On the ground floor are works by Berlin artists (**Adolph Menzel**, Krüger, Schadow) along with Realist landscapes (Constable, Courbet).

Museums of Berlin

The Altes Museum, the first museum in Berlin, was built in 1830 by Karl Friedrich Schinkel on what would become Museumsinsel (Museum Island). It was followed in 1855 by the Neues Museum, in 1876 by the Alte Nationalgalerie, in 1904 by the Bode-Museum and in 1930 by the Pergamonmuseum. Wilhelm von Bode, director of the Berlin museums after 1906, painstakingly organised the city's collections, bringing them to the attention of connoisseurs worldwide.

Reconstruction began after World War II – no small task considering collections had to be gathered from storage or re-acquired from victorious pillagers. Postwar Germany further divided the collections between East and West. The Stiftung Preußischer Kulturbesitz (Foundation for Prussian Cultural Property) preserved those in the West, while in the East artefacts were gathered at the Museumsinsel. In 1992 Berlin's museums rejoined under the umbrella of the Stiftung Preußischer Kulturbesitz – Staatliche Museen zu Berlin.

Bode-Museum★★

Entry via Monbijoubrücke. Open year-round Tue–Sun 10am–6pm (Thu until 8pm). ∞10€. ♿ ✆(030) 266 42 42 42. www.smb.museum.

Housed in a splendid 1904 Neo-Baroque edifice at the northern tip of Museumsinsel, this museum emerged from a thorough renovation in 2006 and once again delights visitors with its stunning **Sculpture Collection**.

Particular strengths lie in medieval Italian sculpture (e.g. *Man of Sorrows* by Giovanni Pisano), Late Gothic German works by such masters as Tilman Riemenschneider and Hans Leinberger, and Rococo sculpture by Ignaz Günther and Jean Antoine Houdon.

The museum also features a sprinkling of objects from the **Museum of Byz**antine Art such as the "Great Berlin Pyx" (around AD 400), a small vessel carved of ivory. Another highlight is the four rooms crammed with the rare and precious coins of the **Numismatic Collection**.

Altes Museum★★ (Old Museum)

Enter from Lustgarten. Open year-round Tue–Sun 10am–6pm (Thu until 8pm). Closed Dec 24 and 31. ∞10€. ♿ ✆(030) 266 42 42 42. www.smb.museum.

Designed by Schinkel and open since 1830, Berlin's first public museum is a Neoclassical architectural masterpiece fronted by 18 Ionic columns. On display is the prestigious **Antikensammlung** (Collection of Antiquities – the monu-

Pergamonmuseum

© visitBerlin / Günter Steffen

mental pieces are in the Pergamon museum), composed of Greek sculpture on the ground floor and Roman and Etruscan works upstairs.

One of the most famous pieces of Hellenic art is the **Praying Boy sculpture** from around 3000 BC on Rhodes. The famous Etruscan collection is one of the largest outside Italy and on display for the first time since 1939. It includes complete tomb finds and magnificent objects of Etruscan art and such objects from everyday life as amphorae, jewellery and coins. Late Hellenistic cremation urns and sarcophagi lead to a section on Roman tomb art that includes the **Medea sarcophagus**.

Other rooms feature Roman mummy portraits, silverware and cosmetic utensils made of glass and jewellery. A portrait gallery of marble busts featuring famous Roman leaders, including Caesar and Caracalla, rounds off the upstairs galleries.

Neues Museum
(New Museum)

Enter from Bodestraße. Open year-round daily 10am–6pm (Thu until 8pm). Closed Dec 24; open Dec 31 10am–2pm. 12€. (030) 266 42 42 42. www.smb.museum.

Shortly after the opening of the Old Museum, **Friedrich August Stüler** (1800–1865) was entrusted with the construction of another building: the New Museum, created in an elegant classical style between 1841 and 1859. Badly damaged during World War II, it remained in a state of ruin during GDR times but was reconstructed as part of the Museum Island masterplan and re-opened in late 2009. The museum houses Berlin's renowned **Egyptian Museum and Papyrus Collection**, including the famous bust of Queen Nerfertiti, as well as the **Museum of Pre- and Early History**.

The building – The building itself is as interesting as the exhibits inside. Architect David Chipperfield sifted through the rubble of the original structure and integrated every usable shard, brick, stone, piece of marble or whatever he

could find into the new structure. As a result, it's a harmonious blend of old and new that instantly won several design awards, including the prestigious "European Award" from the Royal Institute of British Architects (RIBA). The central hall with its grand staircase is the magnificent centrepiece of the museum and gives access to three of the exhibition floors.

Basement – Furniture, utensils, funerary masks and sarcophagi depict life and death in the Nile Valley. Note the unrolled papyrus of the Book of the Dead.

Ground floor – Among Egyptian sculpture, the **"Green Head of Berlin"**★★ (c. 300 BC) is regarded as one of the masterpieces of the late period. Other galleries are devoted to the treasure of King Priam discovered in the late 19C by Heinrich Schliemann in Troy. However, what you see here are all copies: the originals were confiscated by the Red Army in 1945 and are partly on display in the Pushkin Museum in Moscow.

First floor – This floor gets the most visitors thanks largely to one exhibit: the 3 300-year-old, yet timelessly beautiful, **bust of Egyptian Queen Nefertiti**★★★. It is part of the stunning **collection**★★★ of sculptures, figurines and objects dating back to the time of King Akhenaten (Nefertiti's husband, 1353–36 BC) and unearthed between 1911 and 1914 in Tell el-Armana by a team of German archaeologists. The bust was discovered in the workshop of the sculptor Thutmose and served as a model for future effigies of the queen (which explains why only one eye was embedded). Other masterpieces include the representation of Akhenaten's father Amenhotep III wearing a crown; the portrait of his wife Tiye carved from yew that was originally bright orange; reliefs of Akhenaten and other royal family members and an impressive collection of papyri.

Other rooms on this floor are devoted to the Museum of Pre- and Early History. Key items include the exquisite bronze statue of the **Xantener Knabe** (Boy of Xanten; 1C AD), colossal statues of gods from the 2C AD and a coin from the time of Charlemagne (8C).

Upper floor – The Museum of Pre- and Early History continues on this floor. Don't miss the preserved **Neanderthal skull** and the 3 000-year-old **Berliner Goldhut★** (golden hat), a gilded conical ceremonial hat that also functions as a combined lunar and solar calendar. It is the best preserved of four known copies.

KULTURFORUM★★★

A clutch of museums and cultural venues, the Kulturforum was designed, in the late 1950s, to become the West Berlin counterpart to the Museumsinsel in the eastern part of the city.

Gemäldegalerie★★★ (Picture Gallery)

Matthäikirchplatz. Open year-round Tue–Sun 10am–6pm (Thu until 8pm). Closed Dec 24 and 31. ↻8€. ♿ ☏(030) 266 42 42 42. www.smb.museum.

This collection was born of the passion of the Great Elector (1620–1688) and Frederick the Great (1712–1786). But it was **Wilhelm von Bode**, director of the Gemäldegalerie who, beginning in 1890, tirelessly acquired European paintings from the 13C to the 18C. Despite war losses (400 paintings were destroyed), the collection is still considered one of the finest in the world. The modern building's 53 rooms are arranged in a horseshoe around a foyer and provide space for over 1 100 paintings. Works are presented in chronological order and arranged by school:

Rooms I–III, Galleries 1–4: German School, 13C–16C (Late Gothic/ Renaissance). Notably illustrated by Martin Schongauer *(The Birth of Christ)*, Lucas Cranach the Elder (*Venus und Amor, Adam and Eve*), Hans Holbein the Younger *(The Merchant Georg Gisze)* and Albrecht Dürer *(Portrait of Hieronymus Holzschuher)*.

Rooms IV–VI, Galleries 5–7: Dutch School, 15C–16C (Late Gothic/ Renaissance). Features works by Gérard David, Hans Memling, Hugo Van der Goes, Jan Gossaert, Jan Van Eyck,

Gemäldegalerie

Quentin Metsys and Pieter Bruegel the Elder (including his famous painting *Dutch Proverbs*).

Rooms VII–XI, Galleries 8–19: Flemish and Dutch Schools, 17C (Baroque). Extensive section including Peter Paul Rubens *(Child with a Bird, Virgin and Child)*, his pupil Anthony van Dyck *(Portrait of a Wealthy Genoan Couple)*, Matthias Stomer *(Esau Sells his Birth Right)*, Rembrandt *(Self-portrait, Moses Shatters the Decalogue, Susanna and the Two Old Men, The Man with the Golden*

The 5-7-9 Series

The three-naved foyer of the Gemäldegalerie, a wonderfully designed space, boasts a single work of art: a sculpture by the American conceptual sculptor Walter De Maria entitled *The 5-7-9 Series*. It consists of 27 polygonal, highly polished steel staffs ordered in three rows in a granite water basin. The geometric staffs are assembled according to various mathematical combinations. This artwork is a good conclusion to a visit to the Gemäldegalerie: it brings the viewer back to earth, tests his or her imagination and simply permits a rest.

Helmet), Jacob van Ruisdael *(Oaks by the Lake with Water Lilies)*, Jan Bruegel the Elder *(Flower Bouquet)*, Frans Hals *(Singing Child with Flute)* and Jan Vermeer van Delft *(The Glass of Wine)*.

Galleries 20–22: English, French and German Schools, 18C (Rococo/Neoclassical). Artists include Thomas Gainsborough *(The Marsham Children)*, Antoine Watteau *(The Dance)*, Jean-Baptiste-Siméon Chardin *(The Painter)* and Antoine Pesne *(Frederick the Great as Crown Prince)*.

Rooms XII–XIV, Galleries 23–26, 28: Italian School, 17C–18C (Baroque/Mannerism); **French School, 17C; Spanish School, 16C–17C** (Mannerism/Baroque). Exhibits here include Francesco Guardi *(Canal Grande in Venice)*, Canaletto *(Canal Grande with View of the Rialto Bridge)*, Velázquez *(Portrait of a Lady)*, Caravaggio *(Amor as Victor)*, Claude Lorrain *(Ideal Roman Landscape)*, Nicolas Poussin *(Self-portrait)* and Georges de La Tour *(Peasant Couple Eating Peas)*.

Rooms XV–XVII, Galleries 29–32: Italian School, late 15C–16C (late Renaissance/Mannerism). This part of the museum contains works by Correggio *(Leda with the Swan)*, Parmigianino *(Christ's Baptism)*, Titian *(Venus with the Organist, Portrait of a Bearded Young Man)*, Tintoretto *(Virgin and Child)* and several paintings by Raphael.

Gallery 34: Miniatures, 16C–18C, *Katharine of Bora* (Martin Luther's wife) by Lucas Cranach the Elder.

Room XVIII, Galleries 35–41: Italian School, 13C–late 15C (Gothic/Early Renaissance). Includes Botticelli *(Saint Sebastian, Virgin Enthroned)*, Giovanni Bellini, Andrea Mantegna *(Representation of Christ in the Temple)*, Fra Angelico *(The Day of Judgement)* and Lorenzo Monaco *(The Last Supper)*.

Kunstgewerbemuseum★★ (Museum of Decorative Arts)

Matthäikirchplatz. ⚠ Closed until further notice. ♿ ✆(030) 266 42 42 42. www.smb.museum.

The vast treasures of the Museum of Decorative Arts are displayed in two locations. The Kulturforum branch presents a broad overview of European applied arts and design from the Middle Ages to the present. The second part of the collection is at Schloß Köpenick. At the Kulturforum branch, Gallery I *(ground floor)* is devoted to the Middle Ages. Inside the entrance is the Enger-Herford (Westphalia) **Treasure of Dionysius★**, with a remarkable reliquary purse decorated with precious stones (late 8C).

In the centre of the gallery, the **Guelph Treasure★★★** includes a reliquary resembling a Byzantine church (Cologne c. 1175). Gallery II *(ground floor)*: Italian furniture and majolica from the 14C to the 16C, Venetian glassware from the 16C to the 17C. Gallery III *(ground floor)*: **Lüneburg's municipal silver★★★** (late Gothic and Renaissance) and jewellery from Nuremberg. Gallery IV *(first floor)*: the splendid **Pommern Cabinet★** and its contents. Gallery V *(first floor)*: 17C–18C porcelain from China and Germany. Gallery VI *(first floor)*: Biedermeier and Jugendstil objets d'art, a panelled glass cabinet from Schloss Wiesentheid in Franconia (1724). Gallery VII *(first floor)*: porcelain, glazed earthenware and Art Nouveau and Art Deco period glass. Galleries IX and X *(basement)*: modern international design by such practitioners as Charles Eames and Philippe Starck.

Kupferstichkabinett★ (Museum of Prints and Drawings)

Matthäikirchplatz. Exhibition: open year-round Tue–Fri 10am–6pm, Sat–Sun 11am–6pm. Study: open Tue–Fri 9am–4pm. Closed Dec 24 and 31. ⬤6€. ♿ ✆(030) 266 42 42 42. www.smb.museum.

In 1652 the Great Elector laid the foundation for this internationally renowned **collection** of 500 000 prints and 110 000 watercolours, oil sketches, drawings and pastels from the 14C to the 20C. Many famous Italian, Old German and Old Dutch masters are represented, including Rembrandt, Botticelli and Dürer, along with 20C Pop Art, Conceptual Art and Minimal Art.

Neue Nationalgalerie★★
(New National Gallery)

Potsdamer Straße 50. Open year-round Tue–Sun 10am–6pm (Thu until 8pm). Closed Dec 24 and 31. ⊙8€. ⚹. ℘(030) 266 42 42 42. www.smb.museum.

This steel and glass "temple of the arts", designed in 1968 by Ludwig Mies van der Rohe, houses paintings and sculptures from the early 20C to the 1960s. Particularly impressive is the collection of **German Expressionists**, which includes a smattering of works by members of the artist group Die Brücke (⊙see INTRODUCTION: Art), including Kirchner, Schmidt-Rottluff and Heckel. The **Bauhaus** is represented by such artists as Klee and Kandinsky, **Surrealism** by Max Ernst and Dalí, and **Cubism** by Picasso and Gris. The collection ends with **American paintings** from the 1960s featuring works by Frank Stella, Ellsworth Kelly and others.

Philharmonie★★★

Herbert-von-Karajanstraße 1. ⊶Guided tour (1hr) at 1.30pm. Meeting point: stage door. Closed Jan 1, Dec 24–26 & 31. ⊙5€. ⚹. ℘(030) 25 48 80. www.berliner-philharmoniker.de.

The roof of this asymmetrical building designed by **Hans Scharoun** (1963) resembles a giant wave. It is the home base of the Berlin Philharmonic Orchestra, directed by **Sir Simon Rattle**, and surrounded by terraced seats accommodating up to 2 200 people. The **Chamber Music Hall** (1988) next door seats up to 1 150 under a tent-shaped roof.

In an adjacent building (Tiergartenstraße 1, enter via Ben-Gurion-Straße), the **Musikinstrumenten-Museum★** (Musical Instruments Museum) displays keyboards, strings and percussion instruments from the 16C to today, including a mammoth 1929 Wurlitzer theatre organ and flutes played by **Frederick the Great.** (Open year-round Tue, Wed, Fri 9am–5pm, Thu 9am–8pm, Sat–Sun 10am–5pm; ⊙6€; ⚹℘030 25 48 11 78; www.mim-berlin.de.)

Staatsbibliothek Preußischer Kulturbesitz★
(State Library of the Prussian Cultural Heritage Foundation)

Potsdamer Straße 33. Open year-round Mon–Fri 9am–9pm, Sat 10am–7pm. ⊶Guided tour (1hr) at 10.30am, 3rd Sat of month. ⊙Free. ⚹℘(030) 26 60. http://staatsbibliothek-berlin.de.

This huge library, designed by Hans Scharoun and wedged between Potsdamer Platz and the Kulturforum, harbours 3.7 million volumes. Scenes from the Wim Wenders movie Wings of Desire were filmed in the reading room.

POTSDAMER PLATZ★★

East of the Kulturforum, this quarter stands as the largest of Berlin's post-reunification developments. Before World War II, the area was a busy traffic hub and entertainment zone. Completely destroyed, it was bifurcated by the Berlin Wall during the Cold War. After reunification some of the world's top architects collaborated on its reincarnation. Today, Potsdamer Platz is again a lively quarter teeming with hotels, theatres, restaurants, a casino, museums and shops.

Sony Centre★★★

The Sony Centre is dominated by the BahnTower, a glass tower housing the headquarters of the railway company Deutsche Bahn. Designed by Helmut

Sony Centre

Jahn, the massive steel and glass complex centres on a plaza encircled by restaurants, cinemas and beer gardens. Integrated into this postmodern setting is the historic Kaisersaal, one of the few original remnants from the pre-war Potsdamer Platz. In 1996, during construction of the Sony Centre, it had to be moved a few dozen metres in an astonishing technological feat. Another historic section is the façade of the Hotel Esplanade, which can be seen from Bellevuestraße.

Overlooking the central square, the Filmhaus hosts film-related institutions, including the Museum of Film and Television. Also part of the Sony Centre, the **Legoland Discovery Centre** (open year-round daily 10am–7pm; closed Dec 24; ☎14€ up, discounted online; ♿ ℘01806 666 90 110; www.legolanddiscoverycentre.de/berlin) is an indoor theme park that will keep kids under 10 entertained for hours.

Museum für Film und Fernsehen★★ (Museum of Film and Television)

In the Sony Centre. Potsdamer Straße 2. Open year-round Tue–Sun 10am–6pm (Thu until 8pm). Closed Dec 24–25. ☎7€. ♿ ℘(030) 300 90 30. www.deutsche-kinemathek.de.

Germany's film history goes back to the earliest days of the medium. This multimedia museum includes exhibits on such silent-era blockbusters as Fritz Lang's *Metropolis* and *The Cabinet of Dr Caligari* by Expressionist filmmaker Robert Wiene. Leni Riefenstahl's controversial Nazi-era documentary *Olympia* gets examined closely, while the great Marlene Dietrich takes centre stage in one of the largest galleries, complete with lots of personal artefacts such as gowns, luggage, cosmetics and jewellery. Upper floors house the Fernsehmuseum, which takes visitors on a journey through 50 years of TV history in both East and West Germany. On the top floor, catch up on your favourite old-time programmes at private viewing consoles.

Martin-Gropius-Bau★★ (Martin Gropius Building)

Niederkirchnerstraße 7. Open year-round Wed–Mon 10am–7pm. ☎Varies with exhibition. ♿ ℘(030) 25 48 60. www.gropiusbau.de.

A stately Italian Renaissance-style building by Martin Gropius (great-uncle of Walter Gropius) and Heino Schmieden originally served as a museum of decorative arts and now houses travelling exhibitions of international rank.

Topographie des Terrors (Topography of Terror)

Niederkirchnerstraße 8. Open daily 10am–8pm. Closed Jan 1, Dec 24 & 31. ☎Free. ♿ ℘(030) 25 45 09 50. www.topographie.de.

Next to the Gropius-Bau stands a short stretch of the **Berlin Wall★** and beyond it, a largely empty field where once stood the key institutions of oppression and persecution in Nazi Germany: the Gestapo headquarters, the SS central command, the SS Security Service and after 1939, the Reich Security Headquarters. The compound was completely destroyed in World War II, but since 1997 an outdoor memorial exhibit has commemorated the site's fearsome legacy. In 2010, the enlarged exhibit moved into the permanent **Documentation Centre** inside an austere charcoal-grey cube in the middle of the grounds.

Museum für Kommunikation Berlin★ (Museum of Communications)

Leipziger Straße 16. Open year-round Tue 9am–8pm, Wed–Fri 9am–5pm, Sat–Sun & holidays 10am–6pm. Closed Dec 24–25 & 31. ☎4€. ♿ ℘(030) 20 29 40. www.mfk-berlin.de.

Considered the world's oldest postal museum, this exhibit counts an ultra-rare **Blue Mauritius** stamp, entertaining robots and decades' worth of communication devices among its treasures.

👥 Museum Haus am Checkpoint Charlie★ (Berlin Wall Museum)

Friedrichstraße 43–45. Open year-round daily 9am–10pm. 🎫12.50€. ✆(030) 253 72 50. www.mauermuseum.de.

The Berlin Wall Museum houses Wall-related artefacts and illustrates the often hair-raising escapes attempted by East Germans trying to cross over into the West through tunnels, in a hot-air balloon, hidden in the boot of a car, in a suitcase, and even via a chair-lift. Many attempts, of course, ended unsuccessfully, usually resulting in the incarceration of the brave souls. A separate section spotlights human and civil rights movements.

SCHLOSS CHARLOTTENBURG★★★ (CHARLOTTENBURG PALACE)

Schloss Charlottenburg is a summer residence commissioned by King Friedrich I for his wife, Sophie-Charlotte. Designed by Arnold Nering and later expanded by Johann Friedrich Eosander, it is Berlin's most exquisite Baroque palace.

An equestrian statue of the Great Elector by Andreas Schlüter greets visitors arriving in the front courtyard. Allow a full day to see all of Schloss Charlottenburg's buildings and the park, and consider an evening visit for a classical music concert or meal at the Orangery (www.concerts-berlin.com).

Altes Schloss★★ (Old Palace)

Spandauer Damm, ground floor of central block. 🚶Visit by guided tour or audioguide Tue–Sun 10am–6pm (Nov–Mar until 5pm). Closed 24 Dec. 🎫12€. ♿✆(030) 32 09 10. www.spsg.de.

After viewing models of the 18C palace and gardens, visitors approach three small rooms in the **Mecklenburg Apartment**. The official function rooms span 140m/460ft overlooking the gardens. They house family portraits of the Houses of Hohenzollern and Hanover, finely lacquered furniture and Sophie-Charlotte's harpsichord. The famous **Porcelain Room★★** features a magnificent collection of Asian porcelain, while the **Palace Chapel★** (Schloss Kapelle) is occasionally used as a concert venue. Above the royal pew an enormous crown carried by two allegorical figures bears the Prussian eagle. The fine free-standing **staircase** by Eosander (1702) was the first of its kind in Germany.

Passing through the upper rooms overlooking the courtyard and gardens, you then continue to the **apartments of Frederick William IV**, the last king to live at the palace. The painting Parade along Unter den Linden in 1837 by Franz Krüger features some of this avenue's most important buildings, still recognisable today. Adjoining rooms exhibit part of the East Prussian noble Schlobitten Collection, including paintings, tapestries, porcelain and metalwork.

The Crown Prince's Silverware

This masterpiece of 20C German craftsmanship was a gift from 414 Prussian cities at the marriage of Crown Prince William to Duchess Cecilia of Mecklenburg-Schwerin in 1904. Completed in 1914, the dinner service never belonged to the couple. Following the Hohenzollerns' abdication, it became property of the Berlin Senate and is now on long-standing loan to Schloss Charlottenburg. The service originally contained 2 600 pieces for 50 at a 16m/53ft-long table. Tureens, plates and salad bowls are displayed on a magnificent sideboard. Architects, sculptors and the director of the Museum of Decorative Arts supervised the creation of the dinner service, which is in classical and Jugendstil style. The statuettes include elephants surmounted by an obelisk, equestrian statues and candelabras, all part of a long tradition of royal dinner services.

Schloss Charlottenburg

© visitBerlin / Wolfgang Scholvien

The **Crown Prince's silverware★★** is particularly interesting (&see infobox).

Neuer Flügel★★ (New Wing)

East of the central block. Open year-round Wed–Mon 10am–6pm (Nov–Mar until 5pm). Closed Dec 24. ☎6€. &
℘(030) 32 09 10. www.spsg.de.

Also known as the Knobeldorff Wing after its architect, the New Wing was commissioned by Frederick the Great and completed in 1746. This is the most beautiful part of the palace and the one section to see if you're short on time. Stairs lead up to the **White Room** *(Weisser Saal)* used by Frederick II as a dining and throne room. The ceiling painting is a modern work by Hann Trier that replaced the original by Antoine Pesne destroyed in 1943. The 42m/138ft-long **Golden Gallery★★** is a Rococo music room and dance hall restored to its original pastel green, pink and gold hues. Frederick II's apartments, which follow, feature white and gold Rococo décor and important 18C French paintings: **Gersaint's Signboard★★★** (1720) in the concert hall and **Embarkation for Cythera★★★** by Watteau in particular.

Winter Apartments★

Frederick the Great's successor, Frederick William II, lived in these apartments in the late 18C and early 19C. These south-facing rooms display the disciplined elegance of early Prussian Neoclassicism.

Queen Louise's Bedchamber★ is decorated in harmonious mauve tones and draped in white net. The final room contains a fine collection of **portraits★** by court painter Antoine Pesne.

On the ground floor a model shows the **Berlin City Palace** *(Berliner Stadt Schloss)*, blown up in 1950 on the orders of the East German government, but currently being rebuilt. In the adjoining room are Baroque tapestries and portions of Frederick the Great's **antique collection**. The **Chinese Gallery and Chinese Room**, part of Frederick William II's summer apartments, overlook the gardens.

Schlossgarten★★

This English-style park is an oasis of tranquillity and a great place for strolling, picnicking, sunning by the pond or lounging beneath shady trees.

To the west, at the end of a yew and cypress walk, a small **mausoleum** (open Apr–Oct Tue–Sun 10am–6pm; ☎2€) contains the marble sarcophagi of Frederick William III and his wife Queen Louise carved by Christian Daniel Rauch, as well as those of Emperor Wilhelm I and Queen Augusta.

More royal family members are buried in the crypt, which is not accessible to the public.

Designed by Karl Friedrich Schinkel after classical Italian villas, the **New Pavilion★ (Schinkel Pavilion)** *(east of the New Wing)* was built in 1824 as a summer residence for Frederick William III.

North of the lake, toward the Spree, the **Belvedere**★ (open Apr–Oct Tue–Sun 10am–6pm; closed Dec 24 & 31; ⊜3€) is a gleaming white miniature palace overlooking a shaggy meadow. It houses an exhibit of precious historic porcelain made by the *Königliche Porzellan Manufaktur* (KPM), the Prussian royal factory established in 1763.

Museum Berggruen★★

Schloßstraße 1. Open year-round Tue–Fri 10am–6pm, Sat–Sun 11am–6pm. ⊜10€. ♿(partly). ℘(030) 266 42 42 42. www.smb.museum.

Art dealer Heinz Berggruen was an avid collector of **Pablo Picasso**, and his contemporaries and donated a sizable portion of his private collection to this intimate museum in a former royal guard barracks built by Friedrich August Stüler in 1859. On display are about 100 works by Picasso from all his creative periods, including the famous *Horses on a Hill* (1909). These are cleverly juxtaposed with works by Cézanne, Van Gogh, Matisse, Giacometti and others, as well as African tribal art. The second floor features over 60 works by **Paul Klee**, including *Stadtartiger Aufbau (Urban Structure)* (1917), *Betrachtung beim Frühstück* (1925, watercolour) and *Klassische Küste* (1931).

Bröhan Museum★

Schloßstraße 1a. Open year-round Tue–Sun 10am–6pm. Closed Dec 24 & 31. ⊜8€. ♿℘(030) 32 69 06 00. www.broehan-museum.de.

Fine art, furniture and decorative objects from the **Art Nouveau**, **Art Deco** and **Functionalism** periods (1889–1939) get the star treatment at this museum. Downstairs are period rooms by Hector Guimard and Peter Behrens, while the upper floor is dedicated to paintings by artists from the **Berlin Secession** movement, including Willy Jaeckel and Hans Baluschek.

A special exhibition on the third floor shines the spotlight on Belgian multi-talent **Henry van de Velde**.

KREUZBERG DISTRICT★

Kreuzberg has been the hub of counter-cultural Berlin since long before reunification. These days, it is one of the city's liveliest neighbourhoods with a buzzing nightlife; a wide range of restaurants, often in unusual locations; and plenty of galleries, theatres, dance clubs and cultural centres. The eastern section around the Kottbusser Tor U-Bahn station has a large Turkish population and is sometimes nicknamed "Little Istanbul". At the other end, the area around Viktoria Park is considerably more sedate and upmarket.

The Wall

Masterminded by the East German government in 1961, the Berlin Wall divided the city's western districts from East Berlin and the surrounding Brandenburg region for 28 years. Since 1989, the bricks, watchtowers, barbed wire and machine guns have been replaced by new construction and parks, but a few sections of the Wall still commemorate this unique period in history.

The longest stretch, and the most rewarding for visitors, is the **East Side Gallery**, which runs for 1.3km/0.8mi along Mühlenstraße, parallel to the Spree River, just south of Ostbahnhof train station. After reunification, artists from around the world were asked to turn it into an outdoor art gallery. The picture of a Trabi car bursting through the Wall is one of the most iconic images. There are also shorter Wall remnants on Niederkirchner Straße near the Topography of Terror exhibition, on Potsdamer Platz and at the **Berlin Wall Memorial Site** *(Gedenkstätte Berliner Mauer)* on Bernauer Straße, a documentary centre that combines an exhibition, an outdoor installation and a memorial chapel.

Jüdisches Museum Berlin★★ (Jewish Museum)

Lindenstraße 9–14. Open year-round Mon 10am–10pm, Tue–Sun 10am–8pm. Closed Rosh Hashanah, Yom Kippur, Nov 15, Dec 24. ⬛8€. ♿ ✆(030) 2599 33 00. www.jmberlin.de.

American architect Daniel Libeskind designed this spectacular lightning-bolt-shaped museum, which opened in 2001. A veritable labyrinth, with hallways leading into empty spaces called "voids", the building is an architectural metaphor for the torturous experiences of German Jews. The exhibition traces 2 000 years of their history, with special emphasis given to the cultural and artistic contributions made by prominent Jewish Berliners – such as the philosopher Moses Mendelssohn – between the 18C and the 20C. A special section examines the post-reunification renaissance of the local Jewish community.

♟ Deutsches Technikmuseum Berlin★★ (German Museum of Technology)

Trebbiner Straße 9. Open year-round Tue–Fri 9am–5.30pm, Sat–Sun 10am–6pm. Closed May 1, Dec 24–25, 29 & 31. ⬛6€ (child 3.50€). ♿ ✆(030) 90 25 40. www.dtmb.de.

This temple of technology takes you on an eye-opening journey past the milestones of transport, energy, communications and production. It features outstanding exhibits on **aviation and nagivation★★**, an early computer designed by pioneer Konrad Zuse, a historical brewery and an entire hall of **historic locomotives★★**. Interactive displays, live demonstrations and experiments further enliven visits. Kids gravitate to the **Science Centre Spectrum** (*Möckernstraße 26*) where they can playfully learn about scientific phenomena at 250 interactive stations.

Viktoriapark★

Kreuzberg hill, the highest natural elevation in central Berlin (66m/216ft), is entirely covered by the Viktoriapark. The top is crowned by Karl Friedrich Schinkel's monument to the "Wars of Liberation" and delivers fine city views. There is also a children's playground and a leafy beer garden.

TIERGARTEN AND THE CHARLOTTENBURG DISTRICT★

Berlin's oldest public park stretches almost 3km/1.8mi from Charlottenburg Gate to Brandenburg Gate. Originally a royal hunting reserve, it was transformed into a delightful English-style park by landscape architect Peter Joseph Lenné (1789–1866) in the 19C. Further west spreads the vast district of Charlottenburg, which was the centre of West Berlin during the years of division. Its main spine, the Kurfürstendamm, is a popular shopping strip. Outer area sights include the Olympic Stadium and the Funkturm (radio tower).

Olympic Games of 1936

When Germany beat out Barcelona in 1931 to become the host of the 1936 Olympic Games, no one could have predicted that the country would by then have fallen under the rule of Adolf Hitler and his totalitarian National Socialist Party. The US almost boycotted the Games, largely because of the regime's anti-Semitic policies, but was assuaged when Hitler declared that athletes of all races and confessions would be allowed to participate. Ironically, it was African-American runner Jesse Owens who became the star of the show as the winner of four gold medals in the sprint and long jump events. On 1 August 1936 Hitler opened the Games at Berlin's new Olympic Stadium in front of 100 000 people. It marked the second time that the Olympic Flame was used but the first time that it was carried from Olympia, Greece, in a torch relay by thousands of runners.

Siegessäule
(Victory Column)

Open Apr–Oct Mon–Fri 9.30am–6.30pm, Sat–Sun 9.30am–7pm; Nov–Mar Mon–Fri 10am–5pm, Sat–Sun 10am–5:30pm. ⊜2.20€.

At 67m/220ft high, this landmark monument, surmounted by a gilded sculpture of the Goddess of Victory (nicknamed Golden Else), commemorates the successful Prussian campaigns of 1864, 1866 and 1870 against Denmark, Austria and France. From the top *(285 steps)*, views★ extend across Tiergarten Park to the Spree River, the Hansa residential quarter and the Brandenburg Gate.

© visitBerlin / Wolfgang Scholvien

Zoologischer Garten

Schloss Bellevue

Built in the Neoclassical style by Philipp Boumann in 1785, Bellevue was the summer palace of Frederick the Great's younger brother, Prince Augustus-Ferdinand. Today, backed by a lush park that is closed to the public, it is the official residence of the German president.

Bauhaus-Archiv/Museum für Gestaltung★ (Bauhaus Archives/Museum for Design)

Klingelhöferstraße 14. Open year-round Wed–Mon 10am–5pm. Closed Dec 24. ⊜6€ Wed–Fri, 7€ Sat–Mon. ♿ ✆(030) 254 00 20. www.bauhaus.de.

In a building designed by Bauhaus founder **Walter Gropius**, this museum and archive highlights the concepts and philosophy of this early 20C aesthetic movement that greatly influenced modern design and architecture. Exhibits include sculptures, blueprints, models and paintings by Schlemmer, Moholy-Nagy, Feininger, Kandinsky, Klee and other Bauhaus School members.

C/O Berlin

Hardenbergstr. 22-24. Open year-round daily 11am–8pm. ⊜10€. ♿ ✆(030) 28 444 160. www.co-berlin.org.

This well-respected art venue for changing photography exhibits recently moved out of the legendary Postfuhramt in Mitte and into the storied Amerika Haus, near Zoo Station.

♟♟Zoologischer Garten★★★ (Berlin Zoo and Aquarium)

Hardenbergplatz 8. Open Jan–mid-Mar & late Oct–Dec daily 9am–5pm; late Mar–early Sept 9am–7pm; mid-Sept mid-Oct 9am–6.30pm. ⊜13€, combination ticket zoo & aquarium 20€. ♿. ✆(030) 25 40 10. www.zoo-berlin.de.

Some 1 500 species and 20 500 creatures make their home in Berlin's venerable zoo and aquarium. The zoo, the oldest in Germany, opened in 1844. Next door is the aquarium (entry on Budapester Straße; open year-round daily 9am–6pm; ♿; ⊜13€; ✆030 25 40 10; www.aquarium-berlin.de), which has some 650 different species, including some fearsome crocodiles on the first floor.

Knautschke the Survivor

The end of the war was a difficult time for the animals at the zoo; the locals used them for food, just as they used trees from the Tiergarten for heat. One writer, Stefan Reisner (*Stadtfront, Berlin West Berlin*, 1982), recalls his father melting a camel's hump in a frying pan. However, the hippopotamus Knautschke was more fortunate. He stayed underwater during the conflict, re-emerging a true hero once the bombardments were over.

Kurfürstendamm★★

This busy 3.5km/2mi-long boulevard started life as a riding path to the royal hunting lodge in the Grunewald forest. In the 1880s, Bismarck transformed it into the prestigious thoroughfare known as the "Ku'damm". With its many department stores and boutiques, it is still Berlin's major shopping street and also lined by cafés, restaurants, theatres and galleries.

Kaiser-Wilhelm-Gedächtniskirche★ (Kaiser Wilhelm Memorial Church)

Open year-round daily 9am–7pm. &.
℘(030) 218 50 23.
www.gedaechtniskirche-berlin.de.
This neo-Romanesque church was consecrated in 1895 in honour of Emperor Wilhelm I. After World War II its ruined tower was left standing as a reminder of the horrors of war. A much-photographed Berlin landmark, it sits next to a modernistic octagonal house of worship (1961) famous for its deep blue glass walls made by artists from Chartres.

The original church entrance beneath the tower is now a **Memorial Hall**. The entire complex recently restored; the 1961 tower is still under scaffolding, but the complex is open.

Tauentzienstraße

South of the Gedächtniskirche, this fashionable shopping street is home to Europe's second-largest department store, the **"KaDeWe"**. The abbreviation stands for Kaufhaus des Westens: Department Store of the West.

Käthe-Kollwitz-Museum★

Fasanenstraße 24. Open year-round daily 11am–6pm. Closed Dec 24 & 31.
●6€. ℘(030) 882 52 10.
www.kaethe-kollwitz.de.
In a lovely villa, this small museum presents a broad survey of one of the most important German female artists, the Berlin-based Käthe Kollwitz (1867–1945). Highlights include engravings *The Weavers' Revolt* (1893–98) and *The Peasants' War* (1903–08), woodcuts titled *War* (1920–24) and *The Proletariat* (1925), and self-portraits and lithographs labelled *Death*. 1920s-era posters such as *Nie Wieder Krieg (No More War)* underline Kollwitz's pacifist ideals; sculptures on the upper floor include *Muttergruppe (Mother Group)* (1924–37).

Funkturm (Radio Tower)

Messedamm 22. Open year-round Mon 10am–8pm, Tue–Sun 10am–11pm. Closed Jan 1 & Dec 24. ●5€. &
℘(030) 30 38 29 00.
Once known to Berliners as the *Langer Lulatsch* ("lanky laddie"), this 150m/492ft tower looms above the trade show grounds and looks like a smaller brother of Paris' Eiffel Tower. Designed in the 1920s by Heinrich Straumer, it features a viewing platform at 126m/413ft and a restaurant about halfway up.

GREATER BERLIN

Sprawling across nearly 900sq km/ 350sq mi, the city state of Berlin boasts a surprising diversity of landscapes. Lakes and vast forests form a greenbelt around the city, which is also dotted with villages exuding provincial charm.

DAHLEM★★★

The leafy residential suburb of Dahlem is home to the Freie Universität (Free University), which was founded in 1948 and has nearly 35 000 students.
The main visitor attraction, though, is the **Museen Dahlem** (open year-round Tue–Fri 10am–5pm, Sat–Sun 11am–6pm; ●8€; &; ℘030 266 42 42 42; www.smb. museum), a vast museum complex that, aside from collections detailed below, also harbours the child-oriented ▲▲ Junior Museum.

Ethnologisches Museum★★★ (Museum of Ethnology)

Enter on Lansstraße 8.
This museum is home to 400 000 outstanding ethnographic objects divided into several permanent collections.

American Archaeology★★★

This stunning exhibition presents a survey of pre-Hispanic cultures from 2 000 BC to the early 16C. It reveals such treasures as carved stelae from Guatemala, painted stone vessels of the Maya, Aztec stone figures of gods and gold objects from Central America, Colombia and Peru.

North American Indians★

This section showcases the cultural and artistic diversity that developed among Indian cultures throughout North America and also seeks to debunk myths created by western fiction and modern media (films in particular). Items include moccasins, medicine pouches, tomahawks and peace pipes and also contemporary Native American art.

South Seas★★

Among the items gathered during sea voyages since the 18C, some by Captain James Cook, note the painted **masks** and **wooden sculptures** from New Guinea, the spectacular boats from **Oceania** and the **feathered cloak** of the king of Hawaii.

Africa★★

The most interesting objects in this collection include **terra-cotta heads from Ife** (Nigeria), **bronzes** from the ancient kingdom of Benin, and Berber jewellery, along with wooden sculptures from Cameroon. It was recently expanded to include art created by Africans living in Berlin. A standout here is the *ijele* mask created by a Nigerian artist for the local Igbo community.

Music Ethnology

This section documents global music culture and encompasses more than 150 000 **sound recordings**. One of the earliest is from 1900, when the psychologist Carl Stumpf used an Edison phonograph to record a group of Thai musicians performing in Berlin.

Museum für Asiatische Kunst★★ (Museum of Asian Art)

Enter on Lansstraße 8.

The East Asian collections cover art and artefacts from China, Japan and Korea and were recently combined with collections from the Museum of Indian Art. Galleries display objects from the fourth millennium BC to today, including stone sculpture, ceramics, cult objects, Japanese woodcuts and lacquer arts, most notably a **17C imperial throne★★** made of palisander wood with mother-of-pearl inlaid into lacquer and gold. Another highlight is the **Japanese tea room★**, which is occasionally used for tea ceremonies, and a **video installation★** by the late Korean artist Nam June Paik. Folk art from Japan is another focus of the museum.

Museum Europäischer Kulturen★ (Museum of European Cultures)

Focused on everyday European culture from the 18C to the present, this museum features such objects as a 1910 Venetian gondola and a "Christmas Mountain" tower from the Erzgebirge with 328 moveable parts.

Botanischer Garten und Museum★★ (Botanical Gardens and Museum)

Königin-Luise-Straße 6–8. Open year-round daily 9am–sunset (until 9pm at the latest). Closed Dec 24. 6€, incl. museum. (030) 83 85 01 00. www.bgbm.org.

At 43ha/106 acres, Berlin's botanical garden is one of the world's largest and most diverse with more than 22 000 plant species. Vegetation is arranged geographically from mountains to plains. Rare species of trees and shrubs are in the **Arboretum**, while 15 **greenhouses** shelter a wealth of tropical and sub-tropical plants.

The **Botanical Museum★** (Botanisches Museum; open year-round daily 10am–6pm; closed Dec 24; 2.50€, museum only) chronicles the evolution of flora and documents common plant uses.

Botanischer Garten

© visitBerlin / Wolfgang Scholvien

NEAR DAHLEM
Brücke-Museum★

Bussardsteig 9. Open year-round Wed–
Mon 11am–5pm. Closed Dec 24 & 31.
5€. &℘(030) 831 20 29.
www.bruecke-museum.de.

This museum contains works by members of **Die Brücke** (The Bridge), an artist
group of German Expressionists. It was
founded in Dresden in 1905 by architecture students Erich Heckel, Ernst Ludwig
Kirchner, Fritz Bleyl and Karl Schmidt-
Rottluff. Rejecting traditional painting
styles taught at the art academies,
they sought to explore new forms of
expression, especially by employing
bold colour and working with distorted
compositions. In 1911, the group moved
to Berlin where it disbanded two years
later. The small museum, which was
founded by Schmidt-Rottluff himself
and opened in 1967, presents works
by all major Brücke members, including Max Pechstein, Otto Mueller and
Emil Nolde, in addition to those by its
founders.

Grunewald★★

A hunting reserve of the Prince-Electors in the 16C, this mixed forest covers 3 100ha/745 acres and is bounded
by a chain of small lakes. Near one of
them, the Grunewaldsee, is **Jagdschloss
Grunewald★** (open Apr–Oct Tue–Sun
10am–6pm; by guided tour only Nov–

Mar Sat–Sun 10am–4pm; closed Jan–Feb
2015, check website in subsequent years;
5/6€ without/with tour; ℘030 813 35
97; www.spsg.de), an elegant hunting
lodge built in 1542.

Originally a Renaissance palace, it was
converted into the Baroque style for
King Frederick I some 160 years later.
On the ground floor, there's documentation about its most recent overhaul.
Since its completion visitors can again
admire paintings by Dutch and German
masters from the 15C–18C. Highlights
include the famous portraits of the royal
family by Lucas Cranach the Elder and
his son. There's also an exhibit on the
royal hunt in the storehouse.

Grunewald forest is bordered by **Lake
Havel★★**, whose eastern shore is parallelled by the picturesque Havelchaus-
see road. It leads south to the beaches
of the **Wannsee★★**, a hugely popular
recreational area in summer.

Pfaueninsel★★
(Peacock Island)

Ferries leave from the landing at the
end of Nikolskoer Weg, May–Aug daily
9am–8pm; Apr & Sept 9am–7pm; Mar
& Oct 9am–6pm; Nov–Feb 10am–4pm.
3€.

There's a dreamy quality about this
island in the Havel River, which was
turned into a romantic retreat by King
Frederick William II in the 18C.

It is still a popular escape from the city
bustle; its gardens landscaped by Peter
Joseph Lenné invite extensive strolling.
Paths lead to a snowy-white fairytale
castle★ (1794–97) (visit by 30min
guided tour only, Apr–Oct Tue–Sun
10am–5pm; 3€; ℘030 805 86 83 0;
www.spsg.de) that displays souvenirs
of Queen Louise in salons panelled with
exotic woods.

SOUTHEAST OF THE CITY
Kunstgewerbemuseum★
(Museum of Decorative Arts)

In Schloss Köpenick (Schloßinsel).
Open Apr–Sept Tue–Sun 11am–6pm;
Oct–Mar 11am–5pm. 6€. &
℘(030) 266 42 42 42.
www.smb.museum/kgm.

The second branch of the Museum of Decorative Arts (the main one, at the Kulturforum, is currently closed for renovation) occupies a restored 17C Baroque palace on a little peninsula in the southeastern Berlin suburb of Köpenick.

The 16C–19C furniture is especially interesting, as are the **panelled room★** from Haldenstein castle (Switzerland, 16C), the **Treasury★**, with jewellery and 16C Baroque gold- and silverware, the silver **sideboard★★** from the Knights' Room in the old Berlin city palace and the **coats of arms hall★**.

Großer Müggelsee★★

Among the city's most majestic, Berlin's largest lake measures 4km/2.5mi long and 2.5km/1.5mi wide. It is fringed by the Köpenick city forest, which is crisscrossed by pleasant walking trails.

EXCURSIONS

Gedenkstätte und Museum Sachsenhausen (Sachsenhausen Memorial and Museum)

▶ 31km/19.2mi north of Berlin. Open mid-Mar–mid-Oct daily 8.30am–6pm (rest of year 4.30pm); some exhibits closed Mon. Closed Jan 1, Dec 24, 25 & 31. & ℘(033 01) 20 00. www.stiftung-bg.de.

The Nazi-era concentration camp of **Sachsenhausen** near the town of Oranienburg north of Berlin opened in 1936. Tens of thousands of the 220 000 prisoners that passed through its gates until 1945 perished. Exhibits occupy such sites as the camp commander's house, the kitchen, the hospital wing and Baracke 38, where Jewish prisoners were kept. You'll also learn about the organisation of the Nazi concentration camp system, whose cynicism is epitomised by the slogan above the entrance gates: *"Arbeit macht frei"* (work sets you free).

Schloss Rheinsberg★

▶ 87km/54mi northwest of Berlin. Visit by guided tour or audio guide Apr–Oct Tue–Sun 10am–6pm; guided tours only Nov–Mar 10am–5pm. ⌚8€. Closed 24–25 Dec. ℘(033931) 72 60. www.spsg.de.

Frederick the Great spent four years living in this palace, calling them the happiest of his life. Purchased by Frederick's father in 1734, it was remodelled in Rococo style by the architect Knobelsdorff, the painter Pesne and the sculptor Glume. Until German reunification, the palace was used as a sanatorium. Highlights include the Spiegelsaal (Hall of Mirrors), decorated with a ceiling fresco by Antoine Pesne, and the Muschelsaal (Shell Room). On the ground floor the **Tucholsky Literaturmuseum** (⌚4€; combination ticket with palace ⌚10€) portrays the life of journalist, satirist, poet and social critic Kurt Tucholsky (1890–1935).

Ravensbrück

▶ 24km/15mi south of Neustrelitz on the E 251, 1km/0.6mi from Fürstenberg. Open year-round May–Sept Tue–Sun 9am–6pm (until 5pm Oct–Apr). Closed Dec 24–26 & 31. ℘(033093) 60 80. www.ravensbrueck.de.

Construction of Ravensbrück concentration camp on the shores of Schwedtsee lake began in 1938. It was the only major camp for women, and by 1945 had seen 132 000 prisoners from more than 40 nations. Tens of thousands died. The camp is now a memorial site with a permanent exhibit in the old SS camp commander's headquarters that documents the history of the camp and the lives and deaths of its victims. There are also additional smaller exhibits.

Kloster Chorin★★ (Chorin Abbey)

▶ 71km/44mi north of Berlin. Amt Chorin 11a. Open Apr–Oct daily 9am–6pm; Nov–Mar daily 10am–4pm. ⌚4€. ℘(033366) 703 77. www.kloster-chorin.info.

Surrounded by a park, the romantic ruins of Chorin Abbey lie near a small lake. Its building originally constructed in the 13C by Cistercian monks, the abbey was dissolved in 1542, and after centuries of neglect, it was saved by the architect Karl Friedrich Schinkel and the king of Prussia. Now partially restored, it is one of the finest Gothic red-brick structures in northern Germany and hosts a popular summer festival of classical music.

Spreewald★★

◗ The Spreewald region lies about 100km/62mi southeast of Berlin and covers about 260sq km/100sq mi. Lindenstraße 1, 03226 Vetschau. ℘(035433) 722 99. www.spreewald.de. ⌂Don't miss a barge trip from Lübbenau.

A network of hundreds of waterways crisscrosses this lush countryside, painstakingly drained to give it the appearance of a "Venice in the Woods". Another regional interest is its Sorbian minority, western Slavs who settled in Germany's Lausitz area in the 6C and who have managed to retain their language and culture to this day (⌂ see BRANITZ).

Lübbenau

The 18C Parish Church of St. Nikolai★ (open May–Oct Tue–Sun 2pm–4pm; closed public holidays; ⊚donation requested; ♿; ℘03542 26 62; www. kirche-luebbenau.de) is an important example of the Dresden Baroque architectural style. Inside are impressive tombs and epitaphs, most notably the high tomb (c. 1765) of Prince Moritz Carl, count of Lynear. To learn more about the region's cultural history, heritage and traditions, visit the Spreewald Museum (open Apr–Oct Tue–Sun 10am–5pm; Nov–Mar noon–4pm; ⊚5€; ℘03542 24 72).

♙ Barge Trips

Boat trips launch from throughout the Spreewald, but Lübbenau has established itself as the centre. Boats leave from Grosser Hafen or Kleiner Hafen, Mar–Oct (weather permitting; limited service Nov–Feb); 2hrs–9hrs, with stopovers. ⊚10€–25€. ℘(03542) 22 25. www.grosser-kahnhafen.de. A favourite destination is Lehde★, a tiny lagoon village of 150 people. The

Freilandmuseum (Open-air Museum) consists of three 19C farms, complete with living quarters and outbuildings, furniture, folk art, costumes and agricultural tools. The walk from Lübbenau to Lehde takes about 30 minutes.

ADDRESSES

⌂ STAY

⊖**Berlin-Plaza Hotel** – *Knesebeck straße 63, Charlottenburg.* ℘*(030) 88 41 30. www.plazahotel.de. 131 rooms. Restaurant⊖.* This dog-friendly hotel puts you close to Ku'damm shopping and has modern, clean but plain rooms.

⊖ **Transit Loft Hotel** – *Immanuelkirchstraße 14 a, Prenzlauer Berg.* ℘*(030) 48 49 37 73. www.transit-loft.de. 47 rooms.* This former factory building in the stylish quarter of Prenzlauer Berg started out in 2001 as a hostel for young people. Rooms are simple but well-maintained.

⊖⊖ **Am Wilden Eber** – *Warnemünder Straße 19, Grunewald.* ℘*(030) 89 77 79 90. www.hotel-am-wilden-eber.de. 15 rooms.* This simple hotel in a leafy suburb has well-kept and quiet rooms, and a small pool and sauna in the basement.

⊖⊖ **Arte Luise Kunsthotel** – *Luisenstraße 19, Mitte.* ℘*(030) 28 44 80. www.luise-berlin.com. 50 rooms.* This restored building from 1825 houses a unique boutique hotel where the rooms have been designed by different artists who receive a small stipend every time their room is rented. There are also smaller rooms with shared bathrooms.

⊖⊖ **Circus Hostel and Hotel** – *Weinbergsweg 1a, Mitte.* ℘*(030) 20 00 39 39. www.circus-berlin.de. Hostel 247 beds; hotel 62 rooms.* A 10min minute walk from Hackescher Markt, this hostel has clean accommodations, but mostly shared bathrooms. It sits across Rosenthaler Platz from the Circus Hotel, which offers individually designed rooms. Not far away are 23 spacious Circus Aapartments. Services include Internet, bike rental. The hostel has a café and pub; the hotel has a restaurant.

⊖⊖ **Honigmond Garden Hotel** – *Invalidenstraße 122, Mitte.* ℘*(030) 28 44 55 77. www.honigmond-berlin.de. 20 rooms, 4 suites, 3 studios.* Rooms here exude plenty of character with their polished parquet floors and antique furniture. The hotel is in a quiet area close to the historic centre. In summer, breakfast is served in the garden. Not far away is the Honigmond Hotel, with 27 additional rooms, suites and studios.

⊖🛏 **Hotel Am Anhalter Bahnhof** – *Stresemannstraße 36, Kreuzberg. ℰ(030) 251 03 42. www.hotel-anhalter-bahnhof.de. 45 rooms.* The best things about this no-frills property are its convenient location near Potsdamer Platz and a bus stop on its doorstep. Basic rooms are clean and cheap, but only some have private facilities; others must share bathrooms down the hall.

⊖🛏🛏 **Grand Hotel Esplanade** – *Lützowufer 15, Tiergarten. ℰ(030) 254 780. www.esplanade.de. 394 rooms. Restaurant ⊖🛏🛏.* This updated urban designer hotel features elegant rooms dressed in natural hues and accented with wood and chrome. The generous pool and sauna are welcome relaxation zones, while four restaurants feed tummy and soul.

⊖🛏🛏 **Hotel Hackescher Markt** – *Große Präsidentenstraße 8, Mitte. ℰ(030) 28 00 30. http://classik-hotel-collection. com. 32 rooms.* Decorated in English country style, this intimate boutique hotel occupies a modern building concealed by a historic façade. It is located in the Scheunenviertel nightlife district, so get a room facing the small inner courtyard for extra quiet.

⊖🛏🛏🛏 **Hotel Adlon Kempinski** – *Unter den Linden 77, Mitte. ℰ(030) 226 10. www.hotel-adlon.de. 382 rooms. Restaurant⊖🛏🛏🛏.* Adlon is truly a living legend. Since 1997 it has once again been possible to stay in this sumptuous building next to the Brandenburg Gate. It is a close copy of the 1907 original and oozes luxury from every nook and cranny.

⹋/**EAT**

⊖🛏 **Mutter Hoppe** – *Rathausstraße 21, Mitte. ℰ(030) 241 56 25. www.prost mahlzeit.de/mutterhoppe.* This rustic restaurant in the Nikolaiviertel celebrates Old Berlin nostalgia in its warren of rooms filled with faded photographs and yesteryear's memorabilia. On Friday and Saturday nights, live bands play music from the 1920s and 1930s.

⊖🛏 **Vapiano** – *Postdamer Platz 5, Tiergarten. ℰ(030) 23 00 50 05. www.vapiano.de.* At this self-service restaurant, order mix-and-match pasta, salad or pizza, which is then prepared in front of you in the open kitchen. Each table features a basket with fresh basil, rosemary and mint which you can use to add a little spice to your dish.

⊖🛏🛏 **Borchardt** – *Französische Straße 47, Mitte. ℰ(030) 81 88 62 62. www. borchardt-restaurant.de.* With impressive gilded columns, stuccoed ceilings and refined furniture, this stylish restaurant attracts celebrities, politicians and the merely monied. The *Wiener schnitzel* is reportedly the best in town.

⊖🛏🛏 **Diekmann** – *Meinekestraße 7, Charlottenburg. ℰ(030) 883 33 21. www.j-diekmann.de. Closed Sun lunch-time. Reservation necessary.* Josef Diekmann's original restaurant serves upmarket Franco-German fare prepared with locally sourced game, fish and produce. The space itself is old-fashioned with plank flooring and the quaint charm of an early 20C grocers.

⊖🛏🛏 **Lutter und Wegner** – *Charlottenstraße 56, Mitte. ℰ (030) 202 95 40. www.l-w-berlin.de.* Behind a sandstone facade, this popular restaurant is close to Gendarmenmarkt. The cuisine shows a distinct Austrian influence, while the wine menu features 700 choices in all price categories.

⊖🛏🛏 **Marjellchen** – *Mommsenstraße 9, Charlottenburg. ℰ(030) 883 26 76. www.marjellchen-berlin.de.* This homey Berlin restaurant serves substantial dishes from eastern Prussia and Silesia that taste just like in the old days.

⊖🛏🛏 **Schneeweiss** –*Simplonstraße 16, Friedrichshain. ℰ(030) 29 04 97 04. www. schneeweiss-berlin.de.* This chic, all-white restaurant in a lively neighbourhood has great design, and features cuisine from the Alpine region, ranging from Wiener schnitzel to ravioli.

⊖🛏🛏🛏 **Alt Luxemburg** – *Windscheidstraße 31, Charlottenburg. ℰ(030) 323 87 30. www.altluxemburg.de. Closed Sun.* The family Wannmacher has been serving high-level classic cuisine in their colourfully decorated restaurant since 1982.

⊖🛏🛏 **E.T.A. Hoffmann** – *Yorckstraße 83, Kreuzberg. ℰ(030) 780 988 09. www.restaurant-e-t-a-hoffmann.de.*

Named after the German Romantic author and located in the beautiful Riemers Hofgarten complex, this perennial favourite offers traditional dishes with modern flair in a relaxed setting.

CAFÉS

Café Einstein Stammhaus – *Kurfürstenstraße 58, Schöneberg.* ℘*(030) 263 91 918. www.cafeeinstein.com.* This Vienna-style coffeehouse in the former villa of silent-movie star Henny Porten is popular with artists, intellectual types and politicians. Enjoy breakfast, a light lunch, afternoon coffee and cake, or Austrian dishes at dinnertime.

Ephraim's – *Spreeufer 1, Mitte.* ℘*(030) 24 72 59 47. www.ephraims.de.* Nostalgia rules at this café-restaurant in the Nikolaiviertel that serves Berlin specialities, homemade cakes in its warm atmosphere. In fine weather, sit outside for views of the Spree River.

The Bam – *Auguststraße 58, Mitte.* http://barn.bigcartel.com. This trendy cafe in the middle of the Scheunenviertel takes coffee seriously, and offers fine roasts in a minimalist atmosphere. Sit outside on a sunny weekend morning and watch the stylish Mitte crowd go by.

NIGHTLIFE

Useful tips – Berlin's nightlife is decentralised and constantly evolving. Current hotspots cluster in the Scheunenviertel and around Gendarmenmarkt in Mitte; Kollwitzplatz, Kastanienallee and Helmholtzplatz in Prenzlauer Berg; Bergmannstraße, Oranienstraße, Schlesische Straße and Paul-Lincke-Ufer in Kreuzberg; Winterfeldtplatz in Schöneberg; and Savignyplatz in Charlottenburg.

Clärchen's Ballhaus – *Auguststraße 24, Mitte.* ℘*(030) 282 92 95. www.ballhaus.de.* This 19C dance hall draws young and old with tango, swing, ballroom, disco and more. Live bands perform on Friday and Saturday nights and dance lessons are offered, too. German and Italian food (pizza) is served from 12.30pm.

Die Tagung – *Wühlischstraße 29, Friedrichshain, east of Warschauer Straße.* ℘*(030) 29 77 37 88.* This funky been-here-forever bar is a tongue-in-cheek nostalgic celebration with a hodgepodge of retro busts, signs, posters and other memorabilia.

Universum Lounge – *Kurfürstendamm 153, Charlottenburg.* ℘*(030) 3276 4793. www.universumlounge.com.* A cool crowd of cashed-up locals, theatre-goers and hipsters convenes for cocktails and conversation in this sleek, space-age theme lounge. It's right in the Schaubühne theatre, designed by Expressionist architect Erich Mendelssohn in the 1920s.

Zillemarkt – *Bleibtreustraße 48a, Charlottenburg.* ℘*(030) 881 70 40. www.zillemarkt.de.* This Old Berlin hangout with its cobbled courtyard, bric-a-brac décor and earthy cooking is much beloved by tourists and locals alike.

Prater Garten Berlin – *Kastanienallee 7–9, Prenzlauer Berg.* ℘*(030) 448 56 88. www.pratergarten.de.* Dating back to 1873, this is Berlin's oldest, largest and most beautiful beer garden. Quaff a cold one sitting at long blond-wood tables beneath mature chestnut trees.

Philharmonie – *Herbert-von-Karajan-Straße, Tiergarten.* ℘*(030) 25 48 89 99. www.berliner-philharmoniker.de.* Enjoy supreme acoustics, a top-notch orchestra led by Sir Simon Rattle and renowned soloists in one of Germany's finest concert halls, built by Hans Scharoun in the 1960s.

Staatsoper Unter den Linden – *Unter den Linden 7, Mitte.* ℘*(030) 20 35 40. www.staatsoper-berlin.org.* The most prestigious among Berlin's three opera houses, the Staatsoper is helmed by Daniel Barenboim. While the historic 18C opera house is under renovation until 2016, performances take place in the Schillertheater in Charlottenburg *(Bismarckstraße 110).*

SHOPPING

Useful tips – Berlin's main shopping streets are Kurfürstendamm and Tauentzienstraße in Charlottenburg, and Friedrichstraße in Mitte. The biggest shopping centres are the Potsdamer Platz Arkaden, the Alexa mall near Alexanderplatz and newcomer Bikini Berlin, a "concept mall" near Zoo Station. Independent boutiques cluster in the Scheunenviertel in Mitte, along Bergmannstraße in Kreuzberg; on Bleibtreustraße and Fasanenstraße in Charlottenburg; and on Kastanienallee in Prenzlauer Berg.

DEPARTMENT STORES

Berlin's most famous department store is **KaDeWe** on Tauentzienstraße in Schöneberg with a wonderful food hall on the 6th floor. **Galeries Lafayette** brings Parisian style and fashion to Friedrichstraße in Mitte.

On Alexanderplatz, Galeria Kaufhof, redesigned by architect Josef Paul Kleihues, is now an elegant place to max out those credit cards.

Art galleries – Galleries abound around Savignyplatz and along Fasanenstraße in Charlottenburg, on Zimmerstraße and Markgrafenstraße near Checkpoint Charlie and along Auguststraße, Linienstraße and Brunnenstraße in Mitte. An emerging quarter is along Potsdamer Straße and Kurfuerstenstraße in Schöneberg, and for the more adventurous, in Wedding, along Soldiner Straße.

Flea markets – Flohmarkt am Tiergarten, Straße des 17. Juni, Charlottenburg, *Sat–Sun 10am–5pm*; Flohmarkt am Mauerpark, Bernauer Straße 63–64, Prenzlauer Berg, *Sun 8am–6pm*; Flohmarkt am Arkonaplatz, Prenzlauer Berg, *Sun 10am–4pm*; Flohmarkt am Boxhagener Platz, Friedrichshain, *Sun 10am–6pm*.

Farmers' markets – Winterfeldtplatz, Schöneberg, *Wed 8am–2pm, Sat 8am–4pm*; Turkish market Maybachufer, Kreuzberg, *Tue and Fri 11am–6.30pm*; Kollwitzstraße, Prenzlauer Berg, *Thu noon–7pm, Sat 9am–4pm*.

SIGHTSEEING

BUS TOURS

BEX Sightseeing Berlin (*℘880 4190; www.bex.de*); Berolina Sightsseeing (*℘88 56 80 30; www.berolina-berlin.com*); BBS (*℘35 19 52 70; www.bbsberlin.de*); Tempelhofer Reisen (*℘752 30 61; www.tempelhofer.de*) all provide hop-on, hop-off bus tours with taped commentary taking in all major city attractions. Buses run at 15 or 30min intervals (10am–5pm) and leave from Kurfürstendamm and outside the Park Inn Hotel on Alexanderplatz.

WALKING AND BIKING TOURS

For excellent English-language walking and biking tours: *Sandemans New Berlin Tours (℘51 05 00 30; www.newberlintours.com), Original Berlin Walks (℘301 91 94; www.berlinwalks.de), Brewer's Berlin Walking Tours (℘177 38 81 53 7; www.brewersberlin), Insider Tours (℘692 31 49; www.insidertour.com)*. Look for flyers in hotels and tourist offices.

BOAT TOURS

Stern und Kreisschiffahrt (℘536 36 00; www.sternundkreis.de) offers 1hr cruises along the Spree River from various landing docks, including in the Nikolaiviertel and at Friedrichstraße. Longer tours go out to Charlottenburg Palace, along the Landwehrkanal or to Berlin's green suburbs.

SPECIALITY TOURS

Trabi Safari (℘2759 2273; www.trabi-safari.de). Imagine yourself behind the steering wheel of a tinny GDR-era Trabi car exploring Berlin's Wild East following your guide in another vehicle. The ultimate "ostalgia" tour (i.e. nostalgia for the East).

Berliner Unterwelten Bunker Tour (℘030 4991 0518; www.berliner-unterwelten.de). See what Berlin looks like beneath the surface by joining an eye-opening tour of an underground bunker built during World War II.

Fritz Music Tours (℘ 030 3087 5633; www.musictours-berlin.com). Delve into Berlin's popular music history and find out where David Bowie lived, where Depeche Mode and U2 produced some records or where Rammstein keeps their offices. Walking and driving tours.

Berlinagenten (℘030-4372 0701; www.berlinagenten.com). Visit locals in their homes, secret corners and the newest hotspots on lifestyle tours led by clued-in guides. For the culinary scene, **Gastro-Rallye** offers one course each at four restaurant stops, along with insider scoops about the city.

Potsdam★★★

Located just west of Berlin, Potsdam was chosen in the 17C as the residence of the Electors of Brandenburg because of its setting in a natural woodland dotted with lakes and crisscrossed by canals and the River Havel. It is to Frederick the Great that Potsdam owes its renown as "rococo jewel". In 1990, the city's palaces and parks garnered a spot on the list of UNESCO World Heritage Sites.

A BIT OF HISTORY

A Prussian Versailles – Under Frederick William (1713–40), Potsdam became an administrative centre and a garrison town. By contrast, the king's son, **Frederick the Great** (Frederick II) was a devoted patron of the arts.

Most of the sights for which Potsdam is famous were built on his watch, notably Sanssouci Palace and the Neues Palais. Frederick, as fluent in French as in German, welcomed many eminent Frenchmen to his court, among them **Voltaire**.

The Potsdam Conference – The treaty defining the occupation and the future of Germany after World War II was signed at Cecilienhof Palace on 2 August 1945 by the leaders of the Allied powers (Atlee, Truman and Stalin).

SANSSOUCI PALACE AND PARK★★★

This huge complex is a harmonious marriage of architecture and landscape. As you wander around, it is easy to understand why Frederick the Great took such delight in staying here.

Friedenskirche (Peace Church)

Modelled on Rome's basilica of San Clemente, the church contains a fine 18C Murano **mosaic★**. The mausoleum harbours statues of Emperor Friedrich III and his wife and the sarcophagus of Friedrich Wilhelm I (1678–1740), which was hidden during World War II and brought here only in 1991.

▸ **Population:** 157 360

🛈 **Info:** Brandenburgishe St. 3, 14467 Potsdam. (0331) 27 55 88 99. www.potsdam-tourism.com.

▶ **Location:** Potsdam, the capital of the state of Brandenburg, lies just west of Berlin, in the heart of the Havelland, an area of canals and lakes.

🅿 **Parking:** Garages throughout the city, including one near Sanssouci Palace.

☺ **Don't Miss:** Sanssouci Palace.

🕐 **Timing:** Allow at least half a day for a tour of Sanssouci.

Bildergalerie★ (Picture Gallery)

Open May–Oct Tue–Sun 10am–6pm. ✆6€. ☎(0331) 969 42 00. www.spsg.de.

Amid the rich 18C Rococo of the great rooms visitors can admire works mainly from the Italian (Bassano, Tintoretto and Caravaggio), Flemish (Van Dyck, Rubens and Terbrugghen) and French (Simon Vouet and Van Loo) schools, all acquired by Friedrich II.

Schloss Sanssouci★★★

☺ Tours limited to 2 000 a day and often sell out before noon. Admission is by timed ticket. Open Tue–Sun 10am–6pm (until 5pm Nov–Mar). Closed Dec 24. ✆12€, Nov–Mar 8€. ☎(0331) 969 42 00. www.spsg.de.

It is impossible to remain unmoved by the majestic façade as one climbs the great staircase leading to the palace from the park side. Architect Knobelsdorff originally planned for the façade, adorned with 36 atlantes, to encompass the entire terrace area. But Frederick the Great preferred a generous proportion of the space which indeed became one of his favourite places for relaxing. In fact he so loved Sanssouci he gave specific instructions to be buried next to

Schloss Sanssouci

© Jean-Baptiste Rabouan/hemis.fr

his beloved dogs on the highest terrace of the vineyards in front of the palace. A self-guided tour with an audioguide takes in a dozen beautifully decorated rooms. Highlights include the Concert Room, the domed Marble Hall, the king's study and bedchamber and the Music Room, his personal favourite.

Neue Kammern★ (New Chambers)

Open Apr–Oct Tue–Sun 10am–6pm. Closed Nov–Mar. ⊚4€. ♿ ☎(0331) 969 42 00. www.spsg.de.
Designed in 1747 by Knobelsdorff, this former orangery was soon transformed into the palace guesthouse. A highlight of the captivating Rococo interior is the **Ovidsaal★**, decorated with scenes from Ovid's *Metamorphoses*.

Orangerie (Orangery)

Visit by guided tour (30min) only, Apr Sat–Sun 10am–6pm; May–Oct Tue–Sun 10am–6pm. Closed Nov–Mar. ⊚4€. ♿ ☎(0331) 969 42 00. www.spsg.de.
The orangery was built in the style of an Italian Renaissance palace between 1851 and 1860, after plans by Friedrich Wilhelm IV, and served as a guesthouse for visiting royalty. The magnificent apartments where Czar Nicolas I and his wife stayed and the **Raphael Hall★**, which houses 47 copies of paintings by Raphael are highlights of the tour.

Neues Palais★★ (New Palace)

Visit by audioguide or 1hr tour (tour in winter only), Wed–Mon 10am–6pm (Nov–Mar until 5pm). Closed Dec 24, 25 & 31. ⊚8€. ☎(0331) 969 42 00. www.spsg.de.
This imposing building was commissioned by Frederick the Great to demonstrate Prussia's economic power after the Seven Years' War. Some 400 rooms, with excessively lavish decorations and a superabundance of sculpture, testify to the ambitious nature of the project – which was nevertheless completed in just six years.
Only a small section of rooms can be visited, including the Grotto Hall, decorated with shells and fossils; the elegant Marble Hall with its stunning ceiling fresco, and the theatre in the south wing. Separate admission *(⊚5€)* gives you access to a tour of Frederick the Great's **private apartments**. Also here is the **Pesne-Galerie,** with a broad survey of works by this French painter. *The latter two are open only April to October.*

Schloss Charlottenhof★

Visit by guided tour (45min) only, May–Oct Tue–Sun 10am–6pm. ⊚4€. ☎(0331) 969 42 00. www.spsg.de.
Karl-Friedrich Schinkel and his pupil, Ludwig Persius, drew up the plans for this palace, built in the Classical Italian style between 1826 and 1829. Tours include a stop in the bedchamber and in the office of Alexander von Humboldt.

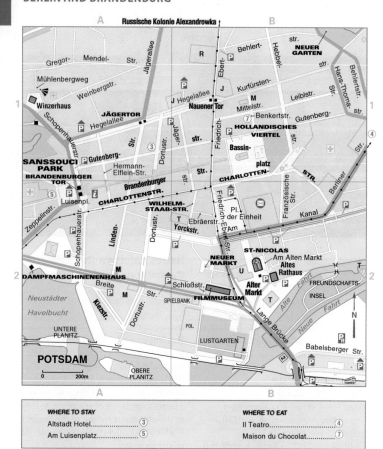

POTSDAM

0   200m

Römische Bäder
(Roman Baths)

Open mid-Apr–Oct, Tue–Sun 10am–6pm.
5€. (0331) 969 42 00.
www.spsg.de.
Schinkel, Persius and landscaper Lenné
made these baths look like an Italian
country estate. The **interior décor★** of
the baths is tastefully done. A pergola
leads to the Tea Pavilion, not unlike a
temple, with a single room decorated
all in blue, which has a good view of the
lake and gardens.

Chinesisches Haus★★
(Chinese House)

Open May–Oct Tue–Sun 10am–6pm.
2€. (0331) 969 42 00.
www.spsg.de.
A circular pavilion decorated with
gilded statues, this structure arose from

the "Sino-mania" so popular in 18C Germany. Inside is an exhibit of Chinese and
Meissen porcelain.

TOWN CENTRE
Alter Markt
(Old Market)

The Church of St. Nicholas (Nikolaikirche) dominates the square. Designed
by Schinkel (1837), it is one of the finest
examples of Neoclassical architecture in
Germany. The dome, completed in 1850
by students of the master, was inspired
by the Basilica of St. Peter's and St. Paul's
Cathedral in London.
Before World War II the "Great Bridge"
(Lange Brücke) led directly to the city
palace (Stadtschloss), the first built in
Potsdam in 1660 by the Great Elector.
Severely damaged by bombing in 1945,
this symbol of the Prussian monarchy

was demolished in 1960 by the East German government. It was recently reconstructed; its entrance gate is topped by a steeple, in place since 2003.

Neuer Markt★★ (New Market)

This tiny square is framed by handsome buildings from the 18C–19C, making it one of the oldest and most beautiful in the city. The most impressive is the Kutschenstall, where the royal carriages used to be stored. Built between 1787 and 1790 according to plans designed by Andreas Ludwig Krüger, it is an early example of Neoclassical architecture and now houses the House of Brandenburg and Prussian History (Haus der Brandenburgisch-Preussischen Geschichte).

Brandenburger Tor★

Luisenplatz.

This monumental gateway was built in the Baroque fashion in 1770, but takes the form of a Roman triumphal arch.

Filmmuseum★

Breite Straße 1a. Open year-round Tue–Sun 10am–6pm. 5€. (0331) 271 81 12. www.filmmuseum-potsdam.de.

Dating from 1685 and modified by Knobelsdorff in 1746, the former royal stables now house this small museum. Exhibits focus on German Expressionist films, émigré film directors and the history of the local Babelsberg film studios. Founded in 1912 as the UFA Studios, it produced such silent-era classics as Fritz Lang's *Metropolis* and *The Blue Angel* starring Marlene Dietrich. Recent productions include Roman Polanski's *The Pianist* and Tarantino's *Inglourious Basterds*.

Holländisches Viertel★ (Dutch Quarter)

The pretty Dutch Quarter is a small grid of lanes lined by gabled red-brick houses. It was built for Dutch artisans who were invited to come to Potsdam by King Frederick William I. Mittelstraße is the main artery.

Dampfmaschinenhaus★★ (Pump House)

Breite Straße 28. Visit by guided tour (30min) only, May–Oct Sat–Sun 10am–6pm. 3€. (0331) 969 42 00. www.spsg.de.

Frederick the Great built the lovely fountains at Park Sanssouci, but it would take another century before they would actually spout water. Under Frederick William IV this steam-powered pump began operating. It allowed jets of water from the great fountain in front of Sanssouci Palace to shoot an impressive 38m/125ft high. Designed by Ludwig Persius, it is nicknamed the "Mosque" and is Potsdam's most exotic building.

NORTH OF THE CITY
Neuer Garten★★ (New Garden)

This park was laid out in the late 18C by Peter Lenné on the shore of the Heiliger See for Frederick the Great, who was a great fan of English-style landscaped gardens. Interesting features in the park include the orangery and a pyramid.

Marmorpalais (Marble Palace)

Visit by guided tour, May–Oct Tue–Sun 10am–6pm, Nov–Mar Sat–Sun 10am–4pm (Apr until 6pm) . Closed Dec 24, 25 & 31. 5€. (0331) 969 42 00. www.spsg.de.

This Neoclassical palace was built by Karl von Gontard and converted into a summer residence for Frederick William II by Carl Gottard Langhans (1744–1797). The king's beautiful private and state apartments are open to visitors. The concert hall and the Oriental Room, which resembles a Turkish tent, are particularly delightful.

Schloss Cecilienhof★

Visit by audio guide or tour, Apr–Oct Tue–Sun 10am–6pm (Nov–Mar to 5pm). Closed Dec 24–25 6€. (0331) 969 42 00. www.spsg.de.

This English-style country residence built during World War I for Crown Prince Wilhelm (1882–1951) and his wife, Cecilia of Mecklenburg-Schwerin (1886–1954), is worth seeing for its own sake. But it is the historic **meeting rooms of the Potsdam Conference** of 1945 that draw the most attention. Members of the Allied delegations signed the Potsdam Agreements here on 2 August 1945, outlining Germany's occupation and future development. The luxury hotel **Relexa Schlosshotel Cecilienhof** *(closed for renovations until 2017; www.relexa-hotels.de)* also occupies space in this palace.

Russische Kolonie Alexandrowka★★ (Russian Colony)

About 1.5km/1mi north of the town centre. Tram 92 or 96 leaves from Hauptbahnhof, Alter Markt and Nauener Tor. Get off at Puschkinallee.

This Russian-style village was commissioned by Frederick William III in honour of his friend Czar Alexander I (1777–1825) and built between 1826 and 1827. It consists of 13 wooden houses arranged in the form of St. Andrew's Cross and surrounded by gardens. The original inhabitants were Russian singers of a Prussian military regiment. Ownership could be passed down through the generations. Descendants of two original inhabitants still live here today. The **Alexandrowka Museum** recounts the history of this curious colony (open Tue–Thu & Sat–Sun noon–6pm, Fri noon–9pm; 3.50€; (0331) 817 02 03; www.alexandrowka.de).

EXCURSIONS
Brandenburg

38km/23.6mi west.

It was in the 14C that this small town in the heart of the Havelland (an area of scattered lakes fed by the River Havel) began to prosper, mainly through the cloth trade. The **Dom St. Peter und St. Paul★**, founded in 1165 and remodelled in the 14C, is furnished with several Gothic altarpieces. In the two-aisle crypt, a mausoleum memorialises the clergy murdered during the Nazi regime.

Rich exterior decoration distinguishes the 15C **St. Katharinenkirche★**, which boasts a hall chancel with an ambulatory typical of red-brick Gothic churches.

Kloster Lehnin★ (Lehnin Abbey)

28km/17.4m southwest. Open Mon–Sat 10am–4pm, Sun 1pm–4pm. Closed Jan 1, Dec 24–26 & 31. (03382) 70 41 51. www.klosterkirche-lehnin.de.

This three-aisle brick basilica, commissioned by Margrave Otto I of Brandenburg and occupied in 1192 by the Cistercian Order, combines Romanesque and Early Gothic elements.

ADDRESSES

STAY

Altstadt Hotel – *Dortustraße 9-10. (0331) 284 990. www.altstadt-hotel-potsdam.de. 42 rooms.* This charming hotel has rooms that are comfortably furnished but don't have much elbow room. Some of them are in the attic. If you need more space, get one of the studios or the apartment.

Bed and Breakfast am Luisenplatz – *Zimmerstraße 1. (0331) 971 90 20. www.bed-breakfast-potsdam.de. 15 rooms.* The relatively central location and reasonable prices make this small hotel a real find. The welcoming guest rooms are modern and furnished in light wood; breakfast is served on the Luisenplatz.

EAT

Maison du Chocolat – *Benkertstraße 20. (0331) 237 07 30. www.schokoladenhaus-potsdam.de.* At this restaurant you can enjoy a French country-style meal and then stock up on all manner of succulent cakes and chocolate truffles in the attached store. A little corner of France in the Dutch quarter of Potsdam.

Il Teatro – *Schiffbauergasse 12. (0331) 200 97 291. www.ilteatro-potsdam.de.* Right next to the Hans-Otto Theatre, this pleasant restaurant is run by an Italian family. In fine weather, the Havel-facing terrace is the perfect spot for enjoying the seasonal cuisine or perhaps just a cup of excellent espresso.

Schloss Branitz★★

The gardens at Branitz Palace were the crowning achievement of Hermann Fürst von Pückler-Muskau (1785–1871), a nobleman, travel writer and one of the most distinguished landscape architects of the 19C. Branitz had been in his family's possession since 1696 but it wasn't until the prince moved here in 1845 that it was transformed into the glorious park and garden you see today.

- 🅘 **Info:** Robinienweg 5. 03042 Cottbus. ℘(0355) 751 50. www.pueckler-museum.de.
- ▶ **Location:** Branitz is less than 5km/3mi east of Cottbus.
- 🅿 **Parking:** Parking is available near the gardens.
- 🕘 **Timing:** Schloss Branitz and its gardens can be seen in half a day.

VISIT
Gardens
Hermann Prince of Pückler-Muskau was born at Muskau Palace, but sold the estate in 1845 and moved to Schloss Branitz, about 37km/23mi to the northwest. He used the proceeds from the sale to transform the surroundings into an exquisite **landscaped park**.

Covering 90ha/222 acres, it is divided into several zones, including a sculpture-studded flower garden adjacent to the Schloss itself. Soil from the excavation of lakes was used to shape hills and pyramids. Pückler placed particular emphasis on the alternation between open spaces, tree groupings, sculpture and pools. He and his wife, Lucie, are buried in the 11m/36ft high pyramid – called **Tumulus** – that rises from one of the lakes.

Palace
Open Apr–Oct daily 10am–6pm; Nov–Mar Tue–Sun 11am–5pm. 🎫5.50€. A combination ticket to the Gutshof, the palace and the Marstall costs 10€.

Approaching the compound, the first building you reach is the **Gutshof** (open Apr–Oct daily 10am–6pm; Nov–Mar Tue–Sun 11am–5pm; 🎫4.50€), which served as Pückler's office and now harbours the visitor centre with an interactive, **multimedia exhibit** on the man, his peers, his life and achievements.

At the park's centre, **Branitz Palace** was completed in 1772 by Gottfried Semper. Inside is an exhibit about Pückler's life and work alongside many original furnishings, especially in the dining room and the library. There's also a gallery featuring the paintings of Carl Blechen (1798–1840), the Romantic painter who was born in nearby Cottbus.

Opposite the palace, the Tudor-style **royal stables** (Marstall) are used for temporary exhibits (open Apr–Oct daily 10am–6pm; Nov–Mar Tue–Sun 11am–5pm; 🎫3.50€). The adjacent **Cavalier's House** (Cavalierhaus) is now a restaurant. Between the two buildings lies the **"Pergola"** with reliefs by the Danish sculptor Berthel Thorwaldsen, zinc copies of antique sculpture and a bronze casting of the Venus Italica by Canova. On the garden side is a terrace featuring two bronze griffins.

Schloss Branitz

© Udo Kruse/Fotolia.com

The Baltic Coast and Inland

Schloss Schwerin, Schlossgarten
© Gabriele Bröcker/Staatliches Museum Schwerin

The Baltic Coast and Inland

Germany's Baltic coast stretches for 2 247km/1 396mi between Denmark and Poland across the *Länder* (states) of Schleswig-Holstein and Mecklenburg-Vorpommern. Thinly populated, the region is rarely overrun with tourists, although its seaside resorts have been a favourite with German holidaymakers since the 19C. Families especially value the shallow and calm waters, wide sandy beaches and relaxing ambience. Hanseatic towns like Lübeck, Stralsund and Wismar are not only picturesque reminders of the region's former power but are also UNESCO World Heritage Sites. Fans of the offbeat can delve into Viking history in Schleswig, climb aboard a World War II submarine near Kiel or ride a historic train in Bad Doberan.

The Lure of Nature

Much of the appeal of Germany's northeast lies in its pristine and diverse landscapes. This is a region where you can truly connect with nature in places where birds and other wildlife outnumber people and where the flora is similar to what it was centuries ago. The seaside itself is a pastiche of narrow fjords with steep banks, flat and sandy beaches, sweeping bays and dramatic cliffs plunging into calm waters. Unspoiled Poel and Hiddensee islands pro-

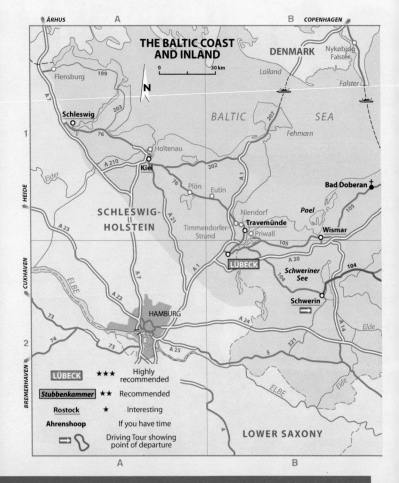

vide quiet retreats, while away from the coast the Mecklenburg lake district offers wide expanses of forest, moorland and an endless string of rivers and lakes, making it a paradise for boaters, birdwatchers, cyclists and nature lovers.

The Legacy of the Hanse

Numerous cities on the Baltic Coast once belonged to the powerful medieval trade alliance called the Hanseatic League (*see sidebar p197*). Its birthplace was Lübeck, whose old quarter, dramatically accessed via the picturesque Holstentor gate, is a must-see (also try delicious local marzipan made from almonds and sugar).

Other Hanseatic cities line up like pearls on a string east of here, most notably Wismar, Rostock, Stralsund and Greifswald. All of them have beautifully restored old towns and blend maritime levity with sturdy Gothic red-brick architectural gems so typical of the Baltic region.

Highlights

1 Exploring the medieval town of **Lübeck** (p164)

2 Gazing at the horizon from the chalk cliffs on **Rügen Island** (p182)

3 Recharging your batteries on car-free **Hiddensee Island** (p184)

4 Admiring the fine palace at **Schwerin** (p190)

5 Boating on **Lake Müritz** (p192)

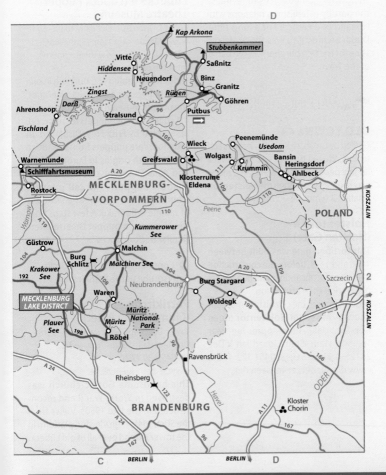

Lübeck★★★

The "queen" of the Hanseatic League, Lübeck is a vivacious town that still retains much of its medieval character despite being badly damaged in World War II. In 1987, its entire Old Town was placed on the UNESCO World Heritage list. Its port, 20km/13mi north in Travemünde, is one of the busiest on the Baltic Sea. Don't miss the marzipan here: it is a local culinary speciality.

▶ **Population:** 210 577

🛈 **Info:** Holstentorplatz 1, 23552 Lübeck. ℘(0451) 889 97 00. www.luebeck-tourism.de.

◖ **Location:** Lübeck is 60km/ 37mi northeast of Hamburg via the A1 autobahn.

🅿 **Parking:** Garages are plentiful in the Old Town.

☺ **Don't Miss:** Strolling the Old Town, or a taste of marzipan.

🕐 **Timing:** Allow a day to do this lovely town justice.

A BIT OF HISTORY

The 14C marked the peak of Lübeck's power as capital of the Hanseatic League. In the 16C, merchants and shipowners joined forces to revitalise the port by establishing relations with Holland and France. For a long time, Dutch architecture was the preferred style for the rich burghers on the banks of the Trave.

🐾WALKING TOUR

OLD TOWN★★★

Girdled by canals, crowned by belfries and towers, the old town of Lübeck sits on a largely pedestrianised island. The nicest way to enter it is through the **Holstentor**, a national symbol in Germany.

Holstentor★★ (Holsten Gate)

This fortified gate was built between 1466 and 1478, before the construction of the city fortification, more as a matter of prestige than protection.
Today it houses the city history museum know as **Museum Holstentor** (open Apr–Dec daily 10am–6pm; Jan–Mar Tue–Sun 11am–5pm; closed Jan 1, Dec 24–25 & 31; ☜6€; ℘0451 122 41 29; www.die-luebecker-museen.de).

👥 Theater Figuren Museum Lübeck★★ (Lübeck Puppet Theatre Museum)

Kolk 14. Open Apr–Oct daily 10am–6pm; Nov–Mar Tue–Sun 11am–5pm. ☜6€. ℘(0451) 786 26. www.theaterfiguren museum.de.

Hidden in a gabled 16C building in one of old Lübeck's most picturesque lanes, the puppet museum has one of the richest collections of puppets in the world, assembled by Fritz Frey. Displayed on four floors are puppets from the 18C to the 20C with origins in Europe, Africa and Asia. Don't miss the Indonesian shadow puppets, the tall puppets from Nigeria or the great characters of Japanese Bunraku. A few steps from the museum, a puppet theatre offers regular performances.

◖ Continue on, then follow Große Petersgrube to the Petrikirche.

Petrikirche (Church of St. Peter)

Tower Open Apr–Sept daily 9am–9pm; Oct–Mar daily 10am–7pm. ☜3€. ℘(0451) 39 77 30. www.st-petri-luebeck.de.

This handsome Gothic church was destroyed in World War II and reconstructed in the late 1950s. Views from the 50m/164ft-high viewing platform in the tower extend over all of old Lübeck.

Holstentor

© M. Hertlein/MICHELIN

▶ Take Schmiedestraße to the Dom (cathedral).

Dom (Cathedral)
The 14C Gothic expansion transformed this Romanesque church. Note the monumental late-Gothic **Crucifix★** by Bernt Notke and the stone screen (early 14C) with a wooden tracery balustrade.

▶ Take Fegefeuer to St. Annen-Straße. Alternatively, extend the walk to the river bank for lovely views of the cathedral.

St. Annen-Museum★ (St. Anne's Museum)
St. Annen-Straße 15. Open Apr–Dec Tue–Sun 10am–5pm; Jan–Mar 11am–5pm. Closed Jan 1, Easter Mon, Dec 24–25 & 31. ✆6€. ✆(0451) 122 41 37. www.die-luebecker-museen.de.
Paintings and sculpture from Lübeck's churches are displayed in this museum alongside German modern art.

▶ Resume on St. Annen-Straße and continue straight until Glockengießerstraße (left turn).

Höfe und Gänge (Courtyards and alleyways)
These open courtyards (*Höfe*) set back from the street are typical for Lübeck. Note the delightful **Füchtingshof**

(no 25) with its Baroque doorway; the **Glandorps-Gang**, a narrow alleyway, at no 41 and, from nos 49 to 51, the **Glandorps-Hof**. The building at no 21 is now the **Günter Grass Haus**.

Günter Grass Haus
Glockengießerstraße 21. Open Jan–Mar Tue–Sun 11am–5pm; Apr–Dec daily 10am–5pm. Closed Jan 1, Dec 24–25 & 31. ✆6€. ✆(0451) 122 42 30. www.die-luebecker-museen.de.
Born in Lübeck, Günter Grass is one of Germany's most famous contemporary writers, author of *The Tin Drum* (1961) and winner of the Nobel Prize for Literature. This exhibit set up in his office and workshop displays manuscripts as well as examples of his work as a sculptor and graphic designer.

▶ At the end of Glockengießerstraße, turn left towards the church.

Katharinenkirche★ (Church of St. Catherine)
Closed for renovation until further notice. ✆(0451)122 4137. www.die-luebecker-museen.de.
Converted into a museum, the lower niches of the façade of this 14C church contain modern **statues★**, the first three on the left being by Ernst Barlach. As you enter, note on the right *The Resurrection of Lazarus* by Tintoretto.

Willy-Brandt-Haus

Open Apr–Dec Tue–Sun 11am–6pm;
Jan–Mar Tue–Sun 11am–5pm. Closed
Jan 1, Dec 24–25 & 31. ☎(0451) 122 42
50. www.willy-brandt-luebeck.de.

This exhibit is dedicated to Willy Brandt,
a native of Lübeck and winner of the
Nobel Peace Prize in 1971 for his policy
of rapprochement with East Germany.
Photos, audio and video tell his life
story, with a particular focus on his work
for human rights. Video screens feature TV
news coverage in East and West Germany
about such events as John F. Kennedy's
visit to Berlin in 1963.

▶ Upon exiting turn right.

Museum Behnhaus Drägerhaus

Open Apr–Dec Tue–Sun 10am–5pm;
Jan–Mar Tue–Sun 11am–5pm. Closed
Jan 1, Easter Mon, Dec 24–25 & 31. ☜6€.
(0451) 122 41 48. www.luebecker-
museen.de.

This 18C former mansion of a wine
merchant houses furniture and paintings primarily from the 18C and 19C
Romantic era, as well as works by Friedrich Overbeck (1789–1869), head of the
Nazarene School. Other artists represented include Max Liebermann, Ernst
Ludwig Kirchner and the Lübeck artist
A Aereboe. There is also a smattering
of paintings by Edvard Munch created
during his time in Lübeck.

▶ Upon exiting, continue straight
up Königstraße.

Heiligen-Geist-Hospital★ (Hospice of the Holy Spirit)

Since the late 13C, the three turreted
gables of this almshouse have stood
above the Koberg. The chapel, a large
Gothic hall embellished with 13C and
14C paintings, is just outside the even
larger Great Hall of the hospice.

▶ Follow Königstraße , which turns
into Große Burgstraße.

Burgtor★ (Castle Gate)

This fortified gateway defended the narrow isthmus, once the only land approach
to Lübeck. The structure is a fine example of 13C–15C military architecture.

▶ Retrace your steps, then turn right.

Haus der Schiffergesellschaft★ (Sailors' Guildhall)

Breite Straße 2.

Behind the stepped Renaissance gable
awaits a handsomely decorated ancient
seaman's tavern with rough wooden
tables, copper lamps and model ships
dangling from the beams. It is now a
restaurant (☜see Addresses).

Jakobikirche★ (Church of St. Jacob)

*Opposite the Haus der Schiffergesell-
schaft.* The magnificent woodwork of
the two organ **lofts★★** (16C–17C) in this
small Gothic hall-church is noteworthy.
Larger than life-size representations of
apostles and saints adorn the pillars of
the central nave.

The chapel north of the tower is now a
memorial to shipwrecked sailors, and
displays a lifeboat from the *Pamir*, the
full-rigged Lübeck ship lost with all
hands aboard in 1957.

▶ Continue south along Breite
Straße, then turn right on Mengstraße.

Buddenbrookhaus

Mengstraße 4. Open Apr–Dec
daily 10am–6pm; Jan–Mar 11am–5pm.
Closed Jan 1, Dec 24–25 & 31.
☜6€. ♿ ☎(0451) 122 4190.
www.buddenbrookhaus.de.

The name derives from Thomas Mann's
1901 novel *Buddenbrooks*, which chronicles the decline of a patrician Lübeck
family. Heinrich and Thomas Mann
were not born in the Buddenbrookhaus.
However, it is true that in 1841 their
grandfather Johann Siegmund Mann
bought the 18C Baroque house, and
the brothers were frequently guests
there during their childhood and ado-
lescence.

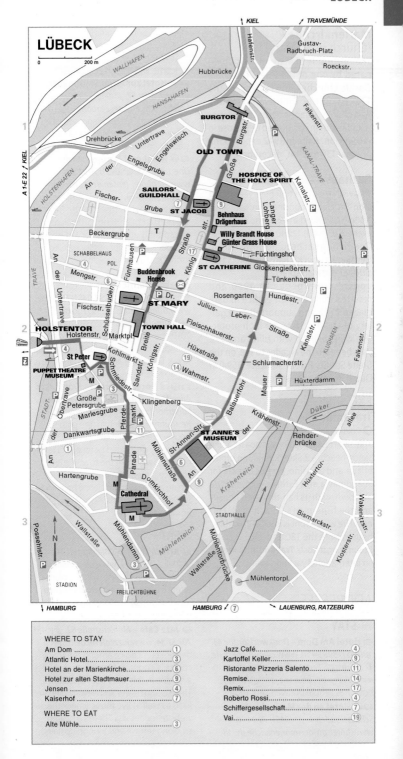

Marienkirche★★ (Church of St. Mary)

The north side of Marktplatz is dominated by one of the finest red-brick Gothic churches in Germany. In the 17C, composer Dietrich Buxtehude was church organist here. The interior is audacious in design and grandiose in proportion. A fire in 1942 exposed the original 13C and 14C decoration.

Rathaus★ (Town Hall)

Visit by guided tour only, year-round Mon–Fri 11am, noon and 3pm; Sat 1.30pm (provided there are no public events). ℘(0451) 122 10 05.

One of the most beautiful town halls in Germany, Lübeck's Rathaus flanks two sides of the Marktplatz.

Construction began in 1250 and resulted in an elegant edifice in dark glazed brick and supported by a gallery of arcades. Note the high protective walls pierced with blind arcades. Pass beneath the arcades to see, on the Breite Straße, a stone staircase (1594) in Dutch Renaissance style.

EXCURSION

Travemünde★

▶ 20km/12.4mi northeast.

This smart Baltic spa resort boasts a fine sandy beach, a 2.5km/1.5mi-long promenade and a casino. Ferries depart for Scandinavia and Estonia. Explore the old town, with its half-timbered houses and the fishermen's Church of St. Lorenz. The waterfront is lined with gabled houses from the 18C and 19C.

In summer, it hosts **Travemünde Week**, an international yachting event.

ADDRESSES

🏨 STAY

⊖ **Hotel Am Dom** – *Dankwartsgrube 43. ℘(0451) 399 94 10. www.cvjm-luebeck.de. 17 rooms.* ☕. Located in a quiet street in the old centre, near the dock, this small hotel has simple but well-kept rooms.

⊖⊖ **Hotel an der Marienkirche** – *Schüsselbuden 4. ℘ (0451) 79 94 10. www.hotel-an-der-marienkirche.de. 18 rooms.* ☕. Some rooms in this charming brick building have views of the Church of St. Mary. Guests receive a warm welcome and a hearty breakfast.

⊖⊖ **Hotel zur Alten Stadtmauer** – *An der Mauer 57. ℘(0451) 737 02. www.hotelstadtmauer.de. 24 rooms.* ☕. This quiet town house has renovated rooms exuding warm family flair. It sits just steps from the bustling Mühlenstraße.

⊖⊖ **Ringhotel Jensen** – *An der Obertrave 4-5. ℘(0451) 70 24 90. www.ringhotel-jensen.de. 42 rooms. Restaurant* ⊖⊖. Located within the historic triangle formed by the Trave, the Holstentor and the Salzspeicher, this comfortably appointed gabled house was built in 1307. It has modernised rooms and a dining room with nautical flourishes.

⊖⊖⊖ **Atlantic Hotel** – *Schmiedestraße 9–15. ℘(0451) 38 47 90. www.atlantic-hotel.de. 135 rooms. Restaurant* ⊖⊖⊖. Open since early 2010, this stylish hotel offers modern comforts in the heart of the historic old town. The sauna and fitness area boast remarkable views across Lübeck.

⊖⊖⊖ **Hotel Kaiserhof** – *Kronsforder Allee 11-13. ℘(0451) 70 33 01. www.kaiserhof-luebeck.de. 58 rooms. Restaurant* ⊖⊖⊖. Two fine patrician houses were united to form this pleasantly decorated hotel only a few minutes walk from the town centre. High-ceilinged rooms and chandeliers create an elegant ambience here and in the classic restaurant. Also of note: the Roman steam bath.

🍴EAT

⊖ **Alte Mühle** – *Mühlendamm 24. ℘(0451) 707 25 92. www.altemühle-lübeck.de.* In a historic mill, this place offers a large choice of *Flammkuchen* (Alsatian pizza), seasonal dishes and a good wine selection.

⊖ **Jazz Café** – *Mühlenstraße 62. ℘(0451) 707 37 34. www.jazzcafe-hl.de.*You will be spoilt for choice among the many cocktails, cognacs, brandies andwhiskeys available in this jazzy bar-restaurant. There is also hearty and cleverly prepared food as well as live music (check the website for details). There's a heated smoking terrace and lounge upstairs.

⊝ **Remix Café** – *Königstraße 26.*
(0451) 709 88 73. www.remix-cafe.de.
Opposite the church of St. Catherine, this bistro serves simple dishes in a cosy atmosphere and has courtyard seating on sunny days.

⊝ **Ristorante Pizzeria Salento** –
Pferdemarkt 19. (0451) 70 98 64 49.
Closed Tue. Enjoy pizza in a charming garden setting with a view of the cathedral. There is a small, tree-shaded playground for children.

⊝⊟ **Kartoffel Keller** – *Koberg 8. (0451)*
762 34. www.kartoffel-keller-hl.de. Enjoy creative regional dishes built around the humble potato. Sit at long tables in the vaulted former wine cellar of the Hospital of the Holy Spirit.

⊝⊟ **Remise** – *Wahmstraße 43–45.*
(0451) 777 73. www.remise-luebeck.de.
The courtyard of this restaurant is ideal for brunch or a light lunch. The kitchen serves mostly Italian-inspired cuisine prepared with seasonal ingredients. Wonderful atmosphere, and on some nights, live music.

⊝⊟⊟ **Schabbelhaus / Roberto Rossi** – *Mengstraße 48–52. (0451)*
720 11. www.schabbelhaus.de. Closed Sun.
This early 20C building is the legacy of local master baker Schabbel. Built as a foundation after his death, it is now an Italian restaurant but retains its original charm. Budget-priced weekday lunches.

⊝⊟⊟ **Schiffergesellschaft** –
Breite Straße 2. (0451) 767 76.
www.schiffergesellschaft.com.
Reservations recommended. This charming tavern, built as a sailors' meeting-house, guildhouse and almshouse back in 1535, is decorated with a maritime-style. Seating is on solid wood benches at long rustic tables.

⊝⊟⊟ **Vai** – *Hüxstraße 42. (0451)*
400 780 83. www.restaurant-vai.de.
Reservations recommended. In a sleek modern interior, Vai offers well-prepared classic German fare as well as an assortment of pasta dishes. Outdoor courtyard.

TRAVEMÜNDE

⊝⊟⊟ **Weinwirtschaft** – *Außenallee 10*
(04502) 307 06 32. www.resort.a-rosa.de.
This bistro and wine shop serves tapas and international cuisine.

Café Niederegger

© Niederegger

TAKING A BREAK

Café Niederegger – *Breite Straße 89.*
(0451) 530 11 26. www.niederegger.de.
This café-shop is *the* place to buy and sample marzipan, although the famous hazelnut-cream cake is just as delicious. Also check out the marzipan museum on the second floor.

Café Utspann – *Wahmstraße 35–37 (in the Hansehof court). (0451) 707 06 77.*
www.cafe-utspann.de. Closed Sun.
Frisian-style décor distinguishes this inviting café specialising in homemade cakes served inside or on the old Hansehof court.

NIGHTLIFE

Brauberger – *Alfstraße. 36. (0451)*
714 44. www.brauberger.de. Closed Sun late Dec–May. This split-level brew-pub opened in 1988 but sits atop cellars dating from 1225. Light snacks and regional fare are available along with daily changing specials. On the first floor is a small terrace.

Im Alten Zolln – *Mühlenstraße 93–95.*
(0451) 723 95. www.alter-zolln.de.
A young and young-at-heart crowd gravitates to this lively pub in a 16C customs post. Pick from several draught beers served in three drinking areas, all with wooden panels and benches.

Kiel★

A key German naval base since 1860, Kiel was obliterated in World War II and post-war reconstruction was done largely in a functional, modern style. Today it has recaptured its role as gateway to Scandinavia and celebrates its maritime tradition with the world's largest sailing event, the annual Kiel Week.

A BIT OF HISTORY

Founded in the 13C, Kiel was always a seafaring town, even if it never achieved more than regional importance as a Hanseatic city. For centuries Kiel led a tranquil existence, until 1871 when it became Germany's main naval base. Within a few years, the little harbour town grew into an industrial metropolis. Today, the capital of Schleswig-Holstein is a quiet, leafy city where you feel the ocean breeze on a walk along the docks and observe the giant container ships passing through its port.

SIGHTS

Harbour★★

A string of resort towns line up along the harbour: Stein, Strande, Schilksee, Schönberger Strand, Laboe and Heikendorf. Kiel has hosted regattas for more than a century and draws as many as 5 000 sailors from around the world to its annual **Kiel Week**.

▶ **Population:** 240 830

▣ **Info:** Andreas-Gayk-Straße 31, 24103 Kiel. ℘(0431) 67 91 00. www.kiel-sailing-city.de.

◖ **Location:** Kiel lies at the end of a 17km/10.5mi deep inlet in the Baltic Sea at the eastern end of the North Sea-Baltic Sea canal (Kiel Canal).

⊗ **Don't Miss:** A leisurely stroll along the picturesque Hindenburgufer.

◷ **Timing:** Allow a day for Kiel and environs.

♟ **Kids:** The U-Boat at Laboe, and Open-Air Museum at Molfsee (◖see Excursions).

Hindenburgufer★★

This promenade extends for almost 4km/2.5mi along the shore, with shady parks on one side and extended **views★** on the other.

Rathaus (Town Hall)

Fleethörn 18–24. ℘(0431) 90 10. Completed in 1911, the Rathaus is dominated by its 106m/347.7ft tower inspired by the Campanile in Venice; a carillon chimes hourly. A lift takes you to the top for splendid **views★** as far as the tall Laboe Memorial.

Parade of sailing ships during Kiel Week

© imagebroker.net/Photoshot

EXCURSIONS

♣ Freilichtmuseum Molfsee★★ (Open-air Museum Molfsee)

▶ Hamburger Landstraße 97. 6km/3.7mi south, in Molfsee. Open Apr–Oct daily 9am–6pm; Nov–Mar Sun 11am–4pm (only some houses open). ⌾8€ (Nov–Mar ⌾3€). ♿ ✆(0431) 65 96 60. www.freilichtmuseum-sh.de.
Some 60 traditional buildings typical of the north Elbe countryside have been relocated to this charming open-air museum. Watch craftspeople as they demonstrate the operation of the forge, the potter's workshop, the old-fashioned bakehouse and the weavers' looms.

♣ Laboe★

▶ 20km/12.4mi north.
This pretty Baltic resort is popular with families for its sandy dunes and calm waters. Overlooking the mouth of the Kiel Firth, the **Marine-Ehrenmal** (German naval war memorial; open Apr–Oct daily 9.30am–6pm; Nov–Mar daily 9.30am–4pm; ⌾5.50€, combination ticket with U 995 8€; ♿; ✆(04343) 49 48 49 30; www.deutscher-marinebund. de/ehrenmal) was built in honour of the 35 000 German navymen who died in World War I; it now serves as a memorial for all naval war casualties. **Views★★** from the 85m/279ft-high tower extend as far as Denmark on clear days.
Next door, you can explore an original World War II submarine, the **U 995** (same hours as Marine-Ehrenmal; ⌾4€; combination ticket 8€).

ADDRESSES

🛏 STAY

⌾⌾ **Consul** – Walkerdamm 11. ✆(0431) 53 53 70. www.hotel-consul-kiel.de. **35 rooms.** Situated close to the harbour and railway station, this hotel has been family-run for three generations. Rooms are individually decorated, clean and well equipped.

⌾⌾⌾ **Kieler Kaufmann** – Niemannsweg 102. ✆(0431) 881 10. www.kieler-kaufmann.de. **39 rooms.** Restaurant ⌾⌾⌾. This historic, ivy-draped hotel sits in a small park upstream from the harbour. Rooms in the main building, a former banker's villa, are particularly elegant and spacious. Bright and cheerful, the restaurant serves upscale international cuisine and has lovely views of the firth.

⚋/EAT

⌾⌾ **Alte Mühle** – An der Holsatiamühle 8 (east bank of the Kiel Firth, follow signs for "Schwentinetal"). ✆(0431) 205 90 01. www.altemuehle-kiel.de. In a former 19C mill on the River Schwentine, this lovely restaurant-café serves modern German cuisine and good-value weekday lunches.

⌾⌾⌾ **Lüneburg-Haus** – Dänische Straße 22. ✆(0431) 982 60 00. www. lueneburghaus.com. **Closed 4 weeks Jul–Aug, Sun & holidays.** In an old town house, above a delicatessen, modern regional fare is served in a relaxed bistro ambience. Hand-selected wine list, attentive staff.

TAKING A BREAK

Werkstatt-Café – Dahlmannstr. 11. ✆(0431) 918 65. Closed Sun. www. werkstattcafe-kiel.de. Try the delicious homemade cakes or daily specials at this congenial garden café.

NIGHTLIFE

Café-Restaurant Schöne Aussichten – Düsternbrooker Weg 16 (north of the town centre, west bank of the Kieler Förde). ✆(0431) 210 85 85. www.schoene-aussichten-kiel.de. Closed Mon.
This restaurant lives up to its name (beautiful views), especially on the summer terrace. Mediterranean-inspired food (mainly fish) dominates the menu, but drop in for cake or beer.

Kieler Brauerei – Alter Markt 9 (town centre). ✆(0431) 90 62 90. www.kieler-brauerei.de. This sociable micro-brewery has a salad bar, lunch specials, and on Sunday, an all-you-can-eat buffet.

Schleswig★

Schleswig-Holstein's oldest town has origins as a Viking village first mentioned in 804 AD. Today, it is a pleasant town on the Schlei, an inlet of the Baltic Sea, with interesting sights and a relaxing, easy-going atmosphere.

A BIT OF HISTORY

Viking traders settled on the south bank of the Schlei by the 9C. Set on major crossroads, the settlement became an important northern European trade centre.

The area, Haithabu, was encircled by a vast defence system of which a portion remains beside the Haddebyer Noor. In the 11C, Haithabu's residents, seeking better defences, crossed to the north bank of the Schlei to found Schleswig.

SIGHTS
Schloss Gottorf (Gottorf Palace)

Open Apr–Oct Mon–Fri 10am–5pm, Sat–Sun 10am–6pm; Nov–Mar Tue–Fri 10am–4pm, Sat–Sun 10am–5pm. ⊕9€. ♿ ℘(04621) 81 32 22. www.schloss-gottorf.de.

Two large museums devoted to Schleswig-Holstein's cultural history are housed in this 16C–18C palace, once the seat of the Holstein-Gottorf ducal family. In 1762, some members married into the Imperial House of the Russian czars.

Landesmuseum für Kunst und Kulturgeschichte★★ (State Museum of Art and Cultural History)

This museum contains extensive cultural and historical collections (arts, crafts and traditions). Note the collection of paintings by **Lucas Cranach the Elder** and the **Renaissance chapel★★** with its ducal loggia and oratory. Another memorable section contains exquisite **Jugendstil★** pieces.

An adjacent building houses Rolf Horn's collection of 20C paintings, from Expressionism to the present. Par-

- ▶ **Population:** 24 000
- **Info:** Wall 55, Kiel. ℘(0431) 60 05 840. www.sh-tourismus.de.
- **Location:** Schleswig was built on low-lying banks at the inner end of a Baltic fjord, the Schlei, which extends for 43km/26.7mi from the coast.
- **Don't Miss:** The Viking Museum, the Nydam Boot and the Globushaus.
- **Timing:** Allow at least half a day to explore Schleswig.
- **Kids:** The Viking Museum.

ticularly striking are paintings by Emil Nolde and Alexei von Jawlensky and sculptures by Ernst Barlach. Another highlight is the extensive collection of works by members of Die Brücke artist group. It is the large
st outside the Brücke Museum in Berlin. On the second floor, admire arts and crafts from throughout northern Germany.

Archäologisches Landesmuseum★ (State Museum of Archaeology)

This museum offers a systematic presentation of Schleswig-Holstein's pre- and early history from the Paleolithic Age to the time of the Vikings.

There are spectacular finds from the 4C (bodies found perfectly preserved, fragments of clothing, shoes, weapons) rescued from the peatbogs.

Housed in its own hall is the **Nydam Boot★★**, an oak-hulled longship from around 320 AD that is 23m/75.4ft long by 3m/9.8ft wide and was powered by 36 oarsmen. It is the oldest surviving Germanic longship, and was probably sunk in the peatbogs as a sacrifice c. 350 AD.

Globushaus★★

In a separate building (about a 5min walk from the palace through a Baroque garden) is the reconstructed **Gottorfer**

Globus (globe; open Apr–Oct Mon–Fri 10am–5pm, Sat–Sun 10am–6pm; ⊚10€). At more than 3m/9.8ft high, it can be entered. The original was created in the 17C and is now in the Lomonosov Museum in St. Petersburg.

Dom St. Petri★ (St. Peter Cathedral)

Thanks to its graceful spire, this brick Gothic hall-church can be easily spotted from far away. The most remarkable work of art is the 1521 **Bordesholm altarpiece★★** in the chancel.

Holm★

This picturesque sailors' and fishermen's quarter with its 18C–19C houses is centred on a small cemetery and chapel.

👥 Wikinger Museum Haithabu (Viking Museum)★

Follow B76 towards Kiel. Open Apr–Oct daily 9am–5pm; Nov–Mar Tue–Sun 10am–4pm (museums only, houses closed). Closed Dec 24 & 31. ⊚7€. ♿ ℘(04621) 81 32 22. www.schloss-gottorf.de/haithabu. Near the Haddebyer Noor lagoon, next to the original Viking settlement, this engaging museum sheds light on the daily lives of the Haithabu residents.

It features re-created huts and displays jewels, weapons and domestic implements along with models of the Viking village. A highlight of the boat hall *(Schiffshalle)* is a Viking longship, reconstructed from fragments dredged from the ancient port.

ADDRESSES

🛏️STAY

⊖⊖ **Zollhaus** – *Lollfuß 110.* ℘*(04621) 29 03 40. www.zollhaus-zu-gottorf.de. 10 rooms. Restaurant* ⊖⊖. In a bustling side street near the Schlei, this small hotel has bright rooms with functional beechwood furniture. The bistro presents changing art exhibits.

🍴EAT

⊖⊖⊖ **Hotel and Restaurant Olschewski's** – *Hafenstraße 40.* ℘*(04621) 255 77. www.hotelolschewski. de.vu. Closed Mon, Tue and Jan–Feb.* This restaurant sits in the heart of Schleswig's historic centre, close to the palace and Holm and with a view of the harbour. It serves international cuisine, including plenty of fish dishes. Lovely terrace. It is attached to a hotel with nicely decorated, comfortable rooms.

Wismar★

Lying midway between Rostock and Lübeck, Wismar is known for its fisheries and naval dockyards. Evidence of the Swedish reign in the 17C and 18C remains throughout the town today. In 2002, the historic town centre, with its characteristic step-gabled red-brick houses and cobblestoned streets, was included on the UNESCO World Heritage List.

▶ **Population:** 44 400
📋 **Info:** Am Markt 1, 23966 Wismar. ℘(03841) 19433. www.wismar.de.
◗ **Location:** Wismar hugs a bay in the Baltic Sea opposite Poel Island to the south. The A20 links the town to Lübeck.
👁 **Don't Miss:** Meandering through the Old Town.
🕐 **Timing:** Allow three hours to explore the Old Town.
👥 **Kids:** A visit to Poel Island.

A BIT OF HISTORY

Wismar dates back to 1229 and enjoyed a heyday as a member of the Hanseatic League. Breweries and wool-weaving were further sources of wealth. Wismar's downfall came at the end of the

Thirty Years' War when it fell under Swedish rule until 1803.

SIGHTS

Marktplatz★ (Market Square)

Situated in the old town, Wismar's Marktplatz – one of the largest town squares in Germany – is dominated by the white Neoclassical **Rathaus** (town hall), built between 1817–19. A permanent **exhibit** (open Apr–Oct Mon–Sat 10am–6pm, Sun 10am–4pm; Nov–Mar daily 10am–4pm; ⊛free) about the town's history can be found in the beautifully vaulted cellars.

Other gabled houses from various eras frame the rest of the square. The most eye-catching is the **Alter Schwede** (Old Swede) on the east side, which dates back to 1380.

On the right is the **Reuterhaus**, a now-UNESCO building where the works of the Mecklenburg writer Fritz Reuter were published. Destroyed during the GDR era, the building was fully reconstructed in the late 1980s and now houses a hotel/restaurant; the house on its left sports charming Jugendstil ornamentation.

On the southeast side of the market stands an artistic pavilion, the **Wasserkunst★** (waterworks).

It was built in 1580–1602 in the Dutch Renaissance style and supplied the town with water for centuries.

Wasserkunst, Marktplatz

© Dagmar Schneider/imageBROKER/age fotostock.com

Marienkirchturm (Church of St. Mary's Tower)

Open Apr–Oct daily 10am–6pm; Nov–Mar daily 11am–4pm.

Only the 80m/262ft-high **tower** remains of the early 13C Marienkirche, which was destroyed during World War II. A carillon comes to life at noon, 3pm and 7pm.

Fürstenhof (Palace)

Originally the seat of the dukes of Mecklenburg, this large building was erected in two phases. The older, western wing dates to 1512–13 and is Late Gothic in style, while the longer "New House" from 1553–55 shows off elements of the Italian Renaissance, including impressive pilasters and terra-cotta friezes. Those facing the road represent the Trojan Wars; those facing the courtyard, the parable of the Prodigal Son.

Grube (Ditch)

The "Grube" is one of Germany's oldest artificial watercourses running through a town (1255). It served as a source of water for drinking and domestic use right up into the 20C.

Schabbellhaus★

⚲Closed for renovation until 2016.
📞(03841) 224 31 10.
www.schabbellhaus.de.

This sumptuously decorated red-brick building was built from 1569 to 1571 as the brewery and home of the later mayor, Hinrich Schabbell; it is one of the oldest Renaissance buildings in the Baltic area. The house is now home to a local history museum with a special section on medical history.

St. Nikolaikirche★

Open May–Sept daily 8am–8pm; Apr & Oct daily 10am–4pm; Nov–Mar daily 11am–4pm. ⊛2€ suggested donation.
📞(03841) 21 36 24.

Built between 1381 and 1487, this brick church's central nave soars skyward for 37m/121.4ft, making it the fourth highest in Germany. The **Altar der Krämergilde★** (Grocers' Guild Altarpiece), a 15C hinged, panelled altarpiece, is worth a closer look. The 1335 bronze font originally stood in the Marienkirche; it depicts the Life of Christ, the Last Judgement and the Wise and Foolish Virgins.

Alter Hafen (Old Harbour)

From the Grube and the idyllic street Am Lohberg, steps lead to the harbour, at the end of which stands an unadorned Baroque building, the **Baumhaus** (tree house). In former times a massive tree was lowered from here into the water at night to prevent harbour access.

EXCURSION

👤👤 Insel Poel (Poel Island)

This little Baltic island north of Wismar can be reached by car, or in the summer, by boat from the old harbour.

Poel makes a pleasant day trip; its charming seaside villages and wild coastal stretches invite exploration.

The flat relief makes a perfect cycling destination; the local tourist office has bikes for hire.

ADDRESSES

🏠 STAY

🛏 **Willert** – *Schweriner Straße 9.* 📞*(0177) 27 29 813. www.hotel-willert.de. 14 rooms.* 🖧. This Jugendstil villa was built in 1910 and meticulously restored in the 1990s. Rooms are modern and elegant; some of the stucco-ornamented ceilings are original.

🛏💰 **Reuterhaus** – *Am Markt 19.* 📞*(03841) 222 30. www.restaurant-reuter haus.de. 10 rooms. Restaurant* 🛏💰💰. This small hotel in a nicely renovated building on the market square has fairly large, comfortable rooms tastefully outfitted with Italian furniture. The elaborately carved wainscoting lends traditional charm to the restaurant.

Rostock★

Once a member of the Hanseatic League, Rostock is the largest city in the northern German state of Mecklenburg-Vorpommern. Its strategic location on the wide Warnow estuary has always favoured its development. Rostock's port plays an important role in international maritime commerce. Though postwar reconstruction was not always pleasing, Rostock still has its charms, especially in its seaside suburb of Warnemünde.

A BIT OF HISTORY

By the 13C, Rostock was already a member of the Hanseatic League, minting its own money and asserting independence from the princes of Mecklenburg. The first Baltic university was founded here in 1419. Such an exalted position drew the envy of powerful neighbours, and the town suffered substantial damage during the Thirty Years' War (1618–

▶ **Population:** 204 000

🛈 **Info:** Universitätsplatz 6 (Barocksaal), 18055 Rostock. 📞(0381) 381 22 22 www.rostock.de.

◉ **Location:** A key Baltic port, Rostock is served by the A19 and A24 autobahn from Berlin (allow 2hrs 30min); the A 20 links the town to Lübeck. The area west of the Kröpeliner Tor is a lively student zone.

🅿 **Parking:** Garages throughout Rostock.

◈ **Don't Miss:** The Baltic resorts of Warnemünde, Fischland, Darß and Zingst.

🕐 **Timing:** Allow half a day to see all the sights.

👤👤 **Kids:** Navigational Museum, beach at Warnemünde.

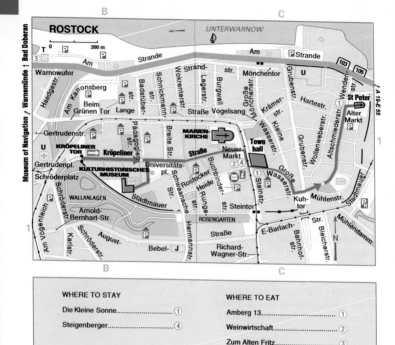

48), the Nordic struggle for supremacy (1700–21) and the Napoleonic Wars (1803–15). In more modern times, until German reunification, Rostock was East Germany's only significant outlet to the Baltic.

👣 WALKING TOUR

OLD TOWN★

Rostock's historic centre forms an oval outline south of the Warnow River. At its centre is the Church of Notre Dame. To the west it is bounded by the Kröpelin Gate, to the south by the Steintor Gate.

Kröpeliner Tor★
(Kröpelin Gate)

At the western end of Kröpeliner Straße, this 14C red-brick gate is six storeys high and houses the local history museum.

Kröpeliner Straße

This pedestrian zone is Rostock's shopping and commercial centre, bordered by gabled houses with façades from

Baroque and Renaissance times. At no 82, the brick façade of the 15C Heilig-Geist-Spital has an unusual gable.

Kulturhistorisches Museum (Cultural History Museum)

Klosterhof 7. Open Tue–Sun 10am–6pm. ✆free. ♿ ☏(0381) 20 35 90. www.kulturhistorisches-museum-rostock.de.
This former 13C Cistercian convent, founded by Danish Queen Margarethe, is the region's only completely preserved abbey complex. It houses medieval art, including the **Altarpiece of the Three Kings★** (late 15C), crafts, toys, coins and Dutch paintings from the 16C to 19C.

Marienkirche★★

Am Ziegenmarkt.
The imposing 13C cross-shaped basilica is one of the biggest churches in northern Germany. The massive tower was not completed until the 18C. From the top unfolds a **panorama★** of the city and the docks. Inside the church, note the 1472 **astronomical clock★★** (its

face was remodelled in 1643), which comprises a calendar valid until 2017.

Rathaus (Town Hall)

Neuer Markt.
Rostock's town hall is a jumble of three 13C–14C gabled houses topped by a brick gallery supporting seven towers. The Baroque façade was added in 1727.

Petrikirche (Church of St. Peter)

Alter Markt. Open May–Sept daily 10am–6pm; Oct–Apr daily 10am–4pm. Tower ⊛3€. ℘(0381) 21 101. www.petrikirche-rostock.de
Rostock's oldest church (14C) is dedicated to St. Peter, the patron saint of fishermen. Its 117m/384ft-high tower long served as a landmark for seafarers. The church was destroyed in World War II and took several decades to restore. The crowning glory is the historic bell tower, which was completed only in 1994.

EXCURSIONS

Bad Doberan

◗ A short drive west via the B105. Severinstraße 6, 18209 Bad Doberan. ℘(038203) 91 50. www.bad-doberan.de.
Doberan was put on the map in 1793 as the summer residence of Grand Duke Friedrich Franz I, who also founded Germany's first seaside resort in nearby Heiligendamm.
Today, the town's principal sight is its superb Gothic brick cathedral. It is also the terminus of a historic narrow gauge train that has delighted young and old since 1886. In July and August the town hosts international thoroughbred horse races.

Münster★★

Open May–Sept Mon–Sat 9am–6pm, Sun 11am–6pm; Mar, Apr and Oct until 5pm; Nov–Feb until 4pm. Closed Good Friday and Dec 24. ⊛3€. ◣Guided tours available. ℘(038203) 627 16. www.muenster-doberan.de.
Consecrated in 1368, this former Cistercian monastery church is a prime example of the northern German red-brick Gothic style. Having been spared wartime ravages, it is one of the best-preserved Cistercian churches in Germany. The design follows the strict order's architectural mandates with such features as mighty windows on the towerless western façade and friezes below the roof line.
Inside, the Münster's sumptuous décor reflects its significance as the burial place of the dukes of Mecklenburg. The church is filled with 13C–14C art worth closer inspection. The magnificent wood-carved **high altar★** from 1300 is considered the oldest winged altar in existence. Note the rood altar (1370), embellished with a **triumphal cross★** (depicted as the Tree of Life). The 11.6m/38ft-high tower-like carved oak **tabernacle★**, the oldest in Germany, dates back to roughly the same period.

Molli-Bahn★★

Departs from Bad Doberan Bahnhof (train station) Apr–Oct daily 8.30am–6.30pm (hourly); Nov–Mar daily 8.30am–4.30pm (every 2hrs). ⊛13€ round trip. ℘(038293) 43 13 31. www.molli-bahn.de.
Kids and nostalgia buffs will love this 1886 steam-powered narrow-gauge railway affectionately known as **"Molli"**. It chugs for 15.4km/9.5mi from Bad Doberan to Heiligendamm *(20min)* and on to Kühlungsborn *(35min)*.

Heiligendamm

◗ 22km/13.5mi northwest of Rostock.
Germany's oldest coastal playground was fashionable with the rich, famous and aristocratic throughout the 19C. In 2007 it again captured the international spotlight when hosting the G8 summit. The architecture is typical of 19C spa resorts with elegant villas, especially along Professor-Vogel-Straße, attesting to the town's illustrious past.

♟ Schifffahrtsmuseum★★ (Navigational Museum)

About 10km/6mi north of Rostock's centre towards Warnemünde's international garden exhibit grounds. Open Apr–Jun & Sept–Oct Tue–Sun 10am–6pm; Jul–Aug daily 10am–6pm; Nov–Mar Tue–Sun 10am–4pm. ☞4€. ℘(0381) 12 83 13 64. www.schifffahrtsmuseum-rostock.de. Exhibits inside a decommissioned 10 000-ton freighter chart the history of maritime travel in the Baltic region from its earliest days to the present. Models of ships, paintings, navigational instruments and photographs document maritime life and work.

Warnemünde★

11km/6.8mi north of Rostock. This former fishing village, bought by its citizens from the Prince of Mecklenburg in 1323, has become Rostock's most popular seaside resort, with charming little streets and a wide beach. The estuary and beach are lined with cafés, restaurants and bars.

Fischland, Darß and Zingst

Northeast of Rostock. The peninsular chain of Fischland–Darß–Zingst is an attractive coastal area alternating with woods, salt-marshes and moorland. The narrow tongue of land extends north and east, parallel to the mainland and separated from it by a lagoon of brackish Baltic sea water and fresh river water. The artists' village of **Ahrenshoop** in the slightly hilly **Fischland** is a popular vacation resort. **Darß** and **Zingst** form part of the Vorpommern Boddenlandschaft National Park. The small villages and seaside resorts feature attractive reed-covered houses and cottages.

Güstrow

50km/31mi south of Rostock. Güstrow became the residence of the dukes of Mecklenburg-Güstrow in the 16C and grew increasingly wealthy over the next centuries. The elegant burghers' houses around the **cathedral** and **market squares** and along surrounding streets are evidence of this period. A highlight is the **Schloss★**(open Tue–Sun 10am–5pm; closed Dec 24; ☞5€; ℘0385 595 80; www.schloss-guestrow.de), a superb 16C Renaissance palace that blends Italian, French and German elements. The **Dom★**, a 14C Gothic brick basilica, is richly endowed with artworks, having been the court church of the dukes of Mecklenburg. Note the **Güstrow Apostles★**, 12 almost life-size oak figures by Claus Berg of Lübeck from c. 1530. A stark contrast to these figures is Ernst Barlach's modernist sculpture *Der Schwebende*.

Ernst Barlach Stiftung★ (Barlach Museum)

Heidberg 15 & Gertrudenplatz 1. Open Apr–Oct Tue–Sun 10am–5pm; Nov–Mar Tue–Sun 11am–4pm, also Mon Jul–Aug. Atelierhaus & Ausstellungsforum. ☞6€; Gertudenkapelle 4€, combination ticket 9€. ♿℘(03843) 84 40 00.· www.ernst-barlach-stiftung.de.

Old Port of Warnemünde

This museum honouring Ernst Barlach (1870–1938) has two locations: his religious works are in the Late Gothic **Gertrudenkapelle**.

Further works are presented at the artist's studio, the **Atelierhaus**, on the shores of the Inselsee.

The **Ausstellungsforum** (exhibition forum), a building (1998) with an attached annex displaying Barlach's graphic work (mostly drawings and prints), sits just a few yards from the studio. It presents largely temporary exhibits.

ADDRESSES

🛏 STAY

🛏 **Die Kleine Sonne** – *Steinstraße 7.* 🖉 *(0381) 461 20. www.die-kleine-sonne. arcona.de. 48 rooms.* 🍽 *13€.* This centrally located hotel is welcoming and well maintained. Rooms are enlivened by paintings and engravings created by Egyptian artists.

🛏 **Steigenberger Hotel Sonne** – *Neuer Markt 2.* 🖉 *(0381) 497 30. www. steigenberger.com/Rostock. 121 rooms.* 🍽 *18€.* Ideally located opposite the town hall, this hotel delivers modern and very comfortable rooms.

🍴 EAT

🍴 **Weinwirtschaft** – *Neuer Markt 2.* 🖉 *(0381) 497 30. http://de.steigenberger. com.* This restaurant resides within Rostock's Steigenberger Hotel Sonne and focuses on Mediterranean cuisine. Dining on the terrace with views of the harbour is also an option.

🍴 **Zum Alten Fritz** – *Warnowufer 65.* 🖉 *(0381) 20 87 80. www.alter-fritz.de.* At this large traditional pub/brewery, you can find hearty German pub food, and even beer soup. Plenty of outdoor seating.

🍴 **Amberg 13** – *Amberg 13.* 🖉 *(0381) 490 62 62. www.altstadt restaurant.de.* At this bistro-style restaurant in the old town the chefs themselves bring out the dishes to the tables. Sunday brunch.

Stralsund★

Stralsund, one of the most agreeable cities on the German Baltic, looks back on a long maritime tradition in fishing and ship building. Tourism is also a backbone of the local economy, thanks in large part to the beautifully restored and UNESCO-protected medieval city centre.

A BIT OF HISTORY

Stralsund was established in the early 13C and quickly found itself competing with Lübeck. After being razed by Lübeck in 1249, Stralsund was fortified with a city wall, and became a member of the Hanseatic League in 1293. Besieged by Wallenstein during the Thirty Years' War, it was liberated by Swedish and Danish troops. In 1815, it became part of Prussia.

▶ **Population:** 57 870

🄸 **Info:** Alter Markt 9, 18439 Stralsund. 🖉 (03831) 246 90. www.stralsundtourismus.de.

◖ **Location:** Stralsund occupies the far northeasterly point of Germany. A causeway and a bridge link the town to the island of Rügen.

🄐 **Don't Miss:** The Old Town or the Ozeaneum.

🄞 **Timing:** Allow two hours.

🄐 **Kids:** The Oceanographic Museum and Ozeaneum.

SIGHTS
Altstadt (Old Town)★

Stralsund's UNESCO-listed old town is anchored by the **Rathaus** (*Town Hall*), a splendid 13C and 14C edifice whose

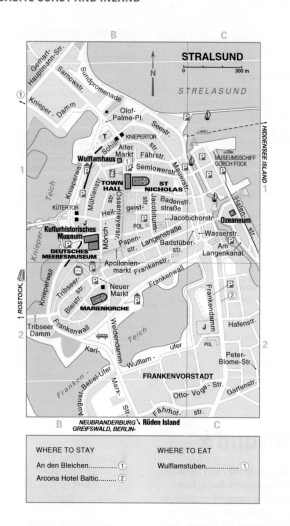

magnificent **north façade★★** was added c. 1450. Arcades open onto a covered market hall leading to the 13C **Nikolaikirche★** (*Church of St. Nicholas*) whose impressive altar has sculptures by Baroque artist Andreas Schlüter.

👥 Deutsches Meeresmuseum★ (German Oceanographic Museum)

Katharinenberg 14-20. Open Jan–Sept daily 10am–5pm (Oct–Dec closed Mon). Closed Dec 24. ♿9€. ℘(03831) 265 02 10. www.meeresmuseum.de.
In a former abbey, this museum concentrates on the flora and fauna of the Bal-

tic Sea. Crowd-pleasers include a massive shark tank and a 15m/49.2ft long fin-back whale skeleton. The museum also operates the **Nautineum** (♿free) on an islet off Stralsund, where you can learn about the local fishing industry, ocean research and boat construction.

👥 Ozeaneum Stralsund★★

Hafenstraße 11. Open Jun–Sept daily 9.30am–8pm (Oct–May until 6pm). Closed Dec 24. ♿16€, with Meeresmuseum 21€. ♿ ℘(03831) 265 06 10. www.ozeaneum.de.
This state-of-the-art museum and aquarium takes visitors on an under-

© OZEANEUM Stralsund / J.-M. Schorke

water journey from Stralsund to the
frigid Polar Sea. Highlights include a
giant tank where 2 500 herring swim
their merry rounds and a huge hall with
life-size whale models.

The museum presents the largest exhibition about the Baltic Sea, and penguins live on the roof-top terrace in a
120 000 litre tank.

Marienkirche★
Neuer Markt.
A Gothic high altar featuring the Coronation of the Virgin Mary (15C) and
an original organ (c. 1659) by Lübeck
builder Friedrich Stellwagen warrant
your attention in St. Mary's.

Kulturhistorisches Museum (History Museum)
Mönchstraße 25-28. ℰ(03831) 253 617.
Open year-round daily 10am–5pm.
∞5–6€. www.museum.stralsund.de.
The museum has displays on Stralsund's
history, Hiddensee island in prehistoric
times and sacred medieval art in rooms,
some with beautiful cross-vaulting.

Ramparts
The best-preserved section of the city
wall lies west of the centre on Kniep-
erteich pond, between Kniepertor and
Kütertor.

ADDRESSES

⌂STAY
⊖ **An den Bleichen** – *An den
Bleichen 45. ℰ(03831) 39 06 75. www.
hotelandenbleichen.de. 23 rooms. �.* In
a residential area, this family-run place

has pretty gardens. It's close to the old
town, port and beach.

⊖⊜⊟ **Arcona Hotel Baltic** –
*Frankendamm 22. ℰ(03831) 20 40.
http://baltic.arcona.de. 133 rooms. ⊟.
Restaurant⊖⊜⊟.* This hotel is located
in a former barracks renovated in
an elegantly modern style. Even the
standard rooms are pretty spacious,
though the décor is rather generic.
The contemporary bistro-restaurant
serves Baltic fish dishes as well as
Spanish tapas.

⁋/EAT
⊖⊜ **Wulflamstuben** – *Alter Markt 5.
ℰ(03831) 29 15 33. www.wulflamstuben.de.*
This restaurant is located in a handsome
14 C Gothic building that is one of
the oldest in northern Germany. It sits
across from the Rathaus (town hall), and
features traditional German "rustic" food
in a pleasant atmosphere.

Rügen Island★

Insel Rügen

The Baltic island of Rügen, Germany's largest, offers a surprising variety of scenery. In the west, the straits widen towards the open sea. Fabled chalk cliffs and sandy beaches in the east attract summer crowds. The southern shores are wooded; and to the north is the deep, jagged Jasmunder Bodden (Gulf).

🚗 DRIVING TOUR

FROM PUTBUS TO KAP ARKONA

75km/46.5mi. Allow half a day.

- **Info:** Ringstraße 113-115. 18528 Bergen auf Rügen. ☎(03838) 80 77 0. www.ruegen.de.
- **Location:** Rügen can be reached by train or car via a long bridge (2.5km/1.5mi) that straddles the straits at Stralsund. Ferries to Scandinavia leave from the port of Saßnitz.
- **Don't Miss:** Chalk cliffs of the Stubbenkammer, Hiddensee Island.
- **Timing:** Allow one or two days to explore Rügen and another half a day to visit Hiddensee (⌚see Excursion).
- **Kids:** Rügen's seaside resorts, Hiddensee Island.

Putbus★

The "white town" in the southeast of the island was founded in 1810 by Prince William Malte of Putbus as a royal seat and bathing resort. The princely castle no longer remains, but the Neoclassical town does, centred on a circular square called the **circus★**. It is anchored by a 21m/69ft-high obelisk from 1845 and surrounded by 16 mansions that are finished in dazzling white and stand out from the green of the oaks. Nearby, the 19C **theatre★** (*Alleestraße*) bears a portico of four Tuscan columns and is endowed with fabulous acoustics. One frieze represents Apollo and the muses. The 75ha/185-acre **Schlosspark★** with its orangery (modified in 1853 by Friedrich August Stüler), royal stables and parish church, is laid out in the style of an English garden.

Störtebeker

Klaus Störtebeker was a notorious pirate said to have been born in Ruschwitz on Rügen in 1360. As a young man, he drank from his master's tankard at work and having been seen by his boss, was promptly chained and beaten. But Störtebeker's strength was such that he broke free and thrashed his tormentor. Then he took off in a fishing boat as far as the Cape of Arkona. There he joined Michael Gödecke and his band of brigands whose reputation struck terror into all who sailed the coast. Störtebeker became one of the most feared buccaneers of his age, scouring the seas until eventually being captured in Hamburg and condemned to the guillotine. As a mark of the respect, his last wish was granted: mercy for the companions arrested with him.

Legend has it that Störtebeker hid his booty beneath the cliffs of the Stubbenkammer, and once a year a ship steered by phantom buccaneers is said to haunt this coast. Every summer, at Ralswiek, islanders put on a play commemorating the adventures of this anti-hero, scourge of the rich and benefactor of the poor.

RÜGEN ISLAND · Old Lighthouse · **Kap Arkona★** · BALTIC SEA · **Stubbenkammer ★★** · Kloster · Grieben · 160 · **Nationalpark Jasmund** · Vitte · **Saßnitz** · Neuendorf · Schaprode · **Hiddensee★** · 96 · Bergen · 196 · Binz · **Granitz** · 84 · Sellin · Baabe · Kubitzer Bodden · 58 · Rasender Roland · 66 · Göhren · **★ Putbus** · 96 · **Stralsund★** · Greifswalder Bodden · 105 · Zudar · ROSTOCK · 105 · N · 0 · 15 km · BERLIN

Jagdschloss Granitz (Granitz Hunting Palace)

12km/7.4mi east of Putbus, south of Binz. Open May–Sept daily 9am–6pm; Nov–Mar Tue–Sun 10am–4pm (Oct & Apr also Mon). Closed Dec 24 & 31 (until 2pm). 6€. (038393) 667 10. www.mv-schloesser.de.

In 1837 Prince William Malte I of Putbus built a neo-Gothic Tudor hunting lodge atop the Tempelberg, the highest point in eastern Rügen. The four crenellated corner towers of the "castle" rise up in the middle of Granitz Forest. A 19C viewing tower and platform are reached via a cast-iron **spiral staircase**. From the top, the **view★★** of Rügen Island is breathtaking. The rooms inside the house are open to the public.

👥 Beach Resorts★

Binz, **Sellin**, **Baabe** and **Göhren** are located in the southwest of the island, luring visitors with sandy beaches, 19C spa architecture and a wooded backdrop. They can be reached via the **"Rasender Roland"** (Racing Roland), a nostalgic steam train shuttling between Putbus and Göhren.

Saßnitz

Ferries bound for Scandinavia embark from this port city that is backed by beech woods.

Jasmund National Park★★

Germany's northernmost national park is famous for its stunning chalk cliffs that border the deep blue sea. This postcard idyll greatly inspired Romantic painter Caspar David Friedrich, especially a spot called the **Stubbenkammer★★**.

The most famous cliff is the 117m/384ft-high **Königsstuhl** (King's chair; 1€). For information, visit the **National Park Visitor Centre** (open Easter–Oct daily 9am–7pm; Nov–Easter 10am–5pm; 7.50€; 038392 66 17 66; www.koenigsstuhl.com), where you can watch a film and peruse exhibits on the park's flora, fauna and geology.

Kap Arkona★

With its 50m/164ft-high chalk cliffs, Kap Arkona is the northernmost point of the island. The **old lighthouse** (038391 41 90; www.kap-arkona.de), a square, three-storey brick building, was built in 1826–29 according to plans by Karl Friedrich Schinkel. There is a wonderful **view★★** from here to the neighbouring island of Hiddensee. The walls located not far from the lighthouse are the remains of the fortress of Jaromars-burg built by the Slavs and destroyed by the Danes in 1168. Near the ramparts stands the watchtower of the navy, built in 1927; it houses an exhibit about the Baltic Coast.

Chalk cliffs of Jasmund National Park

© C. Doerr/Sime/Photononstop

EXCURSION

👥👤 Hiddensee Island★

▶ Ferries depart from Wiek and Schaprode on Rügen (⊜15.30–17.70€; one-way trip duration 30–65min) and from Stralsund (⊜18.90–19.70€; one-way trip duration 95min–2hrs 20min). Reederei Hiddensee, Fährstraße 16, Stralsund. 𝄞(03831) 26 81 0. www.reederei-hiddensee.de.

🚳No cars are allowed on the island; bicycle rental recommended.

Hiddensee Island lies 17km/10mi off the west coast of Rügen and almost entirely within the Nationalpark Vorpommersche Boddenlandschaft. Its gorgeous landscape features towering cliffs, land spits, lagoons and coastal inlets. The highest point is the **Dornbusch peak** (72m/236ft) in the north, site of the island's trademark **lighthouse** (1888). Hiddensee is crisscrossed by trails and bicycle paths.

The village of **Grieben** is famous for its thatched houses. **Kloster** has developed into a bathing resort. The playwright **Gerhart Hauptmann** (1862–1946), best known for his Naturalist dramas, is buried in the churchyard. Hauptmann's summer residence, Haus Seedorn on Kirchweg, is open to the public. The island's administrative centre is at **Vitte**, a fishing village turned tourist resort. South of Vitte, vast dunes are interspersed with marshland *(Dünenheide)*. **Neuendorf**, the island's most southerly village, has fishermen's houses built so that living quarters face the sun.

ADDRESSES

🍽️STAY

⊜🛏️ **Strandhotel Binz** – *Strandpromenade 33, 18609 Binz. 𝄞(038393) 38 10. www.strandhotel-lissek.de. 54 rooms. ⊟.* This hotel offers carefully restored spa architecture with great attention to detail, along with all major mod conveniences. Some rooms have fine views of the Baltic Sea. The restaurant specialises in fish and is often packed to the gills.

⊜🛏️ **Wreecher Hof** – *Kastanienallee 1, 18581 Putbus-Wreechen. 𝄞(038301) 850. www.wreecher-hof.de. 43 rooms. Restaurant⊜🛏️🛏️.* This off-the-beaten-track resort consists of seven reed-thatched buildings in an idyllic location. It is a good place for those needing plenty of elbow room, since most of the accommodations are suites with separate bed and sitting quarters. The international restaurant has a winter garden and lovely terrace.

Greifswald★

There is evidence that Greifswald was granted municipal rights as early as 1250. Once it joined the Hanseatic League in 1281, the town flourished and continued to prosper for the next four centuries. Greifswald boasts a decidedly Scandinavian flavour and a number of historic buildings largely spared destruction during World War II.

▶ **Population:** 55 770
🛈 **Info:** Rathaus am Markt, 17489 Greifswald.
  ℘(03834) 85 36 13 80.
  www.greifswald.info.
▶ **Location:** 30km/18.6mi east of Stralsund and bisected by the little Ryck River.
☺ **Don't Miss:** The Marktplatz, Marienkirche, Museum of Pomerania.
🕐 **Timing:** About half a day.

A BIT OF HISTORY

After the Thirty Years' War, Greifswald became part of the Kingdom of Sweden in 1648. The Swedes granted the town an unusual degree of autonomy. After being absorbed by Prussia in 1815, a busy period of construction began, to which the well-preserved burghers' houses testify.

Germany's greatest romantic painter was the highly influential landscape painter **Caspar David Friedrich**. He was born in Greifswald in 1774 and although he left the town at the age of 20, he remained deeply attached to and inspired by it.

SIGHTS

Marktplatz★
(Market Square)

Greifswald's central square is dominated by the arcaded **Rathaus** (1738) and framed by several architecturally distinguished houses. Standouts include the one at **no 11★** from the 15C.

Marienkirche★

Open Jun–Aug Mon–Fri 10am–6pm; rest of year Sun after mass until 1pm. 🎫1€. ៦℘(038 34) 22 63. www.marien-greifswald.de.

This red-brick hall-church has a 14C east gable whose ornate tracery contrasts with the stocky 13C tower.

Inside, the 1587 **pulpit★**, richly carved and adorned with inlaid wood, merits a closer look, as do the faded 15C frescoes in the southern tower.

Dom St. Nikolai★

Open May–Oct Mon–Sat 10am–6pm, Sun 11.30am–12.30pm & 3pm–6pm; Nov–Apr Mon–Sat 10am–4pm, Sun 11.30am–3pm. ℘(03834) 26 27. www.dom-greifswald.de.

Caspar David Friedrich was baptised in this 13C Gothic hall church with its landmark onion-domed spire. The interior is rather plain thanks to a 19C remodel, although some Late Gothic frescoes remain in chapels 19 and 20.

Klosterruine Eldena
(Eldena Abbey)

Wolgaster Landstraße.

The picturesque ruins of this medieval Cistercian abbey (1199) were a favourite subject of Caspar David Friedrich.

Wieck★

The thatched fishermen's cottages, idyllic harbour and 19C **wooden swing bridge★** (Zugbrücke) of this historic fishing village at the mouth of the River Ryck present a delightful scene.

Pommersches Landesmuseum★
(Museum of Pomerania)

Rakower Straße 9. Open Tue–Sun 10am–6pm (Nov–Apr until 5pm). 🎫5€. ៦℘(03834) 831 20. www.pommersches-landesmuseum.de.

In a converted Franciscan friary, this museum has local history exhibits but is notable for its paintings by Friedrich, Runge and Liebermann.

Usedom Island★

Insel Usedom

Usedom's wonderfully unspoilt natural landscape is a pastiche of moors, estuaries, forests, dunes, sandy beaches and steep cliffs. The island is part of the Usedom-Oderhaff Nature Reserve and is dotted with elegant bathing resorts. For some time the island was known as "Berlin's bathtub" because of the large number of Berliners who came here to relax and recuperate.

Info: Waldstraße 1, 17429 Seebad Bansin. ℘(038378) 477 10. www.usedom.de.

Location: Usedom is Germany's easternmost island, although its far eastern portion, with the town of Swinoujscie, belongs to Poland. The flat northwest contrasts with the hilly southeast, sometimes called "Usedom's Switzerland".

Don't Miss: The 19C beach resort of Heringsdorf.

Timing: Allow one day to soak up the ambience of Usedom.

Kids: Outdoor recreation on sandy beaches and dunes.

SIGHTS

Wolgast

On the mainland.

One point of access to Usedom is in the south at Zecherin; the other lies in the northwest, from Wolgast over the River Peene. The formidable octagonal tower and austere exterior of 14C **Kirche St. Petri** (parish church; open May–Oct 10am–5pm; Nov–Apr check with office; tower ☜2€; ℘038397 202 269; www.kirche-wolgast.de) contrast sharply with the sumptuous interior. Highlights include 15C–16C frescoes and a 1700 *danse macabre* cycle painted by Caspar Sigmund Köppe based on a woodcut by Hans Holbein the Younger.

Krummin

East of Wolgast.

The most beautiful avenue of **lime trees**★ *(Lindenallee)* in Usedom leads to the right off B111 and extends to the little fishing village on the Krummin cove. The surfaced road is just 2km/1.2mi long but is marvellous; the arched canopy of leaves overhead gives the impression of being in a Gothic cathedral formed by Nature.

Peenemünde

In 1936, the German army located its V2 rocket-testing centre to the northeastern tip of Usedom. A rocket museum, the **Historisch-Technisches Museum** (open Apr–Sept daily10am–6pm; Oct–Mar until 4pm; closed Mon Nov–Mar, Dec 24–26; ☜8€; ﹠; ℘038371 50 50; www.peenemuende.de) in the old power station, retraces the history of rocket development and its associated perils. Wernher von Braun developed the V2 rocket here, unveiled in October 1942. It killed thousands of people during World War II but also signalled the beginning of space exploration.

Usedoms "Taille" (Isthmus)

At the island's narrowest point, the white sandy beaches of the resorts of **Zinnowitz**, **Koserow**, **Kölpinsee** and **Ückeritz** lie side by side, protected by steep cliffs. At Koserow, the island is barely 200m/656ft wide.

Bansin, Heringsdorf, Ahlbeck

These "three sisters" in the island's southeast are linked by a 10km/6.2mi-long beach promenade. In the 19C, aristocrats and the merely moneyed convened in these fashionable resorts that were also known as "Kaiserbäder" (imperial spas). Numerous imposing and attractive late-19C beach villas and hotels with frilly white wrought-iron decorations remain to this day.

Heringsdorf★ was especially trendy and often visited by Emperor Wilhelm II, who resided in the still extant Villa Staudt *(Delbrückstraße 6)*. At 508m/1 666ft long, Heringsdorf's pier is the longest on mainland Europe. **Ahlbeck** is also proud of its **historical pier★**, built in 1898. A restaurant was added in 1902. With its white walls, red roof and four green-roofed corner towers, it is one of the most photographed subjects on the island. **Bansin**, the westernmost resort, maintains a more relaxed and family-friendly air.

Mellenthin

Northeast of the town of Usedom, 2km/1.2mi north of the B110.
This seldom-visited village and its Renaissance castle create a rural idyll. Although relatively plain, the three-winged castle surrounded by a moat boasts a colourfully mounted 17C Renaissance fireplace in the entrance hall. The 14C village church in the town cemetery remains a little pearl with its 17C interior **decoration★**.

ADDRESSES

🏠STAY

⊖⊜ **Zur Post** – *Seestraße 5, 17429 Usedom-Bansin. ℘(038378) 560. www.hzp-usedom.de. 170 rooms. Restaurant Zur Alten Post⊖⊜⊜⊜.* A fine example of coastal architecture, this 1901 villa was enlarged with modern guesthouses and an elegant spa centre. There are two restaurants, a casual one serving rib-sticking traditional cuisine, and an elegant dining room specialising in well-prepared international fare.

⊖⊜⊜⊜ **Romantik Seehotel Ahlbecker Hof** – *Dünenstraße 47, 17419 Usedom-Ahlbeck. ℘(038378) 46 20. www.ahlbeckerhof.de. 70 rooms. Restaurant⊖⊜⊜.* Set in a beautifully modernised Neoclassical mansion, this hotel satisfies even the most demanding patrons with its sumptuously outfitted rooms and spa complex. The crystal chandeliers and timeless ambience of the restaurant make this hotel an unforgettable place to stay.

Neubrandenburg

This town, founded in 1248 at the behest of Margrave Johann von Brandenburg, is built on an almost circular ground plan, crisscrossed by a gridlike network of streets. Although 80 percent of the old town was destroyed in 1945, the fortifications, with their four unique gates, were miraculously spared and are now a principal tourist attraction.

SIGHTS
Fortifications★★

Some 50 years after Neubrandenburg was founded in 1248, construction began on the town's defensive fortifications. In the end, the formidable wall was 2.3km/1.4mi long, over 7m/23ft high and 1.4m/4ft 6in thick at the base. It was built using boulders from the vicinity and capped by several rows of bricks. The wall's four gates were closed every evening and only opened in return for payment. They remained the sole access to the town right up to the mid-19C.

The gates are all of the same design, each an individual fortification. So that the town could be safely defended, three- to four-floor sentry posts were built into the wall every 30m/98ft. There were 56 of them in the 16C, 25 of which have been reconstructed. All able-bodied citizens were expected to maintain

- ▶ **Population:** 63 395
- ℹ **Info:** Stargarder Straße 17, 17033 Neubrandenburg, ℰ(0395) 194 33. www.neubrandenburg-touristinfo.de.
- ▶ **Location:** Midway between Berlin and the Baltic Coast, and northeast of the pretty lake of Tollensesee.
- Ⓟ **Parking:** Garages are in the heart of the old city, on Neutorstraße and on Stargarder Straße.
- 🙂 **Don't Miss:** Neubrandenburg's medieval wall.
- 🕐 **Timing:** Plan at least an hour to explore the town wall.
- 👥 **Kids:** Climbing the old wall and towers, and outdoor recreation in the Feldberger Seenlandschaft.

the posts, while defence of the gates was the duty of the four principal guilds: Bakers, Wool Weavers, Blacksmiths and Shoemakers.

The oldest gate, the **Friedländer Tor**, was built just after 1300. It is 19m/62.3ft high. On the outside it is possible to see the transition from the Romanesque to the Gothic period. The **Stargarder Tor**, built during the early 14C, is embel-

Friedländer Tor

© Neppomuk/Fotolia.com

lished with nine terra-cotta figures in long pleated robes, known as "Die Jungfrauen" *(the maids)*. The outer gate is especially sumptuously decorated. The **Treptower Tor**, built around 1400, stands 32m/105ft tall and is the highest of the gate towers. Both the main gate and the outer gate are richly decorated with brick tracery. The **Neues Tor** (New Gate), built after 1550 in the Late Gothic style, combines decorative elements of the other three gates.

Of the two towers that further reinforced the fortifications, only the 19m/62ft-high **Fangelturm** remains. It was used as a prison. The spire was added in 1845.

Konzertkirche (Concert Church)

Formerly the Church of St. Mary, this brick church was completed late in the 13C and was partly rebuilt in Neo-Gothic style in the mid-19C. In the 1990s, Finish architect Pekka Salminen converted the church into a state-of-the-art concert hall. Endowed with supreme acoustics, it is one of the main performance venues of the Neubrandenburg Philharmonic Orchestra *(www.theater-und-orchester.de)*.

St. Johanniskirche (Church of St. John)

Stargarder Straße 2. Open Tue–Sat 10am–4pm. Closed between Christmas and Easter. &♿ℰ(0395) 570 590.
The 13C–14C church of the former Franciscan monastery features a Renaissance **pulpit★** supported by a figure of Moses (1598). It is made of limestone and displays alabaster reliefs of Christ and the Evangelists.

👥 Tollensesee

This lovely lake, which is 10.4km/6.5mi in length and almost 3km/1.8mi wide, lies to the south of the town, in the middle of an attractive landscape. The western bank slopes steeply up to Brodaer Woods. In summer, locals and visitors flock to its shores for swimming, boating, tanning and picnicking. Boat rentals are available, or explore the lake on a leisurely **boat cruise** (May–Sept other months on arrangement; ⚓13–15€; Fahrgastschiff Mudder Schulten; ℰ(0395) 584 12 18; www.fahrgastschiff-mudderschulten.de).

EXCURSIONS
Burg Stargard

⏵ 11km/6.8mi south of Neubrandenburg, via the E251 and L33. The castle ruins dominate their surroundings here.

Woldegk

⏵ 20km/12.4mi further via the B104. This town, with its five windmills, borders the Feldburger Seenlandscaft (✆*see below*).

Seenlandschaft

Southwest of Woldegk, in the Mecklenburg-Strelit district, lies this lovely hilly lake region. It is home to the rare European otter as well as to the sea eagle, osprey and lesser spotted eagle. Woods, meadows, moors and lakes alternate between **Fürstenwerder** and **Feldberg**. The lakes offer plenty of diving opportunities, such as Tauchcenter-Feldberg (ℰ0176 6660 2393; www.tauchcenter-feldberg.de).

Carwitz

⏵ 29.5km/18.3mi southwest of Woldegk along the B198.
In an idyllic lakeside location, the 1848 half-timbered home of the writer **Hans Fallada** (author of *Alone in Berlin,* among many others) contains a museum about the man and his life.

Neustrelitz

⏵ 39km/24.2mi northeast of Carwitz.
The former residence of the dukes of Mecklenburg-Strelitz still bears witness to their proud past.
Admire the **Schlossgarten★** with its graceful buildings and monuments and the orangerie with its remarkable Pompeii-style **paintings★**.
The Baroque town **church** (1768–78), the classical **Rathaus** (1841) and the neo-Gothic **Schloßkirche** (1855–59) are all worth closer inspection.

Schwerin★

The state capital of Mecklenburg-Vorpommern, Schwerin is one of the most pleasant towns in northern Germany. Defined by the numerous lakes surrounding it, the city is endowed with plenty of fine architecture, most famously the lordly castle on an island opposite the old town.

A BIT OF HISTORY

The origins of Schwerin date to the 11C, when the Slavs built a fortress on what is now Schloßinsel. They were soon expelled by Henry the Lion, who colonised Schwerin in 1160 as the first German town east of the Elbe. In 1358 Schwerin was absorbed into the Duchy of Mecklenburg and became the seat of the local dukes from that time onwards.

SCHLOSSINSEL★★
Schloss★ (Palace)
Lennéstraße 1. Open mid-Apr–mid-Oct Tue–Sun 10am–6pm; late Oct–early Apr Tue–Sun 10am–5pm. Closed Dec 24. ⚅6€. ✆(0385) 525 29 20. www.museum-schwerin.de.
Built as the residence of the Grand Dukes of Mecklenburg-Schwerin, the castle is today the home of the state parliament of Mecklenburg-Vorpommern.

▶ **Population:** 91 260
🛈 **Info:** Am Markt 14, 19055 Schwerin. ✆(0385) 592 52 12. www.schwerin.com.
◖ **Location:** Schwerin is surrounded by lakes and forests. The A24 autobahn (Hamburg–Berlin) passes by about 20km/12.4mi to the south.
🅿 **Parking:** Near the Old Town you'll find garages at Reiferbahn and Wittenburger Straße and on Geschwister-Scholl-Straße.
⊛ **Don't Miss:** Schloßinsel and Ludwigslust (☾see Excursion).
🕐 **Timing:** Allow two hours to visit the Schloßinsel.

It is a harmonious hodgepodge of architectural styles ranging from Gothic to neo-Renaissance. Occupying the oldest wing (15C–17C), the **Schlossmuseum** holds a series of rooms richly decked out with 18C and 19C art, furniture and Meissen porcelain. The most impressive are the **Thronzimmer★** (Throne Room) and the **Ahnengalerie** (Ancestors' Gallery), whose paintings are an uninterrupted roll call of all Mecklenburg dukes from the 14C to the 18C.

Schlosskirche★ (Palace Church)
This 16C Renaissance chapel was commissioned in 1560 by Duke Albrecht I. It was the first Protestant church in Mecklenburg and was originally a simple, rectangular, galleried space. The Neo-Gothic choir with splendid stained-glass windows was added in the 19C. A triumphal arch links the choir and the original chapel.

Schlossgarten★ (Palace Garden)
Created in the 19C, this formal Baroque garden is organised around canals, lime trees and ornamental flowerbeds. Lining the canals are statues by Balthazar Permoser.

Schloss Schwerin, Throne Room
© Lothar Steiner / Staatliches Museum Schwerin

OLD TOWN

Markt

Four 17C half-timbered houses are preserved beside the town hall. The 18C Neoclassical **Neues Gebäude** (new building) is fronted by a monument of Henry the Lion.

Dom★ (Cathedral)

This Gothic red-brick cathedral was built in the 14C and 15C on the site of an ancient Roman building. It is filled with wonderful treasures, most notably a **Gothic high altar** (workshop Lübeck, 1480), **tombstones** (14C), a **triumphal cross** of the Church of St. Mary of Wismar (1420) and **frescoes** in the Chapel of the Assumption (14C).

Galerie Alte und Neue Meister Schwerin★ (Gallery of Old and New Masters)

Alter Garten 3. Open mid-Apr–mid-Oct Tue–Sun 10am–6pm (Thu noon–8pm); late Oct–early Apr Tue–Sun 10am–5pm (Thu 1pm–8pm). Closed Dec 24 . ⊗8€. &(0385) 595 80. www.museum-schwerin.de.

This museum houses 17C Flemish and Dutch paintings (Brueghel, Rembrandt, Rubens), European painting from the 16C to the 20C (Cranach, Gainsborough) and contemporary art (Cage, Polke).

EXCURSION

Schloss Ludwigslust★

➤40km/24.8mi south. Open Tue–Sun 10am–5pm (mid-Apr–mid-Oct until 6pm). ⊗3.50€. &(03874) 571 915. www.schloss-ludwigslust.de.

This ducal palace has early 18C origins as a hunting lodge, but was significantly enlarged after Duke Friedrich made Ludwigslust the capital of his duchy in 1764. It is an E-shaped, 18C late-Baroque building with some early Neoclassical elements. The 18 vases and 40 statues adorning the attic parapet represent the arts, sciences and virtues.

The **interior** is dominated by white and gold ornamentation. Paintings, furniture, miniatures and gilded deco-

---

Ludwigslust Cardboard Décor

Duke Friedrich's intensive building activity exhausted his funds, but he was determined to decorate his palace in a manner befitting his social standing. Expensive material was replaced by Ludwigsluster Karton, a type of papier mâché that could be polished and painted and was even weather resistant. The Ludwigslust workshop achieved such mastery that its products were exported as far as Russia. Production ceased in 1835 due to lack of demand. The original formula was closely guarded and remains a secret to this day.

---

rations made from papier mâché reflect the lifestyles of the ducal family. A particular highlight is the **Golden Room**. The sprawling **Schlosspark★** got its naturalistic English landscape design in the 19C under Peter Joseph Lenné. Take a stroll to view streams, monuments, mausoleums and a grotto.

ADDRESSES

🛏 STAY

Niederländischer Hof – *Alexandrinenstraße 12–13. &(0385) 59 11 00. www.niederlaendischer-hof.de. 33 rooms. Restaurant.* In an old building with a listed façade, this hotel fits perfectly into the surrounding urban landscape. The tasteful interior is elegantly furnished.

🍴/EAT

Weinhaus Uhle – *Schusterstraße 15. &(0385) 56 29 56. www.weinhaus-uhle.de.* Located near the market place, this fine town house is home to a well-run, elegant restaurant with an 18C vaulted ceiling and pretty arched windows. The wine list is extensive.

Mecklenburg Lake District★★★

Mecklenburger Seenplatte

Sprinkled with more than 1 000 lakes, the intensely rural Mecklenburg Lake District is also known as Land der Tausend Seen (Land of the Thousand Lakes). Formed during the last Ice Age, it is a peaceful region, untouched by mass tourism. Time seems to move a little slower here, so plan on savouring the area's considerable charms at a leisurely pace. Since only a few lakes have roads along their shores, you will need to get out of the car and onto a trail or the water to truly enjoy this area.

🖹 **Info:** Turnplatz 2, 17207 Röbel/Müritz. ✆(039931) 53 80. www.mecklenburgische-seenplatte.de.

▶ **Location:** The lake district begins about 80km/49.7mi north of Berlin and centres on the Müritz National Park.

☺ **Don't Miss:** Müritz National Park.

🕓 **Timing:** Allow one full day for the Driving Tour.

👫 **Kids:** Outdoor activities at Müritz National Park.

🚗 DRIVING TOUR

FROM SCHWERIN TO MÜRITZ LAKE

150km/94mi. Allow one day.

The **Schweriner See** forms an idyllic backdrop to the provincial capital **Schwerin★** and its castle (🕓*see p170*). The novelist Fritz Reuter (1810–1875), who was born in this region, found inspiration and solace on the peaceful wooded shores of **Krakower See**. Today, the lake is a paradise for birdwatchers. The **Plauer See**, the third-largest lake in Mecklenburg-Vorpommern, offers flat shores to the north and thick forest to the south. Together with the **Müritz**, it forms the heart of the Mecklenburg Lake District.

Northeast of the lakes, **Mecklenburg's "Switzerland"** is a stretch of hills. The road leads through the town of **Malchin**, with its fine brick basilica, to the **Kummerower See**. To the west of the **Malchiner See** *(on the B108)* **Schlitz Castle** is set in a lovely park.

The pearl of the district is **Lake Müritz** with **Waren** on its north shore being the main tourist centre. In addition to the two parish churches of St. Georg and St.

Lake Müritz with boathouses

Canoeing in Müritz National Park

Maria, the old and new town halls and the Löwenapotheke (pharmacy) draw the eye. **Röbel** has a pretty marina with attractive boathouses.

MÜRITZ NATIONAL PARK★

This nature reserve sprawls across 310sq km/120sq mi east of Lake Müritz. Two-thirds of the area is covered with forest, 12 percent is taken up by the lake and 8 percent is wetlands. In East German times, a section was reserved for hunting, but today it is entirely given over to walkers, cyclists and other nature-lovers.

The birdlife here is astonishingly diverse. Bring binoculars to keep an eye out for the rare osprey, which seems to take pleasure in preparing its nest on high-voltage pylons. Chances of encountering osprey, whose territory reaches up to 50sq km/19sq mi, are greatest near the fish pools of Boek. White storks have been seen nesting near Kargowa, and black storks and cranes may also be sighted.

When it comes to fauna, pine and beech trees predominate, but the marshes and sloughs of the eastern Müritz bank are also dappled with alder, birch and ash. All in all, an estimated 150 bird and 700 plant species call this national park home. Take a guided tour in order to gain a more thorough appreciation for this extraordinary natural wealth.

ADDRESSES

▲ STAY

⊖ **Hotel Seestern** – *Müritzpromenade 12, 17207 Röbel.* ℘*(039931) 580 30. www. hotel-seestern-roebel.de. Closed Jan, Feb and Nov. 25 rooms. Restaurant⊖.* This hotel sits on a small tongue of land jutting into the lake. Ask for one of the bi-level rooms with superb views. The restaurant is in a welcoming annex and has a winter garden and a terrace.

⊖⊖ **Der Insulaner Hotel** – *Lange Straße 7, 17213 Malchow.* ℘*(039932) 82 07 40. www.insulaner-malchow.com. 16 rooms. Good size rooms* in the old town, on the edge of a swinging bridge; some have views of Malchow Lake.

⊖⊖ **Hotel Kleines Meer** – *Alter Markt 7, 17192 Waren.* ℘*(03991) 64 80. www.kleinesmeer.de. 30 rooms. Restaurant⊖⊖⊜.* A central location near the harbour and comfortable, modern rooms with a good range of communication devices are among the assets of this hotel. The restaurant exudes contemporary flair and serves ambitious international cuisine.

⊖⊖ **Hotel Paulshöhe** – *Paulshöhe 1, 17192 Waren.* ℘*(03991) 171 40. www.hotel-paulshoehe.de. 7 rooms, 7 bungalows. Restaurant⊖⊜.* In a pleasant location 200m/220yd from the Tiefwarensee lake you'll find lodging with all the mod-cons and a warm and well-presented restaurant.

The Northwest

Hafengeburtstag festival, Hamburg
© www.mediaserver.hamburg.de / C. Spahrbier

The Northwest

This vast region forms a triangle between the windswept beaches of the North Sea, the dense forests of the Harz Mountains and the cycle-friendly expanses of the Münsterland with its moated castles. Aside from natural splendours, historical towns abound. Germany's second-largest city, Hamburg, lures visitors with its cosmopolitan flair, maritime spirit and some of the country's best nightlife. The red-brick architecture that dominates the north gives way to half-timbered gems in such pretty towns as Celle, Hameln and Goslar. Goslar is also a gateway to the Harz Mountains, a paradise for outdoor enthusiasts. Hiking, cycling and even skiing are all popular activities. If water is your element, head to the Frisian Islands for great surfing, swimming and sailing.

Highlights

1 HafenCity and Speicherstadt in **Hamburg** (p205 and p204)

2 Germany's largest- surviving medieval town hall, in **Lüneburg** (p214)

3 Wind-swept beaches and dunes of **Insel Sylt** (p220)

4 Half-timbered towns of **Celle** and **Goslar** (p239 and p243)

5 The annual Libori Festival at **Paderborn** (p258)

Hanseatic Cities

Northwestern Germany's Hanseatic legacy is still evident in several cities, most famously of course its birthplace, Lübeck, the "Queen of the Hanseatic League" (*see BALTIC COAST AND INLAND, p160*). A short drive south, Hamburg on the Elbe River is still a major trading town that is home to Europe's second-largest port. There is also an entire quarter of warehouses called the historic Speicherstadt as well as imposing merchants' houses, such as the eccentric Chilehaus. Finally, there is Bremen, sitting pretty on the Weser River. Shaped both by history and high tech, its port section of Bremerhaven was the launch pad for millions of emigrants bound for the New World.

Historic Heritage

UNESCO World Heritage Sites in northern Germany captivate visitors with religious art treasures, mining monuments and

Old Town, Celle

© Bildagentur RM/Tips Images

Hanseatic League

Long before the European Union, there was the Hanseatic League, a federation of trading cities that dominated commercial activity in northern Europe from the 13C to the 15C. The League's actual origins are hard to determine, although scholars generally agree that its history began in 1159 in Lübeck as a loose alliance of guilds and individual merchants. At its peak, though, it counted as many as 200 member cities and stretched from the Baltic to the North Sea and inland to Münster, Goslar, Hildesheim and beyond. Most towns were located along international trade routes; many were free imperial cities, meaning they reported directly to the Holy Roman Emperor. The member towns had their own system of laws and furnished their own protection, allowing them to influence imperial policy and to prosper economically. Many of the grand medieval houses and public buildings have survived over the centuries and still attest to this phase of great prosperity.

Hanseatic history. Hildesheim for example is blessed with beautiful churches, while fascinating mining and industrial heritage awaits in Goslar. The Hanseatic city of Bremen makes an enthralling destination with its historic old quarters, fine monuments, religious art and traditional brick buildings. Further south, Münster and Osnabrück catapulted to historic fame as the sites where the treaty ending the bloody Thirty Years' War was signed.

Unique and Offbeat

Germany's northwest has plenty in store for those with a penchant for the unusual. How about a walk on the ocean floor at low tide in the Wadden Sea or communing with witches and warlocks in the Harz Mountains? You can pay your respects to Anne Frank at Bergen-Belsen and worship at the altar of the auto in the Volkswagen theme park in nearby Wolfsburg. Delving deep into German folklore comes easy in Hameln, of Pied Piper fame, and in Bremen, whose "Town Musicians" were immortalised in the Brothers Grimm fairytale. Bremen is also home to the bizarre "lead-cellar" where you can gawk at grisly mummified bodies.

Coastal Delights

If you need to rid yourself of the stresses nibbling at your psyche, Germany's North Sea Coast may just be what the doctor ordered.

Remote and tranquil, its sandy, dune-fringed beaches are tailor-made for long walks in the breeze. Flocks of sheep graze

Sign on Rattenfängerhaus, Hamelin

© M. Berg/Fotolia.com

on green man-made dikes that protect the coast from the power of the sea.

The offshore Frisian Islands are hugely popular with holidaymakers, especially families, although the glamorous isle of Sylt is still the darling of the international jet-set. Watch in awe as the water retreats dramatically during low tide, exposing the bottom of the sea and inviting barefoot explorations of the mudflats, which are protected as a national park and as a UNESCO Natural Heritage Site. The windswept landscape dotted with Frisian thatched houses has also inspired many artists, including the Expressionist painter Emil Nolde and the poet Theodor Storm.

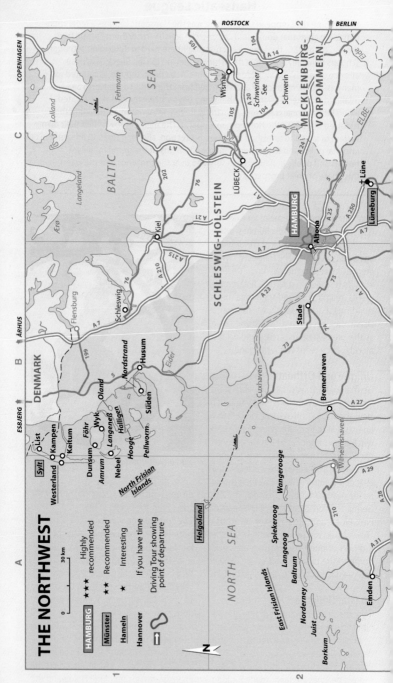

THE NORTHWEST

0 — 30 km

HAMBURG ★★★ Highly recommended

Münster ★★ Recommended

Hameln ★ Interesting

Hannover — Driving Tour showing point of departure

N

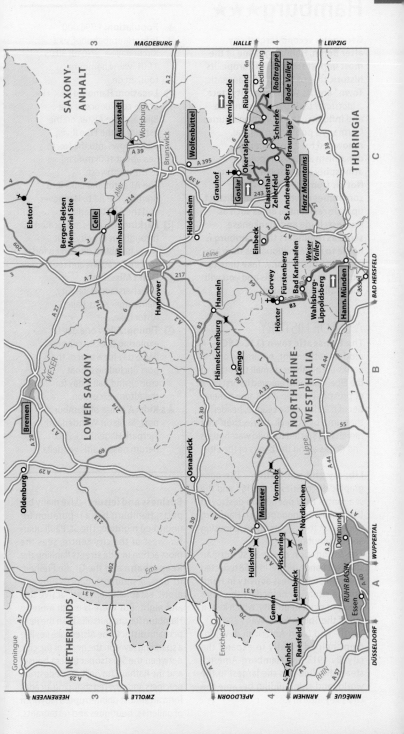

MAGDEBURG

HALLE

LEIPZIG

SAXONY-ANHALT

THURINGIA

LOWER SAXONY

NORTH RHINE-WESTPHALIA

NETHERLANDS

Quedlinburg

Roßtrappe

Bode Valley

Rübeland

Wernigerode

Autostadt

Wolfsburg

Wolfenbüttel

Schierke

Braunlage

Brunswick

Okertalsperre

Harz Mountains

Grauhof

Goslar

Clausthal-Zellerfeld

St. Andreasberg

Bergen-Belsen Memorial Site

Ebstorf

Celle

Wienhausen

Hildesheim

Einbeck

Leine

Bremen

Hannover

Corvey

Fürstenberg

Bad Karlshafen

Weser Valley

WESER

Hämelschenburg

Hameln

Höxter

Wahlsburg

Lippoldsberg

Hann.-Münden

Cassel

BAD HERSFELD

Lemgo

Oldenburg

Osnabrück

Münster

Vornholz

Nordkirchen

Dortmund

Hülshoff

Vischering

Lembeck

RUHR BASIN

Gemen

Essen

Raesfeld

Anholt

Enschede

Lippe

Ems

RHIN

DÜSSELDORF

WUPPERTAL

Groningue

HEERENVEEN

ZWOLLE

APELDOORN

ARNHEM

NIMEGUE

Hamburg★★★

Germany's second-largest city after Berlin, Hamburg is one of the most important ports in Europe. Its historic title of "Free and Hanseatic Town" and its status as a "city state" (*Stadtstaat*) testify to its eminence and influence through the centuries. Germany's publishing capital, renowned for its commercial dynamism and cosmopolitan atmosphere, is a city of contrasts. Not far from the lively – and sometimes rowdy – St. Pauli district, upscale residential areas such as Harvestehude and Blankenese serve as reminders that Hamburg is home to more millionaires than any other city in Germany. Take time to explore the metropolis and you will soon fall under its spell.

A BIT OF HISTORY

The Hanseatic town (13C–15C) – A modest settlement, originally, on the banks of the Alster, a small tributary of the Elbe, Hamburg enjoyed its first taste of prosperity when it became a member of the Hanseatic League, headed at that time by Lübeck. It was then that merchants started to build warehouses and docks along the banks of the Elbe.

Liberty and neutrality – The geographic discoveries of the 16C and the sea routes they opened up destroyed the Hanseatic monopoly, so Hamburg traders set their sights on warehousing and distribution.

The foundation of the first German stock exchange (Börse) in 1558 reflected the intense business activity in Hamburg, a situation helped by the city's policy of strict neutrality, which kept it out of the Thirty Years' War.

North- and Latin-American development helped greatly to expand the city. By 1913, the Hamburg-Amerika steamship line was the largest in the world, and shipbuilding became the city's key industry.

▶ **Population:** 1 796 000

Info: Hauptbahnhof, exit Kirchenallee. ℘(040) 30 05 17 01. www.hamburg-tourism.de.

Location: Hamburg is at the confluence of the Bille and the Alster, on the estuary of the Elbe River, which flows into the North Sea about 100km/62mi to the northwest.
The A1 autobahn links it to Bremen, the A7 to Hannover and the A24 to Berlin.

Parking: Garages are located throughout the city. Visit www.hamburg.de/parken for specific locations and fees.

Don't Miss: Port, Speicherstadt, HafenCity, Hamburger Kunsthalle, Alster Lake.

Timing: Allow one day for exploring the city centre; half a day for a tour of the port (including a boat cruise); and half a day for the Altona Excursion.

Kids: A cruise of Hamburg's port, Miniatur Wunderland; Tierpark Hagenbeck Zoo. Berum nossunditis vendella

Business and leisure – Like many big ports, Hamburg has a reputation for unbridled nightlife. The St. Pauli quarter, west of the city centre, sees the most action in side streets flanking the **Reeperbahn** and the Große Freiheit. Its bars, restaurants, dance clubs and erotic establishments are active day and night. But there is much more to Hamburg leisure pursuits than the Reeperbahn district. The Alster Lake lies like a sparkling jewel in the heart of the city. Between the Staatsoper (opera house) and the Rathaus (town hall), pedestrian precincts and covered shopping arcades form an almost uninterrupted labyrinth of galleries, boutiques and restaurants.

© www.mediaserver.hamburg.de / C. Spahrbier

The Mönckebergstraße, which links the Rathaus with the railway station, is another major commercial artery. Antique shops around the Gänsemarkt specialise in Asian art. Between the Rathaus and the station, a variety of old maps, prints and travel-related items can be found in booksellers' shops, while philatelists and tobacco users frequent the small shops in the printing and counting-house quarter.

The people of Hamburg are said to be very "British" Germans: more reserved and serious than their lively southern compatriots. But Hamburg is among the most welcoming of German cities, and English is spoken in many stores, restaurants and wine cellars.

Culinary specialities – Local dishes often mix area produce with Asian spices, sometimes combining meat, fruit, and sweet-and-sour sauces all in one dish. Typical are *Labskaus*, a seaman's dish of minced meat, herring, chopped gherkins, mashed potato and beetroot topped with fried eggs; as well as *Aalsuppe* – eel soup.

SIGHTS
The Port★★

St. Pauli landing pier. Shops open daily 5/10am–7pm/midnight (Nov–Mar some shops open weekends only).

Exploring the port of Hamburg is one of the highlights of any trip to the city. Apart from St. Michaelis Kirche's tower, the best **viewpoint★** from which to see the port is the **Stintfang**, a raised terrace below the youth hostel *(U/S-Bahn St. Pauli Landungsbrücken)*.

♙♙ Boat Trip of the Port

Boats depart from the dock near the Baumwall U-Bahn station. Duration 1hr. Commentary. ☜18€. ✆(040) 31 99 16 170. www.barkassen-centrale.de.

Visitors will be astonished by the sheer size of the dockyards and the extraordinary activity in the shipyards on either side of the Elbe, where every type of vessel is constructed. Motorised ferries ply back and forth all day long, transporting south bank workers back to the city during the rush hour.

Port of Hamburg

The Hamburg docks comprise 60 basins and more than 68km/42.3mi of quays. The overall surface area is more than 75sq km/29sq mi. Thanks to a relatively small tidefall (3m/9.8ft average), no locks are necessary in the basins accessible to ocean-going traffic able to navigate the Elbe. Some 320 shipping lines call regularly (about 650 departures a month) to transport goods to a thousand ports all over the world.

PRACTICAL INFORMATION

Telephone prefix: ✆ 040

Visitor information: For general information or room and ticket reservations: *Tourismus-Zentrale Hamburg GmbH,* ✆ *(040) 30 05 17 01, www.hamburg-tourism.de. Open Mon–Sat 9am–7pm.* **Information offices:** Main train station (Hauptbahnhof), Kirchenallee main exit, *Mon–Sat 9am–7pm, Sun 10am–6pm*; Harbour, St. Pauli Landungsbrücken between piers 4 and 5, *Sun–Wed 9am–6pm, Thu–Sat 9am–7pm*; Airport, at the Airport Plaza between terminals 1 and 2, *daily 6am–11pm.* All branches distribute the free monthly cultural listings magazine *Vorschau…* (followed by the month), which can also be picked up in many hotels. Newsstands sell the magazines *Prinz* (bi-weekly) or *Szene Hamburg* (monthly).

Internet – www.hamburg.de; www.hamburg-web.de (in German); www.hamburg-information.de (in German).

Daily papers – *Hamburger Morgenpost, Hamburger Abendblatt.*

Post offices with late hours – The post office at Hachmannplatz at the main train station is open Mon–Fri 5am–6pm and Sat–Sun 8am–10pm.

PUBLIC TRANSPORT

Hamburg is best explored using the buses and underground trains (U-Bahn) of the **HVV** *(Hamburger Verkehrsverbund;* ✆ *194 49; www.hvv.de).* There are information offices at the Hauptbahnhof and in many U- and S-Bahn stations. Tickets are available from orange vending machines and bus drivers. Single tickets for rides in the city centre start at 1.45€. Day tickets valid after 9am cost 5.90€ for one person and 9.70€ for groups of up to five people

The one-day **Hamburg Card** costs 9.50€ and is valid for one adult and up to three children under 15; the group version (15.50€) is good for up to five people of any age on the issue date and until 6am the next day. Three- and five-day versions are also available. Benefits include unlimited public transport, free or discounted museum admissions and discounts to sightseeing tours, restaurants and shops. The Hamburg Card is available at tourist offices, in many hotels, at vending machines, in the HVV customer offices and online at www.hamburg-tourism.de.

St. Pauli District

North of the port and west of new town. St. Pauli had its golden age in the 1960s when the Beatles played the Star Club and Kaiserkeller in **Große Freiheit**. Its image was later considerably tarnished by prostitution and drug trafficking, but over the last few years this district, which has the city's biggest police station **(Davidwache)**, has undergone a renaissance.

Although the sex industry is still in full swing, the area is also teeming with trendy bars, cafés and restaurants, many with a genuinely warm atmosphere and popular with locals and non-locals alike. St. Pauli spreads out around the **Reeperbahn**, the main thoroughfare, which runs parallel to the port.

◕ WALKING TOUR

CITY CENTRE

This walk begins at the Jungfernstieg landing dock of the Inner Alster. It explores different aspects of the Alster lakes in the historic city centre and continues to the warehouse district (Speicherstadt), whose stately brick buildings harbour a clutch of interesting museums. Allow an entire day for this tour if you want to include a boat trip and explore some of the museums.

👥 Binnenalster and Außenalster★★★ (Inner and Outer Alster Lakes)

Departures from the Jungfernstieg pier. Alster–Rundfahrt (50min): Apr–Sept daily 10am–6pm, half-hourly; Oct 10am, 11am–4pm half-hourly, 5pm; Nov–Mar 10.30am, noon, 1.30pm & 3pm (Nov–Dec also 4pm, 4.30pm, 5.30pm, 6pm). ⊗14.50€ (child 7€). Alster–Kreuz–Fahrt (hop-on-hop-off at 9 stops): Apr–Oct daily 10.15am–5.15pm. ⊗1.70€ (child 0.80€) per dock or 12€ (child 6€) round trip. ℘(040) 357 42 40. www.alstertouristik.de.

The Alster Lake, north of the old town, is a beautiful stretch of water. It consists of two basins, the Binnenalster and the Außenalster, the latter (the larger of the two) offering sailing and canoeing. A fleet of motorboats ferries passengers regularly between nine landing docks. It is also possible to sail on the Alster canals (past well-kept parks and villas interspersed with undeveloped areas) and on the canals in the old town and port (two locks allow access to the port area from the Binnenalster).

Those with transportation can drive clockwise around the Alster, bordered by luxury apartments on one side and immaculate parks on the other.

Jungfernstieg★

Bordering the southern end of the Inner Alster, the Jungfernstieg is among Hamburg's most cosmopolitan thoroughfares. The crowded terraces of the waterfront Alsterpavillon café-restaurant, the boats crossing the basin, the presence nearby of one of the world's most famous hotels (Vier Jahreszeiten), and the imposing new office blocks lining the Ballindamm all contribute to the spirited ambience.

▷ Leave Jungfernstieg and walk along the Alsterfleet to the Town Hall.

Rathausmarkt

Hamburg's majestic **town hall** (🔍visit by guided tour only; English tours by arrangement); ⊗4€; ♿; ℘ (040) 428 31 20 64) with its 112m/367ft-high clocktower dominates this central square. Rebuilt after the fire of 1842 in neo-Renaissance style and completed in 1887, it is a maze of 647 rooms and boasts a façade adorned with statues of 20 German emperors. The bridge (*Schleusenbrücke*), which forms part of the Alster's lock system, crosses the Alsterfleet, a relic of the city's former canal system. On the far bank the colonnade of the Alsterarkaden shelters elegant shops and cafés.

▷ Turn into Mönckebergstraße.

St. Petri Kirche
(Church of St. Peter)

Mönckebergstraße. Open year-round Mon–Fri 10am–6.30pm (Wed until 7pm), Sat 10am–5pm, Sun 9am–8pm. ℘(040) 325 74 00. www.sankt-petri.de.

This 12C church was rebuilt in neo-Gothic style after the great fire of 1842. The **lion's head door handles★** (1342) on the left west portal are regarded as

Cycling around Alster Lake

© www.mediaserver.hamburg.de/R.Hegeler

Hamburg's oldest surviving work of art. The **tower** can be climbed (Mon–Sat 11am–4.30pm, Sun from 11.30am).

St. Jakobi-Kirche (Church of St. Jacob)

Jacobikirchhof 22. Open Apr–Sept Mon–Sat 10am–5pm, Sun 11.30am–5pm (Oct–Mar from 11am). ℘(040) 303 73 70. www.jacobus.de.

Among the treasures of this 14C–15C hall church are the **reredos★** of St. Luke and the Fishers' Guild; a triptych of the Coopers' Guild on the high altar; Georg Bauman's alabaster and marble pulpit (1610); and the famous 1693 **organ★** by Arp Schnitger.

▷ Cross Steinstraße heading south to Burchardplatz.

Kontorhäuser (Counting House Buildings)

These imposing brick buildings dominate the printing, press and business quarter around Burchardplatz square. Of particular interest is the **Chilehaus** *(between Burgstraße and Meßberg)*. Designed by Expressionist architect Fritz Höger, this 1924 building looms against the sky like the prow of a ship. It was built for a rich local merchant who made his fortune mainly through trade relations with Chile, hence the name. The **Sprinkenhof** (1931) is a town within the town, an office complex complete with roadways open to vehicles.

Fish Market

The Hamburg fish market originated in the early 18C and has become a veritable institution. It is held every Sunday morning in the south of the St. Pauli district along the Elbe from 5am–9.30am (from 7am Oct–Mar). The cheerful fishmongers, crowds of people of all ages who come to buy or browse and musical entertainment in the *Fischauktionhalle* have made it part of living Hamburg folklore.

▷ Continue southwards and cross the canal to explore Speicherstadt.

Speicherstadt★ (Warehouse Quarter)

🚶🚶Guided tours depart Speicherstadt Museum Sat 3pm (Apr–Oct only) and Sun 11pm. ⊛9.50€. ℘(040) 32 11 91. www.speicherstadt-erleben.de

After Hamburg joined the German Customs Federation in 1871, it became necessary to create a free trade zone. An entire district along the Zoll Canal and its side channels was flattened to make room for the Speicherstadt warehouses, set up between 1885 and 1927. Still the world's largest continuous warehouse complex, they store coffee, tobacco, spices, raw silk, oriental carpets and other goods. With its rows of gabled brick buildings topped with green copper roofs, Speicherstadt is an appealing quarter for a stroll or **boat cruise**. For a birds-eye view, catch a flight aboard the **High Flyer hot-air balloon** (Deichtorstraße 1–2; open year-round daily 10am–10pm, weather permitting; 15min; every 15min; ⊛15€; ℘(040) 30 08 69 69; www.highflyer-hamburg.de).

Dialog im Dunkeln (Dialogue in the Dark)

Alter Wandrahm 4. 🚶🚶Guided tours (90min) year-round Tue–Fri 9am–5pm (Fri until 7pm), Sat 10am–8pm, Sun and holidays 11am–6pm. ⊛19€, reservation required. ♿. ℘(040) 309 6340. www.dialog-im-dunkeln.de. English tours on request.

There is really nothing to look at in this unusual museum, but there is certainly plenty to explore. Blind guides lead small groups of people through a world of total darkness. Scents, temperatures, winds and sounds create non-visual experiences that are discovered by passing through various scenarios such as a park, a city centre or a bar. It is also possible to dine in the dark, but you must book well in advance.

Speicherstadt Museum

Am Sandtorkai 36. Open Apr–Oct Mon–Sun 10am–5pm (Sat–Sun until 6pm). Nov–Mar Tue–Sun 10am–5pm. 3.60€. ℘(040) 32 11 91. www.speicherstadtmuseum.de.

In an old red-brick warehouse, this museum chronicles the history of the district and its businesses for more than a century. Measuring instruments and storage tools, bags of coffee and other goods, photos and maps illustrate the various stages of development.

◗ Continue within the Speicherstadt via Zollcanal, where you will find two small museums, or cross the second bridge on your right to get back into the old town.

Hamburg Dungeon

Kehrwieder 2. Open daily 10am–6pm (Jul–Aug until 7pm). Closed Dec 24. 23.95€. &. Not suitable for children under 10. Advance reservation recommended to avoid ticket queue. ℘(1806) 66 69 01 40. www.thedungeons.com/hamburg.

Allow at least 90 minutes for this indoor horror theme park where you encounter graphic scenes related to the history of Hamburg such as the great fire of 1842, the blood-thirsty Thirty Years' War and the execution of the 14C pirate Störtebeker. The visit concludes with a free-fall (Drop Ride) and a boat ride illustrating the deadly flood of 1717.

👥 Miniatur Wunderland★

Kehrwieder 2–4. Open Mon, Wed–Thu 9.30am–6pm, Tue 9.30am–9pm, Fri 9.30am–7pm, Sat 8am–9pm, Sun 8.30am–8pm. 12€. &. Reservation recommended to avoid ticket queue. ℘(040) 300 6 800. www.miniatur-wunderland.de.

At over 4000sq m/43 055sq ft, this is one of the world's largest model railways. Some 700 trains travel through miniature versions of Hamburg, the Alps, the USA, Scandinavia, Switzerland, the Harz Mountains and a town called Knuffingen. Visits include a stop in the control room, where you can watch staff put in motion this ballet of miniatures.

Altstadt (Old Town)

Hamburg's old town is bounded by the Nikolaifleet, the Binnenhafen (docks reserved for river craft and tugboats) and the Zoll Canal.

Highlights of the old town include the **St. Katharinen Kirche**, a 14C–15C Gothic brick church featuring a bulbous openwork tower. It was on **Deichstraße** that the great fire of 1842 erupted.

Many of the 17C–18C merchants' houses have today been converted into bars and taverns. The restored façades of warehouses opposite, lining the curve of the Nikolaifleet canal, recall the Hamburg of yesteryear.

The best view is from the **Hohe Brücke**, which crosses the Nikolaifleet and parallels the Binnenhafen.

◗ Cross the bridge, turn right on Admiralitätstraße, then left on Martin-Luther-Straße.

St. Michaelis Kirche★ (Church of St. Michael)

Open May–Oct daily 9am–8pm; Nov–Apr 10am–6pm. 5€ tower, 4€ crypt and HamburgHiStory, all three 7€. ℘(040) 37 67 80. www.st-michaelis.de.

Designed in 1762 by Ernst Georg Sonnin, this church is one of the finest examples of the Baroque tradition in northern Germany. Its landmark tower (1786) rises high above the Elbe and offers sweeping **views★** from the platform at 132m/433ft.

Another level features **HamburgHiStory** (every 30min, 12.30pm–3.30pm), a multimedia show explaining high and low points of the city's past 1 000 years.

Near the east end of the church, a blind alley off Am Krayenkamp 10 is lined with 17C brick and timber houses, built as **almshouses** (Krameramtswohnungen); today they are mostly art galleries.

HAFENCITY

HafenCity Info Center, Kesselhaus, Sandtorkai 30. Open year-round, Tue–Sun 10am–6pm (May–Sept Thu

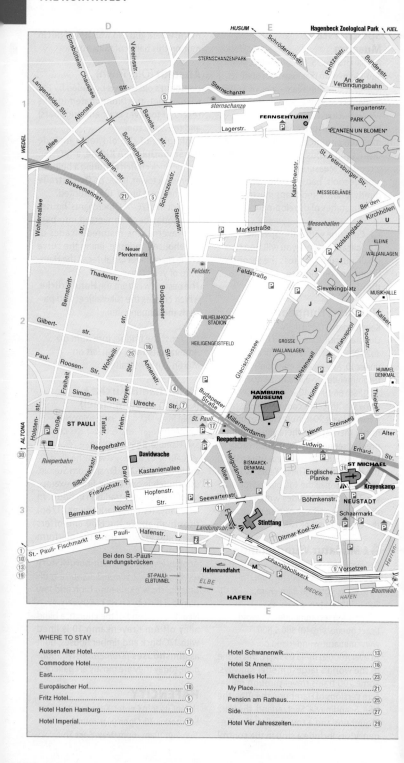

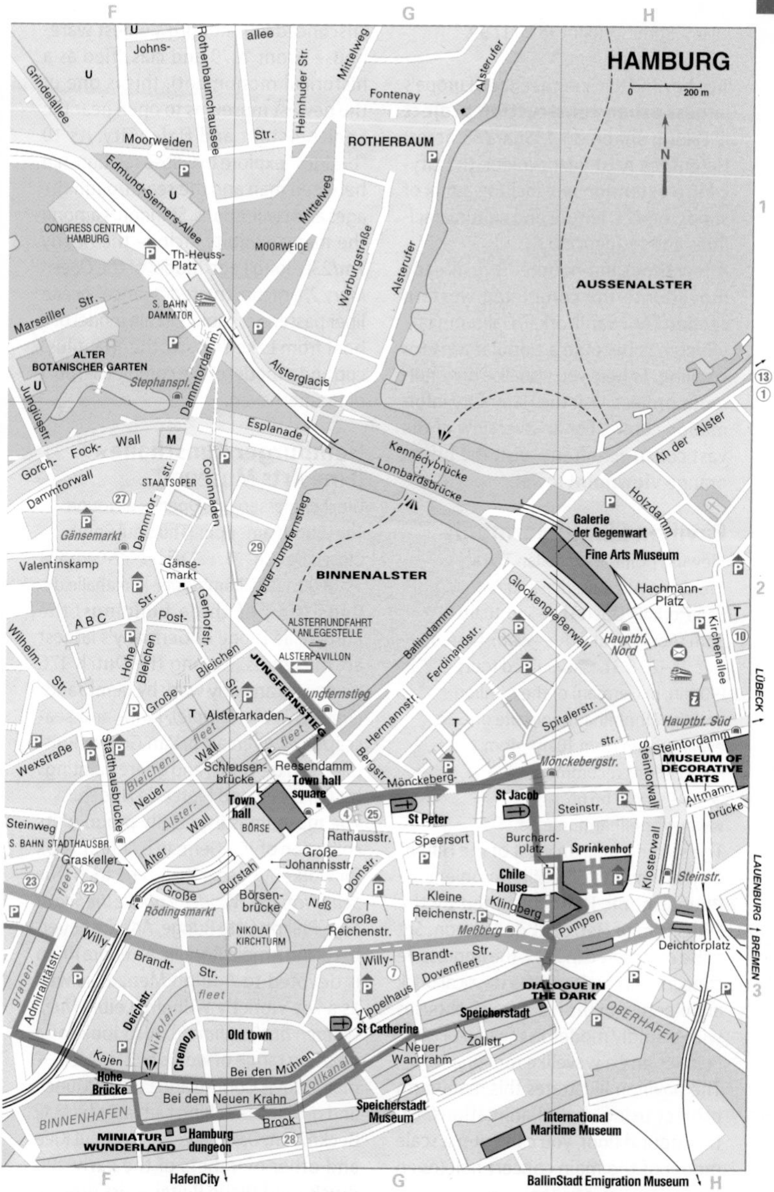

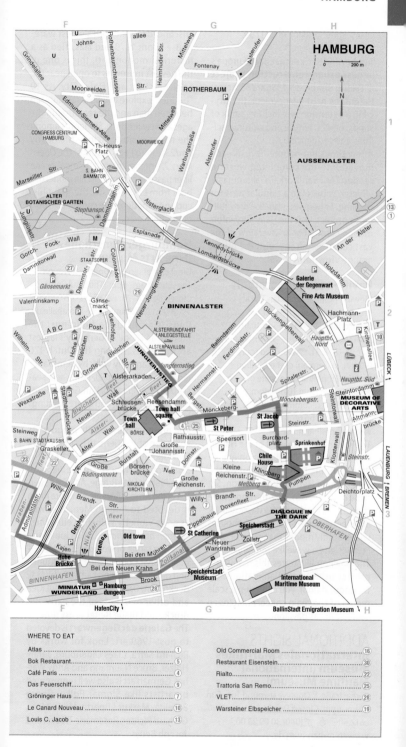

HAMBURG
0
200 m
N
F
G
H
1
2
3
Johns-
allee
Grindelallee
Rothenbaumchaussee
Heimhuder Str.
Mittelweg
Alsterufer
Fontenay
Moorweiden
Str.
ROTHERBAUM
Edmund-Siemers-Allee
CONGRESS CENTRUM HAMBURG
MOORWEIDE
Warburgstraße
Th-Heuss-Platz
AUSSENALSTER
Marseiller Str.
S. BAHN DAMMTOR
ALTER BOTANISCHER GARTEN
Stephanspl.
Dammtordamm
Alsterglacis
Jungiusstr.
Esplanade
Kennedybrücke
Lombardsbrücke
An der Alster
Gorch-Fock-Wall
Dammtorwall
STAATSOPER
Dammtor-str.
Colonnaden
Holzdamm
Gänsemarkt
Neuer Jungfernstieg
Galerie der Gegenwart
Fine Arts Museum
Valentinskamp
Gänse-markt
BINNENALSTER
Glockengießerwall
Hachmann-Platz
Post-
Str.
Gerhofstr.
ALSTERRUNDFAHRT ANLEGESTELLE
ALSTERPAVILLON
Ballindamm
Hauptbf. Nord
Kirchenallee
ABC
Wilhelm-Str.
Hohe Bleichen
Große Bleichen
JUNGFERNSTIEG
Jungfernstieg
Ferdinandstr.
LÜBECK
Alsterarkaden
Hermannstr.
Spitalerstr.
Hauptbf. Süd
Wexstraße
Stadthausbrücke
Bleichen-fleet
Alster-fleet
Schleusen-brücke
Reesendamm
Bergstr.
Mönckeberg-
str.
Mönckebergstr.
Steintordamm
Steintorwall
MUSEUM OF DECORATIVE ARTS
Neuer Wall
Town hall square
Town hall
BÖRSE
St Peter
St Jacob
Steinstr.
Altmann-brücke
Steinweg
S. BAHN STADTHAUSBR.
Alter Wall
Rathausstr.
Speersort
Burchard-platz
Sprinkenhof
Graskeller
Große Johannisstr.
Domstr.
Chile House
Klosterwall
Steinstr.
LAUENBURG
Große Burstah
Börsen-brücke
Neß
Kleine Reichenstr.
Klingberg
Rödingsmarkt
Große Reichenstr.
Meßberg
Pumpen
Deichtorplatz
NIKOLAI KIRCHTURM
Willy-Brandt-Str.
Dovenfleet
BREMEN
graben-
Admiralitätstr.
fleet
Deichstr.
Zippelhaus
DIALOGUE IN THE DARK
Speicherstadt
OBERHAFEN
Nikolai-
Cremon
Old town
St Catherine
Zollstr.
Kajen
Hohe Brücke
Bei den Mühren
Neuer Wandrahm
Zollkanal
Bei dem Neuen Krahn
BINNENHAFEN
Brook
Speicherstadt Museum
International Maritime Museum
MINIATUR WUNDERLAND
Hamburg dungeon
HafenCity
BallinStadt Emigration Museum

WHERE TO EAT

- Atlas 1
- Bok Restaurant 5
- Café Paris 4
- Das Feuerschiff 9
- Gröninger Haus 7
- Le Canard Nouveau 10
- Louis C. Jacob 13
- Old Commercial Room 16
- Restaurant Eisenstein 30
- Rialto 22
- Trattoria San Remo 25
- VLET 28
- Warsteiner Elbspeicher 19

10am–8pm). ℘(040) 36 90 17 99.
www.hafencity.com.

Just beyond the Speicherstadt, Europe's largest **urban construction project** is taking shape on 155ha/383 acres: HafenCity. A 20-year project, the city-centre extension will include a mix of shops, offices, leisure and cultural facilities and residences.

A few thousand people have already moved into the completed western section (Am Sandtorkai/Dalmannkai), which has become a popular area for strolling. To help you visualise this enormous project, visit the HafenCity information centre. For an overview of the vast construction site, visit the bright orange **viewpoint** tower.

Pavillon Elbphilharmonie

Viewing point at Magellan Terraces (between Am Kaiserkai and Am Sandtorkai). Open Thu–Sun 10am–5pm (Apr–Oct also Tue–Wed). Closed Dec 24–26 & 31. Guided tours (90min, in German) of the pavilion and the Elbphilharmonie site on Sun, every 45 min from 10am–4pm. 8€, reservations recommended.
℘(040) 35 76 66 66.
www.elbphilharmonie.de.

The shining beacon west of the Hafen-City will be the Elbphilharmonie (Elbe Philharmonic Hall), designed by the Swiss firm of Herzog & de Meuron. Set to be completed in 2017, the impressive concert hall combines the classical brick architecture of the historic warehouses with a boldly modernist sweep of glass façades and a wavelike roof line.

The pavilion illustrates this mammoth project using digital animations. On the ground floor, you can enter a scale model of the main concert hall (open same hours as pavilion).

ADDITIONAL SIGHTS
Internationales Maritimes Museum (International Maritime Museum)

Koreastraße 1. Open year-round Tue–Sun 10am–6pm. Closed Dec 24 & 31, Jan 1. 12.50€. ℘(040) 30 09 23 00. www.imm-hamburg.de.

Ensconced in Hamburg's oldest warehouse (from 1879 and classified as a historical monument), this is one of the newest museums to open near the Speicherstadt and HafenCity. Its 10 "bridges" explore the close relationship between man and the sea through the ages and civilisations. Standouts among the many exhibits include the nearly 7m/23ft-long Lego model of the *Queen Mary 2*, a reconstructed "France" ocean liner passenger cabin, a scale model of a boat from Lake Titicaca, the "Nautilus" cup and a model of the commercial port of Bremerhaven.

Hamburger Kunsthalle★★ (Fine Arts Museum)

Glockengiesserwall. Open year-round Tue–Sun 10am–6pm (Thu until 9pm). Closed Dec 24–25. 12€. ℘(040) 428 13 13 00. www.hamburger-kunsthalle.de.

Consisting of three buildings, the Kunsthalle is one of Germany's largest art museums. Among the Dutch 17C masters is an early work by Rembrandt *(Simeon in the Temple)*, land- and sea-scapes by Avercamp, Van Goyen, Ruisdael, Van de Velde, and genre paintings by Jan Steen and Pieter de Hooch.

The museum is especially proud of its collection of 19C German painting. Look for works by Caspar David Friedrich *(The Sea of Ice, The Wanderer above the Sea of Fog)*, Philipp Otto Runge, Anselm Feuerbach and Arnold Böcklin. An entire room is devoted to Adolph Menzel as well as a key work by Wilhelm Leibl *(Three Women at the Church)*. Also look for a dazzling range of works by Max Liebermann, Lovis Corinth and Edvard Munch and ground-breaking canvases by Max Beckmann, Oskar Kokoschka, Paul Klee and other members of the early 20C Brücke and Blaue Reiter artist groups.

The **Galerie der Gegenwart** is devoted to post-1960 art. Look for works by Richard Serra, Claes Oldenburg, Jenny Holzer, Bruce Naumann and Andy Warhol. German art is also well represented by artists like Sigmar Polke, Georg Baselitz, Markus Lüpertz, Mario Merz, Gerhard Richter, Rosemarie Trockel and Joseph Beuys.

Museum für Kunst und Gewerbe★ (Museum of Decorative Arts)

Steintorplatz 1, opposite the train station. Open year-round Tue–Sun 10am–6pm (Thu until 9pm). Closed May 1, Dec 24 & 31. ⊚10€. ♿ ✆(040) 428 134 880. www.mkg-hamburg.de.

Situated in a 19C neo-Renaissance palace, this vast museum houses collections of sculptures, ceramics, furniture, jewellery and musical instruments from antiquity to the present. The Jugendstil gallery is outstanding.

Hamburg Museum★

Holstenwall 24. Open year-round Tue–Sat 10am–5pm, Sun 6pm. Closed Jan 1, May 1, Dec 24 & 31. ⊚9€. ♿. ✆(040) 428 132 100. www.hamburgmuseum.de.

Hamburg's fascinating history gets the full treatment at this engaging museum through city models and numerous themed sections (emigration, Jewish Hamburg, the Hanseatic period, etc.).

♟ Tierpark Hagenbeck★★ (Hagenbeck Zoo)

Lokstedter Grenzstraße 2. Open Mar–Jun and Sept–Oct daily 9am–6pm; Jul–Aug daily 9am–7pm; Nov–Mar daily 9am–4.30pm. ⊚20€. ♿. ✆(040) 530 03 30. www.hagenbeck.de.

This delightful animal park (1907) boasts ancient trees, artificial lakes and some 2 500 creatures representing 360 species from five continents.

Next door, the vast **Tropen-Aquarium** (tropical aquarium; open 9am–6pm; ⊚14€, combination with Tierpark 30€) takes visitors on an undersea encounter with 14 000 creatures.

BallinStadt Emigration Museum★★

Veddeler Bogen 2. Open Apr–Oct daily 10am–6pm; Nov–Mar 10am–4.30pm. ⊚12.50€. ✆(040) 31 97 91 60. www.ballinstadt.de. ⊛You can visit by train, car, or boat (which includes a trip around Hamburg Harbour). See the website for details.

On the Elbe island of Veddel, BallinStadt was the embarkation centre for 5 million Europeans headed for America between 1850 and 1938. Multi-media exhibits in three re-created structures vividly portray all phases of emigration – from packing to settling – and bring to life people's hopes and hardships, dreams and realities. You can trace your roots in the Family Research Centre.

EXCURSIONS

Altona

◗3.2km/2mi southwest.

Altonaer Museum★★ (Altona Cultural History Museum)

Museumstraße 23. Open year-round Tue–Sun 10am–5pm. Closed Jan 1, May 1, Dec 24 & 31. ⊚7.50€. ♿ ✆(040) 428 135 3582. www.altonaer-museum.de.

Art, culture and day-to-day life in the lower Elbe valley and Schleswig-Holstein are illustrated here. Exceptional displays are 18C–19C ships' figureheads, models of North Sea boats, ceramics, fine Frisian embroidery, old toys and north German landscape paintings.

Altonaer Balkon (Altona Balcony)

The terrace south of Altona's Town Hall affords a **view★** of the Köhlbrandbrücke and confluence of the two branches of the Elbe. Follow the **Elbchaussee★**, a spacious avenue bordered by fabulous mansions since the early 19C.

Stade★

◗60km/37mi west.

In the Middle Ages, 1 000-year-old Stade boasted a port the size of Hamburg's. Most buildings in the beautiful **old town★★** were built after the great fire of 1659. Note especially: Hökerhaus (*Hökerstraße 27*), Doppelhaus (*Bäckerstraße 1–3*), Haus Knechthausen (*Bungenstraße 20*) and **Bürgermeister-Hintze-Haus** (*Wasser West*).

The **Schwedenspeicher Museum★** (Wasser West 39; open year-round Tue–Fri 10am–5pm, Sat–Sun 10am–6pm; ⊚6€; ✆041 41 79 77 30; www.museen-stade.de) in a late 17C brick granary now houses local history exhibits, including prehistoric **bronze** wheels★ (c. 700 BC), antique jewellery, weapons and pots.

ADDRESSES

⌖ STAY

⊖ Pension Am Rathaus –
Rathausstraße 14. ℘(040) 33 74 89. www.pension-am-rathaus.de. 15 rooms. This small guest house has just a few simple and clean rooms. The cheaper ones share a bathroom in the hallway.

⊖⊟ Commodore Hotel – *Budapester Straße 20. ℘(040) 31 99 96 03. www. hotel-commodore.de. 105 rooms. ⌷9€.* This hotel near St. Pauli station provides classic rooms and warm hospitality.

⊖⊟ Fritz Hotel – *Schanzenstraße 101–103. ℘(040) 82 22 28 30. www.fritz hotel.com. 17 rooms.* This small hotel is ideally located in the heart of the bustling Schanzenviertel neighbourhood and near cafés, restaurants, bars and designer boutiques.

⊖⊟ Hotel Hafen Hamburg – *Seewartenstraße 9. ℘(040) 31 11 30. www.hotel-hafen-hamburg.de. 380 rooms. ⌷20€.* Overlooking the Landungsbrücken pier, this hotel offers comfortable rooms, some with stunning views over the harbour. The restaurant too has panoramic windows and a spacious terrace.

⊖⊟ Hotel Imperial – *Millerntorplatz 3–5. ℘(040) 31 17 20. www.hotel-imperial-hamburg.de. 50 rooms. ⌷.* In the heart of St. Pauli, this hotel has functional rooms with double-glazed windows, although the noise-sensitive should still request one facing away from the Reeperbahn. Comfortable lounge.

⊖⊟ Hotel Schwanenwik – *Schwanenwik 29. ℘(040) 220 09 18. www.hotel-schwanenwik.de. 18 rooms. ⌷.* This charming boarding house (completely non-smoking) occupies a magnificent 18C townhouse on the Alster. The simple, modern rooms face the lake or the back garden.

⊖⊟ Hotel St. Annen – *Annenstraße 5. ℘(040) 31 77 130. www.hotelstannen.de. 36 rooms. ⌷.* Close to St. Pauli and the Reeperbahn, this hotel enjoys a quiet location on a leafy square. Rooms are small but comfortable and service is friendly. In summer, days start with breakfast on a garden terrace. Great value for money.

⊖⊟ Michaelis Hof – *Herrengraben 4, in the Catholic Academy. ℘(040) 35 90 69 12. www.michaelishof-hamburg.de. 22 rooms. ⌷10€ at Baseler Hof.* There are a few well-kept and quiet rooms for rent on the 4th floor of the Catholic Academy. Check-in is 7am to 11am.

⊖⊟ My Place – *Lippmannstraße 5. ℘(040) 28 57 18 74. www.myplace-hamburg.de. 14 rooms. ⌷5€.* This pint-size hotel has lovely, individually decorated rooms named for Hamburg city quarters as well as a few apartments.

⊖⊟⊟ Aussen Alster Hotel – *Schmilinskystraße 11. ℘(040) 284 078 570. www.aussenalsterhotel.de. 27 rooms. ⌷.* Occupying a garden property, this hotel is just 50m/164ft from the Aussenalster. Guest services include a solarium and free bicycle and rowing-boat rentals.

⊖⊟⊟ EAST – *Simon-von-Utrecht-Straße 31. ℘(040) 30 99 30. www.east-hamburg.de. 127 rooms. ⌷19.50€.* Just off the Reeperbahn, this boutique hotel was converted from a former foundry. Every detail speaks of refinement and fits harmoniously into the overall design. Gorgeous dining room, plus several cocktail lounges.

⊖⊟⊟ Europäischer Hof – *Kirchenallee 45. ℘(040) 24 82 48. www.europaeischer-hof.de. 275 rooms. ⌷.* Especially convenient because of its location opposite the train station, this hotel has a wellness centre that spans over four levels and includes a pool and even an indoor slide.

⊖⊟⊟ SIDE – *Drehbahn 49. ℘(040) 30 99 90. www.side-hamburg.de. 178 rooms. ⌷24€.* Located in a business district, this hotel makes sure everything is carefully calibrated for maximum comfort here. An atrium with choreographed lighting effects gives way to clean, stylish rooms. Solid design, a chic bar and a beautiful terrace overlooking the city are other benefits.

⊖⊟⊟⊟ Hotel Vier Jahreszeiten – *Neuer Jungfernstieg 9-14. ℘(040) 3494 31 51. www.hvj.de. 156 rooms. ⌷25€.*

Restaurants ⊖⊟⊟⊟. Unpretentious luxury characterises this lakeside grand hotel with elegant Gründerzeit décor and charming, modern and supremely comfortable rooms. Upscale cuisine is served in this Fairmont property's three separate restaurants.

⊘/EAT

⊖ **Bok Restaurant** – *Schulterblatt 3. ℰ(040) 431 900 70. www.bokrestaurant.de.* This small local chain offers Thai and Japanese dishes in a lively atmosphere and at reasonable prices. Food service is available until 11.30pm.

⊖ **Gröninger Haus** – *Willy-Brandt-Straße 47. ℰ(040) 570 105 100. www.groeninger-hamburg.de. Closed Sat–Sun lunchtime. Reservation recommended.* This private brewery inside the city's oldest hotel (first documented in 1260) is a lovely spot for winding down the day. Meals are hearty and come in belt-loosening portions. Wash them down with the in-house brew.

⊖ **Trattoria Remo's** – *Hein-Hoyer Straße 75. ℰ(040) 31 29 03. www.trattoria-remos.de.* Thumbs up for this friendly trattoria where you can enjoy a varied menu of delicious authentic Italian dishes served in a warm, vaulted room.

⊖⊖ **Atlas** – *Schützenstraße 9a. ℰ(040) 851 78 10. www.atlas.at. Closed Sat lunch, Sun dinner.* A former fish smokehouse has been re-cast as an upbeat bistro/restaurant/cocktail bar with an ivy-covered terrace. It is somewhat hidden away in Phönixhof.

⊖⊟ **Das Feuerschiff** – *City Sporthafen Vorsetzen, station Baumwall. ℰ(040) 36 25 53. www.das-feuerschiff.de.* For something unusual, book a table on the deck of this bright-red lightship, which used to double as a helicopter landing pad. Views of the harbour and the Elbphilharmonie concert hall are truly breathtaking. The on-site bar is a great spot for sunset drinks and has live jazz and blues on Sundays and Mondays.

⊖⊖⊟ **Café Paris** – *Rathausstraße 4. ℰ(040) 32 52 77 77. www.cafeparis.net. Reservation required.* This classic brasserie feels so fantastically French, you half expect to see the Eiffel Tower through the window. Mirrors and

framed prints line the walls, the servers wear crisp white shirts and the menu features *salad Niçoise* and *Côte de boeuf. Très* Gallic, *très* charming.

⊖⊖⊟ **Old Commercial Room** – *Englische Planke 10. ℰ(040) 36 63 19. www.oldcommercialroom.de. Reservation recommended.* A Hamburg institution since 1795, the restaurant was founded by an English shipowner, a possible explanation for the pub décor, with its mahogany and copper accents and maritime pictures. Traditional sailors' dishes dominate the menu *(Labskaus)*, which also features lobster, sole and pork knuckle.

⊖⊖⊟ **Restaurant Eisenstein** – *Friedensallee 9. ℰ(040) 390 46 06. www.restaurant-eisenstein.de.* Located in a converted warehouse in Altona, this restaurant attracts a trendy clientele. In the same building are an art-house cinema, a café and a nice tapas bar (flamenco some nights).

⊖⊖⊟ **Rialto** – *Michaelisbrücke 3. ℰ(040) 36 43 42. www.rialto-hamburg.de.* This elegant dining room overlooks the canal from the Alster port. On sunny days, tables spill out onto the deck, and there is live music some nights. If Rialto is full, try one of the other terrace restaurants surrounding the square.

⊖⊖⊟ **VLET** – *Am Sandtorkai 23/24. ℰ(040) 334 75 37 50. www.vlet.de. Closed Sat lunch, Sun.* This brick warehouse in the Speicherstadt has been nicely renovated, and provides a suitable setting for expertly prepared regional cuisine. To get there, cross the Kibbelstegbrücke bridge.

⊖⊖⊟ **Warsteiner Elbspeicher** – *Große Elbstraße 39. ℰ(040) 38 22 42. www.warsteiner-elbspeicher.de.* Ingeniously converted from an old riverside warehouse, this friendly bi-level establishment is divided into a casual downstairs bistro and a rustic restaurant upstairs where meals come with splendid harbour views. Overall, a fine place for fresh fish and typical Hanseatic dishes.

⊖⊖⊟⊟ **Le Canard Nouveau** – *Elbchaussee 139, Hamburg-Altona. ℰ(040) 88 12 95 31. www.lecanard-hamburg.de. Closed Sun–Mon.*

Alex im Alsterpavillon

© ALEX

Reservation required. New culinary heights are reached in this French restaurant in an elegant white building overlooking the Elbe. Sit in the modern and bright dining room or grab a seat on the plank terrace for sweeping views of the port's container terminal. Gourmets on a budget should come for the affordable lunches.

⊖⊖⊜⊜ **Louis C. Jacob** – *Elbchaussee 401-403, Hamburg-Nienstedten. ☎(040) 82 25 50. www.hotel-jacob.de. Closed Wed lunch, Mon–Tue. Reservation recommended.* Fine dining does not get much more refined than at this elegant hotel-restaurant overlooking the Elbe. The delicious French cuisine is a delight. In fine weather, the most coveted tables are on the terrace with its lime trees; the scene was immortalised in a painting by Max Liebermann in 1902.

TAKING A BREAK

Destille – *Steintorplatz 1 (enter from Brockesstraße). ☎(040) 280 33 54. www.destilleimmuseum.de. Open Tue–Sun 11am–5pm. Free admission if visiting the museum, otherwise 2€.* On the first floor of the Museum of Arts and Crafts, this little self-service café is an excellent lunch stop, and not only for museum goers. Restful views of the leafy courtyard are gratis.

NIGHTLIFE
USEFUL TIPS

Hamburg's nightlife has been synonymous with St. Pauli since time immemorial. In addition to its established temples of eroticism, the area around the Reeperbahn and Große Freiheit has become a rather trendy spot of late with more than 400 restaurants squeezing into these quarters.

The inner centre, too, between the Gänsemarkt and Millerntor (especially around Großneumarkt) offers plenty of opportunities to eat and drink.

The young and alternative crowd congregates in the Schanzenviertel, especially around Susannenstraße and Schulterblatt, and in the Altona district around Spritzenplatz.

Here are some places to enjoy an afternoon or evening in Hamburg:

Alex im Alsterpavillon – *Jungfernstieg 54. ☎(040) 350 1870. www.alexgastro.de.* People of all ages gather throughout the day for a drink or a light meal on this great waterfront terrace.

Amphore – *Hafenstraße 140 (follows the Elbe towards the west from Landungsbrücken). ☎(040) 31 79 38 80. www.cafe-amphore.de.* This friendly little café offers a lovely harbour view from the terrace above the old blockhouses. Breakfast is served until 3pm.

Christiansen's Fine Drinks & Cocktails – *Pinnasberg 60 (in St. Pauli, near the Fischmarkt). ℰ(040) 317 28 63. www.christiansens.de. Closed Sun.* Dedicated drinkers flock to this bar with its array of 250 cocktails, 160 brands of rum and 150 varieties of whisky on offer.

Cotton Club – *Alter Steinweg 10. ℰ(040) 34 38 78. www.cotton-club.org.* Hamburg's jazz institution was founded in 1959, renamed the "Cotton Club" in 1963 and moved to this location in 1971. Performances are stages during most nights.

Grosse Freiheit 36 & Kaiserkeller – *Grosse Freiheit 36. ℰ(040) 31 77 78 10. www.grossefreiheit36.de.* The Beatles rocked the Kaiserkeller back in 1960 and this venue is still going strong.

Laeiszhalle – *Johannes-Brahms-Platz 1. ℰ(040) 357 66 60. www.elbphilharmonie.de.* Until the Elbphilharmonie in HafenCity opens (set for 2017), the neo-Baroque Laeiszhalle (1908) is Hamburg's premier classical music venue.

Staatsoper Hamburg – *Grosse Theaterstraße 25. ℰ(040) 35 68 68. www.hamburgische-staatsoper.de.* One of the world's most renowned opera houses enjoys great popularity and devoted patrons. Seasonal performances often include ballet and contemporary musicals.

SHOPPING
USEFUL TIPS

Department stores and mainstream chain stores line Mönckebergstraße and Spitalerstraße west of the main train station. Deeper pockets are required in the nine exclusive shopping arcades around Jungfernstieg and Neuer Wall, which are the haunts of international designer boutiques and specialty shops. Steer toward the suburb of Eppendorf (Klosterstern to Eppendorfer Markt) to browse through independent boutiques selling trendy fashions, home accessories and gift items.

Harry's Hamburger Hafenbasar – *Sandtorkai 60. ℰ(171) 49 69 169. www. hafenbasar.de. Open Fri–Sun noon-5pm. Admission 4€ (refunded with purchase of 10€ or more).* A jumble of objects

brought back by sailors from the four corners of the world, labyrinthine Harry's has been around for half a century and is really more a museum than a shop. Great for browsing for unique gifts.

Antique dealers – Mainly in the *Quartier Satin* on ABC-Straße and the *Antik-Centre* of the covered arcade at Klosterwall 9–21; the latter has more than 60 stalls selling the best of yesteryear's collectibles.

Flea markets – The best regular flea markets is the Flohschanze Markt in an old slaughterhouse in St. Pauli (every Sat 8am–4pm).

Markets – Hamburg's most famous market, the Fish Market *(www.fischmarkt-hamburg.de)* draws crowds early on Sunday (summer 5am–9.30am, winter 7am–9.30am). A particularly nice farmers' market is held on Monday and Friday around the Eppendorf U-Bahn bridge.

SIGHTSEEING
CITY TOURS

All tours described below depart from the Hauptbahnhof/Kirchenallee exit.

Hop-on-hop-off tours (17.50€) stopping at 11 major landmarks, including St. Michaelskirche and St. Pauli Landungsbrücken, operate Apr–Oct daily every 30min, 9.30am–5pm; Nov–Mar Fri–Sun half-hourly 9.30am–4.30pm, Mon–Thu hourly 10am–4pm. Narrated 2hr 30min city tours depart daily at 10.10am and 2.10pm (22.50€). Details from **Top Tour Hamburg** *(ℰ(040) 641 37 31; www.top-tour-hamburg.de)* or **Hamburger Stadtrundfahrt** *(ℰ(040) 792 89 79; www.die-roten-doppeldecker.de).*

The Hamburg tourist office organises a variety of themed **walking tours** all year round, for instance of the red-light district or in the footsteps of the Beatles. See website for dates and times. www.hamburg-tourism.de.

Lüneburg★★

Lüneburg was quite literally built on salt, a coveted mineral and source of its prosperity since the 10C. The last salt mine closed in 1980, ending a 1 000-year tradition. Lüneburg was spared during World War II, and today is a colourful university town and gateway to the expansive Lüneburg Heath.

SIGHTS

Historisches Rathaus★★ (Historic Town Hall)

Am Markt 1. ☛Guided tours (1hr, in German) Apr–Dec Tue–Sat 11am, 12:30pm, 2:30pm and 4pm, Sun 11am and 2pm; Jan–Mar Tue–Sun 11am and 2pm. Closed Jan 1, Good Friday, Easter, Dec 24–26 & 31. ☜5€. ℘(0800) 220 50 05 04131.

A complex of eight buildings, Lüneburg's municipal headquarters is the largest surviving medieval town hall in northern Germany.

The **Great Council Chamber★★** (*Große Ratsstube*), to the right of the entrance hall, is a Renaissance masterpiece (1566–84). Panelled throughout, it is adorned with intricate wood sculptures carved by Albert von Soest.

The **Fürstensaal** (*Princes' Apartment*) is equally striking. Gothic in style, it has lamps fashioned from stags' antlers and a superbly beamed and painted ceiling.

Marktplatz (Market Square)

Aside from the town hall, other noteworthy buildings framing the market square include the Court of Justice, the former Ducal Palace and the **Heinrich-Heine-Haus**, where the parents of the famous 19C poet lived on the second floor.

Altstadt★ (Old Town)

The houses of the old town are characterised by traditional red-brick architecture and boast steeply stepped gables prevalent throughout northern

▶ **Population:** 72 000

Info: Am Markt, 21335 Lüneburg. ℘(0800) 220 50 05. www.lueneburg.info.

Location: Lüneburg lies about 56.5km/35mi southeast of Hamburg, east of the A7 autobahn (Hannover–Hamburg). Coming from Hamburg, though, the quickest route is via the A255 and A250. The Ilmenau River, a tributary of the Elbe, flows through town.

Parking: Garages are located near the main train station and the Rathaus on Graalwall.

Don't Miss: The Rathaus and the rest of the old town.

Timing: Exploring Lüneburg's charms takes about half a day.

Germany. The nicest ones line a long, narrow square known as **Am Sande★**. Note especially no 1, the 16C **Shwarze Haus** (black house), which was once a brewery and now holds an international chamber of commerce.

At Große Bäckerstraße 10, you'll find the 1598 **Rathsapotheke** (pharmacy), with its fine twisted brick gables.

The Reitende-Diener-Straße is another attractive lane with a double row of identical low houses, each embellished with medallions and curled brick cornices.

St. Johanniskirche (Church of St. John)

Open Mar–Oct Mon–Sat 10am–5pm (Thu until 6pm, Fri until 8pm), Sun 11am–4pm; Nov & Jan–Feb Mon–Fri 11am–5pm (Thu until 6pm, Fri 8pm), Sat–Sun 11am–4pm. Dec daily 11am–6.30pm. Closed Jan–Feb Mon–Wed. ℘(04131) 445 42. www.st-johanniskirche.de.

Am Sande culminates in this hulking 15C church, easily recognised by its leaning steeple. Inside note the high altar with precious sculpted reredos by Heinrich Furnhoff. Its painted panels depict scenes from the lives of St. John the Baptist, St. Cecilia, St. Ursula and St. George (late 15C).

Nikolaikirche (Church of St. Nicholas)

Lüner Straße 15. Open Jan–Mar daily 10am–4pm; Apr–Dec daily 10am–6pm. ℘(04131) 243 0770. www.st-nicolai.eu.
The central nave of this triple-aisled 15C Gothic church soars an impressive 30/90ft high and ends in an intricate star-vaulted ceiling. Have a closer look at the gilded high altar by Hans Bornemann, which depicts 20 carved scenes from the life of Jesus. There is also a bronze baptismal font dating back to 1325. The jaunty church steeple was not added until the 19C.

Wasserviertel★ (Old Port Quarter)

Enjoy a particularly fine view of this district from the bridge across the Ilmenau. On the left you will spot the **Alter Kran** (old boat lift), a crane dating from the 14C and in use until the 19C. Looking upstream, you'll have a good view of the Lüner Mühle, a grand 16C half-timbered mill.

Deutsches Salzmuseum (German Salt Museum)

Open May–Sept Mon–Fri 9am–5pm, Sun 10am–5pm; Oct–Apr daily 10am–5pm. ⊛6€. ℘(04131) 72065 13. www.salzmuseum.de.
Salt has shaped the history of Lüneburg for thousands of years. In the Middle Ages, it supplied a large part of Scandinavia with the precious mineral. Shipments followed the old Salt Road, via Lauenburg, Ratzeburg and Lübeck. Lüneburg's Salt Museum occupies the city's historic salt production plant and was the first in Germany to be installed in a converted industrial site. It traces the history of salt mining in the region and touches on aspects such as extraction technology, the economic importance of salt and the various salt routes.

EXCURSIONS
Kloster Lüne (Lüne Abbey)

◗ 2km/1.2mi northeast via Willy-Brandt-Straße. Am Domänenhof.
◗⚊Abbey visits by guided tour only (75min), Apr–mid-Oct Tue–Sun 10.30am (Sun 11.30am), 2.30pm and 3.30pm. Closed Good Friday. ⊛6€ (8€ with museum). ℘(04131) 523 18. www.kloster-luene.de.
Founded in the 12C as a Benedictine convent, the complex centres on a fountain surrounded by Gothic buildings and a late-Baroque guesthouse. Particularly fine features include the stained-glass windows from the 14C–17C, the frescoed refectory and the muralled nuns' cells. The church boasts a Baroque organ, a Gothic baptismal font and the nuns' choir with a *Lamentation* from the workshop of Lucas Cranach the Elder. The **tapestry museum★** (open Apr–mid-Oct Tue–Sat 10.30am–12.30pm, 2.30pm–5pm, Sun 11.30am–1pm, 2.30pm–5pm; ⊛4€) displays Gothic tapestries and finely worked embroidery.

Bergen-Belsen Memorial Site

◗ 72km/48mi southwest of Lüneburg. Anne-Frank-Platz, 29303 Lohheide. Open Apr–Sept daily 10am–6pm; Oct–Mar 10am–5pm. Closed Jan 1, Dec 24–26 & 31. ℘(05051) 475 90. http://bergen-belsen.stiftung-ng.de.
The **memorial** *(Gedenkstätte)* to the victims of Bergen-Belsen concentration camp was erected in 1946. A recently revamped and award-winning exhibit in a building near the entrance chronicles the history of the camp. Bergen-Belsen started out in 1939 as a POW camp, but was turned into a concentration camp in 1943. Among those incarcerated here was **Anne Frank** whose famous diary is a heart-wrenching personal account of the horrors of the Nazi period. Along with her sister, she died at the camp in 1945 at the age of 15. A tombstone is erected in their honour.
A **monument** (◗⚊45min from the car park) rises beyond the tumulus marking the site of the mass graves. It is a simple obelisk with inscriptions in 13

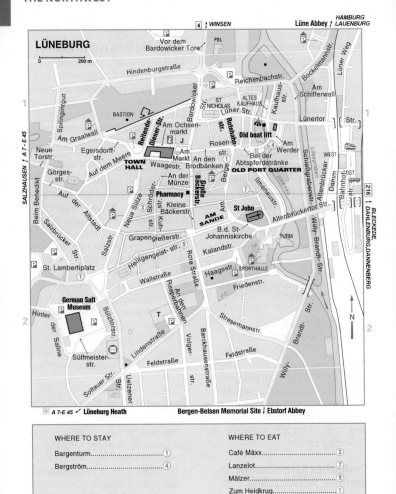

LÜNEBURG

languages honouring the memory of the murdered. From 1945–50, the Allies used the camp to provide shelter and assistance to "displaced persons" (former concentration camp prisoners and slave labourers who had been deported to Germany from all over Europe).

Another section of the exhibit details what happened to the Nazi officers and guards who ran the camp. Arrested by the British Army immediately after its liberation, they were tried before a British military tribunal in Lüneburg in late 1945. Eleven defendants were sentenced to death and 19 received prison sentences.

Kloster Ebstorf (Ebstorf Abbey)

⬤26km/16mi south of Lüneburg, in Ebstorf. ⬤Visit by guided tour (75-90min) only, Apr–Oct Tue–Sun (see website for hours). Closed Good Friday. ⬤4€. ☏(05822) 23 04. www.kloster-ebstorf.de.

The former Benedictine abbey includes the 14C and 15C cloister and the nuns' gallery with its life-size wooden statue of St. Maurice (1300). Don't miss the replica of the **Ebstorfer Weltkarte★**, a circular medieval map of the world with a diametre of 3.57m/11ft; the original was destroyed in 1943.

THE HEATH

In the Middle Ages, the name "Heide" signified the boundary of a village; only later did it come to mean the common heather *(Calluna vulgaris)*, which carpets the ground in August and September. The bell-heather *(Erica tetralix)* blooms in July, if rarely, preferring marshy areas.

The heath is actually a man-made shrubland. Some 5 000 years ago Lüneburg Heath was covered in forest that was eventually uprooted by farmers. To keep the forest at bay, farmers utilised controlled burning, grazed cattle and sheep or lifted the turf with hoes. Only then was the light-hungry heath able to spread.

Flora and Fauna – Juniper *(Juniperus communis)* thrives on the Lüneburg Heath, as well as birch, mountain ash, pine and oak, gorse, broom, silver grass, crowberries, bilberries and cranberries.

Moorland sheep serve as living mowers. They maintain the heather at a height of 20cm/7.8in. Both genders have horns; those of the male are spectacularly coiled. There were 1 million moorland sheep on Lüneburg Heath at the turn of the 19C, when it was much larger, but only a few thousand are left today.

Bees are also an intrinsic feature of the heath. They frequently come with travelling beekeepers who carry their swarms in baskets called *Lüneburg Bogenstülpern*.

The largest bird on the heath is the nearly extinct blackcock or capercaillie. There are plenty of buzzards, red kites, hobbies and kestrels, with herons and snipes in the lowlands and high moors. Autumn sees flocks of fieldfares.

Boulders – Large and small granite boulders are scattered over Lüneburg Heath. They came from Scandinavia as boulder clay and were left behind when the glaciers of the last Ice Age retreated more than 18 000 years ago.

Lüneburg Heide

© Gerhard Köhler/Fotolia.com

ADDRESSES

🏨 STAY

⊜⊜🛏 Bargenturm – *Vor der Sülze 2.* *📞(04131) 72 90. www.hotel-bargenturm.de.* *40 rooms. Restaurant⊜🛏.* Located close to the pedestrian zone, this property exudes contemporary flair from the lobby to the rooms. The restaurant has a friendly, modern ambience and a small inner courtyard.

⊜⊜🛏 Bergström – *Bei der Lüner Mühle.* *📞(04131) 30 80. www.bergstroem.de.* *131 rooms. ⊡15€. Restaurant⊜⊜🛏.* Hugging a scenic stretch of the Ilmenau river, this hotel has tastefully appointed rooms and is well equipped with modern communication devices. Rooms in the ancient water tower are particularly appealing. The brasserie-style restaurant extends to a winter garden, and there is a wine bar as well.

🍴/EAT

⊜ Mälzer Brauhaus – *Heiligengeiststraße 43. 📞(04131) 477 77. www.maelzerbrauhaus.de.* Match your mood to the differently decorated floors of this traditional pub. House specialities on the extensive menu include *Flammkuche* (French pizza), and baked potatoes, best washed down with the tasty homemade brew.

⊜ Café Mäxx – *Schröderstraße 6. 📞(04131) 73 25 05. www.cafe-maexx.com.* Take a trip back to the 1970s in this café decorated with psychedelic wallpaper. Small and big appetites should find something to suit their taste on the varied menu. Good choice of cocktails, shakes and homemade pastries. The terrace has blankets to ward off the chill.

⊜ Lanzelot – *Wandfärberstraße 7. 📞(04131) 40 48 13. www.lanzelot-lueneburg.de.* This cosy, dark-wood-panelled restaurant-bar is the place to stop for pasta, pizza, fish and meat dishes. Vegetarians will also feel well catered for, while the cash-strapped invade for the budget-priced tapas buffet on Mondays and Tuesdays. In summer, the shaded beer garden beckons.

⊜⊜🛏 Zum Heidkrug – *Am Berge 5.* *📞(04131) 241 60. www.zumheidkrug.de.* *Closed 1 week Jan, 1 week Apr, 2 weeks in summer and 2 weeks in fall, Sun, Mon, Tue lunch.* This brick Gothic building was built in the 15C and has been a restaurant since the 19C. The current incarnation is a rustic yet elegant place whose classic dishes show off the chef's considerable talent. The less expensive lunch specials are very popular. A few country-style rooms are available too.

👪 FOR KIDS

Vogelpark Walsrode – *Am Vogelpark, 29664 Walsrode. Open mid-Mar–Oct daily 10am (closing times vary and are posted daily in the park). 19€. 📞(05161) 604 40. www.weltvogelpark.de.* Almost 4 000 feathered creatures live in this family-friendly **bird park**, most of them in their natural habitat and at semi-liberty. Help feed playful penguins, walk through an exotic tropical jungle, visit owls in an abandoned castle, and watch a bird show.

Wildpark Lüneburger Heide – *Am Wildpark, 21271 Nindorf-Hanstedt. Open Mar–Oct daily 8am–7pm (ticket office closes 5.30pm); Nov–Feb daily 9am–4.30pm (ticket office closes 3.30pm). 10€ (child 8€). 📞(04184) 893 90. www.wild-park.de.* The whole family can enjoy a day at this wildlife park, where animals include otters, buffalo, bears and birds of prey. Kids can also let off steam at the adventure and water playgrounds and get close to their favourite creatures in the petting zoo. From April to October big crowds turn out for the bird of prey shows.

Heidepark Soltau – *Heide Park 1, 29614 Soltau. Open late Mar–early Nov daily 10am–5pm (Jul–Aug until 6pm). 32€ (12yrs and up), 26€ (4–11yrs), under-4 free. Online tickets are about 25 percent cheaper. 📞(01805) 91 91 01. www.heide-park.de.* This small amusement park has dozens of rides and attractions centred on themes such as Little America. Thrills include rollercoasters, bird and dolphin shows and water-log rides.

Husum

The birthplace of writer Theodor Storm (1817–1888) has survived the battering of the North Sea since time immemorial. Today this "grey city on the sea", as Storm described it, is the commercial hub of North Friesland as well as a modern holiday region with abundant cultural offerings.

▶ **Population:** 22 000
- **Info:** Großstraße 27, 25813 Husum. ℰ(04841) 898 70. www.husum-tourismus.de.
▷ **Location:** In the far northwestern corner of Germany, close to the Danish border, Husum is linked to the A7 autobahn via the B201 and B202.
- **Don't Miss:** The North Sea Museum.
- **Timing:** Husum can be easily covered in a day.

SIGHTS

Nordseemuseum Husum★ (North Sea Museum)

Herzog-Adolf-Straße 25. Open Apr–Oct daily 10am–5pm; Nov–Mar daily 11am–5pm. Closed Jan 1, Dec 24 & 31. 5€ (child 2€). ℰ(04841) 25 45. www.museumsverbund-nordfriesland. de/nordseemuseum.

This family-friendly museum illuminates various aspects of the North Sea region's cultural history. The exhibits explore the variety of Germany's coastal landscapes as well as the flow of daily life among its inhabitants. The catastrophic consequences of floods are addressed, as are the construction of dikes and the reclamation of land by polders.

Storm-Haus

Wasserreihe 31. Open Apr–Oct Tue–Fri 10am–5pm, Sat 11am–5pm, Sun & Mon 2pm–5pm. 3.50€. ℰ(04841) 803 86 30. www.storm-gesellschaft.de.

Novelist and poet Theodor Storm lived in this typical 1730 merchant's house from 1866 to 1880. Its rooms provide a look at life in the Biedermeier age and include the writer's living room and the study where he penned more than 20 of his novellas. Paintings and documents from the writer's estate are also on view.

Schloss vor Husum (Castle at Husum)

König-Friedrich V.-Allee. Open Mar–Oct Tue–Sun 11am–5pm; Nov–Feb Sat–Sun 11am–5pm. Closed Jan 1, Dec 24–25 & 31. 5€. ℰ(04841) 897 31 30. www.museumsverbund-nordfriesland. de/schloss-vor-husum.

This 16C castle of Duke Adolf von Schleswig-Holstein-Gottdorf was renovated in the Baroque style in the 18C. It now hosts concerts, lectures and art exhibits. The central tract is a museum where you can see the palace's chapel, banquet hall and residential quarters.

EXCURSIONS

Eidersperrwerk★ (Eider Dam)

▷ 35km/21.7mi south.

Skirting a bird sanctuary, the road arrives at the mouth of the River Eider, closed off by a **dam** built between 1967 and 1972. The five colossal steel sluice gates close when the coast is threatened by high seas.

Nolde-Museum★ at Seebüll

▷ 56km/34.7mi north. Open Mar–Nov daily 10am–6pm. 8€. (04664) 98 39 30. www.nolde-stiftung.de.

In 1927, Expressionist painter **Emil Nolde** (born Emil Nansen, 1867–1956), built his private residence in the solitude of the Seebüll marshes based on his own designs. The stark, angular Bauhaus-style structure presents changing exhibits showing all of Nolde's major creative phases. Works with a religious theme are displayed in his former studio. You can also see his living quarters.

North Frisian Islands★

Nordfriesische Inseln

This group of beautiful and windswept islands forms part of the Schleswig-Holsteinisches Wattenmeer (Wadden Sea) National Park, which was created in 1985. The islands' fragile environment, including tall dunes, is protected from the ravages of the North Sea by dikes and artificial banks.

Info: Zingel 5, 25813 Husum. (04841) 897 50. www.nordseetourismus.de.

Location: The North Frisian Islands lie off the west coast of Schleswig-Holstein, in the North Sea, close to Denmark.

Don't Miss: Amrum, mudflat hikes, the megalithic graves of Denghoog near Keitum.

Timing: Spend at least a day relaxing on these islands.

Kids: Island cruising and exploration.

INSEL SYLT★★

Keitumer Landstraße 10 B, 25980 Westerland. (04651) 6026. www.sylt-tourismus.de.

The largest of the Northern Frisian Islands (100sq km/39sq mi), Sylt is a long, narrow island comprising a patchwork of varied landscapes: sandy beaches and dunes, marshes and mudflats, fields and meadows and open heathland.

Its spas and resorts, largely unspoilt nature and North Sea swimming make it popular with holidaymakers. The west coast features a long stretch of fine sandy beach running for miles. A historic attraction is the primeval burial mounds.

Westerland★

Sylt's largest resort is also one of the most popular on the North Sea Coast and is often flooded with visitors. It has the best infrastructure on the island and offers everything from window-shopping (Strandstraße and Friedrichstraße) and gallery-hopping to challenging Lady Luck in the Art Nouveau casino. In foul weather, the boat-shaped water park and health spa called **Sylter Welle** beckon.

On sunny days, the main attraction is of course the 7km/4.3mi-long sandy beach. It is hemmed in by a paved beachfront promenade, where people come to see and be seen or to listen to a concert in the domed shell. On and

Beach near Ratum, Sylt Island

© Sabine Lubenow/Look/Photononstop

GETTING THERE

Since 1927 **Sylt** has been connected to the mainland via rail across the Hindenburgdamm causeway. Cars must be loaded onto the Sylt Shuttle in Niebüll *(30min; car with passengers 90€ round trip; ℘(01806) 22 83 83; www.syltshuttle.de)*.

Car ferries leave from Havneby on the Danish island of Rømø – accessible by road *(7 ferries a day, up to 9 daily Jul–early Sept; 40min; 78€ round-trip per vehicle including passengers, 7.50–10.20€ round trip for pedestrians; ℘(0461) 864 601; www.sylt-faehre.de)*.

Ferries *(℘04667 9 40 30; www.faehre. de)* for **Föhr** and **Amrum** depart from Dagebüll, a small village and harbour on the northwesternmost point of Schleswig-Holstein. Dagebüll–Föhr up to 14 times daily *(13.60€; 50min)*; Dagebüll–Amrum up to 8 times daily *(19.30€; 90min, 2hr via Föhr)*. For **Amrun**, ferries also leave from Schlüttsiel (7km/4.3mi south of Dagebüll) once daily mid-Apr–late Oct *(20.40€; 2hrs 45min)*.

For **Pellworm**, embark from Nordstrand (17km/10.5mi west of Husum). For the **Halligen**, catch a ferry from Husum or Nordstrand.

off the beach there is plenty of action in bars, bistros and nightclubs.

Keitum

This idyllic village with its craft shops presents the most relaxed, unpretentious face of Sylt. Keitum's traditional thatched Frisian houses hidden among trees and lilacs, the embankments of dog roses, and cliffs overlooking the sea and mudflats earn it the nickname "the green heart".

Kampen

This resort is popular with the German jet-set (models, football players, aristocrats, etc.) and international VIPs. It brims with fancy boutiques, while impeccably shiny BMWs and Mercedes patrol the streets.

The main "catwalk" is the Stroenwai, also known as Whiskey Alley. South of town, the **Rotes Kliff** towers above the sea. Embracing it is the **Uwe Dune**, at 52.5m/172ft the highest on Sylt. There are great **views★** over Sylt and neighbouring islands from the top.

Wenningstedt

In Wenningstedt-Braderup, the **Denghoog★** is a 4 000-year-old megalithic grave open to the public. **Morsum-Kliff**, featuring 10 million years of geological history, is an interesting geological feature.

List

Around the port of **List**, where ferries from Rømø drop off Danish day-trippers, the **Wanderdünen** are moving dunes extending 1 000m/3 280ft long and 30m/98.4ft high.

FÖHR

Föhr is a peaceful island blessed with a mild climate. The landscape is largely marshland, dotted with pretty villages (including Nieblum, Süderende and Oldsum). The beaches lie in the south; on the northern end is a windswept forest rich with birdlife.

The port of **Wyk** in the southeast is crisscrossed by well-tended lanes perfect for exploring at leisure. Those interested in local nature, history and culture should drop by the **Friesen-Museum** (open Jul–Aug daily 10am–5pm; mid-Mar–Oct Tue–Sun 10am–5pm; Nov–mid-Mar Tue–Sun 2pm–5pm; closed Dec 24–25 & 31; 4.80€; ℘(04681) 25 71; www. friesen-museum.de).

Dunsum is the departure point for a walk across the mudflats to Amrum.

AMRUM

The smallest of the North Frisian islands, Amrum boasts a west coast that is home to sand dunes, heaths, woods, farmland and mudflats that provide a rich habitat for seabirds, making them a paradise for birdwatchers. Its biggest natural asset is the **Kniepsand**, a gloriously white, fine 12km/7.4mi-long beach. From the **lighthouse** in **Wittdün**, enjoy sweeping views as far as **Sylt**.

The village of **Nebel** grew up around the medieval Church of **St. Clemens** in the 16C. The town also features the **Öömrang-Hüs**, a 19C sea captain's house. The far north of the island is a bird sanctuary and departure point for guided walks across the mudflats to Föhr.

HALLIGEN★

These tiny islands are all that remain of mainland marshes once part of the coastal region. In 1600 there were more than 25 recorded islets, but all save 10 of them have since been swallowed up by the fierce sea. Most of the Halligen are unprotected by sea dikes, resulting in temporary island submersions up to 50 times a year. At these times only a few reed-thatched houses perched on artificial mounds (terps) stay above the water. The prettiest Hallig is **Hooge**, but **Langeneß**, the largest with 18 mounds, is popular also, and Gröde also gets a fair number of visitors, most of them day-trippers. Various shipping companies offer boat trips to the Halligen.

PELLWORM

Pellworm lies below sea level and would be inundated were it not protected by a 25km/15.5mi-long and 8m/26.2ft-high dike. Its main feature is the ruined tower of the 11C–12C **Alte Kirche St. Salvator** church.

The **Friedhof der Heimatlosen** is a nearby cemetery where the bodies of strangers washed up on the island's shores are buried.

NORDSTRAND

Formed of reclaimed farmland (polders) and villages on *terps*, this marshy island is linked to the mainland by a 4km/2.5mi causeway. The main town is charming Süden, where artisans have settled. The north island is a bird refuge.

ADDRESSES

🏨 STAY

🍴🛏 **Ekke Nekkepenn** – *Waasterstigh 19, Nebel, Amrum.* ℘*(04682) 945 60. www.ekkenekkepenn.de. 8 rooms.* ☐. This charming, petite hotel welcomes guests to prettily decorated rooms. Mornings start with an ample breakfast featuring freshly baked bread served in a cheerful room.

🍴🛏 **Duus-Hotel** – *Hafenstraße 40, Wyk, Föhr.* ℘*(04681) 598 10. www.duus-hotel.de. Closed end Nov–mid-Feb. 20 rooms. Restaurant*🍴🛏. A convenient location and well-kept, contemporary rooms (some with harbour views) are among the assets of this family-run hotel. The restaurant serves regional and international meals.

🍴🛏 **Weiße Düne** – *Achtern Strand 6, Wittdün, Amrum.* ℘*(04682) 94 00 00. www.weisse-duene.de. 13 rooms. Restaurant*🍴🛏. Handsomely decorated rooms and self-catering apartments with modern amenities await at this family-run hotel. Enjoy local food with a rustic bent in the traditional restaurant.

♔/EAT

🍴🛏 **Friesenstube** – *Süderstraße 8, Wyk, Föhr.* ℘*(04681) 24 04. Closed mid-Nov–mid-Feb, Mon.* The Frisian décor, complete with cheerful wall tiles, gives this casual inn a winning ambience. The kitchen is known for its fish dishes.

🍴🛏🛏 **Land- und Golfhotel Villa Witt** – *Alkersumstieg 4, Nieblum, Föhr.* ℘*(04681) 587 70. www.hotel-witt.de. Closed Mon–Wed, lunch. Reservations required.* Regional dishes dominate the menu at this elegant restaurant. Rooms are just as pleasant and a 18-hole golf course is close by as well.

Helgoland★★

Only 1sq km/0.38sq mi in size, the island of Helgoland is a mere blip in the North Sea, but its stark red-sandstone cliff silhouette exudes a timeless mystique. Home to unique flora and fauna, it draws thousands of tourists each year who come in pursuit of solitude, natural beauty and duty-free shopping bargains.

A BIT OF HISTORY

Helgoland was originally part of Denmark, but was ceded by the Danes to Britain in 1814 as part of the post-Napoleonic settlements. In 1890, it changed hands again as a result of the Zanzibar Treaty. This time Germany took possession in exchange for commercial rights in the East African island of Zanzibar. Helgoland was subsequently annexed to Schleswig-Holstein (at that time part of Prussia).

Battered by the sea since time immemorial, tiny Helgoland is home to an aquarium, an ornithological observatory and a marine biology station. Blessed with natural beauty, it attracts leisure travellers eager to engage in **outdoor pursuits** like cliff walks, hiking, swimming, birding, biking and more. Shoppers can look forward to bargains on chocolates, cigarettes and spirits because neither duty nor VAT (currently 19 percent) are charged.

SIGHTS

Lange Anna★ (Long Anna)

Helgoland's most famous natural landmark, this 80m/262.4ft-high bright-red rock column stands guard off its northwestern shore like some petrified sentinel. Nearby, the **Lummenfelsen** is Germany's smallest nature reserve (1.1ha/2.7 acres), which draws countless breeding bird species, most notably Helgoland's signature bird, the *Trottellumme* (common murre).

Düne

About 1km/0.6mi from the main island. Turquoise water lapping at white sandy beaches – no, this is not the Caribbean

- ▶ **Population:** 1 300
- **Info:** Rathaus, Lung Wai 28, 27498 Helgoland. ℘(04725) 20 67 99. www.helgoland.de.
- ◐ **Location:** Helgoland lies about 70km/43mi off the coast of Schleswig-Holstein. It is served by ferry from Cuxhaven, Hamburg and the Frisian Islands.
- ◈ **Don't Miss:** Hiking, swimming and other outdoor pursuits.
- ◕ **Timing:** Helgoland can be visited on a day trip.
- ▲▲ **Kids:** The sea voyage to the island, beaches.

GETTING THERE

Ferries leave from Hamburg, Wedel and Cuxhaven to Helgoland. *Katamaran "Halunder Jet"* departs Hamburg Apr–Oct daily at 9am, calling at Wedel at 9.40am and Cuxhaven 11.30am; return trip 4.30pm, arriving at Cuxhaven around 5.45pm, Wedel around 7.30pm, Hamburg around 8.15pm. ℘(0461) 864 44. www.helgoline.de. Reederei Cassen Eils also offers a ferry service from Cuxhaven to Helgoland: www.helgolandreisen.de.

but a small islet that got separated from the main island during a stormy night on New Year's Eve in 1720.

Today, it is a swimmers' and naturelovers' paradise. The southern beaches are particularly family-friendly, while sealions can be observed lazing in the sand on the northern shore. Düne is also one of the few places in the world where you can find carmine-red firestones. Stone Age people used them as tools but today they are turned into precious jewellery. A ferry from Helgoland serves the islet year-round.

Bremen ★★

Bremen, Germany's oldest maritime city, is famous for Beck's beer and the Town Musicians of the eponymous Brothers Grimm' fairytale, *The Town Musicians of Bremen*. Enjoying trade rights from 965, it has a long and proud history of civic independence, joining the Hanseatic League in 1358 and trading directly with America beginning in 1783. Today, Bremen is a compact, congenial city with a charming old town and bustling nightlife districts.

A BIT OF HISTORY

Germany's second-busiest after Hamburg, the twin **ports** in Bremen and Bremerhaven directly or indirectly employ about a third of the city-state's population. Each year some 5 million containers and 1.4 million vehicles pass through port terminals. River and **port tours** (75min) depart the quay by the **St. Martinikirche**. Up to five departures daily Feb–Oct & Dec. 9.90€. ♿. ℘(0421) 33 89 89. www.hal-oever.de.

WALKING TOUR

OLD BREMEN
Allow 2 hours.
MARKTPLATZ ★★ (MARKET SQUARE)

Bremen's market square is one of the most beautiful in Germany. At its centre is the 5.5m/18ft-high canopied statue of the knight **Roland** (1404), a symbol for freedom and civic autonomy; it is listed as a World Heritage Site. Perhaps even more beloved is Gerhard Marcks' bronze sculpture (1951) on the Town Hall's west side. This pyramid formed by a donkey, dog, cat and cockerel represents the characters from the popular Grimm fairytale, **The Town Musicians of Bremen** (*Bremer Stadtmusikanten*). The **Schütting**, an elegant 16C building, used to house Bremen's Guild of Merchants.

▶ **Population:** 547 500

Info: Am Bahnhofsplatz, 28195 Bremen. ℘(0421) 308 00 10. www.bremen-tourismus.de.

Location: Bremen occupies the southern end of the Weser estuary, while its sea port Bremerhaven lies 59km/37mi downstream.

Parking: Look for garages near the Hauptbahnhof and throughout the inner city, including a large 24hr garage on Pelzerstraße (enter on Knochenhauerstraße).

Don't Miss: Marktplatz, Böttcherstraße, German Emigration Centre.

Kids: Universum Bremen, German Emigration Centre, German Maritime Museum.

Timing: Allow at least one full day to see Bremen and another half day for Bremerhaven.

Rathaus ★ (Town Hall)

Am Markt 21. Visits by guided tour (1hr) only, Mon–Sat 11am, noon, 3pm and 4pm, Sun 11am and noon. No tours during official receptions. 5€. ℘(0421) 30 80 01.
www.bremen-tourism.de.

The original town hall was built in Gothic style in the 15C, shortly after Bremen joined the Hanseatic League. A renovation in Weser Renaissance style in the 17C added its decorative gables and a three-story façade rising above an arcaded gallery. Above, tall windows alternate with statues of Charlemagne and the seven Electors (note that these are copies; the Gothic originals are in the Focke-Museum).

Inside, a splendid spiral **staircase ★★** (*Wendeltreppe*) in carved wood (1620) is worth a closer look. The Bremer Rathauskeller (*entrance on the west side*) serves 650 different German wines.

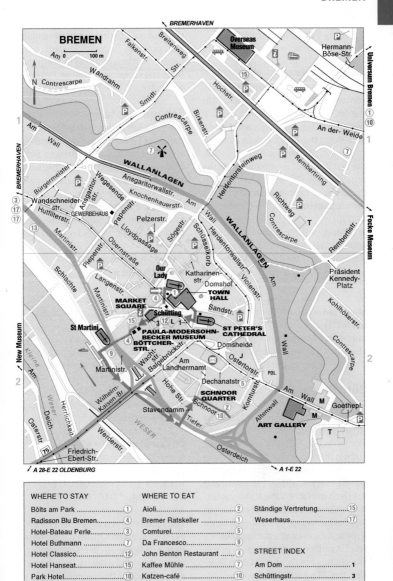

Pfarrkirche Unser Lieben Frauen (Church of Our Lady)

The interior of this 13C hall-church, bare of decoration except for the 1709 chancel, is relieved by rounded ogive vaulting dating to its construction. The four main stained-glass windows, on biblical themes, were executed between 1966 and 1979.

The church's simple **crypt** dates from the preceding church (St. Veit), whose origins have been traced to 1020.

St. Petri-Dom★ (St. Peter's Cathedral)

Sandstraße 10–12. Open year-round Mon–Fri 10am–5pm, Sat 10am–2pm, Sun noon–5pm (until 6pm Mon–Fri

& Sun Jun–Sept). Closed May 1, Oct 3, Dec 24–25 & 31. ☎Tower 1€, Bleikeller 1.40€. ✆(0421) 36 50 40. www.stpetridom.de.

St. Peter's Cathedral (Lutheran) was constructed in the 11C, and updated in the 16C and 19C. Notable religious artworks include a 16C **Virgin and Child**★ and along the organ balustrade, 16C carvings of Charlemagne and Willehad, the first Bishop of Bremen. Beneath the organ loft, the 11C western crypt houses Romanesque capitals and a magnificent bronze **baptismal font**★★ (Taufbecken, c. 1220).

A separate entrance just south of the main portal leads to the hugely popular – if macabre – **lead cellar** (Bleikeller; open Apr–Oct Wed–Fri 10am–4.45pm, Sun noon–4.45pm; Jul–Aug also open Mon–Tue; Jun–Sept to 5.45pm Wed–Mon; ; ☎1.40€), which contains eight perfectly preserved, centuries-old mummified corpses in open coffins. The church tower can be climbed for birds-eye views of the city.

Böttcherstraße★

Running only 110m/360ft from the Marktplatz to the Weser, this narrow street is an architectural gem commissioned in the 1920s by coffee mogul Ludwig Roselius and designed primarily by architect Bernhard Hoetger. Expressionist in style, with Art Nouveau and Art Deco overtones, the buildings feature whimsical design elements, such as façades buttressed by stone sculptures, a spiral staircase and a golden entrance relief. A carillon made of Meissen porcelain chimes hourly noon to 6pm (Apr–Dec; Jan–Mar noon, 3pm & 6pm).

The buildings house galleries and shops as well as the **Paula-Modersohn-Becker-Museum**★ (Böttcherstraße 6–10; open year-round Tue–Sun 11am–6pm; closed Dec 24 & 31; ☎8€; ✆(0421) 338 82 22; www.pmbm.de). It features paintings, drawings and graphic works by the eponymous modern-art pioneer and member of the Worpswede art colony. Tickets are also good for the **Museum im Roseliushaus** (same hours) in the same building. Here you can tour nine period rooms brimming with precious furniture, carpets, porcelain, paintings by Lucas Cranach the Elder and sculpture by Tilman Riemenschneider.

Schnoorviertel★

The cottages in this quarter, once the homes of fishermen and their families, are all that remains of Old Bremen. Built between the 15C and the 19C, they have all been restored and are used as art galleries, antique shops, restaurants and boutiques that are popular with tourists. After dark, night-owls descend on the quarter's bars and restaurants.

ADDITIONAL SIGHTS
Kunsthalle★ (Art Gallery)

Am Wall 207. Open year-round Tue–Sun 10am–5pm (Tue until 9pm). ☎8€. ♿ ✆(0421) 32 90 80. www.kunsthalle-bremen.de.

This museum features an outstanding collection of several centuries' worth of European art. Key artists include Courbet, Delacroix, Monet, Menzel, Leibl, Beckmann, Rubens, Rembrandt and Tiepolo, to name just a few.

Focke Museum★★

Schwachhauser Heerstraße 240. Open year-round Tue 10am–9pm, Wed–Sun 10am–5pm. Closed Dec 24–25 & 31. ☎6€. ♿ ✆(0421) 699 60 00. www.focke-museum.de.

This regional museum presents 1 200 years of Bremen's history. The **Main House** (Haupthaus) covers major milestones in themed exhibits, then follows a chronological trail culminating with displays about modern Bremen. The prehistoric collections are displayed in a thatched annex, the Eichenhof.

Haus Mittelsbüren, a 16C farmhouse, spotlights Bremen's agricultural and industrial development, while exhibits in the 1803 **Tarnstedt Barn** (Tarnstedter Scheune) focus on various agricultural activities, such as animal husbandry, haymaking and dairy farming.

Also part of the complex, the 18C **Haus Riensberg** is a one-time summer resi-

Marktplatz with Rathaus

© Jonas Ginter / BTZ Bremer Touristik-Zentrale

dence for wealthy Bremen families where decorative arts, Fürstenberg porcelain and European glass art are now on display. Kids gravitate to the 🧒🧑 **Children's Museum** *(Kindermuseum)* with its large toy collection, as well as to **Studio Focke**, where they can engage in hands-on experiments and activities.

Neues Museum Weserburg (New Museum Weserburg)

Teerhof 20. Open Tue–Sun 11am–6pm (Thu until 8pm). Closed Jan 1, Good Friday, Easter Mon, May 1, Whit Mon, Dec 24–25 & 31. ⊛8€. ♿ ✆(0421) 59 83 90. www.weserburg.de.

This is one of the largest museums in Germany dedicated to contemporary art. Housed in old red-brick warehouses on an island in the Weser, the museum boasts several private collections and provides a global overview of the past 40 years in contemporary art.

Universum Bremen★★

Wiener Straße 1a, enter via Schaubox. Open year-round Mon–Fri 9am–6pm, Sat–Sun 10am–6pm; last admission 90min before closing. ⊛16€ (5€ during last 90 minutes before closing). ♿ ✆(0421) 334 60. www.universum-bremen.de.

Science gets a fun and entertaining twist at this state-of-the-art park. Visits

start at the **SchauBox**, a rust-coloured cube containing special exhibits, a restaurant and a multimedia theatre. A bridge leads to the **Science Centre**, housed in a silvery building shaped like a closed clam. Inside are 250 experiment and interactive stations divided into three themes: Earth, Humanity and the Cosmos. You can take a virtual journey into space, experience an earthquake or dive 2km/1.2mi below the sea. The outdoor **EntdeckerPark** (Explorer Park) counts a climbing wall and a water playground among its attractions. Skip mornings when school groups invade.

Überseemuseum Bremen★★ (Overseas Museum)

Bahnhofsplatz 13. Open year-round Tue–Fri 9am–6pm, Sat–Sun 10am–6pm. Closed Jan 1, Easter Mon, May 1,

Coffee Bean City

Bremen's close links with coffee date back over three centuries. The first-ever coffeehouse in German-speaking countries was built here in 1673, before those in Vienna and Hamburg. Half of all the cups of coffee drunk in Germany are brewed from beans imported via the port at Bremen.

Whit Mon, Dec 24–25 & 31. ⊛6.50€.
&, ℘(0421)16 03 81 01.
www.uebersee-museum.de.
History, ethnology, culture and trade combine in an exciting journey of discovery back in time and around the world. Learn about colonial trading, admire exotic artefacts from the South Seas or inspect shiny Samurai armour.

EXCURSION
Bremerhaven
◗ 58km/36mi north.

The town's maritime history is given its due at the ♣♣**German Maritime Museum★** (Deutsches Schifffahrtsmuseum; Hans-Scharoun-Platz 1; open Mar–Oct daily 10am–6pm; closed Mon Nov–Apr, Dec 24–25 & 31; ⊛6€; &; ℘(0471) 48 20 70; www.dsm.museum), whose 500 historic boats could keep salty types busy for hours.

Bremerhaven's main draw is the **German Emigration Cente★★★** (Deutsches Auswandererhaus; Columbusstraße 65; open Apr–Oct daily 10am–6pm; Nov–Feb daily 10am–5pm; ⊛12.60€; &; ℘0471 90 22 00; www.dah-bremerhaven.de). This vast centre tells the story of the European emigrants who traded poverty and persecution for hopes of a better life in the New World. Around 7 million embarked from this very spot in Bremerhaven between 1830 and 1974. A tour re-creates every phase of the emigration process, from the quayside farewell to conditions aboard the vessel to the arrival at Ellis Island. Especially moving is the **Gallery of the 7 Millions** that lets you explore the biographies of individuals and learn what prompted them to leave their homelands.

ADDRESSES

🏠STAY

⊜⊜ **Bölts am Park** – *Slevogtstraße 23. ℘(0421) 34 61 10. www.hotel-boelts.de. 15 rooms.* Quiet and family-run, this classic Bremen townhouse offers well-tended rooms and a breakfast nook overlooking the small garden.

⊜⊜ **Hotel Buthmann** – *Löningstraße 29. ℘(0421) 223 80 57. www.hotel-buthmann.de. 9 rooms. ⊑7.50€.* This little inn within walking distance of the train station and the old town has clean and spacious, if fairly non-descript, rooms.

⊜⊜ **Hotel Classico** – *Hinter dem Schütting 1A. ℘(0421) 24 40 08 67. www.hotel-classico-bremen.de. 12 rooms. ⊑6.50€.* This mini-boutique hotel overlooks the market. The charming rooms have evocative names such as "Moulin Rouge" and "Alexander the Great". The café on the ground floor serves homemade pastries.

⊜⊜ **Hotel Hanseat** –*Bahnhofsplatz 8 ℘(0421)146 88. www.hotel-hanseat.com. 33 rooms. ⊑.* Sitting opposite the train station, this hotel has clean and functional rooms. Those facing the courtyard are quieter. Friendly service and hearty breakfast.

⊜⊜⊜ **Hotel-Bateau Perle** – *An der Schlachte 103a. ℘(0421) 33 65 98 50. www.hotelschiff-perle-bremen.de. 2 rooms. ⊑.* For a unique lodging option, book a room aboard this charming little boat moored on the Weser River. Reservations essential. Or contact Hotel Stadt Bremen (*Heinkenstrasse 3–5; ℘(0421) 94 94 10*).

⊜⊜⊜ **Park Hotel** – *Im Bürgerpark. ℘(0421) 340 80. www.hotel-bremen. dorint.com. 175 rooms. ⊑25€. Restaurant*⊜⊜⊜. A sense of luxury embraces you the moment you enter the domed lobby of this elegant manor house right by a little lake within the park. Facilities include a vast spa area and two restaurants.

⊜⊜⊜ **Radisson Blu Hotel Bremen** – *Böttcherstraße 2. ℘(0421) 369 60. www.radissonblu.com. 235 rooms. ⊑12€.* This high-end hotel wraps around a central atrium linked to the Atlantis House on Böttcherstraße.

⊜⊜⊜⊜ **ÜberFluss Hotel** – *Langenstraße 72. ℘(0421) 32 28 60. www.hotel-ueberfluss.de. 51 rooms. ⊑12.50€.* This designer hotel overlooking the Weser River welcomes guests with sophisticated décor, precious woods, beautiful lighting and plenty of attention to detail.

♥/EAT

⊖ Aioli – *Schnoor 3-4. ℘(0421) 32 38 39. www.aioli-bremen.de. Closed Mon lunch.* Warm and welcoming, this tapas bar in the Schnoor district also serves more substantial fish and meat dishes.

⊖ Kaffee Mühle – *Am Wall 212. ℘(0421) 144 66. www.muehle-bremen.de.* This charming restaurant in Bremen's only remaining mill is the place to go for budget lunches, hot drinks and a big Sunday brunch buffet. The staff is generous with smiles.

⊖ Paulaner's – *Schlachte 30. ℘(0421) 169 06 91. www.paulaners.de.* At this pleasant, riverside Bavarian-style beer hall and beer garden you will find efficient, friendly service and a long menu that mixes northern and southern German specialities.

⊖ Ristorante da Francesco – *Martinistraße 12. ℘(0421) 244 26 03. Closed Mon.* On sunny days it's hard to land a table on the lovely riverside terrace of this popular pizza restaurant.

⊖ Ständige Vertretung – *Böttcherstraße 3–5. ℘(0421) 32 09 95. www.staev.de.* The walls of this popular brewery are lined with photographs depicting the history of Germany before reunification. It's the place to come for traditional German cuisine and seafood at reasonable prices.

⊖ Weser Haus – *Hinter der Mauer 5. ℘(0421) 246 390 00. www.weserhaus-bremen.de.* Since this café doubles as a TV studio you may well find yourself included in a programme while sipping your cappuccino. In summer, the large shaded riverside terrace beckons.

⊖⊖ Bremer Ratskeller – *Am Markt. ℘(0421) 32 16 76 . www.ratskeller-bremen.de.* This excellent restaurant sits right below the city hall. For extra privacy, choose a comfortable booth lining the main hall. The excellent wine list includes only German wines (about 600 different bottles).

⊖⊖ Comturei – *Ostertorstraße 30/32. ℘(0421) 32 50 50. www.restaurant-comturei-bremen.de.* Traditional cuisine and fresh fish and crab are on the menu at this rustic and cosy restaurant housed in a 13C vaulted cellar.

⊖⊖ John Benton Restaurant – *Am Markt 1. ℘(0421) 32 30 33. www. johnbenton-bremen.de.* Delicious cuts of aged steak are the main draw at this bi-level restaurant whose terrace offers beautiful cathedral views.

⊖⊖ Katzen-Café – *Schnoor 38. ℘(0421) 32 66 21. www.katzen-cafe.de.* For warm and attentive service, point the compass to this terraced restaurant with cheerful red gingham tablecloths and a menu that hopscotches from schnitzel to spaghetti, steak to coq au vin.

TAKING A BREAK

F. L. Bodes – *Bischofsnadel 1–2 (alleyway leading from Wallanlagen to Domshof). ℘(0421) 32 41 44. www.bodes.de. Closed Sun, Mon.* This fish shop and snack bar is a mere stone's throw from the town centre. Try seafood and fish à la carte, choose from the blackboard menus or make your selection directly from the stalls. Queues are longest at lunchtime.

Konditorei Knigge – *Sögestraße 42–44. ℘(0421) 137 13. www.knigge-shop.de.* Bremen's classic café is the place to try such local specialities as the "Bremer Klaben", a hearty fruitcake.

NIGHTLIFE

Useful tip – Cafés, bars, restaurants and shops cluster in the historic Schnoor district, south of the cathedral. The riverside Schlachte promenade, on the right river bank, is chock-full of trendy restaurants and bars, many with river terraces.

Pannekoekschip Admiral Nelson – *Schlachte Anleger 1. ℘(0421) 3 64 99 84. www.admiral-nelson.de.* Ahoy there. Friendly "pirates" serve sweet or savoury pancakes on this three-masted ship.

SHOPPING

The elegant shopping arcades of **Lloydpassage**, **Domshof Passage** and **Katharinen-Viertel** in the heart of town make for a fun browse. Independent boutiques are located in the historic **Schnoor district** and along **Böttcherstraße**.

Oldenburg

Steeped in tradition, this lively university city is the cultural and economic hub of the region. Seat of government for the Weser-Ems region, Oldenburg is becoming an increasingly popular commercial centre.

SIGHTS
Old Town
The old city embraces Germany's first pedestrian zone and buildings from five centuries, generous parkland and the ancient ramparts.

Landesmuseum für Kunst und Kulturgeschichte (State Museum of Art and Cultural History)
Open year-round Tue–Sun 10am–6pm. Closed Jan 1, Good Friday, Easter Sun, May 1, Pentecost, Dec 24–25 & 31. 6€. &. ℘(0441) 220 73 00. www.landesmuseum-oldenburg. niedersachsen.de.
The collections of the State Museum of Art and Cultural History are spread across three buildings: the Oldenburg Palace, the Augusteum and the Prince's Palace.

- **Population:** 158 000
- **Info:** Schloßplatz 16, 26122 Oldenburg. ℘(0441) 36 16 13 66. www.oldenburg-tourist.de.
- **Location:** Oldenburg lies about 70km/43.5mi west of the Dutch border. Its river port is linked to the Weser and the North Sea by the Hunte, and to the Benelux countries by a coastal canal *(Küstenkanal)*.
- **Parking:** You'll find parking on the Schlossplatz and near the main train station on Willy Brandt-Platz.
- **Don't Miss:** The landscaped castle park.
- **Timing:** Allow half a day to see the main sights of Oldenburg.

Oldenburger Schloss (Oldenburg Palace)
Schlossplatz 1.
Oldenburg's palace was originally built in Renaissance style for Count Anton Günther (1583–1667), but embellished with Baroque flourishes in the 17C. It

Oldenburger Schloss

© fotobeam/Fotolia.com

served as the residence of the grand dukes of Oldenburg until the end of World War I.

Today, it is an extraordinary museum whose permanent exhibit "The Cultural History of an Historical Landscape" shows the variety and cultural heritage of the former grand duchy from the Middle Ages to the 20C. Exhibits are displayed on three floors in lavish rooms that reflect the tastes and wealth of the grand dukes. Highlights include the "Homer Room" and the cycle of 40 miniature idyllic scenes created by court painter Johann Heinrich Tischbein (1751–1829), who is also known as "Goethe-Tischbein" because of his special friendship with the famous poet.

Augusteum
Elisabethstraße 1.
The grand ducal collection of paintings makes a perfect fit for this 19C Italian Renaissance-style edifice. The emphasis is on Italian and Dutch masters from the 16C to the 18C and on 18C–19C paintings by other Europeans. On the ground floor are changing exhibits about the history of painting and contemporary art.

Prinzenpalais
(Prince's Palace)
Damm 1.
This townhouse is filled with two floors of art from the 19C and 20C, starting with the Romantic period. Of particular interest are works by German Impressionists as well as by members of *Die Brücke* (The Bridge) artists' group. There is also a fine selection of canvases by Franz Radziwill (1895–1955), a leading member of the Magic Realists (a style related to Surrealism) that developed in the 1920s.

Stadtmuseum★
Am Stadtmuseum 4–8. Open year-round Tue–Sun 10am–6pm. Closed May 1, Dec 24–25 & 31; ᨑ3€. ᠖ ℘(0441) 235 28 86. www.stadtmuseum-oldenburg.de.
Of interest are rooms from the villas of Francksen (1877), Jürgens and Ballin, with paintings, furnishings and décor dating from the 17C to the early 20C.

There are also departments on local history and an antiques collection.
Next door, the **Horst-Janssen-Museum** (open year-round Tue–Sun 10am–6pm; closed May 1, Dec 24–25 & 31; ᨑ6€; ᠖; ℘(0441) 235 28 91; www.horst-janssen-museum.de) is dedicated to the illustrator and graphic artist (1929–1995) who was born and is buried in Oldenburg.

Schlossgarten★
(Castle Park)
A mild coastal climate favours the growth of magnificent trees and shrubs in this landscaped garden. A nice view of the Lambertikirche unfolds from the weeping willows on the lakeshore.

Landesmuseum Natur und Mensch Oldenburg
(State Museum of Natural and Human History)
Damm 38–44. Open year-round Tue–Fri 9am–5pm, Sat–Sun 10am–6pm. Closed Jan 1, Good Friday, Easter, May 1, Pentecost, Dec 24–25 & 31. ᨑ4€. ᠖ ℘(0441) 924 43 00. www.naturundmensch.de.
These nature exhibits are focused on the northwest region of Germany with its varied landscapes and traces of pre- and early historic settlements. Natural, archaeological and cultural aspects are presented. A huge block of peat, in which ancient bodies were found buried, always attracts attention.

EXCURSION
Museumsdorf Cloppenburg★
◗ 31km/19mi south. Open Mar–Oct daily 9am–6pm; Nov–Feb 9am–4.30pm. Closed Dec 24 & 31. ᨑ7€. ᠖ ℘(04471) 948 40. www.museumsdorf.de.
In an area of about 20ha/49 acres, 53 historic rural buildings from the 15C to the 19C have been moved here and rebuilt around a lake and a church. Most of the buildings come from the region between the rivers Weser and Ems. Large farmsteads, mills and peasants' and tenants' houses illustrate various aspects of the history of Lower Saxony.

East Frisian Islands ★

Ostfriesische Inseln

The East Frisian Islands are part of the Wattenmeer (Wadden Sea) National Park, created in 1986. Due to the prevailing northwesterly tides and winds, the East Frisians are drifting ever further southeast. The northern and eastern coasts of these islands are fringed by sandy beaches dotted with wicker-hooded deck chairs and windbreaks in summer. For visitors the main appeal lies in the island's remoteness, tranquillity and natural splendour conducive to outdoor explorations.

Info: Ledastraße 10, 26789 Leer. ℘(0491) 91 96 96 70. www.ostfriesland.de.

Location: The seven inhabited Eastern Frisian islands lie between the Ems and the Weser deltas off the North Sea Coast of Germany. They are served by ferries whose timetables depend on the tides.

Don't Miss: Quiet exploration of these islands. Take your time.

Timing: Allow 30min–2hrs for the ferry service, depending on the island.

Kids: North Sea cruises and island exploration.

BORKUM

Ferries depart from Emden. 2hrs 10min. ⌖36.20€ round trip. AG EMS: ℘(01805) 18 01 82, www.ag-ems.de.
The largest of the Eastern Frisians boasts an impressive beach promenade and good views of the mainland and a seal bank from the 60m/196.8ft **Neuer Leuchtturm**, a lighthouse from 1879 *(315 steps)*.

JUIST

Ferries depart from Norddeich. 1hr 30min. ⌖20.35–21.25€ same-day return. Reederei Frisia: ℘(04931) 98 70, www.reederei-frisia.de.

Ferry Routes

Emden–Borkum
Norddeich–Juist
Norddeich–Norderney
Neßmersiel–Baltrum
Bensersiel–Langeoog
Neuharlingersiel–Spiekeroog
Harlesiel–Wangerooge

This (17km/10.5mi long) island is home to an interesting **Küstenmuseum** *(Coastal Museum)* in the attractive village of Loog. It documents local coastal

Juist Island

©Martin Sach/istockphoto.com

The Local Brew

Tea-drinking is a way of life in the East Frisian Islands, whose inhabitants consume 14 times more tea per capita than people in the rest of Germany. The beverage was introduced to the region by the Dutch c. 1670 and soon caught on. Frederick the Great attempted to ban tea in 1777, but was forced to reconsider when so many disgruntled people left the region. Even during World War II the East Frisians were allocated a more generous tea ration than others.

East Frisian "tea ceremonies" are full of ritual. First warm the teapot. Then pour boiling water onto the tea leaves in the pot and leave to brew for five minutes. Place a piece of white sugar crystal into a porcelain cup and pour on the strong, hot tea, which crackles pleasantly as it hits the sugar. Finally, add a splash of cream over the back of a special curved spoon made for this purpose. Stirring the tea, however, is a complete no-no – doing so is a grave breach of local etiquette!

living, the history of lifeboat service and the importance of dike building. Beyond the village is the **Bill** nature reserve.

NORDERNEY

Ferries depart from Norddeich. 1hr. ⌖16.60–17.70€ same-day return. Reederei Frisia: ℰ(04931) 98 70, www.reederei-frisia.de.

The most urbanised of the East Frisian islands, Norderney was once the summer residence of the royal House of Hanover. Its main town still has much of its old charm with its well-tended spa gardens and 19C houses. A state-of-the-art thalassotherapy centre called **Bade:haus** occupies the historic Art Nouveau sea-water baths.

BALTRUM

Ferries depart from Neßmersiel. 30min. ⌖17.50–20.50€ same-day return. Reederei Baltrum: ℰ(04933) 99 16 06. www.baltrum-linie.de.

Impressive **sand dunes** (Großes Dünental) line the east side of the smallest of the Eastern Frisians. The main sight here is the **old church** in Westdorf, built a year after the floods of 1826. Its bell was originally a ship's bell, washed up as jetsam.

LANGEOOG

Ferries depart from Bensersiel. 1hr. Up to 8 ferries daily. ⌖24.70€ same-day return. Schiffahrt Langeoog, ℰ(04972) 69 30, www. schiffahrt-langeoog.de.

The **Schifffahrtsmuseum** (Museum of Seafaring) on this island features Langeoog's first rescue ship, in service from 1945 to 1980. From the raised promenade along the chain of sand dunes, near Ebbe, there is a fine view of 14km/9mi of beach and sand banks.

SPIEKEROOG

Ferries depart from Neuharlingersiel. 45min. ⌖24€ same-day return. ℰ(04976) 919 31 01. www.spiekeroog.de.

This car-free island combines state-of-the-art spa facilities with traditional village infrastructure. The **Alte Inselkirche** of 1696 is the oldest surviving church in the Eastern Frisians. A pietà made of wood and fragments of a pulpit are said to have come from a ship in the Spanish Armada that sank in 1588. The unusual **Muschelmuseum** (Mussel Museum) occupies the basement of the seaside hall.

WANGEROOGE

Ferries depart from Harlesiel. 90min. Up to 5 ferries daily. ⌖32.30€ round-trip. ℰ(04464) 94 94 11. www.siw-wangerooge.de.

This easternmost island has belonged to Holland, France, Russia (twice) and the Grand Duchy of Oldenburg. It is now a family vacation destination. The colourful island train runs from the isolated southwest point past lagoons rich in bird life straight to the village centre.

ON THE MAINLAND
EMDEN

Bahnhofsplatz 11, 26721 Emden. ✆(04921) 974 00. www.emden-touristik.de.
Sitting at the mouth of the Ems River across from the Dutch border, this easy-going, pleasant town has remarkable museums, most notably the Kunsthalle gallery of contemporary art. Thanks to the Dortmund-Ems canals, the town has regained its position as Lower Saxony's chief maritime port.

It traces its history back to the 8C and was an important trading place until the 16C. Completely flattened during World War II, Emden was rebuilt in modern but aesthetic fashion with a picturesque harbour, little canals and red-brick houses. Today, the driving force behind its economy is the huge Volkswagen factory.

Kunsthalle Emden★★
(Art Museum Emden)

Hinter dem Rahmen 13; northwest of town. Open year-round Tue–Fri 10am–5pm, Sat–Sun 11am–5pm. Closed Dec 23–25 & 30–31. ⊚8€. ♿ ✆(04921) 97 50 50. www.kunsthalle-emden.de.

This Postmodern red-brick museum houses the sizable private collection of *Stern* magazine founder and local

Kunsthalle Emden

© Kunsthall Emden

boy Henri Nannen. A major emphasis is placed on **German Expressionist** art, with works by *Die Brücke* (Bridge) artists Kirchner, Heckel and Schmidt-Rottluff along with *Blue Rider* members Marc, Macke, Münter and Jawlensky brightening the walls. More recent creativity is represented by the **Neue Wilde** group (New Wild Ones) that included Hödicke, Zimmer, Richter and Damisch – less familiar names, perhaps, but all seminal post-1980 artists.

Ostfriesisches Landesmuseum★
(East Frisian Regional Museum)

Brückstraße 1. Open year-round Tue–Sat 10am–6pm. ⊚6€. ✆(04921) 87 20 58. www.landesmuseum-emden.de.

This modernised museum is a comprehensive treasure trove of all things East Frisian going back to the Stone Age. Pride of place goes to the **Rüstkammer★★** (armoury), one of Germany's largest collections of 16C and 17C weapons. The **mummified body★** of a young man who lived during the early Middle Ages and who was unearthed in a local peat bog always garners good crowds. A fine sampling of Dutch paintings, mostly from the 17C, and graphic arts, including works by Alfred Rethel and Max Liebermann, shows off Emden's artistic heritage.

Port

Ratsdelft.
The oldest section is the **harbour gateway** *(Hafentor)* built in 1635 and bearing the Latin inscription *"God is Emden's bridge, harbour and sailing wind"*. In the historical harbour basin are several **museum ships** *(Museumsschiffe)*.

Pelzerhäuser

Open year-round Tue–Sun 11am–6pm. ✆(04921) 87 20 58. www.landesmuseum-emden.de.

The steeply gabled, red-brick town houses at Pelzerstraße 11 and 12 are the only surviving examples of the 16C Dutch-Flemish Renaissance style that once dominated Emden. One contains period rooms that shed light on upper middle-class lifestyles in the 17C and 18C.

Hannover

Hannover is one of northern Germany's main economic hubs; it hosts important trade shows such as the annual Cebit computer fair. But the city is not all buttoned-down business: visitors will find a wealth of pleasant pastimes, most notably exploring its glorious gardens.

SIGHTS
Herrenhäuser Gärten★★ (Herrenhausen Gardens)

Begun in the 17C, one of Europe's most beautiful public parks comprises four separate and varied gardens linked by the Herrenhäuser Allee.

Großer Garten★★

Open May–Aug daily 9am–8pm; Sept–Apr daily 9am–sunset. ⊕6-8€, includes Berggarten. www.hannover.de/herrenhausen.

Creation of this splendid Baroque garden started in 1666, but it didn't get its finishing touches until Electress Sophie turned her attention to it between 1696 and 1714. The oldest section, a French pleasure garden, features statues of allegorical figures and Roman gods. The first thing you will likely see is the huge **fountain** with its 80m/262.4ft-high plume. An exciting modern highlight is the whimsical **grotto** (open

🛈 **Info:** Ernst-August-Platz 8, 30159 Hannover. ℘(0511) 12 34 51 11. www.hannover.de.

▶ **Location:** Set on a plain on the banks of the Leine and the Mittelandkanal, Hannover lies halfway between the Baltic Sea and the North Sea. The A2 (Dortmund–Berlin) and A7 (Kassel–Hamburg) autobahns intersect here.

🅿 **Parking:** Garages are located throughout Hannover. Those around the Hauptbahnhof are easiest to find.

☺ **Don't Miss:** Hannover's beautiful gardens.

🕐 **Timing:** Allow at least two hours to see the Herrenhäuser Gardens.

👪 **Kids:** Hannover Zoo.

May–Aug daily 9am–7.30pm; Sept until 6.30pm, Oct until 5.30pm; Nov–Mar Sat–Sun 9am–4pm) decorated by the late French artist Niki de Saint Phalle. Illustrating the theme of human life, the octagonal foyer and two adjacent rooms sparkle with coloured glass mosaics, mirrors, pebbles and painted fibreglass figurines.

Southern façade of Neues Rathaus

© Norbert Speicher /istockphoto.com

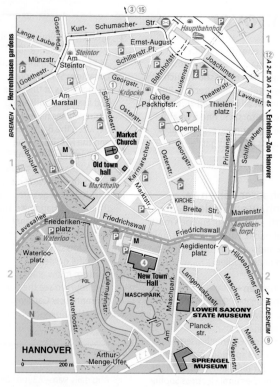

HANNOVER

0 — 200 m

WHERE TO STAY

CVJM City Hotel	①	da Vinci Restaurant	⑨
Kastens Hotel Luisenhof	④	Der Gartensaal	④
WHERE TO EAT		Le Monde	⑫
Basil	③	Neue Zeiten	⑮
Broyhan-Haus	①	Röhrbein Restaurant	⑰

Berggarten★

Open, see Grosser Garten. ☜3.50€.

One of the oldest botanical gardens in Germany, the Berggarten is a charming and colourful riot of 11 000 plant species, including cacti, orchids, and flora native to the Canary Islands. There are some great greenhouses as well as the **Sealife Hannover** (open year-round Apr–early Nov Tue–Sun 10am–6.30pm; mid-Nov–late Dec Mon–Fri 10am–5pm, Sat–Sun until 6.30pm; closed Dec 24; ☜16.50€, combination ticket with Grosser Garten/Berggarten 17.95€; www.visitsealife.com), which takes you on a virtual journey from the local Leine River to the Carib-

bean and the Amazon rain forest. Along the way, visitors are introduced to 5 000 creatures residing in these aquatic habitats. A highlight is the 8m/26.2ft-long glass tunnel "through" the ocean.

At the far end of the garden's principal walk is the mausoleum of the Royal House of Hanover.

Georgengarten

Open 24hrs.

Inspired by English landscape gardens, this romantic patch was laid out between 1835 and 1841 and is distinguished by great expanses of lawn. Enjoy fabulous views from the **Leibniztempel**, a memorial dedicated to the philosopher and scientist, Wilhelm Gottfried Leibniz (1646–1716), on a raised peninsula. The Wallmodenschlösschen is a pavilion housing the **Wilhelm-Busch-Museum** (open year-round Tue–Sun 11am–6pm; closed Dec 24 & 31; ⌒4.50€; &; ℰ(0511) 16 99 99 11; www.karikaturmuseum.de) dedicated to the famous poet, illustrator and humourist (1832–1908) who launched the advent of comic strips with such stories as "Max und Moritz".

Welfengarten
The Welfenschloss (now part of the university) stands in the Welfengarten and is fronted by the trademark of the state of Niedersachsen, the Saxon Steed, created in 1876 by Friedrich Wolff.

Marktkirche
(Market Church)
A four-gabled tower crowned by a sharp pinnacle presides over this Gothic brick church, rebuilt after 1945 to mimic the 14C original. The modern 1957 bronze doors by Gerhard Marcks contrast sharply with the overall style of the church. Inside, note the superb 15C sculpted polychrome **reredos★★** representing the Passion.

Niedersächsisches Landesmuseum Hannover★ (Lower Saxony State Museum)
Willy-Brandt-Allee 5. Open year-round Tue–Sun 10am–6pm (Thu until 8pm). Closed Good Friday, Dec 24 & 31. ⌒4€. &. ℰ(0511) 980 76 86. www.nlmh.de.
This museum is divided into four departments. The **archaeological department★** (Archäologie-Abteilung) travels back in time half a million years and sheds light on the daily lives of our ancestors. One of the most memorable exhibits is a mummified male from AD 300, whose curly red hair has earned him the nickname "Roter Franz" (Red Francis). Fossils, dinosaurs and exhibits on tectonic plates and earthquakes are among the highlights of the **nature department** (Naturkunde-Abteilung). Living fish, amphibians, lizards, spiders and insects from around the world can

be observed in re-created habitats in the attached vivarium.

The **picture gallery** (Landesgalerie) is particularly proud of its extensive collection of German Impressionism and early Expressionism, with a healthy smattering of works by Liebermann, Slevogt, Corinth and Modersohn-Becker.

Names associated with the Middle Ages and the Renaissance include Meister Bertram, Lucas Cranach and Tilman Riemenschneider. Rubens, Rembrandt and Ruisdael represent the Rococo.

Finally, there is the **ethnography department** (Völkerkunde-Abteilung), which features exotic exhibits from New Guinea, Mexico, Indonesia and other non-European cultures.

Sprengel Museum Hannover★
Kurt-Schwitters-Platz. Open year-round Tue 10am–8pm, Wed–Sun 10am–6pm. Closed Good Friday, May 1, Dec 24–25 & 31. ⌒7€. &. ℰ(0511) 16 84 38 75. www.sprengel-museum.de.
A stabile by Calder, the Hellebardier, welcomes you to this first-rate museum of 20C and 21C art.
Key names include Picasso, Klee, Nolde, Beckmann, Hannover-born Kurt Schwitters and Georg Baselitz as well Die Brücke (Schmidt-Rottluff) and Der Blaue Reiter (Kandinsky, Jawlensky, Macke) members. Fans of Niki de St. Phalle will get their fill as well.

👥 Erlebnis-Zoo Hannover★ (Hannover Zoo)
Adenauerallee 3. Open Apr–Oct daily 9am–6pm; Nov–Mar 10am–4pm.

ᴥ14.50-25€ (child 10.50-17€). ℰ(0511) 28 07 40. www.zoo-hannover.de.
The Zoo is divided into seven themed areas, including the arid Outback, where kangaroos and wallabies thrive; Yukon Bay, a peek into the Canadian habitat of polar bears and prairie dogs; and Mullewapp, a fantasy land based on a children's book.

Neues Rathaus (New Town Hall)

Open late Mar–early Nov Mon–Fri 9.30am–6.30pm, Sat–Sun 10am–6.30pm; mid-Nov–mid-Mar 11am–4.30pm. Closed Jan 1, Dec 24–26 & 31. ᴥ3€. ℰ(0511) 16 80.
Anchored in the marshy soil by 6 026 beech poles, Hannover's town hall was completed in 1913. Ride the unique slanted elevator to the dome (ᴥ3€) to enjoy sweeping city views.

The Nanas

Leibnitzufer.
Niki de St. Phalle's colourful if grotesque female doll sculptures caused quite an uproar when first installed along the Leine banks in 1974, but they have since become a beloved landmark.

ADDRESSES

🏨 STAY

ᴥᴥ **CVJM City Hotel** – *Limburgstraße 3. ℰ(0511) 360 70. www.cityhotelhannover.de. 47 rooms.* ⌨. Rooms are functional at this impeccably run hotel in the pedestrian zone. The breakfast room exudes a cheerful Mediterranean mood.

ᴥᴥᴥ **Kastens Hotel Luisenhof** – *Luisenstraße 1-3. ℰ(0511) 304 40.* ⌨. *www.kastens-luisenhof.de. 146 rooms. Restaurant* ᴥᴥᴥ. Comfort reigns in Hannover's oldest hotel (1856), centrally located near the main train station. Rooms are elegantly furnished; the rooftop spa and leisure area offer views.

🍴 EAT

ᴥᴥ **Basil** – *Dragonerstraße 30. ℰ(0511) 62 26 36. www.basil.de. Closed Sun.* The charismatic restaurant specialises in fusion cuisine and is housed in 1867 brick building with vaulted ceilings.

ᴥᴥ **Broyhan-Haus** – *Kramerstraße 24 ℰ(0511) 32 39 19. www.broyhanhaus.de. Reservation necessary.* This 14C building, one of the city's oldest town houses, was bought in 1537 by master brewer Cord Broyhan. Today it offers three floors of cosiness along with hearty German cuisine (schnitzel, roast lamb) best enjoyed with a cold house brew.

ᴥᴥ **Da Vinci** – *Hildesheimer Straße 228. ℰ(0511) 843 65 56. www.rist-da-vinci.de. Closed Sun.* From antipasti buffet to meat and fish dishes and pizza and pasta, this place offers the gamut of Italian fare.

ᴥᴥ **Der Gartensaal** – *Trammplatz 2. ℰ(0511) 16 84 88 88. www.gartensaal-hannover.de.* This bistro has an unusual location in the south entrance of the Neues Rathaus. Obtain superb views of the Maschsee lake from the terrace or through the floor-to-ceiling windows.

ᴥᴥ **Le Monde** – *Podbielskistraße 107. ℰ(0511) 78 12 11. www.le-monde-bistro.de. Closed Sun, Mon.* This classic French bistro delivers meals prepared with quality ingredients.

ᴥᴥ **Neue Zeiten** – *Jakobistraße 24. ℰ(0511) 39 24 47. www.restaurant neuezeiten.de. Closed Sun, Mon.* This restaurant gets plenty of return guests hooked on its Mediterranean-style contemporary cuisine. The walls double as a changing modern art gallery.

ᴥᴥ **Röhrbein** – *Joachimstraße 6. ℰ(0511) 93 66 17 12 00. www.clichy.de. Closed Sun.* This bistro-style restaurant in the Luisenpassage arcade serves regional dishes in a friendly ambience.

TAKING A BREAK

Holländische Kakao-Stube – *Ständehausstraße 2 (Luisenstraße to the southwest). ℰ(0511) 30 41 00. www.hollaendische-kakao-stube. de. Closed Sun and public holidays.* For steamy hot chocolate, try this café decorated with Dutch ceramics. Homemade pastries also figure prominently on the menu.

Celle★★

The former residence of the dukes of Brunswick-Lüneburg, Celle retains the vaunted air of an aristocratic retreat. Its carefully preserved centre of half-timbered houses miraculously escaped war damage and is a joy to explore along with the restored ducal castle and the folklore museum.

▸ **Population:** 70 000

Info: Markt 14-16, 29221 Celle. ℘(05141) 12 12. www.celle-tourismus.de.

Location: Celle is part of the Lüneburg Heath, a region filled with charming villages and lots of opportunities to immerse yourself in nature.

Don't Miss: Celle's old town and its 13C castle.

Timing: Allow half a day to wander.

SIGHTS
OLD TOWN★★

Celle's largely car-free old town boasts some of Germany's most elaborate half-timbered houses, especially along Neue Straße, Zöllnerstraße, Poststraße (note the richly carved Hoppener Haus, dating from 1532) and romantic Kalandgasse, near the church.

Altes Rathaus
(Old Town Hall)

The heavily scrolled and pinnacled north gable (1579) of Celle's imposing Town Hall is a masterpiece of the Weser Renaissance. The *Ratskeller* (council cellar) retains its original Gothic vaulting.

Residenzmuseum
im Celler Schloss★

Schlossplatz 1. Open year-round Tue–Sun 10am–5pm. Closed Dec 24–25. ⊛5€. ℘(05141) 123 73. www.schloss-celle.de.

Begun in 1292, Celle's castle is flanked by massive corner towers and features dormer windows topped by rounded pediments, as is characteristic of the Weser Renaissance style.

Tour highlights include the private rooms of exiled Queen Caroline-Matilde of Denmark (1751–1775), the last royal to live at the palace, and the Renaissance-style **chapel★** (Hofkapelle).

The 17C Baroque *Schlosstheater* (theatre) is still in use. An exhibition from the Bomann Museum in the eastern wing documents the history of the House of Hanover.

Bomann-Museum★

Schlossplatz 7. Open year-round Tue–Sun 10am–5pm. Closed Dec 24–25 & 31 ⊛5€. ⚹. ℘(05141) 123 72. www.bomann-museum.de.

Come here for an in-depth study of the cultural history of Lower Saxony and of Celle. Pride of place goes to heavily detailed period rooms, including the kitchen and a farmhouse.

Stadtkirche★
(City Church)

Open year-round Apr–Dec Tue–Sat 10am–6pm (Nov–Mar until 5pm), Sun after service. www.stadtkirche-celle.de.

Originally Gothic, this church got a 17C Baroque makeover and is noteworthy for its 1613 altar, the 16C *Fürstenstuhl* (Prince's Seat) and the 1610 baptismal font. The tower can be climbed.

EXCURSION
Kloster Wienhausen★

10km/6.2mi south. An der Kirche 1. Visit by guided tour (75min) only, Apr–mid-Oct Tue–Fri 10am, 11am, then hourly 2pm–5pm, Sun hourly noon–5pm. Closed mid-Oct–Mar, Good Friday. ⊛5€. ⚹℘(05149) 186 60. www.kloster-wienhausen.de.

Run by Protestant cannonesses since the Reformation, this 13C abbey counts wooden sculptures of the Virgin and Christ Resurrected among its treasures. The Nuns' Choir is embellished with early 14C **frescoes★**.

Wolfenbüttel★★

For three centuries, until the court transferred to Brunswick in 1753, Wolfenbüttel was the seat of the dukes of Brunswick and Lüneburg. The precise, spacious plan, with perfectly straight streets linking large symmetrical squares, makes it one of the most successful examples of Renaissance town planning in Germany.

▶ **Population:** 53 400

▫ **Info:** Stadtmarkt 7, 38300 Wolfenbüttel. ℘(05331) 862 80. www.wolfenbuettel.com.

◖ **Location:** Straddling the banks of the Oker, Wolfenbüttel is the ideal base for exploring the Harz Mountains.

◈ **Don't Miss:** The city's half-timbered houses.

◷ **Timing:** Allow at least three hours to see everything.

SIGHTS
Fachwerkhäuser★★ (Half-timbered Houses)

The homes of high court officials lining Kanzleistraße, Reichstraße and western Harzstraße, built c. 1600, are distinguished by majestic façades with overhangs flanking the main entrance. At Harzstraße 12, note the grimacing heads above cornices carved with biblical inscriptions. The decoration of smaller houses owned by lesser dignitaries and merchants is, surprisingly, more elaborate. A single gable normally tops their wide, flat façades

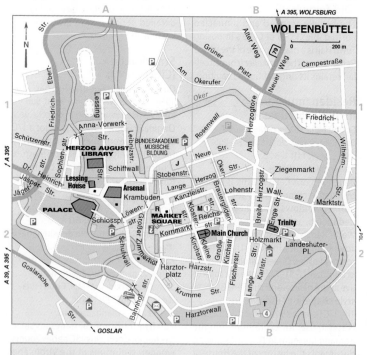

WHERE TO STAY

«Bayrischer - Hof» Hotel..............................①

Parkhotel Altes Kaffeehaus........................④

Fachwerkhäuser on a busy street

(Lange Herzogstraße, Brauergilden-straße, Holzmarkt, Krambuden). Even the simpler, two-storey houses of the less well-to-do (Krumme Straße, Stobenstraße) are ornamented with coloured fan designs. Corner houses with slightly projecting oriels are a particular characteristic of Wolfenbüt-tel and are prevalent around the Stadt-markt (main town square).

Stadtmarkt★ (Town Market Square)

The **Rathaus** (town hall) occupies a number of 16C and 17C buildings on the north and west of the square. The Weights and Measures Office has a dis-tinctive arched doorway surmounted by King Solomon's Edict and the Wolfen-büttel coat of arms.

Schloss★ (Palace)

Open year-round Tue–Sun 10am–5pm. Closed Jan 1, Good Friday, Dec 24–25 & 31. ⊛7€. ♿ ℘(05331) 924 60. www.schlosswolfenbuettel.de.

The palace is reached via an attractive narrow street bordered by arcades known as *Krambuden*. Originally a 12C stronghold conquered by Henry the Lion, the building experienced many transformations before it evolved into Lower Saxony's second-largest palace (after the *Leineschloss* in Hannover).

The **Schlossmuseum** (palace museum) consists of the **Ducal Apartments** as they were in 1690–1750. Rare furniture, tapestries, porcelain and paintings illus-trate Baroque court life. Note the ivory scenes adorning the walls of the small study. *Access via the central courtyard and main stairway.*

Herzog August Bibliothek★ (Library)

Lessingplatz 1. Open year-round Tue–Sun 10am–5pm. Closed Jan 1, Good Friday, Dec 24–26 & 31. ⊛5€, also valid for Lessinghaus. ℘(05331) 80 80. www.hab.de.

Founded in 1572 by Augustus the Young, this was the largest, most impor-tant library in Europe in the 17C. Still a treasure for researchers and scholars, it today houses some 860 000 volumes. Among the priceless manuscripts and illuminated documents from the Middle Ages are a rare example of the 14C *Saxon Mirror*, and a gospel book from 1188 that once belonged to Henry the Lion *(shown periodically in the first-floor Vault Room).*

In the Globe Room are terrestrial and celestial globes from the 16C and 17C, as well as ancient maps. The Malerbuch-kabinett hall contains books illustrated by great artists of the 20C.

Lessinghaus

Lessingplatz 2. Open year-round Tue–Sun 10am–5pm. Closed Jan 1, Good Friday, Dec 24–26 & 31. ⊛5€, also valid for Herzog August Library. ♿ ℘(05331) 80 80. www.hab.de.

Jägermeister Town

Jägermeister (literally, master of the hunt) first appeared in Wolfenbüttel in 1935. This uniquely flavoured alcoholic drink is made from 56 plants, roots and extracts ripened for a year. The stag on the label refers to St. Hubert, patron saint of hunters. Legend has it that 7C King Hubert rejected his wealth when his wife Floribana died, devoting himself to hunting. During one of his solitary outings, a stag with a cross floating between its antlers appeared to him. The vision gave him his calling; he immediately forsook his wealth and title and founded several monasteries.

Gotthold Ephraim Lessing, the great innovator of German drama, spent 11 years working as official ducal librarian in Wolfenbüttel (1770–81) and penning, among other works, *Emilia Galotti* and *Nathan the Wise*. His former home is now a museum with exhibits providing insight into his life, times and work. Beside the Lessing house is the **Zeughaus** (Arsenal, 1613), a distinctive Renaissance building with projecting gables, obelisks and scrolls.

Hauptkirche (Main Church)

Open year-round Tue–Sat 10am–noon & 2pm–4pm, Sun after services until 4pm. 📞(05331) 720 55. www.propstei-wf.de.
Built on Kornmarkt in 1608, this Protestant church was influenced by the Late Gothic hall-church tradition. The massive tower with its Baroque roof resembles the shape of the castle tower. The altar, pulpit and organ case date from the late Renaissance.

Trinitatiskirche (Trinity Church)

Holzmarkt. Open year-round Tue 11am–1pm, Wed 11am–1pm & 2pm–4pm, Thu 3pm–5pm, Sat 11am–4pm. 📞(05331) 75 230. www.propstei-wf.de.

This Baroque church was built in 1719 on top of an existing, twin-towered structure, thus explaining its strangely flat silhouette. Near the church is a **park**, formed from the old city walls.

EXCURSION

🧍‍♂️🧍 Autostadt★★

▶ 40km/25mi northeast, in Wolfsburg. Open year-round daily 9am–6pm. Closed Dec 24 & 31. ⊛15€. ♿. 📞(0800) 288 678 238. www.autostadt.de.
This vast and popular **Volkswagen theme park** sits next to the VW factory where landscaped parkland forms a pleasant backdrop to modernist pavilions. Sections include the **AutoLab**, which explains car manufacturing and vehicle technology.
The **ZeitHaus** tells the history of the automobile and features famous cars such as John Lennon's Beetle. Elsewhere ride a lift to the top of the 48m/157ft **Autotürme** (car towers) where the new cars are stored. Combination tickets with the interactive science centre **Phaeno** (⊛12.50€; 📞05361 890 100; www.phaeno.de), opposite Autostadt, are available as well.

ADDRESSES

🛏 STAY

🛏 **Bayrischer Hof** – *Brauergildenstraße 5.* 📞*(05331) 50 78.www.bayrischer-hof-wf.de. 17 rooms.* ⌑. *Restaurant*🍽. The individually designed rooms occupy a beautiful half-timbered house from the 16C. Some of the rooms overlook the square and the church of Santa Maria.

🛏🛏 **Parkhotel Altes Kaffeehaus** – *Harztorwall 18.* 📞*(05331) 88 80. www. parkhotel-wolfenbuettel.de. 75 rooms.* ⌑. *Restaurant*🍽. Converted from a Turkish coffeehouse, this modern hotel has attractive, comfortable rooms. Dine in the bright restaurant or in the vaulted wine cellar *(Weingrotte)*.

Goslar★★

Goslar is often deluged by day-trippers and for good reason: its historic centre is a wonderful maze of narrow cobbled lanes lined with some of the most richly decorated half-timbered houses in Germany. In 1992, the old town, along with the 1 000-year-old Rammelsberg Mines, became a UNESCO World Heritage Site. In 2010, the 800-year-old Upper Harz mining water management system nearby became a Site.

▶ **Population:** 41 000
🛈 **Info:** Markt 7, 38640 Goslar. ℘(05321) 780 60. www.goslar.de.
◖ **Location:** Goslar lies on the northern edge of the Harz National Park and makes a good base of operations for exploring this mountainous forest region.
⊗ **Don't Miss:** The Old Town.
🕓 **Timing:** Allow three hours for a walking tour of the Old City and another half day if visiting the Rammelsberg Mines.
👪 **Kids:** Rammelsberg Mines.

THE OLD TOWN★★★ (ALTSTADT)

The old town of Goslar is largely a pedestrian zone, making it a pleasant place to wander round.

Marktplatz★ (Market Square)

The market square is surrounded by slate-clad houses. Two Gothic buildings, the Kaiserworth and the Rathaus, stand before the spires of the 12C **Marktkirche**. In the centre of the square is a **fountain** (Marktbrunnen) with two bronze basins (1230). The square also features a chiming **animated clock** with four different scenes (at 9am, noon, 3pm and 6pm) representing the history of mining in the Harz Mountains.

Rathaus★ (Town Hall)

Following the medieval custom, this 15C building was designed with an arcaded gallery opening onto the Marktplatz. On the south side, an exterior staircase leads to the first floor **State Room** (Diele).

Huldigungssaal★★ (Hall of Homage)

Open Apr–Oct and Dec Mon–Fri 11am–3pm, Sat–Sun 11am–4pm. Closed Dec 24. ⊛3.50€. ℘(053 21) 78 060. www.goslar.de.

This room, transformed into the **city council assembly hall** in 1490, was magnificently decorated c. 1520. The wall decorations feature Roman emperors alternating with sibyls in Renaissance costume, while the ceiling depicts biblical figures, including Christ, the prophets and the Evangelists. A tiny side chapel contains an arm-bone reliquary (c. 1300) of St. Margaret.

Hotel Kaiserworth

Opposite the Rathaus, this Gothic edifice (1494) is decorated with statues of eight German emperors along with the irreverent **Ducat Man** (Dukatenmännchen). He is depicted as excreting

Kaiserpfalz

© Kurt Amthor / imageBROKER / agefotostock.com

a gold coin – an allusion to Goslar's ancient right to mint coins.

Fachwerkhäuser★★
(Half-timbered Houses)

The **Schuhhof,** a small square north-west of the Rathaus, is surrounded by half-timbered buildings. Further on, a passageway on the left leads to the narrow Münzstraße, which in turn passes an old inn, **Am Weißen Schwan**, and then the **Alte Münze** (old mint). Now a restaurant, this timbered building dates from 1500. The fine house on the corner of the Münzstraße and the Marktstraße was constructed in 1526.

Facing the Marktkirche, the **Brusttuch** (1521), built for a rich mine owner, is decorated with biblical, mythological and legendary characters. It is now a hotel and restaurant. The tall gable of the **Bäckergildehaus** (bakers' guild hall, 1501–1557) looms not far away.

The **Renaissance houses** at the Markt-straße-Bäckerstraße intersection are adorned with friezes of the fan motif, typical of Lower Saxony.

Siemenshaus★★

Schreiberstraße 12. Admission only with city tour. & (05321) 78 06 20. www.siemenshaus.de.

One of Goslar's most spectacular houses is the ancestral home of the industrial Siemens family, built in 1693. Note the tiled entrance *(Däle)* and picturesque inner courtyard.

ADDITIONAL SIGHTS
Neuwerkkirche★
(Neuwerk Church)

Open Mar–Oct Mon–Sat 10am–noon, 2.30pm–4.30pm, Sun 2.30pm–4.30pm; Nov–Feb after services or by appointment. (05321) 228 39. www.neuwerkkirche-goslar.de.

This former Cistercian collegiate church (12C) is a three-aisled basilica whose tall polygonal towers are exceptionally elegant for a Romanesque church. Heavily ribbed, pointed vaulting characterises the interior. Of particular artistic merit is the former 13C **choir screen★**

festooned with sculptures of Christ, the Virgin Mary, the apostles Peter and Paul and two saints; it now serves as the organ loft. The frescoes in the choir date to the early 13C and depict Mary on the throne and Old Testament scenes.

Pfarrkirche Peter und Paul★
(St. Peter and St. Paul Church)

Enter on Frankenberger Plan.
Open Apr–Oct daily 9am–6pm.
(05321) 225 66.
www.frankenberg-goslar.de

Also known as Frankenberger Kirche (1108), this church was once the principal church of the local miners. The three-nave basilica beautifully preserves its Romanesque features despite Gothic alterations in the choir and southern transept and a lavish Baroque altarpiece. Pillars and vaults are richly decorated with stone carvings, while the frescoes above the choir and upper loft were painted in the early 13C.

The 12C altar bears a splendid Baroque retable dating to 1675, which, like the 1698 chancel, originated in the Goslar woodcarving workshop of Heinrich and Jobst Lessen.

Kaiserpfalz
(Imperial Palace)

Open Apr–Oct daily 10am–5pm; Nov–Mar daily10am–4pm. Closed Jan 1 and Dec 24. 7.50€. & (05321) 311 96 93. www.goslar.de.

One of best-preserved Romanesque palaces in Germany, the Kaiserpfalz was built in the 11C under Emperor Henry III. For two centuries it hosted several imperial diets. It was heavily restored in a Historicist style in the late 19C.

At that time, the gigantic **Reichssaal** *(on the first floor)* was swathed in romanticised paintings depicting significant moments from Goslar's medieval glory days. Beyond the Reichssaal stands the early 12C **Palatine Chapel of St. Ulrich**, where the floorplan transitions from a Greek cross into an octagon. Inside is a tomb holding the heart of Heinrich III (buried in the cathedral at Speyer).

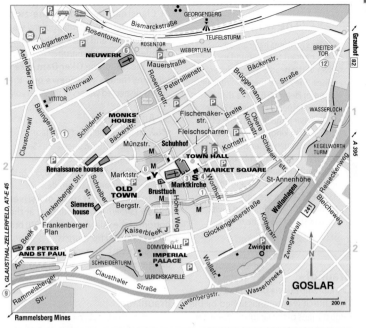

Mönche Haus Museum für Moderne Kunst★ (Monks' House Modern Art Museum)

Mönchestraße 1. Open year-round Tue –Sun 10am–5pm. ⊛5€. ⟨&⟩ ℘(05321) 295 70. www.moenchehaus.de.

A roll-call of such top 20C artists as Beuys, Hundertwasser, Serra, Baselitz, Chilida and de Kooning is the bread and butter of this museum set up in a stately 1528 patrician mansion, adjacent half-timbered buildings and vaulted cellars.

⚒ Rammelsberg Mines★

◗ Bergtal 19, southwest of town via Clausthaler Straße and Rammelsberger Straße. ⟨Guided tours (60–75min) year-round daily 9am–6pm (last tour 4.30pm). Closed Dec 24 & 31. ⊛13€, including museum and one

guided tour. ℘(05321) 75 00. www.rammelsberg.de.

The source of Goslar's prosperity, the 1 000-year-old Rammelsberg mines are now a major tourist attraction.

Spend a little time above ground at the **museum** to gain a better appreciation of their importance before descending deep into the bowels of the earth on a guided tour.

Two types of tours are available. During the "Fire and Water: The Roeder Gallery" you enter an impressive network of galleries, water wheels and shafts and come face to face with the amazing blaze of colour of its minerals. Kids usually prefer the other tour because it involves a ride on an underground railway and noisy demonstrations of old and modern equipment.

The Mines

Goslar's fortunes have always been pegged to the abundance of silver in the nearby Rammelsberg Mines. They were the main reason Emperor Heinrich II made the town an imperial residence in the 11C. Goslar remained a home of the German kings and emperors until 1253 when it became a Free Imperial City and member of the Hanseatic League. Its prosperity peaked during the 15C and 16C, as is reflected in the abundance of the lavish half-timbered town houses still gracing the town centre.

Grauhof★

▶ 3 km/2mi. Exit via Okerstraße.

This church was commissioned by the Augustinians of the Grauhof monastery (1527) and built between 1701–1717 by an Italian architect.

Noteworthy features include a boat-shaped chancel (1721), the splendid organ (1737) and the carved choir stalls where the life of St. Augustine is depicted in 56 scenes.

🚗 DRIVING TOURS

1 THE UPPER HARZ

81km/50mi. Allow half a day.

▶ Leave Goslar on Clausthaler Straße.

This itinerary passes through vast tracts of rolling hills draped in pine.

Clausthal-Zellerfeld

This twin town is the former mining capital of the Harz. At Zellerfeld, the **Upper Harz Mine Museum** (Oberharzer Bergwerksmuseum; Bornhardtstraße 16; open year-round daily 10am–5pm; closed Dec 24; ⊜6€; ℘05323 989 50; www.bergwerksmuseum.de) illustrates mining techniques used until 1930 and documents the history of the region.

At Clausthal the **Pfarrkirche zum Heiligen Geist** (*Hindenburgplatz*) was built in the 17C and is one of the largest wooden churches in Europe.

From the top of the **Oker Dam** (*Okertalsperre*) there is a fine **view★** over the widely dispersed waters of the reservoir.

St. Andreasberg

🕐 Visit by guided tour (1hr) 11am and 2.30pm. Museum open Mon–Sat 8.30am–4pm, Sun after tour. Closed Jan 1 and Dec 24. ⊜5.50€. ℘(055 82) 12 49. www.sankt-andreasberg.de.

The road leads first to an **old silver mine★** (*Silberbergwerk Samson*, at the bottom of the valley), closed in 1910 but since reopened for tourists.

The *Fahrkunst*, a machine of ingenious simplicity, which sent down and brought back the miners, still functions.

Braunlage

Served by the Brocken railway, this spa resort, prized for its climate and ski slopes, lies high up on a plateau overlooked by the wooded **Wurmberg** (971m/3185.6ft).

Schierke★

If you want to climb the summit of the **Brocken** – or at least have a go at it – the Schierke station on the **Brockenbahn** (Brocken narrow-gauge railway) is the place to start. Schierke is a lovely place in its own right and a gateway to the Harz National Park.

Wernigerode★

Wernigerode is one of the most delightful small towns in this region. Its **Rathaus★★** (*town hall, on Marktplatz*) was first mentioned in 1277, and originally served as a courthouse and dance hall. The current model is mostly from the 16C and is considered one of the finest half-timbered buildings in Germany. Breite Straße, as it leaves Marktplatz, is lined with more residential half-timbered beauties. The most admired building is the **Krummelsches Haus** (1674) at no 74, whose timbered front has been covered up with a wooden façade so intricately carved that it resembles a copper-etching.

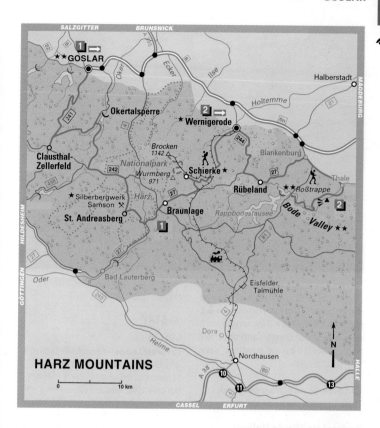

HARZ MOUNTAINS

0 _____ 10 km

Schloss Wernigerode

Open May–Oct daily 10am–6pm;
Nov–Apr by guided tour only, every
full hour Tue–Fri 10am–5pm, Sat–Sun
10am–6pm. ⊛6€. ℘(03943) 55 30 30.
www.schloss-wernigerode.de.
Originally a medieval fortress built to
protect the emperors while on hunting
expeditions, this castle was repeatedly
altered and given a romantic makeover
in the 19C. Rooms are filled with original
paintings and furniture and illustrate
the exalted lifestyle once enjoyed by
the German aristocracy.

② THE EASTERN HARZ

89km/55mi. Allow half a day.

In the eastern stretches of the Harz mountains, pine forests dominate. Although
not quite as dramatic, the landscape still
offers great natural beauty.

> ### ☺ A Bit of Advice ☺
>
> Nostalgia fans will love riding the
> narrow-gauge trains powered
> by steam locomotives that
> crisscross the eastern Harz. The
> Harzquerbahn runs for 60km/37mi
> from Wernigerode to Nordhausen.
> The Brockenbahn chugs up
> Brocken mountain from Drei Annen
> Hohne. And the Selketalbahn runs
> from Quedlinburg to Hasselfelde.

Wernigerode★
(♿See above)

Rübeland

🚶Visit by guided tour (50min) only,
Jul–Aug daily 9am–5.30pm; Feb–Jun
and Sept–Oct daily 9am–4.30pm;
Nov–Jan daily 9am–3.30pm. ⊛8€.
℘(039454) 491 32. www.harzer-
hoehlen.de.

Bodetal near Thale in Spring

© hsvrs/iStockphoto.com

Limestone caving is the chief draw of the Rübeland. Note particularly in 👥 **Hermann's Grotto★** *(Hermannshöhle)*, the Chamber of Crystals and the small pool inhabited by the sightless "cave fish" *(Grottenolmen)*.

▶ Continue via Blankenburg and Thale to reach the Bode Valley.

Bodetal★★ (Bode Valley)

The river here has gouged a passage through a maze of rock masses and now flows along the foot of craggy cliffs. The most spectacular site is the **Roßtrappe★★** (charger's hoofmark), a 10-minute walk from the car park. From the look-out point, which juts out dizzyingly above the river far below, there is an incredible **view★★★** of the cliffs, the tumbling stream, a steep gorge and the distant woods.

The place owes its name to the legend of a horse which, ridden by a princess and chased by a giant, leapt with such force across the chasm that it left an imprint in the rock.

Following the course of the river, the scenic stretch of road twists and turns through the rugged forest landscape as far as the junction with the B81.

ADDRESSES

🏠 STAY

GOSLAR

🛏 **Forest Lodge** – *Clausthaler Straße 19.* ✆*(0394) 68 36 50. www.harz-travel.de 10 rooms.* ⬛*9€.* A bit outside of town, this charming wooden chalet has a just few rooms, but is surrounded by lush greenery. The breakfast is organic and is best enjoyed on the terrace in fine weather.

🛏🛏 **Goldene Krone** – *Breite Straße 46.* ✆*(05321) 344 90. www.goldene-krone-goslar.de. 17 rooms.* ⬛. This small family-hotel occupies a half-timbered house (1733) and makes an excellent launch pad for explorations around the region.

🛏🛏 **Hotel Die Tanne** – *Bäringer Straße 10.* ✆*(05321) 343 90. www.die-tanne.de. 22 rooms.* Behind the shale façade of this cosy hotel in a listed building await bright, modern rooms fitted with all major comforts. The Finnish sauna and hotel bar make good spots to unwind.

🛏🛏🛏 **Hotel der Achtermann** – *Rosentorstraße 20.* ✆*(05321) 700 00. www.der-achtermann.de. 147 rooms.* ⬛. Near the pedestrian zone and railway station, this elegant hotel has nicely decked out rooms with a good range of mod amenities. An indoor pool and a spa are on-site. The restaurant serves traditional German fare.

🛏🪙🛏 **Hotel Kaiserworth** – *Markt 3.*
📞(05321) 70 90. www.kaiserworth.de.
65 rooms. 🛏. This richly decorated
building from 1494 used to belong to
the Guild of Clothmakers and Traders. It
sits on the market square and boasts a
superb restaurant in a series of arcades.

HARZ MOUNTAINS
🛏 **Hotel Zum Brockenbäcker** –
Lindenwarte 20, 38875 Tanne.
📞(0394) 57 97 60. www. harz-hotel-
brockenbaecker.de. Closed 1 week in
Nov. 13 rooms. 🛏. This half-timbered
property was converted into a hotel in
1912. Rustic rooms are comfortable.
The restaurant serves freshly baked
breads for breakfast.

🍴 EAT
GOSLAR
🍽 **Die Butterhanne** – *Marktkirchhof 3.*
📞(05321) 228 86. www.butterhanne.de.
In this brasserie you sit at large tables
and fortify yourself with meaty dishes,
including some game specialities (e.g.
venison, wild boar sausage and steak).

🍽🪙🛏 **Aubergine** – *Marktstraße 4.*
📞(05321) 421 36. www.aubergine-
goslar.de. Modern and sophisticated, yet
warm and welcoming, this restaurant
will charm you with candlelight, fresh
flowers and a trickling fountain and
tempt you with cleverly composed
Mediterranean cuisine.

🍽🪙🛏 **Worthmühle** – *Worthstraße 4,*
📞(05321) 434 02. www.worthmuehle.de.
Closed 1–7 Jan, Mon–Fri lunch.
In summer, this restaurat's beer garden
is the best place for enjoying regional
dishes and locally brewed beers.

Hildesheim★

Founded as a bishopric in 815,
Hildesheim managed to preserve its
beautiful medieval buildings until
an Allied air-raid laid waste to most
of the city in 1945. In the 1980s,
part of the old town was faithfully
reconstructed, especially around
the market square. The cathedral
and the Church of St. Michael are
both UNESCO World Heritage Sites.

▶ **Population:** 103 000
ℹ **Info:** Rathausstraße 20, 31134
Hildesheim. 📞(05121) 179 80.
www.hildesheim.de.
▶ **Location:** Hildesheim is
34km/21mi south of
Hannover, just off the
A7 autobahn.
😊 **Don't Miss:** The Marktplatz
and the Cathedral.
🕐 **Timing:** Allow at least half a
day to do Hildesheim justice.

SIGHTS
Marktplatz★
The historical market square has been
beautifully restored and is framed by
buildings reflecting eight centuries of
architectural styles. The east side is
flanked by Gothic buildings from the
13C, including the **Rathaus** (town hall),
where a carillon is heard several times
daily *(noon, 1pm and 5pm).*

Architectural Gems
Housing the tourist office, the unusual
early 14C Tempelhaus dominates the
south side of the Marktplatz. Its most
distinctive feature is the ornate 16C
Renaissance **oriel★**, which depicts the
parable of the Prodigal Son. The nearby
16C half-timbered **Wedekindhaus** has
bay windows spanning from ground
level up to the roof, a typical feature of
the Weser Renaissance style. Not far off
is the **Lüntzelhaus** (1755), now a local
bank, and the 14C Gothic **Rolandstift**
with a Baroque porch (c. 1730).
The **bakers' guild hall** (*Bäckeramts-
haus, 1451*) and **butchers' guild hall★**
(*Knochenhauer Amtshaus, 1529*) occupy

St. Michaelis-Kirche

© Torsten Krueger / agefotostock.com

the square's west side. The five upper floors house the **Stadtmuseum** (local history museum; open year-round Tue–Sun 10am–6pm; closed Dec 24 & 31; 2.50€; 05121 299 36 85; www.stadtmuseum-hildesheim.de).

The **Rokokohaus** on the north side of the square is wedged between the **Stadtschänke**, a local restaurant, and the **weavers' guild hall** (Wollenweber-gildehaus).

Dom★ (Cathedral)

Open year-round daily 10am–6pm. (05121) 30 77 70.
www.bistum-hildesheim.de.
The reconstructed 11C Romanesque cathedral is endowed with rare and precious artworks. Two bronze casts commissioned by Bishop Bernard in the early 11C are worth closer inspection: the **Christussäule★** (Christ Column) and the **Bernwardstüren★★** (Bernward doors), both depicting biblical scenes. The doors stand almost 5m/16.4ft tall and are 1m/3.28ft wide and were cast as a single piece, an amazing achievement for the time and one of the reasons they are today a UNESCO World Heritage Site. Also note the massive 11C chandelier

and the 13C baptismal font supported by figures representing the rivers of Paradise.

The **legendary rosebush** can be found in the Romanesque **cloister★** (open Mon–Sat 10am–5pm, Sun noon–5pm; 0.50€).

Roemer- und Pelizaeus-Museum★

Am Steine 1–2. Open year-round Tue –Sun 10am–6pm. Closed Dec 24 & 31. 10€. (05121) 936 90.
www.rpmuseum.de.
Named for its 19C benefactors, the lawyer Hermann Roemer and the merchant Wilhelm Pelizaeus, this museum houses one of Germany's richest collections of Egyptian antiquities. Highlights include the life-size figure of Heimunu and the statue of the scribe Heti from excavations near Giza. Rare items from ancient Peru form another focal point.

Medieval Churches

Dating from the 11C, the UNESCO-protected **St. Michaelis-Kirche★** exemplifies Ottonian architecture. The 13C painted ceiling depicts the Tree of Jesse. The 12C **St. Godehardikirche★** sports an elegant silhouette marked by three slender spires. **St. Andreaskirche**, (14C–15C), is a massive Gothic church whose tower can be climbed. Fronted by a Baroque façade, the **Heiligkreuz-kirche** is built on an 11C Early Romanesque church but now has Ottonian, Gothic and Baroque elements jostling for attention.

Einbeck★

In the Middle Ages, no fewer than 600 small breweries in this former Hanseatic town supplied the whole of Germany with "Einpöckisches Bier" (forerunner of Bock beer). Einbeck retains part of its medieval fortifications as well as hundreds of half-timbered houses, richly decorated with multi-coloured carvings.

▶ **Population:** 26 700

🚹 **Info:** Marktstraße 13, 37574 Einbeck. ☏(05561) 313 19 10. www.einbeck-tourismus.de.

◗ **Location:** Einbeck is on the B3, about halfway between Göttingen and Hildesheim.

⊛ **Don't Miss:** The old town.

🕐 **Timing:** Allow at least one hour to see Einbeck's old town.

🐾 WALKING TOUR

OLD TOWN★

The most distinctive building on Einbeck's historic **Marktplatz★★** (market square) is the **Rathaus** (old town hall), dating from 1606 and fronted by a trio of miniature towers reminiscent of witches' hats.

Also looming over the square is the 14C **Marktkirche** (market church), whose off-kilter tower accounts for its nickname "Leaning Tower of Einbeck". Among the church treasures are a 12C Romanesque baptismal font and a 14C Gothic altar.

On the corner of Münsterstraße, the **Brodhaus** (1552) with its jutting upper storey was once owned by the baker's guild. Like most of the old houses, the impressive **Ratsapotheke** (1590) has ventilated attics that served as storage lofts for hops and barley.

◗ Follow Tiedexerstraße, west of the square.

Tiedexerstraße★★

This lane is lined with especially ornate half-timbered houses. The one at no 31 abuts the old town fortifications.

◗ Turn left on Maschenstraße and follow it to Marktstraße.

Marktstraße

The tourist office is housed in the fine **Eickesches Haus★★** (1612–14) at the corner of Knochenhauer Straße. See if you can spot the female figures representing the five senses, the four Evangelists and four of the apostles in the ornate façade.

EXCURSION
Bad Gandersheim

◗ 20km/12.4mi northeast.

The birthplace of Roswitha von Gandersheim, Germany's first (10C) poetess, is best known as a hot spring and salt-water spa. The twin octagonal towers of the **cathedral★** overlook the town centre. Inside you will find two altars, one 15C and the other 16C. The well-preserved half-timbered houses around the market square date from the 16C.

Hann. Münden★★

The famous traveller and naturalist, Alexander von Humboldt, once described Hann. Münden (or Hannoversch Münden) as one of Germany's seven most beautifully sited cities. Built at the confluence of the rivers Fulda, Werra and Weser, this charming town boasts a remarkable historic centre lined with carefully restored half-timbered houses.

SIGHTS
THE OLD TOWN★

This medieval jewel comprises over 700 **half-timbered houses★★** that reflect six centuries of local architecture. The most interesting line the streets between the Rathaus (town hall) and the River Werra. The castle ruins add a picturesque finishing touch to the charming ancient streetscape.

Rathaus (Town Hall)★

The main façade of the town hall is typical of the Weser-Renaissance style (*see HAMELN*), decorated with scrolls, pyramids and statues on its gables.

Städtisches Museum Hann. Münden

Schlossplatz 5. Open May–Oct Wed–Sun 11am–4pm; Nov–Apr Wed–Sun 1pm–4pm. Guided castle tours (70min) May–Sept Fri 2pm (in German only; book in advance for English). Closed Ascension Day. 2.50€; extra 4.50€ with tour. 05541 75 202. www.hann.muenden.de/museum.

The highlight of a visit to the small city history museum is the opportunity to take a tour of the town hall and castle, including its Renaissance and White Horse rooms.

Occasional classical music concerts are held inside the castle.

▶ **Population:** 24 505
🛈 **Info:** Lotzestraße 2 (in the town hall). 055 41 753 13. www.hann.muenden-tourismus.de. Hours vary. Closed Sun May–Sept & Sat & Sun Oct–Apr. Cyclists should ask about special bike maps of the region.
▶ **Location:** Hann. Munden is set at the crossroads of the A7, linking Cassel and Göttingen. The B80 runs through the town along the River Weser.
▶ **Don't Miss:** Old Town.
🕐 **Timing:** Allow at least half a day to see the city.

St-Blasiikirche (St. Blaise Church)

The hexagonal church tower rises proudly from the steep roof. Once inside this converted late-15C Gothic hall church, note in the right aisle, the tomb of Duke William of Brunswick (d. 1503), and to the left of the choir, the epitaph of his son, and a 14C baptismal font.

🚗 DRIVING TOUR

UPPER WESER VALLEY★

67km/42mi. Allow 2hrs. Map p177.

Between Münden and Bad Karlshafen, the Weser winds through a wooded valley. It was settled in the 18C by French Huguenots, under the jurisdiction of the Landgrave (count) of Hesse. The villages bear symbolic names such as Gottstreu (true to God) and Gewissenruh (clear conscience).

Wahlsburg-Lippoldsberg

The ancient abbey church of Lippoldsberg is one of the earliest Romanesque vaulted shrines in Northern Germany.

Where Rivers Meet

Hann. Münden is built deep in a wooded valley where the rivers Fulda and Werra unite to form the Weser ("where the Werra and Fulda kiss, and leave their names behind"). Excavations have revealed that a colony existed here at the time of Charlemagne. The foundation of the city dates back to the late 12C from the time of Henry the Lion. It enjoyed special trading privileges from 1247 to 1823, and this age of prosperity is still reflected today in the many beautiful half-timbered houses in the old town. Originally, the town was called Münden, though by the 18C, it was referred to as Hannoversch Münden, to avoid confusion with the Prussian town of Minden (Minden Preussisch), which is similarly pronounced. With the advent of the railways, in 1870, the name was abbreviated to Hann. Münden, though inhabitants still refer to their town as Münden.

Take the ferry across the river to the left bank.

Gewissenruh

Note the tiny temple (1779) and the French inscriptions on the houses.

Bad Karlshafen

This small town was founded in 1699 by the Landgrave Charles of Hesse, to shelter his French religious refugees; its geometric plan and its uniform buildings lend it a monumental character.

Deutsches Hugenotten-Museum (German Huguenots Museum)

Hafenplatz 9a. Open late Mar–Oct Tue–Fri 10am–5pm, Sat–Sun 11–6pm; Nov–mid-Mar Mon–Fri 9am–noon. ⊚4€. ♿ ℘056 72 14 10. www.hugenotten museum.de.

This small museum is housed in a former tobacco factory. On the first floor, the history of the Huguenots in France is related, with emphasis on the story of the famous potter, Bernard Palissy, and his tragic fate. The second floor is devoted to the reception that the Huguenots received in Germany, and their influence on science and the arts.

Fürstenberg

The famous Fürstenberg porcelain has been manufactured here since 1747. Adjacent to the "factory", in the castle, the **Schlossmuseum** (open Apr–Oct Tue–Sun 10am–5pm; Nov–Mar Sat–Sun 10am–5pm; closed Dec 22–Jan 1; guided tours Apr–Oct Sun 3pm (1hr;

minimum 5 people); ⊚5.50€; guided tour additional 5€; ♿; ℘05271 40 11 61; www.fuerstenberg-porzellan.com) tells the history of porcelain and has hundreds of pieces on show. Films and demonstrations convey local production techniques.

Höxter★

The town's half-timbered houses are decorated in Renaissance and Baroque styles, topped by ancient pink-sandstone roofs. The most picturesque line Westerbachstraße. St. Kilian's Church has a decorated **choir★★** with precious alabaster Renaissance motifs (1597).

Corvey Abbey

Open Apr–Oct Tue–Sun 10am–6pm (May–Sept daily). ⊚6€. ♿℘05271 69 40 10. www.schloss-corvey.de.

In the early Middle Ages, this Benedictine abbey, founded by Ludwig the Pious in 822, was one of the most significant in Germany. Even today, the 9C west end, the only one of its kind in Europe, still reflects the power and splendour of its era. Highlights include the oldest frescoes in Westphalia, the Baroque Imperial Hall, the picture gallery, the cloister with its Romanesque triumphal crucifix, the oldest post-Reformation reliquary shrine (of St. Vitus) in Germany, and the former abbey buildings themselves. *Don't miss the private library of the Dukes of Ratibor (who still own the property), which includes over 74 000 extremely rare volumes.*

Hameln★

Occupying a special spot in German folklore, Hameln is best known as the home of the Pied Piper, the legendary rat charmer who was immortalised in a fairytale by the Brothers Grimm. Hameln glories in fine old houses, most of them in ornate Weser Renaissance style. It is also the starting point for explorations into the surrounding Weserbergland, a pleasant region of rolling hills, golden fields and rivers, all protected as a nature park.

A BIT OF HISTORY

A Jewel of the Weser Renaissance – The Weser Renaissance style (late 16C–early 17C) so well displayed in Hameln is distinguished architecturally by ram's-horn scrollwork and pinnacled gables. Other characteristics include delicately worked stone bands encircling a building, jutting bay windows (Utluchten) and large, well-developed dormers (Zwerch-häuser) with decorated gables.

The Pied Piper of Hameln – In 1284, a mysterious man dressed in multi-coloured clothes promised the townspeople that, for a substantial reward, he would free Hameln of a plague of rats and mice. He played his pipe, and all the rodents emerged to follow him to the banks of the Weser, where they drowned.

When the townspeople didn't pay him, the piper returned and played again in revenge. This time it was the children who emerged from their houses, some 130 of them; they too followed him, never to be seen again. Only two escaped; one was mute, the other blind. The rather less romantic but more accurate version of this tale is that 13C overpopulation led to a troop of young people being sent by the authorities to colonise territories to the east.

But it is the former **👫 Grimm fairytale** that is acted out every Sunday at midday on the terrace of the Hochzeitshaus.

▶ **Population:** 57 800

🛈 **Info:** Deisterallee 1, 31785 Hameln. ℘(05151) 95 78 23. www.hameln.de.

🧭 **Location:** Hameln hugs the banks of the Weser and is located just south of the A2, about halfway between Bielefeld and Hannover. It extends into the Weserbergland, a hilly expanse that becomes a nature park.

🚫 **Don't Miss:** The unique Weser-Renaissance architecture, best seen on foot.

🕐 **Timing:** Allow a couple of hours to see the Altstadt.

👫 **Kids:** Weekly fairytale re-enactments.

👣 WALKING TOUR

OLD TOWN★
Rattenfängerhaus★
(Rat Catcher's House)

This large 1603 building has little to do with rats, but it combines all the major elements of the Weser Renaissance architectural style. The symmetrical façade features sculpted bands of stonework, adorned with carved busts and masks. The two-storey projecting oriel used to feature a crown.

▶ Take the Osterstraße, one of the most well-known streets in Hameln. It was here on 26 July 1284 that the children followed the Pied Piper. Stop at the top of the Kleine Straße to look at the splendid Renaissance houses (Haus Osterstraße 12, Leisthaus and Stiftsherrenhaus).

Stiftsherrenhaus
(Canons' House)

Osterstraße 8. Open year-round Tue–Sun 11am–6pm. Closed Jan 1, Good Friday, Dec 24 & 31. ⌨5€ ♿℘(05151) 202 12 16. www.hameln.de.

Another remarkable house, this one half-timbered and built in 1558, is the only one in Hameln featuring figurative decorations. Represented are Greek and Roman as well as numerous biblical characters, including Christ, the apostles, David and Cain and Abel.

The Stiftsherrenhaus is joined with the adjacent **Leisthaus** via a bridge on the first floor. Rooms in both rambling buildings now harbour the **local history museum**, which counts the world's largest collection of Pied Piper memorabilia among its exhibits.

Dempterhaus
In the market square.
Note the fine Weser Renaissance projecting oriel on this outstanding building from 1607.

Hochzeitshaus (Marriage House)★
The Weser Renaissance-style building, constructed between 1610 and 1617, was used as a reception hall for burghers' weddings. Three elegant gables break the horizontals of the façade.
A **carillon** from 1964 plays the *Rattenfängerlied* (rat catcher song) at 9.35am, the *Weserlied* (by Gustav Pressel) at 11.35am and the *Rattenfängerlied* again at 1.05pm, 3.35pm and 5.35pm.

▶ Take Fischpfortenstraße and pass in front of Wilhelm-Busch-Haus, then continue to the Weser. Retrace your steps until you reach Wendenstraße.

Haus Lücking
Wendenstraße 8.
This rich, half-timbered house of 1638 features a rounded doorway and is lavishly adorned with inscriptions and ornamentation.

▶ At the end of the road, turn right into Bäckerstraße.

Rattenkrug
Bäckerstraße 16.
A projecting bay window and a five-floor-tall gable distinguish this 1568 building.

▶ Continue until the Münsterkirchhof.

Münsterkirchhof (Collegiate Church)
From the gardens to the south, the church appears to cower beneath its massive polygonal tower, once part of a 12C Romanesque basilica. Inside, the columns and their capitals draw attention to the raised transept.

▶ Finish the tour by coming back along Alte Markt-Straße, noticing the Kürie Jerusalem passageway.

EXCURSION
Hämelschenburg★
▶ 11km/6.8mi south in Emmertal.
🐾 Visit by guided tour (50min) Apr–Oct Tue–Sun 11am and 2pm–4pm (May–Sept additional tour 5pm). ☞7€.
&. ℘(05155) 95 16 90.
www.schloss-haemelschenburg.de.
This horseshoe-shaped Schloss (palace), surrounded by a moat and built between 1588 and 1618, is considered a masterpiece of the Weser Renaissance. The wing facing the street is the most ornate, with alternating bands, bay windows and four decorative gables. The interior is filled with furniture, weapons, trophies and paintings.

ADDRESSES

STAY
🛏️🛏️ **An der Altstadt** – *Deisterallee 16.* ℘(05151) 402 40. www.hotel-hameln. de. Closed late Dec–early Jan. 19 rooms. ☕. This small *Jugendstil* hotel in the heart of town is a nice place to unpack your suitcase in comfortably appointed guest rooms furnished in cherrywood.

EAT
🍽️ **Grüner Reiter** – *Kastanienwall 62.* ℘(05151) 92 62 00. www.gruenerreiter.de. This building was erected in 1713 as a chapel for the soldiers of the Hameln Fortress. The bistro-style restaurant is in a glass extension in the courtyard.

Lemgo★

Lemgo was founded in the late 12C at the crossroads of two trading routes and surrounded in 1365 by a still-extant town wall. Its late Gothic and Renaissance town houses still testify to the prosperity of this former Hanseatic town.

▶ **Population:** 41 400

🛈 **Info:** Kramerstraße 1, 32657 Lemgo. ℘(05261) 988 70. www.lemgo.net.

◐ **Location:** Lemgo is in rural eastern North Rhine-Westphalia, a short distance from the A2 (Hannover–Dortmund).

🕓 **Timing:** Allow two hours for the Walking Tour.

SIGHTS

Junkerhaus★

Hamelner Straße 36. Open Apr–Oct Tue–Sun 10am–5pm; Nov–Mar Fri–Sun 11am–3pm. ∞3€. ℘(05261) 66 76 95. www.junkerhaus.de.

Karl Junker (1850–1912) was a painter, sculptor and architect with an eccentric streak, which explains the unusual look of his 1891 half-timbered home that he personally designed and crafted. Organised around a spiral, it offers changing views from every perspective and is adorned with whimsical sculptures, carvings, imaginative furniture and other touches.

Schloss Brake (Brake Palace)

Schlossstraße 18. Open year-round Tue–Sun 10am–6pm. Closed Jan 1, Dec 24–25 & 31. ∞3€. ♿℘(05261) 945 00. www.wrm.lemgo.de.

This mighty palace dates back to the 12C but was repeatedly tinkered with until the 19C, although its predominant style is Weser Renaissance. Inside, the **Weserrenaissance-Museum** is dedicated to art and culture between the Reformation and the Thirty Years' War. Also stop by the palace chapel and climb up the seven-storey tower to take in sweeping views over Lemgo.

👣WALKING TOUR

OLD TOWN★

◐ Head east from the Ostertor gate towards Mittelstraße with its grand half-timbered houses. Note the fine façades of no 17 and no 36, the House of Planets (Planetenhaus).

Rathaus★★ (Town Hall)

The town hall is a hodgepodge of eight joined buildings overlooking the market square. The elegant façade of the old apothecary's shop displays sculpted portraits of 10 famous philosopher-physicians, from Aristotle to Paracelsus. Beneath the central arcades, witchcraft trials were held around 1670.

◐ Bear left into Breite Straße.

Hexenbürgermeisterhaus (Witch Hunter's House)

Breite Straße 19. Open year-round Tue–Sun 10am–5pm. ∞3€. ℘(05261) 21 32 76. www.hexenbuergermeisterhaus.de. This splendid 16C Weser Renaissance building houses the **city museum** with exhibits on everyday culture, trade and witch-hunting. A creepy highlight is the collection of torture and execution instruments from the estate of an actual family of executioners.

Marienkirche (Church of St. Mary's)

A Renaissance 16C organ, among the oldest in German, adorns this triple-aisle Gothic church. Admire, too, the baptismal font (1592), the pulpit (1644) and the Triumphal Cross (c. 1500).

◐ Backtrack to Papenstraße, then turn right.

St. Nicolaikirche (Church of St. Nicholas)

Lemgo's oldest church (13C) is dedicated to the patron saint of merchants and combines Romanesque (three-figure tympanum), Gothic (frescoes) and Renaissance (pulpit) elements; it is often used as a concert venue.

▶ Papenstraße leads back to the starting point.

EXCURSIONS
Herford

▶ 20km/12.4mi west.

This former Hanseatic town between Teutoburger Wald and the Weser River sprouted around an 8C convent and has beautifully preserved half-timbered houses. The convent's Romanesque church, the **Münster** (1220–1280), is one of the oldest in Westphalia and sports a 16C late-Gothic baptismal font and Romanesque capitals. Nearby, the 14C **Johanniskirche** bears fine 17C **carvings★**, both sculpted and painted.

Paderborn★

▶ 71km/44mi north via the A33.

Founded by Charlemagne in the 8C and situated in eastern Westphalia, modern Paderborn is a commercial hub and university town with about 15 000 students. Though badly pummelled during World War II, it boasts a good range of artistic, historical and architectural sights, plus one of the world's largest computer museums.

Birthplace of the Holy Roman Empire – Paderborn's beginnings are tied to Charlemagne who, in 776, established a power base here from which to defeat the Saxons and to oversee their Christianisation. In 799, a deposed Pope Leo III fled to Paderborn to ask for Charlemagne's help in restoring him to the papal throne. In exchange, he was to be crowned emperor, thus laying the foundation for the Holy Roman Empire that lasted until 1806. The coronation took place in Rome on Christmas Day 800.

Clocktower of Dom, Paderborn
©Paul Rüsing/istockphoto.com

Dom★ (Cathedral)

Marktplatz. Open year-round daily 6.30am–6.30pm (Wed & Sat-Sun also open during evening services). www.erzbistum-paderborn.de.

Paderborn's cathedral was built between 1225 and 1270 as a three-aisled Gothic hall-church attached to a Romanesque west tower. The main entrance is through the south portal known as "Paradies". It dates to 1250 and is richly festooned with sculptures of St. Mary, Christ, the apostles and other biblical figures. Inside, the elaborate **tomb of Prince-Bishop Dietrich von Fürstenberg★** and the late-Gothic high altar are artistic highlights.

The crypt is the largest in Germany and shelters the relics of Paderborn's patron saint, St. Liborius (348–398), which were transferred to the city in 836.

Be sure to follow the signs to the cloister to have a look at the endearing **Drei-Hasen-Fenster★** *(Three Hares' Window)*. It shows three hares chasing each other in a circle with each of the ears shared by two animals so that only three ears are shown in all.

Diözesanmuseum (Cathedral Treasury) –

Markt 17. Open year-round Tue–Sun 10am–6pm. ⊜*3.50€.* ♿ ☏*(05251) 125 14 00. www.dioezesanmuseum-paderborn.de.* A modern building next to the cathedral houses religious treasures

Libori Festival

Every year in late July, the people of Paderborn mix up religious tradition and worldly entertainment for one week of fun in honour of the city's patron, St. Liborius. The largely pedestrianised town centre is transformed into a veritable drinking and partying zone where up to a million visitors let their hair down during live concerts, exhibitions, shows and even impromptu singalongs with local nuns!

Thrill-seekers can enjoy carousels and rollercoasters, shopaholics can indulge their addiction at the Pottmarkt arts and crafts market, while night-owls keep the city's dance floors hopping until dawn. See www.libori.de for the full run-down (click on the British flag for the English-language version).

from 20 centuries, including such celebrated items as a Madonna from 1058 and the gilded silver Shrine of Liborius from 1627.

Kaiserpfalzen★★ (Imperial Palaces)

In 1964 archaeologists made a sensational find: just north of the cathedral they discovered the foundations of Charlemagne's 8C palace.

Continued excavations also unearthed the adjacent remnants of Heinrich II's palace from the early 11C. The latter has been meticulously reconstructed and now houses a modern **museum** (open year-round Tue–Sun 10am–6pm; closed Dec 24–25 & 31; ∞3.50€; ℰ05251 10 51 10; www.kaiserpfalz-paderborn.de). Its displays shed light on daily life in the early Middle Ages.

Bartholomäuskapelle (Chapel of St. Bartholomew)

Open year-round daily 10am–6pm.

This tiny chapel next to the imperial palaces is the oldest hall-church north of the Alps (1017). It has splendid acoustics and elaborate capitals.

▲▲ Heinz Nixdorf Museumsforum★★

Fürstenallee 7. Open year-round Tue–Fri 9am–6pm, Sat–Sun 10am–6pm. Closed Jan 1, Dec 24–25 & 31. ∞7€. ♿. ℰ(05251) 30 66 00. www.hnf.de.

The evolution of communication technology gets the spotlight at this engaging and interactive museum. In one section you can travel back 5 000 years to the beginnings of writing in Mesopotamia, then fast-forward into cyberspace in another. In between you come face to face with all sorts of historic calculating machines, typewriters, telephone exchanges and even a full-scale replica of Eniac, a 1940s US Army computer that is the size of an entire room.

Museum für Stadtgeschichte (City History Museum)

Hathumarstraße 7–9. Open year-round Tue–Sun 10am–6pm. ℰ(05251) 882 35 01. www.paderborn.de/stadtmuseum.

City history is chronicled in one of the oldest and prettiest half-timbered buildings in town, the 16C **Adam-und-Eva-Haus**. It is so named because sculptures on the façade depict the expulsion of Adam and Eve from the Garden of Eden.

Rathaus (Town Hall)

This splendid example of Weser Renaissance architecture is one of the most beautiful town halls in the region. Completed in 1616, it sports a triple gable and arcades supported by Doric pillars. In front stands a Baroque fountain decorated with the city's coat of arms.

Paderquellen (Pader Springs)

Paderborn derives its name from the Pader, Germany's shortest river. It originates from 200 springs in a park just north of the cathedral and flows into the Lippe River after a mere 4km/2.5mi.

Münster★★

The historical capital of Westphalia lies at the centre of a wooded plain studded with moated castles and manor houses. Thanks to a busy post-World War II restoration programme, it is an attractive city whose streets are flanked by Renaissance, Gothic and Baroque façades. Münster's key moment in world history came in 1648 with the signing of the treaty that ended the Thirty Years' War. Cyclists will love this pancake-flat university town: its roads are lined with hundreds of kilometres of bike trails. Bicycles, by the way, are called *"Leeze"* in the local dialect.

A BIT OF HISTORY

The Peace of Westphalia – This twin treaty ended the Thirty Years' War: it was signed in two towns: Protestant Osnabrück 15 May 1648, and Catholic Münster 24 October 1648. The treaties involved Emperor Ferdinand III, the kingdoms of Spain, France and Sweden, the Dutch Republic and their respective allies among the princes of the Holy Roman Empire. It recognised and confirmed the cession to France of Alsace, guaranteed the independence of Switzerland and the Netherlands, and favoured the development of Prussia. Protestants and Catholics were redefined as equal before the law, and Calvinism was given legal recognition.

▶ **Population:** 288 900

ℹ **Info:** Heinrich-Brüning-Straße 9, 48127 Münster. ℘(0251) 492 27 10. www.muenster.de.

▶ **Location:** Münster can be reached via the A1 (Dortmund–Bremen), and is one hour by car from the large towns of the Ruhr.

🅿 **Parking:** Garages are located throughout the old city, near the main train station, near the Residenzschloss and near the theatre on Wasserstraße.

☺ **Don't Miss:** The cathedral and the Prinzipalmarkt with the Peace Hall.

🕐 **Timing:** Allow one full day to see the sights of Münster.

SIGHTS
St. Paulus-Dom★★ (Cathedral)

Domplatz 28. Open year-round daily 6.30am–7pm (Sun until 7.30pm). ℘(0251) 495 6700. www.paulusdom.de. Münster's squat twin-towered cathedral reflects the transitional style from Romanesque to Gothic prevalent in the 13C. The entrance is via the 16C south porch decorated with statues of the apostles and overlooked by Christ in Judgement. Inside, don't miss the 1540 **astronomical clock★** in the southern

Prinzipalmarkt in the evening

The Anabaptists

Believed to have originated in Zurich, this radical religious reform movement endorsed adult baptism, polygamy and community of goods. In 1534, its followers attempted to establish a theocracy in Münster, deposing the magistrates and introducing its tenets. The era was brought to an end after a 16-month siege ending with the torture and execution of its leaders in the market square. The Anabaptists, or Rebaptists, were spiritual forerunners of the Mennonites and the Amish.

ambulatory whose hours are struck by metal figurines wielding hammers. A carillon begins at noon daily (12.30pm Sun), and there is also a calendar that goes up to 2071 and a display of the moon phases and planet constellations. The **Chapel of the Holy Sacrament★** is richly furnished (note especially the 18C silver tabernacle).

The cathedral's modern **treasury★★** (Domkammer; open year-round Tue–Sun 11am–4pm; closed Jan 1, Rose Mon, Good Friday–Easter Sun, May 1, Whitsun, Dec 24–26 & 31; €3€; 戊; ℘0251 56 710; www.domkammer-muenster.de) is reached via the cloister. On the ground floor, 15C reliquary busts in copper and silver, the 11C head-reliquary of St. Paul and a 13C Virgin surround a 13C **processional cross.**

Westfälisches Landesmuseum für Kunst und Kulturgeschichte★ (Regional Art and History Museum)

Domplatz 10. Open year-round Tue–Sun 10am–6pm. Closed Jan 1, Dec 24-25 & 31. €8€. 戊. ℘(0251) 590 7201. www.lwl-museum-kunst-kultur.de. This museum's collections span the artistic arc from the Middle Ages to today. Particularly noteworthy are **altarpieces★★** by Conrad von Soest,

Koerbecke and the Masters of Liesborn and Schöppingen.

Prinzipalmarkt★ (Principal Market)

The Prinzipalmarkt is Münster's busiest and most historic street with elegant houses that were once the homes of rich burghers. Under the arcades, attractive shops jostle for attention with cosy pubs and restaurants.

Rathaus (Town Hall)

The dominant building on Prinzipalmarkt is the late 14C town hall, an impressive example of Gothic civic architecture. The diplomatic negotiations between 1644 and 1648 that brought an end to the Thirty Years' War were held in the **Friedensaal★** (Peace Hall; open year-round Tue–Fri 10am–5pm, Sat–Sun 10am–4pm; €2€; 戊; ℘(0251) 492 27 24), a wood-panelled council chamber.

Lambertikirche (St. Lambert's Church)

Groined vaulting lidding the centre nave and star vaults above the side aisles are the striking features of this Gothic hall-church. Dangling from the tower are the iron cages that once held the dead bodies of the Anabaptist rebel leaders displayed to the public following the defeat of their uprising in 1535.

Residenzschloss (Palace)

This Baroque palace was once the residence of the prince-bishops and is now part of the university. The red-brick of the elegant three-part façade designed by Johann Conrad Schlaun is variegated with sandstone facings. The park in the back segues into a botanical garden.

EXCURSIONS
Telgte

▶ 12km/8mi east on B51.

In the centre of Telgte, next to the Baroque pilgrimage chapel with a pietà from 1370, is the local museum, the Heimathaus Münsterland. One of its prize exhibits is a folk-art textile, the

Lenten Veil★ (1623), which measures 32sq m/344.4sq ft.

Freckenhorst

❯ 26km/16mi east on B51.
Freckenhorst's **Collegiate Church**★ *(Stiftskirche)* is a fine example of pre-Romanesque German architecture.

Ostenfelde

❯ 36km/22.3mi east on B51.
The graceful, privately owned **Schloss Vornholz**★ (Vornholz Castle, 1666) stands in a rolling landscape forested with ancient oaks. Built on two islets, it is a typical Münsterland "water castle".

Osnabrück

❯ Osnabrück lies at the northern end of the Teutoburg Forest, about 46km/28.5mi northeast of Münster. Bierstraße 22-23, 49074 Osnabrück. ℘(0541) 323 22 02. www.osnabrueck.de.
The birthplace of writer Erich Maria Remarque *(All Quiet on the Western Front)*, Osnabrück made world history in 1648 with the co-signing of the treaty ending the Thirty Years' War (it was also signed in Münster).
Its other famous native son is the painter Felix Nussbaum, whose work is showcased in a dramatic museum designed by Daniel Libeskind.

Rathaus (Town Hall)

Open year-round Mon–Fri 8am–6pm, Sat 9am–4pm, Sun 10am–4pm. Closed Jan 1, Good Friday, Dec 24 & 31. ⅚ ℘(0541) 323 21 52.
This early 16C building had to be restored after World War II but retains its Gothic look. The Peace of Westphalia treaty of 1648 was announced from its steps. A statue of Charlemagne stands above the entrance.

Friedensaal (Peace Hall) –

The hall in which the peace negotiations took place is adorned with portraits of the heads of state and their delegates. The floor and ceiling have been rebuilt; the 16C wooden seats and chandelier are original. In the **treasury** is the priceless 14C *Kaiserpokal* (Imperial goblet).

Felix-Nussbaum-Haus★★

Lotter Straße 2. Open year-round Tue–Fri 11am–6pm, Sat–Sun 10am–6pm. Closed Jan 1, Dec 24 & 31. ⅚5€. ⅚ ℘(0541) 323 22 07. www.osnabrueck.de/fnh.
This Deconstructivist museum building was designed by **Daniel Libeskind** in 1998 to house 160 works by native son Felix Nussbaum (1904–44). Its broken architectural lines and eccentric details are deliberately meant to be disorienting and are intended to reflect the emotional turmoil experienced by Nussbaum. His work places him under *Neue Sachlichkeit* (New Objectivity).

MOATED CASTLES

The rural, sparsely populated area surrounding the historic town of Münster is an attractive patchwork of flat fields, pastures and meadows dotted with some 100 moated fairytale castles. Most are privately owned and can be viewed only from the outside, but some are open to visitors.

Vornholz★

❯ 36km/22.3mi southeast.
The graceful, privately owned **Schloss Vornholz**★ (Vornholz Castle, 1666) stands in a rolling landscape forested with ancient oaks. Built on two islets, it is a typical Münsterland moated castle.

Burg Hülshoff★

❯ 20km/12.5mi west. Schonebeck 6, Havixbeck. Open late Mar–Oct daily 11am–6.30pm; Nov Tue–Sun 11am–5pm. ⅚5€. ℘(02534) 10 52. www.burg-huelshoff.de.
One of Germany's finest female poets, **Annette von Droste-Hülshoff** (1797–1848) was born in this red-brick Renaissance villa embedded in a lovely park *(admission free)*. Some fully furnished period rooms are open to the public, and exhibits recall her life and work.

Vischering★

❯ 30km/18.5mi south. Berenbrock 1, Lüdinghausen. Open Apr–Oct Tue–Sun 10am–1pm, 1.30pm–5.30pm; Nov–Mar 10am–1pm, 1.30pm–4.30pm. Closed

Burg Vischering

© Heinz Schiffer/Fotolia.com

Jan 1, Dec 24–26 & 31. ⌁2.50€. ✆(02591) 799 00. www.burg-vischering.de.
Built on two islands and protected by a double fortified wall, Vischering is the oldest and still one of the most formidable fortresses in the Münster region. It is essentially a Renaissance building constructed atop the foundations of a medieval castle. The fortress houses a museum displaying furniture through the ages. The wall and ceiling paintings and splendid sandstone fireplaces are particularly impressive.

The Vorburg, on a separate island, once housed farm outbuildings. There is also a richly decorated carriage house.

Lembeck Castle★

◗ 50km/31mi southwest, in Lembeck.
◥Visit of castle museum by guided tour (40min, in German) only, late Mar–Oct Mon–Sun 10am–6pm; Nov–mid-Mar on fair weather days. Park open Mon–Fri 1pm–5pm, Sat–Sun 11am–5pm.
⌁5€. ✆(02369) 71 67.
www.schlosslembeck.de.
The approach to this castle follows a driveway punctuated by Baroque gateways and flanked by arched entrances. The monumental 17C palace features massive towers with onion-domed Baroque steeples protecting each cor-

ner. Guided tours take in splendidly furnished rooms reflecting the styles of the 17C and 18C. **Großer Saal**, the largest room, is embellished with fine panelling and stuccowork.

Raesfeld Castle

◗ 74km/45mi southwest, in Raesfeld.
◥Visit by guided tour (1hr) only.
✆(02865) 609 10. www.raesfeld.de.
Raesfeld Castle, built between 1643 and 1658 by Alexander von Velen, now consists only of a building with two wings, the Vorburg and the castle chapel. It is used as a training centre for various crafts and trades. Visible from afar is the 52.5m/172ft-high **onion-domed tower**, the highest one of the region's moated castles.

Gemen Castle

◗ 63km/39mi west. Schlossplatz 1, Borken. This castle is a church-owned youth centre (Jugendburg) and can be visited only by prior arrangement.
✆(028 61) 93 92 52.
www.muensterland-tourismus.de.
The towers, battlements and buildings of this castle (15C, remodelled in the 17C) are grouped on a fortified islet arising from shaded stretches of water.

Remains of Medieval Wars

The charming **Wasserburgen** – literally "water castles" – are found all over the Münster region. Witness to the incessant defensive battles between rival nobles, they are built on the sites of temporary encampments set up by the Teutonic tribes. The castles first appeared in the 12C in the form of wooden strongholds erected on artificial hills *(Motten)* protected at the base by a surrounding defensive wall and a moat. The invention of firearms in the early 16C made this system of defence precarious, and it was replaced over time with proper fortifications isolated still more by moats or lagoons. Many of these compounds are spread over two islands, joined by a bridge. The first isle, or "Vorburg", was used for outbuildings; the second, or "Hauptburg" was used as the main residence. Their defensive character became less distinct over the centuries, especially after the Thirty Years' War (1618–48). Thereafter, palaces set in formal gardens began to appear.

Anholt Castle★

◗ 100km/62mi west. Schlossplatz 1, Isselburg-Anholt. ↝Visit by guided tour (1hr) only, May–Sept Tue–Sun 11am–5pm; Oct–Apr Sun 1pm–5pm. Closed Jan 1, Dec 24–26 & 31. ⊛6€, combined ticket for guided tour and park 8€. ℘(02874) 453 53. www.fuerst-salm.de.

Surrounded by a landscaped park and restored Baroque garden, this moated castle (*Hauptburg* and *Vorburg* 12C–17C, converted into a Baroque palace c. 1700) frames a square inner courtyard. The museum contains evidence of three centuries of royal home décor. Paintings (Rembrandt, Brueghel, Murillo), furniture, tapestries, porcelain and weapons are on view.

Nordkirchen Castle

◗ 36km/23mi south. Schloss 1, Nordkirchen. ↝Visit by guided tour (1hr) only, May–Sept Sun 11am–5pm; Oct–Apr Sun 2pm–4pm; otherwise by prior arrangement daily 9am–6pm. ⊛2€. Park free anytime, year-round. ℘(02596) 93 30. www.schloss.nordkirchen.net.

Not far from Vischering, this impressive 18C moated castle is the region's largest and is known as "Westphalia's Versailles". The surrounding gardens are sprinkled with splendid sculptures.

ADDRESSES

🛏 STAY

⊜⊜ **Hotel Central** – *Aegidiistraße 1. ℘(0251) 51 01 50. www.central-hotel-muenster.de. 21 rooms. Closed 2 weeks in summer, Dec 22–31.* ⌑. Run by an art-loving couple, this small city hotel has works from Beuys to Warhol decorating the public areas and the modern and good-sized rooms.

⊜⊜ **Hotel Hiltruper Hof** – *Westfalenstraße 148, 48165 Münster-Hiltrup ℘(0251) 278 80. www.hiltruper-hof.de. 17 rooms.* ⌑. For 150 years this family-run hotel has welcomed guests into well-cared-for rooms. Sports and leisure equipment are available locally.

⊰/EAT

⊜⊜ **Spitzner im Oer'schen Hof** – *Königsstraße 42. ℘(0251) 41 44 15 50. www.oerschenhof.ms. Closed Sun–Mon.* This three-floor establishment in an old glazed-brick house boasts a tasteful mix of rustic furniture and modern paintings. The chef ingeniously infuses Westphalian fare with Mediterranean accents.

⊜⊜ **Pinkus Müller** – *Kreuzstraße 4. ℘(0251) 451 51. www.pinkus-mueller.de. Closed Sun.* This classic Westphalian brew-pub exudes rustic flair, makes its own beer and serves hearty meals to mixed crowds sitting around polished wooden tables. The same street has several other restaurants and cafés.

The West

ENGLISH
GUIDED TOURS
SAT, SUN AND
HOLIDAYS!

denkmalpfad@zollverein.de
or +49 201 2 4 6 8 10

ZOLLVEREIN UNESCO WORLD HERITAGE SITE

DENKMALPFAD **ZOLLVEREIN**®
DISCOVER THE "WORLD´S MOST BEAUTIFUL" COAL MINE!

Explore Industrial History / Experience Zollverein / Make Exciting Discoveries

 STIFTUNG
ZOLLVEREIN

www.zollverein.de

The West

Germany's western regions deliver a cornucopia of diverse and awe-inspiring sightseeing opportunities. Soak up cosmopolitan flair and stunning art and architecture in cities such as Düsseldorf, Cologne and Frankfurt or escape to historic villages in the hilly Sauerland or the gentle Eifel. Follow the mighty Rhine or the meandering Moselle rivers past a fairytale setting of medieval castles, steep vineyards and little towns that are veritable symphonies in half-timber. Walk in the footsteps of the Romans in Trier, check out Charlemagne's legacy in Aachen and see for yourself the beauty of Heidelberg, which has inspired so many great poets and artists.

Highlights

1 The buttresses of the mighty **Cologne Cathedral** (p273)

2 Fine art at **Museum Folkwang** in the Ruhr Region (p290)

3 Roman ruins in **Trier** (p307)

4 Wines at Kloster Eberbach in the **Rhine Valley** (p328)

5 Views of **Heidelberg** and its castle from Philosophers' Walk (p350)

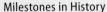

Milestones in History

Two millennia of German history unfold before you as you travel through Germany's western region. The legacy of the Romans survives in Cologne, Bonn and Koblenz, but nowhere more so than in Trier, where you can wander among some of the best-preserved Roman ruins north of the Alps. Aachen also has Roman origins but was most lastingly put on the map by Charlemagne, the "father of modern Europe" who made the town the capital of his enormous Frankish Empire in the 8C. More than 30 German kings were crowned in the chapel he built (now part of Aachen Cathedral) before the ceremony was moved to Frankfurt, where Germany's greatest poet, Johann Wolfgang von Goethe, was born in 1749. A few centuries earlier, nearby Mainz had already given the world Johannes Gutenberg, whose invention of the modern printing press turned the world on its head. Cities that shaped Germany during the Industrial Age can be found in the Ruhr Region and in the Saarland. The former colliery Zollverein in Essen and the Völklinger Ironworks near Saarbrücken are both UNESCO-protected World Heritage Sites.

Great Cathedrals

This region boasts many churches and cathedrals originally built in the Middle Ages. One of the oldest on German soil

In Vino Veritas

The region described in this chapter comprises seven of 13 wine-growing regions in Germany. The smallest and northernmost is the **Ahr Valley** along the Ahr River south of Bonn, which is especially famous for its velvety red Spätburgunder. South of here, Koblenz marks the beginning of the **Moselle** region, where Riesling and Müller-Thurgau grow on some of the steepest slopes in the world, and the **Mittelrhein**, which cuts through the scenic Rhine Gorge. Its slate soil and terraced vineyards are also particularly conducive to growing Riesling. The most refined Rieslings, though, hail from the famous **Rheingau** around Rüdesheim. West of the Rhine, the **Nahe** produces diverse wines from relatively few grape varieties, including the earthy Silvaner. Further south, **Rheinhessen** is Germany's largest growing region with soft, fragrant and medium-bodied wines. Wedged between the Rheinhessen region and France is the **Palatinate**, where smooth Rieslings and mild yet full-bodied Müller-Thurgau dominate.

Museum Folkwang, Essen

© Jens Nober/Museum Folkwang

is the palace chapel in Aachen, a superb example of Carolingian architecture. It was completed in 800, making it the oldest section of Aachen's otherwise largely Gothic cathedral. Driving east, you will soon spot the twin spires of Cologne's magnificent cathedral looming in the distance. The grandeur and loftiness of this French Gothic pile attracts more visitors than any other tourist sight in Germany. For fabulous views, it's worth braving the dizzying climb up the tower. Cologne also preserves a dozen Romanesque churches from the 12C and 13C. Most were destroyed in World War II and have been carefully rebuilt. To see the finest examples of this architectural style in Germany, though, point the compass south and follow the Rhine to Mainz, Speyer and Worms. Each of these cities boasts an awe-inspiring cathedral that exudes solemn ambience and is packed with artistic treasures.

Hubs of Fine Art

Art-ficionados could design an entire itinerary hopping from one museum to the next while exploring Germany's western regions. Düsseldorf especially has a long and distinguished tradition in the art world, ever since Elector Carl Theodor founded the Academy for Painting, Sculpture and Architecture in 1773. Still going strong today as the Düsseldorfer Kunstakademie, it has produced such hotshots as Joseph Beuys, Gerhard Richter, Jörg Immendorf and Andreas Gursky. Their work graces the walls of the Kunstsammlung Nordrhein-Westfalen in Düsseldorf as well as the Museum Ludwig in neighbouring Cologne. Cologne itself also enjoys a stellar reputation in the art world, not only for its museums but also for hosting Art Cologne, one of Europe's most important contemporary art fairs. Cutting-edge exhibits can also be viewed down the Rhine in Bonn's Kunst- und Ausstellungshalle and in Aachen's Ludwig Forum für Internationale Kunst. Away from the Rhineland, the Städel Museum in Frankfurt opened a new subterranean gallery showcasing postwar works by German artists, with Anselm Kiefer, Georg Baselitz and Markus Lüpertz among them.

© Damm Fridmar/Sime/Photononstop

Reliquary bust of Charlemagne in Dom, Aachen

The West

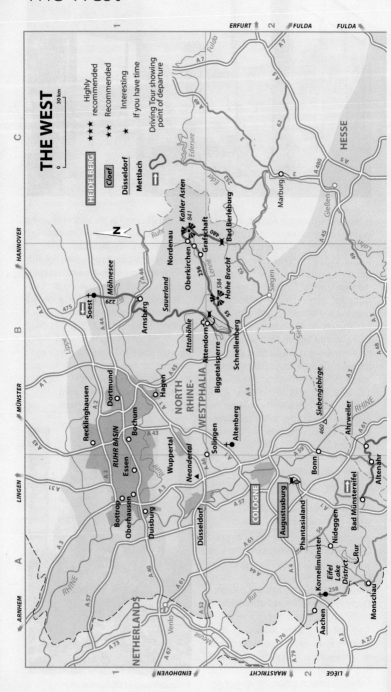

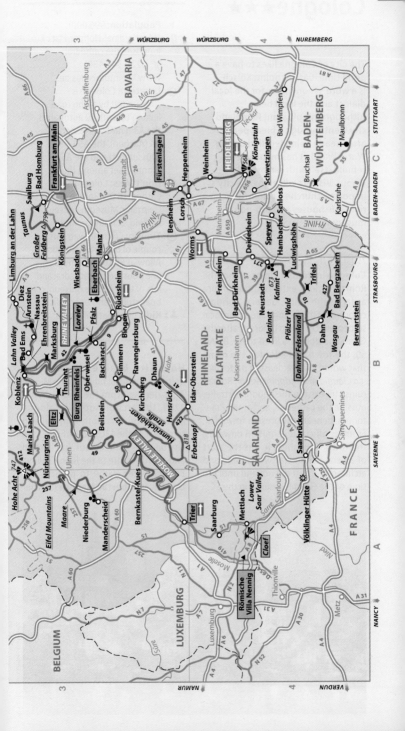

Cologne★★★

Köln

The city of Cologne likes to have a good time. Case in point: Kölsch is a word synonymous for the local dialect and the local beer. Although this pleasant Rhineland city went through a bleak period after nearly being levelled during World War II, it has managed to rebuild itself with remarkable vigour. Visitors will enjoy the city's imposing churches, colourful riverside houses and top-notch museums.

A BIT OF HISTORY

Cologne in Roman Times – Once the Roman legions extended the Empire as far as the Rhine, General Agrippa, coloniser of the region, named the local settlement Oppidum Ubiorum, after the Germanic Ubii who lived there. By AD 50, the town had adopted the name that would stick, at least in part: *Colonia Claudia Ara Agrippinensium*. Roman ruins still exist in the Zeughausstraße, outside the cathedral, and at the Praetorium, beneath the present Town Hall. From its official recognition onwards, the town flourished: it was the start of an era, rich in craftwork, trade and architecture, that did not end until the time of the Great Invasions, in the 5C.

▶ **Population:** 996 000
🛈 **Info:** Kardinal-Höffner-Platz 1 (opposite the cathedral). ℘(0221) 34 64 30. www.koelntourismus.de.
◖ **Location:** Cologne is surrounded by a ring road linking up with 10 autobahns, the A3 (Frankfurt–Essen), A4 (Aachen), the A59 (Düsseldorf) and the A555 (Bonn) chief among them.
⊛ **Don't Miss:** Cologne's Cathedral, the Roman-Germanic Museum, Museum Ludwig, Schnütgen Museum.
🕐 **Timing:** Cologne warrants a couple of days of exploration. Allow at least a minimum of one hour for the cathedral and lots of time for the museums, boat cruises and beer halls.
👪 **Kids:** Chocolate Museum.

Holy City beside the Rhine – Cologne's political power in the Middle Ages derived from the Church. Until 1288, the archbishops of Cologne exercised powers both spiritual and temporal. In the 13C and early 14C, the city became the religious, intellectual and artistic centre of the Rhine Valley. Eminent men came to preach: the Dominican **Albertus Magnus** (teacher

Old Town, Cologne

© KölnTourismus GmbH / Udo Haake

© KölnTourismus GmbH / Dieter Jacobi

CARNIVAL

In Cologne, Carnival is considered the 'fifth season', which officially begins at 11 minutes past 11 on the 11th day of the 11th month. The main celebrations, though, don't actually take place until months later, during the week preceding the beginning of Lent. Normal business essentially shuts down between Fat Thursday and Ash Wednesday when costumed locals are joined by revellers from around the world in a raucous party taking over streets and pubs. The typical greeting during the festival is *Kölle Alaaf!*, a phrase in local dialect that roughly translates as "Cologne alive!"

© KölnTourismus GmbH / Dieter Jacobi

Carnival has been celebrated for centuries, but since 1823 a number of customs and traditions have emerged. Women rule on Fat Thursday *(Weiberfastnacht)* when they demonstrate their cheekiness by indiscriminately cutting off men's neckties. Celebrations on the weekend are more family-oriented and held in the individual districts, leading up to the big School and City Quarter Procession *(Schull-un Veedelszöch)* on Sunday. The biggest parade, though, and the culmination of Carnival, snakes through the city on Rose Monday *(Rosenmontag)*. Organised by the local Carnival associations, it features marching bands, costumed dancers and elaborately decorated floats, often with a political or satirical theme. Hundreds of thousands of merrymakers line the streets cheering them on. It is a huge event that is even shown on German television. Celebrations end on Shrove Tuesday *(Veilchendienstag)* with the burning of straw dolls (called *Nubbel*) at midnight. The traditional way to combat hangovers on Ash Wednesday is with a meal of fish in one of the old-timey brewpubs.

To learn more, visit www.koelnerkarneval.de or, if already in town, the Cologne Carnival Museum (www.koelnerkarneval.de/museum).

of Thomas Aquinas) and **Master Eckhart**, as well as the Scottish Franciscan **Duns Scotus**. It was the work of such religious scholars that led in 1388 to the creation of Cologne University by local citizens.

Trade and commerce – Because of its strategic location on the Rhine and along important trade routes, Cologne soon became a power in the commercial world, imposing its own system of weights and measures over the whole of northern Germany. It held its first major fair in 1360. Elevation to the status of Free Imperial City in 1475 did no more than set an official seal on the dominant role Cologne had in fact been playing since the 13C.

The modern city – Industrialisation in the late 19C quickly expanded Cologne. After World War II, **Konrad Adenauer** continued the process of modernisation begun while he served as the city's mayor from 1917 to 1933. It was on the watch of the man destined to become the Federal Republic's first chancellor that the university (shut down under French occupation in 1798) was reopened in 1919, the Deutz exhibition halls (*Messehallen*) were built; and greenbelts were added throughout the city.

Art and culture – Diversity, above all, marks cultural life in Cologne today. Apart from music and drama, the fine arts hold pride of place: more than 100 galleries are devoted to contemporary art exhibitions alone. Art Cologne is a highly regarded annual international art fair. The Wallraf-Richartz Museum and the Museum Ludwig are among venues mounting important temporary exhibits.

Heinrich Böll (1917–85), one of the pre-eminent German postwar writers and winner of the Nobel Prize for Literature in 1972, was born in Cologne. His work, sparing neither the Church nor society, is inseparable from his birthplace. Publishing houses and printers have been based in Cologne for centuries. Building on this history has been the postwar push into electronic media. Although it's been losing some of its influence to Berlin and Hamburg, Cologne still has a number of broadcasting companies, including several television stations along with recording studios and an Academy of Media Arts.

Town life – There is a strong sense of neighbourhood in Cologne. Each locality centres on its individual parish church, each of which preserves its own traditions. St. Severin is the oldest and most typical. But all Cologne citizens appreciate the old town bordering the Rhine. Remodelled in the 1980s, it is one of the liveliest parts of the city, especially at night. Since the riverside highway has been diverted underground between the Hohenzollern and Deutzer bridges, land has been transformed into attractive gardens (*Rheingarten*) perfect for walking, relaxing or embarking on a leisurely boat cruise.

Stained-glass window of the cathedral

© Philip Lange/Bigstockphoto.com

KÖLNER DOM★★★ (COLOGNE CATHEDRAL)

Self-guided tour pamphlets available in the foyer. Open May–Oct daily 6am–9pm; Nov–Apr daily 6am–7.30pm. ✆Guided tours available. ♿. ✆(0221) 17 94 01 00. www.koelner-dom.de.

This monumental cathedral was built over the course of 600 years. In 1164, when Frederick I Barbarossa donated the relics of the Three Magi to the city, an influx of pilgrims created the need for a larger church. Thus began construction of the first Gothic church in the Rhineland whose design was inspired by the cathedrals at Paris, Amiens and Reims. Builders first set to work in 1248 and by 1320 the chancel was completed. The south tower followed by 1410, but soon after, building was suspended because of lack of funds and political turmoil. When it resumed in the 19C, the original plans were used, and in 1880 the cathedral was finally consecrated before Emperor Wilhelm I. Miraculously, it survived World War II almost intact and was declared a UNESCO World Heritage Site in 1996.

© Vivalapenler/Dreamstime.com

Inside the cathedral

Exterior

The twin-towered western façade marks a high point in the Flamboyant Gothic style. Embellished gables and slender buttresses burst ever upward, in line with tapering spires 157m/515ft high. The bronze doors **(1)** in the south transept entrance (1948–54) are by Ewald Mataré.

Interior

The building's colossal proportions are fully appreciated from the nave, 144m/472.4ft long, 45m/147.6ft wide and 43.5m/142.7ft high.

The five late-Gothic **stained-glass windows**★ in the north aisle (1507–08) depict the lives of the Virgin and St. Peter. In the south transept is a new window by German artist Gerard Richter composed of 11 500 glass

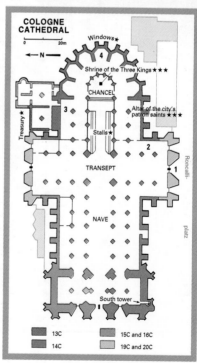

COLOGNE CATHEDRAL

0   20m

← N

Windows★

Shrine of the Three Kings ★★★

CHANCEL

Treasury★

3

Altar of the city's patron saints ★★★

Stalls★

2

1

Roncalli-

TRANSEPT

platz

NAVE

South tower

13C
14C
15C and 16C
19C and 20C

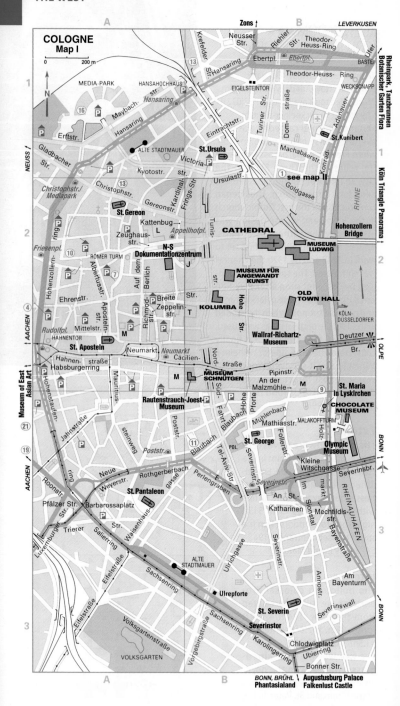

COLOGNE
Map I

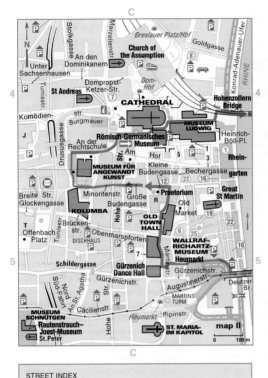

squares in 72 colours, which creates a kaleidoscopic effect when hit by the sun. The same transept houses a Flemish polyptych of 1521 with double side panels known as the **Altarpiece of the Five Moors (2)** (Agilolphusaltar). The Cross Chapel (Kreuzkapelle) off the north ambulatory features the **Gero★ Crucifix** (Gerokreuz) **(3)**, an early example of 10C Ottonian art. In the axial chapel (Dreikönigskapelle) the stained-glass window, the Älteres Bibelfenster **(4)**, was installed in 1265. The shrine behind the high altar contains the relics of the Three Magi: this 12C masterpiece in gold is called **Schrein der Heiligen Drei Könige★★★**. The last chapel in the south ambulatory (Marienkapelle) contains the altar of the city's patrons, the **Altar der Stadtpatrone★★★**.

Painted c. 1440 by **Stefan Lochner**, it illustrates The Adoration of the Magi, St. Ursula and St. Gereon. Finally, the finely carved **choir stalls★** (14C) (Chorgestühl), the most extensive in Germany, contain 104 seats.

For panoramic views, climb the 509 steps of the **south tower** (Südturm; ✑3€) to a platform at 97m/318ft. The belfry (Glockenstube) houses the world's largest swinging church bell: the 24t **St. Peter's Bell** (Petersglocke), which was cast in 1923.

The **cathedral treasury★** (Domschatz-kammer; open year-round daily 10am –6pm; ✑5€; &; ✆0221 17 94 05 55) contains a wealth of religious art. Gold and silver liturgical plates, the shrine to St. Engelbert and a reliquary monstrance with St. Peter's chain are among the highlights.

👣 WALKING TOUR

OLD TOWN

The cultural heart of Cologne extends south of the central station and the super-busy Hohenzollernbrücke.

Several outstanding museums sit in the shadow of the cathedral. The Römisch-Germanisches Museum and Diözesanmuseum rub shoulders with the Museum Ludwig, a 1986 edifice whose distinctive saw-tooth roof contrasts with the Gothic spires of the cathedral. The complex also includes a concert hall, the **Kölner Philharmonie**, at basement level. From Heinrich-Böll-Platz, behind the museums, a series of terraces leads down to the Rheingarten riverside promenade.

Römisch-Germanisches Museum★★ (Roman-Germanic Museum)

Roncalliplatz 4. ⊘Visit afternoons or weekends to avoid school groups. Open year-round Tue–Sun 10am–5pm. Closed Jan 1, Carnival week, Dec 24–25 & 31. ⊚9€. ♿ ℘(0221) 22 12 44 38. www.museenkoeln.de.

As capital of the Roman province of Lower Germania, Cologne enjoyed immense prosperity from the 1C to the 4C, due largely to trade between the Roman colonisers and the Germanic Ubii tribe. Evidence of these exchanges is displayed in this stellar museum. In the basement, the **Dionysius Mosaic★** is an exceptionally well-preserved Roman mosaic made of 1.5 million fragments of stone (measuring 14.5x7m/48x23ft). Belonging to a banqueting hall of a 3C Roman villa, it was uncovered during the construction of an air-raid bunker in 1941 and preserved on its original site. Adjacent rooms evoke funerary rites and the daily lives of the ancient Romans. Exhibits also include the enormous **Poblicius Tomb★★** (AD 40), created for an officer of the Roman Legion; the **Philosophers' Mosaic**; and an array of Roman **glassware★★**.

Museum Ludwig★★

Heinrich-Böll-Platz. Open year-round Tue–Sun 10am–6pm. Closed Jan 1, Carnival week, Dec 24–25 & 31. www.museen-koeln.de. ⊚11€. ♿ ℘(0221) 22 12 61 65. www.museum-ludwig.de.

This spacious museum with its unusual roof houses an important collection of 20C art, with particular emphasis on the Expressionist movement and works by the Brücke and Blaue Reiter groups. There is also a good display of art from between the two world wars: Constructivism, the Bauhaus and New Objectivity. Another strong point is a collection of **Russian Avant-Garde** art. The Surrealist department reveals Dadaism's birth in Cologne and includes a variety of works by **Max Ernst** (he was born nearby in Brühl), Miró, Dalí and Magritte. **Cubism** is represented by Gris, Léger and Delaunay, and **Nouveau Réalisme** by Klein, Tàpies, Burri and Dubuffet. Curators are especially proud of their **Picasso** collection, which encompasses several hundred works.

German postwar and contemporary art includes works by the **Gruppe Zero**, mainly by **Beuys**, Baselitz, Richter, Penck and Kiefer. American abstract painting is represented (Rothko, de Kooning), as is **Pop Art** (Rauschenberg, Warhol and Segal).

Canvases, video, installations and other media by contemporary artists from Europe, America and Asia illustrate the most recent artistic trends.

The museum also has a comprehensive collection of photography; selections are presented in temporary shows.

▷ Cross the bridge going east.

The **Hohenzollern Bridge** (Hohenzollernbrücke) is the world's busiest railway bridge, with one train every two minutes, day and night.

Köln Triangle Panorama

Ottoplatz 1. Open May–Sept daily 11am–10pm (Sat & Sun from 10am); Oct–Apr daily noon–6pm (Sat & Sun from 10am). ⊚3€. ♿ ℘(02234) 99 21 555. www.koelntriangle.de.

The School of Cologne

Manuscript illumination and altar ornamentation were blossoming arts in Cologne in the early 14C. Painting reached its peak in the early 15C with the works of **The Master of St. Veronica** and **Stefan Lochner**, a native of Meersburg (on Lake Constance). From 1450 onward, under the influence of the Dutch schools, the artists of Cologne abandoned the idealistic mysticism of the Gothic period for the gracious realism of the Renaissance.

This later work is characterised by delicate colours and an emotional depiction of subjects. Religious sculpture in Cologne peaked between the 14C and 15C. Many **Madonnas** display this style of tenderness that swept Europe around 1400: the hinted smile, draping fabrics and a relaxed stance.

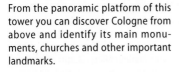

From the panoramic platform of this tower you can discover Cologne from above and identify its main monuments, churches and other important landmarks.

▶ Walk south along the Rhine and cross the Deutzer Bridge to arrive at Heumarkt Square.

Heumarkt (Hay Market Area)

Heumarkt is dominated by an equestrian statue of Prussian king Frederick William III (1770–1840). To the south, across Cäcilienstraße, is the Church of St. Maria-im-Kapitol. From here, continue south to the Rheinauhafen peninsula, where you'll find the Chocolate Museum and the German Sports and Olympic Museum (see description below). The **Church of St. Maria in Lyskirchen**, opposite the island, has beautiful arches and a painted Madonna and Child dating from approximately 1420.

▶ Follow Bolzenstraße west and note the amusing window displays of the costume shop Dieters.

Gürzenich Dance Hall

This structure was one of the first secular Gothic buildings (1441–44) and served as a model for many town houses. The "council's dance hall" was used for banquets in the Middle Ages and then again since the 19C when the modern carnival was born.

▶ Pick up Martinstraße and head north.

Wallraf-Richartz-Museum and Fondation Corboud★★

Obermarspforten. Open year-round Tue–Sun 10am–6pm (Thu until 9pm). Closed Jan 1, Carnival week, Nov 11, Dec 24–25 & 31 ⊛8€. ℘(0221) 22 12 11 19. www.wallraf.museum.

Housed in an angular Postmodern building designed by the late OM Ungers, this museum specialises in fine art from the 13C to the 19C, with a particular emphasis on local artists. The Medieval Painters of Cologne collection culminates with the late-Gothic work of Stefan Lochner. Also of note are the **Master of St. Veronica** and the **Master of Life of the Virgin**. Among the **German Old Masters** on view are **Dürer** and **Lucas Cranach the Elder** (Virgin and Child).

Baroque art is represented by Rubens, Ruisdael, Hals and **Rembrandt**, including a famous late self-portrait. Spanish, Italian and French include Murillo, Tiepolo and Boucher. There are also canvases by 18C–19C German artists Caspar David Friedrich and Cologne-born **Wilhelm Leibl**. French Impressionists Renoir, Monet, Sisley, Cézanne, Van Gogh and Gauguin rank among the perennial crowd-pleasers.

Altes Rathaus★ (Old Town Hall)

This building with its reconstructed 15C Gothic tower (carillon at noon and 5pm) and the Flemish Renaissance pavilion (1569–73) lies at the heart of the old Jewish quarter. In 1349, the ghetto was

Eau de Cologne

The people of Cologne were familiar with Cologne's "aqua mirabile" as early as the 16C, although it did not become widely known until the 18C. Its success is due to the enterprising spirit of an Italian immigrant family, the Farinas, of whom the most famous is **Johann Maria Farina**. "Cologne water" (*Kölnisch Wasser*) was thought to have medicinal properties and to cure a number of ills. In the wake of the Farina family's success, other producers of the miracle water sprang up, making "Eau de Cologne" famous. The new wave of producers included **Wilhelm Mühlens**, who founded a company in Glockengasse in 1792.

Under Napoleon, the use of Eau de Cologne as medicine was banned, so manufacturers began marketing their cure-all as perfume. Mühlens' business was located at no. 4711 Glockengasse, and in 1875 this number was registered as a trade mark for authentic Eau de Cologne (*Echt Kölnisch Wasser*). *The carillon in the gable of no 4711 Glockengasse plays the Marseillaise every hour from 9am to 7pm.*

stormed, its inhabitants killed and their homes torched.

Praetorium

Kleine Budengasse 2. Open year-round Tue–Sun 10am–5pm. Closed Jan 1, Carnival week, Dec 24–25 & 31. ⊶3.50€. ⃠ ✆(0221) 22 13 34 22. www.museenkoeln.de.

Below the town hall lie the foundations of the Roman governor's palace (1C–4C), called the Praetorium. In the antechamber are small sculptures, bricks and receptacles from Roman times. Visitors can also view the old sewer, used as an air-raid shelter in World War II.

Excavations beneath the town hall square have revealed original remnants, ruins and foundations of both Roman Cologne and the Jewish quarter. Pottery, ceramics, sculptures and mosaics are among the displays. A 3D model in the Praetorium illustrates the project.

▶ Follow Kleine Budengasse, then Grosse Budengasse west to Minoritenstrasse, then left on Kolumbastrasse.

Kolumba★

Kolumbaße 4. Open year-round Wed–Mon noon–5pm. Closed Carnival week & Sept 1–14. ⊶5€. ⃠ ✆(0221) 933 19 30. www.kolumba.de.

The Archdiocese of Cologne possesses a stunning collection of 2 000 years of religious art, which is displayed in this evocative modernist space into which Swiss architect Peter Zumthor has integrated the remains of the late-Gothic church of St. Kolumba.

Among the most famous works is Stephan Lochner's **Virgin with Violets**.

▶ Consider making a brief detour to House 4711, where eau de cologne was invented, or continue north on Drususgasse and turn right at An der Rechtschule.

Museum für Angewandte Kunst★ (Museum of Applied Arts)

An der Rechtschule. Open year-round Tue–Sun 11am–5pm. Closed Jan 1, Carnival week, Dec 24, 25 & 31. ⊶6€. ⃠ ✆(0221) 22 12 38 60. www.museenkoeln.de.

This museum contains an extensive collection of furniture, ceramics, glassware, metalwork, jewellery and textiles from the Middle Ages to the present. Of particular interest are tapestries from Basel, a Venetian wedding goblet from the 15C, two life-size animal figures made from Meissen porcelain, and Baroque and *Jugendstil* glassware.

ADDITIONAL SIGHTS
Museum Schnütgen★★

Cäcilienstraße 29-33. Open year-round Tue–Sun 10am–6pm (Thu until 8pm). Closed Jan 1, Carnival week, Dec 24–25 & 31. ⊶6€. ✆(0221) 22 12 36 20. www.museenkoeln.de.

PRACTICAL INFORMATION

Public Transport – The main local transport network in Cologne is the **Kölner Verkehrsbetriebe** *(KVB; 24hr hotline ☏01803 50 40 30)*, which operates buses, subways *(U-Bahn)* and trams *(Straßenbahn)*. The KVB is linked with the regional Rhein-Sieg transport authority (VRS), which extends as far as Bonn. The city is divided into price zones. Short trips cost 1.90€, longer ones are 2.80€. A *Tageskarte* (day pass) costs 8.10€ for one person and 12.10€ for up to five people travelling together. Both are valid for unlimited trips between 9am and 3am the following day. A one-week pass is 23.30€. The most central service centre is in the Neumarkt U-Bahn station, open Mon–Fri 8am–8pm, Sat 8.30am–5pm. *www.kvb-koeln.de.* The **Köln Welcome Card**, available at the tourist office and in hotels, entitles you to unlimited public transport and discounts at museums, attractions, entertainment venues, tours, restaurants, bars and other places. Single cards cost 9€ for 24hrs. Group cards are good for up to five people and cost 19€.

The 12C Cäcilienkirche makes a suitable site for this museum of sacred art of the 6C to the 19C. Since late 2010, some works are also housed in a modern extension. Numerous **Madonnas in wood** illustrate the local "tender" style in statuary. A collection of medieval items in ivory, most of them from Byzantium, France or other parts of Germany, displays particularly fine workmanship. Also note the works in gold, silver and bronze and medieval textiles.

Museum für Ostasiatische Kunst★★ (Museum of East Asian Art)

Universitätsstraße 100. Open year-round Tue–Sun 11am–5pm. Closed Jan 1, Carnival week, Dec 24, 25 & 31. ⊚9€. ♿ ☏(0221) 22 12 86 08. www.museenkoeln.de.

Germany's oldest museum of Asian art (founded in 1909) is surrounded by a Japanese garden laid out by Masayuki Nagare (b. 1923). The permanent exhibition displays works from China, Japan and Korea and covers all periods of artistic endeavour from the Neolithic Age to the present. Among the oldest items are Chinese vessels (16C–12C BC). Other highlights include Buddhist art from China and Japan; Chinese ceramics from all phases; 17C Chinese furniture and writing equipment, as well as Japanese screens.

Rautenstrauch-Joest-Museum (Ethnographic Museum)

Cäcilienstraße 29–33. Open year-round Tue–Sun 10am–6pm (Thu 8pm). Closed Jan 1, Carnival week, Dec 24–25 & 31. ⊚7€. ☏(0221) 22 13 13 56. www.museenkoeln.de.

Now in a new location, this well-respected museum is a treasure-trove of non-European art and culture. Highlights include Thai and Khmer ceramics from the 8C to the 16C, ancient Egyptian art and Native American art.

Japanese Garden, Museum für Ostasiatische Kunst

© Rheinisches Bildarchiv Köln / Marion Mennicken / KölnTourismus GmbH

👥 Schokoladenmuseum★ (Chocolate Museum)

Rheinauhafen. Open year-round Tue–Fri 10am–6pm, Sat–Sun 11am–7pm. Closed Jan 1, Carnival week, Dec 24–25 & 31. ⌑9€. ♿ ✆(0221) 931 88 80. www.schokoladenmuseum.de.

This museum housed in a late-19C customs warehouse and a modern glass annex takes as its subject the tastiest of foodstuffs, chocolate. Inside are displays about the 3 000-year history and production of chocolate, a miniature chocolate factory and a chronology of the local Stollwerck company. A delicious treat from a chocolate fountain completes the visit.

German Sports and Olympic Museum★

Im Zollhafen 1. Open year-round Tue –Fri 10am–6pm, Sat–Sun 11am–7pm. Closed Jan 1, Carnival week, Dec 24–25 & 31. ⌑6€. ♿ ✆(0221) 33 60 90 www.sportmuseum.de.

This museum traces the history of the Olympics, especially the Berlin Games of 1936 and the Munich Games of 1972. Alongside a collection of photos, videos and sound recordings are some interactive stations where you can step into a boxing ring or onto a racing bike. Other sections address the changing role of sport in society and the impact of women, who entered the realm of professional sports relatively late.

NS-Dokumentationszentrum (Nazi Documentation Centre)

Appellhofplatz 23–25. Open year-round Tue–Fri 10am–6pm, Sat–Sun 11am–6pm. Closed Jan 1, Carnival week, Dec 24–25 & 31. ⌑4.50€. ♿ ✆(0221) 22 12 63 32. www.museenkoeln.de.

Between 1935 and 1945, this building served as the headquarters of the local Gestapo. It was used as a prison for regime opponents, who were often subjected to interrogation under torture. The harrowing scribbling on the walls of the narrow cells bear witness to this dark chapter of German history.

ROMANESQUE CHURCHES

The High Middle Ages (1150–1250) saw the construction of numerous churches built in the Romanesque style. Certain design elements, like the clover-leaf chancel, originated in Cologne (ℓsee INTRODUCTION: Art). Most churches were destroyed during World War II, but a dozen were subsequently rebuilt.

St. Maria-im-Kapitol★

Kasinostrasse 6. ✆(0211) 21 46 15. www.maria-im-kapitol.de.

This late Ottonian church (11C) features the oldest **cloverleaf chancel★** in Cologne. The crypt extends beneath almost the entire body of the chancel, the second-largest in Germany after Speyer Cathedral. To the left is an altarpiece of the Madonna of St. Hermann-Joseph (c. 1180). The **Renaissance choir screen** is richly decorated with sculpture (c. 1525). At the west end of the south side aisle are the original wooden **church doors★** from 1065.

St. Severin

Im Ferkulum 29. ✆(0221) 931 84 20. www.sankt-severin.de.

St. Severin is the oldest Christian foundation in Cologne, dating to the 4C and built on a Roman-Frankish burial ground. The present building dates from the 13C (chancel) and 15C (west tower and nave). The chancel in the fine Gothic nave features paintings by the Master of St. Severinus. The tomb of St. Severinus, bishop of Cologne around 400 AD and one of the city's patron saints, is buried in the crypt.

St. Pantaleon★

Am Pantaleonsberg 10a. ✆(0221) 31 66 55. www.sankt-pantaleon.de.

The nave and impressive Westwerk are examples of Ottonian architecture (10C). The **rood screen★** at the chancel is late Gothic.

St. Gereon★

Gereonskloster 2. ✆(0221) 47 45 070. www.stgereon.de.

The originality of this church lies in its elliptical floor plan and the addition, in 1220, of a **decagon**★ between its towers. The crypt with its 11C mosaic floor contains the tomb of St. Gereon. The frescoes date from the 13C.

St. Andreas

Komödienstraße 6–8. ℘(0221) 160 66 0. www.sankt-andreas.de.
Built in the early 13C with a clover-leaf apse, this church teems with remarkable architectural details.
At the beginning of the 15C, the Romanesque chancel was replaced with a Gothic one modelled on that in Aachen.

St. Ursula

Ursulaplatz 24. ℘(0221) 13 34 00.
In the north aisle are 30 plates (1456) by Stefan Lochner depicting the martyrdom of St. Ursula. The daughter of a British king, the saint was murdered by Huns along with 10 of her companions in the 5C. In the south transept, the **Goldene Kammer**★ (Golden Chamber; ⊜2€), contains 120 reliquary busts.

EXCURSIONS

Schloss Augustusburg★★ (Augustusburg Palace)

◗ 13km/8mi south, in Brühl. ☞Visit by guided tour (1hr) only; year-round Tue–Fri 9am–noon, 1.30pm–4pm, Sat–Sun 10am–5pm. ⊜6€. ℘(02232) 440 00. www.schlossbruehl.de.
The town of Brühl developed around a fortress whose foundations, in the 18C, were used to build this fantastic Rococo extravaganza commissioned by Cologne archbishop and Prince Elector Clemens August. With his hunting lodge, **Jagdschloss Falkenschloss**★, it was entered on UNESCO's World Heritage List in 1984.
Clemens August, a member of the Bavarian Wittelsbach ruling family, hired François de Cuvilliés as chief architect of his palatial residence. Cuvilliés in turn drew some of the era's finest artists and craftmen from throughout Europe. Chief among them was **Balthasar Neumann**, the mastermind behind the magnificent **staircase**★★, a riot in greyish-green and yellowish-orange faux marble and elaborate stuccowork

throughout. Crane your neck to study the **ceiling fresco**★, a work of Carlo Carlone that celebrates the prince and the House of Wittelsbach.
Tours take in about two dozen rooms, each one seemingly more lavish than the last. Highlights include the **large new suite**, comprising a garden room with more Carlone frescoes; the **summer suite**, with floors covered in blue and white tiles from Rotterdam; and the **yellow suite**, used principally by Clemens August as his private quarter. The **Schlosspark** (palace gardens) starts out as a French Baroque **garden**★. Designed by Lenôtre student Dominique Girard in 1728, it is sprinkled with reflective ponds and elaborate flowerbeds. It gives way to an English-style park masterminded by Peter Joseph Lenné after 1840.

👪 Phantasialand★

◗ Berggeiststraße 31–41, 50321 Brühl *(shuttles available from Brühl train station, ⬡see website).* Open Apr–Oct daily 9am–6pm, late Nov–mid-Jan daily 11am–8pm. ⊜45€ (child 4-11 22€; child under 4 free). ♿℘(01806) 36 66 00. www.phantasialand.de.
The sprawling amusement park offers thrill rides and attractions within six themed areas. You can take a watery log flume ride, watch a Wild West stunt show or embark on a simulated space flight.
Many adventures are geared towards small children, but there are also hair-raising thrill rides, including the Black Mamba rollercoaster and the Talocan suspended top spin.

Altenberger Dom★

◗ 20km/12.4mi northeast.
This former Cistercian abbey church (known locally as the Bergischer Dom), lies in a lush green valley. The pure Gothic building (1255–1379) has celebrated Roman Catholic and Protestant services alternately since 1857. Its huge (18x8m/59x26ft) coloured canopy (c. 1400) above the west entrance is considered the largest stained-glass window in Germany.

ADDRESSES

🏨STAY

⊜Rhein-Hotel St. Martin – *Frankenwerft 31–33.* 📞*(0221) 257 79 55. www.koeln-altstadt.de/rheinhotel. 40 rooms. ⌧. Restaurant⊜.* All rooms at this central budget hotel have showers but the cheapest ones share toilets down the hall.

⊜Pension Otto – *Richard Wagner Straße 18.* 📞*(0157) 859 52 825 . www. pensionotto.de. 5 rooms. ⌧.* You really feel like family in this small, 1st-floor guesthouse where each room is decorated individually. Those facing the courtyard are quieter.

⊜Hotel Hayk – *Frankenwerft 9.* 📞*(0221) 925 74 40. www.hotelhayk.de. 6 rooms.* You'll get great value for money at this riverside hotel. Expect lots of charm and a warm welcome.

⊜⊜Hotel Im Kupferkessel – *Probsteigasse 6 (north of Christophstraße near St. Gereon's Church).* 📞*(0221) 270 79 60. www.im-kupferkessel.de. 12 rooms. ⌧.* This well-kept hotel on the edge of the old town is a fine budget pick even if rooms are small and some must share a bathroom down the hall. The sunny breakfast room is anchored by a wooden spiral staircase.

⊜⊜Günnewig Kommerz Hotel – *Johannisstraße 30–34.* 📞*(0221) 161 00. www.guennewig.de. 77 rooms.* Located just outside the main train station north exit (opposite the cathedral), this bright orange 1970s building quickly catches the eye. Completely renovated, it has comfortable rooms as well as a sauna.

⊜⊜Hotel Kunibert der Fiese – *Am Bollwerk 1–5.* 📞*(0221) 92 54 680. www.kunibertderfiese.de. 22 rooms. ⌧. Restaurant⊜.* A good compromise between comfort, price and location (near the centre). Other hotels in this category are nearby, all overlooking the Rhine.

⊜⊜Hotel Allegro – *Thurnmarkt 1-7.* 📞*(0221) 240 82 60. www.hotel-allegro. com. 41 rooms. ⌧7.50€.* Choose from modern rooms or traditional ones Bavarian-style (four-poster beds) at this charmer near the Chocolate Museum.

⊜⊜Hotel Krone – *Kleine Budengasse 15* 📞*(0221) 92 59 310. www.hotel-krone-koeln.de. 28 rooms. ⌧.* Housed behind a brown façade, this central hotel has friendly service and clean and functional rooms easily reached by a lift.

⊜⊜Hotel Brandenburger Hof – *Brandenburger Straße 2-4* 📞*(0221) 12 28 89. www.brandenburgerhof.de. 30 rooms.* North of the old town, this reasonably priced hotel has small but functional rooms and a petite garden for relaxing. It is close to the main train station and cathedral.

⊜⊜⊜Lint Hotel – *Lintgasse 7.* 📞*(0221) 92 05 50, (0800) 546 84 68. www.lint-hotel.de. 18 rooms. ⌧.* This contemporary hotel is equipped with all modern conveniences and lies right in the heart of the historic centre.

⊜⊜⊜⊜Excelsior Hotel Ernst – *Domplatz.* 📞*(0221) 27 01. www.excelsior hotelernst.de. 142 rooms. ⌧32€. Restaurants.* Cologne's most illustrious defender of the grand tradition sits directly opposite the towering cathedral. A sumptuous marble lobby leads to refined rooms and grand suites, along with a sauna and fitness facilities.

⊜⊜⊜⊜Hotel Im Wasserturm – *Kaygasse 2.* 📞*(0221) 200 80. www.hotel-im-wasserturm.de. 88 rooms. ⌧28€. Restaurant⊜⊜⊜.* A listed 19C brick water tower has been ingeniously converted into a chic designer hotel with a soaring lobby and rooms boasting the full complement of creature comforts. Enjoy magnificent views from the 11th-floor restaurant.

🍽/EAT

⊜Belgischer Hof – *Brüsseler Straße 54.* 📞*(0221) 54 81 70 17. www.belgischer-hof.de. Closed lunch.* The little table lights lend Mediterranean flair to this place where you'll be tempted by tarte flambee and other French-inspired dishes.

Gilden im Zims – *Heumarkt 77.* *(0221) 16 86 61 10. www.gilden-im-zims.de.* While waiting (briefly) for a snack, schnitzel or traditional regional dish, you can read stories about some of the heroes in Cologne history. In the basement, a nightclub comes alive on weekends.

Paprica – *Zülpicher Straße 46.* *(0221) 271 628 44. www.ichliebeköln.de /paprica/.* Situated in the heart of the lively student quarter, this cosy restaurant is decorated in its namesake colour and serves hearty schnitzel, salads, pastas and pizzas at very reasonable prices.

Hase – *St. Apern-Straße 17. (0221) 25 43 75. www.hase-catering.de. Closed Sun.* Quality ingredients are woven into dishes that are creative without getting too tricky. The chic dining room with its pale wooden tables is great for kicking back at the end of the day.

Heising und Adelmann – *Friesenstraße 58-60. (0221) 130 94 24. www.heising-und-adelmann.de. Closed Sun, Mon and public holidays.* This lively restaurant in fashionable bistro style delivers relaxed flair and modern, international cuisine. Choose from 50 cocktails at the bar or relax on the lovely terrace out back.

Peters Brauhaus – *Mühlengasse 1. (0221) 257 39 50. www.peters-brauhaus.de.* This classic Cologne brewery has woodsy décor that adds warmth and friendliness to the rustic and comfortable place. There are multiple rooms, each one uniquely decorated.

Pfaffen Brauerei – *Heumarkt 62. (0221) 257 77 65. www.max-paeffgen.de. Closed Mon.* One of the few breweries in Cologne where the beer is brewed on site, Pfaffen has retained its traditional, rustic flair and is especially conducive to trying the local *Kölsch* beer alongside regional dishes. In summer you can enjoy the pleasant beer garden.

Em Krützche – *Am Frankenturm 1–3. (0221) 258 08 39. www.em-kruetzche.de. Closed Mon.* This traditional brew-pub has fed stomachs and souls for over 400 years with hearty regional specialities.

Osman 30 Restaurant – *Im Mediapark 8. (0221) 50 05 20 80. www.osman-cologne.de. Dinner only Mon–Sat; Sun brunch only.* This trendy and modern restaurant serves upmarket Mediterranean fare amid fabulous views from the 30th floor of the KölnTurm in the Media Park. There's also a wine bar, weekend brunch and afternoon tea.

Le Moissonnier – *Krefelder Straße 25. (0221) 72 94 79. www.lemoissonnier.de. Closed Sun, Mon, May 1, 3 weeks in summer and around Christmas. Reservation advised.* You will feel like the king of the world at this Art Nouveau bistro in a historic building in the heart of town, especially after indulging in the creative French cuisine.

SIGHTSEEING
CITY TOURS
A hop-on, hop off tour bus *(15€)* with recorded commentary operates Wed–Sun 10.30am–3.30pm (Apr–Oct Fri–Sat until 4pm) . Buses depart up to 15 times daily from outside the tourist office and stop at 13 major attractions. Without getting off, the loop takes 90 minutes.

BOAT TOURS
Boat tours run Apr–Oct and start at 9.50€ for one hour. For all options, tickets and directions to the landing docks, stop by KölnTourimus. Alternatively, just look for operators along the western river bank near Hohenzollern Bridge.

EVENTS
Carnival starts on the Thursday before Ash Wednesday (when Lent begins). A highlight is the parade on Rose Monday (*see Carnival, p271*). April brings art connoisseurs from around the world to town for **Art Cologne**.

PUBLICATIONS
Cultural calendars of events can be found in the monthly publication *Köln im...* (followed by the month) at tourist information offices. Other monthly listings magazines like *StadtRevue* and *Prinz* are sold at news kiosks.

Aachen ★

Aachen snuggles up against the border with Holland and Belgium and has a special place in German history. Its natural hot springs were already popular with Celtic tribes, but it was the Romans who built the first thermal baths. Charlemagne (747–814) made Aachen capital of his Frankish Empire in 794 and, after being crowned emperor in 800, unleashed his military campaigns on Saxony and Bavaria from here. He's buried in the spectacular cathedral that also saw the coronation of 30 German kings between 936 and 1531.

▶ **Population:** 265 208

Info: Elisenbrunnen, Friedrich-Wilhelm-Platz, 52062 Aachen. ✆(0241) 180 29 60 and 180 29 61. www.aachen-tourist.de.

Location: Among the northern foothills of the Ardennes (Hohes Venn), near the Belgian and Dutch borders, Aachen is Germany's most westerly town, easily accessible by road from Cologne, Düsseldorf and Liège, Belgium.

Parking: Public parking is available in garages and car parks near the main train station, the market, the cathedral and Kaiserplatz. Computerised signs throughout town indicate space availability.

Don't Miss: The cathedral and its treasury.

Timing: Allow half day for the cathedral district.

CATHEDRAL DISTRICT
Dom ★★★
(Cathedral)

Open daily 7am–7pm (Jan–Mar until 6pm). ☛Guided tours daily (2pm tour in English). ⌾4€. ♿✆(0241) 47 70 90. www.aachendom.de.

The first German entry on UNESCO's list of World Heritage Sites, Aachen's cathedral soars above the historic district. The oldest part, Charlemagne's palace chapel *(Pfalzkapelle)* was completed around 800 and is a superb example of Carolingian architecture.

The Gothic chancel was added in 1414 to accommodate the growing number of pilgrims wishing to see relics (including Jesus' loin cloth) that Charlemagne had brought to Aachen. They're still displayed every seven years (next in 2014).

Interior

Aachen's cathedral is remarkable for the harmonious design of the domed Carolingian palace chapel, an octagonal structure surrounded by a 16-sided gallery awash with mosaics.

Its other main decorative element is the magnificent 12C wheel-shaped **chandelier ★★**, donated by Emperor Frederick I Barbarossa.

The nave is also a treasure trove of supreme artworks, most notably the 11C **ambo ★★★**, a copper pulpit decorated with precious stones and donated by Henry II. Other highlights are the 13C **Shrine of Mary ★**; the 14C Virgin of Aachen statue; and the high altar adorned with a **Pala d'Oro ★★★**, a gilded panel relief depicting the Passion of Christ (c. 1020).

Behind the altar rests the **Shrine of Charlemagne ★★★** (Karlsschrein: 1200–15), a hand-worked gold and silver reliquary containing the emperor's bones. His **marble throne** in the upper gallery was also used as the coronation throne of 30 German kings (☛*must be seen on guided tours; meet in the treasury*).

Domschatzkammer
(Cathedral Treasury) ★★★

Access via Klostergasse. Open year-round Mon 10am–1pm; Jan–Mar Tue–Sun 10am–5pm; Apr–Dec Tue–Sun 10am–6pm. Closed Jan 1, Carnival, Good Friday, Dec 24–25 & 31. ⌾5€.

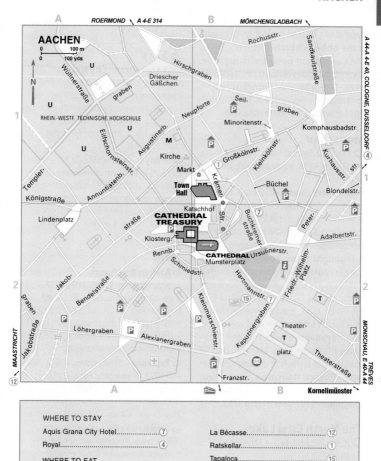

WHERE TO STAY

Aquis Grana City Hotel	⑦
Royal	④

WHERE TO EAT

Aachen Brauhaus	⑦

La Bécasse	⑫
Ratskeller	①
Tapaloca	⑮

Guided tours daily ⊚6.50€.
&, ℘(0241) 47 70 90.
The treasury is one of the most important north of the Alps, with over 100 outstanding artworks arranged in five thematic sections. Highlights include several major silver and gold reliquaries, including the bust of Charlemagne (1349) and the Lothar Cross (c. 1100).

Rathaus (Town Hall)

Markt. Open year-round daily 10am–6pm. Closed major holidays and during special events. ⊚5€. &, ℘(0241) 432 73 10. www.aachen.de.
The Gothic 14C town hall has sprouted from the foundations of Charlemagne's

palace of which only the Granus Tower remains. The palatial building overlooks the market square with its **fountain** and **emperor's statue**. The most important room is the **Reichssaal**, decorated in the 19C by Alfred Rethel with romanticised scenes from Charlemagne's life. The same room also contains replicas of the imperial insignia, including the crown, the orb and several swords (originals in Vienna).

EXCURSION
Kornelimünster

▶ 10km/6.2mi southeast.
This is an enchanting village with slate-roofed, blue and grey stone houses

typical of the Eifel region. Its key sight is the **abbey church★** with origins in the Carolingian period, although the current Baroque version dates from only 1728. The octagonal Kornelius chapel contains the reliquary of 3C Pope Cornelius for whom the town is named.

Monschau

◯ 33km/20.5mi southeast. Coming from Aachen via B258, enjoy a superb view★★ of the town.

Pretty Monschau, with its tall, narrow, slate-roofed houses clustered in a winding river gorge, is lorded over by a ruined medieval castle but is otherwise predominantly Baroque in style.

A highlight is the **Rotes Haus★** (red house; Laufenstraße 10; open Apr–Nov Tue–Sun 10am, 11am, 2pm, 3pm and 4pm; closed Oct 3; ◌3€; ☏ 024 72 50 71) of 1765, a one-time residence of a local cloth-maker and merchant. Rooms provide a peek into the bourgeois lifestyle of the 18C and 19C. Of special note is the free-standing, three-storey **Rococo staircase★**. Nearby Haus Troistorff (Laufenstraße 18) is another magnificent residence from 1783.

The North Eifel Lakes

◯ 85km/52.8mi. Leave Monschau on the B258.

The road rises rapidly, and after a mile there is a **look-out point★** giving a good view of the village.

Leaving the town of Schmidt, the ruined **Burg Nideggen** (Nideggen Castle) lies straight ahead. Until the 15C the rose-coloured sandstone castle was the residence of the counts and dukes of Jülich. The restored 12C church has a Romanesque chancel with frescoes.

Rurtalsperre★
(Rur Dam)

In a wild stretch of countryside, this reservoir forms, with the Urft reservoir to the south, the largest stretch of water in the Eifel. Motorboat services operate on both.

ADDRESSES

🏠 STAY

⊖⊖ Aquis Grana City Hotel –
Büchel 32. ☏(0241) 44 30. www.hotel-aquisgrana.de. 98 rooms. ☐. This cosy hotel is decorated warmly with woodsy elements. Rooms are individually furnished and quiet despite being in the heart of town.

⊖⊖ Royal – Jülicher Straße 10. ☏(0241) 18 22 80. www.royal.bestwestern.de. 35 rooms. ☐15.50€. This modern and comfortable hotel is close to the town centre. Rooms are nicely furnished; those at the back are especially quiet.

🍽 EAT

⊖ Aachen Brauhaus –
Kapuzinergraben 4. ☏(0241) 360 17. www.aachener-brauhaus.de. Closed Sun Jan–Aug. This traditional German brewery-pub in the town centre has a great variety of reasonably priced regional and national dishes.

⊖ Tapaloca – Elisabethstraße 6. ☏(0241) 400 50 78. Dinner only. For tasty tapas make a beeline to this welcoming place with sunny décor and palm trees. There's also a menu for larger appetites.

⊖⊖⊖ Ratskeller – Markt 40. ☏(0241) 350 01. www.ratskeller-aachen.de. This traditional restaurant in the vaulted cellars of the town hall offers traditional German fare updated for the 21C.

⊖⊖⊖ La Bécasse –
Hanbrucher Straße 1. ☏(0241) 744 44. www.labecasse.de. Closed Mon & Sat lunch, Sun. The kitchen of this modern restaurant sources quality products from Belgium. Everything is prepared with expertise and creativity.

Ruhr Region

Ruhrgebiet

Historically, the Ruhr Region is best known as one of the world's largest industrial areas, a conglomeration of 53 cities joined together by coal, steel—and sweat. No more. The Ruhr has been reinventing itself at a steady clip, embracing its industrial past but focusing on a future filled with culture and the arts. Aspiring to undergo a model transformation from industrial to creative powerhouse, it could become a model for other urban areas worldwide. No wonder then that Essen (on behalf of the whole Ruhr Region) was selected as the European Capital of Culture 2010.

A BIT OF HISTORY

Although most of its furnaces and mines are no longer in operation, the Ruhr Region remains one of the world's most important industrial centres. Much of German steel is manufactured here. Duisburg is the largest inland port in Europe and the largest river port in the world. The landscape in the region's north is shaped by the chemical industry and modern mining operations. Former industrial plants have been turned into cultural venues, shopping centres and adventure playgrounds. Old pits and factories have been converted into industrial museums, offering insight into the production methods and social history of the region.

BOCHUM

Kunstmuseum Bochum (Fine Arts Museum)

Kortumstraße 147, opposite the Stadtpark. Open year-round Tue–Sun 10am–5pm (Wed until 8pm). 5€. Closed Jan 1, Good Friday, May 1, Dec 24–25 & 31. (0234) 910 42 30. www. kunstmuseumbochum.de.
The collections in this spacious, airy building concentrate mainly on con-

Info: Am Bergbaumuseum 28, 44791 Bochum. (0234) 587 70. www.ruhr-tourismus.de.

Location: The Ruhr Basin (4 400sq km/1 700sq mi) lies along the Ruhr, Rhine and Lippe rivers and encompasses the cities of Duisburg, Essen and Dortmund plus scores of mid-size and smaller towns.

Don't Miss: Religious art lovers will be impressed by Essen's cathedral and its artworks. About two dozen of the biggest attractions (covering 150 years of cultural heritage) are linked by a 400km/248mi-long **Industrial Heritage Trail**.

Timing: Allow two days to get a flavour of the Ruhr region.

Kids: Westphalian Open-Air Museum and the Schwebebahn.

temporary international art. Exhibits are drawn from the collection, which ranges from works by Josef Albers to those of Ossip Zadkine.

Deutsches Bergbau-Museum★★ (German Mining Museum)

Am Bergbaumuseum 28. Open year-round Tue–Fri 8.30am–5pm, Sat–Sun 10am–5pm. Closed Jan 1, May 1, Dec 24–26 & 31. 6.50€. (0234) 587 70. www.bergbaumuseum.de.
Founded in 1930, this museum examines the evolution of mining from antiquity to the present. A miners' lift descends 20m/65.6ft underground, where the 2.5km/1.5mi of abandoned workings in the **Schaubergwerk** illustrate methods of coal extraction and transport. The tour ends with a trip up the 71m/233ft-high mining tower.

Eisenbahnmuseum★ (Railway Museum)

Dr.-C.-Otto-Straße 191, in northern Bochum-Dahlhausen surburb. Open Mar–mid-Nov Tue–Fri & Sun 10am–5pm. ⊚7€. ℘(0234) 49 25 16. www.eisenbahnmuseum-bochum.de. Founded by railway enthusiasts, this museum is installed in an abandoned station and repair shop on the north bank of the Ruhr. Equipment from as long ago as 1914 is, for the most part, still in working condition. More than 180 steam and electric locomotives trace the evolution of the railway as a form of transportation.

BOTTROP

Josef Albers Museum

Im Stadtgarten 20 (near town centre). Open year-round Tue–Sat 11am–5pm, Sun 10am–5pm. Closed Jan 1, Dec 24–25 & 31. ♿ ℘(02041) 297 16. www.bottrop.de/mq.

Bottrop-born Constructivist painter and Bauhaus theorist Josef Albers referred to his work as *Hommage an das Quadrat* (Homage to the Square). This ultramodern museum displays a survey of his and other Constructivists' work. The adjoining sculpture park contains works by Max Bill, Donald Judd, Norbert Kricke and others. The same complex also harbours the **Museum of Pre- and Local History**. The **Ice Age Hall★** houses Germany's largest Quaternary Era collection.

♟♙ Movie Park Germany★

Warner-Allee 1, in Bottrop-Kirchhellen, via A31, exit Kirchhellen. Open late Mar–Oct daily 10am–6pm, 8pm or 10pm, depending on the day. Call for specific opening times. ⊚37€ (child 4–11, 29€) ℘(02045) 899 899. www.movieparkgermany.de.

This film and amusement park features more than 35 attractions, thrill rides and live shows spread across such themed sections as Old West, Streets of New York and Santa Monica Pier. Scream as you ride the MP Xpress rollercoaster, join SpongeBob on a Back Splash water ride or take in the scene from the Ferris wheel. If you need a little peace and quiet, head for the **Museum of German Film History★**, examining more than 100 years of celluloid history.

DORTMUND★

Max-von-der-Grün-Platz 5-6, 44137 Dortmund. ℘(0231) 18 99 90. www.dortmund-tourismus.de.

Goodbye collieries and steel mills, hello high-tech and culture. Lying on the eastern edge of the Ruhrgebiet (and its largest city), Dortmund has successfully mastered the transition from powerhouse of the Industrial Revolution to future-oriented metropolis. Today, innovation and research, along with trade, insurance and the service sector support the local economy. Also famous for its beer and football team, the city boasts extensive parks and hosts major trade shows. A ring road following the course of the medieval town wall encircles the centre, win which most of the museums and churches are located. The Westfalenpark, football stadium and trade fair grounds lie south of the city centre.

Westfalenpark★

An der Buschmühle, enter from Florianstraße. Open year-round daily 9am–11pm. ⊚3€ until 6pm, 1.50€ after. ℘(0231) 502 61 00. www.westfalenpark.dortmund.de.

Dortmund's "green heart", this huge park was created for the 1959 *Bundesgartenschau* (federal horticultural show), which the city hosted twice more, in 1969 and 1991. Its most prominent feature is the Florianturm television tower, but the vast park is also home to an open-air stage, a puppet theatre, a gallery, a planetarium and the Mondo Mio! interactive children's museum. Another highlight is the **rose garden** *(Rosarium)*, a fragrant oasis with 3 200 varieties of the noble blossom from all over the world.

Florianturm

Open year-round daily 11am–10pm (Sun from 9am). ⊛2.50€. ℘(0231) 502 61 00. www.westfalenpark.dortmund.de.
Dortmund's television tower stands 220m/722ft tall and was named for the patron saint of gardeners. At 141m/462ft, it features a restaurant and a terrace with superb **panoramas★** extending as far as the Sauerland on clear days.

Reinoldikirche★

Ostenhellweg 2. Open year-round Mon–Sat 10am–6pm, Sun 1pm–6pm. ℘(0231) 59 43 51. www.sanktreinoldi.de.
Right in the heart of town, this three-nave basilica was first consecrated in 1280 and was repeatedly damaged and rebuilt in subsequent centuries, the last time after World War II. It houses some outstanding 14C and 15C religious works: a sculpted reredos, probably Burgundian work; the bronze eagle pulpit (Adlerpult); a wooden statue of St. Reinold, patron saint of the town; and a statue of Charlemagne.
The church tower can be climbed for great city views (Sat noon–3pm; ⊛1.50€).

Museum für Kunst und Kulturgeschichte (Museum of Art and Cultural History)

Hansastraße 3. Open year-round Tue–Sun 10am–5pm (Thu until 8pm), Sat noon–5pm. Closed Jan 1, Dec 24–25 & 31. ⊛5€. ℘(0231) 502 55 22. www.mkk.dortmund.de.
Delve into Dortmund history by perusing the paintings, sculptures, furnishings and crafts engagingly displayed inside a converted Art Deco bank building. Keep an eye out for the **Dortmund Treasure★** (Dortmunder Goldschatz), consisting of 444 Roman gold coins, most from the 4C.
The emotive quality of Conrad von Soest's Madonna sculptures is striking, as is the craftsmanship of the Romanesque triumphal cross. Other rooms feature paintings by Spitzweg, Liebermann, Slevogt, Corinth and other 18C and 19C masters.

Museum am Ostwall

Leonie-Reygers-Terrasse. Open year-round Tue–Sun 11am–6pm (Thu–Fri until 8pm). Closed Jan 1, Dec 24–25 & 31. ⊛5€. ℘(0231) 502 47 23. www.museumostwall.dortmund.de.
Fans of 20C and 21C art will be drawn to this fine museum where works by German Expressionists, most notably members of the Blue Rider and Bridge artist groups (Schmidt-Rottluff, Marc, Macke), form the core of the collection. Since late 2010 the museum has occupied three floors of the so-called "Dortmund U", a landmark tower that was once part of the local Union Brewery and has since reinvented itself as a centre for arts and culture.

DUISBURG

Wilhelm-Lehmbruck-Museum★★

Friedrich-Wilhelm-Straße 40, in Duisburg town centre. Open year-round Wed–Sat noon–5pm (Thu until 9pm), Sun 11am–6pm. Closed May 1, Dec 24 & 31. ⊛8€. ℘(0203) 283 32 06. www.lehmbruckmuseum.de.
This museum is home to a prestigious collection of some 700 20C sculptures and objets d'art. Look for emotional works by Barlach and Kollwitz, Cubist and Constructivist sculpture by Archipenko, Duchamp and Brancusi and otherworldly Surrealist contributions by Arp and Dalí. One museum wing showcases works by Duisberg sculptor **Wilhelm Lehmbruck** (1881–1919). The surrounding park contains outdoor sculptures by international artists against a wooded backdrop.

Museum der Deutschen Binnenschifffahrt★

Apostelstraße 84, in Duisburg-Ruhrort. Open Tue–Sun 10am–5pm. Closed Jan 1, Dec 24–25 & 31. ⊛4.50€. ℘(0203) 8088 940. www.binnenschifffahrts museum.de.
The former Art Nouveau swimming pool is one of the country's largest museums devoted to the economic, technological and social aspects of inland shipping.

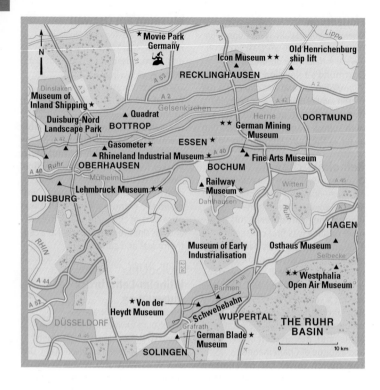

Visitors examine developments from dug-outs to modern tug boats. Two museum ships (⌾2€, accessible May–Sept only) from 1882 and 1922 lie a 10-minute stroll away through the port, near the maritime stock exchange.

Landschaftspark Duisburg Nord

Emscherstraße 71, in Duisburg-Meidrich. ℰ(0203) 429 19 19. www.landschaftspark.de.
This enormous retired iron- and steel-works has been ingeniously recycled into a adventure playground and cultural events venue. You can learn scuba diving in the old gas tank, go rock climbing on its ore bunkers, brave a high-wire parcours suspended between buildings or ascend to the top of the blast furnace for fine views.
The cultural programme includes movie screenings, theatre productions and dance parties.

ESSEN★

Am Hauptbahnhof 2, 45127 Essen. ℰ(0201) 194 33. www.essen.de.
Essen is one of the largest cities in the Ruhr region, wedged between Bochum and Duisburg along the A40 autobahn. The city traces its pedigree back to the 8C but made its biggest mark on history during the Industrial Age. Closely associated with the Krupp family dynasty, its steelworks and collieries were the engines driving the German economy until well into the 1960s. Since then, Essen has been a city in transition, replacing its smokestacks with "clean-air" industries such as administration and finance, a university and plenty of business, commerce and culture.

Museum Folkwang★★★

Museumsplatz 1. Open year-round Tue–Sun 10am–6pm (Fri until 10pm). Closed Rose Monday, Easter Monday, Whit Monday, Dec 24 & 31. ⌾5€. ♿ ℰ(0201) 884 54 44. www.museum-folkwang.de.

An Aladdin's cave of paintings, sculpture, graphic art and photography stretching across the 19C and 20C, this museum is one of Germany's premier repositories of fine art, with particular emphasis on German and French artists. Galleries are filled with a veritable who's who of famous names, from Romantic artist Caspar David Friedrich and modern trailblazers Cézanne, Gauguin and van Gogh to German Expressionists Heckel, Kirchner, Schmidt-Rottluff and postwar bigshots like Baselitz, Kiefer and Pollock. Exhibits are showcased in a glass-fronted building designed by British architect David Chipperfield; galleries (some naturally lit) radiate from inner courtyards and gardens.

Zollverein Site★

Gelsenkirchener Straße 181. Open year-round daily 10am–6pm. Closed Dec 24-25 & 31. ♿8€. ♿🖉(0201) 24 68 10. www.zollverein.de.

A UNESCO World Heritage Site, the Zollverein Coal Mine Industrial Complex is one of the jewels of the Ruhr; at its height, 12,000 tons of coal were extracted here per day. The first coal pit was excavated in 1847, the last coal production took place in 1986 and the coking plant closed in 1993. The brick buildings were built in 1932 by the architects Fritz Schupp and Martin Kremmer. The 100ha site is divided into three areas: the pit XII, 1/2/8 well and the coking plant (2hr English tours Sat–Sun & holidays 3pm; ♿9€). At the main entrance stands the great tower, 55 metres high. Behind the tower is the former coal-washing plant, now a museum.

Ruhr Museum★★

♿🖉(0201) 24 68 14 44. www.ruhrmuseum.de.

Here the history of the Ruhr is engagingly and creatively chronicled. Descend several floors into the depth of the building to explore all facets of Ruhrgebiet culture, from its medieval beginnings on a major trading route to its Industrial Age heyday and the recent metamorphosis into a place of culture, high-tech and logistics.

Münster (Cathedral)★★

Burgplatz 2. Open year-round Mon & Fri 10am–6.30pm, Tue–Thu 6.30am–6.30pm, Sat–Sun 9am–7.30pm. ♿🖉(0201) 220 42 06. www.dom-essen.de.

Just off the main pedestrian shopping strip, Essen's medieval cathedral offers peaceful respite and a bonanza of art treasures, including some from the Ottonian period. The highlights are the **Golden Madonna★★★** (AD 980), one of the oldest surviving sculptures from the early Middle Ages, and a massive **seven-branch candelabrum★** (c. 1000). The **cathedral treasury★★** (Domschatzkammer; open year-round Tue–Sat 10am–5pm, Sun 11.30am–5pm; closed major religious & public holidays; ♿4€; 🖉(0201) 220 42 06; www.dom-schatz-essen.de) holds, among other items, four **processional crosses★★★** (10C and 11C) and a reliquary said to contain a nail from Jesus' cross.

Villa Hügel★

Haraldstraße. Open year-round Tue–Sun 10am–6pm; park open daily 8am–8pm. ♿5€. ♿🖉(0201) 61 62 90. www.villahuegel.de.

This imposing Gründerzeit mansion stands in an attractive park on the north shore of **Lake Baldeney**. Three generations of the industrialist Krupp family lived here from 1873 to 1945. You can tour their private quarters, study company history and stroll around the lovely park. The biggest crowds turn out for the periodic special art exhibits.

HAGEN
Kulturquartier Hagen

Hochstraße 73. Open year-round Tue–Sun 11am–6pm. Closed Jan 1, May 1, Easter Monday, Whit Monday, Dec 24-25 & 31. ♿9€. ♿🖉(02331) 207 31 38. www.kunstquartier-hagen.de.

Hagen's cultural quarter encompasses two museums. The **Osthaus Museum** displays early Modernist works (German Expressionm, New Objectivity) in an Art Nouveau space designed by Belgian artist Henry van de Velde. Next door, the **Emil Schumacher Museum** is dedicated to the Hagen-born artist who was a founder of the German Abstract Art movement after World War II. The exhibit encompasses oil paintings, watercolours, graphic works, ceramics and porcelain.

♠♣ Westfälisches Freilicht-museum★★ (Westphalian Open-Air Museum)

At Hagen-Selbecke. Leave Hagen heading south towards Frankfurt, then take the Eilpe road. At Eilpe, turn right towards Breckerfeld-Halver and continue for just over 1.5km/1mi to Selbecke. 10min walk from parking lot. Open Apr–Oct Tue–Sat 9am–5.30pm, Sun 6pm (last entry 5pm). ⸿7€. ℘(02331) 780 70. www.freilichtmuseum-hagen.de.

Along 2.5km/1.5mi of the Mäcking valley, more than 60 workshops and buildings illustrate the evolution of crafts and trades from the late 18C through the 19C. Exhibits include a working forge, examples of James Nasmyth's steam hammer (c. 1840) and the zinc rolling mill of Hoesch (1841), a printing museum. In the traditional craft village, saddlers, smiths, rope makers, bakers and brewers demonstrate their skills and sell their products.

OBERHAUSEN
Gasometer★

Arenastraße 11, next to CentrO shopping centre. Viewing platform open year-round Tue–Sun 10am–6pm. ⸿Exhibition prices vary. ♿ ℘(0208) 850 37 30. www.gasometer.de.

Europe's largest blast furnace gas storage tank (68m/220ft in diameter, built in 1928–29) has a new life as an exhibition hall. It is an impressive space and worth visiting even when no exhibitions are presented. A lift whisks you to a viewing platform at 117m/350ft for sweeping views across the entire Ruhr region. You can also rent an audioguide (⸿3€) for a self-guided tour.

Next door is the CentrO, one of the largest shopping centres in Germany.

Rheinisches Industriemuseum★ (Rhenish Industrial Museum)

Hansastraße 18, Oberhausen (behind the main train station). Open year-round Tue–Fri 10am–5pm, Sat–Sun 11am–6pm. Closed Carnival week, Easter Monday, Whit Monday, May 1, Nov 1, Dec 22–early Jan. ⸿4€. ℘(02234) 992 15 55. www.industriemuseum.lvr.de.

The Altenberg zinc works were in operation until 1981 and is a rare completely preserved factory site from the early days of industrialisation. The "Heavy Industry" exhibit shows the 150-year history of the iron and steel industry in the Ruhr region and displays such objects as ingot moulds, mill rollers, a steam hammer and a steam locomotive.

RECKLINGHAUSEN
Ikonen-Museum★★ (Icon Museum)

Kirchplatz 2a. Open year-round Tue–Sun 11am–6pm. ⸿6€. ℘(02361) 50 19 41. www.ikonen-museum.com.

Considered the most important museum of icons outside the orthodox world, this museum boasts more than 1 000 works from Russia, Greece and the Balkan countries. Aside from icons, the collection includes embroideries, miniatures, and wood and metal sculptures.

Altes Schiffshebewerk Henrichenburg (Historic Ship Lift)

Am Hebewerk 2, Waltrop. Open year-round Tue–Sun 10am–6pm. Closed major holidays & Dec 24–Jan 1. ⸿4€. ♿ ℘(02363) 970 70. www.schiffshebewerk-henrichenburg.de.

In 1899 Emperor Wilhelm II inaugurated this amazing construction, which lifted river barges travelling on the Dortmund–Ems Canal 14m/46ft high, thereby opening a direct waterway to the North Sea. It was in operation until replaced with a larger, more modern ship lift in 1962. An exhibition illustrates the construction process and technical, political and economic aspects of canal building and river shipping.

Solingen – The Art of Steel

"Cutting edge" is a term that has defined Solingen for centuries, as it is here that steel has been turned into legendary cutting instruments. The town's first mention in history was in 1067, and by the 1600s local craftsmen were creating knives, swords and instruments that were unequalled in quality. Being close to large forests that provided charcoal and being positioned atop rich deposits of iron guaranteed the prosperity of its skilled townspeople. Of course it did not hurt that the key trading centre of Cologne was pretty close by too. Such tradition of excellence continues to this day, through firms such as Henkels and Wüsthof. About 90 percent of all blades made in Germany still hail from this small town.

SOLINGEN
Deutsches Klingenmuseum★ (German Blade Museum)

Klosterhof 4, Solingen-Gräfrath. Open year-round Tue–Sun 10am–5pm (Fri from 2pm). Closed Jan 1, 24–25 & 31 Dec. ⌘4.50€. ♿ ☏(0212) 25 83 60. www.klingenmuseum.de.

In the Baroque former Gräfrath Abbey, this museum traces the cultural history of cutting and eating utensils, showcasing silverware from the Bronze Age to today. A collection of weapons from around the world includes bronze swords from Iran as well as ceremonial rapiers from France.

WUPPERTAL
Von der Heydt-Museum★

Turmhof 8, Wuppertal-Elberfeld. Open year-round Tue–Sun 11am–6pm (Thu until 8pm). Closed Easter Mon, May 1, Whit Mon, Dec 24–25 & 31. ⌘12€. ♿ ☏(0202) 563 62 31. www.vdh.netgate1.net. This museum, housed in a 19C town hall, displays 16C and 17C Flemish and Dutch painting; French and German painting from the 19C to Impressionism, Expressionism (Kirchner, Beckmann), Fauvism, Cubism (Braque) all the way to the present. Sculptures from the 19C and 20C are also on display (Rodin, Maillol).

Museum für Frühindustrialisierung (Museum of Early Industrialisation)

Engelsstraße 10, Wuppertal-Barmen. Open year-round Tue–Sun 10am–6pm. Closed major holidays. ⌘4€. ♿ ☏(0202) 563 43 75. www.historisches-zentrum-wuppertal.de.

Housed in a former factory, this museum is devoted to the economic and social history of the Wupper valley since the mid-18C.

👥 Schwebebahn (Suspended Railway)

The electric cars of the world's oldest suspended passenger railway (1898–1903) travel 12m/36ft above the Wupper River for just over 13km/8mi.

ADDRESSES

🛏 STAY

😴🍽 **Ferrohotel** – *Düsseldorfer Straße 122-124, 47051 Duisburg.* ☏*(0203) 28 70 85.* *www.ferrotel.de, www.sorat-hotels.com.* *30 rooms.* 🍽. This modern boutique hotel sports a streamlined design and stylishly integrated industrial decorations, including historic fire extinguishers. Rooms are comfortable, all with mod-cons. Some rooms have free Wi-Fi.

🍴 EAT

😴🍽 **Livingroom** – *Luisenstraße 9-13, 44787 Bochum.* ☏*(0234) 953 56 85.* *www.livingroom-bochum.de. Closed Sun.* The menu at this trendy lifestyle bistro caters to every taste and diet. Walls have paintings and photographs.

😴🍽🍽 **Bahnhof Nord** – *Am Vorthbach 10, 46240 Bottrop.* ☏*(02041) 98 89 44.* *www.bahnhofnord.de. Dinner only; closed Mon, Tue.* At this converted railway station, market-fresh ingredients headline dishes with modern flair. The terrace and winter garden are coveted seating.

Düsseldorf★

Finance, fashion and fun are the hallmarks of this modern Rhineland city and capital of the German state of North Rhine-Westphalia. Shopping is a major pastime here and the old town is nicknamed the "world's longest bar" for good reason, while a strong tradition in the arts is reflected in a multitude of first-rate museums and cultural institutions.

A BIT OF HISTORY

City of the Arts – Düsseldorf has been an artistic mecca since the reign of Elector **Johann Wilhelm** (1679–1716, also known as Jan Wellem), who surrounded himself with brilliant musicians, painters and architects.

Elector Carl Theodor provided an additional artistic impetus when he founded a prestigious arts academy in 1773, the the Kunstakademie Düsseldorf. Its faculty has included Paul Klee and Joseph Beuys; British artist Tony Cragg served as its director (2009-2013), the position now held by Rita McBride, professor of sculpture at the academy. Düsseldorf also has a few contemporary architectural gems by Frank Gehry and others renowned architects, most notably in the revamped old harbour known as the Mediahafen (Media Harbour).

▶ **Population:** 573 000

ℹ **Info:** Immermannstraße 65b. 40210 Düsseldorf. ℰ(0211) 17 20 28 44. www.duesseldorf -tourismus.de.

◐ **Location:** Düsseldorf straddles the River Rhine and is served by an international airport, long-distance trains and several autobahns. Most of the sights and action concentrate along the river, especially in the Altstadt (old town).

🅿 **Parking:** Garages are plentiful, notably around the Hauptbahnhof and near the Königsallee.

😊 **Don't Miss:** Quaff local *Altbier* in a traditional brewpub; K20 art museum.

🕐 **Timing:** You'll want to devote an entire day to seeing the city.

The World of Fashion – Exhibitions, fairs and collections of haute couture secure Düsseldorf's reputation as one of Germany's fashion capitals. The city hosts several fashion trade shows throughout the year. The graceful **Königsallee★**, with boutiques and arcades on either side of the old royal moat, is the centre of elegance.

Medienhafen

© Mauritius/Photononstop

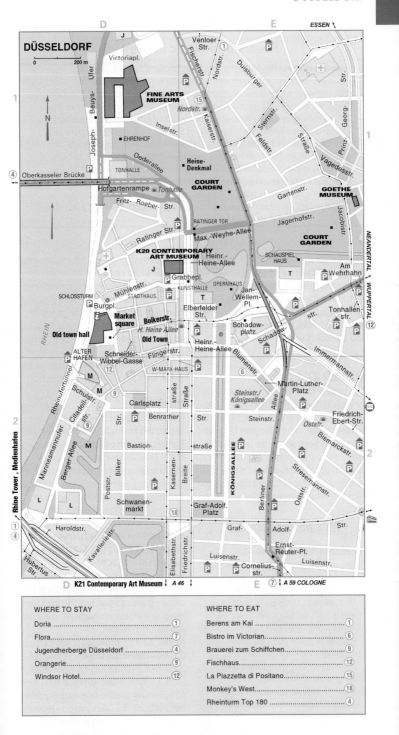

WHERE TO STAY

Doria .... ①
Flora... ⑦
Jugendherberge Düsseldorf ....④
Orangerie..⑨
Windsor Hotel ....⑫

WHERE TO EAT

Berens am Kai ....①
Bistro im Victorian.........................⑥
Brauerei zum Schiffchen................⑨
Fischhaus.......................................⑫
La Piazzetta di Positano.................⑮
Monkey's West...............................⑱
Rheinturm Top 180 ....④

Poetry and Music in the 19C

Heinrich Heine (1797–1856), son of a Bolkerstraße merchant, spent his youth in Düsseldorf, deeply impressed with the French and Napoleon. A poet, pamphleteer, traveller, defender of liberalism and a Francophile, Heine described himself as "a German nightingale which would have liked to make its nest in Voltaire's wig". Among the musicians who have given Düsseldorf its reputation as an artistic centre are Robert Schumann and Felix Mendelssohn-Bartholdy. **Robert Schumann** (1810–1856) was appointed conductor of the municipal orchestra in 1850 and lived on Bilkerstraße for four years. In 1854, he suffered a nervous breakdown and attempted to drown himself in the Rhine. His friend **Felix Mendelssohn** (1809–1847) brilliantly directed the city's Rhine Festival. He made his first journey to England in 1829, conducting his own *Symphony in C Minor* at the London Philharmonic Society.Si vellign ihitas magnis

East Asian connection– Düsseldorf has long played an important role in economic relations linking Germany with East Asia, Japan in particular. More than 500 Japanese firms are based here, including banks, insurance companies, and transport firms.

SIGHTS
Altstadt (Old Town)
This largely car-free riverside quarter is jam-packed with pubs, bars and shops. One of the busiest thoroughfares is **Bolkerstraße**, where the poet Heinrich Heine was born in the house at no 53. The area is also linked with the story of the tailor Wibbel, who attended his own funeral after switching identities to escape a prison sentence. This legend is recalled by the figures of the Schneider-Wibbel-Gasse carillon clock, which operates at 11am, 1pm, 3pm, 6pm and 9pm. The Altstadt is parallelled by a pleasant **riverside promenade** (*Rheinuferpromenade*). Stroll from Burgplatz square, where the medieval castle tower houses a shipping museum, all the way to the 234m/767ft-high **Rheinturm**, a TV tower with a revolving restaurant.

Marktplatz (Market Square)
Separated from the Rhine by the 16C Renaissance **Altes Rathaus** (old town hall), this square is embellished by the bronze equestrian statue (18C) of Elector Jan Wellem. He is buried in the Baroque **Andreaskirche** (Church of St. Andrew), a short walk north of here.

Hofgarten and Schloss Jägerhof★ (Court Garden and Jägerhof Palace)
Hofgarten park is a shady continuation of the Königsallee. Its Napoleon Hill is crowned with a small bronze titled *Harmony*, a modest monument to native son Heinrich Heine.

At the nearby pink Jägerhof Palace, the **Goethe-Museum★** (Jacobistraße 2; open year-round Tue–Fri & Sun 11am–5pm, Sat 1pm–5pm; ∞4€; ℘0211 899 62 62; www.goethe-museum-kippenberg-stiftung.de) takes you on a journey through the life, times and work of this much-revered poet and playwright.

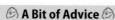

😊 A Bit of Advice 😊

Local Gastronomy - The Altstadt taverns ooze Rhenish earthiness and are perfect for sampling such regional culinary specialties as *Himmel und Erde* (literally "heaven and earth", it is black pudding with onions) and *Halve Hahn* (rye roll with cheese). On Friday evenings, there is a tradition of eating *Reibekuchen* (potato cake). Indigenous to Düsseldorf is the *Altbier*, a copper-coloured, heavily hopped ale served in cylindrical 0.2l/0.4 pint-size glasses.

Museum Kunst Palast★
(Fine Arts Museum)

Ehrenhof 4–5. Open year-round
Tue–Sun 11am–6pm, Thu to 9pm. ◉5€.
& ℘(0211) 566 42 100. www.smkp.de.
This encyclopedic art gallery touches
on all genres from the Middle Ages to
the present. Works by the Düsseldorf
School dominate, but you'll also find
large-scale paintings by Rubens, moody
landscapes by Caspar David Friedrich
and warped Expressionism by Max
Beckmann.
The museum also houses an outstanding collection of vessels from Roman
times via *Jugendstil* to the present day
called the **Glasmuseum Hentrich★★**,
as well as medieval sculpture.

Kunstsammlung
Nordrhein-Westfalen★★
(Art Collection of North
Rhine-Westphalia)

Open year-round Tue–Sun 10am–6pm.
Closed Dec 24–25 & 31. ◉10-12€ or 17€
for both K20 and K21. & ℘(0211) 838
12 04; www.kunstsammlung.de. A free
shuttle bus operates between K20 and
K21 every 20min during opening hours.
This top-rated art collection spans a
century of art history with an emphasis on western European and American
works. Top paintings by Picasso, Chagall, Ernst and Beuys are complemented
by nearly 100 works by Paul Klee, who
taught at the Düsseldorf Arts Academy
from 1930 to 1933. The collection
extends all the way into the 21C with
works by such stellar artists as Andreas
Gursky, Nam June Paik, Candida Höfer,
Thomas Ruff and Thomas Schütte.
Exhibits are distributed across three
locations: the renovated and enlarged
K20 building *(Grabbeplatz 5)* in the
old town; a converted 19C state parliament building known as **K21** *(Ständehausstraße 1)* south of here; and the
Schmela Haus *(Mutter-Ey-Straße 3)*, a
puristic 1970s building by the Dutch
architect Aldo van Eyck opposite K20.

K20 building, Kunstsammlung
Nordrhein-Westfalen

© Walter Klein / Kunstsammlung NRW

Medienhafen★
(Media Harbour)

South of the Altstadt, an old-time river
port has been reborn as a high-tech,
office and entertainment complex that
doubles as a showcase for Postmodern
architecture. The overall design integrates the old with the new, the industrial with the edgy. Red-brick silos and
warehouses have been converted,
while new buildings have sprung
up, most notably the **Neuer Zollhof**
(new customs court). Designed by
Frank Gehry, this three-part complex
is a classic example of his undulating,
organic style. Claude Vasconi's nauti-
cally inspired **Grand Bateau** (big ship)
is another highlight. The tallest building
is the **Colorium** by London-based Will
Alsop with its random patterned façade.

EXCURSION
Neandertal

▶ 14km/8.7mi east, via A46 autobahn,
exit Haan-West, follow signs.
In this deep valley carved by Düssel
creek, the 60 000-year-old skeletal
remains of Neanderthal Man were first
discovered in 1856. The bones are the
star exhibit of **Neanderthal Museum**
(Talstraße 300; open year-round Tue–
Sun 10am–6pm; closed Dec 24-25 &
31; ◉8€; &; ℘02104 97 970; www.
neanderthal.de). Take a virtual journey
through the stages of human evolution broken down into such themes
as "daily life and survival", "tools and
knowledge" and "myth and religion".

ADDRESSES

🏠 STAY

Jugendherberge Düsseldorf –
Düsseldorfer Straße 1. ℘(0211) 55 73 10.
www.duesseldorf.jugendherberge.de.
338 beds. 🚗. Recently renovated, this
youth hostel offers fine river views
and comfortable beds in clean, secure
rooms, each with its own shower and
toilet. It is located opposite the Altstadt
and easily reached on foot via the
Oberkasseler Bridge.

Flora – *Auf'm Hennekamp 37.*
℘(0211) 93 49 80. www.hotel-flora.info.
40 rooms. 🚗€12.50. Close to an S-Bahn
station, this well-kept hotel has modern
and functional rooms, some with a
pleasant, courtyard-facing balcony.

Windsor – *Grafenberger Allee 36.*
℘(0211) 91 46 80. www.windsorhotel.de.
18 rooms. 🚗. Expect a warm welcome
and high-quality rooms in this small
hotel furnished with attention to detail.

Doria – *Duisburger Straße 1a.*
℘(0211) 49 91 92. www.doria.de. 41 rooms.
🚗. A 10-minute walk from the Altstadt,
this mid-range hotel has soundproof
rooms with modern facilities. It is in a
commercial area teeming with cafés
and restaurants.

Hotel Orangerie –
Bäckergasse 1. ℘(0211) 86 68 00.
www.hotel-orangerie-mcs.de. 27 rooms.
🚗. This pretty hotel in a 19C town
palace sits in a quiet corner of the
Altstadt. The bright rooms are
minimalist but comfortable and each
is named after a different artist.

🍴 EAT

Fischhaus – *Bergerstraße 3–7.*
℘(0211) 854 98 64. www.fischhaus-
duesseldorf.de. Fresh fish is the name of
the game at this jolly bistro where you
can watch the goings-on through large
bay windows or, in fine weather, while
perched on the terrace.

Bistro im Victorian –
Königstraße 3a. ℘(0211) 865 50 20.
www.restaurant-victorian.de. Closed Sun
in summer. At this restaurant near the
popular pedestrian zone, Volker Drkosch
is known for well-prepared innovative
cuisine served in a Victorian setting. The
bistro is more modern but just as good.

La Piazzetta di Positano –
Kaiserstraße 5. ℘(0211) 49 46 56. www.
rossini-gruppe.de. This friendly restaurant
not only serves fine Italian cuisine and a
delicious antipasti buffet but also offers
cooking classes in an adjacent space.

Top 180 – *Stromstraße 20.*
℘(0211) 863 20 00. www.guennewig.de.
A lift whisks you up Düsseldorf's
television tower, where you can enjoy
superb views of the city from this slowly
rotating restaurant at a lofty 172m/564ft.

Zum Schiffchen – *Hafenstraße 5.*
℘(0211) 13 24 21 22. www.brauerei-zum-
schiffchen.de. This classic Rhenish brew-
pub has had a loyal following for more
than 350 years. Grab a seat at a polished
wooden table, order a hearty meal and
wash it down with the *Altbier* house
brew. Nice beer garden, too.

Berens am Kai – *Kaistraße 16.*
℘(0211) 300 67 50. www.berensamkai.de.
Closed Sat lunch, Sun. Catering to
business folks and discerning hipsters,
this Medienhafen restaurant affords
splendid views of the Rhine through the
panoramic glass front.

Monkey's West –
Graf-Adolf-Platz 5. ℘(0211) 64 96 37 10.
www.monkeyswest.de. Closed Sun, Mon.
This vibrant blend of trendy bar and
restaurant has some stunning design
elements, such as chandeliers and
sculptures by the late artist Jörg
Immendorf.

TAKING A BREAK

Eis-Café Pia – *Kasernenstraße 1.*
℘(0211) 326 233. Closed mid-Oct–mid-
Feb. Expect queues to snake out of the
door at this hugely popular Italian ice
cream parlour. The café also serves
hot and cold drinks.

NIGHTLIFE

A warren of car-free lanes wedged
between the River Rhine and the
Königsallee boulevard, the Altstadt is
known as "the longest bar in the world".
With all sorts of drinking dens – from
historic brew-pubs to sleek bars – it can
get packed at weekends.

Sauerland★

The meandering Lenne and Ruhr rivers cut through the forest-draped medium-range mountains of the Sauerland – a popular getaway for residents of the heavily urbanised Ruhr Region. In winter, skiers converge on the town of Winterberg while in summer walkers, cyclists and water-sports enthusiasts enjoy the area's many lakes, trails, limestone caverns and charming hamlets.

A BIT OF GEOLOGY

The Sauerland is the most mountainous area of the Rhineland Schist Massif. It is crowned by the **Kahler Asten** (843m/2 766ft), near Winterberg. Lake reservoirs supply water and hydroelectric energy to the Ruhr towns and serve as water-sports centres. The Upper Sauerland, especially the forested Rothaargebirge, is popular with Nordic walkers, hikers and mountain bikers.

🚗 DRIVING TOUR

FROM SOEST TO BAD BERLEBURG

181km/112.4mi. Allow one day.

Soest★

A northern gateway to the Sauerland, the historic town of Soest is still almost entirely encircled by its 16C town wall and is famous as the birthplace of German **Pumpernickel**, a dense black rye bread. The pious and fans of church architecture and religious art will find plenty to like about the town. Dominating its silhouette is the massive 11C–12C Romanesque **Patrokli Dom** (Propst-Nübel-Straße 2; open year-round Mon–Fri 10am–5.45pm, Sun 10am–6.30pm), noted for its elaborate **western façade★★** and perfectly balanced square **tower★★**.

The Romanesque frescoes (c. 1165) in the choir are the originals, while those found elsewhere were restored in 1950.

ℹ Info: Johannes-Hummel-Weg 1, 57392 Schmallenberg. ✆(02974) 20 21 90. www.sauerland.com.

◯ Location: The Sauerland stretches from the south-eastern Rhineland to eastern Westphalia. It is bisected north-south by the A45 autobahn (Hagen–Frankfurt) and is also served by the A4 from Cologne.

☺ Don't Miss: The historic town of Soest and the outdoor pursuits at the Möhnesee.

🕐 Timing: Allow one day for the suggested driving tour.

👥 Kids: The Attahöhle caves and water sports throughout the region.

The 14C Gothic hall-church, **St. Maria zur Wiese★** (Wiesenstraße; open year-round Mon–Sat 11am–6pm, Sun from 11.30am), better known as Wiesenkirche, sports two filigree spires that were added in the 19C. Inside, note especially the 1520 **stained-glass window** depicting a "Westphalian Last Supper" showing Jesus and disciples sitting down for a meal of local food specialities (boar's head, ham, jugs of beer and rye bread loaves).

Finally, there is **St. Maria zur Höhe** (Hohe Gasse; open Mon–Sat 10am–5.30pm, Sun after services–5.30pm; closes 4pm Oct–Mar), also known as Hohnekirche. It contains Romanesque wall paintings, a high altar with paintings of the Passion, and a circular Scandinavian-style cross called a *Scheibenkreuz*.

◯ Follow the B229 south for about 13km/8mi.

Möhnesee★

This lake reservoir on the northern edge of the Sauerland is 10km/6.2mi long. The northern lakeshore is open to visitors and water-sports enthusiasts. The south bank is a well-forested nature reserve known for its birdlife.

▶ Follow the B229 south for about 20km/12.4mi towards Arnsberg.

Arnsberg

The old town is built on a spur of the Ruhr. To the north, a clock-tower commands the approach to the Schlossberg ruins; to the south stands a hunting-themed Rococo gate.

▶ Beyond Arnsberg, the B229 skirts the right bank of the Sorpesee reservoir before crossing the Lennegebirge massif. There are many scenic viewpoints.

� Attahöhle★ (Grotto)

Finnentroper Straße, Attendorn.
Look for signposts just before reaching Attendorn. Visit by guided tour (40min) only May–Aug 10am–4.30pm; Apr & Sept 10am–4pm; Oct 10.30am–4pm; Nov–Mar 11am–3.30pm. Closed Dec 8–25, Mon–Fri mid-Jan–mid-Feb, Mon Nov. 8.50€ (child 4.50€). (02722) 937 50. www.atta-hoehle.de.
Near the north shore of the Biggesee lake lies one of Germany's largest and most impressive limestone caverns with a subterranean network of trails extending for 3km/1.8mi. There are dozens of beautiful stalactite and stalagmite formations, as well as translucent stone "draperies" and an underwater lake.

Attendorn

This typical old Sauerland town boasts a 14C Rathaus (town hall) with stepped gable, an arcaded covered market (Alter Markt), and the **"Sauerland Cathedral"** (Sauerländer Dom). Southeast of Attendorn, high above town, is the 13C **Burg Schnellenberg**, which is now a hotel and a formal restaurant.

Biggetalsperre

This dam, dating from 1964, forms with the **Lister Barrage**, the largest reservoir in Westphalia. It is a popular for swimming, sailing and windsurfing.

▶ About 2km/1.2mi before Olpe, fork left on the B55. Soon after Bilstein, on a small mountain road, turn right turn toward the Hohe Bracht.

Hohe Bracht

Alt 584m/1 916ft.
From the viewing tower (620m/2 034ft above sea level) unfolds a fine panorama that includes the Rothaargebirge massif as far as the Kahler Asten.

▶ After crossing the rural Lenne Valley, the route passes **Grafschaft** and **Oberkirchen**, with charming half-timbered houses, before the landscape becomes wilder and hillier. Beyond **Nordenau**, a typical slate-roofed Upper Sauerland village, is the ski station of Altastenberg. On the far side of a plateau, the road nears Kahler Asten.

Kahler Asten

At 843m/2 765ft above sea level, this is the highest point of the Sauerland region. Views from the look-out tower are superb. To the northeast is the spa and winter-sports centre of Winterberg, where diversions include skiing, snowboarding and tobogganing as well as an indoor skating rink and a 1 600m/5 249.3ft-long bobsled run. In summer, the 5km/3mi trek up the Kahler Asten gets visitors' hearts pumping.

▶ Slate quarries flank the road back down. There are many attractive views towards the south.

Bad Berleburg

This Kneipp spa resort is dominated by **Schloss Berleburg** (Berleburg Palace; visit by 1hr guided tour only May–mid-Oct daily 10.30am and 2.30pm, Jan–Apr Tue, Thu, Sat–Sun 2.30pm, Nov–Dec by appointment; 5€; 02751 93 60 10; www.touristik-bad-berleburg.de), which dominates the historic town centre. Although it has origins in the 13C, the current Baroque structure was built in 1733 and is still owned by the ancestral local rulers, the family of Sayn-Wittgenstein.

Bonn★

In 1949, Bonn beat Frankfurt am Main to become the capital of the newly created Federal Republic of Germany. The decision surprised many people given the town's modest size and provincial character. Bonn, however, rose to the occasion and has maintained an international, cosmopolitan flair ever since the capital was voted to move back to Berlin in 1991. There's plenty to see and do for visitors in the birth town of Ludwig van Beethoven, which has a lovely river location and a wealth of first-rate museums.

A BIT OF HISTORY

Bonn has been inhabited since Roman times, but only achieved importance in the 16C as a residence of the electors and archbishops of Cologne.

Bonn served as West Germany's capital for 50 years and became, in the process, a well-respected seat of government. Since reunification and the transfer of government offices to Berlin in 1999, huge sums of money have been spent redefining the nature of the city. Several United Nations offices have opened here, along with the headquarters of international corporations, and the city is now more vibrant than ever.

●●WALKING TOUR

HISTORIC CENTRE★★
Beethoven-Haus
(Beethoven's Birthplace)

Bonngasse 24–26. Open Apr–Oct daily 10am–6pm; Nov–Mar Mon–Sat 10am–5pm, Sun 11am–5pm. Closed Jan 1, Thu & Mon before Shrove Tue, Good Friday, Easter Sun, Dec 24–26 & 31. ⊕6€. ℘(0228) 98 17 525. www.beethoven-haus-bonn.de.

Visit the room where Beethoven was born in 1770 in this modest town house that chronicles the life and achievements of this great composer. Peruse

▶ **Population:** 312 000

🅸 **Info:** Windeckstraße 1, 53103 Bonn. ℘(0228) 77 50 00. www.bonn.de.

▶ **Location:** Easily accessible from Cologne by the A555 or A59 autobahns, Bonn lies on the left bank of the Rhine River. Historic sights cluster in the old town, while Museum Row stretches along the Adenauerallee south of here.

🅿 **Parking:** Garages are located throughout the city: near the train station, near Beethoven's birth house, and near the old cemetery on Oxfordstraße.

🅰 **Don't Miss:** Beethoven's birth house, House of History, Bonn Museum of Art and the Rhenish Regional Museum.

🕓 **Timing:** Allow one day for Bonn and another half day for the Siebengebirge.

🅰 **Kids:** House of History, and the Siebengebirge (℅see Excursions), especially the funicular.

Beethoven's Formative Years

Precursor of the Romantic music movement, **Ludwig van Beethoven** (1770–1827) was born in Bonn and grew up near the Church of St. Remigius. At 13, Beethoven was already an accomplished musician, playing violin, viola and harpsichord in the court of the elector. At 22 the fervent admirer of Mozart and Haydn left Bonn for Vienna to follow in their footsteps. The **Beethovenhalle** hosts the annual international Beethoven Festival.

portraits, original documents, musical instruments, listening horns and his life and death masks. Tickets also include

Beethoven-Haus

© Beethoven-Haus Bonn

admission to the **Digitales Beethoven-Haus**, a multimedia 3D experience located next door.

▶ Go south on Bonngasse towards the Markt.

Altes Rathaus (Old Town Hall)

This charming Rococo building (1738) with its frilly pink and silver façade dominates the triangular market square.

▶ Head east on Stockenstraße.

Kurfürstliche Residenz (Electoral Princes' Castle)

The lawns of the Hofgarten make a fine backdrop for this imposing Baroque building, completed by Enrico Zucalli in 1702 as a residence for the prince-electors. Since 1818 the palace has been part of the University of Bonn.

▶ From the south end of the Kurfürstliche Residenz, take a right on Am Neutor and walk towards Münsterplatz.

Münster★ (Cathedral)

The former Stiftskirche Sts. Cassius and Florentius beautifully melds 11C–13C Romanesque and Gothic architectural features.

The Romanesque baptismal font and stone carvings are noteworthy, as are the drawings (c. 1200), and fresco (c. 1200) depicting Mary. The quiet **cloister★** (c. 1150) is one of the best preserved from the Romanesque period.

▶ Backtrack to the electoral palace, then head south on tree-lined Poppelsdorfer Allee.

Poppelsdorfer Schloss (Poppelsdorf Palace)

Meckenheimer Allee 171.
About 1km/0.6mi south of the Altstadt, this palace was designed in the early 18C by Enrico Zucalli for the prince-electors of Cologne and completed by Balthasar Neumann in 1756.

In 1818, it became part of the University of Bonn; the extensive park was turned into a **botanical garden**.

ADDITIONAL SIGHTS

Rheinisches Landesmuseum★★ (Rhenish Regional Museum)

Colmanstraße 14–16. Open year-round Tue–Fri & Sun 11am–6pm, Sat 1pm–6pm. Closed Jan 1, Thu before Shrove Tue, Dec 24–25 & 31. ∞8€. ⅁ ℘(0228) 207 00. www.rlmb.lvr.de.

This museum offers an overview of the history, culture and art of the region from prehistory to the present.

Pride of place in the **Neanderthal** section goes to the skull and partial skeleton of a 42 000-year-old locally found hominid.

Other treasures include the *Pietà Roettgen*, a heart-wrenching wooden Madonna sculpture (c. 1360) and stag masks used in prehistoric rituals around 7 700 BC. There are also some impressive Celtic items, including gold jewellery and a bronze helmet.

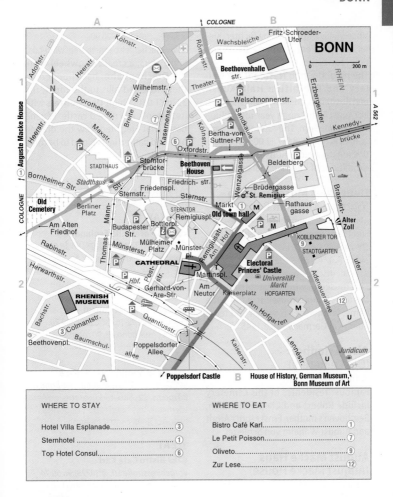

WHERE TO STAY	
Hotel Villa Esplanade	③
Sternhotel	①
Top Hotel Consul	⑥

WHERE TO EAT	
Bistro Café Karl	①
Le Petit Poisson	⑦
Oliveto	⑨
Zur Lese	⑫

Alter Zoll

The panorama of Bonn, the Rhine and the surrounding area as far as the Siebengebirge (⌚ see Excursion) from this bastion is particularly attractive in the late afternoon and early evening.

👥 Haus der Geschichte★★ (House of History)

Willy-Brandt-Allee 14. Open year-round Tue–Fri 9am–7pm, Sat–Sun 10am–6pm. ♿ ℘(0228) 916 50. www.hdg.de/bonn. Germany's first museum of post-World War II history is an intriguing display of original objects, multimedia screens and interactive stations. Highlights include a 1951 Mercedes that belonged to Konrad Adenauer, Germany's first chancellor, an original 1950s ice cream shop and a section of a *Rosinenbomber* (candy bomber) plane used during the 1948–49 Berlin Airlift. A large section of the exhibits trace the history of the former East Germany.

Kunstmuseum Bonn★★ (Bonn Museum of Art)

Friedrich-Ebert-Allee 2. Open year-round Tue–Sun 11am–6pm (Wed until 9pm). Closed Thu and Mon before Shrove Tue, Dec 24. ≈7€. ♿ ℘(0228) 77 62 60. www.kunstmuseum-bonn.de. Expressionism forms the core collection of this excellent art museum, which is especially famous for its works by one-time Bonn resident August Macke. Other rooms emphasise German art

303

since 1945, with works by Richter, Kiefer, Baselitz, Penck, Lüpertz, Beuys and other top artists.

The neighbouring **National Art Gallery and Exhibition Hall** (Kunst- und Ausstellungshalle der Bundesrepublik Deutschland; open year-round Tue–Wed 10am–9pm, Thu–Sun 10am–7pm; ⊛10€; ♿; ℘0228 917 12 00; www.bundeskunsthalle.de) houses temporary exhibitions of international calibre.

Deutsches Museum Bonn
(German Museum Bonn)
Ahrstraße 45. Open year-round Tue–Sun 10am–6pm. Closed Thu before Shrove Tue , Good Friday, Dec 24–25 & 31. ⊛5€. ♿℘(0228) 30 22 55. www.deutsches-museum.de/bonn.
This museum, which is an offshoot of Munich's famous museum of the same name, emphasises research and technology in Germany since 1945.

Alter Friedhof
(Old Cemetery)
Bornheimer Straße.
Famous "residents" of this cemetery include Robert and Clara Schumann, Beethoven's mother, Ernst Moritz Arndt and August Wilhelm von Schlegel.

August Macke Haus
(August Macke House)
Bornheimer Straße 96. Open year-round Tue–Fri 2.30pm–6pm, Sat–Sun 11am–5pm. ⊛5€. ℘(0228) 65 55 31. www.august-macke-haus.de.
Expressionist painter August Macke (1887–1914) lived in this Neoclassical villa from 1910 until 1914. See his re-created studio, examples of his work and a survey of Rhenish Expressionism.

EXCURSION
♟♟Siebengebirge★
⬤15km/9.3mi south on the right bank of the Rhine. Cogwheel train runs May–Sept daily 9am–7pm (every 30min); Jan, Feb & early Nov Mon–Fri noon–5pm (on request), Sat–Sun 11am–6pm (hourly); Mar & Oct 10am–6pm (every 30min); Apr 10am–7pm (every 30min). ⊛10€ (child

5.50€). ℘(02223) 920 90. www.drachenfelsbahn-koenigswinter.de. Since 1883, a creaky cogwheel train, the **Drachenbahn**, has chugged up these forested hills to the top of the 321m/1 050ft-high **Drachenfels** with its romantically ruined castle. Legend has it that Siegfried slew the dragon here and bathed in its blood to become invincible.

ADDRESSES

🛏STAY
⊜⊜🛏**Hotel Villa Esplanade** – *Colmantstraße 47. ℘(0228) 98 38 00. www.hotel-villa-esplanade.de. 17 rooms.* 🍽. This 19C villa has preserved its historic charm, especially in the breakfast room with its high ceilings.

⊜⊜🛏**Top Hotel Consul** – *Oxfordstraße 12-16. ℘(0228) 729 20. www.consul-bonn.de. 90 rooms.* 🍽. Centrally located, this hotel offers functional rooms.

⊜⊜🛏🛏 **Sternhotel** – *Markt 8. ℘(0228) 726 70. www.sternhotel-bonn.de. 80 rooms.* 🍽. Situated near the former town hall, this hotel is part of Bonn's history. Quiet, central location.

🍴EAT
⊜⊜ **Bistro Café Karl** – *Vorgebirgsstraße 50. ℘(0228) 96 50 74 17. www.cafekarl.de.* This bistro has a nice terrace and lovely *Jugendstil* décor, including ornamented ceilings, chandeliers and mirrored walls.

⊜⊜🛏 **Zur Lese** – *Adenauerallee 37. ℘(0228) 22 33 22. www.zurlese.de. Closed Mon.* This restaurant serves international cuisine and offers lovely river views from its summer terrace.

⊜⊜🛏 **Oliveto** – *Adenauerallee 9. ℘(0228) 260 10. www.hotel-koenigshof-bonn.de.* The Mediterranean flair and upmarket Italian cuisine here is best enjoyed on the riverside terrace.

⊜⊜🛏🛏 **Le Petit Poisson** – *Wilhemstraße 23a. ℘(0228) 63 38 83. Closed Sun, Mon. www.lepetitpoisson.de.* Decorated in warm colours, this intimate restaurant serves classic cuisine.

Eifel★

This volcanic central highland region near the Belgian border has lots in store for travellers wishing to get off the beaten track. Roman ruins, a world-class race track, sparkling blue crater lakes, medieval castles and large swaths of quiet and unspoiled countryside await. Take your time: Eifel's charms need to be sipped and savoured like the fine red wine it produces.

 DRIVING TOUR

FROM BAD MÜNSTEREIFEL TO MANDERSCHEID

145km/90mi. Allow one day.

This leisurely drive follows the valley of the Ahr with its popular resorts, climbs to the forested Upper Eifel, and then meanders among the volcanic lakes of the Maare.

Bad Münstereifel★

Hemmed in by massive **ramparts★**, this quaint town is littered with historic houses and monuments. The **Stiftskirche St. Chrysanthus und Daria** is an outstanding twin-towered abbey church with an 11C Romanesque front.

A few miles east of Münstereifel, the road passes a giant **radio-telescope**, rejoins the Ahr at Kreuzberg and continues along the winding valley. The telescope is 100m/328ft in diameter and its parabolic depth is 21m/69ft.

Altenahr

In a rocky valley between two bends in the river, charming Altenahr is dominated by the ruins of the 12C hilltop Burg Are Castle. Ride the chairlift up the Ditschardhöhe hill for sweeping views. Following the valley, with steep vineyards wedged in among rocky outcrops, takes you to pretty, wine-producing villages: Rech with its Roman

- **Info:** Kavalrienbergstraße 1, 54595 Prüm. ✆(06551) 965 60. www.eifel.info.
- **Location:** The Eifel is near the border with Belgium and straddles the German states of Rhineland-Palatinate and North Rhine-Westphalia. It is roughly bounded by Aachen, Koblenz, Trier and Cologne.
- **Don't Miss:** The volcanic lakes called *Maare*.
- **Timing:** Allow one day for the driving tour from Bad Münstereifel to Manderscheid.

bridge, Dernau and its "wine fountain" and Marienthal and its ruined convent.

Bad Neuenahr-Ahrweiler

This twin town has a delightfully split personality. At **Ahrweiler★**, which is still encircled by medieval fortifications, half-timbered houses line narrow, pedestrian-only streets. Study its Roman roots at the **Museum Römervilla**. By contrast, Bad Neuenahr is a bubbly spa town with celebrated mineral springs, a casino and elegant 19C architecture.

▶ Leaving Ahrweiler, the road climbs towards the forest before reaching the highlands.

Hohe Acht★

Take in fine views of deep valleys, rolling hills and the ruined Nürburg Castle from the tower atop the Eifel's highest mountain (747m/2 451ft).

Nürburgring★

✆(0800) 208 3200. www.nuerburgring.de.
This legendary **Formula 1 racetrack** is home to the feared North Loop (*Nordschleife*), nicknamed "Green Hell" by Jackie Stewart. On certain days, you can take your own car along the track or hop aboard a BMW or Viper and let a professional do the driving. Car and

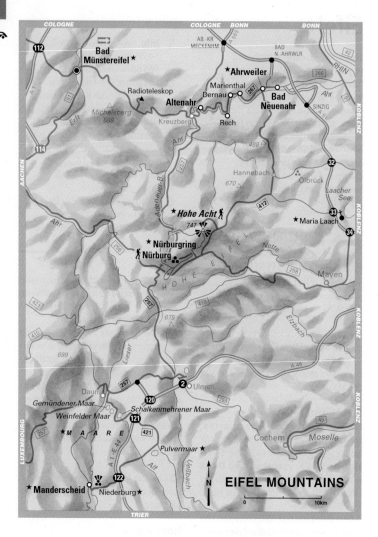

EIFEL MOUNTAINS

motorcycle races take place during the warmer months.

Maare★ (Crater Lakes)

Aeons ago, volcanic activity engulfed the upper reaches of the Eifel, resulting in a series of bright-blue crater lakes. To learn more about this phenomenon, visit the **Eifel Vulkanmuseum** (Leopoldstraße 9; open Mar–mid-Nov Tue–Fri 1pm–4.30pm, Sat–Sun 11am–4.30pm; 3€; 06592 98 53 53; www.vulkaneifel.de/eifel-vulkanmuseum) in Daun and the lakes themselves: the **Gemündener Maar**, the **Weinfelder**

Maar (also known as Totenmaar), the **Schalkenmehrener Maar** and the almost perfectly circular **Pulvermaar★**.

▷ Follow the brown "Maare" signs.

Manderscheid★

From atop the castle keep of the ruined Niederburg, **views★** extend to the Oberburg ruins and the Lieser Valley. In the car park at Pension Burgenblick, a trail leads up to another great **viewpoint★★**, the so-called Kaisertempelchen overlooking the Oberburg and Niederburg ruins.

ADDRESSES

🏨 STAY

⊖ **Hotel Seemöwe** – *Am Obersee 10, 52152 Simmerath-Einruhr. ℘(02485) 271. www.hotel-seemoewe.de. Closed Jan –Feb. 50 rooms. ⌕. Restaurant⊖.* Nice hotel on the edge of the Rursee lake, with clean, well-cared for rooms (many with balcony) and a lakeview terrace. The country-style restaurant offers traditional cuisine.

⊖ **Pension Oos** – *Lieserstraße 16, 54550 Daun-Gemünden. ℘(06592) 29 09. www.pension-oos.de. Closed Nov–mid-Mar. 6 rooms. ⌕.* This simple little B&B near the volcanic lakes has well-kept rooms sleeping two or three, as well as a guest kitchen with fridge and coffeemaker.

⊖⊖ **Burg Adenbach** – *Adenbachhutstraße 103, 53474 Bad Neuenahr-Ahrweiler. ℘(02641) 809 82 97. www.burg-adenbach.de. 7 rooms. ⌕9.50€. Restaurant⊖⊖⊖.* Romance rules at this medieval castle in Ahrweiler. Beautiful, comfortable rooms come with four-poster beds, pleasing colour schemes and large bathrooms. The hearty yet creative home-cooking served in the restaurant pairs well with the red wines from the property's own vineyard.

🍴 EAT

⊖⊖⊖ **Landgasthaus Steinsmühle** – *Kölner Straße 122, 53902 Bad Münstereifel. ℘(02253) 45 87. www.landgasthaus-steinsmuehle.de. Closed Wed, Thu, lunch except Sun.* Feast on international cuisine amid the romantic, brick-walled ambience of this 12C watermill. One room is lit only by candle-light.

Trier★★

Capital of the Western Roman Empire in the 3C, Trier is one of the oldest cities in Germany, along with Worms. Its remarkable collection of Roman ruins earned it a place on UNESCO's World Heritage list in 1986. The city is an ideal starting point to explore the nearby Moselle Valley or Luxembourg.

A BIT OF HISTORY

After the conquest of the Treveri—a Celtic tribe from eastern Gaul—the Roman Emperor Augustus founded on their territory the town of **Augusta Treverorum** (c. 16BC). It evolved into a centre of economic, cultural and intellectual activity until the invasion of Germanic tribes in AD 274.

When Diocletian reorganised the Roman Empire, Trier was retaken and became capital of the western territories (Gaul, Spain, Germania and Britain). As the town regained its former eminence, the Emperor Constantine (306–37) surrounded it with a defensive wall within which magnificent buildings were erected.

▸ **Population:** 100 800

🛈 **Info:** An der Porta Nigra, 54290 Trier. ℘(0651) 97 80 80. www.trier-info.de.

◖ **Location:** Trier straddles the Moselle River, near the Luxembourg border. The Eifel Mountains rise to the north and the Hunsrück massif to the southeast.

🅿 **Parking:** Parking is found in garages throughout town. The Hauptmarkt is convenient for visiting the old city.

◈ **Don't Miss:** The Porta Nigra, the cathedral, the Roman Baths and the Library Treasury.

◷ **Timing:** Allow one day for a tour of the old town.

SIGHTS
OLD TOWN
Porta Nigra★★

Open Apr–Sept daily 9am–6pm; Oct and Mar daily 9am–5pm; Nov–Feb daily 9am–4pm. ☞3€. ℘(0651) 97 80 80.

Porta Nigra

© M. Hertlein/MICHELIN

The **Porta Nigra** (black gate) is Trier's most famous landmark and the largest Roman edifice on German soil. This monumental gateway (2C), built to defend the northern town wall, is made of stones fitted into place without mortar, held together only by iron crampons. The double arcade of the central block leads to an inner court with pierced upper arcades. Assailants who broke through the outer gates would find themselves exposed to attack from all sides.

In the 11C, the fortified gateway was transformed into a church dedicated to St. Simeon. The Romanesque apse and Rococo decoration are still discernible. Napoleon ordered the monument restored to its original form in 1804.

Stadtmuseum Simeonstift
(City Museum)

Open year-round Tue–Sun 10am–5pm. Closed Jan 1, Dec 24–25 & 31. ⊛5.50€. ♿ ℘(0651) 718 14 59. www.museum-trier.de.

This municipal museum occupies a Romanesque convent, the Simeonstift, built beside the Porta Nigra in the 11C. Galleries creatively illustrate the history of Trier through the use of models, maps, paintings, engravings, and sculptures. The museum also encompasses a two-storey Romanesque **cloister**.

Dreikönigenhaus★
(House of the Three Kings)

This early-Gothic town house (c. 1230), with arched windows, recalls the Italianate towers of the patricians of Regensburg.

Hauptmarkt★
(Main Square)

This is one of the finest old squares in Germany, anchored by a **Marktkreuz★** (market cross) from AD 958 and a 16C **Brunnen** (fountain) surrounded by figures representing the cardinal virtues. Standing next to the cross, you are surrounded by 15 centuries of architectural history: to the north is the Porta Nigra; to the east the Romanesque cathedral; to the south the Gothic **Gangolfkirche**, its 16C tower once used as a look-out post; and half-timbered houses to the west. The **Steipe**, a 15C municipal building, is elegantly built over an open gallery. It now houses a café and the privately-owned **toy museum** filled with an abundance of stuffed animals, dollhouses and other childhood delights. Beside it, the 17C **Rotes Haus** (red house) bears the proud inscription: "There was life in Trier for 1 300 years before Rome even existed."

Frankenturm

This sturdy Romanesque tower (c. 1100) is named after one of its early owners, Franco of Senheim (14C).

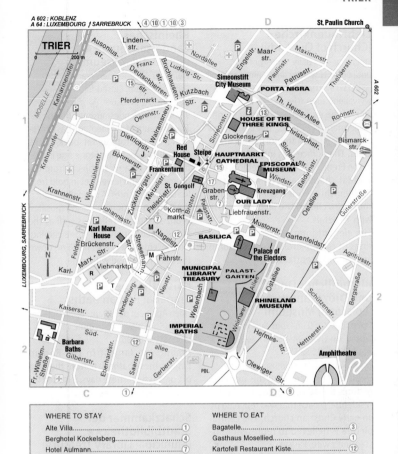

TRIER

A 602 : KOBLENZ
A 64 : LUXEMBOURG / SARREBRUCK ④ ⑩ ① ⑩ ③

St. Paulin Church

0   200 m

MOSELLE

LUXEMBOURG, SARREBRUCK

Simeonstift City Museum

PORTA NIGRA

HOUSE OF THE THREE KINGS

Red House Steipe

HAUPTMARKT

CATHEDRAL

EPISCOPAL MUSEUM

Frankenturm

St. Gangolf

Kreuzgang

OUR LADY

Korn-markt

BASILICA

Karl Marx House

Palace of the Electors

MUNICIPAL LIBRARY TREASURY

PALAST-GARTEN

RHINELAND MUSEUM

Barbara Baths

IMPERIAL BATHS

Amphitheatre

WHERE TO STAY	
Alte Villa	①
Berghotel Kockelsberg	④
Hotel Aulmann	⑦
Hotel Becker's	⑨
Hotel Deutscherhof	⑫
Hotel Deutschherrenhof	⑮
Hotel Petrisberg	⑩
Römischer Kaiser Hotel	⑬

WHERE TO EAT	
Bagatelle	③
Gasthaus Mosellied	①
Kartofell Restaurant Kiste	⑫
Schlemmereule	⑮
Weinstube Kesselstatt	⑦
WeissHaus Restaurant	⑩
Zum Domstein	⑰

Dom★ (Cathedral)

Open Apr–Oct daily 6.30am–6pm;
Nov–Mar daily 6.30am–5.30pm.
www.dominformation.de.

With its six towers, Trier's cathedral looks more like a fortress than a church. A rounded apse projects from a massive, austere façade, which is a fine example of Early Romanesque architecture.

A flattened gable and rectangular plan, visible from the north side, point to the 4C Roman core of the building. West of this central block is the 11C Romanesque section; east of it the 12C polygonal chancel. A Baroque axial chapel crowned by a dome was added in the 18C.

The interior is primarily Baroque. Near the main door, note the fallen Roman **Domstein** (column) that supported part of the former church. A splendid **tympanum★** in the south aisle depicts Christ flanked by the Virgin Mary and St. Peter. Silver and gold plate, valuable ivories and magnificently illuminated Gospels are on view in the **Domschatzkammer★** (cathedral treasury; open Apr–Dec Mon–Sat 10am–5pm, Sun 12.30pm–5pm; Jan–Mar Tue–Sat 11am–4pm, Sun–Mon 12:30pm–4pm; closed Jan 1, Easter Sun, Dec 25; ⊛1.50€; ℰ0651 979 07 90; www.dominformation.de).

Liebfrauenkirche★ (Church of Our Lady)

Open Apr–Oct daily 8am–7pm (Sun until 6pm); Nov–Mar daily 8am–5pm. ℘(0651) 979 07 90. www.liebfrauen-trier.de.
One of the earliest Gothic sanctuaries in Germany (1235–60), this church has a ground plan in the form of a Greek cross. The edifice was inspired by one in the French Champagne region. Four apsidal chapels are flanked by two smaller, three-sided chapels, giving the entire church the layout of a rose with 12 petals.
The elegant interior is enhanced by rings of foliage around each column and the lofty central vault.

Bischöfliches Dom und Diözesanmuseum★ (Episcopal Museum)

Open Tues–Sat 9am–5pm, Sun 1pm–5pm. Closed Jan 1, Dec 24–26 & 31. ⊛3.50€. ⬥℘(0651) 710 52 55. www.bistum-trier.de/museum.
Dedicated to sacred art, this museum features the 4C ceiling frescoes from a residential palace that was replaced by an early Christian church. The central picture is believed to represent Constantine's wife, Fausta.

Basilika★

This large, rectangular building was once the **Aula Palatina** (main hall) of the Imperial palace, built by Constantine AD c. 310. Modified many times over the centuries, it was rebuilt in 1954 and is used today as a Protestant church.

Ehemaliges Kurfürstliches Schloss (Palace of the Electors)

Only the north and east wings remain of the 17C Renaissance electoral palace. The 18C Rococo wings were designed by Johannes Seitz, a student of Balthasar Neumann, whose virtuosity finds expression in a magnificent staircase.

Rheinisches Landesmuseum★★ (Rhineland Museum)

Weimarer Allee 1. Open year-round Tue–Sun 10am–5pm. Closed Jan 1, Carnival, Dec 23–26 & 31. ⊛6€. ⬥ ℘(0651) 977 40. www.landesmuseum-trier.de.
This museum of archaeology has exceptional items from as far back as the **Paleolithic**, featuring Stone Age implements and ceramics; objects from the Bronze Age; and jewels set in gold from Iron Age sepulchres. A major highlight is the **Roman** section, featuring mosaics, bronzes and bas-reliefs as well as the famous Neumagen ship stone carving, a representation of a ship sailing down the Moselle loaded with wine.

Kaiserthermen★★ (Imperial Roman Baths)

Open Apr–Sept daily 9am–6pm, Oct–Mar to 5pm, Nov–Feb to 4pm. ⊛3€. ℘(0651) 97 80 80.
Among the largest in the Roman Empire, these baths date from the time of Constantine. These days, it is used for theatre performances.

Schatzkammer der Stadtbibliothek★★ (Municipal Library Treasury)

Open year-round Mon–Fri 9am–5pm, Sat 9am–4pm, Sun 11am–3pm. ⊛5€. ⬥℘(0651) 718 14 29. www.stadtbibliothek-weberbach.de.
The library counts ancient manuscripts and illuminations, illustrated books and old documents among its treasures.

Karl-Marx-Haus

Brückenstraße 10. Open Apr–Oct daily 10am–6pm; Nov–Mar Mon 2pm–5pm, Tue–Sun 11am–5pm. Closed Jan 1, Mon before Shrove Tue, Dec 23–26 & 31. ⊛4€. ℘(0651) 97 06 80. www.museum-karl-marx-haus.de.
The birthplace of the socialist theoretician Karl Marx has been turned into a museum, displaying letters, manuscripts and a first edition of the *Communist Manifesto*.

NORTH OF PORTA NIGRA
Basilika St. Paulin★
(St. Paulin Church)

Access via Thebäerstraße.
Open year-round Tue 11am–5pm,
Wed–Sat 9am–5pm, Sun 10am–7.30pm.
(0651) 27 08 50.

Tall windows illuminate the single nave of this 18C church whose interior was designed by Balthasar Neumann. The martyrdom of St. Paul, citizens of Trier, and of the Theban Legion (AD 286) are illustrated in ceiling paintings by Christoph Thomas Scheffler of Augsburg. The high altar was based on Neumann's designs with woodcarving by Trier artist Ferdinand Tietz.

SOUTH OF THE OLD TOWN
Amphitheater★
(Amphitheatre)

Open Apr–Sept daily 9am–6pm;
Oct–Mar daily 9am–5pm; Nov–Feb
9am–4pm. ⊛3€. (0651) 97 80 80.
Once seating 20 000 spectators, this hillside arena was used as a quarry in the Middle Ages. The cellars housed theatrical equipment and machinery. Every summer, the amphitheatre hosts the **Antikenfestspiele** (Festival of Ancient Drama).

🚗 DRIVING TOUR

LOWER SAAR VALLEY

57km/35.4mi. Allow two hours.
See region map pp268–269.

South of the Moselle, the Lower Saar Valley parallels the Belgian and French borders. Away mainstream tourist routes, this region remains largely unspoiled. The B51 road links the Saar to Saarburg and Trier. Between Mettlach and Konz, where it flows into the Moselle, the Saar River cuts its way through the Hunsrück massif. Grapes, predominantly Riesling, have been cultivated here since the 18C.

▶ Leave Trier and drive 25km/
15.5mi south.

Saarburg

This picturesque town on the banks of the Saar is dominated by a mighty ruined fortress. Dating from at least 964 and later property of the Prince-Electors of Trier, it was blown up by the French in 1705. The site offers a good view of the town and the Saar Valley. The **old town**, with medieval alleyways, half-timbered houses and a 20m/65ft **waterfall** in the town centre, makes a delightful scene. The **Amüseum am Wasserfall** (Am Markt 29; open Sun–Fri 11am–4pm; ⊛3€; 065 81/99 46 42; www.saarburg.eu) has historic arts and crafts.
Ask at the museum for details of the **Hackenberger Mühle** (watermill).

▶ 21km/13mi south of Saarburg, then a 15min round-trip walk.

Cloef★★

From a viewpoint high above the river, a view of the Montclair loop, a hairpin curve of the Saar River enclosing a wide, densely wooded promontory, unfolds.

▶ From Cloef or Orscholz, a detour (about 30km/18.6mi round-trip via L177 and B406) reaches the Moselle Valley and the town of Nennig.

Römische Villa Nennig★★
(Roman Villa)

Open Apr–Sept Tue–Sun 8.30am–noon and 1pm–6pm; Mar, Oct & Nov 9am–noon, 1pm–4.30pm. ⊛1.50€. &
(06866) 13 29. www.kulturbesitz.de.
In 1852, a farmer accidentally discovered the remains of an enormous Roman villa thought to date from the 2C or 3C. A superb **floor mosaic** (16x10m/52x33ft) survives, consisting of eight medallions framed by intricate geometric designs and gladiator scenes.

Mettlach

The red sandstone Baroque façade of the abbey, now headquarters of Villeroy & Boch ceramics, rises above the road to Merzig. In the abbey gardens stands the 10C "Alter Turm", a ruined octagonal funerary chapel for the Merovingian duke Lutwinus, the abbey's founder.

ADDRESSES

⌂ STAY

⊖⊟ Berghotel Kockelsberg –
Kockelsberg 1, 54293 Trier-Kockelsberg. ℘(0651) 824 80. www.kockelsberg.de. 32 rooms. ⊠5€. Restaurant ⊖⊟, closed Nov–Mar Sun dinner. Enjoy lovely views of Trier from this early 20C hotel with its white façade and turrets. Rooms are charming and comfortable, and the country-style restaurant has perfect pitch as well.

⊖⊟ Hotel Alte Villa – *Saarstraße 133.*
℘(0651) 93 81 20. www.hotelaltevilla.de. 20 rooms. ⊠. This hotel on the outskirts of the city occupies a charmingly restored Baroque villa from 1743. Rooms are well-proportioned and modern.

⊖⊟ Hotel Deutschherrenhof –
Deutschherrenstraße 32. ℘(0651) 97 54 20. www.hotel-deutschherrenhof-trier.de. 15 rooms. ⊠. Close to the pedestrian zone, this hotel has simple rooms.

⊖⊟ Hotel Deutscher Hof – *Südallee 25*
℘(0651) 977 80. www.hotel-deutscher-hof.de. 99 rooms. ⊠8€. Restaurant ⊖⊟. South of the town centre, this professionally managed hotel has spacious rooms as well as a sauna and jacuzzi.

⊖⊟ Hotel Petrisberg –
Sickingenstraße 11-13. ℘(0651) 46 40. www.hotel-petrisberg.de. 35 rooms. ⊠. Well-equipped rooms are charming and have balconies, but it's the idyllic nature-preserve location and trails leading into town that set this property apart.

⊖⊟ Römischer Kaiser Hotel –
Porta Nigra Platz. ℘(0651) 977 01 00. www.friedrich-hotels.de. 43 rooms. ⊠. Restaurant ⊖⊟. This pleasant option in an old building is close to Porta Nigra.

⊖⊟⊟ Becker's Weinhaus –
Olewiger Straße 206. ℘(0651) 93 80 80. www.beckers-trier.de. 17 rooms. ⊠. Rooms at this sophisticated hotel located a few minutes' drive southeast of town are spread within a rustic old building and a more modern one. The latter houses a gourmet restaurant.

⊖⊟⊟ Hotel Aulmann – *Fleischstraße*
47-48. ℘(0651) 976 70. www.hotel-aulmann.de. 36 rooms. ⊠5€. This modern hotel located close to the city offers comfortable accommodation at a reasonable price.

⍾ EAT

⊖ Kartoffel Restaurant Kiste –
Fahrstraße 13–14. ℘(0651) 979 00 66. www.kistetrier.de. Everything revolves around the humble potato *(Kartoffel)*, which here is served fried, mashed, baked and in soups, salads and casseroles or paired with meat or local specialities.

⊖ Weinstube Kesselstatt –
Liebfrauenstraße 10. ℘(0651) 411 78. www.weinstube-kesselstatt.de. The nicest tables at this wine tavern are on the terrace facing the cathedral.

⊖ Zum Domstein – *Hauptmarkt 5.*
℘(0651) 744 90. www.domstein.de. Enjoy a meal prepared with authentic Roman recipes at this original restaurant situated on the market square.

⊖⊟ Gasthaus Mosellied –
Zurlaubener Ufer 86. ℘(0651) 265 88. Closed lunch Nov–Mar. Half a dozen eateries, from snack stand to gourmet restaurant, cluster on the riverbank. All have a terrace. Gasthaus Mosellied is particularly popular with locals.

⊖⊟⊟ Schlemmereule – *Domfreihof*
1b. ℘(0651) 736 16. www.schlemmereule.de. Closed 8–18 Feb and Sun. Modern and elegant, this restaurant in an 18C courthouse delivers a daily changing menu. Courtyard terrace.

⊖⊟⊟ Weisshaus Restaurant –
Weisshaus 1. ℘(0651) 834 33. www.weisshaus.de. Closed Mon, also Tue Jan–Mar. This chic restaurant sitting on the opposite riverbank offers beautiful views over the city. Foodwise, the focus is on delicious meaty fare.

⊖⊟⊟⊟ Bagatelle – *Zurlaubener*
Ufer 78. ℘(0651) 995 69 90. www.bagatelle-trier.com. Casual bistro flair characterises this converted fisherman's house located on the banks of the Moselle River. The cuisine is classic infused with French elements.

Moselle Valley★★★

Moseltal

Scattered with picturesque villages and renowned for its wines, the Moselle Valley is an enchanting region best explored on a leisurely drive or boat cruise. Castles, vineyards and romantic villages line both sides of the river.

🚗 DRIVING TOUR

FROM TRIER TO KOBLENZ

195km/121mi. Allow one day.

Trier★★ – *See TRIER.*

Neumagen-Dhron

This town is known for its Roman discoveries, which can be admired at the Rhineland Museum in Trier. A copy of the famous stone-carved **wine ship** sits next to the chapel, opposite the Am Römerweinschiff café.

Bernkastel-Kues★

This double town straddles the Moselle about 50km/31mi east of Trier. Bernkastel is the prettier of the two with higgledy-piggledy half-timbered houses lining a warren of narrow, cobbled lanes. The nicest surround the **Markt★**, a small, sloping square centred on the 17C **Michaelsbrunnen** (St. Michael's fountain).

South of town, Burg Landshut (Landshut Castle) squats atop a rocky promontory. It was built in the 13C by the archbishops of Trier, but has been in ruins since the 17C War of the Orléans Succession. From up here, panoramic **views★★** take in a bend in the Moselle where even the steepest slopes are planted with vines.

The main draw of Kues across the river is the **St. Nikolaus-Hospital** (chapel and cloisters open year-round Sun–Fri 9am–6pm, Sat 9am–3pm; guided library tours Apr–Oct Tue 10.30am, Fri 3pm; 5€; 06531 22 60; www.

cusanus.de), a hospice founded in 1447 by humanist and theologian Nikolaus Cusanus. The number of lodgers was restricted to a symbolic 33 (the age of Christ Jesus at his death), a tradition that is still respected to this day.

Admire the late-Gothic cloister, the chapel with its fine 15C reredos, and the bronze copy of the cardinal's tombstone (the original is in Rome, at San Pietro in Víncoli). Note the fresco depicting the Last Judgement *(to the left of the entrance)* and the **tombstone of Clara Cryftz**, the prelate's sister.

Wines Full of Character

The slopes of the Moselle Valley are draped in vineyards producing dry and semi-dry white wines, including the main varietal, Riesling. The ground shale plays an important role in the maturation of the grapes as it absorbs the sun's power during the day and continues to radiate the heat back to the grape vines throughout the night. The harvest can be as late as December 6. Light and with a delicate bouquet, the Moselle vines get dryer the further north one goes.

ℹ Info: Kordelweg 1, 54470 Bernkastel-Kues. ✆(06531) 973 30. www.moselland touristik.de.

▶ Location: The peaceful Moselle River enters Germany near Trier and meanders to Koblenz, where it flows into the Rhine.

⊗ Don't Miss: Sampling the famous white wines, Bernkastel-Kues, Burg Eltz.

⊙ Timing: Allow at least one day for the suggested driving tour.

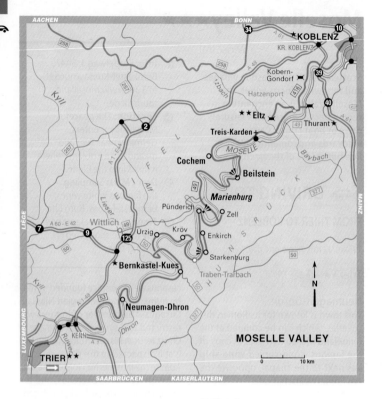

AACHEN — BONN

KOBLENZ
KR. KOBLENZ

Kobern-Gondorf

Hatzenport

★★ Eltz

Treis-Karden

Thurant ★

Cochem

MOSELLE

Beilstein

Marienburg

Pünderich

Zell

ZELL

Wittlich

Urzig

Kröv

Enkirch

Bernkastel-Kues

Starkenburg

Traben-Trarbach

Neumagen-Dhron

TRIER ★★

SAARBRÜCKEN — KAISERLAUTERN

MOSELLE VALLEY

N

0   10 km

LIÈGE · LUXEMBOURG · MAINZ

The **library** houses almost 400 manuscripts as well as astronomical instruments once used by Cusanus himself.

Finish your sightseeing with a wine tasting in the atmospheric cellars of the **Vinothek**.

▶ The road passes through typical wine-growing villages: Ürzig, Kröv, Enkirch (make a 5km/3mi detour to Starkenburg for fabulous valley views) and Pünderich among them. One magnificent vineyard follows another. Some 3.5km/2mi after the bridge at Zell, take the left turn towards Marienburg.

Marienburg

The old convent here enjoyed an exceptional **setting★★**. From the restaurant terrace and the wooden "Prinzenkopf" look-out tower *(follow the trail; 45min round trip)* there are impressive **views★★** of the river and its environs.

Beilstein

This tiny fortified village is nicknamed "Sleeping Beauty of the Moselle" because of its compact shape and fairytale setting amid steeply sloping vineyards. A cluster of half-timbered houses huddles around a picturesque Marktplatz.

Note especially the Zehnthaus, the church of St. Christopher and the 18C wine cellars. The village is lorded over by an enormous Baroque hall-church (1635) and a romantically ruined castle. The latter is reached via a steep staircase *(30min round trip)* and will treat you to sweeping views across the town and the meandering river valley.

Cochem

Cochem is presided over by the playfully turreted and pinnacled **Reichsburg★★** (🚶40min guided tours mid-Mar–Oct daily 9am–5pm, restricted hours in winter, call ahead; ⊙5€; ℘02671 255; www.reichsburg-cochem.de).

Cochem with Reichsburg

The 11C original was badly destroyed by French troops in the 17C, but the castle was elaborately restored in the 19C. It is one of the most celebrated sites in the region thanks to its spectacular setting atop a vine-clad hill.

Views are great from up here but even better from the **Pinner-Kreuz★** hill, comfortably reached by **chairlift** (open late Mar–mid-Nov; 4.30€ one-way, 6.30€ round-trip; 02671 98 90 63; www.cochemer-sesselbahn.de).

Treis-Karden

The Church of St. Castor in the village of Karden represents the transitional stage between the Rhenish Romanesque ("gallery dwarf" in the apse) and Gothic (ribbed vaults).

Inside, note the high altar, the altar of the Magi (1420), and in the chapel of the choir (left), the small Gothic wooden shrine of St. Castor (1490).

Burg Eltz★★

10km/6.2mi from Hatzenport, plus 15min walk or 5min by bus. Guided tours (40min) Apr–Oct daily 9.30am–5.30pm. 9€. (02672) 95 05 00. www.burg-eltz.de.

This romantic 1 000-year-old **castle★★** bristles with towers and turrets rising majestically from the thick forest at the far end of the Eltz Valley. It has been owned by the same family for more than 30 generations. Tours take you into fabulously decorated rooms with wooden and net-vaulted ceilings, a bedroom with 15C frescoes, the splendid Knights Hall and the still-intact medieval kitchen. Another highlight is the painting *Madonna with Child and Grapes* by Lucas Cranach the Elder complemented by other works from the Cranach School. Tickets also give access to the **treasury★**, a feast of gold, silver, porcelain and fancy knick-knacks.

Burg Thurant★

Open May–Oct daily 10am–6pm; Nov–Feb daily 10am–4pm; Mar & Apr daily 10am–5pm. 3.50€. (02605) 20 04. www.thurant.de.

Stroll through the gardens of this small, romantic 12C castle, then soak up medieval flair as you explore its ramparts, chapel and wine cellar, and even the dungeon. Don't miss climbing up the Kölner Turm (Cologne tower) to snap panoramic photographs of the hilly countryside and charming river valley.

Koblenz★ – &*See KOBLENZ.*

EXCURSIONS
IDAR-OBERSTEIN
◐ 37km/23mi south of Bernkastel-Kues. Hauptstraße 419, 55743 Idar-Oberstein. ℘(06781) 64 871. www.idar-oberstein.de.
Twin towns form this municipality: picturesque Oberstein at the foot of a gorge carved by the River Nahe, and Idar on the river's tributary.
Since the Middle Ages, the history of Idar-Oberstein has been linked to the production and sale of gemstones. The abundance of agate, jasper, amethyst and other deposits here has made the town a centre for cutting and polishing of the precious stones. The many jewellery museums and shops bear witness to this trade.

Deutsches Edelsteinmuseum★★ (German Precious Stone Museum)
In the Idar-Zentrum (Diamond Exchange), Hauptstraße 118. Open Feb–Apr daily 10am–5pm; May–Oct, daily 9.30am–5.30pm; Nov–early Jan 10am–5pm. Closed Dec 24–25 & 31, mid to end Jan. ⊕6€. ℘(06781) 90 09 80. www.edelsteinmuseum.de.
The museum houses precious stones from around the world, from agates to diamonds. Its collection has grown to 10 000 glittering objects and includes raw rocks, crystals and cut stones.
Some of the treasures are presented in darkened rooms under black light, making them phosphorescent. Elsewhere you can admire replicas of famous gems, including the legendary Hope diamond.

Felsenkirche★
30min round-trip walk. Access via stairs (214 steps) from Oberstein Marktplatz. Open mid-Mar–Oct daily 10am–6pm; Nov 1–15 daily 11am–4pm. ⊕2€. www.felsenkirche-oberstein.de.
Framed by a rock overhang above the river, this church, restored several times, is worth a visit for the 15C winged altar-piece alone. The scenes of the Passion depict the event with a ferocious realism. According to legend, the church was built in atonement for a fraticide by the surviving brother.

Deutsches Mineralienmuseum (German Mineral Museum)
Hauptstraße 436 at Oberstein Marktplatz (below the Felsenkirche stairway). Open mid-Mar–Oct daily 9am–5.30pm (Jul–Sept until 7pm); Nov–mid-Mar Mon–Fri 11am–5pm, Sat–Sun 11am–6pm. Closed Jan 1, Dec 24–25 & 31. ⊕5.50€. ℘(06781) 246 19. www.deutsches-mineralienmuseum.de.
This museum emphasises the region's minerals and precious stones. Aside from viewing gemstones, you can get a close-up look at an old agate watermill as well as a 19C workshop of a goldsmith. A darkened room features fluorescent minerals sparkling in a rainbow of colours beneath ultraviolet light.

♟♟ Edelsteinminen Steinkaulenberg
Tiefensteiner Straße 87. ☞Visit by guided tour (30min) only, mid-Mar–mid-Nov daily 9am–5pm. ⊕6€. ℘(06781) 474 00. www.edelsteinminen-idar-oberstein.de.
At the only gemstone mine in Europe open to the public, you can see firsthand how the precious minerals are harvested. If you want to dig up your own, head to the **Edelsteincamp** (gemstone camp; sessions by prior arrangement daily 9am–5pm; ⊕10€ (child 7€); ♟sturdy footwear and comfortable clothes required). You get to keep whatever you dig up during the two-hour session.

Industriedenkmal Jakob Bengel★★ (Industrial Monument Jakob Bengel)
Wilhelmstraße 42a. Open year-round Tue–Fri 10am–12pm & 2pm–4pm (also Sat–Sun May–Sept). ℘(067 81) 27 030. www.jakob-bengel.de. ☞Guided tours (1hr) available at extra cost. ⊕3€.

This workshop had its heyday between 1910 and 1920 when Art Deco and Bauhaus jewellery were all the rage. At that time, the house worked for Coco Chanel and Parisian department stores. Today, production is virtually zero, but all the machines (including a 120t press, chain-making machines and polishing stations) are activated during guided visits.

THE HUNSRÜCK

▶ 37km/23mi east of Bernkastel-Kues. The Hunsrück, a low mountain range, forms the southern rim of the Rhine schist massif, a region of low mountains and game-stocked forests slashed by steep valleys.

Erbeskopf

At 818m/2 683.7ft, this is the highest peak in the Hunsrück. Enjoy fine views from the wooden tower as well as the **Hunsrückhöhenstraße★**. The road passes the Stumpfer Turm, an old Roman watchtower.

Kirchberg

Clinging to a hillside, this village is filled with half-timbered houses, especially around the Marktplatz. Also note the pre-Romanesque St. Michaelskirche.

Simmern

The farming centre of the Hunsrück, Simmern is home to the parish church of St. Stephan (15C). The church's **tombs★** of the Dukes of Pfalz-Simmern feature some of the finest Renaissance sculptures in the middle Rhineland.

Ravengiersburg

Tucked into the bottom of a valley, this village boasts a Romanesque church with an imposing west front. Note above the porch Christ in Majesty.

Dhaun

The partly ruined medieval castle perches dramatically atop a steep promontory and is considered the largest in the region. The complex includes the St. George's Chapel (1661) and the kitchen as well as two bastions and defensive towers.

ADDRESSES

🛏 STAY

◒ **Wein- und Gästehaus Port** – *Weingartenstraße 57, 54470 Bernkastel-Kues.* ✆*(06531) 911 73. www.ferienweingut-port.de. 5 rooms, 4 apartments.* 🖃. At this peaceful wine estate, days start with a hearty breakfast in the winter garden and wrap up with a wine tasting, perhaps paired with a robust steak from the grill.

◒◒ **Reichsschenke "Zum Ritter Götz"** – *Robert-Schuman-Straße 57, 54536 Kröv.* ✆*(06541) 816 60. www.reichsschenke.de. Closed 2 weeks in Nov and 3 weeks late Dec–mid-Jan. 16 rooms.* 🖃. *Restaurant*◒◒. This historic inn has smart, uncluttered rooms and a woodsy low-ceilinged restaurant. The menu caters to all tastes with classic German fare, regional dishes and upscale French cuisine.

◒◒ **Römischer Kaiser** – *Markt 2, Bernkastel-Kues.* ✆*(06531) 91 90 04. www.roemischer-kaiser-bernkastel.de. 22 rooms.* 🖃*10€.* Behind its pale pink façade, this centrally located traditional hotel has modern rooms with a good range of amenities.

◒◒◒ **Hotel Bären** – *Schanzstraße 9, 54470 Bernkastel-Kues.* ✆*(06531) 95 04 40. www.hotel-baeren.de. Closed Nov–Mar Sun–Tue. 33 rooms.* 🖃. *Restaurant*◒◒. It's well worth spending a little extra for modern rooms with river-facing balconies at this family-owned hotel. The adjacent restaurant serves everything from snacks to rib-sticking meals.

Koblenz★

Occupying a strategic location at the confluence of the Rhine and the Moselle rivers, Koblenz was established in 9 BC as a Roman camp. It has has grown into a mid-size, modern town dotted with historic buildings and charming wine taverns. The departure point for river excursions, Koblenz is also one of the towns hosting the "Rhine in Flames" summer festival, a celebration of music, fireworks and illuminated boats.

A BIT OF HISTORY

Koblenz came under French influence after the 1789 French Revolution, when it welcomed scores of refugees. Over the coming decades France and Prussia fought repeatedly over this region, alternating control until 1815, when the defeat of Napoleon returned the land to Prussia. The impressive **Rheinanlagen**, a splendid riverside promenade, dates from the 19C French occupation.

SIGHTS

Deutsches Eck★ (German Corner)

A monumental equestrian statue of Wilhelm I presides over this tongue of land marking the confluence of the Rhine and the Moselle rivers. Enjoy fine views from the base of the statue *(107 steps).*

▸ **Population:** 107 500

Info: Zentralplatz 1, 56068 Koblenz. ☏(0261) 194 33. www.koblenz-touristik.de.

◗ **Location:** Located at the confluence of the Rhine and the Moselle rivers, Koblenz also lies at the junction of the Hunsrück, Eifel and Westerwald mountain ranges.

Don't Miss: Deutsches Eck, wine taverns, Ehrenbreitstein Fortress.

🕓 **Timing:** It takes half a day to explore the town and the fortress.

Museum Ludwig

Ballei Building, next to Deutsches Eck. ☏(0261) 30 40 40. www.ludwig museum.org. Open year-round Tue–Sat 10.30am–5pm, Sun & holidays 11am–6pm. Closed Jan 1, Dec 24–25 & 31. ⊙5€.

Designed to support the city's relationship with France in the arts, this museum is dedicated to contemporary art. The collection includes works by Pablo Picasso and Jean Dubuffet as well as big names from North America such as Jasper Johns, Willem de Kooning and Robert Rauschenberg and German artist KO Götz. Also shown are the New

Deutsches Eck at the confluence of the Moselle and Rhine

© Paul Wander/Fotolia.com

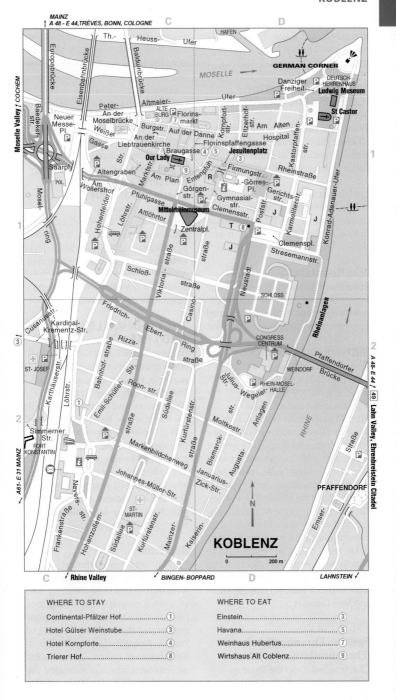

KOBLENZ

0   200 m

WHERE TO STAY

Continental-Pfälzer Hof.....................①
Hotel Gülser Weinstube.....................③
Hotel Kornpforte.............................④
Trierer Hof....................................⑧

WHERE TO EAT

Einstein...③
Havana..⑤
Weinhaus Hubertus..........................⑦
Wirtshaus Alt Coblenz.....................⑨

319

Realists (Arman, César, Tinguely, Martial Raysse) and the famous "Thumb" of Caesar in the garden.

Stiftskirche St. Kastor (Collegiate Church of St. Castor)

The south transept of this Romanesque church features 16 painted wood panels that were once part of a rood screen. St. Castor is depicted on the bottom left.

Liebfrauenkirche

This Romanesque church got its late-Gothic chancel in the 15C and Baroque belfries in the 17C. The modern windows are by HG Stockhausen (1992).

Jesuitenplatz

In the courtyard of a 17C Jesuit College (now the town hall), the *Schängelbrunnen* (fountain) evokes the mischief perpetrated by the city's street urchins.

Mittelrheinmuseum★

Zentralplatz 1. Open year-round Tue–Sun 10am–6pm . Closed Jan 1 & Dec 25. 6€. (0261) 129 25 20. www.mittelrhein-museum.de.

After 48 years at the Florinsmarkt, this museum moved into the stunning new Forum Confluentes in mid-2013, which it shares with other institutions, a tourist information center, cafés, restaurants, and the **Romanticum**, an interactive exhibit about the Middle Rhine Valley. The museum's collections trace the history of the town and environs through paintings, religious artefacts and everyday items dating as far back as the Middle Ages. Forum Confluentes and the Forum Mittelrhein mall are both the work of Dutch architects Jan Benthem and Mels Crouwel.

EXCURSIONS

Festung Ehrenbreitstein★ (Ehrenbreitstein Fortress)

4.5km/3mi. Cross the Rhine on Pfaffendorfer Brücke then turn left. (0261) 66 75 40 00. www.diefestungehrenbreitstein.de.

This strategic hilltop fortress was destroyed by French troops in 1801,

but rebuilt and expanded by the Prussians between 1817 and 1828. **Views★★** from the top are great, and the compound also harbours a youth hostel and a restaurant.

A chairlift operates during the warmer months (mid-Apr –Oct daily 10am–6.30pm, Jun–Sept Thu–Sat until 10pm; 9€ round trip; (0261) 20 16 58 50; www.seilbahn-koblenz.de).

Kloster Maria Laach★ (Maria Laach Abbey)

20km/12.4mi west.

Near a volcanic lake, this well-preserved 12C Romanesque basilica is part of a Benedictine abbey. The cloister-style **entrance portico★** has very intricately worked capitals and the hexagonal baldaquin over the altar suggests a possible Moorish influence.

THE LAHN VALLEY AND LIMBURG

The tourist offices of Nassau and Diez offer many activities: hiking, bike and boat rides, kayaking and wine tasting.

The valley cuts through the Taunus-Rhine massif and meanders through the forests of the Nassau Natural Park east of Koblenz. The winding course of the lower Lahn is characterised by wild scenery and steeply wooded banks.

The valley holds a number of castles and the historic town of Limburg. The following towns, all located east of Koblenz, may be explored on a 60km/37mi-long loop.

Bad Ems

17km/10.5mi from Koblenz.

The Lahn Valley, separating the Westerwald and the Taunus-Rhine schist massif, is rich in mineral springs. A flagstone bearing the date 13 July 1870, commemorates the Bad Ems meeting of Prussian King Wilhelm I and the French Ambassador to Prussia, Count Vincent de Benedetti, which precipitated the outbreak of the Franco-Prussian War of 1870–71.

Nassau

❯ 25.9km/16mi from Koblenz. 🚉☏0260 495 250. www.nassau-touristik.de.
This health resort in the Lahn Valley was the cradle of the counts of Laurenburg, from whom Dutch royalty, including William of Orange, William III of England and the current Dutch royal family, are descended. Points of interest include the Adelsheimer Hof (town hall), the Stammburg (ancestral castle) and the Steinisches Schloss.

Kloster Arnstein

❯ 1km/0.6mi by a steep uphill road from the Obernhof Bridge.
The Premonstratensian church bears one Romanesque chancel (west) and one Gothic (the east).

Diez

❯ 56.8km/35.3mi from Koblenz. 🚉☏06 432 501 275. www.urlaubsregion-diez.info.
Dominating this small town, the 17C **Schloss Oranienstein** is an early Baroque edifice that was the ancestral seat of the House of Nassau-Orange. It boasts stucco ornamentation by Castelli and Genone and ceiling frescoes by Jan van Dyck. In the 19C the palace served as barracks for Prussian cadets; today sections are used by the German army. Some rooms house the **Oranien-Nassau-Museum** (👁visit by 1hr guided tour only, Apr–Oct Tue–Fri 9am, 10.30am, 2pm, Sun 10.30am and 2pm, Sat also 3.30pm; Nov–Mar Tue–Fri 9am, 10.30am, 2pm and 3.30pm; ☜3€; ☏06432 940 16 66; www.museumdiez.de). Tours visit the **Blue-Golden Hall** with its copper etchings and paintings. The Calvinist chapel is decorated with rich stucco ornamentation and frescoes.

Burg Runkel★

❯ 62.5km/38.8mi from Koblenz.
The picturesque **setting★★** of the castle, built into the rock face, and the ancient village below it can best be appreciated from the 15C bridge over the river.

LIMBURG AN DER LAHN★

❯ Bordering Hessen and Rheinland-Pfalz, Limburg is south of Koblenz via the A3. Bahnhofsplatz 2, 65549 Limburg. ☏(06431) 61 66. www.limburg.de.
The powerful yet elegant silhouette of the cathedral dominates the Limburg skyline. The town centre consists largely of half-timbered houses dating from the 13C to the 18C.

Dom★
(Cathedral)

Limburg's St. Georgsdom enjoys a picturesque **setting★★** on a rocky spur and is especially noted for its striking architecture, which is a classic example of the Romanesque-Gothic transitional style. The exterior remains Romanesque and closely resembles the Rhineland Romanesque-style cathedrals, but its interior is already Gothic. Look for Gothic hallmarks: galleries, arcades, a triforium and clerestory windows. Artistic highlights include the 13C stone rood screen and the frescoes in the nave. From the cemetery terrace there is a good **view★** of the Lahn River.

Staurothek
Diözesanmuseum★

Domstraße 12. Open Apr–Nov Tue–Sat 10am–1pm & 2pm–5pm, Sun 11am–5pm. ☜3€. ☏(06431) 29 54 82. www.staurothek.de.
The 10C Byzantine reliquary cross known as the Limburger Staurothek is the jewel of the religious art collection displayed in this museum. The most precious exhibit though is the so-called 15C "Dernbacher Beweinung", a group of sculptures representing the lamentation over Christ's Passion and Death.

Old Town★
(Altstadt)

Take time to discover the beautiful old houses along Limburg's winding alleys and pretty squares, most notably Domplatz, Fischmarkt, Brückengasse, Römer, Rütsche and Bischofsplatz. Walderdorffer Hof (Fahrgasse) is an impressive Renaissance construction.

ADDRESSES

🛏 STAY

KOBLENZ

⊖⊜ Hotel Gülser Weinstube – *Moselweinstraße 3. ℰ(0261) 988 64 10. www.hotelguelserweinstube.de. 14 rooms. ⌸.* This small family hotel in a beautiful half-timbered house sits right on the banks of the Moselle and has a restaurant/wine bar where you can taste the local wines.

⊖⊜ Hotel Kornpforte – *Kornpfort-straße 11. ℰ(0261) 311 74. www.hotel-kornpforte.de. 19 rooms. ⌸.* Pleasant and affordable accommodation in the city centre. Expect a friendly welcome and pleasantly furnished, high-ceilinged rooms.

⊖⊜ Trierer Hof – *Clemensstraße 1. ℰ(0261) 100 60. www.triererhof.de. Closed late Dec–late Jan. 35 rooms. ⌸.* Beautiful house close to the city centre and the River Rhine.

⊖⊜⊜ Continental-Pfälzer Hof – *Bahnhofsplatz 1. ℰ(0261) 301 60. www.continental-koblenz.de. 32 rooms. ⌸.* This modern hotel is close to the train station. Double-glazed windows ensure a good night's sleep. There are several other hotels close by, although all are a fair distance from the town centre.

LIMBURG AN DER LAHN

⊖⊜ Martin – *Holzheimer Straße 2-3. ℰ(06431) 948 40. www.hotel-martin.de. 26 rooms. ⌸.* This family-run hotel opposite the train station welcomes guests with handsome rooms sporting wooden floors and soothing hues.

⊖⊜⊜ Hotel Zimmermann – *Blumenröder Straße 1. ℰ(06431) 46 11. www.hotelzimmermann.de. 20 rooms. ⌸.* With English-inspired furnishings, rooms exude an air of luxury at this centrally located hotel near the train station. Huge breakfasts are served in a lovely room.

🍴/EAT

KOBLENZ

⊖ Havana – *Kornpfortstraße 6. ℰ(0261) 100 46 84.* This restaurant serves snacks as well as Mexican cuisine in a relaxed atmosphere. Happy hour extends from 6pm to 8pm.

⊖ Einstein – *Firmungstraße 30. ℰ(0261) 914 49 99. www.einstein-koblenz.de.* This busy restaurant in the pedestrian zone serves international fare. The Sunday brunch is worth a linger. Some terrace tables available.

⊖⊜ Weinhaus Hubertus – *Florinsmarkt 6. ℰ(0261) 311 77. www.weinhaus-hubertus.de.* The dining room in this beautiful half-timbered house is panelled in dark wood and decorated with hunting trophies. It's one of the best addresses in the old town.

⊖⊜ Wirtshaus Alt Coblenz – *Am Plan 13. ℰ(0261) 16 06 56. www.alt-coblenz.de. Closed Mon lunch.* The rustic setting is perfect for enjoying a traditional German meal or tasting the local wines.

LIMBURG AN DER LAHN

⊖ Bella Cittá Vecchia – *Fischmarkt 8. ℰ(06431) 210 608. www.bella-citta-vecchia.de.* Situated in the heart of the old town, this charming restaurant serves authentic Italian cuisine, including pastas, pizzas, meat and fish dishes. Some rooms available, too *(92€)*.

⊖⊜⊜ Himmel und Erde – *Joseph-Heppel-Str. 1a. ℰ(06431) 584 7208. www.kapelle-himmelunderde.de. Closed Tue & Sat lunch, Sunday dinner & Mon.* This restaurant housed in an ancient chapel has maintained its rustic character over the years.

CRUISES

Cruises run between Koblenz and Cochem Jun–Sept. ⛴31€ one way.

KD Deutsche Rheinschiffahrt *ℰ(0221) 208 83 18; www.k-d.com.*

Rhine Valley★★★

Few rivers have captured the imagination of artists and travellers as much as the Rhine, a 1 320km/820mi ribbon rushing northwards from the Swiss Alps to the North Sea. Along the nicest stretch between Mainz and Koblenz, dreamy wine villages with dainty half-timbered houses are lorded over by legend-shrouded medieval castles. In 2002, the region became a UNESCO World Heritage Site.

A BIT OF HISTORY

Rhine legends – There is not, along the whole length of the Rhine, a castle, an island, or even a rock without its tale of chivalry or legend. **Lohengrin**, the Knight of the Swan, appeared at the foot of the Castle of Kleve (Cleves); at the **Loreley**, the Rock of Lore, a beautiful enchantress bewitched boatmen with her song, leading their vessels to disaster.

But the single outstanding Rhine legend is the story of the Nibelungen (*see INTRODUCTION: Literature*), which provided composer Richard Wagner with inspiration for his *Ring* cycle. Probably composed late in the 12C, the epic **Nibelungenlied** (Song of the Nibelungen) tells of murder, the splendours of the 5C Burgundian court

- ☒ **Info:** Loreley Besucherzentrum, 56346 St. Goarshausen. ℰ(06771) 95 93 80. www.romantischer-rhein.de.
- ▷ **Location:** Roads parallel both river banks, but there are no bridges – only ferries – between Koblenz and Mainz. A more leisurely way to experience the region is by tour boat with service from nearly all the nearby villages.
- ⊛ **Don't Miss:** A boat tour or drive along the river, Loreley Rock, Marksburg, Burg Rheinfels, Bacharach.
- ◷ **Timing:** Allow four hours for suggested driving tour ☐1☐ and one day for driving tour ☐2☐.
- ☙ **Kids:** Marksburg, Burg Rheinfels.

at Worms, and of the passions inflaming the hearts of its heroes. The tribal treasure is rumoured to be buried in the Rhine near Worms.

From the Alps to the North Sea – The Rhine rises in the Swiss Alps. Gushing down the mountains, it quickly reaches

The Loreley, Burg Katz and the Rhine

© Dominik Ketz/Romantischer Rhein Tourismus GmbH

the Bodensee (Lake Constance). After the river exits the lake, rock outcrops and the foothills of the Jura produce the famous Rhine Falls at Schaffhausen (⊙ see Michelin Green Guide Switzerland). Further downstream, limestone strata cause Laufen (rapids). At Basel, the Rhine abruptly changes direction, veering north towards the Vosges Mountains and the Black Forest.

From Bingen to Neuwied, north of Koblenz, the Rhine cuts its way through the Rhineland schist massif, where the rock can foment dangerous whirlpools. This "romantic" stretch of river valley, with its pastiche of steeply terraced vineyards, woods, escarpments and castle ruins, is the most picturesque part of the River Rhine.

Later, having passed through the industrial region around Duisburg, the river turns west and curls slowly across the plain towards the sea.

An exceptional shipping lane – The Rhine is navigable over almost 1 000km/620mi between Rotterdam and Rheinfelden and has always been an important European waterway. The world's largest river port is in Duisburg.

⊙ DRIVING TOURS

1 THE LORELEY★★

From Rüdesheim to Koblenz.
75km/47mi. Allow 4hrs.

This route, following the Rhine's east bank, passes through the wildest and steepest part of the Rhine Gorge, with splendid views of the castles and fortresses lining the river.

Rüdesheim★

Rheinstraße 29A, 65385. ℘ (06722) 90 61 50. www.ruedesheim.de.
The wine town of Rüdesheim am Rhine lies at the gateway to the "Romantic Rhine" and is a key tourist centre in the valley. Its narrow streets, most famously the Drosselgasse, are crammed with traditional wine taverns where you can

sample the celebrated local Riesling and other varietals.

Rheingauer Weinmuseum Brömserburg (Wine Museum)

Rheinstraße 2. Open mid-Mar–Oct daily 10am–6pm. ⊙5€. ℘ (06722) 23 48. www.rheingauer-weinmuseum.de.
This museum is housed in a medieval castle that has seen stints as a 13C residence of the Mainz bishops, as a stronghold of the knights of Rüdesheim, and as a meeting place for brigands. Exhibits include old winepresses and Roman amphorae (vases and jars for storing or transporting wine).

Niederwalddenkmal (Niederwald Memorial)

Access on foot, by road (2km/1.2mi) or by cable-car (terminal on Oberstraße: 20min round trip; ⊙7€ round trip). www.niederwalddenkmal.de.
Built in 1883 to commemorate the 1871 founding of the German Empire, this memorial comprises a massive statue of Germania sitting on a bronze plinth featuring Bismarck, Emperor Wilhelm I, German princes and their armies.

After Rüdesheim the road runs beneath terraced vineyards overlooked by the ruins of **Burg Ehrenfels**. This fortress was built by the archbishops of Mainz at the same time as the Mäuseturm on the opposite bank, which served as a tollbooth.

After Aßmannshausen, silhouetted high up on the oposite bank, the crenellated towers of Rheinstein, Reichenstein and Sooneck appear one after the other. The tower of Fürstenberg, on the wooded slopes facing Lorch, marks the start of an open stretch of vineyards and the towers of **Bacharach**, followed by the fortified isle of Pfalz.

The Pfalz at Kaub

The village of Kaub is dominated by the ruins of Gutenfels castle, and has a picturesque main street called Metzgerstraße. More interesting though is the fortress that sits on a spit of land in the middle of the Rhine. This medieval toll castle is called the **Pfalz★** (open Mar–Oct Tue–Sun 10am–6pm, Mar until 5pm; Jan–Feb & Nov Sat–Sun 10am–5pm; closed Dec; ✆0172 262 28 00; ≈3€) and also known as Pfalzgrafen-stein. Its main tower is surrounded by a wall evoking the shape of a ship. Its location and the thickness of its walls kept it out of reach of attackers.

Before arriving at a right bend in the river, note the castle of Schönburg above Oberwesel on the opposite river bank. This is the starting point of the valley's most romantic section.

The Loreley★★

This legendary spur, 132m/433ft high, symbolises the Romantic Rhine and enjoys a special place in German literature. The outcropping reduces the river's width by one quarter. According to legend, the Loreley was a water sprite who bewitched boatmen with her beauty and melodious songs at the river's narrowest and thus most dangerous spot.

St. Goarshausen

The town, strung out along the riverbank, is dominated by **Burg Katz** (Cat Castle), said to have been built to neutralise **Burg Maus** (Mouse Castle), a little further downstream.

Loreley Viewpoint★★

From St. Goarshausen take the road signposted "Loreley-Burgenstraße". From Apr to Oct, shuttle buses leave from St. Goarshausen boat landing. There are impressive **views★★** of the romantic gorge from several accessible spurs here. On the plateau a landscape garden with marked trails is laid out, and a **visitor centre** (open Mar–Oct daily 10am–6pm; ≈2.50€; ☞; ✆06771 59 90 93; www.loreley-besucherzentrum.de) has interactive displays about the Loreley legend and local geology, flora and fauna.

Wellmich

Dolkstraße 6. ✆(06 771) 940 00. www.kath-kirche-loreley.de.
Have a peek inside the parish church with its nicely restored 15C frescoes depicting the Crucifixion, the Last Judgement and the martyrdom of the apostles.

▷ Continue to Kamp-Bornhofen, turn right towards Dahlheim, then right again at the sign "Zu den Burgen".

The Rival Brothers

The hill slopes become wild again. Beyond Kestert there is a **panorama★★**; from the ruins of **Liebenstein Fortress**, the castle of **Sterrenberg** and the valley below come into view. The two castles are traditionally linked to a legend concerning two rival brothers.

From Boppard on, where the Rhine swings into a huge double loop, the landscape becomes densely cultivated with vines. Soon the fortress of Marksburg emerges on its promontory above the town of Braubach.

▷ At Braubach, take the road to Nastätten.

♟♙ Marksburg★

🗪Visit by guided tour (50min) only, mid-Mar–Oct daily 10am–5pm; Nov–mid-Mar daily 11am–4pm. (English-language tours 1pm–4pm). Closed Dec 24 & 25. ≈6€. ✆(02627) 206. www.marksburg.de.

The **castle**, the only one in the entire Rhine Valley not to be destroyed, is spectacularly sited on a craggy hilltop. Tours take you inside a Gothic assembly hall, the medieval kitchen and the torture chamber. Also note the medieval garden and a collection of armour from 600 BC to the 15C.

Burg Lahneck

3km/1.8mi from Lahnstein, near the confluence of the Rhine and the Lahn.
🗪Visit by guided tour (40min) only Apr–Oct daily 10am–5pm. ≈5€. ✆(02621) 91 41 71. www.burg-lahneck.de.

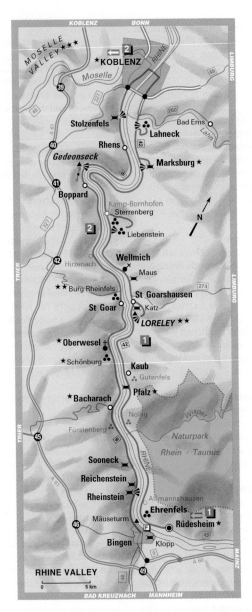

The ruins of this fortress, originally built in the 13C to protect neighbouring silver mines, were reconstructed in neo-Gothic style in the 19C.

From the keep a **view** is obtained of the junction of the two rivers and the turreted fairytale castle of Stolzenfels, across the Rhine.

2 THE RHINE CASTLES★★★

From Koblenz to Bingen. 63km/39mi. Allow one day.

This itinerary retraces the previous one, in the opposite direction, on the west bank of the river. Soon after leaving Koblenz, Lahneck comes into view again, its tower overlooking the river confluence. Above, on the right, rises Stolzenfels.

Schloss Stolzenfels (Palace)

Open Mar–Nov Tue–Sun 10am–5pm (Apr–Sept until 6pm); Jan–Feb Sat–Sun 10am–5pm. Closed Dec. 4€. (0261) 516 56. www.schloss-stolzenfels.de
This enormous **castle** was recon-structed in 1842 in neo-Gothic style. From the terrace you can enjoy a love-ley view of Koblenz and the citadel of Ehrenbreitstein.

Rhens

This town is known for its many painted half-timbered houses.

Gedeonseck

1hr round-trip, including 20min on a chairlift. Apr 1–15 daily 10am–5pm; mid-Apr–Sept daily 10am–6pm; Oct 1–15 daily 10am–5.30pm; holidays until 6.30pm. 7€ round-trip. (06742) 25 10. www.sesselbahn-boppard.de.
In fine weather, a trip up this 240m/ 787ft-high rock outcrop will treat you to superb **views★** of the Rhine's hair-pin curve near Boppard. The **Four Lake View★** gives you the illusion of looking at four separate lakes rather than a con-tinuous river.

Boppard

Originally a Roman camp, Boppard became a Free Imperial City in the Middle Ages. Sights include the late-Romanesque Severuskirche and the Gothic Carmelite Church with its 15C choir stalls and Renaissance tombs. The **museum** in the 14C fortress displays, among other things, bentwood fur-niture by native son Michael Thonet. There is also a pleasant riverside walk and the Römerkastell, where you can see a section of the 4C Roman town wall and graves from the Frankish period in the 7C. The beginning of the "romantic" Rhine Gorge is marked by the two Rival Brothers fortresses (*see above*) on the opposite slopes. After Hirzenach, the Cat and Mouse castles loom above St. Goarshausen.

The Rhine Valley Castles

The Rhine Valley boasts an impressive number of castles. Stately residences, defensive forts, toll gates, travellers' refuges, each served a purpose. While many were severely damaged in fighting during the 17C and 18C, many castles were rebuilt following the creation of the German Confederation in 1815.

St. Goar

The village, clinging to the hillside at the foot of the impressive **Burg Rheinfels★★** (open mid-Mar–mid-Oct daily 9am–6pm; late Oct–early Nov daily 9am–5pm; 4€; 06741 7753; www.st-goar.de) stands guard over the Loreley passage along with St. Goarshausen across the river. Rheinfels was, until it fell to the French in 1797, the valley's most powerful fortress. Climb the clock-tower for panoramic views of the river and the Cat and Mouse castles. Kids love exploring Rheinfels Castle's maze of towers, gates and courts. Bring or borrow a torch to go inside the under-ground defensive tunnel network.

Beyond St. Goar, the river banks are steep and heavily wooded until Ober-wesel.

Oberwesel

Sixteen towers survive of the original town wall hemming in this appealing wine-growing village. It is possible to walk along sections of it, from which there is a good view of the Rhine.

South of the town, the Gothic **Lieb-frauenkirche★** has a fine 14C altar-piece, one of the oldest in Germany, a Gothic rood screen and an unusual 1510 triptych illustrating the 15 cataclysms presaging the end of the world.
From the terrace of **Schönburg Castle★**, you can spot Kaub and the fortified Isle of Pfalz in the distance. The castle itself

consists of three forts with a common defensive wall.

Bacharach★

Surrounded by vineyards, protected by an ancient town wall, Bacharach is one of the prettiest – and thus most popular – towns in the Rhine Valley. The row of half-timbered houses on Marktplatz and along Oberstraße are a delight, especially when decked out with flowers during the warmer seasons. The Peterskirche has one of the last Romanesque naves built in Germany. From here, a trail leads up to the romantically ruined Gothic Wernerkapelle (chapel) and the medieval Burg Stahleck, now a youth hostel.

The ruined towers of Nollig and Fürstenberg mark the end of the valley's most grandiose stretch. The road runs past a trio of audaciously perched castles.

Burg Sooneck

At Niederheimbach. Open year-round Tue–Sun 9am–5pm (Apr–Sept until 6pm). Closed Dec. ☜4€. ℘(06743) 60 64.

This restored **fortress** clings to a steep slope of the Soonwald outcrop, and is

---

The Name of the Rose

The cameras began rolling at Eberbach in 1986 for the filming of the monastic whodunnit *The Name of the Rose*. Director Jean-Jacques Annaud allegedly chose the Cistercian abbey of Eberbach from a list of 300 abbeys as the primary setting for Umberto Eco's novel. The dispute between the papal envoy and the Franciscan monk William of Baskerville, played by Sean Connery, was filmed in the chapter-house, where monastic law was once laid down.

The scriptorium was reconstructed in the monks' dormitory. In the film, sentences were passed by the Holy Inquisition where people now gather to taste wine, in the monastery cellar. The abbey church and hospice also feature in the film.

---

tiered to suit the terrain with a maze of staircases, platforms and terraced gardens beneath the turrets.

Burg Reichenstein

Open year-round daily 10am–6pm. ☜5€. ℘(06721) 61 17. www.burg-reichenstein.de.

Strategically situated at the mouth of a valley, this 10C **castle** has a collection of arms and hunting trophies. After serving as an imperial tollhouse, it was converted into a summer residence in the 19C. Inside is a hotel and restaurant.

Burg Rheinstein

Open mid-Mar–Oct daily 9.30am–6pm (last entry 5.30pm). ☜5€. ℘(06721) 63 48. www.burg-rheinstein.de.

This **castle** is perched on a rock spur, in a commanding position above the Rhine. From the foremost watchtower extends a birds-eye **view★★** of the valley. Rheinstein was the first of the Rhine castles to be rebuilt by the Hohenzollerns (after 1823).

Once past the **Mäuseturm**, balanced on its tiny islet in the middle of the river, the valley widens and the east bank becomes covered with terraced vines.

Bingen

Bingen started out as a strategic Roman camp set up at the confluence of the Rhine and the Nahe *(Castellum Bingium)*. Nowadays, tourism and wine-growing are the town's main sources of income. Sights include the landmark **Burg Klopp** and the **Historisches Museum am Strom** (open year-round Tue–Sun 10am–5pm; closed mid-Jan–mid-Feb, Dec 24–25 & 31; ☜3€; ♿; ℘06721 18 43 53) with exhibits on local history and on the 12C abbess, artist and author Hildegard von Bingen.

EXCURSION
Kloster Eberbach★★

◗ 20km/12mi northeast of Rüdesheim am Rhein. Open Apr–Oct daily 10am–6pm; Nov–Mar daily 11am–5pm. Closed Mon before Shrove Tue, Dec 24–25 & 31. ☜7.50€.

🐾 Audio-guides and guided tours available. Tours 🎧10€ (includes admission fee) ♿ ℘(06723) 917 81 00. www.kloster-eberbach.de.

Founded by Bernard of Clairvaux in 1136, this former Cistercian abbey existed for nearly 700 years before its secularisation in 1803. During the Middle Ages, it evolved into one of the region's finest wine estates and even had its own fleet of ships plying the Rhine. It is still a famous wine producer today.

Abbey Church

Built in two stages, in 1145–60 and in 1170–86, this three-nave Romanesque basilica reflects the understated and elegant austerity typical of Cistercian architecture. Gothic side chapels with tracery windows were added in the 14C, and there are remarkably elaborate **tombs★** dating from the 14C to the 18C.

Abbey Buildings

Outlying 13C–14C buildings wrap around the **cloister★** which, on the north side, gives access to the **monk's refectory★★**.

Only the Romanesque portal remains of the original dining room; the rest was rebuilt in Baroque style and lidded by a magnificent stucco ceiling by Daniel Schenk, a court artist from Mainz.

The refectory is flanked by the **abbey museum** *(Abteimuseum)* on the left and the **monks' dormitory★** to the right. Dating to c. 1250–70, the double-naved, rib-vaulted room has a slightly rising floor and shortened pillars to create the illusion of length.

Monks usually gathered in the adjacent **chapterhouse★** *(Kapitelsaal)*, which got its beautiful star-ribbed vaulting in the middle of the 14C and stylised plant ornamentation around 1500.

The lay brothers slept and ate in the area west of the cloister. Their old refectory now contains a collection of mighty **winepresses★**, documenting the abbey's 800-year-old history of wine-producing. The oldest press dates from 1668. Wine tastings, food and lodging are also available in the complex.

ADDRESSES

🛏 STAY

🍽 **Altkölnischer Hof** – *Blücherstraße 2, 55422 Bacharach.* ℘*(06743) 13 39. www.altkoelnischer-hof.de. Closed Nov–Mar. 20 rooms.* 🍴 *Restaurant*🍽. Rooms at this family-run hotel in a half-timbered building ooze charm and history. Rhenish specialities are served in a panelled dining room.

🍽 **Bacharacher Hof** – *Marktstraße 8, 55422 Bacharach.* ℘*(06743) 14 22. www.bacharacher-hof.de. Open mid-Mar–mid-Nov. 25 rooms.* 🍴 *Restaurant*🍽, *closed Wed.* This family-run establishment offers comfortable rooms, some with Rhine views, and regional dishes in the *Pfalzgrafen* room.

🍽 **Flairhotel Landsknecht** – *Aussiedlung Landsknecht 4–6 (B9), 56329 St. Goar-Fellen.* ℘*(06741) 20 11. www.hotel-landsknecht.de. Closed late Dec–Feb. 21 rooms.* 🍴 *Restaurant*🍽 *closed Nov & Mar, Mon–Wed.* This modern family-run property with attached wine estate has comfortable rooms facing the Rhine or a lovely garden. The restaurant serves modern, regionally sourced cuisine.

🍽 **Schloss Rheinfels** – *Schlossberg 47, 56329 St. Goar.* ℘*(06741) 80 20. www.schloss-rheinfels.de. 63 rooms.* 🍴 *Restaurant*🍽. Across from the Loreley Rock, next to Rheinfels Castle, this hotel and villa offer comfortable rooms, an extended spa centre, a fine-dining restaurant and a castle tavern with a panoramic river terrace.

🍴 EAT

🍽 **Gasthaus Hirsch** – *Rheinstraße 17, 56154 Boppard-Hirzenach.* ℘*(06741) 26 01. www.gasthaus-hirsch.net. Closed Mon, Tue.* A tasteful, rustic establishment with a panelled dining room adorned with paintings. The kitchen uses market-fresh regional ingredients whenever possible.

🍽 **Zum Turm** – *Zollstraße 50, 56349 Kaub.* ℘*(06774) 922 00. www.rhein-hotel-turm.com. Closed Tue & Jan–Mar Mon–Thu & Nov.* This establishment near the old tower has housed an upscale family-run restaurant for over a century. The menu includes roast pork and dove *pot au feu*.

Frankfurt am Main★★

Germany's financial and commercial capital, Frankfurt is characterised by a forest of skyscrapers in its centre, filled with international companies, government organisations and banks. Some of the world's biggest trade shows, including the famous Frankfurt Book Fair, take place in high-tech halls near the airport, the largest and busiest on the continent. But Frankfurt isn't all business. Join the locals in the traditional cider taverns, visit Goethe's birth house or take in the stellar exhibits in the string of museums hugging the south bank of the Main River.

▶ **Population:** 643 000
🔲 **Info:** Lobby of Hauptbahnhof (main train station). ℘(069) 21 23 88 00. www. frankfurt.de.
◑ **Location:** Two major autobahns join near Frankfurt: The A3 (Köln– Nuremburg) and the A5 (Karlsruhe). The city is 2hrs from Köln and 2hrs 30min from Nuremburg.
🅿 **Parking:** Garages are located throughout the city. Visit www.frankfurt.de for specific locations and fees.
◉ **Don't Miss:** Städel Museum, Römerberg, the cathedral and a glass of apple cider in a traditional Sachsenhausen tavern.
🕐 **Timing:** Allow a day to take in the major sights.
👥 **Kids:** Zoo; Senckenberg Natural History Museum.

A BIT OF HISTORY

The second coronation city – Built in the 8C on the site of a Roman military camp, Frankfurt rose to prominence in 1152 with the election of Frederick I Barbarossa as German king. All subsequent royal elections until 1796 took place here, a status officially confirmed in 1362 by the Golden Bull issued by Emperor Charles IV. In 1562 Frankfurt replaced Aachen as the **coronation place** of the Holy Roman emperors – a privilege it retained until the dissolution of the Reich in 1806.

The young Goethe – Johann Wolfgang von Goethe was born in Frankfurt in 1749. From 1772 to 1775, he penned many of his classics here, including *The Sorrows of Young Werther*, which allegedly took him only four weeks.

Capital of finance and economy – In the 16C Frankfurt was granted the right to mint money. The money market flourished and the **stock exchange** followed. German banks dominated the economy in the 18C; in the 19C they acquired a worldwide reputation, thanks to financiers such as **Bethmann** and above all, **Rothschild**, whose sons, "the Five Frankfurters", established branches throughout Europe. Industry quickly followed in the wake of such a favourable climate.

Frankfurt has always been a trade show city, starting in 1240 with the first Autumn Fair. Since the 20C, the Fur Fair *(Pelzmesse)*, the Motor Show *(Automobilausstellung)* and the famous Book Fair *(Buchmesse)* have underscored Frankfurt's role as Germany's capital of commerce and finance as did the EU's decision to base the European Central Bank here.

City life – Despite its cosmopolitan character, this metropolis on the Main has preserved an easygoing flair. The **Hauptwache** is a lively square dating from 1729, while the adjacent **Zeil** is said to be Germany's busiest shopping strip. To the north, the Westend quarter is losing the fight to stave off office blocks encroaching from the commercial centre. Cafés, cabarets, bars and

View of Frankfurt from the rooftop of Zeil Galerie

© Lubenow Sabine/Sime/Photononstop

BASIC INFORMATION

Telephone prefix: ☎069

VISITOR INFORMATION

The Frankfurt tourist office can help with room reservations (☎21 23 88 00; *www.frankfurt-tourismus.de; open Mon–Fri 8am–9pm, Sat–Sun 9am–6pm)*. There are two walk-in branches: Hauptbahnhof, central station foyer, *open Mon–Fri 8am–9pm, Sat–Sun 9am–6pm*; and Römer, Römerberg 27, *open Mon–Fri 9.30am–5.30pm, Sat–Sun 10am–4pm. Both offices are closed Jan 1 and Dec 25–26.*

Post Offices with late Hours – Zeil 90 branch *(Mon–Sat 10am–8pm)*; main train station – Hauptbahnhof, 1st floor *(Mon–Fri 7am–7pm, Sat 9am–4pm)*; airport branch *(Mon–Fri 8am–7pm, Sat–Sun 11am–6pm)*.

Daily Papers – *Frankfurter Allgemeine Zeitung; Frankfurter Rundschau; Frankfurter Neue Presse.*

Internet – *www.frankfurt.de; www.rhein-main.net; www.frankfurt-tourismus.de.*

GETTING AROUND

The largely pedestrianised city centre is a pedestrian zone, meaning that the best way to get around is on foot.

Public Transport

Regional services are offered by **RMV** (☎*(01801) 768 46 36 (.04–0.42€/ min); www.rmv.de; 24 hours daily)*. Local public transport is provided by **VGF** (☎(069) 194 49; www.vgf-ffm. de; Mon–Fri 8am–5pm). Information kiosks are at Kurt-Schumacher-Straße 8 *(Mon–Fri 8am–5pm)* and at Konstablerwache, Passage B level *(Mon–Fri 8am–5pm)* as well as in many other U-Bahn and S-Bahn stations. The tariff rate 3 is valid for all rides within Frankfurt. Single tickets are 2.60€; day tickets costs 6.60€, or 8.50€ for day tickets valid for travel to the airport. Tickets are sold at vending machines and from bus drivers but not aboard trams and U-Bahn and S-Bahn trains.
Useful Tip: For S-Bahn rides to the airport you need a ticket at tariff rate 4.

SIGHTSEEING

The **Frankfurt Card** costs 9.90€ (valid for 24hrs) and 14.50€ (valid for 48hrs) for travel within the VGF network (Tariff rate 3, plus to the airport). It also entitles you to a 50 percent discount on admission to 30 museums and other attractions, such as the zoo and the airport visitor terraces, and 20–25 percent off selected boat and coach tours. The Frankfurt Card is available at www.frankfurt-tourismus.de, selected hotels, Hauptbahnhof and Römerberg tourist information offices and the Frankfurt airport.

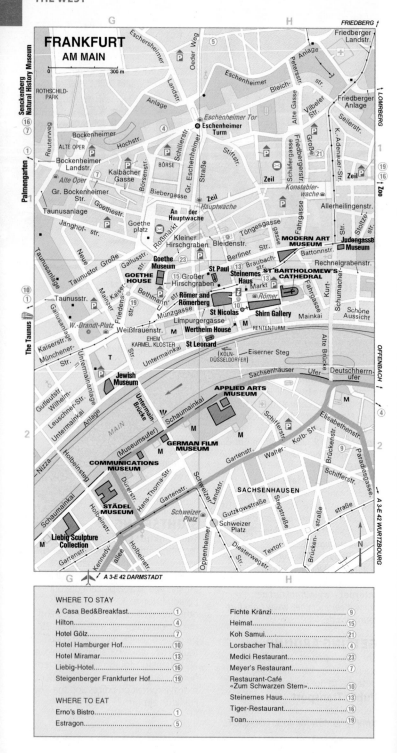

FRANKFURT
AM MAIN

restaurants are grouped around the central station, while the taverns of the olde-worlde Sachsenhausen quarter, on the south bank of the Main, specialise in the celebrated **Äppelwoi** or **Ebbelwei** (slightly bitter cider), and *Handkäse mit Musik* (a small yellow cheese served with onions and vinegar sauce).

A general view – Frankfurt suffered tremendous destruction in World War II and was rebuilt as a modern city. Its distinctive skyline of skyscrapers has even garnered it the nickname "Mainhattan". The silhouette is most striking from the **Untermainbrücke** bridge. For the best birds-eye view, take the lift up the **Main Tower** *(Neue Mainzer Straße)*, which has an open-air platform at 200m/656ft.

SIGHTS
Römer and Römerberg

The Römerberg, Frankfurt's historical central square, is ringed by a collection of step-gabled, half-timbered houses, built in the 15C by rich merchants. What you see today, however, are faithful postwar reconstructions.

The most imposing building is the Römer itself, on the western side of the square, which is a jumble of three joined buildings. The block has served as town hall since 1405. After 1562, its banquet hall was used to celebrate the election and coronation of the emperors. The hall in which the coronation itself took place – the **Kaisersaal** (open year-round daily 10am–1pm, 2pm–5pm; closed Jan 1, 24–25 & 31 Dec and during official functions; ♿2€; ♿; ☎069 21 23 48 14) – doubles as a gallery of oil portraits depicting all 52 emperors, from Charlemagne to Franz II (1806).

Other reconstructed buildings encircling the Römerberg include the 13C **Alte Nikolaikirche**, the half-timbered **Haus Wertheim**, the 1464 Italianate **Steinernes Haus** and a row of half-timbered 15C–18C mansions.

The **Gerechtigkeitsbrunnen** (Fountain of Justice, 1543) is In the centre of the square. Contrasting with the historical architecture is the Postmodern starkness of the **Schirn Kunsthalle**, a con-temporary art gallery on the south side of Römerberg.

Kaiserdom St. Bartholomäus★ (Cathedral St. Bartholomew)

Open year-round Mon–Thu 8am–8pm, Fri noon–8pm, Sat–Sun 9am–8pm. www.dommuseum-frankfurt.de.

Though technically not a cathedral (it is not a bishop's seat), Frankfurt's Dom played a key role in German history. The elections of all German kings from 1356 onwards took place in what is called the *Wahlkapelle*, an austere chapel attached at the south end of the choir. Between 1562 and 1792, the church also hosted 10 imperial coronations.

The Dom's outstanding feature is the tall **west tower★★** *(Westturm)*, orna-mented with a gabled polygonal crown and lantern.

Inside are several artworks worth noting: the 16C sandstone **Crucifixion** by Mainz artist Hans Backoffen; the 14C finely worked **choir stalls★** crafted in the Upper Rhine; and **mural paintings** from 1427, of the Cologne School, illus-trating the legend of St. Bartholomew. In the north chancel is the **Altar of Mary Sleeping** *(Maria-Schlaf Altar)*, from 1434, also of the Cologne School, and the sole surviving altar from the ori-ginal church. The large **Descent from the Cross** on the west wall was painted by Anthony van Dyck in 1627.

Dommuseum★ (Cathedral Museum)

Open year-round Tue–Fri 10am–5pm, Sat–Sun 11am–5pm. Closed Jan 1, Dec 24–25 & 31. ♿4€. ♿; ☎(069) 13 37 61 86. www.dommuseum-frankfurt.de.

This small museum is accessed from the cathedral cloister. Besides the treasury *(Domschatz)*, preserving precious gold works and vestments from the high Middle Ages, the late-Merovingian tomb of a young girl merits special attention.

West of the cathedral is an **Archaeo-logical Garden** *(Historischer Garten)*, with remains of Roman, Carolingian and Baroque fortifications.

Museum für Moderne Kunst★ (Modern Art Museum)

Domstraße 10. Open year-round Tue–Sun 10am–6pm (Wed until 8pm). Closed Good Friday. ◉12€, free admission last Sat of month. ♿ ✆(069) 21 23 04 47. www.mmk-frankfurt.de.

Viennese architect Hans Hollein designed this triangle-shaped museum, dubbed "a slice of cake" by locals. It is a suitably edgy setting for an impressive collection of 20C art with particular emphasis on the New York School (Claes Oldenburg, Andy Warhol) and German contemporary artists (Joseph Beuys, Mario Merz, Katharina Fritsch and Gerhard Richter). Displays from the permanent collection rotate every few months.

Leonhardskirche

The exterior of this 15C Gothic church conceals its Romanesque origins. Two octagonal towers remain at the east end, along with a doorway embellished with fine carvings by **Master Engelbert**. The central nave is surrounded on three sides by a gallery. Stained-glass windows illuminate the chancel. To the left of the chancel are a superbly carved reredos representing scenes from the life of the Virgin and a painting by Holbein the Elder depicting the Last Supper. The baptismal chapel is located in the north aisle.

Paulskirche

It was in this circular building that the German National Assembly, elected after the revolution of March, met from 1848 to 1849. Originally a church, it now houses an exhibit devoted to the history of the German democratic movement.

Goethe-Haus★ and Goethe-Museum

Grosser Hirschgraben 23–25. Open year-round daily 10am–6pm (Sun until 5.30pm). Closed Jan 1, Good Friday, Dec 24–25 & 31. ◉7€. ✆(069) 13 88 00. www.goethehaus-frankfurt.de.

Fans of poet, playwright, diplomat and scientist Johann Wolfgang von Goethe (1749–1832) flock to this large town house where the great man first saw the light of day. You can see the study on the top floor where he penned many of his early works – usually standing at a high desk. It has been re-created as it was in his lifetime. Right by the door hangs a silhouette portrait of Charlotte Buff, the object of his youthful passion and the inspiration for the character of Lotte in *The Sorrows of Young Werther*. A separate exhibit examines the lives of the Goethe family in 18C Frankfurt. The adjoining **museum** is in fact a picture gallery dedicated to works by Goethe's contemporaries, including Tischbein, Graff, Hackert and Friedrich.

Jüdisches Museum and Museum Judengasse

Kurt-Schumacher-Str. 10. Jüdisches Museum open Tue–Sun 10am–5pm (Wed until 8pm). ◉4€. ♿ ✆(069) 21 23 50 00. www.juedischesmuseum.de. Museum Judengasse is closed for renovation until at least fall 2015.

The Jewish Museum occupies the 1821 Palais Rothschild (1821) and traces the history of the Jewish community of Frankfurt (one of Germany's most important) from the Middle Ages to today.

MUSEUMSUFER (Museum Bank)

Frankfurt's delightful "Museum Row" extends along the Schaumainkai between the Eiserner Steg and Friedensbrücke bridges.

Städel Museum★★

Schaumainkai 63. Open year-round Tue–Sun 10am–6pm (Wed–Thu until 9pm). Closed Dec 24 & 31. ◉12€. ♿ ✆(069) 605 09 80. www.staedelmuseum.de.

This stronghold of art houses 700 years' worth of European masters, making it one of the biggest and most important such collections in Germany. All the famed artists are here, from Old Masters such as Holbein the Elder, Grünewald, Altdorfer, Dürer, Vermeer, Rembrandt, Rubens and Tiepolo to French and German Impressionism, German Expressionism, Fauvism, Cubism, Surrealism, the Bauhaus and contemporary art. Part of the collection is displayed in a stately 19C neo-Renaissance building; the rest in more modern wing. Yet another annex, situated beneath the Städel garden, houses post-war art by such German artists as Anselm Kiefer, Georg Baselitz, Markus Lüpertz und Gerhard Richter.

Museum für Angewandte Kunst★ (Museum of Applied Arts)

Schaumainkai 17. Open year-round Tue–Sun 10am–5pm (Wed until 9pm). ⊛9€. ⸜ ℘(069) 21 23 85 30. www.museumangewandtekunst.de. The museum (1985) was designed by New York architect Richard Meier and consists of a modern building wrapped around a Neoclassical villa from 1803. Artefacts include furniture from the Middle Ages, Renaissance, Baroque and *Jugendstil* periods; 15C and 16C glassware; Islamic porcelain and carpets; and a book and calligraphy section.

Liebieghaus Skulpturen-Sammlung★ (Liebieg Sculpture Collection)

Schaumainkai 71. Open year-round Tue –Sun 10am–6pm (Thu until 9pm). ⊛7€. ℘(069) 605 098 200. www.liebieghaus.de. This museum is a fine place to trace the evolution of sculpture through the ages. The oldest works are from ancient Egypt, Greece and Rome, but there are also fine examples from the Middle Ages (Tilman Riemenschneider), the Renaissance (Giambologna) and Rococo and Neoclassical (Thorvaldsen) periods. A sprinkling of Asian works provides an interesting contrast.

Deutsches Filmmuseum★ (German Film Museum)

Schaumainkai 41. Open year-round Tue–Sun 10am–6pm (Wed until 8pm). ⸜ ⊛6€. ℘(069) 961 220 220. www.deutsches-filminstitut.de. The permanent exhibit of this museum is divided into two sections: one illustrates the origins of the cinema and displays such early inventions as a *laterna magica* and Edison's Kinetoscope (1889). The other

focuses on the magic of film-making and the many steps involved in the production of both silent movies and "talkies". Special exhibits and daily screenings of rare films in the on-site cinema are also on view.

Museum für Kommunikation★

Open year-round Tue–Fri 9am–6pm, Sat–Sun 11am–7pm. ⊛3€. ⸜ ℘(069) 606 00. www.mfk-frankfurt.de. Tracing the history of communications from clay tablets to computers and the telegraph to MP3 players, this museum is a great place for kids and teens. One of the world's first telephones by Philip Reis and a VCR the size of a suitcase are among the displays.

GREATER FRANKFURT

♟♟ Zoo★★

Open year-round Apr–Oct daily 9am–7pm; Nov–Mar 9am–5pm. ⊛10€ (8€ during the last 2hrs). ⸜ ℘(069) 21 23 37 35. www.zoo-frankfurt.de. Germany's second-oldest animal park (since 1858) is home to 4 800 denizens representing 565 species, including such endangered species as black rhinos and okapis. The bird section with its huge free-flight aviary is also quite impressive. Penguins, reptiles, fish and insects inhabit the Exotarium, while nocturnal animals such as koalas and the desert fox can be observed In the artificially darkened Grzimek-Haus. Kids especially love the simulated tropical storm in the crocodile enclosure.

♟♟ Senckenberg Naturmuseum★ (Senckenberg Natural History Museum)

Senckenberganlage 25, via Bockenheimer Landstraße. Open daily 9am–5pm (until Wed 8pm, Sat–Sun until 6pm). ⊛9€ (child 6–15yrs 4.50€). ⸜ ℘(069) 754 20. www.senckenberg.de. Germany's largest natural history museum takes visitors on an eye-opening trip back in time and around the world. It is especially famous for its extensive **dinosaur collection★★**

(nearly 20 specimens) that includes a triceratops skull and a complete Edmontosaurus skeleton with preserved sections of scaled skin. Other highlights include the 50-million-year-old fossils of a **primitive horse★★** and other prehistoric animals dug up in the UNESCO-recognised pit mine of Messel.

The shrunken head from the Ecuadorean Shuar Indian culture and the mummified bodies of two boys from Ancient Egypt are among the more macabre (and memorable) objects on display.

Palmengarten★

Siesmayerstraße 61, via Bockenheimer Landstraße. Open Feb–Oct daily 9am–6pm; Nov–Jan until 4pm. ✆7€. ♿ ✆(069) 21 23 39 39. www.palmengarten.de.

If you need a break from the city bustle, head to these lovely gardens that put on a dazzling display of plants and flowers throughout the year. The eponymous subtropical palms are housed in the 1869 **Palmenhaus**, one of the oldest greenhouses in Germany. The gardens are part of the Westend greenbelt and segue into the city's botanical garden and the vast Grüneburgpark, which is immensely popular with joggers.

🚗 DRIVING TOUR

TAUNUS

62km/39mi. Allow 4hrs. ♿ See region map pp268–269.

These slate Rhenisch mountains are covered by beautiful forests and dotted with numerous mineral springs; the tallest peak in the range is the Großer Feldberg, reaching a modest 880m/2 887ft.

▶ The first stop is 24km/15mi northwest of Frankfurt.

Königstein★

This attractive spa town boasts a number of historic buildings, including the old 13C town hall and the *Burgruine* (castle ruins). All that remains of the town's 16C feudal castle is its original round bastions and 17C Vauban fortifications, set on massive foundations (open Mar–Oct daily 10am–7pm; Nov–Feb Sat–Sun 10am–5pm; ✆3€; ✆061 74 20 22 51; www.kur-koenigstein.de). Climb the 166 tower steps for views over the town and the slopes of the Taunus.

Großer Feldberg★

Open 9am (Sun 8am) until dusk. Closed Nov. ✆2€. ✆061 74 93 35 84.

The Aussichtsturm (lookout tower; 163 steps) of this important telecommunications hub offers a wide-ranging **panorama★★** taking in the Westerwald plateau to the northwest, the Wetterau depression to the northeast, and the plains of the Lower Main, including the encroaching Frankfurt, to the southeast. On a clear day you can see the spires of the cathedrals of Cologne and Strasbourg.

Römerkastell Saalburg (Saalburg Roman Fort)

Open Mar–Oct daily 9am–6pm; Nov–Feb Tue–Sun 9am–4pm. ✆5€. Closed Dec 24 & 31. Last admission 30min before closing. ✆06175 93740. www.saalburgmuseum.de.

This fort is claimed to be the world's only fully reconstructed Roman fort, complete with all the buildings, fixtures and fittings used in that period. It lies adjacent to the Limes Straße, once the ancient frontier between the Roman Empire and the Germanic tribal territories, now a UNESCO World Heritage Site. Once beyond its striking exterior, the buildings in the central courtyard house an archaeological museum.

Bad Homburg★

This small spa town was transformed into one of Europe's elite gambling centres by the Blanc brothers, when they opened a casino here in 1840. Today Bad Homburg is a modern city but retains its exclusive character. Visitor activity revolves around the Kurpark (hydrotherapy spa), designed by Peter Joseph Lenne, which, with its fountains, Kaiser-Wilhelm Spa, casino, Russian church and Siamese temple, lends the town a somewhat exotic air.

Bad Homburg Schloss (☎06172 9262 148; www.schloesser-hessen.de), dominated by the tall tower that survives from the previous White Castle, was originally the palace of the Landgrave (count) of Hesse-Homburg. It then became the summer residence of the Prussian kings, who, from William I (1871) onwards, ruled as emperors of Germany. The castle possesses the only surviving furnished apartment of the last German Imperial couple, and was also the home of Landgrave Frederick II (1633–1708), immortalised as the hero of Kleist's drama, "Prince Friedrich of Homburg". The count's wooden leg is still here, on show to visitors.

EXCURSIONS
Offenbach
⬤ 7km/4.3mi east. Leave from the Deutschherrn-Ufer.

This town on the south bank of the Main is the centre of the German leather industry and hosts an International Leather Fair twice yearly.

DLM Ledermuseum★★
(DLM Leather Museum)
Frankfurter Straße 86. Open year-round Tue–Sun 10am–5pm. Closed Jan 1, Dec 24–25 & 31. ◉8€. ♿☎(069) 829 79 80. www.ledermuseum.de.

This museum unites three collections under a single roof: the **Shoe Museum** featuring four millennia of foot fashion from around the world; the **Museum of Applied Arts** with crafts and design from the Middle Ages onwards, leather in particular; and the **Ethnological Museum** with objects from Africa, America and Asia.

Friedberg★
⬤ 28km/17.4mi north via Friedberger Landstraße.

Friedberg is an attractive example of a medieval community with two distinct centres: the town enclosed within the Imperial castle and the bourgeois town grouped at the foot of the church, at either end of the main street (Kaiser-straße). The **castle** (Stauferburg) erected by Frederick Barbarossa in 1180, together with its outbuildings, follows the pattern of a Roman camp and still has the air of a small, self-sufficient town. The ramparts, now a promenade, have been made even more attractive with the addition of bays of greenery and look-out points. The 54m/177ft-high **Adolf's Tower★** (Adolphsturm, 1347) with its four watchtowers overlooks the assembled buildings and contains a local history museum. The **Jewish Baths★** (Judenbad, 13C) at Judengasse 20 in the bourgeois sector, consist of a 26m/85ft-deep domed well used by Jewish women for ritual ablutions required by Jewish law. The **church** (Stadtkirche) is a 13C–14C building with a typically Hessian exterior: transverse attics with separate gables jutting from the roof above the aisles. Inside, an unusually tall **ciborium★** (a chalice-like vessel that contains the sacrament) from 1462 looms in the chancel. On the left of the late-Gothic rood screen is the **Friedberg Madonna** (c. 1280), expressively carved from sandstone.

Darmstadt
⬤ 30km/18.6mi south of Frankfurt on the A5. Luisen-Centre, Luisenplatz 5, 64283 Darmstadt. ☎(06151) 13 45 13. www.darmstadt.de.

The former capital of the grand duchy of Hesse-Darmstadt, Darmstadt has a pedigree as an intellectual and cultural centre thanks to a succession of art-loving princes, but it was practically obliterated by Allied bombs during World War II.

During reconstruction, function often won out over aesthetics, although the former artists' colony of Mathildenhöhe continues to delight fans of Art Nouveau design and architecture.

Mathildenhöhe★★
Olbrichweg 13. ☎(06151) 13 27 78. www.mathildenhoehe.info.

In 1899 Grand Duke Ernst Ludwig invited seven artists, including Peter Behrens and Joseph Maria Olbrich, to build an

artists' colony *(Künstlerkolonie)* on the eastern edge of the city. The result: one of the world's finest *Jugendstil* (Art Nouveau) architectural ensembles. Studios and villas were grouped around a Russian Orthodox Chapel built between 1897 and 1899 at the behest of the last Russian czar Nicholas II, whose wife Alexandra was a member of the ducal family.

Olbrich's Ernst-Ludwig-Haus, which opened in 1901, today houses the **Museum Künstlerkolonie** (open year-round Tue–Sun 11am–6pm; ☞5€). Fronted by monumental sculptures of Adam and Eve, it showcases products designed by colony artists – silverware, furniture, jewellery – along with temporary exhibits.

The **Ausstellungsgebäude** (exhibition hall; closed for renovation until at least late 2016) is devoted to changing displays. Next to this spacious hall looms the 48m/157ft-high **Hochzeitsturm** (open Mar–Oct Tue–Sun 10am–6pm; Nov–Feb Fri–Sun 11am–5pm; ☞3€; www.hochzeitsturm-darmstadt.eu). Its distinctive roofline resembles the outline of a hand, which has become the city's emblem. There's a viewing platform on top.

ADDRESSES

🏠 STAY

⊜⊜ A Casa Bed & Breakfast – *Varrentrappstraße 49. ℘(069) 97 98 88 21. www.hotel-acasa.de. Closed late Dec to early Jan. 6 rooms. ☞6€.* This small B&B in an old villa has tasteful, individually decorated rooms, each reflecting a theme: Miami, Goethe, Rose Garden, Montparnasse, Bahama and Piccolo.

⊜⊜ Hotel Gölz – *Beethovenstraße 44. ℘(069) 74 67 35. www.hotel-goelz.de. 12 rooms. ☞.* A stone's throw from the city centre and trade fair grounds, this family-run hotel in a 19C villa has spacious doubles and basic singles.

⊜⊜⊜ Hotel Hamburger Hof – *Poststraße 10-12. ℘(069) 27 13 96 90. www.hamburgerhof.com. 62 rooms. ☞.* Light and airy rooms with stylish contemporary touches make this business hotel opposite the Hauptbahnhof north exit a good base.

⊜⊜⊜ Hotel Miramar – *Berliner Straße 31. ℘(069) 920 39 70. www.miramar-frankfurt.de. 39 rooms. ☞.* This modern hotel with comfortable rooms is located close to the historic centre.

⊜⊜⊜ Liebig-Hotel – *Liebigstraße 45. ℘(069) 24 18 29 90. www.hotelliebig.de. Closed Dec 22–Jan 2. 19 rooms. ☞16€.* This small hotel in a villa in the bank district offers charming and luxurious rooms sporting Italian- and English-style furniture and beautiful fabrics.

⊜⊜⊜⊜ Hilton – *Hochstraße 4. ℘(069) 133 80 00. www.hilton.com. 342 rooms. ☞33€. Restaurant⊜⊜.* A spacious, open atrium-style lobby provides access to rooms with all mod-cons, reached via a glass lift. The fitness club boasts a 25m/82ft-long swimming pool. The restaurant serves American and international fare.

⊜⊜⊜⊜ Steigenberger Frankfurter Hof – *Am Kaiserplatz. ℘(069) 215 02. www.steigenberger.com/frankfurt. 261 rooms. ☞35€. Restaurants⊜⊜⊜.* This 1876 grand hotel has been perfectly renovated. Luxury reigns throughout, from the elegant lobby to the rooms. Dining options are the bistro-style Oscar, the pan-Asian Iroha and gourmet restaurant Français.

🍴 EAT

⊜ Fichte Kränzi – *Wallstraße 5. ℘(069) 61 27 78. www.fichtekraenzi.de.* This café has served cider since 1849 along with local fare, all at reasonable prices. The shaded beer garden is lovely on a hot summer day.

⊜ Koh Samui – *Grosse Friedberger Straße 32. ℘(069) 29 28 28. www.kohsamui24.net.* Choose from a huge selection of Thai dishes in an exotic setting accented with orchids and lilies.

⊜ Lorsbacher Thal – *Große Rittergasse 49–51 (descends southeast from Deutschherrnufer near Alte Brücke). ℘(069) 61 64 59. www.lorsbacher-thal.de.* This is a particularly charming cider restaurant that serves traditional, hearty food and has a beautiful garden tucked away at the back.

Steinernes Haus – *Braubachstraße 35.* *(069) 28 34 91. www.steinernes-haus.de. Reservation necessary.* This pleasant, rustic establishment is more than 500 years old. Typical Frankfurt cuisine and specialities grilled on lava stone can be sampled here.

Toan – *Friedberger Anlage 14.* *(069) 44 98 44. Closed Sat lunch, Mon. www.restaurant-toan.de.* Located near the zoo and Frankfurt's greenbelt, this modern restaurant serves excellent Vietnamese food. Garden terrace.

Estragon – *Jahnstraße 49.* *(069 597 80 38). www.estragon-ffm.de. Closed Sun.* This pretty restaurant is decorated in warm colours and serves international cuisine infused with the flavours of the Mediterranean.

Heimat – *Berliner Straße 70.* *(069) 29 72 59 94. www.heimat-frankfurt.com.* The menu at this simple and relaxed place is small but changes with the seasons. The bar overlooks the open kitchen. Good wine choices.

Medici – *Weißadlergasse 2.* *(069) 21 99 07 94. www.restaurant medici.de. Closed Sun.* This family business in the city centre, near the Zeil, serves international cuisine.

Meyer's Restaurant – *Grosse Bockenheimer Straße 54.* *(069) 91 39 70 70. www.meyer-frankfurt.de. Closed Sun.* At this small bistro-restaurant near the old opera house, you can see the chefs at work in the open kitchen.

Restaurant-Café Zum Schwarzen Stern – *Römerberg 6.* *(069) 29 19 79. www.schwarzerstern.de Reservation recommended.* This half-timbered house was painstakingly rebuilt after the war and sports pleasant, rustic décor. Upscale seasonal German cuisine dominates the menu.

Erno's Bistro – *Liebigstraße 15.* *(069) 72 19 97. www.ernosbistro.de. Closed Sat, Sun and holidays.* A comfortable ambience reigns at this West End restaurant that delivers classic cuisine injected with a creative, personal touch. The list of French wines is superb.

Tiger-Restaurant – *Heiligkreuzgasse 16-20.* *(069) 920 02 20. www.tigerpalast.com. Closed 6 weeks in summer & Sun.* This modern restaurant shares space with the Tigerpalast variety theatre and serves classic cuisine with a Mediterranean inflection. Candlelight and brick vaulting create a relaxed atmosphere.

TAKING A BREAK

The section of Grosse Bockenheimer Straße between Opernplatz and Börsenstraße (nicknamed the *Fressgasse* or "eating alley") is lined with casual eateries and is a good place to grab a quick bite to eat.

NIGHTLIFE

After dark, Frankfurt's liveliest quarter is the Sachsenhausen, on the left bank of the Main. It is laced with olde-worlde cobblestone streets lined with traditional taverns serving *Äppelwoi*, the dry cider that is a local speciality. To keep the cider cool, it is usually served in grey-blue earthenware jugs called *Bembel*. Look for taverns along Grosse Rittergasse (one block south of Deutschherrnufer) and along Schweizer Straße.

SHOPPING

Frankfurt's **main shopping street** (department stores, mainstream chains) is the Zeil. More exclusive boutiques have set up along Große Bockenheimer Straße and Goethestraße, while independent stores line the streets of Sachsenhausen, Schweizer Straße in particular.

A fun **flea market** is held along the Museumsufer on Saturdays.

Wiesbaden★

Lying at the foot of the Taunus mountains and favoured by the mild climate of the Rhine Valley, the capital city of Hessen has the refined atmosphere of a spa town and the flair of an elegant city.

OLD TOWN

The largely pedestrianised town centre wraps around the Schlossplatz. Shop-lined Landggasse and Neugasse are two particularly lively streets.

Schlossplatz (Palace Square)

This elegant and well-proportioned square lies in the heart of the town. It is lined with beautiful buildings and hosts a market twice weekly.

The former residence of the dukes of Nassau, the 19C **Schloss** was built in the unadorned Neoclassical style and today is the seat of the Hessen Parliament.

Altes Rathaus (Old Town Hall)

Built in 1609–10 and the city's oldest surviving building, the old town hall retains its late-Renaissance features on the ground floor. The upper storey dates from 1828 and bears the Romantic Historicist style.

Neues Rathaus (New Town Hall)

Georg Hauberisser, architect of the Munich town hall, erected this building in the German Renaissance style in 1886–87. It was destroyed in World War II and has been rebuilt since.

Marktkirche (Market Church)

This first brick-built church in the Nassau region was erected in the mid-19C. Its architect, Carl Boos, copied the Schinkel-designed Friedrichwerder Church in Berlin. A carillon chimes daily at 9am, noon and 5pm.

▶ **Population:** 276 750

▯ **Info:** Marktplatz 1, 65183 Wiesbaden. ℘(0611) 172 99 30. www.wiesbaden.de.

◗ **Location:** Some 40km/24.8mi west of Frankfurt and across the Rhine from Mainz. Take the A66 if you are coming from Frankfurt.

🄿 **Parking:** Old City parking garages can be found near the market on Bahnhofstraße and at Neugasse and Friedrichstraße.

⊘ **Don't Miss:** A peek at the Kurhaus.

🕔 **Timing:** Allow one hour each for the old town and the Spa Quarter.

SPA QUARTER

The spa quarter has developed west of the old town.

Kaiser-Friedrich-Therme (Emperor Friedrich Baths)

Langgasse 38–40. Open year-round daily 10am–10pm (Sept–Apr Fri–Sat until midnight). ⊛4.50€ per hr May–Aug, 6€ per hour Sept–Apr. ℘(0611) 31 70 60. This *Jugendstil* building boasts impressive frescoes in the entrance hall and a Roman-Irish steam bath festooned in glazed tiles. It is a fantastic place for visitors to enjoy Wiesbaden's famous thermal springs.

Kochbrunnen

This fountain is made up of 15 springs. Its hot salty water contains iron, evident from the reddish deposit on the granite basin. The octangular Kochbrunnen Temple dates from 1854.

Kurhaus★ (Casino and Conference Centre)

A lawn as flat as a bowling green is flanked by colonnades and lofty plane trees, and leads up to what Emperor Wilhelm II called "the most beautiful *Kurhaus* in the world". Built in 1907, the casino has a sumptuous interior that has always been a social gathering spot for spa visitors. Today it is used as a conference centre, but to enjoy its special ambience, you need to visit the casino, where Dostoyevsky allegedly found inspiration for his novel *The Gambler*. 😊 Men must wear a jacket and tie to get inside the casino.

Staatstheater

The impressive 19C Renaissance-style building lies south of the theatre colonnades. The taste for lavish decoration is evident in its Rococo foyer.

Kurpark★ (Spa Gardens)

A vast park, laid out in 1852, stretches east behind the Kurpark. Sonnenberger Straße *(to the north)* and Parkstraße *(to the south)* are flanked by magnificent villas from the Gründerzeit (late 19C).

WILHELMSTRASSE AND NEROBERG AREA

The main street, **Wilhelmstraße**, is lined by upscale shops and the "Warmer Damm" park.

Museum Wiesbaden

Friedrick-Ebert-Allee 2. Open year-round Tue & Thu 10am–8pm, Wed & Fri–Sun 10am–5pm. Closed Jan 1, Shrove Mon, May 1, Dec 24–25 & 31. 6€. ♿ 0611 335 22 50. www.museum-wiesbaden.de This museum comprises collections of the **natural sciences**, **Nassau antiquities**, and **art**, including the world's largest **Jawlensky collection★** (the artist lived in Wiesbaden from 1921 until his death in 1941).

👥 Nerobergbahn★

Runs every 15min May–Aug daily 9am–8pm; Apr and Sept–Oct daily 10am–7pm; 3.30€ round-trip (child 1.65€). 📞 (0611) 236 8500. www.eswe-verkehr.de. The water-powered funicular railway still runs as smoothly as when it was built in 1888. It leads up the Neroberg, Wiesbaden's local mountain (245m/804ft), which affords panoramic views★.

An International Spa Town

The Romans were the first to become aware of the benefits of Wiesbaden's hot sodium chloride springs, and Pliny noted with surprise that the water stayed warm for three days. In the 9C, Wiesbaden was first called "Wisibada" (spa in the meadows), but it was not until the 19C that it evolved into a famous spa town and gathering-spot for higher nobility and the crowned heads. Modern Wiesbaden enjoys an excellent reputation as a spa resort specialising in rheumatism.

Russisch-Orthodoxe Kirche (Russian Orthodox Church)

Christian-Spielmann-Weg 2. Open May–Oct Mon–Sat 10am–8pm (Sat until 4:45pm, Sun 12.30pm–6pm; Nov–Apr 10am–4pm. 1€. 📞 (0611) 52 84 94. Atop the Neroberg, this church (also known as the Greek Chapel) was built by Duke Adolf of Nassau in 1847–55 in memory of his wife, a Russian grand duchess who died at age 19. The central building has five gilded cupolas.

ADDRESSES

🛏 STAY

Drei Lilien – *Spiegelgasse 3.* 📞 *(0611) 99 17 80. www.dreililien.com. 15 rooms.* ☐. In a *Jugendstil* villa, this hotel offers individually furnished rooms mixed with historical details and a high degree of comfort. Lavish breakfast.

🍽 EAT

Käfer's Bistro – *Kurhausplatz 1 (inside the Kurhaus).* 📞 *(0611) 53 62 00. www.kurhaus-gastronomie.de.* This restaurant is inside the *Kurhaus* and casino constructed in 1907 in Wilhelminian style. Paintings and wood dominate the décor of the beautiful dining room. The sunny terrace is an ideal spot for balmy summer days.

Mainz★

The capital of the federal state of Rheinland-Pfalz, Mainz is Germany's largest and most important wine market as well as the birthplace of Johannes Gutenberg, the inventor of moveable type. Its historic centre was nicely reconstructed after World War II and brims with handsome buildings housing atmospheric taverns.

CATHEDRAL QUARTER

▶ From Liebfrauenplatz square walk west to Markt and enter the cathedral from the north side.

Dom★★ (Mainz Cathedral)

Dedicated to Sts. Martin and Stephen, Mainz' Romanesque cathedral is one of the most magnificent in Germany. There are lovely **views★★** of its complex ridge roof and six towers from the **Leichhof** square. The adjoining square, the Höfchen, segues into Gutenbergplatz on the south and Markt to the northeast.

▶ **Population:** 197 630

Info: Brückenturm am Rathaus, 55116 Mainz. ℘(06131) 24 28 88. www.touristik-mainz.de.

Location: Mainz lies near the confluence of the Rhine and the Main rivers, across the river from Wiesbaden and not far from Frankfurt. It is the eastern gateway to the Romantic Rhine wine region.

Parking: Garages are located throughout the city. Visit http://wap.parkinfo.com for fees and locations.

Don't Miss: The Dom; Gutenberg Museum.

Timing: Allow up to a day to see Mainz' highlights.

The cathedral has a double choir linked by pillars affixed with **stone funeral monuments★** honouring 44 of Mainz' 84 archbishops. In the second chapel **(1)** is a moving 15C tomb, and a multi-

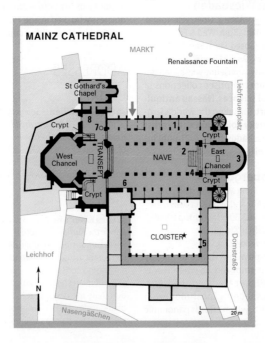

coloured Gothic funerary monument is attached to one of the main pillars **(2)**. In the east crypt, beneath the chancel, you'll find a modern **gold reliquary (3)** of the saints of Mainz. A pillar **(4)** in the east chancel bears another funerary monument surrounded by statuettes of St. Benedict, St. Catherine, St. Maurice and St. Clare.

A door in the south aisle leads to the Gothic **cloister★** *(Kreuzgang)*. Besides the tombstones, note the bas-relief **(5)** of the 14C master-singer Heinrich von Meißen.

Fine statues adorn the doorway **(6)** of the former chapter-house *(Kapitelsaal)*, built in the 15C in an elegant Rhineland style. In the opposite wing is a fine 1328 pewter baptismal font **(7)**. Beyond, a Romanesque doorway **(8)** leads to the Gotthardkapelle.

OLD TOWN

South of the cathedral, the picturesque Kirschgarten square is framed by pretty half-timbered houses. From Augustiner-straße, small side streets lead to ancient houses that used to shelter artisans and craftspeople. Kapuzinerstraße leads to the Church of St. Ignatius past historic houses with sandstone portals and Rococo doors.

Ignazkirche
(Church of St. Ignatius)

Kapuzinerstraße 36. Open year-round daily 9:30am–7pm.

Built by Johann Peter Jäger between 1763–75, this church illustrates the transition from Rococo to Neoclassicism. Outside is imposing 16C group of the **Crucifixion★** *(Kreuzigungsgruppe)* by Mainz artist Hans Backoffen (1519), who designed it as his own funerary monument.

Stephanskirche★
(Church of St. Stephen)

Kleine Weissgasse 12. Open year-round Mon–Sat 10am–4:30pm, Sun noon–4:30pm (Mar–Oct until 5pm).

This late 13C church is the oldest Gothic hall church on the Middle Rhine. Though severely damaged in World War II, it has been beautifully rebuilt and is one of Mainz' must-see sights, thanks to Marc Chagall's remarkable **stained-glass windows★★**. Created between 1978–85, they depict biblical themes such as the salvation history of the Israelites and the Crucifixion. There are a further 18 colourful windows by Charles Marq, a close friend of Chagall's.

▶ Along the Ballplatz and the Schillerplatz note the lavish mansions.

Schillerplatz and Schillerstraße

The Baroque mansions in this square and street house the ministries of the state of Rheinland-Pfalz. The fountain in the centre of Schillerplatz is decorated with carnival scenes.

MUSEUMS
Gutenberg-Museum★★★

Liebfrauenplatz 5. Open year-round Tue–Sat 9am–5pm, Sun 11am–5pm. Closed most public holidays. 5€. ♿ ☎(06131) 12 26 44.

The art of the printed word is revered in the Gutenberg Museum as in no other place. Exhibits trace the evolution of printing from the beginnings in Asia, but focus primarily on the achievements

Gutenberg-Bible, the "Shuckburgh-exemplar," Mainz between 1452-1455

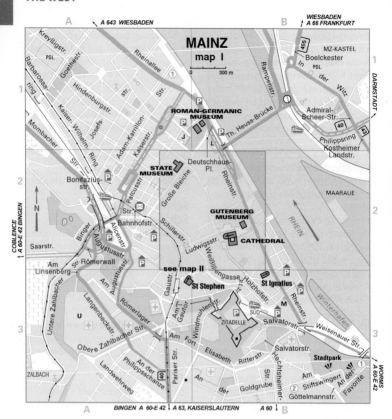

MAINZ
map I

0 ──── 300 m

A 643 WIESBADEN
WIESBADEN
A 66 FRANKFURT

DARMSTADT

MZ-KASTEL

ROMAN-GERMANIC MUSEUM

STATE MUSEUM

GUTENBERG MUSEUM

CATHEDRAL

St Stephen

St Ignatius

ZITADELLE

Stadtpark

see map II

COBLENCE
A 60-E 42 BINGEN

Am Linsenberg

ZALBACH

MAARAUE

RHEIN

Winterhafen

WORMS
A 60-E 42

BINGEN A 60-E 42 A 63, KAISERSLAUTERN   A 60

WHERE TO STAY

Favorite......................①
Stiftswingert................②

WHERE TO EAT

Geberts Weinstuben....①
Weinhaus Schreiner.....②

map II

0 ──── 100 m

STATE MUSEUM

GUTENBERG MUSEUM

Renaissance fountain

Leichhof

CATHEDRAL

Altstadt

CASINO RHEINGOLDHALLE CCM

EISERNTURM

ALTE UNIVERSITÄT

Schillerplatz

of native son Johannes Gutenberg. The most prized items are two original **Gutenberg Bibles★★★** (1452–55). Other interesting displays include incunabula and 16C–19C books, ancient presses and typesetting machines, and a section on modern book production and paper.

Set up in the basement is Gutenberg's re-created workshop, while at the **Druckladen** (printshop) you can learn how to print your own books using the ancient technology.

Römisch-Germanisches Zentralmuseum★ (Roman-Germanic Central Museum)

Ernst Ludwig Platz 2. Open year-round Tue–Sun 10am–6pm. Closed Jan 1, Carnival week, Easter Monday, Whit Monday, Dec 24–25 & 31. &(06131) 912 40. http://web.rgzm.de.

In the former Electors' Palace (15C–17C), this rambling museum houses collections on European prehistory, the advanced Mediterranean civilisations, and Ancient Roman and early medieval archaeology. Five original Roman ships are displayed in the nearby **Museum für Antike Schiffahrt** (Museum of Ancient Shipping; Neutorstraße 2b; same hours).

Landesmuseum Mainz★ (State Museum Mainz)

Große Bleiche 49–51. Open year-round Wed–Sun 10am–5pm, Tue 10am–8pm. Closed most public holidays. ⊗6€. &(06131) 285 70. www.landesmuseum-mainz.de.

The Department of Antiquities traces the cultural history of the Rhineland from prehistory to the present.

Of particular interest is the Steinhalle with 300 Roman-era stone memorials, including the **Jupitersäule** (Jupiter's column). The museum's medieval and Baroque sections and its Höchst porcelain and *Jugendstil* glassware are also impressive.

Gutenberg

Johannes Gutenberg (c. 1394–1468), the father of modern printing, is Mainz' most famous son. After honing his skills in Strasbourg as a young man, he returned to Mainz where he devised a groundbreaking printing technique using moveable type. It allowed large volumes of books to be printed at low cost. Gutenberg did not profit from his invention, however. Unable to repay his creditors, he died in poverty in 1468.

ADDRESSES

🛏STAY

⊜⊜ **Stiftswingert** – *Am Stiftswingert 4. &(06131) 98 26 40. www.hotel-stiftswingert.de. 30 rooms. ⌇.* This well-managed hotel has cherry-wood furnished guest rooms and modern bathrooms and facilities.

⏶/EAT

⊜⊜ **Weinhaus Schreiner** – *Rheinstraße 38. &(06131) 22 57 20. Closed Sun, Mon (except Jul–Aug & Dec), Tue–Fri lunch and public holidays. www.weinhausschreiner.de.* This classic wine tavern has rustic décor and a lively atmosphere. Featured are seasonal dishes with regional flavour.

⊜⊜⊜ **Geberts Weinstuben** – *Frauenlobstraße 94. &(06131) 61 16 19. www.geberts-weinstuben.de. Closed Mon.* Patrons share laughs over a glass of wine or earthy regional fare at this cosy, family-run wine tavern founded in 1887. Sit inside or in the vine-draped inner courtyard.

⊜⊜⊜⊜ **Favorite**– *Karl-Weiser-Straße 1. &(06131) 801 50. www.favorite-mainz.de. Closed Mon–Tue. Reservation recommended.* With its panoramic windows and warm furnishings, this restaurant exudes supreme elegance without being stuffy. The kitchen is expert in putting modern spins on traditional recipes. Nice terrace and separate smokers' lounge.

Mannheim

Mannheim's city layout is a rarity among European towns: its centre is essentially a chessboard of 142 identical blocks (Quadratstadt), each identified by a letter and a number. But it would be wrong to think this is a staid, inflexible city. Local enthusiasm for the arts is, and always has been, strong. It was at Mannheim's theatre that many of Schiller's plays premiered back in the 18C.

▶ **Population:** 308 400

🅱 **Info:** Willy-Brandt-Platz 3, 68161 Mannheim. ✆(0621) 293 87 00. www.tourist-mannheim.de.

▶ **Location:** 23km/14.3mi southeast of Worms, Mannheim sits at the confluence of the Rhine and the Neckar rivers.

🅿 **Parking:** Car parks and garages are located throughout the city. Visit http://wap.parkinfo.com for fees and locations.

😊 **Don't Miss:** The Fine Arts Museum, Reiss-Engelhorn-Museen.

🕐 **Timing:** Plan two hours to view the Fine Arts Museum.

SIGHTS
Kunsthalle Mannheim★★ (Fine Arts Museum)

Friedrichsplatz 4. Open year-round Tue–Sun 11am–6pm (Wed until 8pm). Closed Dec 24 & 31. ⬤5€. ♿ ✆(0621) 293 64 30. www.kunsthalle-mannheim.com.

In a 1907 Jugendstil building, this acclaimed art museum concentrates on works of the 19C and 20C. The exceptional **sculpture collection** includes works by Rodin, Lehmbruck, Barlach, Brancusi, Giacometti, Moore, Nam June Paik, Richard Long, Mario Merz and other well-known sculptors.

Another focus belongs to such crowd-pleasing **French Impressionists** as Manet, Monet and Cézanne. **German Secession** artists are represented by Slevogt and Corinth; Beckman and Heckel are artists included among the **Expressionists**.

Reiss-Engelhorn Museen★★

Open year-round Tue–Sun 11am–6pm. Closed 24 & 31 Dec. ⬤Permanent collections 2.50€, special exhibits 6€–12€. ♿ ✆(0621) 293 31 50. www.rem-mannheim.de.

Mannheim's REM encompasses four museums in different locations. Housed in the former arsenal, the **Museum Zeughaus** (in grid C5) takes you on a journey of discovery through the region's art and cultural history, theatre and music history, natural history and international photography in modern and playful yet substantial exhibitions.

A highlight is the collection of **European porcelain and faïence★**.

The **Museum Weltkulturen** (Museum of World Cultures) occupies a modern cube opposite the arsenal (D5). It presents archaeology collections, including artifacts from the Paleolithic and Mesolithic eras, the Carolingian period, and from ancient Greece and Rome.

The **Schillerhaus Museum** (B5) takes visitors on a multimedia tour of the life of Germany's famous poet and playwright, Friedrich Schiller, who lived in Mannheim from 1783-85. Finally, **ZEPHYR – Room for Photography** (C4) presents outstanding works of contemporary photography.

Schloss Mannheim★ (Palace)

Bismarckstraße 1. Open year-round Tue–Sun 10am–5pm. Closed 24–25 & 31 Dec. ⬤6€, including audioguide. ♿ ✆(062) 21 65 88 80. www.schloss-mannheim.de.

Construction of this Baroque palace, the largest in all of Germany (400 rooms, 2 000 windows), lasted from 1720 to 1760 and drew upon the talents of the period's finest artists, including Balthasar Neumann and Cosmas Damian Asam. Today, the building is largely used by the university but the opulent living quarters are accessible to the public. Furniture, paintings, tapestries, porcelain and clocks are among the items reflecting the illustrious lifestyle of the Prince-Electors.

A highlight on the ground floor is the Rococo library of Princess Elisabeth Augusta, which is the only room that has been barely altered.

Jesuitenkirche (Jesuit Church)

Open year-round daily 9am–7pm.
℘(0621) 12 70 90. www.jesuitenkirche.de.
Built at the same time as the palace, this massive edifice is said to be the biggest Baroque church in southwest Germany. The façade, though, is Neoclassical.

Technoseum★

Museumsstraße 1. Open year-round Tue-Sun 9am–5pm. Closed Dec 24 & 31. 6€. ℘(0621) 429 89. www.technoseum.de.
The Technoseum is one of Germany's largest technology museums. The modern presentation chronicles developments in the fields of natural science and technology from the 18C to today and highlights the social and economic changes brought on by Industrialisation. Machines are not merely shown but arranged in context and put through live demonstrations. In one room, for instance, you can gain an insight into the inner workings of a steam engine. Scattered about the floors are several experimentation stations, where you can playfully explore scientific principles.

Heidelberg★★★

A source of inspiration for many poets and artists, each charmed by the town's natural beauty and its castle, Heidelberg symbolises German Romanticism. Hölderlin wrote a famous ode to Heidelberg, and Brentano, Eichendorff and Von Arnim were among the Romantics who gathered here in the early 19C. But this jewel of the Neckar is also a lively university town with a vibrant cultural scene.

A BIT OF HISTORY

The political capital of the Palatinate – The *Pfalz* (Palatinate), of which Heidelberg was the political centre, owes its name to the "palatines", the highest officers in the Holy Roman Empire. These functions no longer existed in the 14C, but their vestiges remained with the hereditary family. The governing prowess of these Palatine-Electors *(Kurfürsten)* made the Palatinate *(Kurpfalz)* one of the most advanced states of Europe.

▶ **Population:** 143 000

Info: Willy-Brandt-Platz 1 (central station), 69115 Heidelberg. ℘(06221) 584 4444. www.heidelberg-marketing.de.

Location: Heidelberg is 20km/12.4mi east of Mannheim and reached via the A5 autobahn (Frankfurt–Freiburg).

Parking: Heidelberg has several garages in the old town. Especially convenient are those on Neue Schlossstraße, near the castle, and below Karlsplatz, near the Rathaus.

Don't Miss: Heidelberg Castle, a walking tour of the old city and a panoramic stroll along the Philosophers' Walk.

Timing: Allow half a day for the castle and another half-day for the rest of the city.

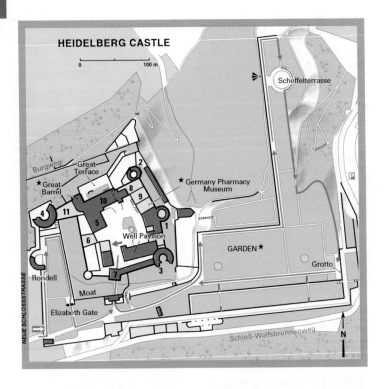

HEIDELBERG CASTLE

The "Orléans War" (1688–97) – In the 16C, Elector Karl-Ludwig, hoping to ensure peace, married off his daughter **Liselotte** (Elisabeth-Charlotte) to Duke Philip of Orléans, brother of Louis XIV. The marriage alliance proved disastrous to both the Palatinate and to Heidelberg: political infighting resulted in the town's destruction and the sacking of the castle; total disaster followed in 1693, when it was completely destroyed by fire. Before long the Electors abandoned the partly ruined castle, but today it is precisely this ivy-draped red-sandstone pile that gives Heidelberg its romantic flair.

SCHLOSS★★★

Open year-round daily 8am–5.30pm.
6€, guided tour supplement 4€.
(06221) 888 0. www.service-center
-schloss-heidelberg.com.
Looming above the town, Heidelberg Castle is a superb example of a fortress with both Gothic and Renaissance features. For an **overview★** of the town

and the Neckar Valley, visit the Rondell promontory. Enter the castle through the **Elisabethentor**, a gate built by Friedrich V (allegedly in a single night in 1615) as a surprise for his wife Elizabeth Stuart.

Two gates separated by a moat lead to the inner courtyard. The **gardens★** were laid out under Friedrich V in the 17C. The east face of the castle, with its three towers, is visible from the Scheffel Terrace.

Courtyard and Buildings

The courtyard is on the far side of a fortified bridge guarded by the **Torturm** (7; gate tower). The simple residential building, the **Ruprecht**, was built by Ruprecht III who became German king in 1400; above the crown are two little angels, thought to be the architect's twins who died just before completion of the work.

The 14C **Apothekerturm (1)** tower is even older and forms part of the **Deutsches Apothekenmuseum★**

© R. Schmid/Sime/Photononstop

Karl-Theodor Bridge towards Church of the Holy Spirit

(German pharmaceutical museum; open year-round daily 10am–5.30pm; included in general admission), with 18C–19C apothecaries' equipment and an alchemist's laboratory complete with ancient instruments.

Gothic and Renaissance Additions

Immediately off the courtyard is the Gothic **Brunnenhalle** (Well Wing), whose granite Roman columns came from Charlemagne's palace at Ingelheim. The **Library (6)**, set back from the west wing, is awash with light and was once home to the royals' personal library, art collections and treasure. Only slightly more recent is the **Hall of Mirrors Wing (8**; Gläserner Saalbau). Following a fire, only a shell remains of this tiered, Italian Renaissance building. The **Ottheinrich Wing (9**; Ottheinrichsbau), built by Elector Otto-Heinrich, an enlightened Renaissance ruler, inaugurated the late-Renaissance period in German architecture.

Horizontals predominate in the façade, bearing biblical and mythological ornamentation. The famous sculptor, Alexander Colin of Mechelen (1526–1612), helped design the entrance, a triumphal arch festooned with the Elector's coat of arms.

Transitional Renaissance-Baroque Additions

The **Friedrich Wing★★ (10**; Friedrichsbau), whose façade retains the classical Renaissance design, also bears elements pointing towards the coming Baroque. The statues represent the ancestors of Friedrich IV, who added the wing. The rear of the building and views over Heidelberg are best seen from the **Great Terrace** (Altan), accessed via a passageway to the right of the Friedrich Wing.

Grosses Fass★ (Great Vat)

This colossal 18C cask, with a capacity of 221 726l/48 780gal, still serves up wine to visiting customers. The platform above the Fass hosts tastings and occasional dancing. The guardian of this extravagance, an enduring idol of local folklore, is a statue of the dwarf court jester **Perkeo**, celebrated for his astonishing drinking feats.

VIEWS

From the north bank of the Neckar, which you reach either via the Alte or the Karl-Theodor bridges, are **views★★** of the castle ruins and the old town clustered around the Heiliggeistkirche. Further views of the castle and the town can be seen from the **Philosophenweg★** (Philosophers' Walk *see below*), reached by crossing the Alte Brücke and climbing the Schlangenweg.

👣 WALKING TOUR

Philosophenweg★
(Philosophers' Walk)

Start your tour of the city by climbing the hill on the north bank of the Neckar to enjoy spectacular views of Heidelberg and its castle. The nicest time to visit is later in the day when the setting sun bathes the city in intense colours.

▷ Retrace your steps to the Alte Brücke.

Alte Brücke★

The 18C bridge is flanked by two medieval fortification towers. The west tower contains three prison cells.

▷ Follow Steingasse to Marktplatz.

Heiliggeistkirche
(Church of the Holy Spirit)

This late-Gothic church is distinguished by covered market stalls set up between the building's buttresses as they have been for centuries. The galleries in the apses were used for the Biblioteca Palatina, once Europe's finest library, which ended up as war booty at the Vatican in 1623. The chancel was formerly the sepulchre of the Palatine Electors, but only the tomb of Ruprecht III and his wife remains.

Haus zum Ritter★
(Knight's House)

This magnificent bourgeois house owes its name to a bust of St. George in knightly armour on a richly scrolled pediment. Built in 1592 for the Huguenot merchant Charles Bélier, it was the only late-Renaissance masterpiece to survive the devastating Orléans War.

▷ Follow Hauptstraße to Universitätplatz and the Baroque Old University (Alte Universität).

Studentenkarzer★
(Student Prison)

Augustinergasse 2. Open Apr–Oct daily 10am–6pm; Nov–Mar Tue–Sat 10am–4pm. 3€. ℘(06221) 54 35 54.
One of Heidelberg's most popular tourist attractions, the old student jail was in use from 1712 and 1914. A stint here was practically a rite of passage for male students. Walls are covered in inscriptions and graffiti.

Jesuitenkirche

This 18C Baroque church bears a façade based on the Gesù Church in Rome. The luminous triple nave is supported by pillars decorated with Rococo stuccowork. Accessed via the church is the **Museum of Sacred and Liturgical Art** (Museum für sakrale Kunst und Liturgie; Richard-Hauser-Platz; open Jun–Oct Tue–Sat 10am–5pm, Sun 1pm–5pm; Nov–May Sat 10am–5pm, Sun 1pm–5pm; closed Jan 1, Easter Mon, Pentecost, Dec 25–26; 4€; ℘06221 16 63 91).
It houses religious artefacts from the 17C–19C, most notably an oversized silver Madonna by J Ignaz Saller (1736).

▷ Follow Hauptstraße west to the Palais Morass, which houses the Electorial Palatinate Museum.

Kurpfälzisches Museum★
(Palatinate Museum)

Hauptstraße 97. Open year-round Tue–Sun 10am–6pm. Closed Jan 1, Shrove Tue, May 1, Dec 24–25 & 31. 3€. ℘(06221) 583 40 20. www.museum-heidelberg.de.
The highlight of this museum is the jawbone of the prehistoric "Heidelberg Man" (500 000 BC). Other key displays are the **Altarpiece of the Twelve Apostles★★** (Zwölfbotenaltar) carved

---

"Homo Heidelbergensis"

In 1907, the jaw of a man who lived some 500 000 years ago was found in Mauer near Heidelberg. Called **Heidelberg Man** (Homo heidelbergensis), this hominid is considered to be an ancestor of Homo sapiens, the species of modern humankind.

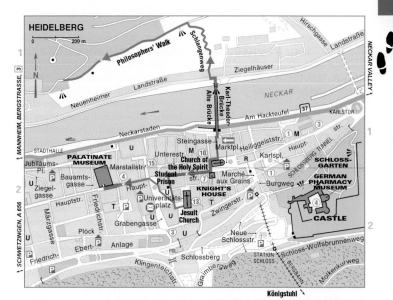

WHERE TO STAY		Weißer Bock	⑮
Am Kornmarkt	①	Zum Pfalzgrafen	⑬
Arthotel	③		
Backmulde	④	**WHERE TO EAT**	
Romantik Hotel Zum Ritter St. Georg	⑦	Herrenmühle	③
		Kulturbrauerei Heidelberg	①
Schnookeloch	⑩	Schlossweinstube	④

by Tilman Riemenschneider in 1509 and
several **works**★★ from the Romantic
Period.

EXCURSIONS
Königstuhl

◎ 5km/3mi southeast, via Neue
Schlossstraße, Molkenkurweg and then
Gaiberger Weg. Or take the funicular,
which stops at four stations: Stadt
(near Kornmarkt), Schloss, Molkenkur
and Königstuhl. Funicular: mid-Apr–
Sept 9am–8.30pm, Oct–mid-Apr
9am–5.45pm. ◎12€ round-trip from
Kornmarkt station. ℘(06221) 513 21 50;
www.bergbahn-heidelberg.de.

The 550m/1 804ft-high Königstuhl
marks the highest point in Heidelberg
and can be ascended by funicular from
Kornmarkt via the *Schloss* to the Molkenkur viewpoint. There you switch to
the nostalgic *Königstuhlbahn*, which
rumbles to the top for even more

sweeping views of the Neckar Valley.
The total trip takes about 20 minutes.
Aside from hiking trails, kid-friendly
diversions include a **falconry** and a
fairytale-themed amusement park
(open Mar–early Nov).

Schwetzingen★

◎ 10km/6.2mi west via the Friedrich-
Ebert-Anlage.

During the spring asparagus season
(Spargelzeit), gourmets flock to Schwetzingen, while music fans descend on
this sweet little town during the May
and June festival season.

Schwetzingen's **Schloss**★★ (closed for
renovation until at least the end of 2015)
was destroyed in the 17C but rebuilt in
1700–1717 as a Baroque palace. About
40 of the palace rooms are open to
the public. The 18C **Rococo theatre**★
(Rokokotheater) is open throughout the
summer and hosts concerts and plays

during the Schwetzingen Festival (open year-round; ☏(06202) 814 82).

The 72ha/178-acre **Schlossgarten★★**, which blends formal French and English gardens, is dotted with mock ancient temples and ruins popular during the Late Rococo.

🚗 DRIVING TOUR

BERGSTRASSE

From Heidelberg to Darmstadt
58km/36mi Allow approx 3hrs.

The *Bergstraße*, or mountain road, follows an ancient Roman trading route *(strata montana)* winding through gentle forest- and vineyard-covered hills and sunny escarpments sloping towards River Rhine. This is the place "where Germany starts to turn into Italy" is Emperor Joseph II's description of the lovely landscape. Dotted with castles and half-timbered villages, orchards and wineries, it holds much appeal for hikers, cyclists and others seeking outdoor pursuits.

Weinheim

Sun-splashed Weinheim is the first town on the *Bergstraße* to see springtime. The 13C agricultural community has a charming **old town** centred on a romantic market square with a 16C *Altes Rathaus* (old town hall). Nearby, the Büdinger Hof *(Judengasse 15–17)* is another attractive building. The **Schloss** (castle) abuts an English-style park that segues into the 19C **Exotenwald★** (exotic forest), blessed with a wonderful variety of trees. The castle ruins of **Burg Windeck** and **Wachenburg** stand watch over the town.

Heppenheim

The charming **Marktplatz★** is framed by the medieval Liebig pharmacy, the 16C town hall and the vast neo-Gothic "Bergstraße Cathedral".

Lorsch

A key stop on the *Bergstraße*, tiny Lorsch is home to **Kloster Lorsch**, an 8C Carolingian abbey that once ranked among the most important in Europe. In 1991 it was listed as a UNESCO World Heritage Site, largely because of the well-preserved 8C **Königshalle★★** (royal hall, also known as *Torhalle*). Presumed to be a gatehouse, it sports arches and an elaborate façade. It is one of the few surviving pre-Romanesque architectural relics in Germany. The building opposite houses a trio of **museums** (Museumszentrum Lorsch; Nibelungenstraße 35; open year-round Tue–Sun 10am–5pm; closed Jan 1, Shrove Tue, Dec 24; ⊕5€; ♿; ☏06251 51 44 6; www.kloster-lorsch.de). One details the history of the abbey; another presents Hessian folklore and traditions and the third focuses on tobacco.

From behind the church you can enjoy a panorama over the Rhine Valley towards the Odenwald forest region.

Bensheim

This "town of flowers and wine" is proud of its **old town**. Quaint half-timbered houses line the Marktplatz, the Haupstraße and Wambolterhofstraße.

Located in a sheltered valley, the **Fürstenlager★★**, once the summer residence of the landgraves of Hessen, is now surrounded by a park.

To the north, the imposing **Auerbacher Schloss** (Auerbacher castle; open Mar Wed–Sun noon–6pm; Apr–Sept Wed–Sun 11am–10pm; Oct–Nov Sat–Sun noon–6pm; Dec–Feb only by request; ☏06251 729 23; www.schloss-auerbach.de) commands a view of the entire region.

ADDRESSES

🛏 STAY

Hotel Am Kornmarkt – *Kornmarkt 7. ℰ(06221) 90 58 30. www. hotelamkornmarkt.de. 20 rooms. ⌷9€.* This charming small hotel sits in the heart of the old city. Staying here entitles you to a discount at the nearby car park 12.

Hotel-Restaurant Schnookeloch – *Haspelgasse 8. ℰ(06221) 2 41 64. www. hotel-schnookeloch.de. 11 rooms. ⌷. Restaurant.* The Schnookeloch's history is intertwined with the history of this university town, the restaurant having been a traditional student hangout.

Weißer Bock – *Grosse Mantelgasse 24. ℰ(06221) 900 00. www.weisserbock.de. 23 rooms. ⌷12€. Restaurant.* This historic charmer in the old town has one of the best restaurants in the region that is especially known for its hand-picked selection of German and international wines.

Zum Pfalzgrafen – *Kettengasse 21. ℰ(06221) 536 10. www.hotel-zum-pfalzgrafen.de. 22 rooms. ⌷.* In a city where rates are rather steep, this mid-size hotel delivers comfortable, reasonably priced rooms. Some have views of the castle.

Hotel Backmulde – *Schiffgasse 11. ℰ(06221) 536 60. www. gasthaus-backmulde-hotel.de. 25 rooms. ⌷. Restaurant.* This old sailors' lodging has pleasant rooms dressed in soothing browns and reds with crisp linens and brass chandeliers. Rustic dark wood beams and curtains give the dining room a rustic country flair.

Romantik Hotel Zum Ritter St. Georg – *Hauptstraße 178. ℰ(06221) 13 50. www.ritter-heidelberg.de. 37 rooms. ⌷12€. Restaurant.* Behind the sandstone façade of this 1592 Renaissance building, visitors are welcomed with tradition and history. For fine dining, visit the Restaurant Belier; for an elbows-on-the-table atmosphere, enter the Ritterstube.

Arthotel – *Grabengasse 7. ℰ(06221) 65 00 60. www.arthotel.de. 24 rooms. ⌷12.90€. Restaurant.* This beautifully restored hotel has an elegant atmosphere and a restaurant renowned for its top-notch cuisine. Unwinding spots include a cocktail lounge and a sunny arched courtyard.

🍴 EAT

Kulturbrauerei Heidelberg – *Leyergasse 6 (between Hauptstraße and Am Hachteufel). ℰ(06221) 50 29 80. www.heidelberger-kulturbrauerei.de.* Though updated, this restaurant exudes old-style charm with coffered ceilings and cast-iron chandeliers. Beer brewed on-site goes down well with the regional specialities. Rooms in the adjacent hotel are spacious and luxurious.

Herrenmühle – *Hauptstraße 239. ℰ(06221) 60 29 09. www.herrenmuehle-heidelberg.de. Reservation recommended. Closed lunch, Sun.* This lovely spot adds rustic flair with its wooden furniture and beamed ceilings. Enjoy a glass or two of the excellent local wines inside or on the romantic terrace.

Schlossweinstube – *Schlosshof 1. ℰ(06221) 872 70 10. Closed Tue–Wed.* With a coveted setting inside the world-famous Heidelberg Castle, this restaurant sprawls across several historic rooms. In summer, the terrace facing the courtyard is also a pleasant spot.

TAKING A BREAK

Strohauer's Café Alt-Heidelberg – *Hauptstraße 49. ℰ(06221) 18 90 24. www.strohauer.de.* An unhurried ambience envelops this traditional café with its several-metres-long counter of homemade cakes and pastries, complemented by seasonal snacks.

NIGHTLIFE

Zum Roten Ochsen – *Hauptstraße 217. ℰ(06221) 209 77. www.roterochsen.de. Closed Sun, public holidays and 3 weeks after Christmas.* Once frequented by Bismarck, Mark Twain and John Wayne, this student pub offers rib-sticking German fare served on tables carved with autographs. After 8pm, it becomes a piano-bar and a pleasant place to enjoy a beer or glass of wine.

Pfalz★

The Palatinate is a lovely patchwork of thick forests (Pfälzer Wald), endless vineyards, castle-crowned hills and small towns where time seems to move a little slower. The German Wine Route runs through this region, which is blessed with a mild climate that even permits the growth of figs, lemons and exotic fruit.

A BIT OF HISTORY

The Palatinate, Germany's largest wine-growing region, produces almost one-third of the country's total output. The most famous vintages come from the villages of Bad Dürkheim, Deidesheim and Wachenheim.

⬤ DRIVING TOUR

FROM WORMS TO BAD BERGZABERN

151km/91mi. Allow one day.

This route runs partly along the German Wine Route (Deutsche Weinstrasse), which connects Schweigen at the French border with Bockenheim.

Worms★

20km/13mi north of Mannheim. Neumarkt 14, 67547 Worms. ℘(06241) 853 73 06. www.worms.de.
Worms is one of Germany's oldest cities and, along with Speyer and Mainz, was an Imperial residence on the banks of the Rhine. Its history is closely associated with the 5C kingdom of the Burgundians, whose fate was immortalised in the 12C Nibelungenlied epic (⬤see INTRODUCTION: Literature). Surrounded by vineyards, Worms makes an ideal base for exploring the region.

Dom St. Peter★★ (Cathedral)

Open Apr–Oct daily 9am–6pm; Nov–Mar daily 10am–5pm. ℘(062 41) 61 15. www.wormser-dom.de.

ℹ Info: Hetzelplatz 1, 67433 Neustadt an der Weinstraße. ℘(06321) 926 80. www.neustadt.eu, www. deutsche-weinstrasse.de.

▶ Location: The Palatinate Mountains stretch from the Rhine plains to the Vosges. The main access route is the A65 autobahn from Mannheim or Karlsruhe. The German Wine Route starts 15km/9.3mi to the west of Worms (⬤see German Wine Route).

🕐 Timing: Allow at least one day for the suggested Driving Tour.

Worms Cathedral, completed in 1181, is one of the finest Romanesque edifices in Germany. Entering through the south portal, you see a splendid Christ in Judgement statue from the 12C. In the older east chancel note the Baroque **high altar★** by Balthasar Neumann. The elegant west chancel sports rose windows, a chequered frieze and arched blind arcades. In the north aisle, the five **Gothic relief sculptures★** represent biblical scenes.

Lutherdenkmal (Luther Monument)

Unveiled in 1868, this monument shows Luther before the Diet of Worms surrounded by early Reformers, such John Wycliffe, Jan Hus and Savonarola, as well as Reformist theologians including Melanchthon and Reuchlin.

Museum Heylshof★

Stephansgasse 9. Open May–Sept Tue–Sun 11am–5pm; Oct–Apr Tue–Sat 2pm–5pm, Sun 11am–5pm. Closed Jan 1–Feb 15, Good Fri, Dec 24–25. ⬤3.50€. ℘(06241) 220 00. www.museum-heylshof.de.
This Gründerzeit mansion showcases a collection of 15C–19C **paintings★**, including works by Rubens, Van Loo and

Tintoretto, alongside precious ceramics, glassware and porcelain.

Jewish Sites

Worms was one of Germany's great centres of Jewish culture and is home to Europe's oldest Jewish **cemetery** (open Jul–Aug daily 8am–8pm; rest of the year until dusk) in use since the 11C.

The old **synagogue** (Judengasse; open Apr–Oct daily 10am–12.30pm, 1.30pm–5pm; Nov–Mar 10am–noon and 2pm–4pm) dates to the same period but was destroyed in World War II and rebuilt in 1961. Steps lead down to the **Mikwe** (bathhouse).Behind the synagogue, the modern Raschi-Haus houses a **Jewish Museum** (Hintere Judengasse 6; open Apr–Oct Tue–Sun 10am–12.30am, 1.30pm–5pm, Mar & Nov until 4.30pm; ⊕1.50€; ℘06241 853 47 01) which traces Jewish life in the Rhineland.

Museum der Stadt (City Museum)

Weckerlingplatz 7. Open year-round Tue–Sun 10am–5pm. Closed Jan 1, Good Fri, May 1, Dec 24–26 & 31. ⊕2€. ℘(06241) 94 63 90.

Five thousand years of artefacts are displayed in this former Romanesque monastery. The Ancient Roman section boasts one of Germany's largest collections of glassware from this period.

Nibelungen Museum★★

Fischerpförtchen 10. Open year-round Tue–Fri 10am–5pm, Sat–Sun until 6pm. ⊕5.50€. ℘(06241) 853 41 20. www.nibelungenmuseum.de.

This modern multimedia exhibit brings to life the epic Nibelungen legend in two medieval towers and along a section of the old town wall.

▶ South of Worms, the Rhine plain becomes progressively devoted to viticulture.

Freinsheim

This large wine town is still encircled by its medieval ramparts. The Baroque town hall, beside a 15C church, has an overhanging roof that protects an outside staircase.

Rhine-Main-Danube Canal

Ever since Roman times, emperors, kings, engineers and visionaries have dreamed of linking the Rhine and Danube rivers. Charlemagne made the first attempt at this great enterprise, called Charlemagne's Ditch (Fossa Carolina). Bavaria's Ludwig I made another attempt 1 000 years later with the building of the Ludwig Canal. But it would not be until the late 20C that the amazing feat of engineering would finally be completed. In 1992, the inauguration of the 177km/110mi Rhine-Main-Danube Canal created the final link between the North Sea and the Black Sea.

Bad Dürkheim

Sheltered by the Pfälzer Wald, this spa town has thermal springs and enjoys a mild climate in which fig, almond and chestnut trees thrive. A couple of miles west (via Schillerstraße and Luitpoldweg) is the ruined **Limburg abbey**.

Deidesheim

This is one of the most prosperous and prettiest towns on the German Wine Route, with its half-timbered houses, a wine museum and numerous galleries.

Neustadt an der Weinstraße

The commercial hub of the German Wine Route, Neustadt has a pretty **old town★** that boasts the largest number of historic houses in the region. Its narrow, picturesque lanes surround a pretty market with an 18C town hall.

Hambacher Schloss

Guided tours (45min) Apr–Oct daily 11am, noon, 2pm, 3pm and 4pm; Nov–Mar Sat, Sun and holidays 11am, noon, 2pm. ⊕8€. ℘(06321) 92 62 90. www.hambacher-schloss.de.

Founded by the Salian Franks in the 11C, the castle is considered "the cradle of German democracy". In 1832, some

30 000 freedom-loving citizens from all parts of Germany demonstrated here for the freedom and unity of Germany. The black, red and gold flag, which was adopted as the German national emblem in 1919 and again in 1949, was first raised. An exhibit marks the event.

Kalmit
8km/5mi.
The highest outcrop (673m/2208ft) in the Rhineland-Palatinate offers a **view★★** of the Rhine plain and Speyer Cathedral from the Kalmithaus terrace.

▶ Return to the Wine Route via charming **St. Martin★**.

Schloss-Villa Ludwigshöhe★
Villastraße, 2km/1.2mi from Edenkoben. Historic rooms ☛ visit by 45min guided tour Mar–Nov Tue–Sun 10am–5pm (May–Oct until 6pm); Jan–Feb Sat–Sun 10am–5pm. Closed Dec. Max-Slevogt-Galerie: Apr–Sept Tue–Sun 9am–6pm; Oct–Nov & Mar 9am–5pm; Jan–Feb Sat–Sun 10am–5pm. Closed Dec. ☞6€. ☎(06323) 930 16. www.max-slevogt-galerie.de.
Built by Ludwig I of Bavaria, this stately Italianate villa houses a **gallery★** devoted to the German Impressionist painter Max Slevogt (1868–1932). The apartments are also open to the public. A chairlift goes up to the Rietburg (550m/1804ft) for forest walks.

Trifels★
7km/4.3mi from Annweiler. Open Apr–Sept daily 9am–6pm; Oct–Mar 9am–5pm. Closed Dec. ☞3€.
☎(06346) 84 70. www.burgen-rlp.de.
Once a Hohenstaufen stronghold, the castle held the crown jewels in the 12C and 13C, but is really best known as the place where **Richard the Lionheart** was imprisoned on returning from a crusade in 1193. He was eventually ransomed and returned to England in 1194.

Dahner Felsenland★★
The resort of **Dahn** is surrounded by hiking terrain with red sandstone outcroppings. The **castle ruins★** of Altdahn feature staircases and guard rooms hewn into the rocks.

Burg Berwartstein★
Turn off toward Erlenbach (B427). Open Mar–Oct daily 9.30am–5pm; Nov–Feb, Sat–Sun, 1pm–6pm. ☞4€. ☎(06398) 210. www.burgberwartstein.de
This former robber baron's lair sits 100m/328ft above the village of Erlenbach. Much of the castle is open to the public, including subterranean passages.

Bad Bergzabern★
This charming health resort brims with half-timbered houses. The **Gasthaus zum Engel★** (1579) is said to be the finest Renaissance building in the region.

ADDRESSES

🛏 STAY
😴 **Hotel Zum Lam** – *Winzergasse 37, Gleiszellen, 5km/3mi north of Bad Bergzabern.* ☎(06343) 93 92 12. www.zum-lam.de. 11 rooms. Jan 2–23. ☐. *Restaurant* 😴🍽. This 18C house has a garden terrace and rooms with mod cons.

😴🍽 **Hotel Deidesheimer Hof** – *Am Marktplatz 1, Deidesheim.* ☎(06326) 968 70. www.deidesheimerhof.de. Closed Jan 1–15. 28 rooms. ☐21€. This elegant inn has tasteful rooms and a gourmet restaurant serving regional specialities.

🍴 EAT
😴 **Reuters Holzappel** – *Hauptstraße 11, 76889 Pleisweiler-Oberhofen.* ☎(06343) 42 45. www.reuters-holzappel.de. Closed Sun eve, Mon, Tue Nov–Mar. This traditional wine cellar occupies a 250-year-old farmhouse with a courtyard. Cosy ambience.

😴 **Weinstube Ester** – *Triftweg 21, 67098 Bad Dürkheim.* ☎(06322) 98 90 65. www.ester24.de. Closed Mon and Tue. This typical Palatinate tavern serves regional specialities and local wines.

Speyer★

The old imperial city of Speyer lies in the Rhine plain; it was founded around 10 BC as a Roman camp, and gained in importance during the Middle Ages. Its main sight is the magnificent Romanesque cathedral, one of the largest in Europe and burial site of several Holy Roman Emperors.

A BIT OF HISTORY

An episcopal seat since the 4C, Speyer grew in importance from the 11C onwards under the Salian emperors. It was made an Imperial city in 1294 and hosted more than 50 Imperial diets (parliament sessions) until 1570. The city was razed in 1689 by French troops. As a result, the only remaining evidence of Speyer's medieval splendour is the Kaiserdom, fragments of the town wall and the Altpörtel, a former city gate.

KAISERDOM★★

Open Apr–Oct daily 9am–7pm; Nov–Mar daily 9am–5pm. &. ℰ(06232) 10 23 97. www.dom-speyer.de.

Founded by Konrad II in 1030 and remodelled at the end of the 11C, Speyer's Kaiserdom is the largest Romanesque building in Europe. It has been a UNESCO World Heritage Site since 1981.

▶ **Population:** 50 000

Info: Maximilianstraße 13, 67346 Speyer. ℰ(06232) 14 23 92. www.speyer.de.

Location: Lying south of Heidelberg, Speyer is located between the wooded mountains of the Odenwald and those of the Pfalz.

Parking: Garages are located throughout Speyer. The main train station has a garage convenient for travellers.

Don't Miss: The Kaiser-dom or the excellent Palatinate Museum.

Timing: Allow at least half a day to see the main sights.

Kids: Sea Life.

The **interior★★** is a masterpiece of unity and balance. The **Chapel of the Holy Sacrament** *(Afrakapelle, on the left, before the north transept)* houses two 15C low-relief sculptures, the Bearing of the Cross and the Annunciation. The two-tier central rotunda contains the **baptistry** (Chapel of St. Emmeram) and, above, a chapel dedicated to St. Catherine.

The Kaiserdom's **crypt★★** is the finest and largest Romanesque crypt in Ger-

Kaiserdom

© fab400/Fotolia.com

many. Groined vaulting features transverse arches of alternate pink and white sandstone. Four Holy Roman emperors and four German kings, along with some of their wives, are buried in the **Royal Vault**.

In the gardens south of the cathedral the 16C **Ölberg** was once the centre of the cloister. A large stone trough, the **Domnapf**, stands in the forecourt. In former times, each time a bishop was installed, it was filled with wine and anyone who wished to do so could drink until he dropped.

SIGHTS
Maximilianstraße
Speyer's main historic thoroughfare runs west from the cathedral to the 12C–13C **Altpörtel★**, a gateway tower. The lively street is lined by ornate Baroque buildings, most notably the **Rathaus** (town hall) and the "Alte Münze" (old mint).

Judenhof
(Jewish Courtyard)
South of the town hall, the Judenhof sits at the centre of the medieval Jewish quarter. Remains of the 12C synagogue and a ritual bath (Mikwe) are reminders of this once-vibrant community.

Historisches Museum der Pfalz★
(Palatinate Museum)
Domplatz. Open year-round Tue–Sun 10am–6pm. Closed Jan 1, Dec 24 & 31. ⊛7€. ⅋(06232) 62 02 22. www.museum.speyer.de.
This excellent museum is filled with treasures that illustrate the region's often-tumultuous history. The rarest and most precious item on view is the gold-plated, cone-shaped **Golden Hat of Schifferstadt★★** from the 12C BC. In the basement, the **Cathedral Treasury** (Domschatzkammer) houses tomb furnishings of the emperors, notably the funerary crown of Konrad II, the first Salian emperor. Also note the Imperial orb of Heinrich III and the crown

worn by Heinrich IV during his penance walk to Canossa. In the cellar, the **Wine Museum** (Weinmuseum) presents 2 000 years of wine history, including a bottle of **Roman wine★** from the 3C AD, the world's oldest wine in a liquid state.

Technik Museum Speyer★
(Museum of Technology)
Am Technik Museum. Open year-round Mon–Fri 9am–6pm, Sat–Sun 9am–7pm. ⊛14€. ⅋(06232) 670 80. http://speyer.technik-museum.de.
Planes, trains and automobiles make up the bulk of the exhibit at this engaging museum. Highlights include a tour of a U-9 submarine from World War I, the maritime displays and the musical instruments.

👥 Sea Life★
Open year-round Mon–Fri 10am–5pm, Sat–Sun until 6pm. Closed Dec 24. ⊛15.50€. ⅋(06232) 697 80. www.visitsealife.com/speyer.
Kids especially love this walk-through aquarium where they get acquainted with marine denizens from the Arctic to the tropical seas.

ADDRESSES

🛏STAY
⊜⊜ **Hotel Goldener Engel** – Mühlturmstraße 5-7. ⅋(06232) 13260. www.goldener-engel-speyer.de. Closed late Dec–early Jan. 46 rooms. ⊑. This hotel in the centre of town features individually decorated rooms ranging from rustic to modern in style.

🍽EAT
⊜⊜⊜**Kutscherhaus** – Am Fischmarkt 5a. ⅋(06232) 705 92. www.kutscherhaus-speyer.de. Closed Wed, 3 weeks in Aug. Behind the half-timbered façade of this old house, meals are enjoyed in comfortably furnished dining rooms. The Biergarten is one of the most charming in town.

Saarbrücken★

Although pummelled by bombs during World War II, the capital of the Saarland has developed into a regional metropolis infused with subtle French flair, a host of museums and a large number of beautifully restored Baroque buildings by master architect Friedrich Joachim Stengel.

OLD TOWN
Schloss (Palace)

The medieval fortress was replaced in the 17C by a Renaissance castle, which in turn was demolished in 1738 to make way for a Baroque palace designed by Stengel. Since then, the palace has suffered various forms of destruction, including war and fire, but was completely renovated in 1989 by Gottfried Böhm. It now has a modern look and is used by the city administration and as a cultural venue.

The **Historisches Museum Saar** (open year-round Tue–Fri & Sun 10am–6pm Thu until 8pm, Sat noon–6pm; ≈5€; ♿; ℘0681 506 45 01; www.historisches-museum.org) adjoins the right wing of the castle. Its permanent exhibition deals with World War I and National Socialism in the Saar region.

▶ **Population:** 182 000

Info: Rathausplatz 1, 66111 Saarbrücken. ℘(0681) 9590 9200. www.saarbruecken.de.

◖ **Location:** Saarbrücken lies in the Saar valley, on the French border and at the crossroads of the A6 autobahn to Mannheim and the A4 to Metz, France.

🅿 **Parking:** Garages in the Old City are at Tal- and Reeppersbergstraßen and at Roon- and Stengelstraßen.

🚸 **Don't Miss:** The Ludwigsplatz and its yellow and red Ludwigskirche.

🕐 **Timing:** Allow three to four hours for all the sights.

Museum für Vor- und Frühgeschichte (Museum of Early and Prehistory)

Am Schlossplatz 1. Open year-round Tue–Sun 10am–6pm (Wed until 10pm). Closed Dec 24–25. ≈5€. ♿ ℘(0681) 95 40 50. www.kulturbesitz.de.

Housed in the neo-Baroque former parliament building, this museum presents archaeological items from the beginning of the Stone Age to the early Middle Ages.

Saarbrücken Schloss (Palace)

© KonTour Saarbrücken

Political Ping-Pong

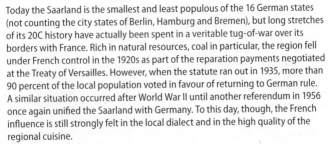

Today the Saarland is the smallest and least populous of the 16 German states (not counting the city states of Berlin, Hamburg and Bremen), but long stretches of its 20C history have actually been spent in a veritable tug-of-war over its borders with France. Rich in natural resources, coal in particular, the region fell under French control in the 1920s as part of the reparation payments negotiated at the Treaty of Versailles. However, when the statute ran out in 1935, more than 90 percent of the local population voted in favour of returning to German rule. A similar situation occurred after World War II until another referendum in 1956 once again unified the Saarland with Germany. To this day, though, the French influence is still strongly felt in the local dialect and in the high quality of the regional cuisine.

A highlight is the **Celtic princess's grave**★★ from Reinheim, which dates to 400 BC. The find is considered one of the most important in Central Europe from the early Celtic period. The princess' jewellery and tomb furnishings, including a gilded bronze jug, are well-preserved.

Museum in der Schlosskirche

Am Schlossberg 6. Open year-round Tue–Sun 10am–6pm (Wed until 8pm). Closed Dec 24–25. ⊛5€. ℘(0681) 954 05 0. www.kulturbesitz.de.
The renovated palace-church now houses a museum of religious art from the 13C to the 19C. Note the three Baroque tombs of the Saarbrücken princes and the colourful stained-glass windows by Georg Meistermann (1950s).

Ludwigsplatz★★

The square is bordered in the north, south and west by eight magnificent town houses of various sizes. All with three storeys and mansard roofs, they illustrate the transition from the late Baroque to the Neoclassical style. Their white and silver-grey colouring enhances the effect of the Ludwigskirche, built in yellow and red sandstone in the centre of the square. The governor of the Saarland has his offices in Ludwigsplatz.

Ludwigskirche (Church of St. Louis)

Open Apr–Dec Tue–Sun 10am–6pm; Jan–Mar Tue noon–5pm, Wed–Sat 10am–5pm. ♿ ℘(0681) 525 24. www.ludwigskirche.de.
After a full restoration, this Baroque Protestant church – a Stengel masterpiece – radiates its former glory. The east end exhibits a degree of splendour unusual in a Protestant church, with statues of the Evangelists by Franziskus Bingh.

ADDITIONAL SIGHTS
St. Johanner Markt★

The old town around the market square is the true heart of Saarbrücken.
The focal point is the beautiful fountain (designed by Stengel), with its obelisk and cast-iron railing, built in 1759–60. Life pulses in the crooked, mostly car-free lanes and in the numerous pubs and bistros around here.

Basilika St. Johann★

Open year-round Mon, Fri–Sat 9.30am–7.15pm; Tue, Thu, Sun 8.30am–7.15pm; Wed 8.30am–5pm. ℘(0681) 90 68 80. www.pfarrei-st-johann.de.
This Stengel-designed Baroque church has an onion tower and lantern.

Stadtgalerie (City Gallery)

St. Johanner Markt 24. Open year-round Tue–Fri noon–6pm, Sat–Sun 11am–6pm. ℘(0681) 905 18 42. www.stadtgalerie.de.

This first-floor gallery displays contemporary and conceptual art, new media, installations, performances and video art. In summer, concerts and exhibitions take over the charming courtyard.

Saarland Museum – Alte Sammlung (Old Collection)

Am Schlossplatz 16. Open year-round, Tue–Sun 10am–6pm (Wed until 10pm). Closed Dec 24–25. 5€. ♿ ℘(0681) 95 40 50. www.kulturbesitz.de.

Completely overhauled and expanded, this museum now presents an extensive overview of artworks covering all periods from the Renaissance to the Baroque and into the 19C. Besides paintings, rooms are also filled with a collection of furniture (including a remarkable Renaissance cabinet from the Abbey of Limburg), sculpture, silver and ceramics.

Saarland Museum – Moderne Galerie (Modern Gallery)

Bismarckstraße 11–15, on the banks of the Saar. Open year-round Tue–Sun 10am–6pm (Wed until 10pm). Closed Dec 24–25. 5€. ♿ ℘(0681) 996 40. www.kulturbesitz.de.

The diversity of European art from the late 19C to the 21C is featured in this museum. The collection's particular strengths lie with **German Impressionism★** (Liebermann, Slevogt, Corinth) and **Expressionism★** (Kirchner, Jawlensky). Other major artists include Picasso, Léger, Tàpies and Beuys. The museum also owns the estate of the sculptor Alexander Archipenko.

Stiftskirche St. Arnual★ (Collegiate Church of St. Arnual)

In the St. Arnual suburb, via Talstraße and Saargemünder Straße.

Named after 7C bishop Arnual of Metz, this 13C–14C Gothic church was given a Baroque dome in 1746 based on plans by Stengel. As the burial place of the dukes of Nassau-Saarbrücken, the church houses 50 **tombs★★** dating from the 13C to the 18C, some of them remarkably artistic.

EXCURSION
Völklinger Hütte★

▶ 10km/6.2mi west of Saarbrücken. Rathausstraße 75, Völklingen. Open mid-Apr–mid-Oct daily 10am–7pm; mid-Nov–late Mar daily 10am–6pm. Closed Dec 24–25 & 31. 15€ (child free). ℘(06898) 910 01 00. www.voelklinger-huette.org.

This iron- and steelworks was established in 1873 and at its peak employed 16 000 people. It remained in operation until 1986 and in 1994, became the first industrial monument to be included on UNESCO's list of World Heritage Sites. Today it is essentially a giant adventure playground where guides take you on a tour through the labyrinths of blast furnaces and air heaters, coking gas pipes and suspended railways.

You can climb to the top of the 30m/98ft-high charging platform where the blast furnace was once fed with coke and ore. High-calibre special exhibits take place in the blast furnace house, while kids gravitate towards the interactive **Ferrodrom**, where exhibits demystify scientific principles.

ADDRESSES

STAY

☞ Hotel Schlosskrug – *Schmollerstraße 14. ℘(0681) 367 35. www.hotel-schlosskrug.de. Closed Dec 24–early Jan. 20 rooms. 5€. Restaurant.* This traditional, family-run guesthouse in an old town house has functional rooms, some with their own bath, as well as larger family rooms with several beds. The restaurant is a good place to try regional home-cooking paired with freshly poured Pilsner.

EAT

Restaurant Quack – *Gersweiler Straße 43a. ℘(0681) 521 53. www. restaurant-quack.de. Closed Fri–Sat lunch, Sun. Reservation recommended.* This 19C villa delivers modern fine dining on the 1st floor, more casual international fare in the downstairs brasserie and a bar in the basement. In summer, sit on the terrace beneath a canopy of old trees.

The Southwest

Augustinermuseum - Städtische Museen Freiburg
© Thomas Eicken

The Southwest

Germany's southwest covers the *Land* (state) of Baden-Württemberg and embraces one of Europe's top-ranked holiday regions, the Black Forest. Its romantic valleys, fir-clad highlands, crystal-clear lakes and rushing waterfalls weave a magical alchemy of natural beauty. This is great hiking and cycling terrain, of course, punctuated by half-timbered villages, traditional farmhouses and vibrant towns like Baden-Baden and Freiburg. East of here, Lake Constance beckons with a storybook setting characterised by expansive views, a warm climate and stunningly elaborate Baroque churches. Stuttgart, the state capital, exudes cosmopolitan flair and is also the gateway to the thinly populated Swabian Jura region traversed by the Neckar River.

Highlights

1. The narrow medieval streets of **Schiltach** (p369)
2. The stunning view from **Mount Belchen** (p372)
3. A dip in the warm waters of **Baden-Baden** (p379)
4. Glamourous exhibits at the car museums in **Stuttgart** (p406)
5. Celestial architecture along the **Upper Swabian Baroque Road** (p425)

The Black Forest

The Black Forest stretches north–south for about 200km/124mi from Baden-Baden to the Swiss border and east–west for 60km/37mi from France to the Swabian Alps. It is divided into three distinct areas. In the northern Black Forest streams have carved deep valleys between fir- and pine-studded plateaus. There are plenty of natural mineral springs here, whose healing properties have been cherished since Roman times. Today, the area boasts Germany's highest concentration of spas, health resorts and hotels with beauty and fitness facilities.

The central Black Forest is classic cuckoo-clock country. Don't miss the world's biggest "cuckoo-clocks" in Triberg and Schonach or the German Clock Museum in Furtwangen. Schiltach is a symphony in half-timber, while Gutach has the impressive Vogtbau-ernhof Open-air Museum, where historic regional houses and farm buildings have been assembled in a mock village. Germany's biggest theme park, Europa-Park Rust, is west of here near the French border. The gateway to the southern Black Forest is Freiburg, a lively university town with a fantastic brick minster. Be sure to drive up Schauinsland (1 284m/4 212ft) for knock-

Kloster Maulbronn, near Karlsruhe

© Willi Wilhelm/Fotolia.com

Black Forest Treats

The Baden Wine Route cuts through the sun-kissed foothills of the entire Black Forest, with each area specialising in different varietals. Ortenau is famous for its Riesling; the Markgräflerland cultivates mostly Gutedel, while in Breisgau and the Kaiserstuhl the focus is on Grauburgunder (pinot gris) and pinot blanc (Weißburgunder).

Famous throughout the world is the Black Forest ham, which is still smoked in traditional farmhouses and eaten with bread, often as part of a light supper. The region is also home to Germany's most famous cake, the Schwarzwälder Kirschtorte (Black Forest gateau). This waist-expander is a three-layered chocolate sponge cake filled with cream and morello cherries marinated in *kirsch* (cherry) schnapps. With more than 14 000, the Black Forest has the world's highest density of distilleries. Aside from cherries, all sorts of other fruit, including pears and plums, are turned into this potent liquor.

out views of the Rhine Valley, the Vosges and the Alps. Further south, the peaks gets higher, culminating in the Feldberg at 1 493m/4 899ft.

Lake Constance

Aside from its size, one of the most remarkable aspects of Lake Constance is its stunning Alpine backdrop. The B31 skirts the northern shore, meandering past orchards, vineyards, golden fields and lovely Baroque churches such as the one in Birnau. Admire the bonanza of plants and flowers on the garden island of Mainau, then hop over to Reichenau Island for an immersion in the early Middle Ages at the 9C UNESCO-protected abbey. Other stops include Friedrichshafen, famous as the birthplace of the Zeppelin airship, and romantic Lindau with its picture-perfect old town.

The Cities

The area described in this chapter is largely rural, but there are four larger cities worth a closer look. The state capital Stuttgart is often undeservedly perceived as all buttoned-up business. Its true that Bosch, Daimler and Porsche all have headquarters here, but Stuttgart also boasts a lively cultural landscape with world-class opera and ballet and a hot hip-hop scene. The locals truly let their hair down during the Cannstatter Volksfest, a festival often compared to Oktoberfest in Munich.

West of Stuttgart, Karlsruhe on the Rhine has a unique fan-shaped city layout and also scores points with its outstanding art

museums and a renowned Centre for Art and Media.

Baden-Baden is the northern gateway to the Black Forest and has been one of the most elegant spa resorts since the 19C when the famous, royal and wealthy started to arrive to cure their ailments in the town's warm mineral springs.

In the south, Freiburg is one of Germany's most charming towns. Surrounded by tree-covered mountains, anchored by a medieval centre with its famous minster, and enlivened by 20 000 students, it is a great launch pad for explorations into the southern and central Black Forest.

Todtnau Falls, Black Forest

© Christoph Hähnel/Fotolia.com

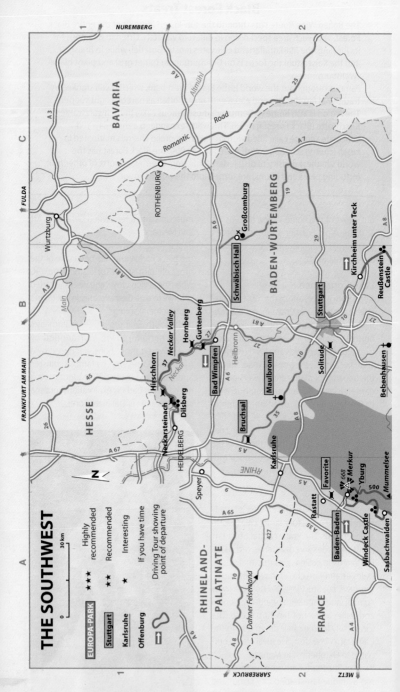

THE SOUTHWEST

0 — 30 km

★★★ Highly recommended
★★ Recommended
★ Interesting

EUROPA-PARK
Stuttgart
Karlsruhe
Offenburg
⬆ Driving Tour showing point of departure

BAVARIA
BADEN-WÜRTEMBERG
HESSE
RHINELAND-PALATINATE
FRANCE

NUREMBERG
FULDA
Wurtzburg
ROTHENBURG
Romantic Road
Altmühl
FRANKFURT AM MAIN
Main
Hirschhorn
Neckarsteinach
Dilsberg
Neckar Valley
Hornberg
Guttenberg
Bad Wimpfen
Neckar
Heilbronn
HEIDELBERG
Speyer
Bruchsal
Maulbronn
Schwäbisch Hall
Großcomburg
Solitude
Stuttgart
Kirchheim unter Teck
Reußenstein Castle
Bebenhausen
Karlsruhe
RHINE
Favorite
Rastatt
Merkur 668
Yburg
500
Mummelsee
Baden-Baden
Windeck Castle
Saßbachwalden
Dahner Felsenland
SARREBRUCK
METZ

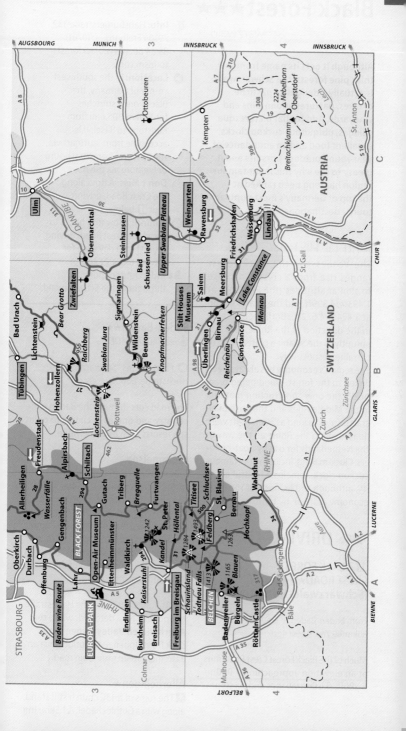

Black Forest★★★

Schwarzwald

Although it gets its name from the thick pine forests, the Schwarzwald is actually a delightful pastiche of lakes, pastures, mountains and vineyards. Add to that picturesque villages, ubiquitous cuckoo clocks, excellent food and an abundance of year-round outdoor pursuits and it is easy to see why this mountainous region has long been ranked at the top of Germany's most popular tourist destinations.

A BIT OF HISTORY

The Vosges and the Black Forest ranges rise from a crystalline base to similar altitudes (the Feldberg at 1 493m/4 899ft and the Grand Ballon at 1 424m/4 672ft). Both drop steeply in the direction of the Rhine, and less abruptly to the Swabian plateau and to Lorraine, respectively.

The region's **economy** has always been linked to the forest, wood being practically the only construction material in the Middle Ages and the base of all crafts. Trees as long as 50m/164ft were floated along the Rhine all the way to the Netherlands for use by boat-builders. Clock-making, including the famous cuckoo clock, remains a fruitful activity, although today much of the local economy is driven by tourism.

🚗 DRIVING TOURS

1 BLACK FOREST CREST ROAD★★★ (Schwarzwald-Hochstraße)

From Baden-Baden to Freudenstadt. 80km/49.7mi. Allow 4hrs.

Much of the Black Forest Crest Road runs at an elevation approaching 1 000m/3 280ft, skirting villages and ski slopes.

Info: Habsburgerstraße 132, 79104 Freiburg. ℘(0761) 89 64 60. www.blackforest-tourism.com.

Location: In the southwest corner of Germany, the Black Forest stretches for 170km/105.6mi from Karlsruhe to Basel. It is accessible from Stuttgart via the A81, and from Strasbourg or Freiburg via the A5.

Don't Miss: A drivealong the Crest Road, driving tour 1 below.

Timing: Allow four hours to travel the Crest Road, driving tour 1, one day each for driving tours 2 and 3.

Kids: Outdoor pursuits throughout the Schwarzwald.

Baden-Baden★★

See BADEN-BADEN.

▷ Follow signs "Schwarzwald-Hochstraße/B500".

The road cuts through the Baden wine country and gradually climbs to quiet spa resorts such as Bühlerhöhe.

Mummelsee

This small, dark glacial lake at the foot of the **Hornisgrinde** (1 164m/3 819ft), the highest point of the northern Black Forest, is named after the *"Mümmeln"* (water sprites) that inhabit its icy depths, according to local legend. In former times, Black Forest breweries obtained blocks of ice chopped out of the frozen lake until well into spring.

▷ At Ruhestein, leave the Hochstraße temporarily for a detour down to the **Allerheiligen Valley★**, then climb back from Oppenau to Zuflucht via an extremely steep mountain road.

Allerheiligen★

The ruins of a 13C church still stand, along with a Gothic chapel. A 1.5km/1mi trail leads from the abbey ruins to the **Allerheiligen-Wasserfälle★**, a celebrated series of seven waterfalls with a total drop of 90m/295ft. Allow about 45 minutes for the round-trip walk.

◗ Continue along the Hochstraße towards Freudenstadt.

Freudenstadt★

Lying at the crossing of several tourist routes, this 17C town was destroyed by fire in 1945. It now follows a chessboard plan centred on the **Marktplatz★**, a huge square surrounded by Italianate arcaded buildings. The two naves of the 17C **Stadtkirche** (parish church), built at right angles, form one corner of Marktplatz. Inside, note the carved and painted 12C Romanesque **lectern★★** supported by the Four Apostles. A further treasure is the 12C **baptismal font★** with intricate animal decorations.

2 CENTRAL BLACK FOREST★★

From Freudenstadt to Freiburg. 152km/94.4mi. Allow one day.

The itinerary meanders through the Kinzig and Elz valleys, passing through bustling tourist villages before reaching the Upper Black Forest at Freiburg.

◗ Drive about 18km/11mi south of Freudenstadt.

Alpirsbach★

Alpirsbach is worth a stop for its 11C red sandstone **Kloster Alpirsbach★** (open mid-Mar–Oct Mon–Sat 10am–5.30pm, Sun 11am–5.30pm; Nov–late Mar Thu, Sat–Sun 1pm–3pm; ⊛4€; ℘07444 510 61; www.kloster-alpirsbach.de), a former Benedictine abbey and the oldest Romanesque structure in the Black Forest. Inside the church the painted apse, ornate pillars, Romanesque choir and late-Gothic high altar are noteworthy. The attached museum showcases 16C objects from daily life at the monastery, unearthed during excavations in 1958.

Schiltach★★

This postcard-pretty town gets its idyllic character from its beautifully restored half-timbered houses and its scenic location at the confluence of the Schiltach and Kinzig rivers.

Schwarzwälder Freilichtmuseum Vogtsbauernhof★★ (Black Forest Open-Air Museum)

In Gutach. Open Apr–Oct daily 9am–6pm (Aug until 7pm). ⊛8€. ℘(07831) 935 60. www.vogtsbauernhof.org.
Black Forest construction, craftwork, culture and agriculture are imaginatively presented in this outdoor museum in the Gutach Valley. The museum's namesake, the 1612 Vogtsbauern farm, is set amid other farmhouses along with such outbuildings as a bakery, a smithy, a chapel and a granary. All buildings were moved and re-assembled here from throughout the region.

◗ Continue towards Triberg, enjoying fine **views★** from the Landwassereck pass. Upstream from Oberprechtal, the beautiful cascades of the Elz parallel the route.

Triberg★

🚶The romantic (if busy) **Waterfall Walk★** (1hr round-trip; ⊛3€) follows

Half-timbered houses, Schiltach
© Mauritius/Photononstop

Of Clocks and Trains

For a unique travel experience, travel the **German Clock Road** (*Deutsche Uhrenstraße*), covering about 320km/198.8mi and taking in various cuckoo-clock sites: museums, factory tours and remarkable clocks themselves (details available from information offices in the region). For railway fans, the **Black Forest Train** (*Schwarzwaldbahn*) negotiates a 670m/2 198ft elevation change following the landscape on a route that avoids bridges. Despite the 39 tunnels required to manage the largest natural obstacles, the journey encompasses magnificent scenery; the most interesting section (27km/16.7mi) lies between Hornberg and St. Georgen.

the Gutach as it cascades over boulders and past tree-lined mossy banks. Back in town, **Maria der Tannen (Our Lady of the Firs)**★ is one of the most popular pilgrimage churches in the Black Forest. The **Schwarzwald Museum** (Wallfahrtstraße 4; open Apr–Sept daily 10am–6pm; Oct–Mar 10am–5pm; closed Mon Oct–Mar, Dec 24–25; ⌾5€; ℘07722 44 34; www.schwarzwaldmuseum.de) exhibits traditional costumes and local craftwork, including one of Europe's largest collections of barrel-organs. Another attraction, the **World's Biggest Cuckoo Clock** (Schonachbach 27; open Easter–Oct Mon–Sat 9am–6pm, Sun 10am–6pm; Nov–Easter Mon–Sat 9am–5.30pm, Sun 11am–5pm; ⌾2€; ℘07722 962 20; www.uhren-park.de) contains a clock shop and is even listed in the *Guinness Book of Records*. Its claim, however, is disputed by the world's "other" biggest cuckoo clock about 1km/0.6mi further along in Schonach.

Furtwangen

The **Deutsches Uhrenmuseum** (Robert -Gerwig-Platz 1; open Apr–Oct daily 9am–6pm; Nov–Mar daily 10am–5pm; ⌾5€; ⅋; ℘07723 920 28 00; www. deutsches-uhrenmuseum.de) displays the world's largest collection of Black Forest clocks and explains the ingenuity that artisans brought to the simple telling of time.
From here you can visit **Bregquelle** (the source of the Breg), a small stream that eventually feeds into the Danube.

▶ Soon after leaving Furtwangen, turn right for Hexenloch, a deep wooded gorge enlivened by

waterfalls. Between St. Märgen and St. Peter, the twisting road treats you to plenty of fine **views**★★.

St. Peter★

Two onion-domed towers top the splendid Rococo **church**★ of this 18C former Benedictine abbey. Johann Anton Feuchtmayer carved the marvellous statues representing the Dukes of Zähringen, who founded Freiburg. Several hiking trails leave from the car park.

Kandel★

From the viewpoint (*30min round-trip walk*) unfolds a beautiful **panorama**★ of the Vosges, Feldberg and Belchen.

Waldkirch★

Clustered around the collegiate church of St. Marguerite are pretty 18C houses. The church **interior**★ has preserved its original furniture and fittings.

Freiburg★★ – ⌾ See FREIBURG.

③ UPPER BLACK FOREST★★★ (Hochschwarzwald)

Round-trip leaving from Freiburg im Breisgau. 142km/88mi. Allow one day. ⌾See maps pp366, 367 and 371.

This circuit skirts the three main peaks of the Black Forest (Schauinsland, Belchen and Feldberg) and also takes in its two best-known lakes (Schluchsee and Titisee).

Schauinsland★

🅐 An extremely twisty mountain road leads to the upper cable-car station. From the parking lot, follow the signs

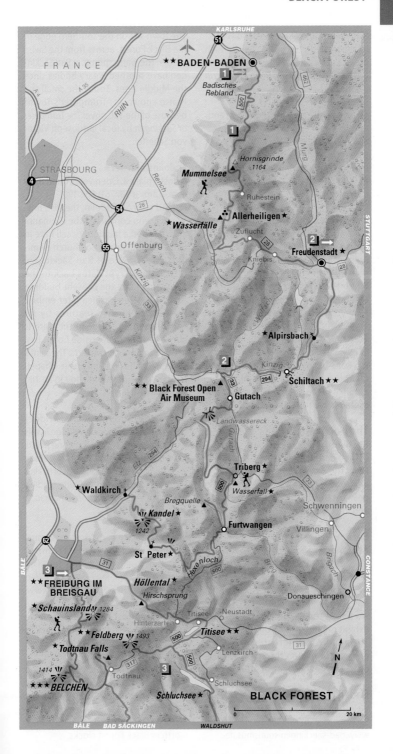

KARLSRUHE

51

★★ BADEN-BADEN ◉

FRANCE

1

Badisches Rebland

500

1

462

Murg

△ *Hornisgrinde*
1164

STRASBOURG

Mummelsee

4

● Ruhestein

▲▲ **Allerheiligen** ★

RHIN

54

28

STUTTGART

★ *Wasserfälle*

Zuflucht ○

2

28

55   Offenburg

Kniebis   **Freudenstadt** ★

◉

28

Rench

Kinzig

A 5

Wolfach

★ **Alpirsbach** ●

2

Kinzig

33   294

Schiltach ★★

▲

★★ **Black Forest Open**
Air Museum

Gutach ○

Landwassereck

Gutach

Elz   294

Triberg ★

○

★ **Waldkirch** †

Bregquelle

▲

Wasserfall ★

Schwenningen ○

\\|/ **Kandel** ★

1242

Furtwangen ○

Villingen ○

Breg

62

31

\\|/

St Peter ★

Höllenloch

500

CONSTANCE

Brigach

BÂLE

3

Höllental ★

★★ **FREIBURG IM**
BREISGAU

Hirschsprung

▲

Donaueschingen ●

★ *Schauinsland* \\|/ 1284

Titisee ○   Neustadt ○

Hinterzarten ○

Titisee ★★

N

★★ **Feldberg** \\|/ 1493

500

★ **Todtnau Falls**

▲

Lenzkirch ○

31

1414 \\|/

317

3

500

★★★ *BELCHEN*

Todtnau ○

Schluchsee ★

Schluchsee ○

BLACK FOREST

0   20 km

"Rundweg" and "Schauinsland Gipfel" to the viewing tower *(91 steps)*, which offers a **view**★ across upland meadows to the **Feldberg**★★ *(30min round-trip walk)*.

◑ Follow the road for 1km/0.6mi and take the right fork towards Stohren and the Münstertal. Meandering through meadows, the route finally plunges once more into the forest. At Wiedener Eck, turn right towards the Belchen.

Mount Belchen★★★

🚶 30min round-trip walk from the car park to the observation platform.
Dominating the Wiesenthal, the Belchen rises to a height of 1 414m/4 637ft. When the skies are clear, **views**★★★ extend all across the Rhine plain, the High Vosges and the Alps.

Todtnau Falls★

🚶1.5km/1mi from Todtnau, 1hr round-trip walk.
Climbing through a wooded combe, a trail leads to an impressive series of cascades plunging down 97m/318ft.

The Hochkopf Massif
Hochkopf

🚶1hr round-trip walk.
From the parking lot, a trail leads to a look-out with **views**★★ of the barren peaks of the Belchen and the Feldberg and, on clear days, the Alps.

Bernau★

At Bernau-Innerlehen, the **town hall** *(Rathaus)* houses the **Hans-Thoma-Museum** (open Mon–Fri 10.30am–noon and 2pm–5pm, Sat–Sun 2pm–5pm; closed Nov 15–Dec 10; ⊛7€; ℘07675 16 00 40; www.hans-thoma-museum.de) with an exhibit of paintings by this local artist. The road runs high above the Alb gorges, tunnelling through the cliffs on its way to the Rhine at Albbruck.

Bad Säckingen★

Waldshuter Straße 20, 79713 Bad Säckingen. ℘(07761) 568 30. www.bad-saeckingen-tourismus.de.

The town sits on the southern edge of the Black Forest, across from the Swiss border. The warm springs at Bad Säckingen have soothed weary bodies since the Middle Ages. Today the small spa is also known as "Trumpeter's Town" because of the 19C novel *The Trumpeter of Säckingen* by local lad Joseph Victor von Scheffel.

Fridolinsmünster★

Münsterplatz 8. Open year-round daily 8am–7pm. ℘(07761) 568 190.
Named after St. Fridolin, the Irish missionary who converted the Alemanni and founded a missionary cell here in 522, this twin-towered church dominates the skyline of Bad Säckingen. Although its crypt dates back to the Carolingian era, the present building is a 14C Gothic basilica later embellished with Rococo features by JM Feuchtmayer. A statue of the saint is above the porch alongside Count Ursi of Glarus, one of his converts. The saint's relics are in the Fridolinkapelle (chapel) on the right side of the choir in an 18C **silver shrine**★.

Gedeckte Brücke★ (Covered Bridge)

There has been a wooden bridge in this spot since the 13C, but its stone pillars were not erected until 1575. The bridge is 200m/656ft long, the longest of its kind in Europe, and spans the Rhine, leading to Stein in the Swiss *canton* of Aargau.

Schloss Schönau

The local palace harbours the unusual **Trompetenmuseum** (Trumpet Museum; open year-round Tue, Thu & Sun 2pm–5pm; May–Sept also Wed 2pm–5pm; ⊛3€; ℘07761 22 17; www.trompetenmuseum.de). It boasts Europe's largest collection of these instruments, the oldest dating back to 1664. The original 1900 trumpet workshop came from the town of Oldenburg. The palace itself was built c. 1600 by the lords of Schönau and is surrounded by pleasant gardens. It also contains the local history collection, pre- and early history exhibits and several centuries' worth of Black Forest clocks.

Waldshut

Situated halfway up a wooded slope rising from the Rhine, this small town sparked the Black Forest peasant revolt of 1524. Today it retains two fortified 13C gateways: the Lower (or Basle) Gate to the west and the Upper (or Schaffhaus) Gate to the east. The heart of the **old town★** is **Kaiserstraße**, a street lined by houses with overhanging eaves. Buildings of note include the 18C late-Baroque **town hall;** the **"Wilder Mann"**, a 16C town house; and the 16C **"Alte Metzig"** (Butcher's Gateway), now a **local museum** (Heimatmuseum; open year-round Sun 2pm–5pm; ℘07751 833 200; www.waldshut-tiengen.de)

St. Blasien★

Am Kurgarten. ℘(07652) 1260. www.hochschwarzwald.de.
The majestic domed church comes into view in the southern part of the Black Forest. Dedicated to St. Blaisen, It stands in the grounds of a medieval monastery founded in 835 by hermit monks.

Dom★★ (Cathedral)

Inspired by the Pantheon in Rome, French architect Pierre-Michel d'Ixnard designed this early Neoclassical church. Completed in 1772, its central copper dome (33.5m/110ft in diameter) is the third largest in the world after those of St. Peter's in Rome and Les Invalides in Paris. Inside is a splendid Rococo high altar by Christian Wenzinger.

Schluchsee★

This glacial lake became the largest body of water in the Black Forest when it was dammed in 1932.

Feldberg★★

The **Feldbergbahn chairlift** (open Jul–Sept daily 9am–5pm; May, Jun & Oct 9am–4.30pm; ⊕9.50€ round-trip; ℘07676 940 9110 ; www.feldbergbahn.de) conveys sightseers up the Black Forest's highest mountain, which is crowned by the Bismarck monument. Various █ **hiking trails** start near the top, taking in tremendous **views★** as far as the Alps and down to the Feldsee, a small lake in the hollow of a glacial cirque. In winter, downhill and cross-country skiing are popular outdoor pursuits.

Titisee★★

This clear glacial lake sits at the junction of several tourist routes and is popular for swimming, boating and windsurfing. In winter, cross-country skiing is the main outdoor activity. The name is derived from Roman emperor Titus.

Returning to Frieburg, you travel through **Höllental★** (Valley of Hell). The route at times is hemmed in by towering cliffs, particularly at **Hirschsprung** (deer's jump), its narrowest point.

ADDRESSES

🛏 STAY

⊖ **Berggasthaus Gisiboden** – *79674 Todtnau-Gschwend. ℘(07671) 99 98 21. www. berggasthaus-gisiboden.de. 18 rooms. ☲. Restaurant⊖.* If you don't mind simple rooms and shared bathroom facilities, you will definitely enjoy the peace and quiet of this rustic mountain inn at an altitude of 1 200m/3 937ft. It is an ideal base for hiking and mountain-biking excursions. The pleasant restaurant serves rib-sticking regional fare.

⊖ **Gasthof Gedächtnishaus** – *Fohrenbühl 12, 78730 Lauterbach. ℘(07422) 44 61. www.king-gastro.de. Closed 6 weeks from Jan 6. 7 rooms. ☲. Restaurant ⊖⊖. Closed Wed and Thu.* An ideal destination for tired hikers, this historic inn has newly renovated, modern rooms with a welcome degree of comfort. The rustic restaurant serves energy-restoring local fare.

⊖ **Hotel Belchen-Multen** – *79677 Schönau-Aitern-Multen. ℘(07673) 209. www.belchen-multen.de. Closed mid-Nov–mid-Dec. 22 rooms. ☲. Restaurant ⊖.* This well-kept hotel in the wilds of the Black Forest has simple rooms and an indoor swimming pool, which comes in handy on those days when the sun is a no-show.

⊖⊖ **Hotel Alemannenhof** – *Bruderhalde 21, 79856 Hinterzarten am*

Titisee. ℰ(07652) 911 80. www.hotel-alemannenhof.de. 60 rooms. ☷. Restaurant ⊜❸❸. On the shores of the Titisee, this modern Black Forest hotel boasts a private beach and dock. In addition to the comfortable rooms, the establishment has a pleasant restaurant and a lakeside terrace.

⊜❸**Hotel Bären** – Langestraße 33, 72250 Freudenstadt. ℰ(07441) 27 29. www.hotel-baeren-freudenstadt.de. 25 rooms. ☷. Restaurants ⊜❸, closed Sun, lunch. Owned by the same family since 1878, this central inn has a homey feel and spacious rooms with rustic flair. The restaurant serves creative Black Forest cuisine. Even vegetarians will not feel left out.

⊜❸ **Hotel Sonne** – Krumlinden 44, 79244 Münstertal-Obermünstertal. ℰ(07636) 319. www.sonne-muenstertal.de. Closed mid-Nov–mid-Dec. 16 rooms. ☷. Restaurant closed Tue eve and Wed. This pleasant intimate hotel snuggles into the romantic Münstertal valley and gets a high charm quotient from blond wood furniture and good-size balconies. Regional home cooking beckons in the traditional restaurant.

⊜❸ **Schwarzwaldhaus** – Am Kurpark 26, 79872 Bernau-Innerlehen. ℰ(07675) 365. www.sbo.de/schwarzwaldhaus. Closed Nov. 14 rooms. ☷. Restaurant⊜❸. Sample classic Black Forest flair in this cosy farmhouse

covered in wooden shingles typical of the region. After enjoying a delicious meal in the former stables, retire to handsome rooms decorated either farmhouse- or country-style.

⛙ EAT

⊜ **Löffelschmiede** – Löffelschmiede 1, 79853 Lenzkirch. ℰ(07653) 279. www.sbo.de/loeffelschmiede. Closed Nov–mid-Dec., Tue eve–Wed. This little family-run restaurant is set in a valley near Lenzkirch. Trout and simple regional dishes are served in the bright restaurant with its earthenware oven. Also lets out a few inexpensive rooms.

⊜❸ **Jägerstüble** – Marktplatz 12, 72250 Freudenstadt. ℰ(07441) 23 87. www.jaegerstueble-fds.de. The rustic setting and relaxed atmosphere make this central restaurant a popular choice with both locals and visitors. Rooms are decked out in blond-wood furniture and cheerful colours.

⊜❸❸❸ **Bareiss** – Hermine-Bareiss-Weg 1, 72270 Baiersbronn-Mitteltal. ℰ(07442) 470. www.bareiss.com. 99 rooms. Restaurants ⊜–⊜❸❸. Charming décor and creaking wood make this upscale establishment a delightful refuge. Restore energies in the pool and spa, or play golf, hunt or hike. A farmhouse-style tavern serves Black Forest specialities. The gourmet restaurant is among the region's best.

Karlsruhe★

Karlsruhe had its genesis in 1715 as the residential retreat of Margrave Karl Wilhelm of Baden-Durlach. It evolved into a modern city with a grand palace and fine museums. It is home to the country's oldest school of technology (1825), whose graduates include Heinrich Hertz, discoverer of electromagnetic waves, and pioneering auto engineer Karl Benz. Karlsruhe is also the seat of the Bundesverfassungsgericht, Germany's highest court.

▶ **Population:** 290 740
▤ **Info:** Bahnhofplatz 6. ℰ(0721) 37 20 53 83. www.karlsruhe-tourismus.de.
▶ **Location:** Karlsruhe occupies the right bank of the Rhine, close to the French border. It is served by the A5 and A65 autobahns.
☺ **Don't Miss:** Art lovers should head for the Fine Arts Museum and the ZKM.
◷ **Timing:** Allow at least half a day for Karlsruhe's museums.

Staatliche Kunsthalle Karlsruhe

© Norbert Miguletz / Staatliche Kunsthalle Karlsruhe

A BIT OF HISTORY

Karlsruhe is one of Germany's earliest masterplanned cities, laid out in the 18C with the palace at its centre and a network of streets radiating away from it. It became the capital of the Grand Duchy of Baden in 1806.

SIGHTS

Staatliche Kunsthalle Karlsruhe★★ (Fine Arts Museum)

Open year-round Tue–Sun 10am–6pm. Closed Dec 24 & 31. 8€. (0721) 926 33 59. www.kunsthalle-karlsruhe.de.

One of Germany's finest and most comprehensive art museums is particularly famous for its **Old German Masters★★**. Among the displays are an emotionally wrenching *Crucifixion* by Matthias Grünewald, a small tablet depicting *Maria and Child* by Lucas Cranach the Elder and several works by Dürer and his pupil Hans Baldung Grien. The Golden Age of Flemish and Dutch painting is represented by Rubens, Jordaens and Rembrandt.

The 19C collection on the ground floor showcases romantic landscapes by Caspar David Friedrich as well as boldly pigmented canvases by Cézanne.

The adjacent **Orangery** focuses on classical, modern and contemporary art. Paintings by German Expressionists (Marc), Cubists (Léger, Delaunay) and works by Ernst and Dix are hung alongside sculptures by Barlach, Lehmbruck and Henry Moore. Contemporary artists include Richter, Klein and Tàpies.

Schloss★ (Palace)

The palace served as the grand-ducal residence until 1918; it got a major drubbing in World War II. Only the tall **octagonal tower** (Schlossturm; open year-round Tue–Thu 10am–5pm, Fri–Sun 10am–6pm; 4€; 0721 926 65 14) survived and can now be climbed for sweeping views of the city and the Black Forest.

The palace park gives access to the **Botanical Garden**(Botanischer Garten; grounds open year-round 6am–sunset, greenhouses Tue–Fri 10am–4.45pm; closed Dec 24; 2€; 0721 926 30 08; www.botanischer-garten-karlsruhe.de), which is a fine place to relax among a profusion of flowers, trees and plants, many of them rare and exotic.

Badisches Landesmuseum★ (Baden Regional Museum)

Open year-round Tue–Thu 10am–5pm, Fri–Sun 10am–6pm. Closed Jan 1, Shrove Tue, Dec 24–25 & 31. 4€. (0721) 926 65 14. www.landesmuseum.de.

This palace museum covers all major historical periods of the last 2 000 years with paintings, furniture, uniforms, crowns and jewellery, statues and other objects of cultural significance.

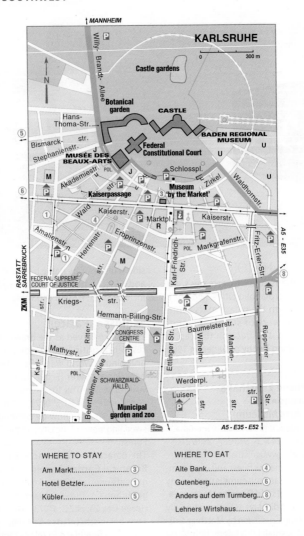

WHERE TO STAY

Am Markt.........................③
Hotel Betzler....................①
Kübler.............................⑤

WHERE TO EAT

Alte Bank........................④
Gutenberg......................⑥
Anders auf dem Turmberg...⑧
Lehners Wirtshaus.............①

Museum beim Markt (Museum by the Market)

Karl-Friedrich-Straße 6. Open year-round Tue–Thu 11am–5pm, Fri–Sun 10am–6pm. Closed Jan 1, Shrove Tue, Dec 24–25 & 31. 2€. & (0721) 926 65 14. www.landesmuseum.de.

Applied arts since 1900 are the main theme of this museum, which exhibits exceptional collections of **Jugendstil★** (Art Nouveau) and Art Deco.

Zentrum für Kunst und Medientechnologie★ (ZKM) (Centre for Art & Media)

Lorenzstraße 19. Open year-round Wed–Fri 10am–6pm, Sat–Sun 11am–6pm. 6€ per museum or 10€ for both. & (0721) 810 00. www.zkm.de.

This early 20C weapons and ammunition factory now unites teaching, research, workshops and museums revolving around art and electronic media technologies under a single roof. In the **Museum für Neue Kunst** (Museum for New Art), European and American works since 1960 take centre stage along with rotating shows featuring paintings, graphics, sculpture, photography and installations.

The **Medienmuseum** (Media Museum) is the world's first repository focused exclusively on interactive art. *Access at the level of the blue cube.*

EXCURSIONS
Schloss Bruchsal★★

◐ 20km/12.5mi north of Karlsruhe. Open year-round Tue–Sun 10am–5pm. Closed Dec 24–25 & 31. ◉6€ for palace and museums. ⅙ ℘(07251) 74 26 61. www.schloss-bruchsal.de.

Bruchsal was the residence of the last four Prince-Bishops of Speyer. Their Baroque palace was commissioned in 1720 by Prince-Bishop Damian Hugo von Schönborn, who brought some of the finest architectural and artistic talent to the Rhine. Most notable among these was Balthasar Neumann, whose magnificent **staircase★★** (1731), lidded by elaborate stucco ornamentation, is a true Rococo masterpiece. The **state apartments** are filled with original furnishings as well as silver, porcelain and portraits. The vaulted Gartensaal (Garden Room) with its marble floor opens onto the park that used to extend all the way to the River Rhine 16km/10mi away.

♣♣ Deutsches Musikautomaten Museum★ (German Museum of Musical Instruments)

In the main building. ➳ Guided tours (1hr) with musical demonstrations 11am, & 3pm. ℘(07251) 74 26 52. *www.dmm-bruchsal.de.*

This fun collection includes 200 musical instruments from the 18C to the 20C, most of them worked by cylinders or perforated cardboard or rolls of paper. It is well worth taking the guided tour to experience the musical recitals. Cinema organs, "Barbary organs" and pianolas (mechanical pianos operated by perforated "piano rolls") are also on view. Note the "household" organs and orchestrations (in 19C England Aeolian Orchestrelles, machines resembling oversize, upright pianos with manual keyboards

and stops). Many instruments hail from Leipzig and the Black Forest.

Museum der Stadt Bruchsal (Local History Museum)

Southern part of the main block. ℘(07251) 79 253.

This local history museum in the palace presents the city's paleontological collection, including minerals from Bruchsal and the surrounding area.

The prehistoric department brims with fossil finds and excavations from the Stone Age to the Middle Ages. There's also a sparkling collection of coins and medals, many of them ancient and rare, that is sure to delight numismatists.

Another focus is the history of the local penal system from 1848 until the end of World War II. There are displays about the bombing raids on 1 March 1945 that obliterated the town.

Kloster Maulbronn★★ (Maulbronn Abbey)

◐ 38km/23.5mi east of Karlsruhe. Klosterhof 5. Open Mar–Oct daily 9am–5.30pm; Nov–Feb Tue–Sun 9.30am–5pm. Closed Dec 24–25 & 31. ◉7€. ⅙ ℘(07043) 92 66 10. www.klostermaulbronn.de.

Founded in 1147, Maulbronn is considered the best-preserved medieval monastery complex north of the Alps. The abbey sits right in the middle of Salzach Valley, within a small, fortified medieval village that is approached by a rampart walk.

One of the earliest Cistercian foundations in Germany, this enormous abbey remains intact with all its outbuildings inside a perimeter wall. The school established here in 1557 has seen the flowering of such diverse talents as Johannes Kepler, Friedrich Hölderlin, Justinus Kerner and Hermann Hesse. The main buildings were constructed between the 12C and 14C in transitional Romanesque-Gothic style. The structure was instrumental in paving the way for Gothic architecture throughout northern and central Europe. The abbey was added to the UNESCO World Heritage list in 1993.

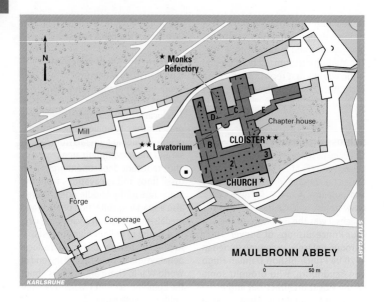

MAULBRONN ABBEY

The Cistercians – This Benedictine order traces its name to the monastery of Cîteaux in Burgundy, France, founded by Robert of Molesmes in 1098. The order grew rapidly; and by the 13C maintained 742 monasteries from Ireland to Syria. In Germany, early foundations include the abbeys of Ebrach in Bavaria and Altenberg near Cologne. Monasteries in Roman Catholic regions got Baroque makeovers in the 18C, while those in Protestant regions, such as Maulbronn, survived unaltered.

Abbey Church★

Consecrated in 1178, the church is entered via a 13C Paradise Porch **(1)**, an early German example of the Romanesque-Gothic transition. Inside, a Romanesque rood screen **(2)** topped by a dog-tooth frieze divides the nave into separate sections for the monks and the lay brothers. A large Crucifix (1473), impressively sculpted from a single stone, stands before the screen. Note the richly carved choir stalls, made c. 1450, and the beautiful 14C **Virgin** *(to the left of the high altar)* **(3)**, probably from the Cologne School.

Cloister★★

The west gallery leads to the **refectory for lay brothers (A)** (rebuilt 1869–70), and to the Romanesque **storeroom (B)**, now a lapidarium. Completed c. 1220–30, the **monks' refectory★** is flanked by the calefactory **(C)** and the kitchens **(D)**. A charming **lavatorium★★** (c. 1350) juts out into the cloister garden. Off the east gallery are the **chapter-house** and a **connecting building (E)**.

Monastery Buildings★

Behind the cloister stands a three-storey Gothic palace with its picturesque **Faustturm** (Faust Tower). The famous Doctor Faust, who inspired Goethe, Wagner and many others, was supposedly summoned here in 1516 for alchemy experiments.

Back in the main courtyard, the **museum** and information centre are housed in the Frühmesserhaus and on the first floor.

ADDRESSES

🛏 STAY

🛏 **Hotel Betzler** – *Amalienstraße 3.* ℘*(0721) 91 33 60. www.hotel-betzler.de. 34 rooms.* ⌑*7€.* In the heart of Karlsruhe, the Betzler is good value, particularly for easy access to public transport. Rooms are clean and functional. The pedestrian zone and most sights of interest are within walking distance.

Am Markt – *Kaiserstraße 76.* *℘0721 91 99 80. www.hotelammarkt.de. 38 rooms.* ⌷. This hotel on the market square enjoys a panoramic view of the town. Rooms are simple, modern and comfortable with the usual international-class facilities.

Kübler – *Bismarckstraße 39-43.* *℘0721 1440. www.4a-hotelwelt.de. 200 rooms.* ⌷. Set in a lush garden in the heart of the city, the Kübler offers a stylish, rustic and intimate atmosphere. Rooms are well equipped, and some have a traditional faïence oven.

⚟ EAT

Alte Bank – *Herrenstraße 30.* *℘0721 183 28 18. www.altebank.de.* Pub food is the focus in this high-ceilinged venue

that is particularly suited to lunchtime. A laid-back atmosphere prevails.

Lehners Wirtshaus – *Karlstraße 21a.* *℘(0721) 249 57 20. www.lehners-wirtshaus.de.* For solid German cuisine, make a beeline to this buzzy brasserie in the town centre. The wooden tables and large bar exude a low-key feel which, in summer, extends to the lively, 300-seat beer garden.

Gutenberg – *Nelkenstraße 27.* *℘0721 985 15 16. www.gasthaus-gutenberg.de.* This attractive and atmospheric rustic restaurant serves regional specialities either indoors or in its beer garden.

Anders auf dem Turmberg – *Reichardstraße 22, Karlsruhe-Durlach (7km/4.5mi east). ℘0721 414 59. www. anders-turmberg.de.* Nestled below the Turmberg, this modern bistro-style restaurant offers wonderful views across the city from its terrace. Local fare and international cuisine are served here.

Baden-Baden★★

From Brahms to Queen Victoria to Bill Clinton, the spa resort of Baden-Baden has long been a favourite playground of the wealthy, famous and powerful. There's plenty to lure them, including an idyllic location on the little Oos River, hot mineral springs that worked miracles on the aching joints of ancient Roman generals and superb cultural institutions. A highlight is the casino, a lavish Belle Epoque extravaganza that inspired Dostoyevski's novel *The Gambler* and Prokofiev's eponymous opera.

▶ **Population:** 54 780

Info: Kaiserallee 3, *℘(07221) 27 52 00.* www.baden-baden.de.

Location: Wedged into the Oos Valley on the edge of the Black Forest and surrounded by the Baden vineyards, Baden-Baden is 60km/37.3mi from Strasbourg via the A5 Autobahn.

Don't Miss: Lichtentaler Allee, the casino or the Museum Frieder Burda.

Timing: Allow two days. City-Bahn **trolley tours** are offered mid-March to October *(55min, ⊛5.50€).*

👣 WALKING TOUR

Kurhaus and Casino★

👣 Casino tours (25min, in German) Apr–Oct daily 9.30am–11.40am; Nov–Mar daily 10am–11.30am. Closed major holidays. ⊛7€. ℘(07221) 302 40.

www.casino-baden-baden.de. Enquire about tours in English. If you plan to gamble, dress well (men in tie and jacket) and bring your passport.

GETTING AROUND

Baden-Baden is linked to Karlsruhe by city train line S 4 and regional RE trains. Check ticket prices and schedule with **Stadtwerke Baden-Baden** (*&(072 21) 27 70; www.stadtwerke-baden-baden.de*) or with **Deutsche Bahn** (*www.bahn.de*). **Airport** – Karlsruhe/Baden-Baden Airport (10km/6mi west of town) has flights serving Berlin, London, Hamburg and other destinations. *&(07229) 66 20 00 or www.baden-airpark.de.*

The majestic 19C Kurhaus hosts balls, festivals, concerts and society events but it is most famous for its elegant casino. A symphony of red velvet and gilded chandeliers, the Belle Epoque venue was designed by Benazét to resemble a French palace.

Lichtentaler Allee★★

This riverside promenade has been the place to see and be seen for over a century. Napoleon III, Queen Victoria, Bismarck and Dostoevsky all whiled away the hours here and in the equally enchanting **Gönneranlage★** nearby.

▶ The route passes Museum Frieder Burda and the State Art Gallery.

Museum Frieder Burda★

Lichtentaler Allee 8b. Open year-round Tue–Sun 10am–6pm. Closed Dec 24 & 31. ⊚12€. *&(07221) 39 89 80. www.museum-frieder-burda.de.*

Situated in the Kurpark, a stunning building by New York-based architect Richard Meier houses this equally stellar art collection. The focus is on 20C works by Max Beckmann, August Macke, Picasso, Jackson Pollock, Mark Rothko, Georg Baselitz and Gerhard

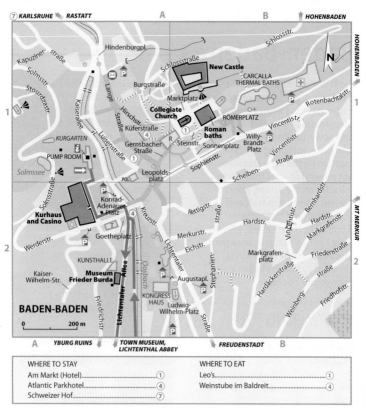

WHERE TO STAY		WHERE TO EAT	
Am Markt (Hotel)	①	Leo's	①
Atlantic Parkhotel	④	Weinstube im Baldreit	④
Schweizer Hof	⑦		

Richter. The white aluminium facade integrates beautifully with the park and sits next to the **State Art Gallery** (Staatliche Kunsthalle; same hours as museum; ⊜12€; ☎07221 30076 400; www.kunsthalle-baden-baden.de), which also hosts important exhibitions.

Stadtmuseum★ (Town Museum)

Lichtentaler Allee 10. Open year-round Tue–Sun 11am–6pm. Closed major holidays. ⊜5€. ☎(07221) 93 22 72. www.stadtmuseum-baden-baden.de. Two thousand years of town history are engagingly chronicled in this glass pavilion. Keep an eye out for rare coins, gambling paraphernalia, sculpture from across the epochs and an enchanting assortment of historical toys.

Abtei Lichtenthal★ (Lichtenthal Abbey)

Hauptstraße 40. ☛Guided tours Sun, Wed, Sat 3pm. ⊜4€. ☎(07221) 50 49 10. www.abtei-lichtenthal.de. Cistercian sisters have run this abbey for more than 750 years. The courtyard and the abbey itself are open to the public. The Princes Chapel (Fürstenkapelle) contains the tombs of the margraves of Baden.

ADDITIONAL SIGHTS
Neues Schloss (New Castle)

The former hilltop residence of the local margraves is closed to the public but is still a great place to enjoy a signature **panorama** of the town and surrounding hills.

Stiftskirche (Collegiate Church)

Climb the stairs up to Marktplatz (the market square) to visit the burial place of the Baden margraves of the 14C to the 18C. Several of their epitaphs are remarkable works of art that invite inspection. Of particular note is the 5.6m/18ft-high sandstone **Crucifix★**, a 1467 masterpiece by Nicolaus Gerhaert von Leyden and a fine example of late medieval sculpture.

Spa

Sample the restorative powers of Baden-Baden's mineral springs in two spa complexes: the **Friedrichsbad**, a neo-Renaissance style bathing palace with a Roman-Irish Bath; and the modern **Caracalla-Therme** with pools, saunas, whirlpools, grottoes and other relaxation stations. Both are open daily but the admission price depends on the length of your stay and treatment menu.

Römische Badruinen★ (Roman Bath Ruins)

Römerplatz 1. Open mid-Mar–mid-Nov 11am–noon and 3pm–4pm. ⊜2.50€. ☎(07221) 27 59 40. www.badruinen.de. Excavations beneath the Friedrichsbad have unearthed the remains of baths once used by Roman soldiers, including the ingenious floor heating systems and the well-preserved walls. Computer animation helps you visualise how it all looked originally.

EXCURSIONS
Yburgruinen★ (Yburg Castle Ruins)

▶6km/3.5mi SW via Friedrichstraße. The tower is all that survives of this 13C castle. From the top there are great **views★★** of the Rhine plain and the Baden vineyards.

Mount Merkur

▶2km/1.2mi east via Markgrafenstraße or bus 204 or 205 to Leopoldsplatz. Funicular (Merkurbergbahn) open daily 10am–10pm; ⊜4€ round-trip. From the top of the mountain, you have panoramic **views★** over Baden-Baden, west towards the Vosges Valley and east to the Murg Valley.

Rastatt★

▶19km/12mi N. Herrenstraße 18, 76437. ☎(07222) 972 1220. www.rastatt.de. Less than 10km/6.2mi from the French border, Rastatt straddles the Murg River just before it flows into the Rhine.

Schloss★ (Palace)

🎧 Guided tour (45min) Apr–Oct Tue–Sun 10am–5pm; Nov–Mar Tue–Sun 10am–4pm. Closed Dec 24–25 & 31. ⊜7€. 𝄞(07222) 97 83 85. www.schloss-rastatt.de.

This harmonious U-shaped palace was built in 1698–1707 by Italian master architect Domenico Egidio Rossi, who was replaced by **Michael Ludwig Rohrer** after Ludwig the Turk's death in 1707.

Royal Apartments – The margravial apartments are embellished with frescoes and stuccowork. **Ahnensaal** (Hall of Ancestors) sports column capitals decorated with stucco figures representing Turkish prisoners.

Wehrgeschichtliches Museum (Military Museum) – *(access via the south wing)*. Weapons, uniforms and pictures illustrate German military and general history from 1500 to 1918 (open Apr–Oct Tue–Sun 10am–5.30pm; Nov–Mar Tue–Sun 10am–4.30pm; closed Dec 24–25 & 31; ⊜7€; ♿; 𝄞07222 342 44; www.wgm-rastatt.de).

German Freedom Movements Memorial Museum – *(access via the north wing)* displays document German freedom movements from 1500 to the resistance in former East Germany up to 1990 (open year-round Sun–Thu 9.30am–5pm, Fri 9.30am–2pm; closed Jan 1, Dec 24–25 & 31; ♿; 𝄞07222 77 13 90; www.bundesarchiv.de/erinnerungsstaette).

Schloss Favorite★★

⊙ 5km/3mi southeast of Rastatt. 🎧 Guided tours (1hr) mid-Mar–Sept Tue–Sun 10am–6pm; Oct–mid-Nov Tue–Sun 10am–5pm. ⊜8€. 𝄞(07222) 412 07. www.schloss-favorite.de.

Margravine Sibylla Augusta of Baden-Baden commissioned this Baroque pleasure palace in 1710, partly to display her famous china, glass and faïence collections. The exterior is coated with a matrix of gravel and granite chips. The sumptuous **interior★★** sports floors of brilliant *scagliola* (stucco imitating encrusted marble) as well as mirrors, mosaics and precious chinoiserie.

ADDRESSES

🛏️ STAY

⊜⊜ **Hotel Am Markt** – *Marktplatz 18.* 𝄞07221 270 40. www.hotel-am-markt-baden.de. Closed 1–2 weeks mid-Dec. 23 rooms. ⬚. This attractive, quiet hotel-pension in the heart of the old town offers lovely bright rooms. Good value.

⊜⊜ **Schweizer Hof** – *Langestraße 73.* 𝄞07 221 30 460. www.schweizerhof.de. 42 rooms. ⬚. Set in the city centre, next to the opera house, this traditional hotel features rooms furnished in modern style, some with a balcony or terrace.

⊜⊜⊜⊜ **Atlantic Parkhotel** – *Goetheplatz 3.* 𝄞07 221 36 10. www.atlantic-parkhotel.de. 49 rooms. ⬚. Restaurants⊜⊜. Dating from 1836 (when it was the Englischer Hof), the Atlantic is a historic hotel with large and luxurious, but pricey, rooms. Breakfast can be taken on the pretty terrace.

🍴 EAT

⊜⊜ **Leo's** – *Luisenstraße 8–10.* 𝄞07221 380 81. www.leos-baden-baden.de. Open 10am–1am (2am Fri–Sat). A café, restaurant and wine bar in one, stylish, hip Leo's is the place to eat, drink and be seen in Baden-Baden, particularly as the night wears on. Mediterranean-inspired menu and wine list.

⊜⊜ **Weinstube im Baldreit** – *Küferstraße 3.* 𝄞07221 231 36. Open Tue–Sat 5pm. Closed Sun, Mon. Tucked away in a dead-end alley in the old town, this traditional Weinstube serves generous portions of local food with a French accent (the chef comes from just over the Rhine). Reduced menu at lunchtime.

TAKING A BREAK

Café König – *Lichtentaler Straße 12.* 𝄞(07221) 2 35 73. www.chocolatier.de. This legendary coffeehouse has counted Tolstoy and Liszt among its patrons. It is the best place in town to sample the famous liqueur-laced Black Forest gateau. In summer, sit outside on the lime-tree shaded terrace.

Baden Wine Route★★

The **Badische Weinstraße★★** winds sinuously for 400km/250mi through the vineyards on the lower slopes of the Black Forest, from Heidelberg to the Swiss border, crossing nine wine regions, which together comprise the third-largest wine-producing area in Germany. Ruby-red Pinot Noir, fruity Riesling, spicy-aromatic Pinot Gris, sweet Muscat and crisp Müller-Thurgau wines all hail from the soils of this diverse region. The driving tour below travels through the Ortenau district, where vineyards surround charming villages, sheltered from the peaks of the Black Forest. The mild climate, long hours of sunshine and spectacular views of the Rhine Valley and its imposing castle ruins make exploring the Baden Wine Route a joy.

- **Michelin Map:** 718 and 545 R 12–13 H 58–P62.
- **Info:** www.blackforest-tourism.com.
- **Location:** For a description of the entire Wine Route, see Michelin *Green Guide Alsace-Lorraine*. The tour here runs south from Baden-Baden.
- **Don't Miss:** Oberkirche or Durbach.
- **Timing:** Allow a day for the driving tour described, which follows minor roads.

DRIVING TOUR

L'ORTENAU

100km/62mi. Allow one day.

▷ Leave Baden-Baden on the B3 heading for Offenburg.

The sandstone hills of the northern Black Forest, south of Baden-Baden, allow the vineyards and orchards to flourish.

Steinbach

This enchanting village lies at the foot of the hills crowned by the ruined castle of Yburg. Note the monument in memory of Erwin von Steinbach, one of the architects of Strasbourg Cathedral.

Neuweier

Set at the foot of the castle, Neuweier vineyard produces a special variety of Riesling known as *mauerwein* (literally, "wall wine" as the ripest grapes come from vines planted next to the wall). The owners are descended from French nobility, who were originally authorised to bottle the wine by the Prince Arch-bishop of Würzburg (they also granted this privilege to the villages of Steinbach and Umweg Varnhalt). A special short-necked, fat-bellied *bocksbeutel* distinguishes the wines.

▷ At Altschweier, turn off the Wine Route to visit the town of Bühl.

Bühl

This small, busy market town is famous for its dark red plums and its Affental wine. The town's *Zwetschgenfest* (plum festival) takes place every year in September, during which delicious plum tarts and pies are on sale everywhere. The neo-Gothic collegiate church of St. Peter and St. Paul features beautiful modern stained glass (1955–1958) by Albert Burkart.

▷ Head back towards Altschweier as far as Bühlertal.

Bühlertal

The surrounding vineyards and forests provide a romantic setting for this small resort town that thrives, thanks to its mild climate.

▷ The road rises to Hof (the residential area of town). Turn right towards Neusatz and its 13C Waldsteg castle.

Windeck Castle★

This ancient circular castle was built in 1200 but was mostly destroyed in the 16C. Two towers, two rooms and a curtain wall survive. In the shadow of the towers, in the leafy castle grounds, is the modern but very charming Burg Windeck hotel-restaurant (*www.burg-windeck.de*), which enjoys a lovely **view**★ over the Rhine plain.

▶ Continue south for 7km/4.5mi to the L83a.

Sasbach

🚶 15min on foot; round trip.
Leave your car and enter the park.
An obelisk and a stele with inscriptions in French, German and Latin mark the spot where, in 1675, the Captain of Turenne (one of Louis XIV's commanding officers during the Imperial conquest of Franche-Comte) died from a bullet wound.
The Baroque-style parish church, dedicated to St. Bridget, retains some parts of an older Gothic building.

▶ Continue southeast via the L86a then turn left onto the L86.

Sasbachwalden★

This pretty spa village, which specialises in the Kneipp form of hydrotherapy, is a past winner of the national best-kept village competition. The historic centre features beautiful flower-decked half-timbered houses that have been lovingly conserved.
🚶 *Footpaths lead to the* **Mummelsee** *and the* **Hornisgrinde**.

▶ Retrace your steps then take the L86a south.

Kappelrodeck

This small wine-producing village of beautiful half-timbered houses lies in the Acher Valley. It can be reached on the **tourist railway** line from Achern to Ottenhöfen. **Schloss Rodeck** (11C, though remodelled in the Renaissance period) is the emblem of the village. According to local legend, in the 14C, the Hex vom Dasenstein (Witch of Dasenstein) lived below the castle. Her name has been adopted by the local wine cooperative: if you get the opportunity, try a bottle of the local red.

▶ Continue along the L86a south for 10km/6.5mi.

Oberkirch★

This charming town, owned by the bishops of Strasbourg from 1303 to 1803, is surrounded by orchards, vineyards and forests. Stroll along the Mühlbach (millstream) to see its quaint half-timbered houses, which go back as far as the 17C. Oberkirch holds two records: the largest strawberry market

Windeck Castle

© Jens Schmitz/imagebroker/age fotostock.com

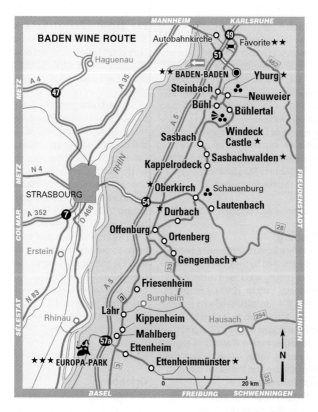

in Germany and the largest number of distilleries. Its raspberry, cherry and plum brandies have become famous.

The city is dominated by the ruins of Schauenburg Castle, which was founded in the 11C by the Dukes of Zähringen; from the castle, there are panoramic views of the Rhine Valley towards Strasbourg.

The Zum Silbernen Stern, now a historic guesthouse *(www.silberner-stern.de)*, in Oberkirch-Gaisbach, was the home of the great 17C writer **Hans Jakob Christoffel von Grimmelshausen**, who wrote his famous novel, *Der Abenteuerliche Simplicissimus Teutsch*, here. He also lived in the nearby village of Renchen, where he became mayor.

▷ Follow the B 28 east for 3.5km/2mi.

Lautenbach

Set among meadows, vineyards and forests in the Rench Valley, Lauten-bach is known for its various kinds of stone fruits and strawberries. From the town there are good views from several points over the valleys of the Rhine and the Rench.

The late-Gothic pilgrimage **Church of Maria Himmelfahrt** contains one of the few surviving medieval rood screens in Germany. It also has a superb altar, with one of the finest Gothic triptychs in the region. Created in the late 15C, it is attributed to the Strasbourg School and is a brilliant combination of sculpture and painting. In the central part, the polychrome statues of St. John the Baptist and St. John the Evangelist frame a Madonna on a crescent moon. The two early 16C side altars hold 15C stained glass from the workshop of Peter Hummel Andlau.

▷ Return towards Oberkirch then take the K5369 south.

Durbach★

The municipality of Durbach has been growing vines, most notably Traminer and Riesling varieties, since the Middle Ages. Since 1836 they have also been cultivating Sauvignon following an exchange with the owners of the famous Chateau-Yquem vineyards. The village of Durbach enjoys a pretty **location**★ surrounded by vineyards. Its picturesque centre is dominated by the 11C **Schloss Staufenberg** and is a popular tourist destination.

▶ Continue east on the K5369.

Offenburg

Originally a Roman settlement, but re-founded in 1148 by the Dukes of Zähringen, Offenburg was raised to the status of Imperial City in 1240 by Emperor Frederick II. Unfortunately its development was abruptly halted in 1689 when the troops of Louis XIV burnt the city down during the War of the League of Augsburg. Today it functions as the administrative and industrial centre of the Ortenau region.

The **Hauptstraße** and adjacent alleyways (in the pedestrian zone) are lined with interesting houses and picturesque squares. A Baroque building from 1720, the Unicorn Pharmacy (Einhornapotheke) has a scrolled façade on which stands a unicorn. Note also the Fountain of Neptune dating from 1783; the Fischmarkt (fish market); the Hirschapotheke (Stag Pharmacy) of 1698; and before it the Lion Fountain (Löwenbrunnen) of 1599.

The **Heilig-Kreuz-Kirche**★ (Church of the Holy Spirit) in Pfarrstraße is an elegant if sober Baroque building. It dates from 1700, built on the foundations of a 13C church destroyed by the fire of 1689. The interior exudes a feeling of great harmony. The main altar and side altars are the work of Franz Lichtenauer (1740); the altar table is by Joseph Esperlin (1737). Note the remarkable Neoclassical pulpit of marble and stucco by Johann Nepomuk Speckert (1795), and the superbly carved gate of the Rococo organ loft.

The Baroque **Franziskanerkloster** (Church of the Franciscan Monastery), built in 1702, has a richly decorated altar and Silbermann organ. In the cloister chapel is an early 16C statue of the Virgin.

In **Spitalstraße**, near the fish market, Sankt-Andreas-Hospital (St. Andrew's Hospital) dates from the 18C. Note on the outside of the adjoining church buildings the 14C Gothic Madonna. Also on the same street is the imposing Old Granary, a large and impressive space, home to exhibitions and cultural events. Dating from 1741, the **Rathaus** (town hall) is a well-proportioned building. The city coat of arms and the double eagle on the balcony above are reminders that the city belonged to Austria from the mid-16C until 1706 and again, from 1771 to 1805. The town hall carillon, which consists of 25 bronze bells, delights both locals and visitors with its repertoire of 100 tunes.

▶ Head southeast on the L99.

Ortenberg

This "village of wine, flowers and fountains" is dominated by the **Schloss Ortenberg**. Built in the 12C by the Dukes of Zähringen to protect the entrance to the Kinzig Valley, it was destroyed in 1678 by the French and rebuilt in 1838 by Friedrich Eisenlohr, who created a building in the Gothic Revival style of the period.

The castle is now home to one of the most modern youth hostels in Germany. Just outside the village at Ortenberg-Käfersberg, the **Bühlwegkapelle Mariä Ruh** (Mariä Ruh Chapel) dates from 1497 and is renowned for its remarkable early 15C Flamboyant-Gothic style murals.

▶ Continue 7.5km/4.5mi on the L99.

Gengenbach★

Set on the banks of the River Kinzig, in the heart of the Ortenau district, Gengenbach is a charming, well-preserved historic city. Here, the medieval and the Baroque happily rub shoulders, having avoided the ravages of the Thirty Years'

War. Gengenbach was raised to the status of Free City in 1360, and became a Protestant stronghold after the Reformation in 1525. However, from 1547, the town, now under Austrian law, again embraced the Catholic faith.

The picturesque streets of the **Old Town★** are lined with half-timbered houses and gabled Baroque buildings. The Hochtor and the Kinzigtor (city gate) towers are two remnants of the town's medieval fortifications. The late-18C Rathaus stands on the market square. Next to the Old Town, Gengenbach's huge 18C convent conceals an ancient Benedictine foundation, predating it by a thousand years.

The Romanesque early 12C **Church of St. Mary** features a chancel rebuilt in the Gothic period and surmounted by an elegant Baroque tower by Jakob Risch. The interior was remodelled in the Romanesque Revival style between 1892 and 1906 and decorated with many paintings. Note too the beautiful baroque stalls, baptismal font and altar of St. Joseph. Near the church is the old abbey mill and overhead, the millrace that once supplied it. Two museums worth a visit are the **Flößerei- und Verkehrsmuseum** (Timber Rafting and Traffic Museum), housed in an old gate-keeper's lodge that is classified as a historical monument, and the **Carnival Museum** in the Niggelturm.

The town and its surrounding area are also popular with visitors on account of its mild weather and sports facilities, particularly fishing, horseback riding, hiking and biking.

▷ Head south out of Gengenbach, on the B 33 and go back (north) in the direction of Offenburg. Turn left off the B 33 towards Zunsweier, head south through Diersburg, then turn left onto the B 3.

Friesenheim and Schuttern

Friesenheim is a small town with handsome half-timbered houses. Between Friesenheim and Schuttern *(2km/1mi west)*, the remains of a Roman city have been excavated.

At **Schuttern**, visit the Convent Church of Mariä Himmelfahrt. During the Middle Ages Schuttern was home to the wealthy monastery of **Offoniscella**, founded in 603. It was completely destroyed in the 19C (only the rectory remains), but the site has been excavated to reveal the oldest **mosaic** in Germany; it dates from the 11C, is in the shape of a 3m/20ft diameter medallion and covers the tomb of the abbey founder, an Irish-Scottish monk named Offo.

▷ Continue south on the B3.

Lahr

Don't be put off by the industrial suburbs of this city of 42 000 inhabitants. It boasts a fine old historic centre. Highlights are the early 17C **Altes Rathaus** (old town hall) and the **Storchenturm**, a remnant of its 13C castle.

The **Burgheim** church dates back to the Carolingian period, though its belfry is Romanesque. In the nave are frescoes (1463) depicting St. Christopher and the Holy Trinity, while the murals in the choir were completed in 1482.

▷ Continue south on the B3.

Kippenheim

The church of St-Maurice was built between the 16C and 18C with a fan-vault ceiling and late-Gothic interior. The town hall is decorated with a stepped gable roof and a Renaissance oriel window. Note the two pretty houses adjacent to it that date from the 16C to 19C.

▷ Leave the Wine Route and make a 6km/3.5mi-round-trip detour.

Mahlberg

This small town is home to a 13C castle, a Baroque chapel dedicated to St. Catherine and the interesting **Oberrheinisches Tabakmuseum** (Museum of Tobacco; ✆078 25 71 42; open May–Sept Sun and holidays 10am–5pm; ⌾3.50€; www.tabakmuseum-mahlberg.de).

▷ Get back on the B3.

Ettenheim

Ettenheim owes its name to the Duke of Alsace (Etichon II), and until 1803 was part of the bishopric of Strasbourg. The **old town** is separated from the rest of the city by two 18C gates, and spreads around the large parish church. Opposite the town hall rises the gable of the former palace of **Cardinal de Rohan**, one of the main protagonists in the Affair of the Diamond Necklace, a scandal that rocked late 18C France and shook the faith of the people in the monarchy. The church further along Rohanstraße holds the tomb of the Cardinal.

The **Mühlenwanderweg** (Mills Trail, 2hrs 30min) leads to the mills of Ettenbach, Ettenheim and Ettenheim-münster.

Take the L103 east for 6km/3.5mi.

Ettenheimmünster★

The town nestles in the picturesque Münster Valley, and was formerly the seat of a Benedictine monastery, dissolved in 1803. Today only its well-proportioned pilgrim church remains.

Built between 1687 and 1689, the church of **St. Landelin** was enlarged in the 18C, and its Gothic tower added in the middle of the 19C. The interior, and in particular the altar, is heavily decorated with some notable sculptures, stuccowork and ceiling frescoes. The most precious treasure is a reliquary **bust★** of the Celtic missionary saint and martyr St. Landelin, created by a Strasbourg silversmith in 1506. It contains the skull of Landelin, who was murdered here in 640. The splendid **organ★**, built in 1769 by **Johann Andreas Silbermann**, is the best-preserved organ on the whole east bank of the Rhine (concerts are held during the summer months).

ADDRESSES

🛏 STAY

FRIESENHEIM

Mühlenhof – Oberweierer Hauptstraße 33, 77948 Friesenheim-Oberweier. ℰ078 21 63 20. www.land hotel-muehlenhof.de. 32 rooms. ☲. Restaurant☺☺, closed Tue. Closed 2.5 weeks Feb and 2.5 weeks Aug. This hotel-restaurant in a rustic setting serves carefully prepared regional dishes.

SASBACHWALDEN

Tannenhof – Murberg 6, 77887 Sasbachwalden. ℰ078 41 640 70. www.relaxhotel-tannenhof.de. 18 rooms. ☲. This small, traditional hotel surrounded by vineyards offers modern rooms with traditional wooden furnishings. Wellness centre. Dinner for residents only.

GENGENBACH

Hirsch – Dorfstraße 9, 77791 Gengenbach-Berghaupten. ℰ078 03 939 70. www.hirsch-berghaupten.de. 23 rooms. ☲6€. Large bedrooms and regional specialities are hallmarks.

🍴 EAT

KAPPELRODECK

Zum Rebstock – Kutzendorf 1, 77876 Kappelrodeck-Waldulm. ℰ07842 94 80. www.rebstock-waldulm.de. Closed Mon–Wed lunch (open Mon–Tue for hotel guests only). This quintessential local inn has been family-run since 1750. Tasty regional dishes. Also has rustic, country-style rooms for overnight stays.

OBERKIRCH

Haus am Berg – Am Rebhof 5, 77704 Oberkirch. ℰ078 02 47 01. www.haus-am-berg-oberkirch.de. Closed Tue. This traditional Landhaus enjoys a superb panorama across the vineyards; its terrace has views as far as Strasbourg. International cooking with local flavours in a family atmosphere.

LAHR

Grüner Baum – Burgheimer Straße 105, 77933 Lahr. ℰ078 21 222 82. www.gruenerbaum-lahr.de. This traditional rural hotel has bright, modern rooms. Regional dishes are prepared according to the season and have a Mediterranean accent. Pleasant courtyard terrace.

Europa-Park★★★

In this theme park dedicated to Europe, more than 100 attractions and shows take visitors on a tour of 12 European countries: the character of each country, from the architecture to the vegetation and the gastronomy, is brought to life in great detail. In addition, the park, famous for its rollercoasters, offers excitement for every member of the family.

Use the map given to you at the entrance to find your way among the various countries.
You might also like to get an overall view on board the panoramic EP-Express with main stations in Germany, England, Greece, Russia and Spain. The woodland and lake setting greatly enhances the appeal of the park. (⊙Note that there may be long queues at the main attractions.)

Germany

Your tour of Europe starts with the host country. Stroll along the German Alley lined with typical architecture from the different regions of Germany. Enjoy the rose garden of the medieval Balthasar Castle, and then take a look at a piece of the Berlin Wall.

▷ **Location:** Europa-Park is on the outskirts of Rust, between Freiburg and Strasbourg: *Europa-Park-Straße 2, 77977 Rust-bei-Freiburg. ℘018 057 766 88. www.europapark.de.*

France

For a breathtaking view of the Park and the Rhine Valley as far as the Vosges and the Black Forest, take a glass lift up the Euro-Tower (75m). The super-fast and high Silver Star rollercoaster offers guaranteed thrills, as does Eurostat, a roller coaster speeding "through space" in the dark. Take a 10-minute break to enjoy a 4D movie experience accompanied by tactile, sound and olfactory effects. Follow up with an easy stroll past the charming bistros and old-fashioned boutiques of the *"quartier français"*.

Switzerland

The Swiss village with its old watermill and wooden chalets sets the scene. Take a thrilling bobsleigh ride down a metal run at 50km/hr/30mph, then maybe a spinning plane ride or a Wild Mouse ride featuring a vertical lift and a hair-raising nose dive.

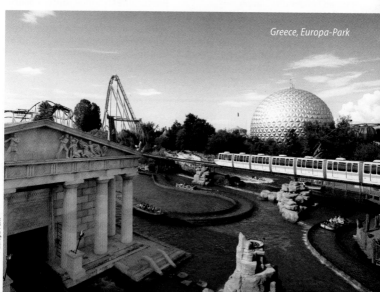
Greece, Europa-Park

© Europa-Park

PRACTICAL INFORMATION

☎ *(0180) 577 66 88. www.europapark.de*.
♿. Hours change daily; call or check
the website. Closed 3 weeks in Nov &
mid-Jan–Mar. ☜35-41€ (child 30-36€),
including train; multi-day tickets are
available.

GETTING THERE

By car from Strasbourg, follow the
road to Kuhl and take exit 57b to Rust,
or drive along D468 then D5 and take
the ferry at Rhinau. Small parking
charge. By shuttle from Strasbourg
(Gare de Strasbourg) (info: ☎07723 96
990; www.expressdrive.de)*.

VISITOR INFORMATION

Three information offices (ATM
machines, lost property) located by
the lake, at the main entrance (locker
and buggy rental) and in Spain.
Nestlé Schöller meeting points can be
found in every themed area.

WHERE TO STAY

Possibilities in Rust include the
peaceful, comfortable Pension Kern
(Franz-Sales-Straße 30, 77977 Rust;
☎*07822 61 278; www.pensionkern.de;*
7 rooms; 80€; ☕).
For accommodation in Europa-Park
see the next page.

Greece

Welcome to Mykonos, one of the Greek
islands. At "Cassandra's Curse" you can
discover the power of illusions, followed
by a thrilling trip on the Poseidon water
rollercoaster through Greek mythology.
Wrap up by venturing into the legendary world of the sunken city of Atlantis.

Russia

Discover a country full of contrasts from
the traditional craftsmen's village to the
Mir Space Station, and test your nerves
on the Euro-Mir ride with spinning gondolas hurtling towards the ground at a
speed of 80km/hr/50mph.

Spain

Do not miss the spectacular stunts
of the Duel of the Brothers featuring
knights on horseback fighting it out in

the arena or the flamenco show staged
by the "Ballet Español".

Other Countries

Plunge into a gigantic wave in Portugal,
experience the famous Venice Carnival
in Italy, race along the Silverstone racetrack or book a seat at the Globe Theatre
in England, get caught up in a pirates'
attack on a Dutch colony in Holland,
take a refreshing fjord-rafting ride in
Scandinavia or float in a tree trunk down
a fast-flowing river in the Austrian Tyrol.

👥 Children's World

Boats, slides, roundabouts, a beach,
climbing walls, a Viking ship, the
Children's Lighthouse and other attractions keep kids busy here and in the
Adventure Land.

Success Story

The Mack family, which has produced fairground vehicles since 1780 and
rollercoasters for the largest theme parks in the world since 1921, set up Europa-
Park in 1975 as a showcase for its various ride models. The chosen location in the
small border village of Rust was a surprise for many, but the grounds of Balthasar
Castle (1442) offered 60ha/148acres of beautiful greenery. The European theme
adopted in 1982 asserted the originality of the park. Since then, the park has
consistently expanded and won many awards. Can we then speak of a model
company? Maybe. Today the park sets itself apart from similar ventures by its
concern for the environment (use of electric vehicles, solar panels).

ADDRESSES

🏠 STAY

Accommodation inside the park includes themed hotels, a guesthouse, a campsite and a tipi village. *Hotel and guesthouse reservation:* 📞 *07822 8600.*

Portugiesisches Kloster – Enjoy upmarket comforts within the setting of a historical monastery.

Hotel Colosseo – This is one of the largest hotels in Germany; designed in the style of Ancient Rome, it features opulent décor, 324 family rooms and 22 luxury suites, typical Italian restaurants, cafés and bars and a wellness area.

Hotel El Andaluz, Hotel Castillo Alcazar – Both hotels are steeped in Andalusian atmosphere: the first is designed in the style of a Spanish *"finca"* with terra-cotta floors and arcades, whereas the second suggests the grander style of a Spanish castle at the time of the Reconquista.

Circus Rolando – This guesthouse in the German area is convivial and offers good value for money (23 rooms, swimming pool and sauna).

Campsite – The campsite has an idyllic location by a lake (200 pitches for camping cars and caravans; vast meadow for tents; playground, breakfast room and boutique; no prior reservation).

Tipi village – A Wild West atmosphere prevails: heated tipis, log cabins and covered wagons *(bring sleeping bags and towels – breakfast in the Western Saloon – reservation:* 📞 *+49 (0) 7822 860 5566, camp-resort@europapark.de).*

🍽 EAT

Inside the park, dozens of restaurants and fast-food places reflect the diversity of European cuisine: French flavour at Marianne's, Scandinavian-style fish at the Fiskhuset, tapas at the Bodega or Greek specialities at the Mykonos.

Freiburg im Breisgau★★

Sunny Freiburg is one of the most attractive cities in southern Germany. Its 500 year-old university, the old town's cobbled lanes lined by half-timbered houses, a majestic cathedral and an easy-going Mediterranean flair make it a perfect base for exploring the Black Forest. Freiburg is a leader when it comes to alternative energies, especially solar energy and energy-efficient structures.

▶ **Population:** 219 670

🛈 **Info:** Rathausplatz 2–4. 📞 (0761) 388 18 80; www.freiburg.de.

▶ **Location:** Midway between Basel and Strasbourg, on the Rhine plain.

🅿 **Parking:** Garages are located throughout the city.

👁 **Don't Miss:** The Münster and Augustinermuseum.

🕐 **Timing:** Allow a day for the cathedral and the old town.

A BIT OF HISTORY

Freiburg was founded in the 12C by the Dukes of Zähringen, who conferred upon it a number of special privileges, hence the town's name, which literally means "free town". When the dynasty died out in 1388, the town passed under Habsburg rule (until 1798). It was here in 1770 that the Archduchess Marie-Antoinette said farewell to Austrian territory and set out for Strasbourg, and her life as the bride of the future Louis XVI, and later, victim of the guillotine in 1773. Napoleon ended five centuries of Austrian rule. In the second half of the 19C, Freiburg won renewed importance as a place of research and learning, thanks to its university.

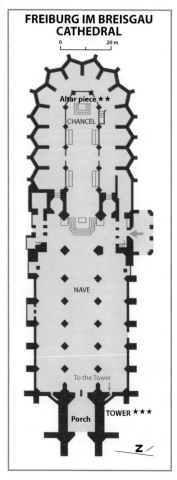

FREIBURG IM BREISGAU CATHEDRAL

0   20 m

Altar piece ★★

CHANCEL

NAVE

To the Tower

Porch   TOWER ★★★

Z

SIGHT
Münster★★ (Cathedral)

Pick up an English-language brochure in the information centre, Herrenstraße 30 (behind the cathedral). Open year-round Mon–Sat 10am–5pm, Sun 1pm–7.30pm. & ℘(0761) 208 5963. www.freiburger-muenster.info.

Work on Freiburg's magnificent cathedral began around 1200 in Romanesque style, but today all that remains from this period is the transept crossing and the two "Cockerel Towers" flanking it. In 1354, work started on a Gothic chancel. The grand design and severity of the times meant that construction was not finished until 1513. The cathedral's **north side** features an interesting 14C

tympanum above the door illustrating the theme of Original Sin. The **West Tower★★★** is surmounted by a delicate spire. Four sharply jutting projections form a star at the foot of the tower house. On the **south side,** statues of the apostles and the Old Testament kings stand on the buttresses of this richly ornate façade.

The cathedral's **west porch and doorway** feature late 13C figures. On the left wall, Satan, disguised as a knight, leads a procession. The doorway, guarded by statues representing the Church (left) and the Synagogue (with eyes covered, right) deals with the mystery of the Redemption.

The **nave** is embellished with graceful galleries and statuary: **(1)** the Virgin at the pillar (1270–80); **(2)** a late-Gothic pulpit (1560); **(3)** a statue of Berthold V, last of the Dukes of Zähringen and founder of Freiburg; **(4)** the Holy Sepulchre, from c. 1330; **(5)** 13C stained-glass medallions in the windows; and **(6)** a 1505 group sculpture, the Adoration of the Magi.

The **chancel** includes many more works of note, including **(a)** a Rococo baptismal font and **(b)** a 1521 Oberried altarpiece in the University Chapel. The two side panels, the *Nativity* and *Adoration of the Magi*, are by Hans Holbein the Younger. Also worth closer inspection are: **(c)** in the second Imperial Chapel *(Kaiserkapelle)*, an altarpiece depicting Rest during the Flight to Egypt by Hans Wydyz on the central panel; **(d)** a painting of the Crucifixion, in back of the large Hans Baldung Grien altarpiece; **(e)** the Romanesque Locherer Crucifix in beaten silver by Böcklin; and **(f)** an altarpiece in the Locherer Chapel by Sixt von Staufen (1521–24). The carved portion depicts the Virgin. The central panel of the **Hochalter★★** (high altar) by **Hans Baldung Grien** (1512–16) portrays the Coronation of the Virgin.

Ascend the **West Tower** (open year-round Mon–Sat 9.30am–4.45pm, Sun 1pm–5pm; ∞1.50€; ℘0761 285 37 11) along the stairway leading to the tower room. The upper platform beneath the beautiful spire offers **views★** over the city, Kaiserstuhl and the Vosges.

👣WALKING TOUR

Allow 1hr 30min not including visits.

Rathausplatz★

The pleasant town hall square has flowered balconies and a fountain featuring Berthold Schwarz, said to have invented gunpowder in Freiburg in 1350.

Haus zum Walfisch (House of the Whale)

Franziskanerstraße 3.

This building (1516) boasts an ornamented late-Gothic façade topped by an oriel. It served as the refuge of the Humanist philosopher Erasmus, one of the key figures of the Reformation.

◗ Cross Kaiser-Joseph-Straße and follow Marktgasse.

Münsterplatz

The buildings facing the cathedral across this central square were all designed with municipal or ecclesiastical prestige in mind. They include: the **Erzbischöfliches Palais** (Archbishop's Palace from 1756); the **Historisches Kaufhaus★** (Historical House of Trade) the centre of commercial life in the Middle Ages; and the **Wentzinger-**

haus (1761) with a splendid Rococo staircase. Originally the private residence of renowned local artist Johann Christian Wentzinger, it now houses a local history museum, the **Museum für Stadtgeschichte** (open year-round Tue–Sun 10am–5pm; closed Jan 1, Dec 24–25 & 31; 3€; 0761 201 25 15; www.freiburg.de).

▷ Exit the square by the Buttergasse alley next to Wentzingerhaus Kaufhaus and then turn left into Schusterstraße to join Konviktstraße, a pleasant shopping street that was rebuilt in the 1960s.

Schwabentor (Swabian Gate)

From the Swabian Gate, which is a rare relic from the medieval fortifications, follow along the *Gewerbekanal* (canal). This "Insel" quarter was home to the artisans who depended on water or watermills to pursue their work: tanners, tailors, gemstone cutters and millers.

▷ Walking along the canal which, according to legend, hides the head of a crocodile, you pass close by the local modern art museum (Marienstraße 10a) to arrive at Augustinerplatz.

Augustinermuseum★★

Augustinerplatz. Open year-round Tue–Sun 10am–5pm. Closed Jan 1, Dec 24–25 & 31. 7€ (valid for all municipal museums). (0761) 201 25 31. www.freiburg.de.

Housed in a former monastery church, this museum contains an exquisite but small collection of art from the Middle Ages to the 19C. Key attractions include the original stone figures and stained-glass windows from Freiburg's Cathedral, as well as wooden sculptures and panel paintings by Matthias Grünewald, Lucas Cranach the Elder and Hans Baldung Grien. The choir is dedicated to Baroque works, while the top floor displays 19C paintings by such practitioners as Anselm Feuerbach, Franz Xaver Winterhalter and Hans Thoma.

▷ Follow Grünwälderstraße. At no 2 is the entrance to the market hall (Markthalle). Arriving at Kaiser-Joseph-Straße, continue left to return to the centre.

ADDITIONAL SIGHTS
Schlossberg★

On this last foothill of the Black Forest (456m/1 500ft), woods have almost completely enshrouded Zähringen Castle. A trail leads from the Schwabentor to the summit, where you can enjoy panoramic views from the lookout tower. *(Cable-car service.)*

Archäologisches Museum Colombischlössle★ (Archaeological Museum at Colombi Palace)

Rotteckring 5. Open year-round Tue–Sun 10am–5pm. Closed Jan 1, Dec 24–25 & 31. 4€. (0761) 201 25 74. www.freiburg.de.

This neo-Gothic villa in the heart of town and surrounded by vineyards houses extensive archaeological displays. Female statuettes from the Stone Age, mysterious moon idols from the Bronze Age and treasures from Celtic royal tombs are among the highlights.

EXCURSIONS
Kaiserstuhl★

▷ Around 31km/19mi northwest of Freiburg. Leave Freiburg on Lessingstraße and go to Breisach via Gottenheim.

A small volcanic massif rising from the Baden plain, the Kaiserstuhl (the Emperor's Throne; 557m/1 828ft) enjoys a warm, dry climate particularly suitable for orchards and vineyards. In fact, the wines of Achkarren, Ihringen, Bickensohl and Oberrotweil are considered among the finest in the region.

Villages along the route that are worth a stop include **Endingen★**, with its fine old market square, and **Burkheim★**, occupying a picturesque spot on the southwest slope of the Kaiserstuhl.

Breisach★ – During the 17C Breisach was at the core of a system of fortifications that were among the most powerful in Europe. However the city was mostly laid waste by French Revolutionaries in 1793 and during the Allied Invasion in 1945, it was again 85 percent destroyed.

The most important building to survive is the **Münster St. Stephan★** (St. Stephen's Cathedral). Its nave, transept and towers are Romanesque; the richly decorated Gothic choir includes an exquisitely carved **altarpiece★** (1526). In the first bay (west), note the late 15C Last Judgement mural by Colmarien Schongauer.

From the **Burgplatz★**, there is a fine view of the peaks of the southern Black Forest, the heights of Sundgau, the Grand Ballon (highest point of the Vosges massif) and the terraces of Kaiserstuhl.

Badenweiler

❍ 36km/22mi south, take the B3 out of Freiburg. Ernst-Eisenlohr-Straße 4. ✆07 632 79 93 00. www.badenweiler.de. This relaxing small Black Forest spa village is set amid orchards and vineyards on a sunny south-facing hillside. As well as its famous spa there are natural hot springs here.

Parc Thermal (Kurpark)★★ – This modern spa enjoys a lovely setting in the grounds of the old castle (Schlosspark), surrounded by tropical plants, cedars, cypresses and huge redwoods. The park includes the remains of Roman baths, once the largest complex north of the Alps, now protected by a large glass tunnel (open Apr–Oct daily 10am–7pm; Nov–Mar 10am–5pm; ⊚2€). From the castle ruins, **views★** stretch over the Rhine Valley and the Vosges Mountains.

Blauen★

❍ 45km/28mi southwest of Freiburg and 8km/5mi southeast of Badenweiler. Blauen look-out tower offers a fine **panorama★★** of the Rhine plain. At a height of 1 165m/3 822ft, this peak of the southern Black Forest provides a sweeping view that takes in the highest point of the Vosges massif to the west, the summit of the Belchen (the third-highest mountain in the Black Forest) to the northeast, and on a clear day, the Alps to the south. Down below, the two parallel ribbons of the Rhine and the Rheinseitenkanal (Alsace Grand Canal) are a rewarding sight.

Schloss Bürgeln★ (Bürgeln Castle)

❍ 46km/28.5mi south of Freiburg, 10km/6mi south of Badenweiler. ☞Guided visits (1hr) Mar–Oct daily 11am, 2pm, 3pm, 4pm, 5pm; Nov–Feb Fri–Sun, 2pm, 3pm, 4pm. Also by appointment year-round. ⊚6€. ✆(076 26) 2 37. www.schlossbuergeln.de. Surrounded by neat, terraced gardens, this country manor, built in 1762 for the abbots of St-Blasien, dominates the foothills of the Black Forest. The interior features fancy Rococo plasterwork.

Burg Rötteln (Rötteln Castle)★

❍ 63km/39mi south of Freiburg, at Lörrach; 27km/16.5mi south of Badenweiler. Open mid-Mar–mid-Oct daily 10am–6pm; mid-Nov–early Mar Sat–Sun and holidays 11am–4pm. ⊚2€. ✆(07621) 564 94. www.burgruine-roetteln.de. Ruins are all that remain of this 14C complex, destroyed during the Palatinate War of Succession. Only the upper parts of the castle – its defensive core – with ramps and a bridge, are accessible. The Grüner Turm (Green Tower), which now dominates the scene, has been restored and converted into a look-out tower. The view embraces the valley of the Wiese (right up until it disappears into the Basel area); the wooded Blauen Mountains; the gentle hills of the Black Forest; and on the horizon, the Swiss Alps.

ADDRESSES

☺ STAY

☺☺ Schwarzwälder Hof –
Herrenstraße 43. ☎0761 380 30. www. shof.de. 40 rooms. ☐. Restaurant☺☺ (closed Sun & 2–3 weeks in Aug). This smart hotel marries modern comforts with Black Forest charm and discreet service.

☺☺☺ Hotel Am Stadtgarten –
Karlstraße 12. ☎0761 28 29 002. www. hotelamstadtgarten.de. Closed Jan. 35 rooms. ☐14€. A 5-minute walk from the centre, this new design hotel is nothing to look at from the exterior, but inside are chic, fashionable bedrooms (some with a balcony) and stylish public areas.

☺☺☺ Hotel Zum Roten Bären –
Oberlinden 12. ☎(0761) 38 78 70. www.roter-baeren.de. 25 rooms. ☐. Restaurant ☺☺☺, closed Sun. If you want to stay in Germany oldest hotel, book a room in this gem near the Schwabentor. Don't worry, rooms have all the mod-cons you'd expect, while the cosy restaurant is a fine place to enjoy Swiss-influenced cuisine.

☺ EAT

☺ Hausbrauerei Feierling –
Gerberau 46. ☎(0761) 24 34 80. www.feierling.de. This micro-brewery brews its own organic beer in copper vats still visible from the gallery. Regional cuisine is served here and in the beer garden across the road.

☺ Osteria Freiburg – *Grünwälderstraße 2. ☎0761 32054. Closed Sun– Mon. www. osteria-freiburg.de.* Parma hams and strings of garlic hang from the ceiling in this Belle-Epoque decorated informal restaurant. Wash down the excellent antipasti with Italian and Portuguese wines.

☺☺ Gasthaus Kybfelsen –
Schauinslandstraße 49, 79100 Freiburg-Günterstal, 5km/3mi south of Freiburg. ☎0761 21 11 99 26. www.kybfelsen-freiburg.de. Closed weekdays lunch. This smart, recently renovated brasserie is a landmark on the main road. Regional specialities are served in its two rustic dining rooms or in its beer garden.

☺☺ Schlossbergrestaurant Dattler –
Am Schlossberg 1 (follow Wintererstraße or take the Schlossberg cable-car). ☎(0761) 13 71 700. www.dattler.de. Closed Tue. Enjoy fabulous views over Freiburg's rooftops from this hilltop fine-dining restaurant. Ask about their value-priced lunch specials.

☺☺ Zur Tanne – *Altgasse 2, 79112 Freiburg-Opfingen, 9km/5.5mi west. ☎766 418 10. www.tanne-opfingen.de. Closed Mon–Tue. 10 rooms, from 59€. ☐.* An abundance of carved woodwork and an old tiled oven characterise this typical 100-year old Black Forest restaurant. Its guest rooms have been simply but tastefully furnished.

TAKING A BREAK

Markthalle – *Grünwälderstrasse 4. ☎(0761) 45 15 30 00. www.markthalle-freiburg.de. Closed Sun.* With piles of fruit and vegetables, mountains of bread, buckets of olives, Freiburg's market is a smorgasbord of culinary delights from the world over. Stock up, eat in, take out.

NIGHTLIFE

Kagan – *Bismarckallee 9 (in the building beside the central station; take the lift). ☎(0761) 7 67 27 66. www.kagan-lounge.de.* At German-American designer Vladimir Kagan's posh party palace, you can sip your cocktails with a view from the 17th floor, then hit the dancefloor on the 18th.

UC Café – *Niemensstr. 7 (between Bertoldstraße and Kaiser-Joseph-Straße). ☎(0761) 38 33 55.* Sit below a shady maple tree at this popular café in Freiburg's pedestrian zone, where visitors stop for coffee and snacks.

Constance★

Konstanz

Presumed to have been founded by Roman Emperor Constantius Chlorus (AD 292–306), Konstanz (Constance) has an enviable location right on the shores of its namesake lake. It has a well-preserved old town and a lively vibe, thanks to a large student population. It is also the gateway to the "flower island" of Mainau and charming Reichenau Island with its ancient abbey.

A BIT OF HISTORY

Council of Constance – From 1414 to 1418, a council convened in Koblenz to resolve the Great Schism that had led to the simultaneous existence of three popes. The only conclave ever held north of the Alps concluded in 1417 with the election of Pope Martin V.

Two years earlier this same council had summoned before it the Bohemian religious reformer **Jan Hus**, rector of the University of Prague. Regarded as a threat to the Church's hold on power, Hus was declared a heretic and burned at the stake; his Reformist ideas were categorically rejected. A precursor of Protestantism, he was hailed in his native Bohemia as a national hero.

◣◆◗WALKING TOUR

Allow 90min. Leave from the tourist office, crossing the railway tracks via the underground passageway.

Seeufer★ (Lake Shore)

The easy-going, almost Italianate charm and ambience of Konstanz is particularly evident along its lakeside. Just beyond the boat dock *(near the tourist office)* is the **Konzilgebäude** (council building), the warehouse where the Council of Constance convened in the 15C; it is now used as a concert and congress hall.

At the bottom of the jetty, the 10m/32.8ft-high **Imperia** is a slowly rotating

▶ **Population:** 82 600

▉ **Info:** Bahnhofplatz 43. ℰ(07531) 13 30 30. www.konstanz-tourismus.de.

◗ **Location:** Bordering Switzerland, Konstanz sits at the point separating Lake Constance (Bodensee in German) from its picturesque prolongation (Untersee). The islands of Mainau *(to the north)* and Reichenau *(to the west)* are linked to the town by a causeway.

◉ **Don't Miss:** The beautiful islands of Mainau and Reichenau.

◔ **Timing:** Allow two hours to tour Mainau Island.

♟ **Kids:** Outdoor activities on Mainau and Reichenau islands (◖see Excursions).

monumental female sculpture created by artist Peter Lenk in 1993. It satirises the influence the Italian courtesan Imperia wielded as the lover of members of the Council; she was immortalised by Honoré de Balzac in his novel *Ribald Tales (Contes drôlatiques)*.

Across the road, in the municipal gardens *(Stadtgarten)*, stands a monument to Count Ferdinand von Zeppelin (1838–1917), the celebrated airship inventor. He was born in Constance on the Insel, a tiny island in the Stadtgarten that is reached via a footbridge.

Across the Rheinbrücke (bridge) and along the Rheinsteig rise the old **defence towers** (Rheintorturm, Pulverturm). On the opposite bank, the Seestraße *(to the right)* is lined with Jugendstil villas.

◗ Follow Rheingasse, which takes you past an elegant early-17C building with a striking red façade housing the cathedral priory. Go left on Inselgasse and right on Brückengasse to return to the cathedral on Münsterplatz. Wedged

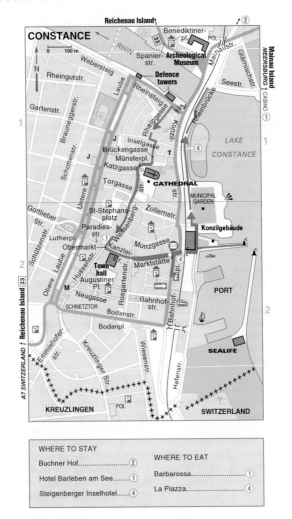

between the cathedral and the Rhine is the maze-like Niederburg, the town's oldest quarter, where craftsmen and artisans clustered in the Middle Ages.

Münster★ (Cathedral)

Since its construction lasted from the 11C to the 17C, this **cathedral** lacks any architectural unity. The **panels★** (*Türflügel*) of the porch doors in the main façade are decorated with bas-relief sculptures representing scenes from the life of Christ (1470). The 13C Mauritiuskapelle (chapel) houses the most prized piece of sculpture, the

Holy Tomb★, a vaulted dodecagon containing three statuary groups. It is one of the few examples of its kind from the High Middle Ages, bearing a stylistic resemblance to the sculptures of Bamberg and Naumburg.

Known as **Konstanzer Goldscheiben**, four gilded 11C–13C plaques In the crypt represent Christ in Majesty, the Eagle of St. John, and St. Conrad and St. Pelagius, patrons of the diocese.

The tower (open Mon–Sat 10am–5pm, Sun 12.30pm–5.30pm; ∽2€) can be climbed for sweeping city and lake views.

▶ Follow Wessenbergerstraße, a pedestrian zone lined with painted houses. Pass by Obermarkt before turning left into Kanzleistraße.

Rathaus (Town Hall)

The façade of this Renaissance building is embellished with paintings illustrating the history of Constance.

ADDITIONAL SIGHTS

Archäologisches Landesmuseum (State Museum of Archaeology)

Benediktinerplatz 5. Open year-round Tue–Sun 10am–6pm. Closed Jan 1, Fat Thu (Thu before Lent), Dec 24–25 & 31. ⌚4€, free 1st Sat of month. ♿ ☎(07531) 980 40. www.konstanz.alm-bw.de.

This museum is housed in the old former Peterhausen Abbey. History comes to life in 3 000sq m/32 291sq ft of exhibition space, spanning an arc from 6 000-year-old stilt buildings to recent industrial activity.

▲▲ Sea Life

Hafenstraße 9. Open year-round daily 10am–6pm. Closed Dec 24. ⌚16.50€ (child 12.95€). ☎(01806) 66 69 01 01. www.visitsealife.com.

Follow the flow of the Rhine from its source to the North Sea in this imaginatively designed aquarium and encounter some 3 700 aquatic creatures along the way. A 8m/24ft-long tunnel, where sharks, skates and turtles dart around you, is a highlight, as are touch pools where sea anemones and starfish bring big smiles to visitors.

EXCURSIONS

Insel Mainau★★ (Mainau Island)

▶ 7km/4.3mi north via Mainaustraße. Open year-round sunrise–sunset. ⌚18€. ♿ ☎(07531) 30 30. www.mainau.de. Allow 2hrs.

Friedrich I, the duke of Baden, sowed the seeds (quite literally) for this garden island in 1853. Now owned by a Swedish aristocratic family, the Bernadottes, it is a lavish symphony of scent and colour and one of the most popular destinations in the lake region.

The palace, Baroque church and exotic and tropical flowers and plants contribute to the island's magic. ▲▲ The petting zoo, playground, pony rides and butterfly house are magnets for kids.

Insel Reichenau★ (Reichenau Island)

▶ 7km/4.3mi west. Take B33 in the direction of Radolfzell. ☎(07534) 920 70. www.reichenau.de.

Reichenau traces its origins to 724 when St. Pirmin founded the first Benedictine monastery in Germany on this petite island in the Untersee section of Lake Constance. It was a renowned centre of learning and arts for centuries. During the Ottonian period (9C), Reichenau monks were particularly noted for producing outstanding illuminated manuscripts as well as brilliant frescoes.

Thanks to its three ancient churches, Reichenau has enjoyed UNESCO World Heritage Site status since 2000. Note especially the 9C Carolingian church in Oberzell with its wall paintings, and the Romanesque former abbey church in Mittelzell. Here, a wooden vaulted apse, a Gothic chancel and a 1477 altar with relics of St. Mark are among the treasures deserving closer inspection.

ADDRESSES

🏨 STAY

⊜⊜⊜ **Buchner Hof** – *Buchnerstraße 6 (via Mainaustraße).* ☎*(07531) 810 20. www.buchner-hof.de. 13 rooms. ⌚. Closed Dec 20–Jan 10.* In a quiet location, this little hideaway near the lake and the old town is run with a personal touch. Rooms are bright and furnished in a pleasing palette of colours.

⊜⊜⊜⊜ **Hotel Vill aBarleben am See** – *Seestraße 15, 78464 Konstanz-Staad. ☎(07531) 94 23 30. www.hotel-barleben.de. 9 rooms. ⌚. 15€.* This 1872 villa turned boutique hotel draws lots of regulars to its lovely, personalised rooms. The location in the heart of parkland adjacent to the lakeside promenade boosts its appeal as a romantic getaway.

🛏🛏🛏🛏 **Steigenberger Inselhotel** – *Auf der Insel 1. ☎(07531) 12 50. www.steigenberger.de. 102 rooms.* 🍽. *Restaurants* 🍴🍴🍴🍴. Still boasting details of its former reincarnation as a monastery, this hotel envelops guests in a tasteful, upmarket ambience that moves smoothly from the public areas to the rooms. Dine in the elegant restaurant or on the splendid terrace with lake views.

🍴/EAT

🍴 **La Piazza** – *Marktstätte 2. ☎(07531) 91 79 27. www.lapiazza-kn.de.* A relaxed atmosphere and a modern setting for Italian cuisine and outstanding desserts.

🍴🍴 **Barbarossa** – *Obermarkt 8–12. ☎(07531) 12 89 90. www.barbarossa-hotel.com. 50 rooms.* 🍽. *Restaurant*🍴🍴. This upstairs dining room decked out in dark wood delivers attentive service and a delicate cuisine. A speciality is locally caught fish, which is sometimes given an exotic treatment. In winter, locals get together for wine and tapas accompanied by live music *(Wed–Sat 6pm–1am)*.

Lake Constance★★

Bodensee

With its expansive horizons and a climate mild enough for tropical vegetation, Lake Constance (*Bodensee* in German) attracts a multitude of German holidaymakers who regard it as their local "Riviera". In addition to the vistas, which encompass the Alps to the south in clear weather, tourists love the lake's clear waters, medieval towns and boat cruises.

🚗 DRIVING TOURS

FROM ÜBERLINGEN TO LINDAU

56km/35mi. Allow 4hrs.

Überlingen★
Am Landungsplatz 5, 88662 Überlingen. ☎(07551) 947 15 22. www.ueberlingen.de.
This former Free Imperial City on Lake Constance was founded around 1180 by Frederick I Barbarossa and achieved great prosperity in the Middle Ages thanks to its vineyards and leading

▪ **Info:** Bahnhofsplatz 43. ☎(07531) 13 30 30. www.konstanz-tourismus.de.

▸ **Location:** The Rhine flows into the Bodensee as it spills out of the Alps and shares borders with Switzerland and Austria. Due to its vast size, the lake creates its own microclimate especially conducive to fruit cultivation. Boat services ply the lake's waters, frequently linking Constance, Überlingen, Meersburg, Friedrichshafen, Lindau and Bregenz (in Austria).

▸ **Don't Miss:** Lake cruises from Constance or Friedrichshafen. The Stilt Houses Museum (🕯 *see the Driving Tour*).

🕐 **Timing:** Allow half a day for a leisurely boat cruise. The entire region easily warrants a full day or two.

👪 **Kids:** Swimming or cruising on the lake.

role in the salt and grain trade. Since the mid-19C, the tourist industry has become the local economic engine, especially after Überlingen became an official Kneipp spa resort in 1956.

Lying on the northwest shore of Bodensee (Lake Constance), the town is surrounded by orchards and blessed with a mild climate. West of the centre, a pleasant walk along the ancient moat leads to the **Seepromenade**.

Münsterplatz (Minster Square)
The square is bordered by the Gothic cathedral, the north façade of the town hall and the Renaissance **Alte Kanzlei** (municipal chancellery).

Münster (Minster)★
This Gothic cathedral (1350–1562) is the mightiest in the region. Inside the harmonious five-nave basilica all eyes are drawn to the magnificent wooden high altar carved by local artisan Jörg Zürn (1613–1616). A 16C Swabian work, the Virgin of the Crescent Moon, stands in St. Elizabeth Chapel.

Rathaus (Town Hall)
Münsterstraße 15. Visit by guided tour Wed–Thu 11am. ✆(07551) 991 011. www.ueberlingen.de.
The first-floor Gothic **Ratssaal**★ (council chamber) is beautifully decorated with panelled walls and a carved frieze with 41 statuettes representing members of the Guilds of the Holy Roman Empire. The council still convenes here.

Städtisches Museum (Municipal Museum)
Krummebergstraße 30. Open year-round Tue–Sat 9am–12.30pm, 2pm–5pm (Apr–Oct also Sun 10am–3pm). Closed Thu after Easter and Pentecost. ✆5€. ✆(07551) 99 10 79.
www.museum-ueberlingen.de.
Exhibits in this late-15C mansion with Baroque touches include paintings and sculpture by local artists from the Gothic period to classicism, a collection of 18C crèches (Krippen) and 50 dollhouses from the Renaissance to Jugendstil.

GETTING AROUND
FERRY: Between Constance and Meersburg (20min). Daily departures every 15min from 6am–8pm (fewer at other times). ✆7.90€ with car, 2.80€ per passenger. ✆(07531) 80 30. www.stadtwerke.konstanz.de.
CRUISES: Hafenstraße 6 (behind the tourist office). ✆(07531) 364 00. www.bsb-online.com. Trips available to Mainau, Uhldingen and the Zeppelin Museum in Friedrichshafen.

Birnau
An important stop on the Upper Swabian Baroque Route, this 18C pilgrimage church overlooks the Bodensee and was an exuberant collaboration of master artists of the day. Peter Thumb designed the building, Gottfried Bernard Göz was responsible for the richly detailed frescoes, while Joseph Anton Feuchtmayr carved the altars, stucco ornamentation and sculptures. The church's most famous sculpture is the adorable "Honey Sucker", a cheeky cherub caught with his fingers inside a beehive.

Salem★
Founded by the Cistercians in 1137, Klosters Salem (Salem Abbey) was, for more than 650 years, one of the most important abbeys in Germany, and its abbot was answerable only to the emperor and the Pope. Under Abbot Anselm II (1746–1778), builder of the pilgrimage church of Birnau, the abbey reached its apogee. In 1802 it passed to the Margrave (Counts) of Baden and is still under their ownership.
Today the 7ha/17acre abbey complex is a striking architectural ensemble that combines the Gothic, Renaissance, Baroque and Classical. It resembles a small village, complete with private college, craftworkers, a café-restaurant and shop. Seek out the pharmacy, in the Untertor-Haus, an elegantly designed Baroque pavilion.
Münster★ (Cathedral) – Construction of this fine Gothic building began in

1297, though it was not consecrated until the Council of Constance in 1414. The splendid Gothic windows are pierced by gables east and west. The interior is typical of Cistercian architecture, with its large choir and high arches. It owes its splendid alabaster decoration to Abbot Anselm II.

Schloss★ (Castle) – (open Apr–Oct by 1hr guided tour Mon–Sat 9.30am–6pm, Sun and holidays 10.30am–6pm; 7€; 07 553 916 5336; www.schloesser-magazin.de). The highlight is the old refectory, which has retained its stucco ceiling, executed by the Schmuzer brothers. The same artists are also responsible for the superb vaulting in the library.

Also worth a visit are the Bernhardus-gang (Bernard Gallery), the Kaisersaal (Emperors' Hall) completed in 1707 – the first large reception room in a Baroque abbey in Germany – and the Rococo study of Abbot Anselm II.

In the old convent part of the castle, the Feuerwehr Museum (Firemen's Museum) is a reminder that this section was constructed after the devastating fire of 1697 (by Franz Beer, from the school of Vorarlberg). Its size and decoration reflect the wealth of the Abbey at that time.

▷ Return to the B 31 and head in the direction of Uhldingen to reach the lakeside village of Pfahlbauten.

Pfahlbaumuseum★★ (Stilt Houses Museum)

Strandpromenade 6, 88690 Uhldingen-Mühlhofen. 07 556 92 89 00 . www.pfahlbauten.de. Open Apr–Sept daily 9am–6.30pm; Oct 9am–5pm; Nov Sat–Sun 9am–5pm. Guided tours (in German) 9€ (child 5.50€).

This spectacular open-air Lake Village museum, constructed in 1922 near the original excavation site, comprises 20 stilt houses that vividly evoke the Bronze Age period (between 4000 and 1000 BC.). The architectural reconstructions (the most recent were added in 2002) are wholly convincing, as are the costumed actors who play out the daily lives of the village inhabitants. Even if you don't understand German, both parents and children will enjoy pretending to be archaeologists, or having a go at stone carving, or perhaps making fire, using only the primitive techniques of our ancestors.

Meersburg★

A former residence of the Prince-Archbishops, Meersburg is now a picturesque village on a rocky outcrop overlooking the lake and surrounded by vineyards and orchards. The historic upper town (Oberstadt) centres on the **Marktplatz★**, from which the **Steigstraße★**, bordered by half-timbered houses, offers delightful views. Dominating the Unterstadt (lower town) from its perch is the massive medieval **Burg Meersburg** (Meersburg Castle; open Mar–Oct daily 9am–6.30pm; Nov–Feb daily 10am–6pm; 9.50€; 07532 800 00; www.burg-meersburg.de) For seven years until her death in 1848, this was the home of **Annette von Droste-Hülshoff**, a poet born in Westphalia in 1797 and famous for the 1842 novella Die Judenbuche (The Jew's Beech). Annette's rooms are among the 28 that can be seen on a self-guided tour. Others include the kitchen, baths, private and representational rooms. The prison, the torture chamber and the treasury, however, can be seen only on guided tours (included in admission).

▷ The itinerary continues along the Grüne Straße (Green Route), famous for its apple orchards, whose fruit is exported throughout Europe.

Friedrichshafen

Friedrichshafen is a lively if industrial port town and the birthplace of the dirigible at the turn of the 19C.

Aside from the Zeppelin Museum (described below), the Baroque **church** (Schlosskirche) near the castle (still occupied by the ducal family of Württemberg) is worth a visit. Designed by Christian Thumb between 1695 and 1701, it features a richly detailed ceiling and fanciful choir stalls.

Meersburg

© BasieB/iStockphoto.com

Friedrichshafen is the departure point for boat excursions to the Rhine falls in Schaffhausen, to the "flower island" of Mainau and to the stilt houses in Unteruhldingen (👓*see Überlingen*).

👥 Zeppelin Museum

Seestraße 22. Open May–Oct daily 9am-5pm; Nov–Apr Tue–Sun 10am–5pm; last entry 30min before closing. Closed Dec 24–25. ⊛8€. ♿ 𝒫(07541) 380 10. www.zeppelin-museum.de.

Housed in a converted railway station on the eastern promenade of Lake Constance, the Zeppelin Museum is a must-see for technology buffs. In six major departments, it presents the entire history of airships first developed in Friedrichshafen by Count Ferdinand Zeppelin at the turn of the 19C. Among the museum's main attractions is a 33m/108ft-long reconstructed walk-through section of the *LZ 129 Hindenburg* that tragically crashed in New Jersey in 1937.

Upstairs, an art exhibition demonstrates regional works from the Middle Ages to today. Look for works by Otto Dix, Max Ackermann and Karl Caspar.

Wasserburg

Often deluged by day-trippers, this village is wedged into a narrow spit of land jutting into the lake. Walk to the tip for beautiful views over the river banks with the Alps as a backdrop.

Lindau★★

(👓*see LINDAU IM BODENSEE*)

ADDRESSES

🛏 STAY

⊖**Gasthof Auer** – *Stockacher Straße 62, 78359 Orsingen-Nenzingen.* 𝒫(07771) 24 97. www.auer-nenzingen.de. 5 rooms. ⌁. *Restaurant*⊖, *closed Mon.* Simple but welcoming, this inn combines a rustic restaurant serving seasonal, regional cuisine with a few basic but nicely decorated rooms.

⊖⊖**Bodensee-Hotel Kreuz** – *Grasbeurer Straße 2, 88690 Uhldingen-Mühlhofen.* 𝒫(07556) 92 88 90. www. bodensee-hotel-kreuz.de. 46 rooms. ⌁. *Restaurant*⊖⊖. This family-run hotel on a quiet side-street offers rooms in a historic main building and a modern annex. In either, the interior is warm and traditional with spacious, homey rooms, many with a balcony.

⊖⊖**Gästehaus Hagnauer Hof** – *Hauptstrasse 19, 88709 Hagnau.* 𝒫(07532) 441 10. www.hagnauer-hof.de. 8 rooms. ⌁. Situated just a few minutes' walking distance from the lake, this guesthouse has simply furnished rooms and a restaurant serving international cuisine, with the bonus of views of the lake. Sun-worshippers will love the common terrace overlooking Lake Constance.

⊖⊖**Landgasthof Zum Sternen** – *Schienerbergstraße 23, 78345 Moos-Bankholzen.* 𝒫(07732) 24 22. www.zum-sternen.de.18 rooms. ⌁. *Restaurant* ⊖⊖, *closed Tue lunch (Oct–May, closed Tue).* This congenial country inn is a great place to lay low in well-proportioned, charmingly furnished rooms. The restaurant is justly popular for its fresh fish and meat dishes.

🍴🍴🛏 **Villa Seeschau** – *Von-Laßberg-Straße 12, 88709 Meersburg. ℰ(07532) 43 44 90. www.hotel-seeschau.de. 18 rooms. 🍽.* This pretty villa is surrounded by lush gardens and has elegant, good-sized rooms in neutral hues and with balcony views of the lake. The panorama terrace is the perfect spot for breakfast.

🍴 EAT

🍴 **Pfälzer Hof** – *Lindenplatz 3, 88142 Wasserburg. ℰ08 382 98 85 30. www.pfaelzer-hof-wasserburg.de. Closed Nov–Mar & Wed throughout the year.* This family-run hotel-guesthouse has a friendly atmosphere. Simple, rustic.

🍴🍴 **Winzerstube zum Becher** – *Höllgasse 4, 88709 Meersburg. ℰ(07532) 90 09. www.winzerstube-zum-becher.de. Closed 1 week in Jan & Mon.* This rustic establishment has been welcoming thirsty visitors since 1610 and been run by the same family for the past 120 years. The kitchen specialises in regional cuisine with international accents.

🍴🍴🍴 **Bürgerbräu** – *Aufkircher Straße 20, 8862 Überlingen. ℰ07551 927 40. www.buergerbraeu-ueberlingen.com. Closed Mon–Tue, Wed–Fri lunch.* This charming half-timbered historic lakeside inn serves high-quality local and regional dishes in a cosy rustic dining room.

TAKING A BREAK

Strandcafé – *Strandbadstraße 102 78315 Radolfzell. ℰ(07732) 16 50. www.strandcafe-mettnau.de.* This modern glass pavilion has an enviable lakeside location with first-rate views. Come for pre-dinner sunset drinks.

SPORTS AND LEISURE

Swimming – There are numerous beaches with swimming pools around the lake, most notably at Überlingen and Meersburg.

Cruises – *Bodensee-Schiffsbetriebe, 88045 Friedrichshafen. ℰ07 541 923 80. www.bsb-online.com.* Cruises cover several parts of the lake: Überlingen See cruises depart from Meersburg *(2hr–3hrs 30min, 18€)* allowing guests to enjoy the lakeside village, Birnau church and Mainau Island. Evening cruises depart from Unteruhldingen, Mainau, Friedrichshafen, Meersburg, Lindau and Konstanz.

Lindau im Bodensee★★

Lindau is Bavaria's westernmost town. Its old town sits on an island in Lake Constance and exudes a casual, almost Mediterranean flair. Its lanes brim with fine gabled burghers' houses reflecting its past prosperity as a trading partner with Italy. Alas, its lanes are often deluged with visitors, but simply wander off into a quiet side-street or hidden courtyard and the magic of Lindau will quickly reveal itself.

A BIT OF HISTORY

A former Free Imperial City (1275-1802), Lindau – im Bodensee (in the lake) and not am Bodensee (by the lake) – boasts several churches; gabled burghers' houses testify to its bygone wealth as an important trading centre.

▶ **Population:** 24 700
🛈 **Info:** Alfred-Nobel-Platz 1, opposite the train station. ℰ(08382) 26 00 30. http://lindau-tourismus.de.
▶ **Location:** Lindau sits on the far eastern edge of Bodensee (Lake Constance). Ferries link the town to Konstanz and Bregenz (Austria) several times daily (www.bsb-online.com).
😊 **Don't Miss:** A stroll through the old town.
🕐 **Timing:** Allow one hour for a walking tour of the old town.

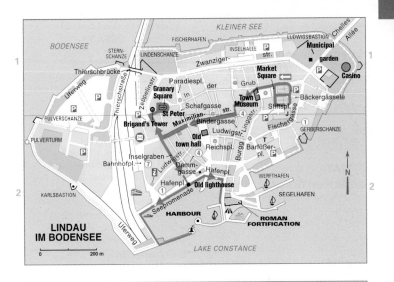

WALKING TOUR

OLD TOWN★★

Marktplatz (Market Square)

A large circular fountain anchors Lindau's handsome market square, which is dominated by two churches. The Baroque **Haus zum Cavazzen★**, on the west side, houses the **Town Museum** (Stadtmuseum; open year-round Mon–Sun 10am–6pm; ∞7.50€; ℘(08382) 94 40 73).

Follow **Maximilianstraße★★**, old town's picturesque main artery, then turn right into the Zeppelinstraße.

Schrannenplatz

The landmark Brigands' Tower *(Diebsturm)* is part of the medieval fortifications. The nearby **Peterskirche**, the oldest church in town (AD 1000), serves as a war memorial and is adorned with **frescoes** (15C) by Hans Holbein the Elder.

Lindau harbour

▶ Backtrack on Zeppelinstraße.

Hafen★ (Harbour)

This is the departure point for boat trips on Lake Constance. Contact Bodensee-Schiffsbetriebe (Schützingerweg 2; ℰ(08382) 27 58 40; www.bsb-online.com).

ADDRESSES

🛏 STAY

⊖⊜🖲 **Hotel Vis à Vis** – *Bahnhofplatz 4–6. ℰ08 382 39 65. www.visavis-lindau.de. 72 rooms.* ☒. Opposite the station, this smart, fairly new hotel offers spacious rooms with warm colours and light airy contemporary designs, plus a bistro.

⊖⊜🖲🖲 **Hotel Bayerischer Hof** – *Bahnhofplatz 2. ℰ(08382) 91 50. www.bayerischerhof-lindau.de. 97 rooms.* ☒. *Restaurant*⊖⊜🖲🖲. Sporting a classical façade, this elegant hotel has plush yet traditional décor and flair. Views of the harbour channel are a major perk of the stylish restaurant.

⊖⊜🖲🖲 **Hotel Lindauer Hof** – *Dammgasse 2. ℰ(08382) 40 64. www.lindauer-hof.de. 30 rooms.* ☒. *Restaurant* ⊖⊜🖲🖲. This hotel is a winning marriage of history and modern sophistication and is pleasantly close to the lake. Meals are served on the first floor or on the pretty terrace.

🍽 EAT

⊖⊜ **Alte Post** – *Fischergasse 3. ℰ08 382 934 60. www.alte-post-lindau.de Closed Nov, late Dec–Mar. 11 rooms.* Traditional local cooking with attention to detail is served either in the *Biergarten*, on the terrace in the square or in the formal dining room of this long-established city centre hotel.

⊖⊜ **Zum Sünfzen** – *Maximilianstraße 1. ℰ08 382 58 65. www.suenfzen.de.* The restaurant in this beautiful 14C historic house is something of a local institution. In summer you can dine out, under the sunshades, on its pretty terrace on the pedestrianised street.

Stuttgart★★

The capital of Baden-Württemberg is a city in transition. No longer purely defined by its urbanity, it is gradually becoming increasingly green and pedestrian-friendly and more in sync with the forested hills surrounding it. As the hub of Mercedes Benz, Stuttgart is naturally associated with cars, but fans of art and modern architecture will also have plenty to see and explore. Originally called "Stutengarten", the name derives from a seigniorial 10C stud farm. In the 14C Stuttgart became the home of the dukes and kings of Württemberg, and centuries later hit its full stride during the Industrial Revolution.

A BIT OF HISTORY

Two auto pioneers – An engineer born in Bad Cannstatt, **Gottfried Daimler**

▶ **Population:** 600 000

🛈 **Info:** Königstraße 1a. ℰ(0711) 222 80. www.stuttgart-tourist.de.

▶ **Location:** Stuttgart lies in a valley surrounded by vineyards and wooded hills opening onto the Neckar. The finest city **view★** is from the upper platform of the 400m/1 312ft-high **Fernsehturm** (TV tower).

🅿 **Parking:** There is ample parking throughout Stuttgart. Visit www.stuttgart.de/parken for fees and locations.

☺ **Don't Miss:** The world-class fine arts gallery. Car buffs should make time for the Mercedes-Benz and Porsche museums.

👪 **Kids:** Wilhelma Park and Zoo.

(1834–1900) invented the internal combustion engine needed to power vehicles. **Karl Benz** (1844–1929) envisaged an entire motor vehicle, which he elaborated in every detail at Mannheim. Soon he was able to start manufacturing cars in larger numbers; in 1899 he sold his 2 000th vehicle and thus became the world's leading automobile manufacturer.

In 1901, Daimler's company marketed the **Mercedes**, a name that would make an automotive dynasty as well as no small fortune. Today, the night sky over Stuttgart blazes with the illuminated three-point-star within a circle, the firm's world-famous trademark.

Urban landscape – The only remnants of Stuttgart's medieval core are apparent on **Schillerplatz**, flanked by the **Stiftskirche** (Collegiate Church) and the **Altes Schloss** (Old Castle). The statue of Schiller in the centre of the square is the work of the Danish sculptor Thorwaldsen (1839). The Baroque **Neues Schloss** (New Palace) is now the home of regional ministerial departments.

WALKING TOUR

TRAIN STATION TO SCHLOSSPLATZ

Allow 2hrs.

From the tourist office take Schillerstraße to the train station. Built between 1917 and 1924, it has a tower topped with a Mercedes star (free access). From here, have a look down Königstraße.

Schlossgarten (Castle Gardens)

A lovely spot for a picnic, these gardens are crisscrossed by more than 11km/8mi of walkways and form part of the vast green belt cinched around the central city. The original "Stutengarten" was located here.

Keep right to get to the Staatstheater (State Theatre), then

hook a left after the opera house to go through a subway to emerge onto Konrad-Adenauer-Straße.

Kulturmeile Konrad-Adenauer-Straße

Stuttgart's main cultural institutions conveniently line up along an 800m/ 2 625ft stretch of Konrad-Adenauer-Straße in what has come to be known as the "Boulevard of Culture" (Kulturmeile). On your left looms the immense **Staatsgalerie** (state gallery), the vast art museum that displays its fine collections in the original Neoclassical 19C building and in modernist additions by Sir James Stirling (1984) and Wilfrid and Katharina Steib (2002).

Walking south on Konrad-Adenauer-Straße takes you past the **Conservatory of Music and Dramatic Arts** and the **House of History** (Haus der Geschichte) to the **Wilhelmspalais**, where the last king of Württemberg, William II, lived until his abdication in 1918. A statue of the monarch and his little dog stands in front of the Neoclassical building.

Cross Konrad-Adenauer-Straße, then walk past the New Castle on your right to Schlossplatz (Castle Square).

Schlossplatz (Castle Square)

This green square is the heart of the city. It is dominated by the **Neues Schloss** (New Castle), a royal residence built between 1746 and 1807 and now the seat of the Baden-Württemberg state parliament. Opposite, the Classical columns of the **Königsbau** (Royal Pavilion) conceal a large new shopping centre called Königsbau-Passagen. The glass cube on the left houses the **Kunstmuseum Stuttgart** (Museum of Art).

Head south from Schlossplatz to Schillerplatz.

Altes Schloss (Old Castle)

The most prominent building flanking Schillerplatz is the Old Palace, a largely 16C Renaissance ducal residence that consists of four wings flanked by round towers. Its **courtyard★** (with access to *the Schlosskirche church)* is surrounded by three floors of arcaded galleries. It now houses the regional history museum (☞*see next*).

Landesmuseum Württemberg★ (Württemberg State Museum)

Schillerplatz 6, inside Altes Schloss.
Open year-round, Tue–Sun 10am–5pm.
☞5.50€. ✆(0711) 89 53 51 11.
www.landesmuseum-stuttgart.de.
This museum chronicles regional history from prehistoric times to today. Its collections from the Bronze and Iron Ages include important finds from a from mid-6C BC Celtic **royal tomb★** excavated near Ludwigsburg.

Upstairs Roman artefacts mingle with **religious statuary★★** of southern Germany. Funerary objects (weapons, jewels and household items) are displayed in the **Franks and the Alemanni Section**, tribes that dominated wide parts of Europe between the 3C and 8C.

Additional exhibits include a coin gallery; collections of furniture, clocks, scientific instruments and weapons; and the crown jewels of the kings of Württemberg.

A fine collection of musical instruments is on display in a nearby building, the Fruchtkasten on Schillerplatz.

Stiftskirche (Collegiate Church)

Also on Schillerplatz, the Collegiate Church strikes a fine silhouette and combines architectural elements from the Romanesque (base of the south tower, 12C), early Gothic (chancel, 14C) and late Gothic (the nave, 15C). A **memorial★** to the Dukes of Württemberg stands in the chancel.

Kunstmuseum Stuttgart (Stuttgart Fine Arts Museum)

Kleiner Schlossplatz 1. Open year-round Tue–Sun 10am–6pm (Thu until 9pm). Closed Good Fri, Dec 24–25 & 31. ☞6€. ✆(0711) 216 19600. www.kunstmuseum-stuttgart.de.
North of Schillerplatz, this gallery possesses prized canvases by famous artists from the classical, Modern and contemporary periods. Pride of place goes to *Neue Sachlichkeit* artist **Otto Dix**, who was famous for the ferocity of his social critique and anti-war sentiment.

The museum building itself is in an impressive glass cube that glows from within at night. The mobile out the front is by Alexander Calder.

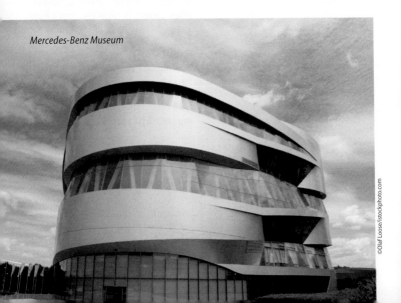

Mercedes-Benz Museum

©Olaf Loose/istockphoto.com

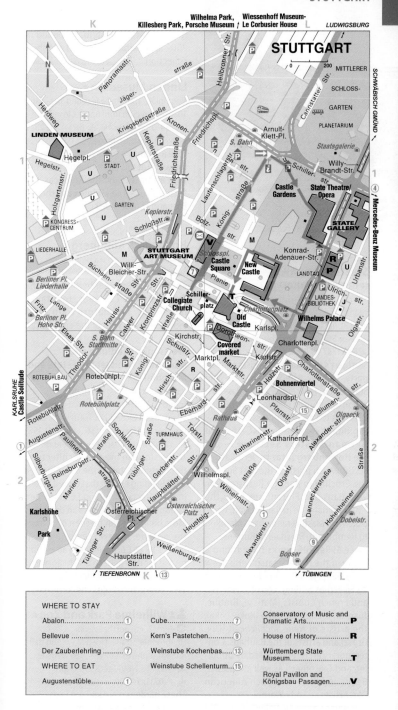

STUTTGART

Wilhelma Park,   Wiessenhoff Museum-
Killesberg Park, Porsche Museum   Le Corbusier House   *LUDWIGSBURG*

SCHWÄBISCH GMÜND

KARLSRUHE
Castle Solitude

TIEFENBRONN   (13)   *TÜBINGEN*

WHERE TO STAY		
Abalon............(1)	Cube............(7)	Conservatory of Music and Dramatic Arts............**P**
Bellevue ....(4)	Kern's Pastetchen............(9)	House of History............**R**
Der Zauberlehrling ....(7)	Weinstube Kochenbas.....(13)	Württemberg State Museum............**T**
WHERE TO EAT	Weinstube Schellenturm....(15)	
Augustenstüble............(1)		Royal Pavillon and Königsbau Passagen..........**V**

Schloss Solitude

© Olaf Loose/istockphoto.com

SIGHTS

Staatsgalerie★★ (Fine Arts Gallery)

Konrad-Adenauer-Straße 30–32. Open year-round Tue–Sun 10am–6pm (Thu until 8pm). Closed Good Fri, Dec 8, 24 & 25. ⊙5€, special exhibitions 12€. ௸ ℰ(0711) 47 04 00. www.staatsgalerie.de.

Stuttgart's state gallery consists of three parts. The 19C Alte Staatsgalerie (Old State Gallery) presents a world-class collection of European painting from medieval times to late 19C Impressionism.

Highlights include the 14C–16C **Old German Masters Section★★** and the **Herrenberg Altar** by Jerg Ratgeb (1519), which portrays the Last Supper, the Crucifixion and the Resurrection. Venetians and Florentines from the 14C dominate the Italian section, while Dutch Old Masters range from Memling to Rembrandt, Ruisdael to Rubens.

Since 1994, 20C works have found a home in the Neue Staatsgalerie (New State Gallery), a Postmodern building by Sir James Stirling. Look for Fauvists and French Cubists (Matisse, Braque, Juan Gris), Expressionists (Kokoschka), the artists of *Neue Sachlichkeit* (Dix, Grosz) and artists of the Bauhaus. Contemporary art is represented by Dubuffet, and Giacometti as well as Baselitz, Beuys and Kiefer and such American Pop Artists as Andy Warhol.

A separate annex is linked to the Old State Gallery by glass bridges. Designed by the Basel architectural team of Wilfrid and Katharina Steib, it opened in 2002 and harbours a prized graphics collection.

Linden Museum★★

Hegelplatz 1. Open year-round Tue–Sat 10am–5pm (Sun until 6pm). Closed Dec 24–25 & 31. ⊙4€. ௸ (0711) 202 23. www.lindenmuseum.de.

Take a journey back in time and around the world at this ethnographic museum with artefacts from the Americas, the Pacific, Africa, the Middle East, the Far East and southern Asia.

EXCURSIONS

Höhenpark Killesberg

▶ 4km/2.5mi north via Heilbronner Straße.

This part of the greenbelt around the inner city has cascades, fountains, flowerbeds, a **miniature train** and a look-out tower with of the entire city.

Weissenhofsiedlung and Museum★ (Weissenhof Estate and Museum)

Rathenaustraße 1–3. Open year-round Tue–Fri 11am–6pm, Sat–Sun 10am–6pm. Closed Jan 1, 4th week of the year and Dec 24. ⊙5€. ℰ(0711) 257 91 87. www.stuttgart.de/weissenhof.

A milestone in modern architecture, this housing estate is the outcome of a 1927 building exhibit that drew 17 leading architects, including Le Corbusier, Walter Gropius and Mies van der Rohe. Most buildings can be seen only from the outside, but two semi-detached homes by Le Corbusier hold an exhibit on the estate's genesis and history and a restored interior to reflect the original 1927 floorplan, colours and furnishings.

▲▲ Wilhelma Park and Zoo★

▶ 4km/2.5mi northeast via Heilbronner Straße. Open May–Aug daily 8.15am–6pm; rest of year, see website. ⊙14€; 10€ Nov–Feb & after 4pm. ௸ ℰ(0711) 540 20. www.wilhelma.de.

These gardens were laid out in the 19C. Don't miss the **aquarium**, **terrarium** and **Amazonian house**.

Mercedes-Benz Museum★★

⊙ Mercedesstraße 100, 6km/3.5mi east. Open year-round Tue–Sun 9am–6pm. Closed Jan 1, Dec 24–25 & 31. ⊛8€. ⧖. ℘(0711) 173 00 00. www.mercedes-benz-classic.com.

This museum sits mere paces from the garage where Gottlieb Daimler first developed the gasoline engine some 120 years ago. Exhibits are in a spectacular building designed like a giant double helix wrapped around a towering, triangular atrium. Visitors descending from the top take a journey through time, encountering prototype, racing and luxury car fantasies along the way.

Porsche Museum★★

⊙ Porscheplatz 1, Zuffenhausen. 8km/5mi north via Heilbronner Straße. Open year-round Tue–Sun 9am–6pm. Closed Jan 1, Dec 23–25 & 31. ⊛8€. ⧖ ℘(0711) 91 12 09 11. www.porsche.com/museum.

Porsche stands for glamorous sports cars, but did you know it was Daimler-Benz engineer **Ferdinand Porsche** who also invented the Volkswagen Beetle in 1934? Since 2009 a futuristic "temple of torque" has paid homage to the man and the brand. The building is stunning: a gravity-defying triangle hovering on concrete stilts. Behind its gleaming white walls await 80 of the company's most dazzling legends of prowess and style, including the legendary Roadster 356.

Schloss Solitude★

⊙ 9km/5.6mi southwest via Rotebühlstraße. ⟜Guided tours (30–45min) Apr–Oct Tue–Sat 10am–noon & 1.30pm–5pm, Sun 10am–5pm; Nov–Mar Tue–Sat 1.30pm–4pm, Sun 10am–4pm. Closed Dec 24 & 31. ⊛4€. ℘(0711) 69 66 99. www.schloss-solitude.de.

This 18C royal summer residence wraps around a domed oval pavilion, the lower outbuildings spreading out in an arc. The interior is Neoclassical, although a few apartments are French Rococo. The most opulent room is the White Hall *(Weisser Saal)*, whose ceiling fresco depicts Duke Carl Eugen.

ADDRESSES

🛏 STAY

⊖⊜ **Bellevue** – *Schurwaldstraße 45. ℘0711 48 07 60. www.bellevue-stuttgart.de. ⌦. Restaurant closed Tue–Wed and Aug.* This traditional 100-year-old family-run hotel-restaurant will give you a warm welcome. Ask for a room with a view.

⊖⊜ **Hotel Abalon** – *Zimmermannstraße 7–9 (access via Olgastraße 79). ℘(0711) 217 10. www. abalon.de. 42 rooms. ⌦.* This modern building is in the city centre but has comparatively quiet rooms that are spacious and functionally furnished. Views are great from the leafy rooftop terrace.

⊖⊜⊜⊜ **Der Zauberlehrling** – *Rosenstraße 38. ℘0711 237 77 70. www.zauberlehrling.de. 17 rooms. ⌦ 7.50–19€. Restaurant closed Sun.* Rooms are spacious and modern in this hotel with a chic design, and carefully decorated in every detail. Each has its own flair and atmosphere.

🍴 EAT

⊖ **Weinstube Kochenbas** – *Immenhofer Straße 33. ℘0711 60 27 04. www.kochenbas.de. Closed Mon.* This is one of the oldest wine bars in the city. Enjoy its rustic atmosphere and hearty Swabian dishes.

⊖⊜⊜ **Cube** – *Kleiner Schlossplatz 1. ℘0711 280 44 41. Reservation advised. www.cube-restaurant.de.* This light and airy dining room, on the top floor of the Kunstmuseum (Museum of Art), serves excellent international cuisine, and offers good value at lunchtime. The wine list is extensive.

⊖⊜⊜ **Weinstube Schellenturm** – *Weberstraße 72. ℘0711 236 48 88. www.weinstube-schellenturm.de. No lunch. Closed Sun, holidays, Dec 24–Jan 6.* Housed in a fortified tower that originally dates from the 16C (but twice rebuilt), this atmospheric restaurant serves fine wines and Swabian food that includes homemade *Maultaschen* ("Swabian ravioli") and *käsespätzle* (cheese noodles). In summer, dine on the lovely terrace.

⊖⊜⊜ **Augustenstüble** – *Augustenstraße 104. ℰ0711 62 12 48. www.augustenstüble.de. No lunch. Closed Sun–Mon.* For dinner, this bistro-style restaurant serves regional cuisine, accompanied by an extensive wine list, right up until midnight.

⊖⊜⊜ **Kern's Pastetchen** – *Hohenheimer Straße 64. ℰ0711 48 48 55. www.kerns-pastetchen.de. No lunch. Closed Sun and 3 weeks in Jun.* This elegant rustic restaurant serves quality regional and international cuisine with French and Austrian influences.

TAKING A BREAK

Weinhaus Stetter – *Rosenstraße 32 (south of and parallel to Charlottenstraße). ℰ(0711) 24 01 63. www.weinhaus-stetter. de. Closed Sun, holidays, Dec 25–Jan 8, 2-3 weeks late Aug–mid-Sept.* For more than 100 years this rustic establishment has been offering an excellent choice of mainly regional wines to accompany its small selection of hearty local dishes.

NIGHTLIFE
USEFUL TIPS

The **Bohnenviertel** between Charlottenstraße and Pfarrstraße brims with charming restaurants and bars. The mainly cobbled streets are pedestrian friendly.

EVENTS
PUBLICATIONS

The annual *Highlights* brochure lists events taking place year-round. Pick it up at the tourist office or download it as a free PDF file from www.stuttgart-tourist.de. The monthly magazines *Lift Stuttgart* and *Prinz* highlight current happenings and are on sale in bookshops and newspaper kiosks.

SHOPPING
USEFUL TIPS

Stuttgart's main shopping district centres on Königstraße and its side streets. The main department store is *Breuninger* (on Marktplatz). South of the Altes Schloss, the *Markthalle* is an Art-Deco covered market. Craft shops and antique dealers are found in the *Bohnenviertel* (between Charlottenstraße and Pfarrstraße).

Bad Wimpfen★★

This small fortified town with its web of half-timbered houses along narrow streets overlooks the River Neckar. Buttressing the hill are the Ludwigshalle saltworks, which once brought prosperity to the entire region.

▶ **Population:** 6 900
▦ **Info:** Hauptstraße 45. ℰ(07063) 972 00. www.badwimpfen.de.
▶ **Location:** Bad Wimpfen is a short distance from the A6 (Mannheim–Nurremberg). From Heidelberg, travel along the Neckar via the scenic B37.
⊛ **Don't Miss:** The suggested driving tour through the Neckar Valley.
⊙ **Timing:** Allow one and a half hours for the walking tour, four hours for the excursions.

 WALKING TOUR

WIMPFEN AM BERG★★
(Upper Town)
Start on Marktplatz.

Kaiserpfalz
(Imperial Palace)

Behind the Rathaus (town hall) are remains of the Kaiserpfalz with the **Blauer Turm (Blue Tower)** from which views extend over the town and the Neckar Valley. Further on is the 16C Romanesque **Steinhaus (Stone**

BAD WIMPFEN

Neckar Valley ①

0   100 m

NECKAR

Sailer- Str.

Erich-

Mathildenbad- straße

Kirchgasse

Badgasse

Rappenauer Str.

Eagle Fountain

Markt- platz

POL

R

Blue Tower

Imperial Palace

Stone House

Burgviertel

Red Tower

Schwibbogengasse

Salzgasse

HAUPTSTR.

HOHENSTAUFEN GATE

Marktrain

Langgasse

Spitalhof

HAUPTSTR.

Spitalgasse

Carl- Ulrich- Str.

Neuerweg

Neutor- Str.

Schiedstraße

Schulstraße

Klostergasse

Steinweg

Bollwerkgasse

Wallstraße

Schiedstraße

Str.

Alte Heilbronner Str.

Biberacher Str.

N

P

A 6-E 50

† Collegiate Church

House), in which a museum traces the history of Bad Wimpfen since Roman times.

◐ Continue along the wall to the staircase on the right, which leads to the spur on which the town is built, below the **Roter Turm (Red Tower)** – the fortress' final defensive point. Follow Schwibbogengasse to Hauptstrasse and then Klostergasse.

Historic Streets

Klostergasse is lined by half-timbered houses, including the former bath-houses, easily recognisable by their exterior galleries. You can explore more of the town's streets via Langgasse, leading to **Hauptstraße★** by way of a narrow alley (*Spitalgasse*), which runs past a former hospital (*Spitalhof*) whose cluster of half-timbered houses is among the oldest buildings in town. It is now a gallery.

Bad Wimpfen

© www.badwimpfen.de

▶ Continue west along Hauptstraße, with its picturesque, eloborate signs, past the 1576 **Adlerbrunnen (Eagle Fountain)** before returning to Marktplatz via Salzgasse.

WIMPFEN IM TAL (Lower Town)

The Gothic **Stiftskirche St. Peter und St. Paul** (parish church) has retained a strikingly plain west façade from an earlier Romanesque building. The **cloister★★** shows the evolution of the Gothic style. The north gallery (c. 1350), already more angular in design, marks the transition to the Renaissance. ➴Guided tour (1hr) by prior appointment. ℘(07063) 970 40.

🚗 DRIVING TOUR

NECKAR VALLEY★

74km/46mi. Allow 4hrs.

▶ Leave Bad Wimpfen on the B27 N.

Downstream from Bad Wimpfen, the **Neckartal** cuts through the sandstone massif of the Odenwald, many of whose hills are crowned by castles.

Burg Guttenberg (Guttenberg Castle)

9km/5.6mi north of Bad Wimpfen. Open Apr–Oct daily 10am–6pm; tours by request year-round. ➾4€ (➾5€ if tour) ℘(06266) 228. www.burg-guttenberg.de. A massive defensive wall protects this castle, which shelters rare collections of **objets d'art★** and archives. Note the 18C "Library-Herbarium" in which plants are encased in 92 "wooden books".

▶ Drive towards Neckarzimmern, then 1.5km/1mi to Burg Hornberg.

Burg Hornberg

Open year-round daily 10am–5pm. ➾3€. ⬥ ℘(06261) 50 01. www.burg-hornberg.de. Crowning a vine-covered hill, this **castle** is easily recognised from afar by its tall keep. A **museum** features the armour of Götz von Berlichingen, who died here in 1562. This knight, popularised in German folklore as a Robin Hood figure, was immortalised in a play by Goethe.

▶ Return to the B27 and continue towards Neckarzimmern, skirting Eberbach.

Hirschhorn am Neckar★

38km/23.6mi northwest of Burg Hornberg. The castle stands on a fortified spur. From the terrace and tower (121 steps) the **view★** encompasses the wooded slopes of the Neckar Valley.

▶ Follow the B37 southwest.

Neckarsteinach

Four castles stand on a narrow ridge overlooking the village: the Vorderburg and Mittelburg castles are privately owned. Hinterburg Castle (c. 1100) is the oldest and is now in ruins. Burg Schadeck, also in ruins, is a small 13C castle known as "swallow's nest".

▶ Continue on the B37.
After 4km/2.5mi take a left over the bridge at Neckarggemünd. Follow the K3200 for 4.5km/3mi.

Dilsberg

Dilsberg is noteworthy for its romantically ruined castle reached by following the signs to Burgruine. From the **tower★** (97 steps) unfolds a fantastic panorama of the Neckar. The route ends with a scenic approach to Heidelberg (▶ see HEIDELBERG).

ADDRESSES

🛏STAY

➾➾ **Am Kurpark** – Kirschenweg 16, Bad Wimpfen. ℘(07063) 93 42 46. www.dashotel amkurpark.de. Closed mid-Dec–mid-Jan. 10 rooms. ⬚. This hotel-guesthouse has a quiet location near the spa park. You will find comfortably furnished guestrooms (including six double rooms with a balcony) and a friendly welcome.

⊜⊜ **Sonne** – *Langgasse 3, 74206 Bad Wimpfen.* ✆*(07063) 96 11 60. www.arkus-heilbronn.de/gaestehaus-sonne. 12 rooms.* 🍴. *Restaurant*⊜ ⊜⊜. This old town hotel delivers modern comforts in historic surroundings. The rustic but comfortable rooms occupy two handsome half-timbered buildings. The restaurants Friedrich and Feyerabend are on the premises.

🍴 EAT

⊜⊜⊜ **Friedrich** – *Hauptstraße 74, Bad Wimpfen.* ✆*(07063) 2 45. www.friedrich-feyerabend.de. Closed Mon, Tue.* This bright and convivial restaurant at the beginning of the pedestrian zone serves international fare.

Schwäbisch Hall★★

This town, built in tiers up the steep flank of the Kocher Valley, grew up around salt springs already known in Celtic times. In the Middle Ages, it was famous for the *Heller*, the Imperial silver coins, minted here. The town's well-preserved half-timbered houses and tranquillity make it a pleasant stopping point.

▸ **Population:** 36 800

Info: Am Markt 9. ✆(0791) 75 12 46. www.schwaebischhall.de.

▸ **Location:** Schwäbisch Hall is tucked into the Kocher Valley, south of the Hohenlohe plain, in northeastern Baden-Württemberg.

SIGHTS

Marktplatz★★ (Market Square)

This sloping central square is dominated by the monumental stone steps of the **Michaelskirche** (Church of St. Michael), which hosts a popular open-air theatre festival in summer. It is flanked by houses in a variety of architectural styles from Gothic to Baroque.

Dating from 1509, the **Marktbrunnen** (fountain) stands against a decorative wall adorned with statues of Samson, St. Michael and St. George (originals, copies are in the Hällisch-Fränkisches Museum). The rectangular design, unusual in a Gothic work, incorporates the old pillory post. The elegant 18C late Baroque **town hall★** and its beautiful clock-tower stand opposite the church. The two parallel streets of **Obere** and **Untere Herrengasse**, linked by stone stairways, are bordered by numerous 15C and 16C half-timbered houses.

Michaelskirche

Originally Romanesque, this church was transformed into a Gothic hall-church in the 15C and is reached via 53 steps.

The Flamboyant chancel was added in the 16C.

Hällisch-Fränkisches Museum (Regional Museum)

Keckenhof 6. Open year-round Tue–Sun 10am–5pm. Closed Good Friday, Dec 24-25 & 31. ⊜2.50€. ♿ partly. ✆(0791) 75 14 26. www.schwaebischhall.de.

This museum is housed in seven historical buildings, one of which is the eight-storey **Keckenturm** (tower) from the 13C. Collections concentrate on the art, culture and everyday life of the townspeople, delving into the history of the *Heller* coins and the region's role in the salt trade. Highlights include the hand-painted wainscoting from a 18C synagogue and ivory carvings created during the Thirty Years' War.

Kunsthalle Würth (Fine Art Museum)

Lange Straße 35. Open year-round daily 10am–6pm. Closed Dec 24 & 31. ✆(0791) 94 67 20. www.kunst.wuerth.com.

The White Gold of Hall

The word Hala means "salt" in old German. The Celts found a salt-water spring here and were using it as long ago as 500 BC. Rediscovered in AD 800, the saltworks quickly brought fame and fortune to the town of Hall. Green brine was pumped from a well that was dug where Hallplatz now stands, then processed by "distillers" who fed huge wood fires to evaporate the water. The resulting salt, said to be very white, very fine and of high quality, was used until 1924. The town was renamed Schwäbisch Hall in 1934.

Open since 2001, this ultra-modern art temple created from a 19C brewery presents often exemplary changing exhibits of works created after World War II.

Along the Banks of the Kocher★

Attractive views of the half-timbered buildings across the river unfold from the **Henkersbrücke** (Hangman's Bridge). The view is perhaps even better from the junction of Am Spitalbach lane and the Salinenstraße quay, from which you can also spot the Church of St. John. **Views★** of the stepped silhouette of the old town lorded over by the Michaelskirche are especially appealing from Unterwöhrd Island. Attractive roofed wooden bridges span the river.

EXCURSION

Benediktinerkloster Großcomburg★ (Benedictine Abbey of Grosscomburg)

◗ 3km/1.8mi south. ☙ Guided tours (30min) Apr–Oct Tue–Fri 11am, then hourly 1pm–4pm; Sat–Sun hourly 2pm–4pm; Nov–Mar by appointment. ⊛4€. ℘(0791) 93 81 85. www.kloster-grosscomburg.de.
Dating from 1130, the crown-shaped **chandelier★★** in the church is made of copper-plated and gilded iron. An **antependium★** of the same period in front of the high altar shows Christ surrounded by the apostles. The supporting framework is treated with filigree work and *cloisonné* enamel.

Tübingen★★

Tübingen escaped World War II with nary a shrapnel wound and is therefore a 3D history textbook of the Middle Ages to the 19C. The maze of narrow, sloping lanes lined with ancient half-timbered houses and its animated student life create a delightful atmosphere.

☙WALKING TOUR

OLD TOWN★★
Eberhardsbrücke (Bridge)

This bridge gives a scenic **view★** over the Neckar with the Hölderlin Tower rising behind weeping willows. The **Platanenallee** is a beautiful walkway

▸ **Population:** 85 350

🛈 **Info:** An der Neckarbrücke 1 ℘(07071) 913 60. www.tuebingen-info.de.

◗ **Location:** Tübingen lies near Stuttgart, on the banks of the Neckar and Ammer rivers, between the slopes of Schlossberg and Österberg.

🅿 **Parking:** Garages are located throughout Tübingen. Visit http://wap.parkinfo.com for fees and locations.

☺ **Don't Miss:** A walking tour of the old town.

🕐 **Timing:** Allow a full day to absorb the history of Tübingen.

along the Neckar. Gondolas travel from Hölderlin Tower past the riverfront.

▶ Right after crossing the bridge, take the staircase down to the riverbank.

Hölderlinturm (Tower)

Bursagasse 6. Open Tue–Fri 10am–noon & 3pm–5pm, Sat–Sun 2pm–5pm. ∞2.50€. ✆(07071) 220 40. www.hoelderlin-gesellschaft.de. Once part of the fortifications, this tower was the residence of Friedrich Hölderlin from 1807 until his death in 1843. Now a museum, it has displays on the life and work of the poet.

▶ Turn right at the front of the tower, then left on Bursagasse. The route skirts Tübingen's first university hospital (Burse) with its double staircase. Also here is the protestant seminary (Evangelisches Stift), where Hegel, Hölderlin and Schelling once studied. Climb up to the palace via Burgsteige and note the interesting fraternity house at no 20.

Schloss Hohentübingen (Palace)

The present Renaissance building was constructed on the foundations of an 11C fortress built by the archdukes of Tübingen. It is now a **museum**★ (open year-round Wed–Sun 10am–5pm, Thu

The University

They say that rather than having a university, Tübingen *is* a university, so closely linked are the town and its *alma mater*. It all began in 1477, when Count Eberhard founded the institution in a town of only 3 000. Tübingen University now has 7 faculties and 28 500 students registered in 280 different fields of study. The university and the Protestant seminary of 1536 have educated such important figures as the poets Hölderlin, Mörike and Uhland, the philosophers Hegel and Schelling, the astronomer Kepler, the theologian Melanchthon, and Swiss biologist, Friedrich Miescher – discoverer of DNA. It has also produced nine Nobel Prize winners, most in the field of chemistry.

until 7pm; closed Jan 1, Dec 24 & 25; ∞5€; ✆07071 297 73 84; www.uni-tuebingen.de/museum-schloss) on pre- and early history. A favourite exhibit is the tiny **Vogelherdpferdchen**★, an ivory horse figurine named for the cave near Ulm where it was discovered in 1931. It is one of the oldest works of art from the New Paleolithic Age. There are also outstanding exhibits from Classical Antiquity, Ancient Egypt and the

Neckar riverfront

© Jens Hilberger/Fotolia.com

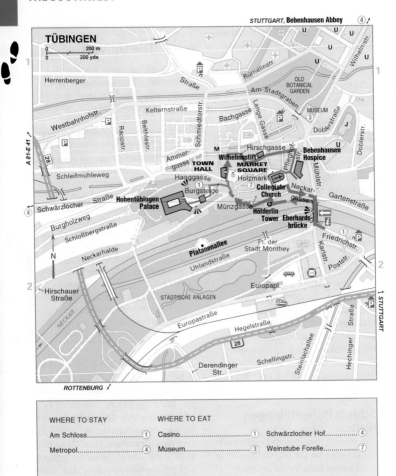

TÜBINGEN

STUTTGART, Bebenhausen Abbey

WHERE TO STAY		WHERE TO EAT			
Am Schloss	①	Casino	①	Schwärzlocher Hof	④
Metropol	④	Museum	③	Weinstube Forelle	⑦

Ancient Orient. Note in particular the **religious chamber★** from an Old Kingdom tomb (third millennium BC), completely covered in bas-relief sculptures. There is a good **view★** of the Neckar and the roofs of the old town from the castle terrace.

◗ Backtrack, then turn left on Wienergäßle towards Marktplatz.

Marktplatz★
(Market Square)
This charming historic square is surrounded by half-timbered houses and accented by a Renaissance fountain and a statue of Neptune. It comes alive on market days (*Mon, Wed and Fri*). The 19C graffito decoration on the 15C **Rathaus** (town hall) depicts the allegories of Justice, Agriculture and Science. The astronomic clock dates from 1511.

Wilhelmsstift
At Collegiumgasse 7, this late 16C stone building was once home to a renowned academy for young Protestant noblemen who came here from throughout Europe. Note the coat of arms of Baden-Württemberg above the portal.

◗ Continue via Hafengasse, then turn right into Pfleghofstraße and enter the old hospital through the arched porch.

Friedrich Hölderlin in Tübingen

Friedrich Hölderlin was born at Lauffen am Neckar in 1770. He studied theology at Tübingen'sn Protestant seminary, where he befriended philosophers Hegel and Schelling, in preparation for the ministry. Poetry continued to interest him in Tübingen, a craft he began while studying in Maulbronn. Finally rebelling against a career in the church, he worked as a tutor in Frankfurt, Switzerland and Bordeaux. The first sign of mental illness (thought to be schizophrenia) manifested itself in 1802. In 1806, he returned to Tübingen where he was promised recovery under the care of medical professor Autenrieth at a residential home. When treatment failed, Hölderlin resided in the tower room at the home of the Zimmers, a family of carpenters, at Bursagasse 6, for the remainder of his life.

Bebenhausener Pfleghof (Bebenhaus Hospice)

The Bebenhausen Hospice was erected in the 15C and served as the tithes barn for the abbey. Jutting out from the tall, steep roof is a three-storey dormer through which the grain was passed.

▶ Go around the building, then descend via Schulberg to arrive at Holzmarkt.

Holzmarkt

This square owes much of its attractiveness to the fountain of St. George.
In the old Heckenhauer bookshop the writer and poet Hermann Hesse spent his apprenticeship from 1895 to 1899. At the northern end of the church, note the sculpture of St. George, who was martyred on the wheel. It inspired John Heartfield, an artist famous for his photomontages denouncing Nazism.

Stiftskirche (Collegiate Church)

Am Holzmarkt. Open year-round daily 9am–4pm. ◉1€. ☎(07071) 431 51. www.stiftskirche-tuebingen.de.
This 15C Gothic hall-church boasts a Flamboyant rood screen and pulpit. For centuries the chancel was the burial place of the Württemberg princes. Note the funerary monument of university founder Eberhard the Bearded and the **Renaissance tombs★★** of Duke Ludwig and his wife, adorned with fine alabaster relief work. An altar was created by a student of Dürer (1520)

and choir stalls are adorned with Bible figures. Climb the tower for sweeping views over the Neckar, castle and the Swabian Jura.
West of the church, the **Cottahaus** is the former home of Johann Friedrich Cotta (1764–1832). A leading publisher of the Enlightenment, he was the first to print the works of Goethe and Schiller.

EXCURSION
Kloster Bebenhausen★

▶ 6km/3.7mi north via the Wilhelmstraße. Open Apr–Oct daily 9am–6pm (closed Mon noon–1pm); Nov–Mar Tue–Sun 10am–noon, 1pm–5pm. Closed Jan 1, Dec 24–25 & 31. ◉4.50€. ☎(07071) 60 28 02. www.kloster-bebenhausen.de.
Along with Maulbronn and Eberbach, this 12C abbey ranks among the best preserved Cistercian monasteries in Germany. Located in the peaceful Schönbuch Forest, it is an interesting example of Romanesque-Gothic architecture. The landmark roof **turret★** dates from the monastery's 15C heyday. Also note the Flamboyant-style cloister (1475–1500) with its net-vaulted ceiling.

Schloss Bebenhausen

☛Guided tour (45min) Apr–Oct Tue– Fri 11am–6pm, Sat–Sun 10am–5pm; Nov–Mar Tue–Fri 2pm–4pm, Sat–Sun 11am–5pm. Closed Jan 1, Dec 24–25 & 31. ◉6€.
On the monastery grounds, this palace is the former hunting lodge of King Charles of Württemberg, to which the

last king of Württemberg, Wilhelm II, retired after his abdication. His widow, lived here until her death in 1946.

ADDRESSES

🏨 STAY

🛏️ Hotel Metropol – *Reutlinger Straße 7. 𝒫(07071) 910 10. www. metropol-hotel-garni.de. 12 rooms. ⛶.* This small hotel sits on the edge of town within walking distance of the historic centre. Rooms are rather basic but clean and modern.

🛏️ Hotel Am Schloss – *Burgsteige 18. 𝒫07071 92 940. www.hotelamschloss.de. 37 rooms. ⛶. Restaurant🛏️🍽️.* Housed next to the castle in two old wooden houses, this hotel serves national and Swabian specialities in its cosy restaurant. In summer dine on the terrace.

🍽️ EAT

🍽️ Schwärzlocher Hof – *Schwärzloch 1 (2.5km/1.5mi west of town, via Schwärzlocher Straße between Schleifmühleweg and Burgholzweg.* 𝒫(07071) 433 62. www.hofgut-schwaerzloch.de. Closed Mon–Tue, Jan 1.* The chancel of a 12C church has been incorporated into this farm inn. The terrace, shaded by lime trees, has a stunning view. Sample the *Most* (dry cider) with traditional dishes.

🍽️ Casino – *Wöhrdstraße 25. 𝒫07071 65 07 50. www.casino-am-neckar.de. Closes Sun 8pm.* This modern, lively brasserie on the banks of the River Neckar specialises in fish and Swabian dishes. Dine in the *Biergarten* in summer.

🍽️ Museum – *Wilhelmstraße 3. 𝒫07071 228 28. www.restaurant-museum.de. Tue–Sat 11.30am–3pm, 6pm–midnight, Sun 11.30am–3pm. Closed Mon.* The elegant restaurant serves fresh, light, creative Mediterranean-inspired cuisine. Or you can dine informally downstairs in the *Weinstube*.

🍽️ Weinstube Forelle – *Kronenstraße 8. 𝒫(07071) 240 94. www.weinstube-forelle. de. Closed Mon lunch & Dec 23–25.* This restaurant is popular with students and tourists in the evenings for its friendly staff and creatively updated Swabian dishes.

Swabian Jura★

Schwäbische Alb

East of the Black Forest, between Stuttgart and Lake Constance, the Swabian Jura region is a paradise for walkers, cyclists and history buffs. From the highest point at Lemberg (1 015m/3 330ft), the Jura plateaux drop 400m/1 312.3ft to the Neckar basin in the northwest. Mountain outcrops form natural fortresses; some were chosen as castle sites by such famous dynasties as the Hohenstaufens and Hohenzollerns.

- 🛈 **Info:** Marktplatz 1, 72574 Bad Urach. 𝒫(07125) 94 81 06. www.schwaebischealb.de.
- ▶ **Location:** East of the Black Forest, between Stuttgart and Lake Constance, the Swabian Jura is punctuated by caves, dry valleys and steep-sided gorges.
- 🏛️ **Don't Miss:** Burgruine Reußenstein and Burg Hohenzollern.
- 🕐 **Timing:** Allow one day for driving tour 1 and half a day for driving tour 2.
- 👥 **Kids:** Urwelt-Museum Hauff, Bärenhöhle caverns.

🚗 DRIVING TOURS

1 FROM KIRCHHEIM UNTER TECK TO BURG HOHENZOLLERN

125km/77.6mi. Allow one day.

Kirchheim unter Teck
The tower of the 18C half-timbered Rathaus (town hall) overlooks the central crossing in town.

▶ Drive E on the L 1200 to Holzmaden.

Holzmaden
👥 Urwelt-Museum Hauff★
Aichelberger Straße 90. Open year-round Tue–Sun 9am–5pm. Closed Jan 1, Dec 24–25 & 31. ∞7€. ♿ ℘(07023) 28 73. www.urweltmuseum.de.
This prehistoric collection showcases fossilised dinosaur bones, fish, sea lilies and ammonites found locally in the 180 million-year-old Jurassic slate strata.

Burgruine Reußenstein (Castle Ruins)
🚶 45min round-trip walk.
Head for the edge of the escarpment to appreciate the setting★★ of Reußenstein as it dominates the Neidlingen Valley. From the look-out point built into the castle ruins a view★ encompasses the whole valley and beyond it, the plain of Teck.

▶ After Wiesensteig, which is characterised by its many half-timbered houses, the route follows the Schwäbische Albstraße, marked by blue-green arrows.

Bad Urach
This is a pretty town, enclosed deep in the Erms Valley, with half-timbered houses surrounding the picturesque central Marktplatz (market square).

Uracher Wasserfall (Urach Falls)
🚶 15min round-trip walk. Leave from the parking area marked "Aussicht 350m".

At the end of the walk unfolds an impressive view★ of the valley and the waterfall (flow reduced in summer).

Schloss Lichtenstein
Open Apr–Oct daily 9am–5.30pm; Feb–Mar & Nov Sat–Sun 10am–4pm. ∞6€. ℘(07129) 41 02. www.schloss-lichtenstein.de.
Built on a rock spur, Lichtenstein looks medieval but in fact only got its fairytale looks in the 19C. Before crossing the entrance bridge, turn right for two viewpoints: one overlooks the Echaz Valley, the other the castle itself.

Bärenhöhle (Bear Grotto)
Near the town of Erpfingen.
🐾 Guided tour (30min) Apr–Oct daily 9am–5.30pm, Mar & Nov Sat–Sun 9am–5pm. ∞4€. ℘(07128) 635. http://hoehlenwelten.sonnenbuehl.de.
This popular cavern was once home to prehistoric bears; it contains well-preserved fossilised bones.

▶ At Onstmettingen, follow the signs Nädelehaus and Raichberg.

Raichberg★
🚶 30min round-trip walk.
Park at the hotel and walk past a stone tower, across the fields to the lip of the plateau. From here views★ extend over the downward sweep of the Jura. In the

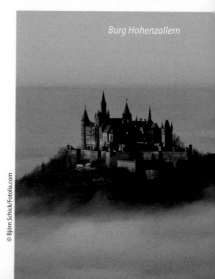
Burg Hohenzollern

© Björn Schick/Fotolia.com

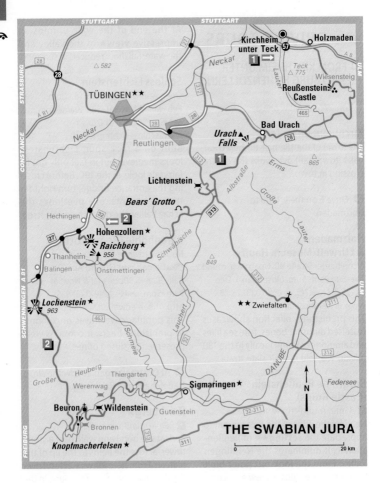

THE SWABIAN JURA

distance, you can spot the turrets of Burg Hohenzollern.

◯ Continue to Burg Hohenzollern (*see BURG HOHENZOLLERN*) via Tannheim and Hechingen.

② FROM HOHENZOLLERN TO THE DANUBE GAP★

89km/55.3mi. Allow half a day.

Burg Hohenzollern★

Open year-round mid-Mar–Oct daily 10am–5.30pm; Nov–mid-Mar, 10am–4.30pm. Guided tours of the treasury. Closed Dec 24. 5-10€.
ℰ (07471) 24 28.
www.burg-hohenzollern.com.

The ancestral home of the royal Hohenzollern family stands tall and turreted on a hill bordering the Swabian Jura; from any angle, it looks like a fortress plucked straight from a fairytale.
Draped over a hillside, the massive castle projects medieval flair, thanks to its many turrets and towers and crenellated walls, but actually dates to only the 19C.
The chapel of **St. Michael** (*Michaeliskapelle*) and the casemates alone survived from the old castle, which was built between the 11C and 15C and fell into disrepair in the 18C. The chapel's **stained-glass windows** are considered to be the oldest in southern Germany. Another chapel held the coffins of Friedrich-Wilhelm I, the Prussian Soldier

Cradle of the Hohenzollerns

The Hohenzollern dynasty goes back to the Counts of Zollern, rulers of Hechingen; the dynasty was subsequently divided into several branches. In 1415, the Hohenzollerns of Franconia became margraves, then Prince-Electors of Brandenburg. In 1618 they succeeded to the Duchy of Prussia. In the 18C the Kingdom of Prussia became a leading power in Europe, and so it was a Hohenzollern, Wilhelm I, who became head of the German Empire, founded in 1871 at the instigation of Prussia. Less than 50 years later, military defeat in World War I ended the domination of the Hohenzollern dynasty: on 9 November 1918, Kaiser Wilhelm II was forced to abdicate.

King, and his son Frederick the Great from Potsdam from 1952 to 1991 when they were returned to Potsdam.

Guided tours provide access to the castle **treasury** (Schatzkammer), a treasure chest of crowns and gowns, uniforms, snuff boxes, flutes and porcelain.

Before leaving the castle, tour the ramparts (start on the left, after the drawbridge) and enjoy the **panorama★** of the Swabian Jura and the Upper Neckar Valley.

Lochenstein★

🚶 30min round-trip walk.

Park at the Lochenpaß saddle and climb to the Lochenstein summit (alt 963m/3 159ft) topped by an iron cross. From here a **view★** of the Balingen–Hechingen depression, and in the distance, Hohenzollern Castle, is possible.

Beyond the pass, the road corkscrews downhill and then crosses the bare, rolling uplands of the Großer Heuberg plateau.

Knopfmacherfelsen★

Below the car park, make your way to a **viewpoint★** over the Danube Valley as far as Beuron Abbey and on the right, Schloss Bronnen.

Kloster Beuron (Beuron Abbey)

Open year-round daily 5am–8pm.
♿ ℘(07466) 170.
www.erzabtei-beuron.de.
This flourishing Benedictine congregation contributed to the revival of monastic life, the liturgy and the use of the Gregorian chant in Germany. The **Gnadenkapelle** (chapel of mercy), added in 1898, is decorated in the so-called "Beuron style" inspired by a 19C Byzantium-influenced school of sacred art.

Burg Wildenstein

7km/4.3mi from Beuron via Leibertingen. This small citadel commanding the Danube has a defence system made up of two moats and two towers linked by a fortified wall.

Below Beuron, the road follows the **Danube Valley★** past Wildenstein and Werenwag castle, towards Sigmaringen. As you approach the town, the cliffs give way to whimsical rock pinnacles between Thiergarten and Gutenstein.

Sigmaringen★

🛈 Leopoldplatz 4. ℘(07571) 106 224. www.sigmaringen.de. Open Apr–Sept Mon–Fri 10am–1pm & 2pm–6pm, Sat–Sun and holidays 10am–1pm; Oct–Mar Mon–Fri 10am–1pm & 2pm–4pm.

Thanks to its strong natural defensive site, Sigmaringen prospered as the capital of the small principality of Hohenzollern-Sigmaringen. The castle, perched on the cliff above, dominates the town.

Schloss (Castle)

Guided visit (1hr) Apr–Oct daily 9am–6pm; Nov–Mar daily 10am–4pm. Closed Jan 1, Shrove Tue, Dec 24–25 & 31. ⊚9€. ℘(07 571) 729 230.
http://schloss-sigmaringen.de.

The oldest parts of the castle date back to 1200, though many alterations and rebuilding took place during the 17C and 19C. In fact the rooms are decorated in 16C style with coffered ceilings and tapestries and contain valuable furniture and large paintings. The Armoury is home to one of the largest weapons collections in Europe, dating from the 15C to the 19C.

Museum Marstall
Carriages, sleighs and sedan chairs are on display, alongside fine collections of 15C and 16C Swabian paintings and sculptures.

Katholisch Pfarramt St. Johann (Catholic Parish Church of St. John)
Standing fast on the castle rock, the church boasts bright stuccowork. Note in the transept chapel *(to the left)*, the alleged cradle of St. Fidelis of Sigmaringen (1577–1622), who was the first martyr and patron of the Capuchin order, as well as patron saint of Hohenzollern.

Upper Swabian Plateau★★

The enormous prosperity and cultural influence of the Benedictine abbeys of the 18C resulted in a flurry of beautiful Baroque churches scattered across the Upper Swabian Plateau. Some of the finest artists of the period were brought in to create magnificent buildings whose fluid decorations harmonise with their surroundings "so that God may be glorified in all things", according to the inscription on the Weingarten façade.

Info: Neues Kloster 1, 88427 Bad Schussenried. ℰ(07583) 33 10 60. www.oberschwaben-tourismus.de.

Location: Between Ulm and Bodensee (Lake Constance), this tour crosses the Upper Swabian Plateau through gentle hills and soft light.

Don't Miss: The abbey churches in Weingarten, Steingaden and Oberschwäbische Barockstraße.

🚗 DRIVING TOUR

RAVENSBURG TO ZWEIFALTEN

85km/52.8mi. Allow half a day.

Ravensburg
This ancient Swabian town, and onetime Free Imperial City, still hides behind a city wall of towers and fortified gateways. The road from Wangen passes beneath the Obertor, a gateway with stepped gables. At the end of Marktstraße, a block of old buildings comprises the **Rathaus** (town hall, 14C–15C) and the weigh-house with the Blaserturm, a 15C–16C tower. Another stone tower, the **Mehlsack** (sack of flour), originally whitewashed, looms 50m/164ft above the southern part of the old town. A steep staircase *(240 steps)* leads up to the Veitsburg for even more spectacular views.

Follow the B30 towards Weingarten.

Weingarten★★
Consecrated in 1724, the abbey church in Weingarten rivals Ottobeuren as the largest Baroque sanctuary in Germany,

102m/334.6ft long and 44m/144.3ft wide at the transepts. Various architectural elements reflect an Italian influence transmitted by way of Salzburg.

The interior is a collaboration of the masters of the day. The frescoes on the vaulted ceiling by Cosmas Damien Asam are full of virtuosity, as are the choir stalls carved by Joseph Anton Feuchtmayer. The **organ**★★ was crafted by Joseph Gabler (1700–1771) and fits perfectly with the rest of the decoration: its 6 666 pipes follow the line of the windows and blend with the pink marble.

▶ The tour continues along the **Upper Swabian Baroque Road** (signposted "Oberschwäbische Barockstraße") via the B30 until Bad Waldsee. Turn left onto the L 275.

Bad Schussenried

Abbey: open Apr–Oct Tue–Fri 10am–1pm, 2pm–5pm, Sat–Sun 10am–5pm. Nov–Mar Sat–Sun 1pm–5pm. Church: Easter–Oct daily 1.30pm–5.30pm (Sat from 10am); closed Nov–Easter. Closed Jan 1, Dec 24, 25 & 31. ☞5.50€. ✆(07583) 92 69 140. www.kloster-schussenried.de.

This pleasant town's **abbey buildings** (now partly used as a psychiatric hospital and for art and cultural events) and abbey church owe their sumptuous Baroque appearance to Premonstratensian abbots. In the **church**, the upper panels of the intricately decorated choir stalls (1717) are separated by 28 statuettes representing men and women who founded religious orders. The most spectacular part of the complex is the light-flooded Baroque **library**★ with two storeys of bookcases canopied by a ceiling fresco by Franz Georg Herrmann depicting the Apocalypse, Scholarship, Education and Craft.

Steinhausen★

Designed by Dominikus and Johann Zimmermann, this hamlet's beautiful little pilgrimage church comprises a single nave and a small chancel, both oval. Capitals, cornices and window embrasures are adorned with birds,

The Devil to Pay

Of the 66 stops (sets of pipes) of the Weingarten organ, the 46th is called "Vox Humana". Joseph Gabler's ambition was to build an organ combining man and machine in resounding praise of God. After countless attempts to re-create a human sound, he is said to have sold his soul to the devil, who supplied him with a piece of metal that he melted to make the pipes. The monks were so enthralled by the beauty of the organ's song that they were unable to pray, whereupon the abbot ordered an enquiry. Gabler was found out, confessed and sentenced to death. But since the only sounds produced by the organ now resembled wailing, Gabler was reprieved.

insects or flowers. Also note the 1415 Pietà above the altar.

▶ Follow the L275 until Riedlingen, then join the B312 to Zwiefalten.

Zwiefalten★★

This village has a remarkable 18C **church**, built by **Johann Michael Fischer** and considered a late Baroque masterpiece.

Church façade, Zwiefalten

© Imagebroker.net/Photoshot

Behind a comparatively plain façade hides a lavish interior accented by a profusion of colours, exuberant details and artistic virtuosity. The eye finally settles on the details: ceiling paintings of the Virgin Mary by Franz Joseph Spiegler, a pulpit decorated by Johann Michael Feuchtmayer (uncle of the sculptor and stuccoworker, Joseph Anton Feuchtmayer), angels and cherubs galore.

▶ Go back to Riedlingen, then take the B311 to the left.

Obermarchtal

☏Tour on request. ✆(07375) 95 050. Built by Michael and Christian Thumb and Franz Beer, this 17C **abbey church** is an example of the early Baroque. Gems include white Wessobrunn stuccowork, elaborate carved choir stalls by Paul Speiegger and a famous organ.

Ulm★★

The royal palace of "Hulma", recorded for the first time in 854, was one of Europe's most important medieval cities. Blessed with an exceptional cathedral and walks along the Danube, the old city delights visitors. Ulm's most famous local figure is Albert Einstein, born here in 1879.

MÜNSTER★★★

Open Jul–Aug daily 9am–7.45pm; Apr–Jun & Sept until 6.45pm; Mar & Oct until 5.45pm; Nov–Feb until 4.45pm (tower closes 1hr earlier). Tower ⊛4€. www.ulmer–muenster.de.

▶ **Population:** 121 650
🛈 **Info:** Münsterplatz 50. ✆(0731) 161 28 30. www.tourismus.ulm.de.
▶ **Location:** Ulm is separated from Neu-Ulm by the river Danube and lies about midway between Munich and Stuttgart on the A8 autobahn.
🅿 **Parking:** Garages can be found near the main train station and the town hall.
☺ **Don't Miss:** Ulm's cathedral and the suggested walking tour.
🕐 **Timing:** Allow at least an hour to tour Ulm's cathedral, including a climb up the world's tallest church spire.
👥 **Kids:** Ascending Ulm Cathedral's spire (older children).

Nave, Münster

© Reinhold Mayer/Ulm/ Neu-Ulm Touristik GmbH

At a height of 161m/528ft, Ulm's cathedral spire is the tallest in the world and the most distinctive feature of the city skyline. Although the foundation stone was laid in 1377, the two towers and spire were added only in 1890.

The minster's **interior** also draws the eye skyward. The chancel arch bears the largest fresco north of the Alps, a 1471 work depicting the Last Judgement. To the right on the chancel arch stands the 15C *Man of Sorrows*, an early work by native Ulmer, Hans Multscher. The pulpit is canopied by a splendid wooden sounding board from 1510, the work of Jörg Syrlin the Younger. A second pulpit in the late-Gothic style further up is intended for the Holy Spirit, the invisible preacher. The four side aisles feature fine late-Gothic fan vaulting.

Left of the entrance to the chancel is the **tabernacle★**, at 26m/85ft the tallest in Germany. This masterpiece (c. 1460–70) was chiselled out of limestone and sandstone. Three rows of wooden figures depict the prophets and lawmakers. Note the small figures of people and animals carved into the handrail of the banister on which the artist has allowed his imagination to run riot.

The **choir stalls★★★** are a marvellous example of wood carving, executed by Jörg Syrlin the Elder between 1469 and 1474. Two series of characters, from the Bible and from pagan Antiquity, face one another. Men are grouped on the left, women on the right, the upper gables being devoted to the Church's apostles and martyrs, and the high backs of the stalls to Old Testament figures.

For many cathedral visitors, the highlight is a 768-step **ascent of the spire**. The structure resembles stone lacework in its upper reaches, and reveals a **panorama★★** of not only the town and the Danube but also the plateaux of the Swabian Jura and the Alps.

SIGHTS
Stadthaus (Town Hall)
Ulm's town hall is a daring construction by American architect Richard Meier. His Modernist design uses white stone, stucco and concrete in curving forms to serve as a backdrop to the venerable cathedral. It generated a lot of controversy upon its completion in 1993. However, it does lend a casual air to the Münsterplatz, and has since been accepted as an attractive link between the past and the present.

Ulmer Museum★
Marktplatz 9. Open year-round Tue–Sun 11am–5pm (Thu until 8pm for special exhibits). Closed Shrove Tue, Good

The Iconoclasts
Konrad Sam, a virulent preacher, brought the Swiss Reformation to Ulm in 1530, advocating the destruction of religious imagery. Following a referendum approved by 87 percent of the population, he made the cathedral Protestant. Private donors removed their altars and sealed the cathedral's central door, the stalls and the tabernacle. Some altars were given to neighbouring villages, where they remain today. The full rage of the iconoclasts was unleashed on 21 June 1531 when the remaining cathedral icons (60 altars, numerous statues, altarpieces and hangings) were destroyed.

Friday. 5€, combination ticket with Kunsthalle Weishaupt 10€. (0731) 161 43 30. www.ulmer-museum.ulm.de.

This rambling museum has some great works by local masters. Note especially the *Virgin Mary of Bihlafingen* by Hans Multscher and the charming 13C *Mary of Sorrows*, edged in blue and gold, by a master from the Lake Constance area. The archaeological department boasts the 30 000-year-old Stone Age "Lion Man" statuette, masterfully carved from a mammoth tusk.

Also part of the museum is the late-Renaissance **Kiechelhaus**, which is the only suviving Patrician mansion from the 16C–17C; it provides insight into the lifestyle of a wealthy merchant family. A new modern building makes a suitable setting for the **Kurt Fried Collection** of 20C art, including works by Kandinsky, Klee, Kirchner and Rothko.

Kunsthalle Weishaupt
Hans-und-Sophie-Scholl-Platz 1. Open year-round Tue–Sun 11am–5pm (Thu until 8pm). 6€ or 10€ in combination with Ulmer Museum. (0731) 161 43 60. www.kunsthalle-weishaupt.de.

A spectacular, modern glass-and-steel building, designed by Richard Meier

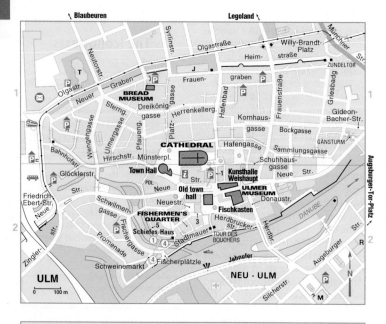

Map of Ulm

Olympic Designs

Pictograms representing each of the Olympic disciplines were designed at the Ulm School of Design by German designer Otl Aicher for the Olympic Games in Munich in 1972. They have been used at each game and are reproduced on the medals, to the great pride of the city.

student Wolfram Wöhr, houses one of Germany's most important private collections of 20C art. Feast your eyes on Concrete art (Albers, Richard Paul Lohse), American Colour Field paintings (Rothko, Kenneth Noland), Pop Art (Warhol, Rauschenberg) as well as sculptures and installations by such high-profile practitioners as Keith Haring and the late Nam June Paik.

Altes Rathaus
(Old Town Hall)

This elegant Gothic and Renaissance building features painted façades and an astronomical clock on its west façade. It borders the market square with the Fischerkasten fountain, thus named because fishermen would cool their wares in it. The spiral pedestal was fashioned by Jörg Syrlin the Elder in 1482.

Museum der Brotkultur★
(Bread Museum)

Salzstadelgasse 10. Open year-round daily 10am–5pm. Closed Good Friday, Dec 24–25 & 31. ⊕4€. & ℘(0731) 699 55. www.museum-brotkultur.de.

The cultural and social history of 8 000 years of bread is explored in this unique museum. Exhibits range from ovens, models, guilds, coins and stamps to specially selected works of art (by Brueghel, Corinth, Kollwitz and Picasso), all

Museum der Brotkultur

© Museum der Brotkultura

related to grain or bread. The world's food supply is also critically examined.

Fischerviertel★
(Fishermen's Quarter)

Ulm is most lovely in the narrow alleys emanating from the Blau River in the quarter once inhabited by millers, fishermen and tanners.

From Fischerplätzle, a small, lime-tree-shaded square, turn left into a narrow street and pass over the little bridge, which leads to the so-called mid-15C **Schiefes Haus** (crooked house) on the banks of the Blau. The tiny alley opposite is known as the **Kußgasse** (kissing alley) because the roofs of the houses touch one another.

In the nearby 17C **Schwörhaus** (house of oaths), the town mayor swears allegiance to the 14C constitution and renews his oath of office on the first Monday of July. The town **walls** afford a wonderful close-up of the gables of the old houses. The crooked **Metzgerturm** (butcher's tower), erected in 1349, stands out since it rises nearly 2.05m/6.7ft off-centre. Go through the rose garden to reach the **Adlerbastei** (eagle bastion), where the unfortunate "Tailor of Ulm" attempted to fly in 1811.

South Bank of the Danube★

In fine weather, stroll along the pretty *Jahnufer* (the south bank of the Danube) to take in enchanting views of ornately gabled houses, the Metzgerturm and the cathedral.

ADDRESSES

🛏️STAY

🛏️ **Pension Rösch** – *Schwörhausgasse 18.* 🕿*(0731) 657 18. 16 rooms.* This simple little hotel provides good value and clean rooms at the entrance to the picturesque fishermen's quarter.

🛏️🛏️🛏️ **Schiefes Haus** – *Schwörhausgasse 6.* 🕿*(0731) 96 79 30. www.hotelschiefeshausulm.de. 11 rooms.* 🛏️. This restored medieval house harmoniously marries historic and modern touches. Some beds even sport water-filled mattresses.

🍴EAT

🍴🍴 **Zunfthaus** – *Fischergasse 31.* 🕿*(0731) 644 11. www.zunfthaus-ulm.de. Reservation recommended.* Set in the heart of the old town, this 600-year-old half-timbered building once served as the guild of the fishermen and ship builders. Today its three floors house a country-style restaurant serving regional cuisine, including locally caught fish.

NIGHTLIFE

Barfüßer – *Paulstraße 4, 89231 Neu-Ulm* 🕿*(0731) 97 44 831. www.barfuesser-brauhaus.de.* On balmy summer days, there are few places more idyllic than this riverside beer garden. Sample the homemade brews along with tasty nibbles and traditional dishes.

Munich and Southern Bavaria

*Viktualienmarkt maypole
and Peterskirche*
© A. Mueller/Munich City Tourist Office

Munich and Southern Bavaria

Germany's southernmost region bewitches visitors with gorgeous scenery, quaint villages, ancient traditions and art-filled cities. Whether you want to raise a mug of beer at Munich's Hofbräuhaus, cheer on the championship football team FC Bayern München, ski the slopes above Garmisch-Partenkirchen, soar to the "top of Germany" called the Zugspitze, or go underground in a Berchtesgaden salt mine, Munich and southern Bavaria have it all. A more sobering visit can be made to confront the darkest chapter in German history at Dachau concentration camp memorial site.

Highlights

Capital of Bavaria

The magic of Munich and southern Bavaria best unfolds when the Föhn blows in from the mountains. A warm and gusty wind, it creates crystal-clear air and generates the illusion that the Alpine peaks are actually within arm's reach when, in fact, they are over 90km/56mi away! Locals claim the wind makes them cranky, but photography enthusiasts will have a field day. Just climb up any tower to see for yourself.

City for All Seasons

Any time of year is a fine time to visit Munich. Springtime brings longer days, raucous carnival celebrations, potent beers and traditional dancing during the *Starkbierzeit* (strong beer festival). Summer is best for carousing in beer gardens or listening to live music at the Tollwood Festival against the backdrop of the landmark Olympic Stadium. The biggest lure in autumn is, of course, Oktoberfest, the world's biggest drink-up. Winter, too, is lovely with its aromatic Christmas markets, a busy cultural calendar and cosy beer taverns serving hearty fare.

Munich Museum Mania

Museums are in season year-round, naturally, and there's truly something for everyone. Art fans can spend days feasting on canvases from Tintoretto to Twombly by just touring the three Pinakothek museums. Sculpture lovers should steer towards the

---

Bavaria's "Dark Ages"

If Berlin was the head of the Nazi government (1933–45), its heartbeat was in Bavaria. After Hitler came to power in January 1933, Munich became the official "Capital of the Movement", and Nuremberg was chosen for staging the Nazi party's mass rallies. In Dachau, north of Munich, Germany's first concentration camp was built in 1933. In 1935 the party brass ushered in the systematic repression of the Jews by passing the notorious Nuremberg Laws. Many leading Nazis were Bavarian, including Heinrich Himmler and Hermann Göring. Hitler himself was born just across the border, in Austria's Braunau. The Alpine resort of Berchtesgaden served as the southern party headquarters, and the Winter Olympic Games of 1936 were held in Garmisch-Partenkirchen. Although the Nazis enjoyed almost universal support in Bavaria, there were also some pockets of resistance, most notably from the Munich-based student group, Die Weisse Rose (The White Rose).

Glyptothek and the Antiquity Collection, while technology lovers should put the German Museum, the Transport Museum and the BMW World at the top of their list. Those who are interested in the history of the former German royal family will want to make the pilgrimage to the Residence and its many treasures as well as the Wittelsbach's summer retreat, Nymphenburg Palace, with its expansive and lushly landscaped gardens.

Schloss Linderhof

© Bergfee/Fotolia.com

Legacy of Ludwig II

The most famous Wittelsbach ruler was Ludwig II, the late 19C fairytale king whose life ended young, tragically and mysteriously in Lake Starnberg, just south of Munich. An idealist and a dreamer, Ludwig quite literally built his legacy in stone. The palaces he conceived – Neuschwanstein, Herrenchiemsee, Linderhof – are as lavish as they are theatrical and thus a perfect reflection of the king's fantasies and longings for a time long gone.

Bewitching Scenery

What all three of Ludwig's palaces have in common is their stunning locations: surrounded by forest, in a romantic valley and on an island in a huge lake. But then it's hard to find any less than breathtaking scenery in southern Bavaria. The rugged peaks of the mighty Alps give way to rolling foothills, thick forests, rippling mountain streams, moody moorland and majestic lakes that are havens for outdoor adventurers. Through it all run rivers like the Isar and the epic Danube, which has captured the imagination of poets, painters and composers and delivered power and prosperity to the region.

Roman Metropolises

When Munich was created in the 11C, Passau, Augsburg and Regenburg had already been on the map for over 1 000 years. Founded by the Romans, they reached their zenith in the Middle Ages, especially Augsburg, where the Fugger family financed European wars, and Regensburg, whose UNESCO-listed old town is still an enticing blend of medieval architecture and 21C vitality fuelled by a sizable student body.

Königssee Berchtesgaden National Park

© Stefan Baum/Bigstockphoto.com

Munich and Southern Bavaria

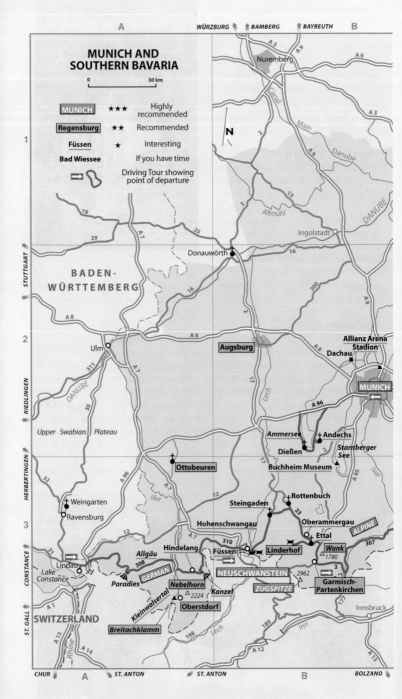

WÜRZBURG BAMBERG BAYREUTH

MUNICH AND SOUTHERN BAVARIA

0   30 km

MUNICH   ★★★   Highly recommended

Regensburg   ★★   Recommended

Füssen   ★   Interesting

Bad Wiessee   If you have time

Driving Tour showing point of departure

N

Nuremberg

Canal   Main   Danube

Altmühl   Ingolstadt   DANUBE

STUTTGART   Donauwörth

BADEN-WÜRTTEMBERG

Ulm   DANUBE

RIEDLINGEN   **Augsburg**   Allianz Arena Stadion   Dachau

Upper Swabian Plateau   Lech

A 96   **MUNICH**

Ammersee   Andechs

HERBERTINGEN   Weingarten   **Ottobeuren**   Dießen   Starnberger See

Ravensburg   **Buchheim Museum**

Iller   Steingaden   **Rottenbuch**

Hohenschwangau   Oberammergau

Allgäu   Hindelang   Füssen   **Linderhof**   Ettal   ALPINE

GERMAN   **NEUSCHWANSTEIN**   **Wank** △1780

CONSTANCE   Lindau   Paradies   **Nebelhorn** △2224   Kanzel   2962   **ZUGSPITZE**   Garmisch-Partenkirchen

Lake Constance   Kleinwalsertal   **Oberstdorf**   Lech   Innsbruck

ST. GALL   **SWITZERLAND**   **Breitachklamm**   Inn

Rhine   198   A 12

CHUR   ST. ANTON   ST. ANTON   BOLZANO

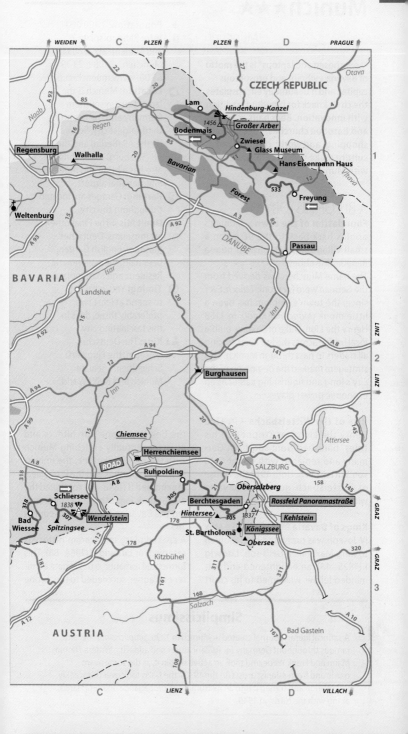

Munich★★★

München

"Lederhosen and laptops" is the motto of Bavaria's vibrant and prosperous capital, and it beautifully encapsulates the city's knack for blending tradition with innovation. Beer halls, gardens and Baroque churches, superb shopping, and world-class art and culture make it easy to fall in love with Munich.

A BIT OF HISTORY

Foundation of the town – Munich's origins hark back to the 9C when a small village was established near a Benedictine abbey.

The name München was derived from the German word for monk: *Mönch*. Ever since, the town's emblem has been a little monk *(Münchner Kindl)*. In 1158 Henry the Lion, Duke of Saxony, built a local bridge across the Isar River, forcing all traders to pass through Munich. This stratagem marked the beginning of the city's long and flourishing career as an economic power player.

Rise of the Wittelsbachs – In 1180 Henry the Lion was stripped of his titles, banished from southern Germany and replaced with Count Otto von Wittelsbach. Until 1918 the House of Wittelsbach governed Bavaria without interruption.

Kings of Bavaria – In 1806 Duke Max IV Joseph was promoted by Napoleon to King Maximilian I. His son, **Ludwig I** (1825–48), an enlightened and art-minded fellow, welcomed to his court

▶ **Population:** 1 400 000

▪ **Info:** Bahnhofsplatz 2 and Marienplatz 2, 80335 München. ☏(089) 23 39 65 00. www.muenchen.de.

▶ **Location:** Munich is the largest city in southern Germany and the country's third-largest city. Served by the A9 (Berlin) and the A8 (Salzburg) autobahns, it also has a huge and modern international airport.

P **Parking:** Garages are located throughout the city.

🐾 **Don't Miss:** The Pinakothek art museums, Deutsches Museum, English Garden, beer halls, Viktualienmarkt, Residenz and Marienplatz.

🕐 **Timing:** You will want to spend at least two, preferably three, days in this fascinating city.

👥 **Kids:** The Deutsches Museum, the Flugwerft Schleißheim, SeaLife Munich and BMW World.

the best of Europe's architects and artists, eventually enriching Munich with the Alte Pinakothek, the university, the Glyptothek and the Propylaea. **Maximilian II** (1848–64) continued the artistic traditions of his father by founding the Bavarian National Museum in 1855.

A special place in Bavarian history is reserved for **Ludwig II** (1864–86). This tormented romantic, a passionate admirer of Wagner, succeeded to the throne

Simplicissimus

A satirical literary journal created in Munich in 1896, *Simplicissimus* became famous throughout Germany for its caricatures and audacity. Writers Thomas Mann and Frank Wedekind took an active part in it, as did some avant-garde and Expressionist artists. In the 1930s, the Nazis took over this weekly publication and turned it into an instrument of propaganda. It disappeared, along with the Nazis, in 1945.

PRACTICAL INFORMATION

TELEPHONE AREA CODE: ℰ089

TOURIST INFORMATION

Tourist Offices: *Bahnhofsplatz 2 (main train station);* Neues Rathaus *(Marienplatz 2).*

PUBLICATIONS

Several publications including listings of current events. Check out the free publication *In München* and the glossy for-purchase *Prinz.* Thursday's *"SZ-extra"* supplement of the *Süddeutsche Zeitung* newspaper also has listings.

TICKETS

Book tickets well in advance by phone, online or in person from the tourist offices or at commercial ticket vendors such as www.muenchenticket.de.

POST OFFICES WITH LATE HOURS

Bahnhofsplatz 1: Mon–Fri 8am–8pm, Sat 9am–4pm; Postfiliale 24 at the airport *(central area level 3)* in McPaper: Mon–Sat 7.30am–9pm.

DAILY PAPERS

Süddeutsche Zeitung, Münchner Merkur.

INTERNET

www.munich-touristinfo.de; www.muenchen.de; www.munichfound.de.

AIRPORT

ℰ*(089) 975 00. www.munich-airport.de.* Munich International Airport, 34km/ 21mi north, is linked to the city by S-Bahn lines S1 and S8 *(departures every 10min around the clock, 10.80€),* and by the Lufthansa Airport Bus *(www.airportbus-muenchen.de; departure every 20min from 6.20am to 9.40pm, 10.50€).*

GETTING THERE AND AROUND

Central Munich is compact, and large sections of it are pedestrianised. Many sights are within walking distance; the city's main museums can be reached by tram or U-Bahn, from Karlsplatz, Marienplatz or Hauptbahnhof (main railway station).

Public Transport – Munich and its surroundings are divided into four ring-shaped price zones. The network consists of subways (U-Bahn), buses and trams *(Straßenbahn),* and light rail (S-Bahn). The main local transportation authority is **MVV** *(Münchner Verkehrs-und Tarifverbund; ℰ(089) 41 42 43 44; www.mvv-muenchen.de).* Information by phone, online or at the MVV office on the mezzanine level of the main train station, open Mon–Fri 8am–8pm, Sat 9am–4pm. Tickets are available from vending machines at any U-Bahn or S-Bahn rail station, in trams and from bus drivers. Tickets must be stamped on the station platform or aboard buses and trams. The fine for riding without a valid ticket is 40€.

Tickets for the central zone *(Münchner Innenraum),* which includes Munich city centre: single tickets *(Einzelfahrt)* 2.60€; stripe card *(Streifenkarte)* 12.50€ consists of 10 stripes, stamp two stripes for rides within the central zone, more stripes for longer trips; card can be used by more than one person and transfers are allowed. Single day tickets *(Single-Tageskarte)* 8.10€.

CityTourCard – There are six versions: one-day single *(Single 1 Tag)* 10.90€; three-day single *(Single 3 Tage)* 20.90€; four-day single *(Single 4 Tage)* 25.90€; one-day "Partner" (for five adults – two children between six and 14 years old equal one adult) *(Partner 1 Tag)* 17.90€; three-day "Partner" *(Partner 3 Tage)* 30.90€; and four-day "Partner" *(Partner 4 Tage)* 39.90€. The ticket entitles you to unlimited public transport in the central city and to discounts of 10–50 percent for more than 70 sights, museums, castles, tourist attractions, as well as city tours and bicycle hire. It is available from MVV offices, U-Bahn and S-Bahn ticket vending machines and in some hotels.

Bicycle rental – Munich is a bicycle-friendly city. *Radius Bike Tours (Arnulf-straße 3; ℰ(089) 54 34 87 77 30; www.radiusmunich.com)* rents bikes for 17€ per 24hrs (50€ deposit) and also conducts bike and walking tours. The office is located opposite track 32 of the Hauptbahnhof and is open Apr–Oct daily 8.30am–6pm (May–Sept until 8pm on weekends); Nov–Mar dependent on weather or by request.

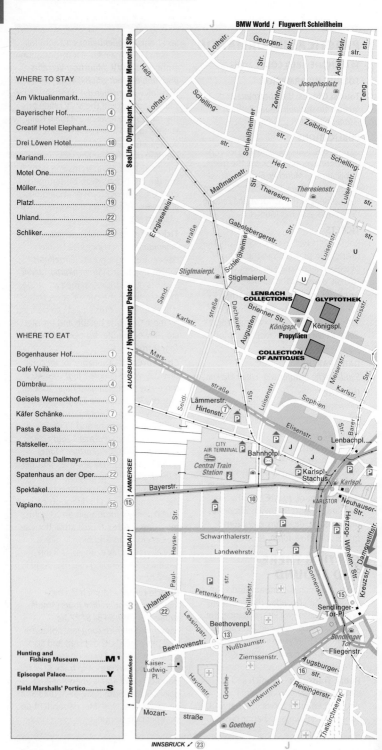

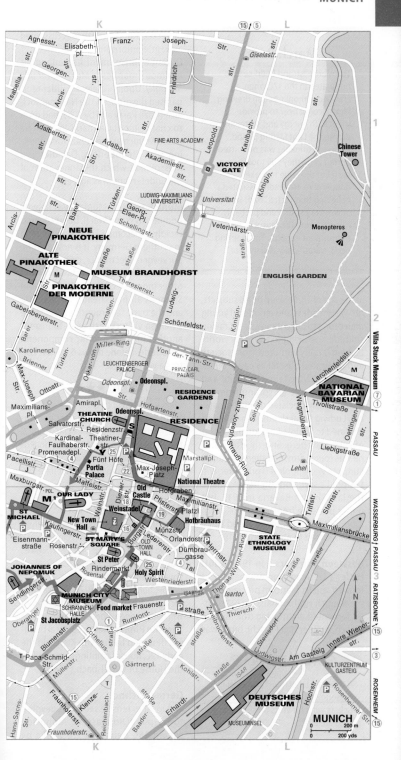

March Beer

The March "strong beer" season originated in the 17C when Franciscan monks began brewing high-alcohol beer to provide them with energy and sustenance during the Lent fasting period. Although drinking was permitted during Lent, they still took a barrel to the Pope to make doubly sure. He readily assented, believing that such a "bad" beer (it was very strong and probably ruined during the journey) was punishment enough. These spring beers traditionally end in "ator".

at the age of 18. Beloved by his subjects, he was a restless and emotional young man prone to deep depression. Craving solitude and living in a fantasy world, Ludwig largely withdrew from society and dedicated himself to castle building: Neuschwanstein, Linderhof and Herrenchiemsee all sprang from his fevered brow. Declared mentally unstable, Ludwig II was deposed in 1886 and confined to Schloss Berg, on the shores of Lake Starnberg. Shortly afterwards he was found drowned there. His uncle Luitpold was appointed prince regent. Luitpold's son, **Ludwig III**, was made the last king of Bavaria in 1912, but under pressure from a workers' revolutionary movement after World War I, he was forced to abdicate in 1918.

Between two wars – In 1919, **Adolf Hitler**'s German Workers' party was formed and its platform proclaimed at the Munich Hofbräuhaus. In 1923, Hitler fomented an uprising (the Munich Putsch, or Beer Hall Putsch), but it was

unsuccessful, the party was dissolved and Hitler imprisoned.

During imprisonment he penned his infamous manifesto *Mein Kampf (My Struggle)*. Upon his release, Hitler reorganised the group as the National Socialist (Nazi) Party and by 1933, had risen to chancellor of Germany. In 1938, he chose Munich as the venue for a meeting with Chamberlain, Daladier and Mussolini at which the annexation of the Sudetenland was agreed.

Munich today – Munich was heavily bombed in World War II, but recovered rapidly to become a key economic zone in southern Germany. It is now a prime purveyor of electronics, cars, insurance services, information technology and other industries. Microsoft, BMW and Siemens all have headquarters here and the trade fairgrounds attract some 2 million visitors each year. Tourism is another major economic component: Oktoberfest alone draws 6 million visitors a year.

KUNSTAREAL★★★ (ART QUARTER)

Munich's famous Art Quarter encompasses the Alte Pinakothek (14C to 18C), the Neue Pinakothek (19C), the Pinakothek der Moderne (early 20C) and since 2009, the Museum Brandhorst (late 20C and 21C).

Alte Pinakothek★★★

Barer Straße 15. Open year-round daily 10am–6pm (Tue until 8pm). Closed Shrove Tue, May 1, Dec 24, 25 & 31. ✆4€, Sun 1€. ♿ ℘(089) 23 80 52 16. www.pinakothek.de.
Renovations through 2017 will close some sections of the museum, but other sections will remain open. Check the website.
The **Alte Pinakothek**, a colossal building designed by Leo von Klenze in the early 19C, houses paintings amassed by the House of Wittelsbach.

German School

The most extensive section is devoted to German Old Masters. Alongside sacred 15C paintings are works by

☺ **A Bit of Advice** ☺

A Day Pass to all four Kunstareal museums is 12€. Combination tickets valid for visits on separate days are 29€.

Neue Pinakothek

painters inspired by the Italian Renaissance. Masterpieces include **Albrecht Dürer**'s *Four Apostles* (1526); **Albrecht Altdorfer**'s *Landscape* (1528); and **Hans Holbein the Elder**'s *St. Sebastian Altarpiece* (1516).

Dutch and Flemish Schools
Among the most important works in this section are *The Land of Milk and Honey* (1566) by **Pieter Brueghel the Elder** and *The Last Judgement* (c. 1614–16) by **Peter Paul Rubens**. Early Dutch masterpieces include the *Altarpiece of the Three Magi* (1455) by **Rogier Van der Weyden**; *Seven Joys of Mary* (c. 1480) by **Hans Memling**; and *Last Judgment* by **Hieronymus Bosch**. **Rembrandt**'s Passion Cycle constitutes the heart of the collection of 17C Dutch paintings.

Italian School
Here the spotlight is on Renaissance masters: **Sandro Botticelli**'s *Lamentation of Christ* (post 1490); three major works by **Raphael**, including the *Madonna Tempi* (1507); *The Crowning of Thorns* (1560) by **Titian**; **Tiepolo**'s *Veneration of the Holy Trinity* by Pope Clemens (1739) and the *Adoration of the Magi* (1753); and works by **Antonio Canaletto** and **Francesco Guardi**.

French School
French Classicism is represented by **Claude Lorrain**'s *Sea Port at Sunrise* (1674) and by paintings of **Nicolas Poussin**, who takes his subjects from Ovid's *Metamorphoses* (1627). Among the 18C paintings, **François Boucher**'s *Madame Pompadour* is on display, commissioned by her in 1756.

Spanish School
This school is notably represented by **Murillo**'s lively genre paintings alongside epic canvases by **El Greco** and **Velázquez**.

Neue Pinakothek★★
Barer Straße 29, enter from Theresienstraße. Open year-round daily 10am–6pm (Wed until 8pm). Closed May 1, Dec 24, 25 & 31. 7€, Sun 1€. &. (089) 23 80 51 95. www.pinakothek.de.
The **Neue Pinakothek** is a well-proportioned Postmodernist work by Alexander von Branca, completed in 1981. It replaced the original building by Friedrich von Gärtner that suffered irreparable damage during World War II. The collection focuses on works from the 19C and early 20C.

Early 19C
Galleries **1, 2 and 2a** are devoted to European art from around 1800. Canvases worth focusing on include: **Thomas Gainsborough**'s portraits and landscapes, works by **Jacques-Louis David**, including the *Marquise de Sorcy*, **Joshua Reynolds** (*Captain Pownall*), **William Turner** (*Ostend*) and **Francisco Goya** (*Marquesa de Caballero*).

The Collection

The Pinakothek collection was started in the 16C by Duke Wilhelm IV, who commissioned historical scenes from the most eminent painters of his time, Altdorfer and Burgkmair. In the 17C, the Elector Maximilian I founded the Kammergalerie which, under King Ludwig I, developed into the finest exhibition of art in the whole of Europe. The building suffered severe damage in 1943, but the paintings had already been moved to a safe location.

Early 19C German painters

On display in Galleries **3 and 3a** are early-Romantic works from Dresden, Berlin and Munich, including the highly spiritual landscapes of **Caspar David Friedrich**. Johann Christian **Dahl** (*Frederiksholm Canal in Copenhagen*, 1817) and Karl **Blechen** (*View of Assisi*, 1830) are also represented. Ludwig I of Bavaria was a great patron of the arts who commissioned many paintings, including those on display in Galleries **4 and 4a**. Galleries **5 and 5a** are devoted to the German Neoclassicists in Rome, including a well-known landscape by **Ludwig Richter**, *The Night-Watchman* (*Watzmann*, 1824).

The following galleries focus on two early 19C trends: the spiritual Nazarenes, who sought to reconcile northern and southern painting by hearking back to Raphael and Dürer; and artists of the **Biedermeier** style.

Romanticism to Realism

Pride of place is given to French painters in Galleries **10 and 10a**. The Romantics are represented by **Théodore Géricault** and his admirer **Eugène Delacroix**. In Galleries **11 and 11a**, **Andreas Achenbach** and **Carl Spitzweg** (*The Hussar*, *The Poor Poet*, 1839, *The Writer*, 1850) represent late German Romanticism.

Late 19C German painters

Gallery **15** is entirely devoted to **Hans von Marées** (1837–1887), a great portrait painter inspired by Renaissance art. Gallery **16** contains works by a group of German painters who went to live and work in Rome: Arnold Böcklin, Hans Thoma, **Anselm Feuerbach** and **Wilhelm Leibl**.

Impressionists, post-Impressionists and Symbolists

Gallery **18** focuses on **Wilhelm Liebl**, while **19** is devoted to French Impressionists **Manet, Degas and Cezanne**. German Impressionists, plus a few sculptures by **Auguste Rodin**, occupy Gallery **20**. Rodin's marble bust of *Helene von Nostitz* is surrounded by several works by **Ferdinand Hodler** (*Landscape on Lake Geneva*).

Gallery **21** is devoted to French Impressionists such as **Paul Gauguin** and Paul Sérusier. **Vincent Van Gogh**'s *Sunflowers* series (1888) is also on display. Symbolism and *Jugendstil* provide the theme of Gallery **21a**.

Gallery **22** is reserved for modernists such as **Pablo Picasso** (bronze *Head of a Jester*, 1906), **Lovis Corinth** (*Self Portrait*, 1924), Giovanni Segantini (*Ploughing*, 1890) and Hodler.

Gallery **22a** holds works of early 20C contemporaries such as **Gustav Klimt** (*Margarethe Stonborough-Wittgenstein*, the philosopher's sister and the subject of Klimt's famous portrait of 1905) and **Egon Schiele** (*Agony*, 1912).

Pinakothek der Moderne★★

Barer Straße 40. Open year-round Tue–Sun 10am–6pm (Thu until 8pm). Closed Shrove Tue, May 1, Dec 24, 25 & 31. ⊚10€, Sun 1€. &ℓ(089) 23 80 53 60. www.pinakothek.de.

Designed by Munich architect Stephan Braunfels, the building is known as the "Cathedral of Light" because of its glass rotunda and glazed saw-tooth roofs. It unites four museums with collections of 20C paintings, sculpture, graphics, design and architecture under a single roof.

Sammlung Moderne Kunst
(Collection of Modern Art)

3rd floor. The question of form and content in modern art is the underlying theme of the permanent exhibition, arranged in chronological order and by cross-influence.

"Classic" Modern Art (Galleries 1–17) – A large section is devoted to German Expressionism. The artist group *Die Brücke (The Bridge)*, which was led by **Ernst Ludwig Kirchner** and whose tortured subjects set them apart from the Fauves, is well represented. So are members of *Der Blaue Reiter (The Blue Rider)*, who focused on abstraction and spiritualisation of form; Franz Marc and **Wassily Kandinsky** were at the visionary helm of this group. Another Expressionist, **Max Beckmann**, is represented by the *Temptation of St. Anthony*. The Cubists and Futurists moved towards autonomous art, as illustrated in numerous works by **Pablo Picasso** (including *Madame Soler*) and **Georges Braque**. Surrealism is represented by Max Ernst, René Magritte and Salvador Dalí, and Bauhaus by Feininger and Paul Klee.

Modern Art (Galleries 20–36) – Important themes in art during the second half of the 20C – informal art, celebration of the trivial, rise of pop culture, etc.– are broached in artists' monographs. One can follow the works of **Joseph Beuys**, **Francis Bacon** *(Crucifixion)* and Willem de Kooning. The museum also displays some remarkable works by American artists, with paintings by **Andy Warhol**, photographs by Jeff Wall and videos by Bruce Nauman.

Other Departments

Neue Sammlung *(New Design Collection, basement)* – In addition to objects of industrial design, accessories, cars and computer equipment, the museum presents prototypes of items designed since the industrial revolution up to the 1960s.

Selections from the **Grafische Sammlung** (Graphic Arts Collection) are shown in temporary exhibits on the ground floor owing to their great sensitivity to light.

Finally, the **Architekturmuseum** (Architecture Museum) is the largest of its kind in Germany with a rich collection of models, photographs, blueprints and computer prints dating from the 16C to today. The focus is on architecture in Germany in the 19C and 20C with particular attention given to the genius of Leo von Klenze, Le Corbusier and Peter Zumthor.

Museum Brandhorst★★

Theresienstrasse 35a. Open year-round Tue–Sun 10am–6pm (Thu until 8pm). Closed Shrove Tue, May 1, Dec 24–25 & 31. ᷛ7€, Sun 1€. ᴽᴽ(089) 238 05 22 86. www.museum-brandhorst.de.

In a stunning, eco-friendly building by the Berlin architectural firm Sauerbruch Hutton, the Museum Brandhorst has enriched Munich's cultural landscape since 2009. It presents masterpieces by key contemporary artists, including the largest collection of works by Cy Twombly outside of Houston. The artist's 12-canvas *Lepanto* cycle, which is displayed in its own polygonal room, is especially fine. Pop-Artist Andy Warhol also gets plenty of wall space alongside ground-breaking German practitioners Joseph Beuys, Mario Merz, Sigmar Polke, Georg Baselitz and Gerhard Richter. Select works by Damien Hirst, Dave LaChapelle and Bruce Nauman complete the collection.

Sammlung Schack★★

Prinzregentenstraße 9. Open year-round Wed–Sun 10am–6pm. Closed Shrove Tue, May 1, Dec 24–25 & 31. ᷛ4€, Sun 1€. ᴽᴽ(089) 238 05 22 86. www.pinakothek.de.

Literary critic, lawyer and diplomat Count Adolph Friedrich von Schack began collecting art in the mid-19C, focusing on young, unknown artists, and later adding Renaissance Italian works. He bequeatherd his collection to the German emperor. A gallery in which to display it was built in Munich in 1909, where it has remained ever since, comprising the fifth of the Pinakothek museums.

Among the displays are three galleries devoted to Austrian saga painter **Moritz von Schwind** (1804-1871), such as his *Captive Princess*, (1860) in which the chained maiden is guarded by a giant.

DEUTSCHES MUSEUM★★★
👥 Main Museum★★★

Museuminsel 1. Open year-round daily 9am–5pm. Closed 1 Jan, Shrove Tue, Good Friday, May 1, Nov 1, Dec 24, 25 & 31. ⊜8.50€. ✆(089) 217 91. www.deutsches-museum.de.

Founded in 1903, this museum – one of the most important in the world for scientific and technical matters – is built on an isle in the Isar **(Museumsinsel)**. It traces the history of science and technology from the beginning of time to the present and explains physical processes and phenomena. Besides a large number of original items and reconstructions are dioramas and scale models. According to the wishes of founder and Bavarian electricity pioneer **Oskar von Miller**, the displays invite visitors to enquire, touch and discover.

☺*This is a huge museum, so be selective and don't expect to see everything on a single visit. Ongoing renovations will close individual sections at times; check the website for details.*

Ground Floor

Oil and gas, electricity, metallurgy and civil engineering are among subjects addressed on the ground floor.

The Aeronautical Section exhibits early planes, including the Messerschmitt Me-262 (the first fighter jet made on a production line), helicopters, glid-

ers and vertical take-off machines. The bulk of flying machines, though, are at the museum's branch in Schleissheim, the **Flugwerft Schleißheim** (☺*see opposite)*. An Elbe sailing ship (1880) and an Italian steam tug (1931) stand at the entrance to the Navigation Department *(continued in the basement)*. There's also a fine collection of model trains, although to see the big engines, you have to visit the museum's **Verkehrszentrum** near Theresienwiese (☺*see opposite)*.

Basement

Among many other displays, the Navigation Section highlights naval construction, warships (including U-1, the first German submarine, built in 1906), methods of navigation, fishing techniques, and Jacques Picard's 1958 bathysphere. An exhibit on mining techniques follows, including a model salt mine.

👥 Young children (ages 3-8) will be stimulated and entertained in the **Kinderreich**, an educational play zone.

First Floor

This floor is dominated by the Physical Science section (optics, mechanics, nuclear physics, electronics, etc.). The Old Aeronautics Hall presents pioneering flying machines, such as gliders built by Otto Lilienthal (c. 1885) and a 1917 Fokker Dr I Triplane, made famous by Baron von Richthofen's "circus" in World War I.

Note also the Wright Brothers' Type-A Standard (USA, 1909), a Blériot Type XI (1909) and a Junkers F-13 (the first successful commercial airliner, 1919).

Second Floor

The main draw here is the re-created Altamira Cave with its famous Stone Age paintings, but there is plenty more to keep you engaged: glass and ceramics, printing techniques, photography (Daguerre's apparatus, 1839), space travel, textiles and environmental science.

☺ A Bit of Advice ☺

Combination tickets for the three Deutsches Museum branches (Museumsinsel, Flugwerft und Verkehrszentrum) cost 15€ and are valid on separate days.

Deutsches Museum

Third Floor

Exhibits on weights and measures, tele-communications, agriculture, micro-electronics and computer science fill this floor.

Fourth to Sixth Floor

The upper floors are dedicated to astronomy and present everything from ancient equipment to solar system models. **Tickets** *(⊜2€)* for shows in the sixth-floor **Planetarium** must be purchased at the information booth in the entrance foyer.

👥 Verkehrszentrum (Transport Museum)

Theresienhöhe 14a. Open year-round daily 9am–5pm. Closed Jan 1, Shrove Tue, Good Friday, May 1, Nov 1, Dec 24, 25 & 31. ⊜6€ (child 3€). ♿ ✆(089) 500 80 67 62. www.deutsches-museum.de.

Housed in the former exhibition centre near Theresienwiese, this interesting museum traces the evolution of mobility in three large halls. Historical coaches and steam locomotives take you back to the beginning, while exhibits such as the ultra-speedy Transrapid train offer a glimpse of the present.

👥 Flugwerft Schleißheim★

Effnerstraße 18, Oberschleißheim, next to Schloss Schleißheim. Open year-round daily 9am–5pm. Closed Jan 1, Shrove Tue, Good Friday, May 1, Nov 1, Dec 24, 25 & 31

Dec. ⊜6€ (child 3€). ♿ ✆(089) 315 71 40. www.deutsches-museum.de.

A 1920s Bavarian air corps hangar now houses the aviation department of the Deutsches Museum. Aside from gliders, helicopters and small planes, it also has several military aircraft from the Cold War era, including a 1959 Lockheed F-104F Starfighter and a Soviet MiG-23BN from 1980. Behind a glass wall, engineers are busy restoring historical craft. Children can even get their own "pilot's licence".

RESIDENZ★★ (THE RESIDENCE)

Combined ticket for the Residenzmuseum and Schatzkammer ⊜11€. With Altes Rezidenztheater 13€.

After the ruling Wittelsbachs had outgrown their original residence *(Alter Hof, on Burgstraße)*, construction of a new royal palace began in 1385. The complex was expanded considerably in subsequent centuries and today consists of seven structures enclosing eight inner courtyards.

Schatzkammer★★ (Treasury)

Open Apr–mid-Oct daily 9am–6pm; late Oct–Mar daily 10am–5pm; last entry 1hr before closing. Closed Jan 1, Shrove Tue, Dec 24, 25 & 31. ⊜7€. ✆(089) 29 06 71. www.residenz-muenchen.de.

Bavarian rulers had a passion for collecting precious things, as you will see on a tour of the treasury, which brims

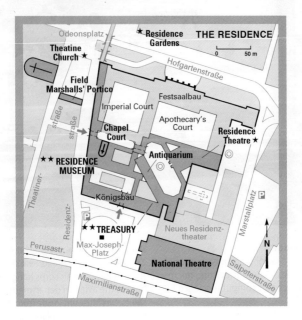

with gold works, enamels, crystalware, carved ivories and other fanciful items. Among the highlights are an 11C cross made for Queen Gisela of Hungary, Heinrich's crown from 1280 and dazzling jewellery inlaid with precious stones.

Residenzmuseum★★

Open Apr–mid-Oct daily 9am–6pm; late Oct–Mar daily 10am–5pm; last entry 1hr before closing. Closed Jan 1, Shrove Tue, Dec 24, 25 & 31. ⌖7€. ℘(089) 29 06 71. www.residenz-muenchen.de.

Allow at least two hours to visit this vast museum. An audioguide, available in multiple languages, is included in the admission price.

On your tour you will see **Die Reichen Zimmer** (state rooms, 1730–37), which illustrate early Rococo style. Highlights include the **Königlichen Appartements** (royal apartments) in the **Königsbau** (king's wing), which were built under Ludwig I between 1826 and 1835. One of the most important rooms is the **Antiquarium** (c. 1570). Inlaid with marble and embellished with ceiling

frescoes, it is a treasure trove of original and copied statues from ancient Greece. Also noteworthy are the **Special Collections** with porcelain masterpieces from Meissen, Nymphenburg, Frankenthal and Sèvres.

The 17C **Hofkapelle** (court chapel) is dedicated to the Virgin Mary, patron saint of Bavaria.

The **Reiche Kapelle** (ornate chapel, 1607) was the private chapel of Duke Max I and is a lavish kaleidoscope of coloured marble and gilded reliefs.

Altes Residenztheater★★
(Cuvilliéstheatre)

Enter via Brunnenhof courtyard. Open Aug–mid-Sept daily 9am–6pm; Apr–Jul & late Sept–mid-Oct Mon–Sat 2pm–6pm Sun 9am–6pm; late Oct–Mar Mon–Sat 2pm–5pm, Sun 10am–5pm; last entry 1hr before closing. ⌖3.50€.

This enchanting red-and-gold Rococo theatre was masterminded by **François de Cuvilliés**, built in 1750s and recently restored. The Prince-Elector's box is set apart by the elegance of its hangings, marble and stuccowork.

ᮁᮁ WALKING TOUR

OLD TOWN★★
⏱ See itinerary on the city map.
Allow half a day.

Marienplatz★
(St. Mary's Square)
This square is the heart of Munich and centres on the **Mariensäule**, a column erected in 1638 by Prince-Elector Maximilian in honour of Mary, patron saint of Bavaria. On the square's north side looms the fantastic neo-Gothic **Neues Rathaus** (new town hall, 1867–1908) with the tourist office on the ground floor. Its enchanting **carillon** (Glockenspiel) has tourists craning their necks daily at 11am and noon (Mar–Sept, also 5pm) when brightly coloured figurines emerge accompanied by merry chimes. Two scenes are represented: the upper level shows a knights' tournament held in 1568 in celebration of the marriage of Duke Wilhelm V to Renata of Lothringia; the lower half re-enacts the **Schäfflertanz** (Dance of the Coopers), first held to celebrate the end of the plague in the 16C.

The **Altes Rathaus** (old town hall) on the square's eastern side is decorated with stepped gables and bell turrets and now houses the **Spielzeugmuseum** (toy museum).

Peterskirche
(Church of St. Peter's)
This 13C three-aisle Gothic church acquired a Baroque look in the 17C and 18C. Note Erasmus Grasser's statue of St. Peter (1492) in the centre section of the high altar. Affectionately nicknamed "Old Pete", the bell-tower can be ascended (306 steps, ☜1.50€) to obtain splendid city views.

▷ Continue via Burgstrasse, which follows the route of the medieval town wall.

Weinstadel
Burgstrasse 5.
Munich's oldest surviving building (1552) used to be the office of the Clerk of the Court; it now sports a colourful *trompe-l'œil* façade.

▷ At the end of Burgstrasse, the route passes under the tower of the Old Castle.

Alter Hof (Old Castle)
This building was the official Wittelsbach residence from 1253 to 1474. The south wing has an elegant tower with half-timbered corbelling (late 15C), known locally as the *Affenturm* (monkey tower). In recent times, sections of the building have been controversially turned into apartment and office buildings.

The complex also contains a **central information office** about Bavarian castles and palaces and a free **multimedia exhibit** (open Mon–Sat 10am–6pm; ☎089 21 01 40 50) about the Alter Hof and general Munich history.

▷ Exit Alter Hof to the east and continue on Münzstraße.

Hofbräuhaus
Now owned by the Bavarian state government, Munich's best-known beer hall has stood on **Platzl Square** since 1589. Every day, servers deliver virtual rivers of beer in one-litre (1.75 pint) tankards (Masskrug) to a thirsty crowd cheering on raucous brass bands performing popular songs. The huge vaulted **Bierschwemme**, on the ground floor, is the rowdiest section. Head to the beer garden for less noise.

▷ From Platzl head north to Hofgraben, turn left and continue to Max-Joseph-Platz.

Nationaltheater
(National Theatre)
Built between 1811 and 1818 by Leo von Klenze, the national theatre is home to the Bavarian State Opera and can seat up to 2 100 people.

Residenz★★ (⏱ See above)

For an exterior tour of the Residence, you can walk from courtyard to courtyard. Coming from either Residenzstrasse or Max-Joseph-Platz, the first one you enter is the Königsbauhof, followed by the Grottenhof (grotto courtyard), the Kapellenhof (chapel courtyard), Brunnenhof (fountain courtyard), Apothekenhof (apothecary courtyard) and the Kaiserhof (Imperial courtyard).

▶ Follow Residenzstraße north along the west side of the Residence.

Odeonsplatz
(Odeon Square)

On the west side of this square stands the 19C Leuchtenberg-Palais, built for Eugène de Beauharnais, Count of Leuchtenberg, and now home to the Bavarian Finance Ministry.

To the south, the **Feldherrnhalle** (1840–44) by Andreas Gärtner marks the southern terminus of grand Ludwigstraße built under Ludwig I; the northern end culminates in a triumphal arch *(Siegestor)*.

Theatinerkirche★

A fine example of Baroque architecture, this church was built between 1663 and 1688, first under the direction of the Italian Agostino Barelli and later by Enrico Zuccalli from Graubünden, Switzerland. The particularly lavish interior stucco ornamentation is primarily by Nicolo Petri. Several Bavarian rulers, including King Max I and Crown Prince Ruprecht are buried in the south transept.

▶ Follow Theatinerstraße south until to see the entrance to the Fünf Höfe arcades on your right.

Fünf Höfe
(Five Courtyards)

The Fünf Höfe is a well-designed shopping complex consisting of arcades linking five interior courtyards. Each passageway is lined with high-end boutiques, cafés and restaurants.

The glass-and-steel complex was designed by Herzog & de Meuron and completed in 2003. Do not miss the **Kunsthalle Munchen**, an exhibition space that hosts changing high-calibre art shows (open year-round daily 10am–8pm; closed Dec 24; admission varies; ✆ 089 22 44 12; www.kunsthalle-muc.de).

▶ Exit the Fünf Höfe via the Pranner passageway to emerge on Kardinal-Faulhaber-Straße.

Erzbischöfliches Palais
(Episcopal Palace)

Kardinal-Faulhaber-Straße 7.
Cuvilliés' finest palace was built between 1733–37 and still serves as the residence of the local archbishop. It boasts a magnificent pink-and-white façade with a rounded balcony supported by cherubs.

Palais Portia

Kardinal-Faulhaber-Straße 12.
This pink-and-grey mansion was originally designed by Enrico **Zuccalli** (1694), with a façade by **Cuvilliés**, for one of Karl Albrecht's favourites, Countess Portia.

▶ Take the alley at the end of Kardinal-Faulhaber-Straße.

Siegestor, Theatinerkirche and Frauenkirche backed by the Alps

© Rudolf Sterflinger/Munich City Tourist Office

Frauenkirche★★
(Church of Our Lady)
Altes Rathaus architect **Jörg von Halspach** also designed this vast late Gothic hall-church (1468–88). The two onion-domed towers were added in 1525 and are a city landmark.

In striking contrast to the austere, red-brick façade, the **interior** is brilliant white and makes a stunning impression. Eleven pairs of octagonal pillars support the reticulated vaulting. Seen from the entrance, the perspective of these columns forms a continuous line, effectively hiding the aisles.

In the south aisle is a monumental black marble **cenotaph★** to Emperor Ludwig of Bavaria, by Hans Krumper (1619–22). All the chapels contain high-quality paintings and altarpieces, and those off the ambulatory sport extraordinary 15C **stained-glass windows**. For views of Bavaria and the Alps, climb the stairs in the south tower to a **viewing platform★** (open Apr–Oct Mon–Sat 10am–5pm; ⌚3€).

⊳ Follow Liebfrauenstraße, then turn right into the Kaufingerstraße, which becomes Neuhauserstraße.

Deutsches Jagd- und Fischereimuseum
(German Hunting and Fishing Museum)
Neuhauserstraße 2. Open year-round daily 9.30am–5pm (Thu until 9pm). Closed Shrove Tue, Dec 24 & 31. ⌚3.50€. ℘(089) 22 05 22. www.jagd-fischerei-museum.de.

Housed in a former Augustinian church, the museum displays three floors of ancient and modern arms, trophies, paintings and drawings of hunting scenes, along with a veritable zoo's worth of stuffed animals.

⊳ Walk a few steps west on Neuhauserstraße to the Michaelskirche.

Michaelskirche★
(Church of St. Michael's)
This 16C Jesuit sanctuary is considered the oldest Renaissance church north of the Alps. The façade is decorated with pilasters, bands of script and a statue of the church's patron, the Archangel Michael.

The single nave inspired many Baroque builders in southern Germany. The pulpit and seven side altars date from 1697. Thirty of the Wittelsbach rulers, including King Ludwig II of Bavaria, are buried in the crypt (*Fürstengruft*).

⊳ Head south on Eisenmannstraße which turns into Damenstiftstraße. After crossing Brunnstraße, take the Asamhofpassage on your left to Sendlinger Straße. Turn right and the Asam Church will be on your right.

Asamkirche★
(Church of St. Johannes Nepomuk)
The church, built in 1733, is usually referred to by the name of the men who constructed it, the **Asam Brothers**: the painter Cosmas Damian Asam and the sculptor Egid Quirin Asam. The church's remarkable unity of style is due to the fact that the brothers not only drew up the plans but also supervised every stage of the building process. The result is Rococo artistry run amok with colour, stuccowork, gilding, statuary and embellishments of every sort covering every single square inch of wall space.

⊳ Turn left on Sendlinger Straße as you exit the church, then turn right on Hermann-Sack-Straße, then cut across Oberanger.

St. Jacobsplatz
Opened in 2007, Munich's **Jewish Museum★** (open year-round Tue–Sun 10am–6pm; closed Jan 1, Shrove Tue, Rosh Hashanah, Yom Kippur, Dec 24, 25 & 31; ⌚3€; ℘089 23 39 60 96; www.juedisches-museum-muenchen.de) is part of an architectural ensemble on St. Jakobsplatz that also includes a **community**

A Little Exercise

The people of Munich enjoy all kinds of sports in the English Garden: jogging, cycling, basketball playing – and surfing. Yes, surfing! Go to the bridge on Prinzregentenstraße at the southern tip of the park and see them "hang ten" on an artificial wave.

centre and a **synagogue**. The small permanent exhibit in the basement delivers impressions of the city's Jewish history and cultural contributions, while the upper floors are devoted to changing presentations.

Münchner Stadtmuseum★ (City Historical Museum)

St. Jakobsplatz 1. Open year-round Tue–Sun 10am–6pm. Closed Shrove Tue, Dec 24 & 31. ⊛7€, Sun free. & ℘(089) 23 32 23 70. www. muenchner-stadtmuseum.de. In the stables of the old arsenal, this museum illuminates all aspects of the city's cultural history. Themes covered include puppetry, musical instruments, photography and film. A separate exhibit chronicles Munich during the Third Reich. The most important artistic item is a sculpture ensemble by Erasmus Grasser called the *Moriskentänzer* (morris dancers).

▷ Continue to Sebastiansplatz and walk past the Schrannenhalle, a former granary turned event-location, to the central food market.

Viktualienmarkt (Food Market)★

Fruit and vegetables, meat and fish have been sold in this market daily except Sunday since 1807. Stalls, kiosks and a beer garden *(in suitable weather)* crowd around a colourful maypole, ensuring a lively atmosphere and making a fun lunch spot. Two of the six fountains recall local comedian Karl Valentin and his partner Liesl Karlstadt.

Heiliggeistkirche (Church of the Holy Spirit)

This Gothic hall-church at the top of Viktualienmarkt went Baroque in the 1720s and got a neo-Baroque façade in 1888. The mid-15C Virgin in the north aisle, said to be by Hammerthal, hails from the Benedictine abbey at Tegernsee.

▷ Turn left on Im Tal to return to Marienplatz.

ADDITIONAL SIGHTS
NORTH OF THE OLD TOWN
Englischer Garten★ (English Garden)

Just north of the historic centre, in the district of Schwabing, this vast park was designed in the late 18C. Characterised by broad, tree-bordered lawns, streams and lakes, it is particularly popular in summer for sunbathing, strolling and picnicking. There are also several beer gardens, most notably the one below the **Chinese Tower** (*Chinesischer Turm*), which seats up to 7 000. From the **Monopteros**, a circular temple built by Klenze, gaze over Munich's old town.

Propyläen

West side of Königsplatz.
This imposing gateway by Leo von Klenze (1784–1864) was inspired by the Acropolis in Athens and completed two years before the architect's death. The frieze represents the Greek war of liberation against the Turks.

Glyptothek★ (Antique Sculpture Collection)

Königsplatz. Open year-round Tue–Sun 10am–5pm (Thu until 8pm). Closed Shrove Tue, Nov 1, Dec 24, 26 & 31. ⊛3.50€, Sun 1€. & ℘(089) 28 61 00. www.antike-am-koenigsplatz.mwn.de. One thousand years of Greek and Roman sculpture are gathered under the roof of this museum, buttressed by a colonnaded Neoclassical porch. The **Tenea Apollo** (*Gallery I*), with his handsome, smiling face, is among the more memorable pieces, as is the

Barberini Faun (c. 220 BC) *(Gallery II)*, which appears sated with drink and half asleep. Also note the **bas-relief by Mnesarete** *(Gallery IV)*, said to have adorned the tomb of Socrates' daughter, and the statue of *Irene*, the Goddess of Peace *(Gallery V)*.

Antikensammlungen★ (Collection of Antiquities)

Opposite the Glyptothek. Open year-round Tue–Sun 10am–5pm (Wed until 8pm). Closed Jan 1, Shrove Tue, Good Friday, Nov 1, Dec 24, 25 & 31. ⊛6€, Sun 1€. ℘(089) 59 98 88 30. www.antike-am-koenigsplatz.mwn.de.

Greek, Etruscan and Roman art is the focus of this famous collection. Displays on the ground floor trace the evolution of pottery in Greece, which reached its zenith during the 6C and 5C BC. Geometric decoration was succeeded by the representation of black figures on a red background (illustrated by an amphora and a goblet by the painter Exekias). The transition towards the use of red figures against a background of varnished black can be seen on another amphora, in which a single subject – Hercules' banquet in the presence of Athena – is treated in the two styles *(Gallery III, showcase 6)*. **Bronzes** on the first floor and **Etruscan jewellery** in the basement *(Galleries VII and X)* testify to the high-quality craftsmanship of these metalworkers.

Städtische Galerie im Lenbachhaus★ (Lenbach Collections)

Luisenstraße 33. Open year-round Tue–Sun 10am–6pm (Tue until 9pm). Closed Shrove Tue, Dec 24. ⊛10€, depending on exhibitions. ♿ ℘(089) 23 33 20 00. www.lenbachhaus.de.

Housed in a 19C villa, the Lenbach collections are devoted primarily to the works of **19C Munich painters**. The landscapes of EB Morgenstern and portraits by FA von Kaulbach and F von Defregger stand out, as do the powerful portraits created by **Franz von Lenbach** himself *(King Ludwig I, Bismarck, Wagner)*.

The gallery's international reputation is built, above all, on the avant-garde **Blaue Reiter** collection. Born in the tumultuous period just before World War I, the movement is represented by its founding members, Kandinsky and Marc, and by paintings of Jawlensky, Klee and Macke. **Contemporary art**, including works by Joseph Beuys and Anselm Kiefer, is usually shown in the Kunstbau annex.

EAST OF THE OLD TOWN
Bayerisches Nationalmuseum★★ (Bavarian National Museum)

Prinzregentenstraße 3. Open year-round Tue–Sun 10am–5pm (Thu until 8pm). Closed Shrove Tue, May 1, Pentecost, Nov 1, Dec 24, 25 & 31. ⊛7€. ♿℘(089) 211 24 01. www.bayerisches-nationalmuseum.de.

Maximilian II created this museum in 1885 with the aim of preserving Bavaria's artistic and cultural heritage. The rooms on the ground floor offer a survey of Bavarian arts and crafts from **Romanesque to Renaissance** *(Galleries 1–19)*, including silver and gold plate and religious statuary. The interior of an **Augsburg weaver**'s studio is re-created in Gallery 9; the **Renaissance and Baroque** periods are represented by tapestries *(Gallery 22)*, medieval town representations and Italian bronzes *(Gallery 25)*. The first floor houses musical instruments, board games, silverware and porcelain, while the basement is dedicated to folklore exhibits.

Museum Villa Stuck

Prinzregentenstraße 60. Open year-round Tue–Sun 11am–6pm (first Fri until 10pm). Closed Shrove Tue, Dec 24. ⊛9€. ℘(089) 455 55 10. www.villastuck.de.

Franz Stuck (1863–1928) was a professor at the Munich Academy of Fine Arts from 1895 and a founding member of the Munich Secession. He personally drew up the plans for this exquisite *Jugendstil* villa along with its custom-made furniture, panelling, bas-reliefs, sculptures and coffered ceilings. Today the rooms house temporary art exhibits.

Museum Fuenf Kontinente (State Ethnology Museum)

Maximilianstraß 42. Open Tue–Sat 9.30am–5.30pm. Closed Shrove Tue, Good Friday, May 1, Nov 1, Dec 24–25 & 31. ☞5€. ⟁ ℘(089) 210 13 61 00. www.museum-fuenf-kontinente.de.

Amassed by the Bavarian royal family, this collection of more than 200 000 objects from the Americas, India, Middle East and Oceania was first displayed in 1836 and has taken up this museum since 1868. It is considered the second-largest of its kind in Germany.

SCHLOSS NYMPHENBURG★★ (NYMPHENBURG PALACE)

6km/3.7mi west of the city centre. Open Apr–mid-Oct daily 9am–6pm; late Oct–Mar daily 10am–4pm. Closed Jan 1, Shrove Tue, Dec 24, 25 & 31. ☞6€. A combination ticket to all palaces and exhibitions in and around Nymphenburg Palace is 11.50€. ℘(089) 17 90 80. www.schloss-nymphenburg.de.

The oldest part of this former summer residence of the Bavarian rulers is the 17C five-storey central pavilion, built in the style of an Italian palazzo. Prince-Elector Max Emmanuel (1679–1726) added two side wings, while his successors Karl-Albrecht (1726–45) and Max III Josef (1745–77) commissioned various outbuildings. From 1701 onwards, the surrounding park was enlarged with formal French gardens and several park pavilions: the Pagodenburg (1719), Badenburg (1721), Magdalenenklause (1728) and Amalienburg (1739).

Schloss★★ (Palace)

The splendid **banqueting hall** (*Steinerner Saal*, or Stone Hall) is a symphony of white, gold and pale green. It was richly adorned with coloured stucco-work and frescoes by Johann Baptist Zimmermann and his son, Franz. The panelled rooms in the north wing are decorated with tapestries and paintings. One of the most fascinating rooms is devoted to **Chinese lacquer**. In the south pavilion, the apartments of Queen Caroline contain the famous **Schönheitengalerie** (Gallery of Beauties). King Ludwig I commissioned

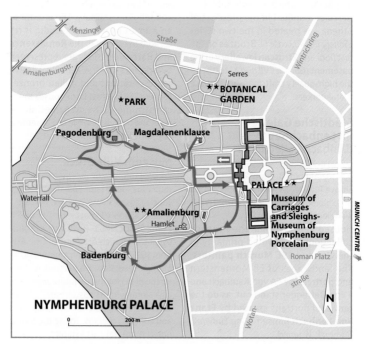

NYMPHENBURG PALACE

Midway, Oktoberfest

© fotoman_65/Fotolia.com

MUNICH FESTIVALS

Servers at Oktoberfest

© Wilfried Hösl/Munich City Tourist Office

Oktoberfest – The world's biggest public party is held on the Theresienwiese mid-September to the first Sunday in October. It originated in 1810 as part of the celebrations surrounding the marriage of Crown Prince Ludwig I of Bavaria to Princess Therese of Saxe-Hildburghausen. Each year 6 or 7 million locals and visitors flock to the huge beer halls and the thrill rides on the midway. The party kicks off Saturday with the Brewer's Parade, followed by the Costume Procession on Sunday. But mostly Oktoberfest is about beer drinking: visitors consume around 7 million l/1850 000 gal of *Wiesenbier,* brewed especially for the event and delivered by horse-drawn drays. It is served in a 1l/0.2gal tankards called a *Mass*. For sustenance, revellers gorge on roast chicken and beef (two oxen are cooked on a spit each day). Hotels usually fill up, so book as early as a year in advance. If you show up during Oktoberfest, hope for cancellations but expect to pay top euro.

Fasching – Carnival is celebrated with high spirits and much merriment and ends with the traditional market women's dance at the Viktualienmarkt.

Corpus Christi – The religious festival of *Fronleichnam* involves a procession of clergy, Roman Catholic personalities, Catholic student organizations and guild representatives through streets garlanded with young birch branches.

Other festivals – *Starkbierzeit* ("strong beer" festival) in March; *Auer Dult* (local festival) in late Apr/early May, late Jul and mid-Oct; *Tollwood Festival* (global music and theatre) from late Jun to mid-Jul and Nov–Dec; *Opernfestspiele* (opera festival) in Jul; and the *Christkindlmarkt* (Christmas market) in Dec.

Cultural activities in Munich are listed in *Offizielles Monatsprogramm* (in German) and *Munich Found* (in English), both available at the tourist office.

Joseph Karl Stieler (1781–1858) to immortalise on canvas the epoch's most beautiful women.

Park★

From the top of the palace steps you have a sweeping view over the formal flower gardens and the Grand Canal ending in a waterfall in the far distance.

Amalienburg★★ – This Rococo hunting lodge is one of **Cuvilliés'** most accomplished designs. The simplicity and sobriety of the exterior contrasts vividly with the extraordinarily elaborate interior. The **Hall of Mirrors** is a case in point: the combination of blue walls and ceiling, silver-plated stucco and wood-framed glass forms a marvellous ensemble.

Badenburg – A luxurious heated swimming pool, its ceiling decorated by mythological motifs, is the centrepiece of this 18C bathhouse.

Pagodenburg – The 18C fascination with Asia is exemplified in the design of this octagonal teahouse, in which a drawing room, a Chinese room and a boudoir occupy the first floor.

Magdalenenklause – A "hermitage" built in the popular mock-ruin style, this pavilion is dedicated to St. Mary Magdalene.

Marstallmuseum und Porzellansammlung (Carriage Museum of Carriages and Sleighs and Porcelain Collection) – The museum is housed in the palace's former stables. Besides superb 18C and 19C harnesses, the Wittelsbachs' broughams, coaches, sledges and sedan chairs are on display. Note especially the coronation coach of Emperor Karl VII, and the state coach and personal sleigh of Ludwig II.

Upstairs, the **Bäuml Collection of Nymphenburg Porcelain** includes painted figurines by Franz Anton Bustelli, factory master from 1754 to 1763. The **reproductions in porcelain★** – miniature copies of paintings in the Alte Pinakothek – were commissioned by King Ludwig I.

Botanischer Garten München-Nymphenburg★★ (Botanical Gardens)

Menzinger Straße 65. Open Jan, Nov & Dec daily 9am–4.30pm; Feb, Mar & Oct until 5pm; Apr & Sept until 6pm; May–Aug until 7pm. Closed Dec 24 & 31. 4€. (089) 17 86 13 10. www.botmuc.de.

Situated next to Schloss Nymphenburg, one of Europe's finest botanical gardens boasts more than 14 000 plant species. The Scmuckhof (opposite the main building), Spring Garden and Rose Garden are particularly memorable. Rhododendrons brighten the Alpine Garden; orchids and sub-tropical beauties bloom in the greenhouses. The garden celebrated its centennial in 2014.

Schloss Nymphenburg

© J. Lutz/Munich City Tourist Office

OLYMPIAPARK QUARTER
Olympiapark

5km/3mi north of the city centre via Dachauer Straße. Guided tours Apr, May and Jun, including: Olympic Stadium tour at 11am (7.50€), park tour aboard miniature train at 2pm (9.50€). Olympic Stadium: open Apr–mid-May & late Sept–Oct 9am–6pm, late May–mid-Sept 9am-8pm, Nov–Mar 11am–4pm, closed on events days. 3€. (089) 30 670. www.olympiapark.de.

Munich hosted the 20th Olympic Games in 1972. The grounds continue to be used for sporting events, festivals and concerts. They can be explored on guided tours or by renting an audio-guide (7€) from the Info Pavilion.

The lift ride up the 290m/951ft-high **Olympiaturm** (television tower; open 9am–midnight; 5.50€) offers a scenic **panorama★★** with views often extending as far as the Alps.

Your ticket also lets you visit the small and private **Rock 'n' Roll Museum** at the tower level. It features guitars, fan mail, letters and photographs of such giants as Jimi Hendrix and Jim Morrison. Other activities include ice skating, inline skating, tennis and miniature golf. Visitors can climb the stadium roof (while harnessed) and ride a zipline from the rooftop.

SeaLife München

Open Apr–Aug daily 10am–7pm; Mar, Sept and Oct until 6pm; Nov–Jan until 5pm. Closed Dec 24. 15.95€ (child 9.95€, online 9.50€). (089) 45 00 00. www.visitsealife.com/Munchen.

This interactive aquarium is home to some 10 000 marine and freshwater creatures. The order of the tanks simulates the habitats encountered if following the flow of the Isar into the Danube, which itself flows into the Black Sea before spilling into the Mediterranean.

BMW World

Petuelring 130. Northeast corner of Olympiapark. Open year-round Mon–Sat 7:30am–midnight, Sun 9am–midnight. Museum: Tue–Sun 10am–6pm. Closed Jan 1, Dec 24, 25 & 31. 9€ (child 6€). (089) 38 22 56 57. www.bmw-welt.com.

The famous car maker's flagship **museum** is housed in a giant silver bowl docked to a pavilion. Inside, floating ramps lead visitors on a dynamic multimedia journey past shiny cars and motorcycles, from vintage wheels to concept cars and the latest production models.

The museum sits next to the BMW headquarters, plant and stunningly designed **BMW Welt** car pick-up centre, which also has free exhibits open to the public. For a tour of the **BMW plant** (Mon–Fri; 8€), you must pre-register by calling (089)125 016 001.

EXCURSIONS
Dachau Concentration Camp Memorial Site★

19km/11.8mi northwest. Alte Römerstraße 75, Dachau. Follow signposts to Dachau Ost and "KZ-Gedenkstätte". Open year-round daily 9am–5pm. Free entry; parking 3€. Audioguide recommended (3.50€). (08131) 66 99 70. www.kz-gedenkstaette-dachau.de.

Allow at least two hours to visit Nazi Germany's first concentration camp, built in March 1933 near the pleasant town of Dachau on the orders of Heinrich Himmler. Originally designed for the detention of German political opponents of the Nazi regime, the camp was soon flooded by tens of thousands of deportees, mostly Jews of diverse nationalities. More than 35 000 people died there, plus at least 6 000 Russian prisoners-of-war killed on the nearby SS firing range.

Visitors are sobered by the **ruins and commemorative monuments**. Two prisoner barracks have been faithfully reconstructed and the foundations of 32 others are still visible. They offer a glimpse of a camp that was designed for 5 000 prisoners-of-war but was crammed with 30 000 people by 1944. At the rear camp entrance one can still read the inscription *"Arbeit macht frei"* (Freedom Through Work). A Jewish memorial, a Protestant commemorative sanctuary and a Catholic chapel have been built within the precincts of the old camp. Just beyond its borders are the crematorium and a gas chamber, although the latter was apparently never used.

A **museum** presents (in English and German) a sobering and comprehensive look at life in the camp. Exhibits deal with the organisation of the KZ system and use photographs and documents to illustrate the Dachau camp's history, daily life, medical experiments, mass executions, and its liberation.

Allianz Arena Stadion★

10km/6.5mi north near intersection of A9 and A99. Guided tours (1hr 15min) daily except on game days 9.30am–4.30pm, English tour at 1pm. 10€ (child under 12, 5€). (089) 350 948 350. www.allianz-arena.de.

Built for the FIFA World Cup 2006, this gigantic 66 000-seat stadium is an architectural stunner designed by Herzog & de Meuron. Each of the 2 760 transparent inflatable panels can be lit up in a particular colour: white for international games, blue for local club 1860 München, red for Bayern Munich. A **museum** (open daily 10am–6pm; 12€). devoted to FC Bayern has exhibits about star players and the club's 2013 Champions League title.

DRIVING TOUR

AROUND AMMERSEE

Round trip of 116km/72mi

Ammersee★

This glacial lake sits framed by wooded hills at an elevation of 533m/1749ft; it is popular for swimming, sailing and boating.

Follow the western lakeshore.

Dießen

Built in 1730, Diessen's Rococo **Marienmünster★** (St. Mary's Church) was a collaboration between architect **Johann**

Michael Fischer, the Asam brothers and Cuvilliés.

The road climbs from Fischen to Andechs, offering fine lake views.

Kloster Andechs★ (Andechs Abbey)

Guided tours (60min) year-round by reservation only: church Mon–Fri; brewery Mon–Wed. (08152) 37 60. www.andechs.de.

This 10C abbey overlooks the Ammersee. Its Gothic **church★★** got a Rococo remodel in 1750 by Johann Baptist Zimmermann. Bavarian composer Carl Orff (of Carmina Burana fame) is buried in the Chapel of Suffering. Still an active abbey, the monks brew their own beer, which can be sampled in the beer garden and beer hall.

Return to Munich via Herrsching and Seefeld or detour to Bernried.

Buchheim Museum der Phantasie★ (Buchheim Museum of Imagination)

45km/28mi southwest. Am Hirschgarten 1, Bernried. Open Tue–Sun 10am–6pm (Nov–Mar 5pm). Closed Dec 24 & 31. 8.50€. (08158) 99 700. www.buchheimmuseum.de.

Situated on the shores of Lake Starnberg, this museum presents the private art collection of Das Boot author Lothar-Günther Buchheim. Its main strength is in German Expressionism, with members of Die Brücke, such as Kirchner, Heckel, Pechstein and Schmidt-Rottluff particularly well represented.

ADDRESSES

STAY

Creatif Hotel Elephant – Lämmerstraße 6. 089 55 57 85. www.creatif-hotel-elephant.com. 45 rooms. Close to the Hauptbahnhof, this colourful and buzzy budget hotel was renovated in 2006 and features hypoallergenic rooms and English TV channels.

⊖**Motel One** – *Orleansstraße 87; Landsberger Straße 79; Michael-Haslbeck-Straße 26a; Herzog-Wilhelm-Straße; 28, Daimlerstraße 5a. www.motel-one. com/de/hotels/hotels-muenchen.html.* This modern chain hotel has several locations in Munich, and provides good value for the money.

⊖⊖**Hotel Drei Löwen** – *Schillerstraße 8. ℘(089) 55 10 40. www.hotel3loewen.de. 97 rooms. Restaurant⊖⊖.* This welcoming hotel near the main train station has bright, and modern rooms, whimsically decorated two-room suites and a wood-panelled lobby.

⊖⊖**Hotel Müller** – *Fliegenstraße 4. ℘(089) 232 38 60. www.hotel-mueller-muenchen.de. Closed Dec 23–Jan 6. 44 rooms.* In a quiet spot in the happening Glockenbachviertel, steps from the historic centre, this hotel includes such perks as free Wi-Fi and a generous breakfast buffet in its room rates.

⊖⊖**Hotel Uhland** – *Uhlandstraße 1 ℘(089) 54 33 50. www.hotel-uhland.de. 25 rooms.* Run by a multi-generational family, this charming hotel sits in a century-old neo-Renaissance mansion on a quiet side street near the Oktoberfest grounds. It has rooms that suit all tastes; some have modern water beds, some have rustic furniture. Service is bend-over-backwards friendly.

⊖⊖**Mariandl** – *Goethestraße 51. ℘089 5529 100. www.mariandl.com. 30 rooms. Restaurant⊖⊖.* Situated close to the station, but away from the bustle, this grand late-19C castle-like building houses a hotel with Belle Époque and Art Nouveau furniture and décor. It has a restaurant and a popular *Konzertcafé* that regularly hosts live classical musicians and adds to the agreeable atmosphere.

⊖⊖**Am Viktualienmarkt** – *Utzschneiderstraße 14. ℘089 231 10 90. www.hotel-am-viktualienmarkt.com. Closed Dec 20–Jan 7. 27 rooms.* Ideally located in the city centre, this inviting family-run hotel offers bright, modern, minimalistic designer-style rooms in colour schemes of beiges, creams and browns. Some of the rooms are small but all offer good value for the money.

⊖⊖⊖**Hotel Platzl** – *Sparkassen-straße 10. ℘(089) 23 70 30. www.platzl.de. 167 rooms. Restaurants⊖⊖ – ⊖⊖⊖.* Tradition marries modern comforts in this Bavarian-style hotel that sits within walking distance of the famous Hofbräuhaus and Munich's main historic sights. Dining options include the elegantly vaulted Pfistermühle restaurant with its leafy terrace and the restaurant Wirtshaus Ayingers.

⊖⊖⊖**Hotel Schlicker** – *Tal 8. ℘(089) 242 88 70. www.hotel-schlicker.de. Closed Dec 23–Jan 7. 69 rooms.* Located in the heart of the old quarter, this hotel in a 16C building offers personalised service and well-kept and spotlessly clean rooms. Some rooms have views of the new town hall with its world-famous carillon, but those in back are usually quieter.

⊖⊖⊖⊖**Hotel Bayerischer Hof** – *Promenadenplatz 2. ℘(089) 212 00. www.bayerischerhof.de. 345 rooms. ⊑30€. Restaurant⊖⊖⊖.* Hospitality doesn't get more luxurious than at this traditional grand hotel that has kept an illustrious guest list since 1841. The rooftop pool and spa offer the ultimate in relaxation plus a view of the Frauenkirche.

¶⁄EAT

REGIONAL SPECIALITIES

The most famous local specialities include the veal sausages known as *Weißwurst*, roast knuckle of pork *(Schweinshaxe)* and *Leberkäse*, a meat loaf. At beer festivals, a favourite offering is *Steckerlfisch*, which are small fish grilled on a skewer. *Pretzels* and white radishes *(Radi)* are often served with beer. And speaking of beer: Munich is Germany's beer capital. Five and a half million hectolitres (110 000 000 gallons) of beer are brewed every year, most of it consumed in the beer halls and gardens *(Biergarten)* within Munich.

⊖**Café Voilà** – *Wörthstraße 5. ℘089 48 91 654. www.cafe-voila.de.* This popular locals' place is perfect for brunch, or a beer or two.

⊖**Pasta e Basta** – *Fraunhoferstraße 19. ℘089 1393 9446. www.pastaebastaweb.de.* Good-value budget Italian food.

Ratskeller – *Marienplatz 8.*
℘089 21 99 89 0. Popular and stylish, this huge labyrinthine tavern lies beneath the Gothic arches of the town hall; it is a real city institution. While you are tucked away in a cosy wooden cubicle, savour a dish of crispy pork hock or on Ratskeller's trademark tasty sausages.

Spektakel – *Pfeuferstraße 32, Sendling.* *℘089 76 75 83 59. www.spektakel-muenchen.de.* This typical Bavarian pub-restaurant is a favourite of the locals.

Vapiano – *Salvatorpassage, Fünf Höfe, Theatinerstraße 15. ℘089 20 60 658 60. www.vapiano.de. No reservations.* Enjoy top-quality all-fresh fast food, such as made-to-order fire-roasted pizzas, homemade pasta and gourmet salads in smart-casual surroundings. Other city addresses include: *Kaflerstraße 4; Richard-Strauss-straße 80, Hackerbrücke 4.*

Zum Dürnbräu – *Dürnbräugasse 2. ℘(089) 22 21 95.* Oozing traditional Bavarian flair from every nook and cranny, this inn is a great spot for hearty meals and cool brews. Enjoy the terrace or courtyard garden in fine weather.

Spatenhaus an der Oper – *Residenzstraße 12. ℘089 290 70 60. www.kuffler.de.* This beautifully designed traditional restaurant is famous for its game dishes. The upstairs dining room is more formal. Lovely bedrooms in the hotel upstairs are available to overnight guests.

Käfer Schänke – *Prinzregentenstraße 73. ℘(089) 416 82 47. www.feinkost-kaefer.de. Closed Sun and public holidays.* This fine-food emporium blends a delicatessen shop, a catering service and a pleasant warren of a restaurant with stylish but relaxed décor. The globally inspired menu is likely to contain a favourite for everyone.

Bogenhauser Hof – *Ismaninger Straße 85. ℘(089) 98 55 86. www. bogenhauser-hof.de. Closed Dec 24–Jan 8, Sun and public holidays.* This former 19C hunting lodge is now a modern gourmet restaurant serving inspired seasonal cuisine. The idyllic summer garden is ideal for lounging over leisurely dinners on balmy summer nights.

Geisels Werneckhof – *Werneckstrasse 11. ℘(089) 388 795 68. www.geisels-werneckhof.de. Closed Sun, Mon.* This culinary shrine practices a farm-to-table philosophy, and melds Bavarian cuisine with golbal influences such as Asian and Spanish. The results, for example, sturgeon flamed in hay with a lemon-tea sauce, can be astounding.

Restaurant Dallmayr – *Dienerstrasse 14-15. ℘(089) 2135 100. www.dallmayr.com. Closed Sun, Mon and public holidays.* Though it dates back to the 18C, this stylish fine-dining establishment focuses on modern interpretations of continental classics such as lake fish with hempseed sauce or grilled sweetbreads in broccoli coulis. The adjacent **Cafe-Bistro** (⊜⊜⊜) serves lighter portions of lighter fare like leek polenta and apple-filled ravioli.

TAKING A BREAK

Café Arzmiller – *Theatinerstraße 22. ℘(089) 29 42 73, www.cafe-arzmiller.de.* This café is a good place to relax and forget the stress of the tourist track. Coffee, cakes and daily specials are served in the lovely, peaceful Theatinerhof. The house speciality, *Strudel*, is not to be missed.

Café Luitpold Palmengarten – *Brienner Straße 11. ℘(089) 242 87 50. www.cafe-luitpold.de. Closed public holidays.* This café offers a choice of more than 300 different cakes and tarts. The house speciality is *Luitpoldkuchen*, which can be enjoyed beneath a glass dome in the palm-filled inner courtyard or on the terrace facing Maximilianplatz.

Chocolaterie Beluga – *Viktualienmarkt 6. ℘(089) 2323 1577. www.chocolaterie beluga.de.* Hot chocolate is the main draw at this café and shop in old town, but truffles, pralines and ice cream are found in abundance as well.

Viktualienmarkt – *Viktualienmarkt. ℘(089) 890 682 05. www.viktualien markt.de. Closed Sun.* This traditional market offers delectable victuals like handmade sausages, artisanal cheeses, smoked fish, fine olive oils and hearty loaves of bread.

NIGHTLIFE

USEFUL TIPS

Beer gardens are an integral part of Bavarian life, especially in Munich. These chestnut tree-shaded gardens and terraces open at the first ray of spring sunshine. Prices can be high and the service limited, but the atmosphere is unique and the surroundings delightful.

Munich's best-known café and bar scene is in the district of **Schwabing**. Around the university you will find a number of student bars, while south of the Münchner Freiheit U-Bahn station, Leopoldstraße is lined with posh establishments where people go to "see and be seen". Other parts of town with good nightlife are Haidhausen (around Pariser Platz and Weißenburger Platz) and the Gärtnerplatzviertel quarter. For online information: www.munig.com, www.nightlife-munich.de and www.munichx.de.

SIGHTSEEING

WALKING TOURS

The tourist office organises tours with English-speaking guides for groups, upon request (✆ *(089) 233 32 34)*. **Stattreisen** (✆ *(089) 54 40 42 30; www. stattreisen-muenchen.de)* also offers dozens of themed walking tours (beer, architecture, on foot, tram or bike) in German. Regular guided tours in English are offered by **New Munich Tours** *(www.newmunich.com)*, **Radius Bike Tours** (✆ *see Practical Information)* and **Munich Walk Tours** (✆ *(089) 24 23 17 67; www.munichwalktours.de)*.

BUS TOURS

SIGHTseeing Gray Line
(Schützenstraße 9 ✆ (089) 54 90 75 60, www.stadtrundfahrten-muenchen.de) –
Hop-on, Hop-off Express Circle: Buses depart every 20 minutes and follow a one-hour loop taking in all major sights. You are free to get on and off as often as you wish. Tickets cost 18€ (child 8€). An extended route *(Grand Circle)* taking in Nymphenburg Palace and the Olympic Park costs 20€. Buses depart from Bahnhofplatz *(in front of Karstadt department store)*. Tickets are available aboard.

FINDING YOUR WAY

The liveliest part of Munich is in the pedestrianised old town around Marienplatz and Karlsplatz (or "Stachus") via shop-lined Neuhauser Straße and Kaufingerstraße. Elegant boutiques cluster in Maffeistraße, Pacellistraße, Maximilianstraße and Brienner Straße; antique dealers in Ottostraße near Maximilianplatz; art galleries under the arcades of Hofgartenstraße. Schwabing, around Leopoldstraße, enjoyed its fame as the city's artistic and intellectual hub at the turn of the 19C and remains one of Germany's liveliest after-hours destinations.

SHOPPING

USEFUL TIPS

Many people consider Munich Germany's best city for shopping. The old town has numerous arcades and boutiques catering to all budgets. *Ludwig Beck* and other department stores line Neuhauser Straße and Kaufingerstraße between Marienplatz and Karlsplatz (Stachus).
Another good shopping district is Schwabing (along Leopoldstraße and smaller side streets such as Türkenstraße), which is home to small and funky boutiques. International labels are found in Residenzstraße, Brienner Straße and Maximilianstraße. The *Fünf Höfe* shopping centre is a visual stunner in stylish Theatinerstraße and is also filled with high-end boutiques and shops. Independent designers cluster in the charming Gärtnerplatzviertel along such streets as Reichenbachstraße and Hans-Sachs-Straße.

Art galleries – Munich's key galleries are in Maximilianstraße and nearby streets, in Residenzstraße and on Odeonsplatz. In the old artists' district of Schwabing, interesting avenues are Türkenstraße, Schellingstraße and Franz-Joseph-Straße.

Antiques – Munich antiques range from elegant pieces offered by exclusive dealers to bargain-basement wares sold in bric-à-brac shops. Schwabing boasts a wealth of antique stores, as does the city centre around Maximilianplatz, Lenbachplatz and Promenadenplatz.

Augsburg★★

Bavaria's third-largest city (after Munich and Nuremberg) and a stop on the Romantic Road, Augsburg has long been associated with luminaries, including 16C artist Hans Holbein the Younger, Mozart's father, Leopold (1719–1787), and the dramatist Bertolt Brecht (1898–1956). Today, the Renaissance city continues to enchant visitors with its artistic beauty and lively cultural scene.

▶ **Population:** 280 000
🛈 **Info:** Rathausplatz. ℰ(0821) 50 20 70. www.augsburg-tourismus.de.
◐ **Location:** Augsburg is one hour west of Munich by the A8 and 30 minutes by train. The river Lech, a tributary of the Danube, crosses the town and feeds into a canal in the lower town.
🅿 **Parking:** Public car parks and garages are located throughout the city, including near the main train station and the Rathaus. Electronic signs indicate car park locations and space availability.
☻ **Don't Miss:** Maximilianstraße and the cathedral.
◷ **Timing:** Allow about one day to see Augsburg.

A BIT OF HISTORY

Roman origins – Founded in 15 BC by Drusus and Tiberius, stepsons of Emperor Augustus, Augsburg is, along with Trier and Cologne, one of Germany's oldest cities. It became a trading centre en route to Italy and, at the fall of the Roman Empire, an Episcopal see. By the late 13C it was a Free Imperial City and the seat of the Diet.

The Fuggers – Augsburg reached its historical peak at the end of the 15C, when it became a European financial centre, thanks to two wealthy merchant families, the Fuggers and the Welsers. History has preserved the name of Jakob Fugger the Rich (1459–1529), renowned as the Empire's banker and the financier of the Habsburgs. He was powerful enough to rebuke Charles V, reminding him: "It is well known that, without my help, Your Majesty would no longer wear the crown of the Holy Roman Empire" The unpaid debt of the Habsburgs to their Augsburg bankers has been estimated at 4 million ducats.

SIGHTS

Rathausplatz (Town Hall Square)

Augsburg's hulking **town hall** ranks among the most important secular Renaissance buildings north of the Alps. Built by Elias Holl between 1615 and 1620, it has two onion-domed towers framing a pediment adorned with the traditional pinecone.

Inside, the Golden Hall (Goldener Saal; open year-round daily 10am–6pm; ⊜2€), with its restored coffered ceiling, can be visited.

The **Perlachturm** was originally a Romanesque watchtower and can be climbed in summer. A yellow flag is flown when views extend all the way to the distant Alps.

St. Anna-Kirche

Fuggerstraße 8. ℰ(0821) 450 17-5100. When Martin Luther came to Augsburg in 1518 to defend his reformed thesis, he stayed at what was then a Carmelite monastery. The rooms, accessed via a flight of wooden stairs (Lutherstiege) now house a small exhibition about the man and his times. The **Fugger Chapel★** (Fuggerkapelle), where Jakob Fugger and his brothers are buried, is a prime example of Renaissance architecture. Note the three works by Lucas Cranach the Elder in the east chancel.

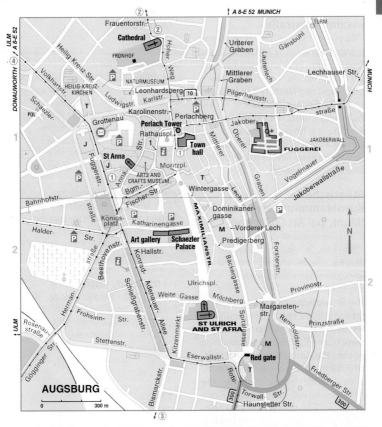

AUGSBURG

0   300 m

WHERE TO STAY	WHERE TO EAT	STREET INDEX
Dom Hotel............................②	August.....................................②	Philippine-Welser-Straße........1
Ost am Kö.............................①	Die Ecke................................①	
Unterbaarer Hof....................④	Haupt im Prinz Karl Palais.....③	

Fuggerei★

Enter via Jakoberstraße. Open Apr–
Sept daily 8am–8pm; Oct–Mar daily
9am–6pm. ⌨4€. ♿ ℘(0821) 31 98 810.
www.fugger.de.
Known as the "town within the town",
the Fuggerei was founded in 1516 by
Jakob Fugger the Rich and is the world's
oldest social housing compound.
To this day it provides simple but permanent housing for impoverished local
Catholics in exchange for a symbolic
annual rent of 0.88€ and three daily
prayers for the souls of the founders.

Dom St. Maria (St. Mary's Cathedral)

Hoher Weg. ℘(0821) 316 63 53.
Augsburg's cathedral has origins in the
10C, but didn't get its Gothic shape until
the 14C. Noteworthy features include
the **Jungfrauenportal★★** (Virgin's
Door), as well as 11C Romanesque
bronze door **Türflügel★** (panels). Four
of the nave altars are adorned with
paintings★ by Holbein the Elder.
Outside the cathedral, look for remains
of the Roman city.

Maximilianstraße★

This elegant street is flanked by the mansions of wealthy Renaissance-era Augsburgers (including the Fuggers at no 36). Two monumental 16C fountains depicting Mercury and Hercules grace the **Schaezlerpalais** at no 46, Augsburg's most important Rococo building. It is home to several art collections as well as a grand **Festsaal★★** (ballroom) canopied by a lush ceiling fresco and stuccowork.

Städtische Kunstsammlungen★ (Municipal Art Collection)

Maximilianstrasse 46. Open Tue–Sun 10am–5pm. Closed Good Friday, Dec 24–25 & 31. ✆7€. ℰ(0821) 324 41 02. www.kunstsammlungen-museen. augsburg.de.

The Schaezlerpalais harbours several art collections, most importantly the **German Baroque Gallery** (Deutsche Barockgalerie). The same building also houses the **Collection Haberstadt**, which was amassed over decades by a local art dealer and his wife. The collection includes paintings by Paulo Veronese, Giovanni Battista Tiepolo, Antonius van Dyck, Jacob Ruisdael und Lucas Cranach the Elder.

Many more famous canvases grace the walls of the **State Gallery of Old Masters** in the nearby Church of St. Catherine (Katharinenkirche). Highlights include a portrait of Jakob Fugger the Rich by Albrecht Dürer and Hans Holbein's paintings of Roman basilicas.

Basilika St. Ulrich und Afra★

Ulrichsplatz 19. ℰ(0821) 34 55 60.
This former Benedictine abbey was built in 1474 in late-Gothic style with Renaissance and Baroque additions. It boasts the shrines of the town's patron saints, gilded Baroque altars and a bronze Crucifixion (1607). St. Simpert's chapel features a gallery topped by terra-cotta **Statues of the Saints★**.

The Catholic basilica hugs the much smaller Protestant **Ulrichkirche** in reflection of the religious compromise achieved at the Peace of Augsburg.

ADDRESSES

🛏 STAY

⊜ Unterbaarer Hof – *Ulmer Straße 218. ℰ(0821) 43 13 00. www.unterbaarer-hof.de. 6 rooms. Restaurant⊜⊑.* This good-value hotel has modern if fairly basic rooms and a large self-catering apartment. The restaurant specialises in specialities from Swabia and Bavaria served in a cosy ambience with plenty of wood and curtained windows.

⊜⊜ Dom Hotel – *Frauentorstraße 8. ℰ0821 34 39 30. www.domhotel-augsburg.de. Closed mid-Dec–early Jan. 54 rooms.* Elegant rooms and apartments in a historic town house near the cathedral. In summer, breakfast is served under the chestnut trees.

⊜⊜ Ost am Kö – *Fuggerstraße 4. ℰ089 50 20 40. www.ostamkoe.de. 49 rooms. ⊑.* Set in the centre of Augsburg, 300m/330yd from the station, this smart traditional-modern hotel offers well-equipped bedrooms; most look onto a tranquil courtyard. Facilities include a sauna.

🍴 EAT

⊜⊜ Die Ecke – *Elias-Holl-Platz 2. ℰ(0821) 51 06 00. www.restaurant-die-ecke.de.* This historic restaurant once hosted such luminaries as Mozart and Bertolt Brecht. It ingeniously melds rustic and modern styles in an elegant setting. Great for special occasions.

⊜⊜⊜ Haupt im Prinz Karl Palais – *Schertlinstraße 23. ℰ0821 589 84 75. www. prinzkarl-restaurant.de. Closed Sun evenings.* Housed in a former barracks, with vaulted ceilings, and a garden, this modern restaurant serves delicious local and international dishes.

⊜⊜⊜⊜ August – *Frauentorstraße 27 ℰ0821 352 79. Dinner only. Closed Sun–Tue, 1st week Jan, Easter Week and late Aug–mid Sept. ⊡.* This Michelin two-star restaurant, overseen by chef Christian Grünwald, lives up to its reputation with carefully selected dishes that reflect Grünwald's individual style of creative cuisine. In summer dine out on the lovely roof terrace.

Ottobeuren★★

The Benedictine abbey of Ottobeuren, founded in 764 under the patronage of Charlemagne, was transformed into the Baroque style in the 18C. The abbey church is undoubtedly one of the most visually stunning churches in Germany.

▶ **Population:** 8 000
Info: Marktplatz 14.
🖉(08332) 92 19 50.
www.ottobeuren.de.
Location: Ottobeuren is a charming village surrounded by forests and pastureland. The A96 autobahn (Memmingen–Munich) is 11km/6.8mi north.
Don't Miss: The abbey church.
Timing: Allow at least two hours to view the church and other buildings.

SIGHTS
Abbey Church★★
Open year-round daily 9am–sunset, 8.30pm at the latest (Thu 1pm–3pm).
🖉(08332) 79 80.
www.abtei-ottobeuren.de.

In 1748, **Johann Michael Fischer**, the great architect of southern Germany, put the finishing touches on this jewel of the German Baroque style, which was to be his masterpiece. When it came to the church's interior ornamentation, he was assisted by equally gifted Rococo masters: Johann Jakob Zeiller and Franz Anton Zeiller for the frescoes, Johann Michael Feichtmayr for the stuccowork, and Johann Joseph Christian for the figurative sculptures.

The church's astonishing dimensions are evident only once inside. The impression of space is enhanced by the unusual amount of light, a result of the church's north–south orientation. The architecture of the entire church is focused on the flattened central dome, amid a proliferation of paintings, stuccowork and sculptures with wonderfully depicted cherubs, draperies and lighting.

The four altars, of St. Michael – patron saint of the Ottobeuren area and the Empire – of the Holy Guardian Angels, of St. Joseph and of St. John the Baptist, are remarkable features, as are the outstanding **pulpit** and opposite, the representation of the **Baptism of Christ** in red and marble stucco.

On the altar of the Holy Sacrament stands a much venerated **crucifix** dating from 1220, the Ottobeurer Gnadenheiland (Merciful Redeemer). The **high altar**, with paintings of the Holy Trinity by Zeiller and larger-than-life figures of the Apostles and saints is outstanding. The walnut **choir stalls★★** (1764) are masterpieces of the woodcarver's art. The high backs to the stalls are adorned with gilded lime-wood reliefs by Joseph Christian.

Karl Joseph Riepp, a pupil of the famous organ builder Silbermann, built the **chancel organs ★★** in 1766.

Abbey Buildings
Open Palm Sun–Oct daily 10am–noon, 2pm–5pm; limited hours rest of the year.
4€. 🖉(08332) 79 80.

The abbey's buildings were constructed between 1711 and 1725. Inside the **museum★** admire the superb decoration that echoes the splendour of the church. The museum also houses interesting medieval artworks and 15C–17C paintings.

Note the magnificent **library**, the theatre and the **Kaisersaal** (Emperor's Hall), with a frescoed ceiling depicting the coronation of Charlemagne.

German Alpine Road★★★

Deutsche Alpenstraße

Splendid mountain scenery combined with such landmarks as the Wieskirche and the castles of Ludwig II of Bavaria make the Alpenstraße an unforgettable journey. When passing through the region's villages, where life goes on much as it has for centuries, stop to sample local culinary and cultural traditions, or head off for a walk in the woods or across alpine meadows.

🚗 DRIVING TOURS

1 THE ALLGÄU★

From Lindau to Füssen 112km/69.6mi. Allow half a day.

The Allgäu is home of the Swabians, an Allemanic tribe that settled in the area around the 2C AD. It is a fairytale landscape where lazy cows graze on steep mountain pastures and farmers still produce wonderful artesanal cheeses.

Lindau★★ – 👀See LINDAU.

▶ Leave Lindau on the A96 (towards Memmingen), then join the B308.

Paradies

Engineers gave this name to a viewpoint between Oberreute and Oberstaufen, along a sweeping curve, from which the distant Swiss Appenzell Alps can be seen.

Oberstaufen

This charming ski resort sits at the foot of the Hochgrat massif (1 832m/6 010ft). From the mountain station at 1 708m/5 600ft, you'll have a 360-degree **panorama★★** across the Allgäu, Lake Constance and into Switzerland.

▶ The road now climbs the alpine valley of the Iller, which runs to the foot of Grünten.

🛈 **Info:** Deutsche Alpenstraße, 81243 Munich. ✆(089) 8025 924 49 52. www.deutsche-alpenstrasse.de.

▶ **Location:** Running from Lindau on Lake Constance (Bodensee) to Berchtegaden near the Austrian border, this 450km/279.6mi scenic route traverses spectacular high-mountain country accented by pristine Alpine lakes. It meanders along the foothills of the Allgäu and the Bavarian Alps, parallelling the southern German border and linking world-famous ski resorts, bucolic villages, onion-domed churches, royal castles and the lofty peaks of the Zugspitze (2 964m/9 724.4ft) and the Watzmann (2 712m/8 897.6ft).

😊 **Don't Miss:** Beautiful panoramas appear around every corner, but the best lie atop the Wendelstein and along the final part of tour 4 below.

🕐 **Timing:** Allow at least three days to explore this alpine region.

👪 **Kids:** Hohenschwangau and Neuschwanstein castles; cable-car rides up the Wendelstein.

Bad Hindelang★

Together with its neighbour, Bad Oberdorf, this romantic flower-decked village is a popular spa and holiday resort perfectly suited for mountain walks in summer and skiing in winter.

Above Bad Hindelang, climbing the **Jochstraße★** delivers idyllic views over the jagged summits of the Allgäu Alps. From the **Kanzel★** viewpoint, near the summit, take in the splendid panorama embracing the Ostrach Valley and surrounding mountains.

On its descent, the road crosses the Wertach Valley, skirts the Grüntensee and passes the sprawling Pfronten ski resort before arriving at Füssen.

Füssen★

Kaiser-Maximilian-Platz 1. ℘(08362) 938 50. www.stadt-fuessen.de.
Tucked into the *Königswinkel* ("royal corner") in the Allgäu mountains, Füssen is surrounded by the lakes of Forggensee, Hopfensee and Weißensee. With a spectacular setting in the Alpine foothills, this historic town is like the dot of the exclamation mark at the end of the Romantic Road (Romantische Straße). Most visitors use it as a base from which to visit Ludwig II's fairytale palace of Neuschwanstein and his ancestral home of Hohenschwangau, but the town is actually worth a stop in its own right. Attractions include an ancient abbey, art museums and the surrounding lakes.

Museum der Stadt Füssen im Kloster St. Mang★ (Füssen Heritage Museum at Abbey of St. Mang)

Open Apr–Oct Tue–Sun 11am–5pm; Nov–Mar Fri–Sun 1pm–4pm. ☞6€. ℘(08062) 938 50. www.fuessen.de.
This ancient Benedictine **abbey** looks back on more than 1 000 years of history. It honours the work of St. Magnus, an 8C missionary who founded a monk's cell here and is buried in the church's crypt.

In the 18C, the medieval complex got a complete Baroque makeover reflecting the skill and vision of Johann Jakob Herkomer, who had learned his craft in Venice. The monastery was secularised in 1802.
The southern wing, with *trompe l'œil* paintings in the cloister, now houses a modern **museum** containing exhibits on the history of the abbey, Füssen's violin-making tradition and milestones from the town's past. Most impressive are the richly decorated rooms themselves, notably the festive **Kaisersaal★★** (Imperial Hall), a large banquet hall embellished with fanciful frescoes and stucco ornamentation. In summer it hosts classical concerts. The **Annakapelle★** (St. Anna Chapel), from 850, has a macabre Dance of Death fresco from 1602 that vividly depicts the ravages of the Black Plague.

Stadtpfarrkirche (Parish Church)

Open year-round daily 8.30am–6pm.
Herkomer's Baroque design displays astonishing harmony and rich décor that encompasses an elaborate fresco cycle with scenes from the life of St. Magnus. An artistic and spiritual highlight is the high altar with statues by Anton Sturm. Various reliquaries of the saint, including his staff, dot the church.

Along the German Alpine Road

© Alpin Consult

Hohes Schloss (High Palace)

The ramp to the castle entrance starts behind the parish church. Open Apr–Oct Tue–Sun 11am–5pm; Nov–mid-Mar Fri–Sun 1pm–4pm. Closed Dec 24 & 31. 6€. (08362) 90 31 46.

Looming above the town, the fortified late-Gothic palace became the summer residence of the Prince-Bishops of Augsburg in the late 15C.

Today, the former apartments house two collections. The **Staatsgalerie** (Bavarian State Gallery) holds Swabian art from the 15C and 16C. The octagonal **Rittersaal★** (Knights' Hall), which is lidded by a sumptuous coffered ceiling, is the most impressive room. On the lower floor, the **Städtische Gemäldegalerie** (Municipal Picture Gallery) presents paintings by Spitzweg, Lier, Defregger and other Munich School members working around 1900. A rotating selection of graphics by Franz Graf von Pocci (1807–1876) supplements the paintings. For a dazzling **panorama★**, climb the clock-tower, which is accessible via the gallery. Surrounding the castle is a public park called the Baumgarten.

Lechfall (Lech Gorge)

500m/547yd south.

The river Lech leaves the Alps in Füssen and cascades down a small, rocky gorge spanned by a footbridge.

Forggensee (Lake Forggen)

Boats depart from Füssen landing docks, Jun–mid-Oct daily 10am–5.25pm. Commentary. 7€ (50min tour), 11€ (2hr tour). Forggensee Schiffahrt (08362) 92 13 63. www.fuessen.de.

The Forggensee reservoir measures 12km/7.4mi long and up to 3km/1.8mi wide. It was created in 1954 to regulate the waterflow of the Lech River. In summer it is swarmed by watersports enthusiasts and cyclists enjoying the paved trails around its perimeter.

Cruise boats ply its waters, allowing breathtaking views of the mountains, Neuschwanstein Castle and historic Füssen. In winter, the lake is drained and you can walk on the dry bottom to look for remnants of Stone Age and Roman settlements.

2 THE AMMERGAU★

From Füssen to Garmisch-Partenkirchen. 95km/mi. Allow one day.

The road bypasses the Ammergau Alps to the north, then crosses countryside seamed and broken by the moraines deposited by the ancient Lech glacier. This rolling land is punctuated by villages with onion-domed churches.

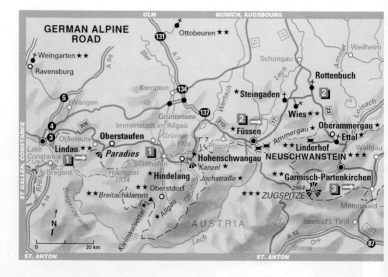

Interior of Wieskirche, Steingaden

♠♠ Hohenschwangau and Neuschwanstein★★★
⚫*See NEUSCHWANSTEIN.*

Steingaden★

Long before you reach the village of Steingaden, the distinctive onion-domed silhouette of its 12C Premonstratensian abbey church rises from the misty horizon. Numerous alterations have all but obscured its Romanesque origins. The Gothic entrance bears a painted genealogy of the Welf family, who founded the abbey in 1147. But first and foremost it is luxuriant Baroque flourishes that now give the interior its dynamic and uplifting character. Ten gleaming pillars guide the eye towards the pastel-coloured ceiling fresco depicting the ascension of Mary and enhanced with spectacular stuccowork. Only the cloister, where the architect Dominikus Zimmermann is buried, retains its comparatively austere 13C Romanesque columns.

Wieskirche★★

Wies 12, 86989 Steingaden. Open May–Oct daily 8am–8pm; Nov–Apr until 5pm. ⚪By donation. ♿.✆(08862) 93 29 30. www.wieskirche.de. To avoid the largest crowds, visit early morning or at

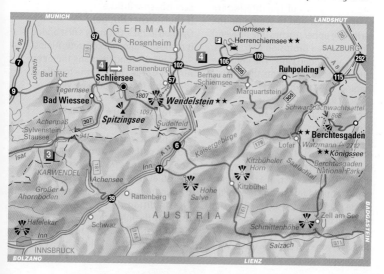

Der Blaue Reiter

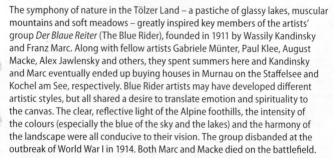

The symphony of nature in the Tölzer Land – a pastiche of glassy lakes, muscular mountains and soft meadows – greatly inspired key members of the artists' group *Der Blaue Reiter* (The Blue Rider), founded in 1911 by Wassily Kandinsky and Franz Marc. Along with fellow artists Gabriele Münter, Paul Klee, August Macke, Alex Jawlensky and others, they spent summers here and Kandinsky and Marc eventually ended up buying houses in Murnau on the Staffelsee and Kochel am See, respectively. Blue Rider artists may have developed different artistic styles, but all shared a desire to translate emotion and spirituality to the canvas. The clear, reflective light of the Alpine foothills, the intensity of the colours (especially the blue of the sky and the lakes) and the harmony of the landscape were all conducive to their vision. The group disbanded at the outbreak of World War I in 1914. Both Marc and Macke died on the battlefield.

day's end and avoid Sundays. No visits or walking around during church services.

The Wieskirche, whose full name is Pilgrimage Church of the Scourged Saviour, is a masterpiece of Bavarian Rococo masterminded by the architect Dominikus Zimmermann in the 18C. It has been on UNESCO's World Heritage list since 1983.

Exterior – The elegantly understated church exterior leaves visitors unprepared for the splendour of the interior.
Interior – Gilded stucco, wood carvings and vivid frescoes stand out from the white walls, bathed in subtle light entering the windows.

The lower parts of the interior are sparsely decorated to symbolise the earth. The upper reaches (the heavens) vibrate with a profusion of frescoes, stucco and gilded work. The immense **cupola fresco** represents the Second Coming, the Last Judgement and the Gates of Paradise (still closed).

The decoration of the **choir** is unparalleled: columns, balustrades, statues, gilded stucco and frescoes form a glorious symphony of colour.

In the centre of the church is a figure of the flagellated Christ. In 1738, a local farmer noticed tears in the eyes of the statue. This prompted such a pilgrimage rush that the local abbot commissioned this magnificent church to accommodate everyone. To this day, up to 1 million people visit every year.

Rottenbuch

First built as an Augustinian monastery, the **Mariä Geburt Kirche★** (Church of the Nativity of the Virgin) was remodelled in Baroque and Rococo styles in the 18C. The School of Wessobrunn, of which Joseph and Franz Schmuzer were masters, crafted the magnificent stucco. Matthäus Günther's ceiling fresco depicts the death of St. Augustine in perfect visual harmony with the extravagantly sculpted décor. The pulpit, organ loft and altars by Franz Xaver Schmädl are heavily adorned with statues and giltwork in pure Rococo tradition.

Echelsbacher Brücke (Echelsbacher Bridge)

Opened in 1929, Germany's first bridge is made of reinforced concrete. Almost 90m/295.3ft long, it spans the deep Ammer Gorge. Walk to the middle of the bridge for an impressive view.

Oberammergau★

This small town of farmers and craftspeople, encircled by the wooded foothills of the Ammergau, is internationally famous for its Passion Play, staged every 10 years (next in 2020) by hundreds of local amateur actors. The tradition derives from a vow made by the inhabitants in 1634 after being spared by a plague epidemic. Performances are held at the **Passionstheater** (👣 45min guided tours Apr–Oct 10am–5pm; Dec Sat–Sun 11am and 3pm; ∞6€; ℘8822 945 88 33; www.passionstheater.de), where tours give you insight into the play's history, meaning and production. Oberammergau is also renowned for its *trompe-l'oeil* façades painted in a style called *Lüftlmalerei* (roughly "air painting"). These are colourful frescoes depicting both secular and religious themes, from fairytales to biblical scenes.

Linderhof★★
Ġ*See Schloss LINDERHOF.*

Ettal★
A blossoming of the Benedictine tradition and the local veneration of a Virgin statue explain the vast dimensions of **Ettal Abbey★**, founded by Emperor Ludwig the Bavarian in 1330. The original Gothic church succumbed to a fire in 1774, after which it was rebuilt by Baroque star architect Enrico Zuccalli and Joseph Schmuzer of the Wessobrunner School. The dazzlingly detailed dome **fresco** showing St. Benedict and his followers is a masterpiece by Johann Jakob Zeiller.
The monastery is still active today with several dozen monks busy running a hotel, a brewery, a distillery and other ventures.

▷ The road rejoins the Loisach Valley. To the south, the cragged Wetterstein range reveals the peaks of the Zugspitze, Alpspitze and Dreitorspitze. Continue to Garmisch-Partenkirchen.

Garmisch-Partenkirchen★★
Ġ*See GARMISCH-PARTENKIRCHEN.*

③ THE UPPER ISAR VALLEY AND THE LAKE DISTRICT★

From Garmisch-Partenkirchen to Schliersee. 105km/65mi. Allow 1 day.

The first part of the route traverses the upper Isar Valley, which here runs wide and wild. It is among the most scenic stretches of road in the Alps.

▷ From Garmisch-Partenkirchen, take the B2 (E533) towards Mittenwald, then follow signs to Krün and Wallgau. On leaving Wallgau, turn right on Risserstraße, a small road that runs through the upper Isar Valley, continuing as the B307 past Vorderriss and skirting the Sylvenstein reservoir. Continue on the B307 over the Achenpass all the way to Tegernsee.

Tegernsee
Splendidly embedded in forested Alpine foothills, Tegernsee has long been popular with the rich, famous and powerful. It is surrounded by four villages, each with its own flair.
Bad Wiessee on the western shore is a fashionable spa resort with a sparkling casino. Rottach-Egern in the south is the ritziest enclave and has the best restaurants and posh houses. On the eastern shore, the village of Tegernsee is the most historical with origins as a Benedictine monastery founded in 746. Its beer hall, the Bräustüberl, is famous. Finally, **Gmund** in the north is the most low-key village and popular with families.

▷ Continue on the B307 to Schliersee.

Schliersee
Beside the lake of the same name, this small community – together with Fischhausen, Neuhaus and Spitzingsee (Ġ*see itinerary below*) – offers interesting day trips.
The **St. Sixtus Parish Church★** (Pfarrkirche) was styled in the Baroque between 1712 and 1714. The interior frescoes and delicate stucco were executed by Johann Baptist Zimmermann (1680–1758), brother of the architect of the Wieskirche (Ġ*see WIESKIRCHE*).

④ THE SUDELFELD AND THE CHIEMGAU MOUNTAINS★

From Schliersee to Berchtesgaden. 172km/1076.8mi. Allow one day.

◐ Continue on the B307 until Neuhaus to catch the road climbing up to Spitzingsee (10km/6.2mi round-trip).

Spitzingsee

Less than 0.6km/0.4mi from the summit, the steep access road offers views of the Fischhausen–Neuhaus plain and Schliersee.

Soon after, the road stops at the Spitzingsee, a lovely lake.

◐ Continue on B207. About 3km/1.8mi before Bayrischzell, the road passes the cable-car terminal to the Wendelstein summit.

Wendelstein★★

Cable-car operates daily 9am–5pm (Jun–Sept until 5pm); ⊜round-trip 31€. Cogwheel train runs daily 9am–2pm (Nov–Apr until 2pm); closed Nov–Dec 20. ⊜Round-trip 21€. ☏(08034) 30 80. www.wendelsteinbahn.de.

👥 To ascend the Wendelstein, take either the **cable-car** from Bayrischzell-Osterhofen *(7min)*, or the **cogwheel train** *(Zahnradbahn)* from Brannenburg *(25min)*. From the mountain station at 1 738m/5 702ft, a trail leads another 100 vertical metres (328ft) to the peak.

Crowned by a solar observatory and an 18C chapel, it offers an unforgettable **panorama★★** and access to four trails (Geo-Wanderwege). The Gipfelweg circles the summit in about 2hrs 30min.

◐ From Wendelstein follow the A8 Munich–Salzburg autobahn to the shore of Lake **Chiemsee★**. Turn south onto the B305, which winds through the Chiemgau, a region of lakes, moors, valleys and lakes with top skiing, hiking and mountain biking in the villages of Reit im Winkl, Inzell and Ruhpolding.

Ruhpolding★

This popular cross-country skiing resort also has a famous art work: a 12C Romanesque statue of the Virgin Mary in the twin onion-domed parish church of **St. George**.

◐ The Schwarzbachwacht pass reveals the contrast between the austere wooded Schwarzbach alley and the open pastures on the Ramsau slopes. The drive offers **panoramas★★** of the Watzmann peak and the Hochkalter with its Blaueis glacier. The German Alpine Road ends at Berchtesgaden.

View from Wendelstein towards Munich

ADDRESSES

🏠STAY

THE CHIEMGAU

⊖ Gästehaus Weißes Rössl – *Dorfstraße 19, 83242 Reit im Winkl. ☎(08640) 982 30. www.weissesroessl-riw.de. 10 rooms. ☐* This low-key inn in the Chiemgau Alps offers self-catering apartments perfect for families along with comfortable rooms, all with balconies. Cool off in the outdoor pool or wrap up your day in the sauna or gym.

THE AMMERGAU

⊖ Gasthaus Zum Fischerwirt – *Linderhofer Straße 15, 82488 Ettal. ☎(08822) 63 52. www.zum-fischerwirt.de. Closed end-Nov–Dec. 10 rooms. Restaurant (⊖⊖).* A pleasant traditional hotel with charmingly decorated and sparkling rooms. The restaurant serves reasonably priced regional favourites.

⊖ Alpengasthof Winklmoosalm – *Dürrnbachhornweg 6, 83242 Reit im Winkl. ☎(08640) 974 40. www.winklmoosalm.com. Closed Nov–Dec. 18 rooms. Restaurant (⊖⊖)☐.* You'll sleep well in the fresh mountain air of this well-maintained inn in a famous ski area. Enjoy panoramic views and organic dishes in the cheerfully decorated restaurant.

THE ALLGÄU

⊖⊖ Hotel Hirsch – *Kaiser-Maximilan-Platz 7, 87629 Fuessen. ☎(08362) 93 980. www.hotelfuessen.de. 52 rooms. ☐ Restaurant (⊖).* Operated by the same family for four generations, this early 20C property in the small town of Fuessen sits in the shadow of the Alpine foothills across the river. Various "motif" rooms honour local personalities or sights, such as King Ludwig and the Schwansee.

⊖⊖ Parkhotel Maximilian – *Bannwaldweg 11, 87724 Ottobeuren. ☎(08332) 92 370. www.parkhotel-ottobeuren.de. 111 rooms. Restaurant (⊖).* Though it's a fairly large complex at the edge of Ottobeuren, this vacation resort emits a relaxed pastoral atmosphere, with a pool, spa (complete with ice grotto), and hiking opportunities in the wooded hills; golf, tennis, cycling and horseback riding are nearby.

⊖⊖ Hotel Geiger – *Uferstraße 18, 87629 Füssen-Hopfen am See. ☎(08362) 70 74. www.hotel-geiger.de. Closed Nov–mid-Dec. 24 rooms. Restaurant ⊖⊖⊖.* Recently renovated, this long-standing family hotel on the lakeside promenade features chic designer décor, a small spa with Finnish sauna and mint steam room plus two restaurants one rustic, one à la carte.

⊖⊖⊖ Hotel Sonne – *Prinzregentplatz 1 ☎(08362) 90 80. www.hotel-sonne.de. 50 rooms.* Champagne breakfast and free fitness centre passes are among the extra perks at this luxurious and centrally located hotel with cheerful, spacious and modern rooms, many with balconies.

🍴EAT

THE CHIEMGAU

⊖⊖ Schlosswirt – *Kirchplatz 1, 83098 Brannenburg. ☎080 34 707 10. www.schlosswirt.de. Closed Wed.* This family-run restaurant specializes in fresh local game and meats, and sources its produce, baked goods and more from the village or nearby sources.

THE AMMERGAU

⊖⊖ Moosbeck-Alm – *Moos 38, 82401 Moos. ☎08867 912 00. www.moosbeck-alm.com. Closed mid-Nov–mid Dec and Tue.* Dine either in the rustic König-Ludwig-Stube or in the conservatory of this Landhotel with outdoor pool and wellness facilities.

THE ALLGÄU

⊖ Zum Schwanen – *Brotmarkt 4. www.schwanen-fuessen.de. Closed Mon, Sun dinner, mid-Jan–mid-Mar. ☎(08362) 61 74.* The welcoming hosts serve specialities from the Allgäu such as roast pork with spaetzle and sauerkraut in a well-kept setting with a rustic flair.

Oberstdorf★★

A well-known mountain, skiing and spa town in the Allgäu Alps of southern Germany, this charming resort is presided over by the Fellhorn and Nebelhorn peaks. It is the departure point for walking and hiking tours. Note that vehicles are banned from the centre of town.

SIGHTS

Nebelhorn★★

🏃 Take the Nebelhorn cable-car (45min) via three stations: Seealpe (1 280m/4 200ft), Höfatsblick (1 932m/6 338.5ft) and Summit (2 224m/7 296.5ft) every 10min mid-May–early Nov 8.30am–4.30pm (until 4.15pm Feb–Apr; 3.45pm Dec and Jan) Closed 4 weeks in Apr–May and Nov 5–mid-Dec. Round-trip summer 19€ Seealpe, 26.50€ Höfatsblick, 30.50€ Summit; ski day pass 40.50€. ℘(08322) 960 00. www.das-hoechste.de.

The highest cable railway in the Allgäu leads to the 2 224m/7 300ft-high summit of the Nebelhorn. In clear weather, the **panorama★★** extends over 400 Alpine peaks, from the Zugspitze in the east to the Säntis in the west. Laced by numerous hiking trails, the Nebelhorn is also the departure point for the demanding "Hindelang climb". In winter, it morphs into a popular ski resort.

Fellhorn★★

🏃 Take the Fellhorn cable-car in two stages to the summit (2 037/6 683ft) mid May–mid-Jun daily 9am–4pm, late Jun–Oct daily 8.30am–4.30pm; Dec–Jan daily 8.30am–15.30pm; Feb–mid Apr daily 8.30am–4pm. Round-trip summer 26€, ski day pass 42€. ℘(08322) 960 00.

There is a superb **view★★** over the Allgäu, the Austrian and Swiss Alps from the 2 037m/6 683ft-high summit of the Fellhorn. The mountain has an easily accessible network of hiking paths, including an interesting **Blumen-und Wanderlehrpfad** (flower walk) with rare Alpine blooms.

▶ **Population:** 10 000

ℹ **Info:** Prinzregenten-Platz 1. ℘(08322) 70 00. www.oberstdorf.de.

◐ **Location:** Midway between Bodensee (Lake Constance) and the castles of Ludwig II, deeply incised into the Allgäu Alps, and seven other valleys, the town lies at the junction of the valley of the Iller River.

✦ **Don't Miss:** A trip to the Nebelhorn or the Fellhorn.

🕐 **Timing:** Allow a full day to explore this Alpine resort.

👥 **Kids:** Riding the cable-car up the Nebelhorn or Fellhorn.

EXCURSIONS

Breitachklamm★★

◖ 6.5km/4mi southwest, plus 1hr 30min round-trip walk. Open May–Sept daily 9am–5pm; Oct–Apr daily 9am–4pm. Closed Nov, Dec and during snowfall. 3.50€. ℘(08322) 48 87. www.breitachklamm.de.

In the lower gorge, galleries lead into sheer, polished walls, where the turbulent mountain creek has carved a course 100m/328ft deep into the bedrock. You can return via a series of stairways leading to Walserschanze, on the Kleinwalsertal road, from which there is a frequent bus service back into town.

Kleinwalsertal★

◖ 17km/11mi southwest.

A high valley of the Breitach River, this mountain area was settled in the 13C by the **Walsers**, Germanic emigrants from the Upper Valais.

Today the Kleinwalsertal has Austrian police, German customs, a German postal service and Austrian stamps. (Adopting the euro simplified money matters.) **Riezlern**, **Hirschegg** and **Mittelberg** are the most popular resorts.

Schloss Neuschwanstein★★★

With its forest of playful towers and turrets, Neuschwanstein is the quintessential fairytale castle and a product of the imagination of King Ludwig II of Bavaria (1845–86). Set against the splendid backdrop of the Alps, it is a top tourist attraction in Germany and is deluged with visitors every day. A friend and sponsor of the composer Richard Wagner, Ludwig II regarded this palace as a tribute to his operas and German heroic legends in general. Escape the crowds by walking the forest trails surrounding the castle.

- **Info:** Neuschwansteinstraße 20, 87645 Schwangau. ℘(08362) 93 98 80. www.neuschwanstein.com.
- **Location:** About 5km/3mi east of Füssen, the castle sits on a rocky ridge 200m/656ft above the Pöllat Gorge, making an impressive sight.
- **Don't Miss:** The view of the castle from the Marienbrücke.
- **Timing:** Allow half a day for your visit, including waiting time.

A BIT OF HISTORY

The construction – King Ludwig II found the ideal location for "Neu-Hohen-schwangau" (the name "Neuschwanstein" was adopted only in 1890) not far from Hohenschwangau Castle, where he had spent part of his childhood and youth. Ludwig came up with the design of the new palace himself. To some extent it was inspired by the medieval Wartburg in Thuringia (*see EISENACH*), which he had visited in 1867.

The end of a dream – Ludwig II lived at Neuschwanstein for a mere 170 days. The palace construction had put a serious strain on the royal coffers, and the king's increasingly eccentric behaviour led a government commission from Munich to bring him news of his dethronement on 10 June, 1886. Just three days later, he was found dead, floating in Lake Starnberg.

The true circumstances of his death and that of his doctor, who had accompanied him on a walk that fateful evening, remain a mystery to this day.

Schloss Neuschwanstein (foreground) and Schloss Hohenschwangau (on the left)

© photo75/iStockphoto.com

Ludwig II's Castles

The term *Königsschlösser* generally refers to Ludwig's ancestral home of Hohenschwangau and his romantic fantasy castle of Neuschwanstein. But the king's passion for palaces didn't end here. His favourite retreat was actually the comparatively intimate Schloss Linderhof, in an idyllic valley near Garmisch-Partenkirchen. By contrast, Herrenchiemsee Palace in Chiemsee was less a residence than a tribute to his idol, French King Louis XIV. No surprise then that Ludwig spent only 10 days living there.

VISIT

Guided tours (35min) Apr–mid-Oct daily 9am–6pm; late Oct–Mar daily 9am–4pm. Ticket booths open 1hr prior. Closed Jan 1, Dec 24, 25 & 31. www.neuschwanstein.de. 12€, same-day combination ticket with Schloss Hohenschwangau 23€. Buy tickets at the **Ticketcenter** (Alpseestraße 12, Hohenschwangau; 08362 93 08 30; www.hohenschwangau.de/ticketcenter) in Hohenschwangau village before embarking on the 30-40min walk up to the castle (horsedrawn carriage rides available: 6€ uphill, 3€ downhill). Advance tickets (1.80€ booking fee) available by phone and online.

The interior, with its profusion of gilded panelling and wall paintings, reflects Ludwig's fertile imagination and fantasies. The most distinctive chambers are on the third floor: the **throne room★** (unfinished), the **bed chamber★** furnished with Gothic pieces, the **living room★** with its Lohengrin-inspired decorations, and the artificial stalactite cave with the adjacent winter garden, evoking the Tannhäuser legend. The design of the **Sängersaal** (*minstrels' hall*) is based on the Wartburg, where the legendary poetry contest featured in the Wagner opera *Tannhäuser* was

said to have taken place in the early 13C. For dreamy **views★★** of the castle, take the short but steep 10-minute trail up to Marienbrücke bridge above the cascading Pöllat River.

SCHLOSS HOHENSCHWANGAU★

Guided tours (35min) Apr–Sept daily 8am–5.30pm; Oct–Mar daily 9am–3.30pm. Closed Dec 24. 12€, same-day combination ticket with Schloss Neuschwanstein 23€.
For advance tickets, see Schloss Neuschwanstein.

It is about a 15-minute walk to the castle from Hohenschwangau village.

In the 1830s, when **Maximilian II** of Bavaria was still crown prince, he commissioned this castle as a summer residence; it stands atop the foundations of a 12C fortress. The flamboyant neo-Gothic style was in accordance with current taste and reflected Maximilian's predilection for chivalric romance. Ludwig II spent most of his largely unhappy youth in this castle, which stands in a picturesque setting on a wooded hill overlooking the deep-blue Alpsee.

In comparison with Neuschwanstein – and in spite of the almost compulsive repetition of the swan motif – Hohenschwangau has retained a romantic, comfortable feel. Queen Maria, Ludwig II's mother, spent much time here, which explains the welcoming, lived-in atmosphere.

After the maniacal decoration of Schloss Neuschwanstein, the clean lines of the maple and cherrywood Biedermeier furniture here may come as a relief. Still, some rooms also sport elaborate wall paintings, usually depicting scenes from German history or mythology.

One of Ludwig II's favourite rooms was the upstairs music room, where he would listen to Richard Wagner playing the piano, still in situ today.

Don't miss the king's bedchamber, where the ceiling is painted to represent night stars. Follow your visit of the castle with a stroll to a **viewpoint★** on a shaded rocky spur of the **Pindarplatz** on the Alpsee.

Garmisch-Partenkirchen★★

Germany's most famous winter sports resort snuggles against the massive peaks of the Wetterstein chain, most notably the Zugspitze, which soars to a lofty 2 962m/9 717ft and is the highest mountain in the country. The twin town hosted the fourth Winter Olympics in 1936 and the World Alpine Ski Championships in 1978.

▶ **Population:** 26 000

🛈 **Info:** Richard Strauss Platz 2. ℰ(08821) 18 07 00 www.garmisch-parten kirchen.de.

◖ **Location:** Garmisch-Partenkirchen is a highlight on the Deutsche Alpenstraße and lies less than 15km/9.3mi from the Austrian border.

☻ **Don't Miss:** A trip up the Zugspitze as well as Linderhof Palace.

👪 **Kids:** Snow sports, cable-car ride up the Wank, Leutasch Ghost Gorge

SIGHTS

Alte St. Martin-Kirche (Old Church of St. Martin)

Garmisch's original parish church is a 13C Gothic pile in a picturesque neighbourhood with carefully preserved chalets on the west bank of the River Loisach. Several of its medieval murals have been uncovered and restored, most notably a 7m/22ft-high image of St. Christophorus and scenes depicting the Crucifixion and the Last Judgement.

Neue St. Martin Kirche (New Church of St. Martin)

Garmisch's "new" parish church is an 18C work by the famous Wessobrunn architect Josef Schmuzer, with ceiling frescoes by Matthias Günther and a chancel carved by Frank Hosp.

LOCAL WALKS

Wank★★

🚶 cable-car ride (20min) operates May–Oct daily 8.45am–5pm at least half-hourly; Nov–Apr 9am–4.30pm. ☜20€ round-trip. ℰ(08821) 79 70. www.zugspitze.de.

From the summit (1 780m/5 840ft) of sunny Wank mountain **views★★** open up across the entire Wetterstein range and the Zugspitze peak, extending all the way to Munich on clear days. Enjoy varied vistas while following the two easy and bench-lined panoramic trails along the top.

Philosophenweg (Philosophers' Way)

🚶 The early 18C church of St. Anton is the departure point for this easy and panoramic walk along the icy Loisach River. Enjoy clear **views★** of the surrounding massifs, including the Zugspitze looming behind the Waxenstein.

Partnachklamm★★

🚶 About 90min round-trip. Bring rain gear. Open summer daily 8am–6pm; winter daily 9am–5pm. ☜3.50€. ℰ(08821) 31 67. www.partnachklamm-info.de.

The splendour of this deep, narrow gorge, some 800m/2 624ft-long and carved by a rushing creek into solid rock, will probably etch itself into your memory forever. The route passes two spectacular bottlenecks amid the thunder of falling water and clouds of frothy spray. In winter it is decorated with icicles. The trailhead is about 2km/1.2mi south of the Olympic ski stadium.

Kramerplateauweg

🚶 Upon leaving Garmisch, cross the Loisach River.

At the foot of the Kramerspitz, this almost entirely flat trail leads to the mountain restaurant Almhütte *(45min)*

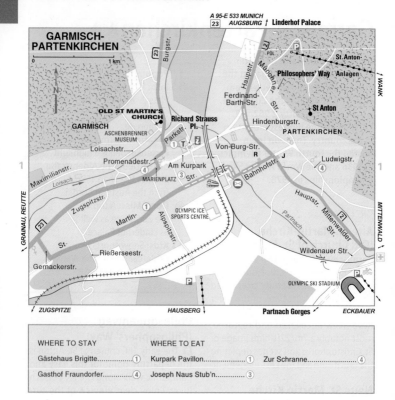

WHERE TO STAY	WHERE TO EAT	
Gästehaus Brigitte................(1)	Kurpark Pavillon...................(1)	Zur Schranne.......................(4)
Gasthof Fraundorfer.............(4)	Joseph Naus Stub'n.............(3)	

and the Pflegersee lake *(90min)*, which is a great place for swimming.

EXCURSIONS

Mittenwald★

⊙ 20km/11.8mi east.

Mittenwald is intensely popular, thanks to its gorgeous location below the Kranzberg and Karwendel massifs and the beauty of the town itself. Its biggest claim to fame is its abundance of intricately frescoed **house façades★★** in a style called *Lüftlmalerei*. The ones on Obermarkt are especially spectacular.

ZUGSPITZE★★★

☎(08821) 79 70. www.zugspitze.de.

The Zugspitze is the northwest pillar of the Wetterstein limestone massif, a rocky barrier enclosing the valley of the Loisach and on the border with Austria. With a summit at 2 964m/9 724ft above sea level, the Zugspitze is the highest peak in Germany.

Its matchless panorama and extensive ski slopes keep the mountain well supplied with tourist facilities. On clear days views extend to Germany, Italy, Switzerland and Austria.

🧗 Summit Ascent

⊙ Wear appropriate (warm) clothing.

Getting to the Zugspitze summit involves either a cogwheel-train ride followed by a short cable-car ride, or a steep cable-car ride straight up from Eibsee Lake. Many people ascend the summit on the cogwheel train and return by cable-car, or vice versa.

Coming from Ehrwald on the Austrian side, use the **Tyrolean Zugspitz Railway** (www.zugspitzbahn.at).

From Garmisch-Partenkirchen

Duration 1hr 15min by cogwheel train and cable-car. Departs hourly 8.15am–8.15pm. ⊛50€ round-trip in summer, 41.50€ in winter. Last train to Garmisch 4.30pm. ☎(08821) 79 70. www.zugspitze.de.

The high-tech cogwheel trains depart from their own station behind the main train station in Garmisch, and travel along the foot of the mountain past the Eibsee lake before starting their steep ascent through a 4.6km/2.8mi tunnel to the Zugspitzplatt station. From here, a cable-car *(Gletscherbahn)* ascends the last 350m/1 148ft to the summit in 4min.

From the Eibsee

Duration 10min by cable-car. Departs at least every 30min 8am–4.45pm (until 4.15pm in winter). ☎51€ round-trip, 60€ in winter. ☎(088 21) 79 70. www.zugspitze.de. Service reduced or suspended in bad weather.

The cable-car makes the intensely steep trip to the summit in a mere 10 minutes; the ride is not really suited for those suffering from fear of heights.

Zugspitzgipfel★★★ (Summit)

The upper terminals of the *Gletscherbahn* and the Eibsee cable-car are on the German side, while the Tyrolean Zugspitzbahn terminates on the Austrian side.

The **panorama★★★** to the east reveals the Kaisergebirge, the Dachstein and

Steep ride to Zugspitzgipfel
© Adam Bukolt/Bigstockphoto.com

the Karwendel, the glacial peaks of the Hohe Tauern, the High Alps of the Tirol and the Ortler and the Bernina massifs. Nearer are the mountains of the Arlberg before the Säntis in the Appenzell Alps; further away, to the west and northwest, are the Allgäu and Ammergau ranges. To the north, the Bavarian lowlands are visible, along with the Ammersee and Starnberger See lakes. On good days, you can even spot Munich in the distance.

In fine snow conditions (usually Oct–May), the lower Zugspitzplatt offers a **skiing** area and a terrain park with half-pipes, kicker and rail areas.

View of Zugspitze from Eibsee
© Vadim Shtral/Bigstockphoto.com

SCHLOSS LINDERHOF★★ (LINDERHOF PALACE)

▶ 27km/16.7mi north of Garmisch-Partenkirchen. ●Guided tours (25min) Apr–mid-Oct daily 9am–6pm; late Oct–Mar daily 10am–4pm. Closed 1 Jan, Shrove Tue, 24, 25 & 31 Dec. Outbuildings closed May–mid-Oct. ◎Summer 8.50€, winter 7.50€. ✆(08822) 920 30. www.linderhof.de. Allow at least two hours and prepare for long waits in high season.

Ludwig II's most whimsical palace is tucked deep into the forest in one of the most secluded and idyllic valleys of the Ammergau Alps. Though not particularly large, it was the young king's favourite retreat and reflects his romantic fantasies.

Schloss★★ (Palace)

Ludwig II had this intimate palace built between 1874 and 1879 in a style blending Italian Renaissance and Baroque elements and inspired by his idol, French King Louis XIV. The lavish **state bedchamber** surpasses even the luxury of Versailles, while the dining room has a table that disappears into the floor.

Park★★

The Italianate terraced gardens complement the natural slopes of the landscape. Views from the **Temple of Venus** rotunda are especially pleasant when the fountains are in action.

⊛ Do not miss the **Moorish Kiosk**, an exotic extravaganza of stained glass, feathers, painted wood and even an enamel throne. The **Venus Grotto** is just as lavish, and features an artificial lake complete with waterfall and a gilded shell-shaped boat. The setting was inspired by the Wagner opera *Tannhäuser*.

ADDRESSES

🛏 STAY

⊜ **Gästehaus Brigitte** – *St. Martin-Straße 40, Garmisch-Partenkirchen.* ✆(08821) 739 38. www.brigittegarmisch.de. *11 rooms* ⌑. This spotless guest-house

is located near the cable-car station and just around the corner from trails and the Olympic skating rink.

⊜◉ **Gasthof Fraundorfer** – *Luswigstraße 24, Partenkirchen.* ✆08 821 92 70. www.gasthof-fraundorfer.de. *Closed Nov. 30 rooms.* ⌑ Some of the bedrooms may be small here but the balconies, with views over the Waxenstein, help to compensate. Expect oompah music, yodelling and folk dancing at the convivial Bavarian restaurant.

MITTENWALD

⊜ **Hotel Garni Edlhuber** – *Innsbrucker Straße 33, Mittenwald.* ✆08 823 13 89. www.edlhuber-mittenwald.de. *6 rooms.* ⌑ This traditional wooden family-run hotel, at the foot of the Karwendel Mountain, is an idyllic location for outdoors holidays. Comfortable, pretty rooms and a warm welcome await.

⏹ EAT

⊜ **Gasthaus zur Schranne** – *Griesstraße 4.* ✆(08821) 16 99. www.zurschranne.de. *Closed Tue.* Sample Bavarian comfort food, served in particularly belt-loosening portions, at this typical regional eatery. Sit inside or on the covered terrace.

⊜ **Kurpark Pavillon** – *Richard Strauss Platz 1.* ✆08 821 31 77, www.adlwaerth.de. Regional specialities are served in this attractive glass pavilion in the centre of Garmisch; ideal for dinner after an evening at the casino or the theatre.

⊜◉◉ **Joseph-Naus Stub'n** – *Klammstraße 19.* ✆(08821) 90 10. For a more refined, modern take on local cuisine, grab a table at this graciously rustic restaurant named for the man who first reached the Zugspitze summit in 1820.

MITTENWALD

⊜ **Gasthaus zur Römerschanz** – *Innsbrucker Straße 30.* ✆08 823 15 31. This inviting Bavarian-style establishment offers local specialities such as pork roasted in beer, expertly prepared, as well as a good list of regional beers.

Chiemsee★

Known as the "Bavarian Sea", the Chiemsee is the largest of the province's lakes. Its calm waters offer plenty of recreation options, including swimming, boating and windsurfing. The lake's two islands are both worth a visit: steer towards Herreninsel (Gentlemen's Isle) to tour King Ludwig II's extraordinary palace and to the Fraueninsel (Ladies' Isle) to view its ancient Benedictine abbey. In the background are the Chiemgau Alps, a popular winter-sports area.

THE ISLANDS

Ferries leave from the Prien-Stock docks (exit the A8 at Bernau). Round-trip to Herreninsel (15min) 7.40€; combination tickets for Herreninsel and Fraueninsel (25min) 8.40€. Boat tours on the lake 11.90€. (08051) 60 90. www.chiemsee-schifffahrt.de.

Herreninsel

King Ludwig II of Bavaria bought this island in 1873 to save it from deforestation but built a sumptuous palace.

Schloss Herrenchiemsee★★

20min walk from the dock. Visit by guided tour (30min) only Apr–Oct daily 9am–6pm; Nov–Mar daily 9.40am–4.15pm. Closed Jan 1, Shrove Tue, Dec 24, 25 & 31. 8€. (080 51) 688 70. www.herrenchiemsee.de.
It was to be the grandest of Ludwig II's palaces, modelled on Versailles in honour of his idol, French king Louis XIV. Ludwig poured funds into the construction of the **Neues Schloss** (New Palace) on Herreninsel, but when he died in 1886 it was still only partly finished. Tours start in the entrance hall with its **double state staircase** (Prunktreppenhaus). Especially dazzling are the **state bedroom★** and the 77m/252ft-long **Hall of Mirrors★**.The south wing houses the **König Ludwig II Museum** (entrance included in Schloss ticket), with

Info: Felden 10, 83233 Bernau. (08051) 96 55 50. www.chiemsee-alpenland.de.

Location: Prien, on the western shore, is the busiest and most central of the Chiemsee resorts. The A8 autobahn (Munich–Salzburg) skirts the lake's southern shore.

Don't Miss: Schloss Herrenchiemsee, the view of the Alps from the northern lake shore between Rimsting and Seebruck.

Timing: Allow at least half a day to visit Schloss Herrenchiemsee.

portraits, busts, historical photographs and original clothing.

Augustinian Monastery at Altes Schloss (Old Palace)

The first Augustinian monastery was founded on the island in 1130, but the current incarnation dates to the Baroque era. The four wings enclose a large, almost rectangular courtyard with a rose garden. Also known as Altes Schloss (Old Palace), it is now partly a **museum** tracing 1 200 years of Bavarian history. Highlights include the Baroque library designed by Johann Baptist Zimmermann and King Ludwig II's private quarters, including the Blue Bedroom. Almost as impressive are the state rooms in the Princes' Tract, especially the Imperial Hall and the Garden Room.

Fraueninsel

This small islet is home to the Benedictine **Frauenchiemsee Monastery**, founded in 782 by Duke Tassilo III. One of the oldest women's abbeys in Germany, it was secularised in 1803 and revived in 1837 by King Ludwig I.
The three-aisled church is Carolingian at its core, but sports Romanesque frescoes as well as Gothic and Baroque

touches. Copies of its ceiling frescoes grace the upper chapel of the nearby **Torhalle** (gatehouse), now a museum surveying early sacred art in Bavaria.

ADDRESSES

🏨 STAY

⇔ **Gruber-Alm** – *Almweg 18, 83370 Seeon-Roitham.* ℘*(08667) 696. www.gruber-alm.de. 19 rooms. Restaurant⇔🍴🍴.* This pleasant hotel on a little hill affords views of the Chiemgau Alps. The "Wedding Room" has a handpainted ceiling, while others brim with rustic Bavarian hospitality. The restaurant serves regional dishes.

⇔🍴 **Alter-Wirt** – *Kirchplatz 9, 83233 Bernau am Chiemsee.* ℘*(08051) 965 69 90. www.alter-wirt-bernau.de. 41 rooms. Restaurant⇔🍴.* The half-timbered Alter Wirt inn has rustic charm and country furnishings; balcony rooms overlook the town.

⇔🍴 **Inselhotel Zur Linde** – *on the Fraueninsel. 5min boat ride from Gstadt.* ℘*(08054) 903 66. www. linde-frauenchiemsee.de. 14 rooms. Restaurant⇔🍴🍴.* A romantic island getaway, this inn dates from 1396 and was once the haunt of artists and writers. Rooms and public areas lend a sense of unhurried charm, while the dining room, still with its original layout, adds yet more character to the place.

🍽 EAT

⇔🍴 **Kloster-Wirt** – *Frauenchiemsee 50, Fraueninsel. 5min boat ride from Gstadt.* ℘*(08054) 77 65. www.klosterwirt-chiemsee.de.* Part of the island's Benedictine abbey, this dockside restaurant is a nice spot for a hearty meal or coffee and cake. In fine weather, relax in the tree-shaded beer garden.

Berchtesgaden★★

Journey's end of the German Alpine Road (Deutsche Alpenstraße), Berchtesgaden has a sublimely beautiful setting embraced by half a dozen mountain ranges and anchored by the painterly Königssee lake. Much of the landscape is protected as the Berchtesgaden National Park and is a year-round outdoor playground. The only stain on the region's legacy came during the Nazi years when Adolf Hitler chose the Obersalzberg as the site of his southern headquarters.

SIGHTS

Schlossplatz★

This triangular square is the heart of Berchtesgaden. On the western side is the Getreidekasten, the former granary furnished with an arcade in the 16C. Lombard influence is evident in the multi-colour stone façade of the **Church of St. Peter and St. John** (*Stiftskirche St. Peter and Johannes*).

▶ **Population:** 8 000

🛈 **Info:** Königsseer Straße 2, ℘(08652) 944 53 00. www. berchtesgaden.de and www. berchtesgadener-land.de.

▶ **Location:** Berchtesgaden is the main town of the Berchtesgadener *Land* (region), which also includes the Schönau on Königssee 5km/3mi south of town, Obersalzberg 4km/2.5mi east, Marktschellenberg 9km/6mi north, Ramsau 9km/6mi west, and Bischofswiesen 5km/ 3mi north.

👁 **Don't Miss:** Königssee, Eagle's Nest, Rossfeld-Panoramastraße.

🕐 **Timing:** Allow a full day, preferably two, to enjoy this region's outstanding natural beauty.

👪 **Kids:** The salt mines.

Schloss (Palace)

Guided tours (50min) mid-May–mid-Oct Sun–Fri 10am–noon, 2pm–4pm; rest of the year Mon–Fri 11am–2pm. Closed Shrove Tue, Dec 24 & 31. 9.50€. (08652) 94 79 80. www.schloss-berchtesgaden.de.

Once a monks' priory, this sumptuous palace is still owned by the Wittels-bachs, Bavaria's former royal family. The palace museum displays weapons, religious art, French tapestries and Nymphenburg porcelain. A **guided tour** allows a closer look at the palace. Visit the highest terrace for memorable views of the Watzmann.

Salzbergwerk (Salt Mines)★★

Bergwerkstraße 23. Guided tours (2hrs) May–Oct daily 9am–5pm; Nov–Apr daily 11am–3pm. Closed Jan 1, Good Friday, Pentecost, Dec 24,25 & 31. 16€. (08652) 60 02 20. www.salzzeitreise.de.

The Berchtesgaden salt mines, which started operating in 1517, brought prosperity to a once very poor region. The salty rock is washed by water and the resulting brine *(Sole)* is piped to Bad Reichenhall to be refined.

On the **tour**, visitors get to dress in miner's overalls, take a small train, whoosh down wooden slides and raft across an illuminated underground lake.

Dokumentationszentrum Obersalzberg★★

Salzbergstraße 41. Open Apr–Oct daily 9am–5pm; Nov–Mar Tue–Sun 10am–2pm. Closed Jan 1, Nov 1, Dec 24, 25 & 31. 3€. (08652) 94 79 60. www.obersalzberg.de.

After the American military handed the Obersalzberg back to the Bavarian government in 1996, the decision was made to document the area's sinister past in a multi-lingual, multimedia exhibition centre. Open since 1999, it stands on the foundations of the former Nazi guesthouse "Hoher Göll". A visit here is an essential, if disturbing, experience.

EXCURSIONS
Kehlsteinhaus★★ (Eagle's Nest)

4km/2.5mi east. Buses operate mid-May–Oct daily 8.55am–4pm every 25min. 15.50€. (08652) 2969. www.kehlsteinhaus.de.

One of the region's most impressive **panoramas**★★ unfolds from the Eagle's Nest lodge atop Mount Kehlstein at 1 834m/6 020ft. A restaurant today, it was originally a gift from the Nazi party to Hitler on his 50th birthday; it is the only remaining Third Reich-era building. It took 3 000 workers 13 months to build the steep **road**★★★ leading all the way up the mountain. Today, special shuttle buses make

Chapel of St. Bartholomä by Königssee

Obersalzberg

Adolf Hitler first visited and fell in love with the Obersalzberg area in 1923 and began spending summers in the Wachenfeld House in 1928. After seizing power in 1933, he had the property enlarged and turned into the elegant Berghof chalet. Many of the party brass built their own estates, including Martin Bormann and Hermann Göring, thus gradually turning the Obersalzberg into the southern Nazi party headquarters alongside Berlin. Most of the compound was destroyed by British and American bombs in April 1945. The Bavarian government demolished the remaining ruins in 1952; a year later the American military made the area a recreation zone.

the vertigo-inducing ascent from the parking lot at Hintereck. At the end of the road, a lift hewn straight through the rock ascends the final 100m/328ft. **Views★★★** extend across the German and Austrian Alps, while the Königssee shimmers below like an emerald jewel.

Königssee★★

⊙ 5km/3.1mi south. Boats leave year-round every 30min. Allow 1hr 45min round-trip, plus 1hr for short walks ashore. ⊛13.90€ to St. Bartholomä, 16.90€ to Salet. ℘(08652) 963 60. www.seenschifffahrt.de.
This long, narrow lake lies within Berchtesgaden National Park. With the Watzmann, Germany's second-highest mountain (2 713m/8 900ft) looming above, the lake narrows at St. Bartho-

lomä, where you can visit the onion-domed pilgrimage **Chapel of St. Bartholomä**. From here, a moderate trail *(1hr)* leads to the **Eiskapelle★★**, an ice grotto (⊛do not enter – dangerous!). From the final boat stop at Salet an easy 15min trek reaches the **Obersee** and Röthbach Falls.
For bird's-eye views, take the Jennerbahn **cable-car** up the 1 800m/5 900ft Mount Jenner (⊛20.80€ round-trip). Maps can be picked up at the **Nationalpark-Haus** (Franziskanerplatz 7; open Mon–Sat 9am-5pm; ℘08652 643 43; www.nationalpark-berchtesgaden.de) in central Berchtesgaden.

Hintersee★

⊙ 12km/7.4mi west via B305.
The road climbs the narrow Ramsau Valley to reach this lake framed by the domes of the Reiteralpe and the teeth of Hochkalter.

Almbachklamm (Almbach Gorge)★★

⊙ 5km/3mi north via the B305.
Considered one of the prettiest gorges in the Bavarian Alps, this one is carved into the cliffs behind a traditional inn and 17C marble mill that still grinds big chunks of rocks into smooth balls.
A trail follows the creek past waterfalls and pools, crossing more than two dozen iron footbridges along the way. From the top of the gorge, return either the same way or continue via a steepish trail to the village of Ettenberg with its lovely pilgrimage chapel. Allow about 90min for the gorge only or 2hrs30min for the trek to Ettenberg.

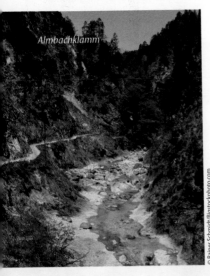

Almbachklamm

© Rainer Schmidt/Bigstockphoto.com

🚗 DRIVING TOUR

ROSSFELD PANORAMASTRAßE★★

Round-trip of 29km/18mi east of Berchtesgaden (anticlockwise) 1hr 30min. Toll 🅿5€ car & driver, 2€ per passenger. 📞(0861) 574 15. www.rossfeldpanoramastrasse.de.

The road *(open year-round)* ascends the crest of the Austrian valley of the Salzach and overlooks the Tennengebirge. The Dachstein with its glittering glaciers fills the background. On the other side of the ridge is a view over Berchtesgaden, Salzburg and the peaks of Hoher Göll, Kehlstein and Untersberg. From the Hennenkopf car park, climb to Hennenkopf Cross at 1 551m/5 089ft. The road descends from the crest after the Rossfeldhütte (inn) and winds through the charming valleys of the Oberau region.

Regensburg★★

Regensburg is among the most delightful towns in eastern Bavaria. It has a history going back 2 000 years. Its remarkably well-preserved medieval centre is punctuated by a stunning cathedral, an ancient stone bridge and Italianate patrician towers. In 2006, it made UNESCO's list of World Heritage Sites.

A BIT OF HISTORY

Preserved by time – Regensburg began in 179 AD as a Roman garrison guarding the empire's natural frontier of the Danube at its most northerly point. The town was converted to Christianity in the 7C, and St. Boniface founded a bishopric there in 739, making it a centre of religious life in the Middle Ages. As the seat of the Bavarian dukes (6C–13C), the town developed into an important trading post. It became part of Bavaria in the 19C and lost influence to Munich, a circumstance that spared it from bombardment during World War II. Today its city centre is one of the best-preserved medieval towns in Germany.

The city of diets – Once a Free Imperial City, Regensburg hosted plenary sessions of the Imperial Diet charged with responsibility for the internal peace and external security within the Holy Roman Empire. From 1663 to 1806 the

- ▶ **Population:** 137 000
- ℹ **Info:** Altes Rathaus. 📞(0941) 507 44 10. www.regensburg.de.
- ◐ **Location:** Regensburg is located in eastern Bavaria and spans the Danube at the crossroads of the A3 and A93.
- 🅿 **Parking:** Garages are located throughout Regensburg.
- 👁 **Don't Miss:** The cathedral, the view from the left bank.
- ◷ **Timing:** Allow at least a full day for this lovely city.

city was the seat of a permanent diet, which drew representatives from 70 states to Regensburg.

👣 WALKING TOUR

OLD TOWN
Allow half a day.

Kathedrale St. Peter★

Domplatz 1. Open Apr–Oct daily 6.30am–6pm; Nov–Mar daily 6.30am–5pm. 📞(0941) 597 10 02. www.bistum-regensburg.de.
Construction of this cathedral began after 1260, but was essentially brought to a halt in 1525; the spires were not added until the 19C.

The Gorges of the "Donaudurchbruch"

Between Kelheim and Kloster Weltenburg, the Danube narrows as it "breaks through" steep, narrow limestone cliffs in a series of meanders. The best way to view this beautiful gorge is on a boat cruise. Up to 20 tours depart from Kelheim daily from mid-March to October. Drop by the tourist office or visit www.schiffahrt-kelheim. de for a timetable. The round-trip cruise costs ↺8€.

The **Eselsturm** (Donkey Tower), above the northern transept, is all that remains of the original Romanesque sanctuary. The **west front**, richly decorated, is the work of a local family of sculptors named Roritzer. The main entrance, flanked by two neo-Gothic towers, is unusual, with a triangular, jutting porch. A statue of St. Peter can be seen on the pier.

Inside, the huge late-Gothic nave houses two 13C masterpieces of local Gothic statuary: the archangel Gabriel and opposite, Mary at the Annunciation. The three chancel windows are adorned with beautiful 14C stained **glass★★**.

Detail of Kathedrale St. Peter

The cathedral is home to a famous boys' choir, the Regensburger Domspatzen.

Domschatz (Cathedral Treasury)

Krauterermarkt 3. In the south wing of the bishops' residence (Bischofshof), entrance via the courtyard. Open Apr–Oct Tue–Sat 10am–5pm, Sun noon–5pm; Dec–Mar Fri–Sat 10am–4pm, Sun noon–4pm. Closed Jan 1, Nov 2–30, Dec 24–Jan 6. ↺2€. ℘(0941) 576 45. www.domschatz-regensburg.de.
The cathedral's treasury displays liturgical items, reliquaries and vestments from the 11C to the 18C.

Kreuzgang (Cloister)

Access via the cathedral garden.
Inside the cloister, traces of ancient frescoes adorn the walls of the Romanesque **Allerheiligenkapelle** (All Saints Chapel). The old 11C Stefanskapelle is another highlight with an altar reliquary thought to date from the 5C–8C.

▶ Move towards the apse of the cathedral for a closer look at the stonemasonry.

Museum St. Ulrich★

Domplatz 2. Open Apr–Oct Tue–Sun 10am–5pm. ↺2€. ℘(0941) 516 88. www.domschatz-regensburg.de .
This newly renovated museum in the early Gothic **Ulrichskirche** presents religious art from the 11C to the 20C, including bishops' crosses, reliquaries and paintings. The church itself is decorated with murals from the 13C to the 16C.

▶ Make your way to Alter Kornmarkt via the Romanesque Römerturm (Roman Tower), which is connected to the ducal residence (Herzogshof).

Alte Kapelle★ (Old Chapel)

St.-Kassians-Platz 7.
The Basilica of Our Lady associated with this chapel stands on the south side of Alter Kornmarkt. Originally Carolingian, the Alte Kapelle was completely transformed in the Rococo style in the 18C. The splendid reredos, the painted

© M. Hertlein/MICHELIN

ceiling and the gilded stuccowork are accented by the light penetrating the tall windows. It is open only during services, but you can see the interior through a glass pane.

Porta Praetoria

On your left are remnants of the ancient wall and the north gate of the 2C Roman camp (25 ha/62 acres).

▶ Turn right and go down to the Danube.

Steinerne Brücke (Stone Bridge)

This 310m/1 017ft-long bridge from the 12C rests on 16 arches. For many centuries it was the only crossing over the Danube River for a long distance. From the middle of the bridge, there is a fine **view★** of the old town.

In the foreground is the 14C Brückturm gateway, flanked by the huge roof of the 17C Salzstadel (salt loft).

Beside this building, on the quayside, the **Historische Wurstkuchl**, a 500-year-old sausage kitchen, is still serving up local fare.

Goliathstraße

Goliath House, with its monumental 16C frescoes, stands out among several interesting houses flanking this street. At Watmarkt 4, a fine Gothic patrician tower has a private chapel on the ground floor (now the Scandinavian-themed, Michelin-starred restaurant Storstad), a first-floor balcony and a residential wing.

Altes Rathaus and Reichstagsmuseum★ (Old Town Hall and Imperial Diet Museum)

🔊 Guided tours (1hr) Apr–Oct daily 9.30am–4pm, every half-hour (3pm tour in English); Nov, Dec & Mar daily 10am, 11.30am, 1.30pm, 2pm, 3pm and 3.30pm (2pm in English); Jan–Feb daily 10am, 11.30am, 1.30pm and 3pm. Closed Jan 1, Shrove Tue, Dec 24 & 25. ☜7.50€. 𝄞(0941) 507 34 40. www.regensburg.de.

The eight-storey tower of the old town hall dates from 1250. The Gothic western section was built c. 1360. The façade includes a gabled doorway and a pedestal supporting a charming oriel window.

Tours include a stop in the *Reichssaal* (Imperial Hall), where the delegates of the permanent diet once gathered.

Haidplatz★

This square is surrounded by historic buildings, including the **Zum Goldenes Kreuz** inn (at no 7) with a stone tower and façade. In the centre of the square is the 1656 **Justitiabrunnen** (Justice Fountain).

Schottenkirche St. Jakob (Scottish Church of St. Jacob)

Protected by a glass roof, the portal of this ruined church, founded by Irish Benedictine monks in 1090, is a Romanesque masterpiece (1183).

Its complex iconography is still not fully understood, although it is possible to identify scenes from the Last Judgement: note the representations of the good deeds on the left and the bad deeds on the right.

Bismarckplatz

In Roman times and in the Middle Ages, warehouses stood on this lively square on the edge of the city centre. Today, it is dominated by two 19C Neoclassical buildings.

Sporting a columned portico, the Präsidialpalais (Presidential Palace) at the southern end was home to the French delegation in town for the Imperial Perpetual Diet. The imposing building on

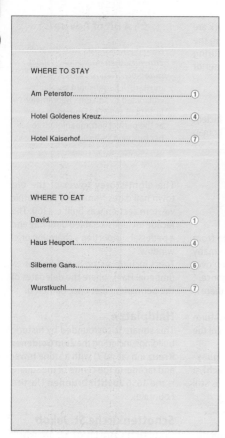

WHERE TO STAY

Am Peterstor......................................①

Hotel Goldenes Kreuz........................④

Hotel Kaiserhof...................................⑦

WHERE TO EAT

David...①

Haus Heuport....................................④

Silberne Gans....................................⑥

Wurstkuchl..⑦

the square's north side is the municipal theatre (*Stadttheater*).

The former embassy of Württemberg stands at the corner of Gesandtenstraße (street of the envoys). Further down this street, the Trinity Church (Dreieinigkeitskirche) is surrounded by ornate Baroque epitaphs of several of these ambassadors.

▶ From Gesandtenstraße, turn left on Rote-Hahnen-Gasse, then right on Hinter der Grieb.

Hinter der Grieb

This alley and the surrounding lanes are flanked with patrician houses from the Middle Ages. At the bottom a beautiful view of the cathedral is obtained.

▶ Upon arriving in Untere Bachgasse, head down an alleyway at no 7 that leads to Wahlenstraße 16. Turn right to get to Kramgasse alley that leads back to the cathedral.

ADDITIONAL SIGHTS
Kunstforum Ostdeutsche Galerie (Art Forum East German Gallery)

Dr. Johann-Maier-Straße 5.
Open year-round Tue–Sun 10am–5pm (Thu until 8pm). Closed Jan 1, Shrove Tue, 1 May, 1 Nov, Dec 24–25 & 31.
⊛6€. ✆(0941) 29 71 40 .
www.kog-regensburg.de.
Smartly presented in 15 bright galleries organised by style or subject matter, this collection presents a thorough survey of Eastern European art from the

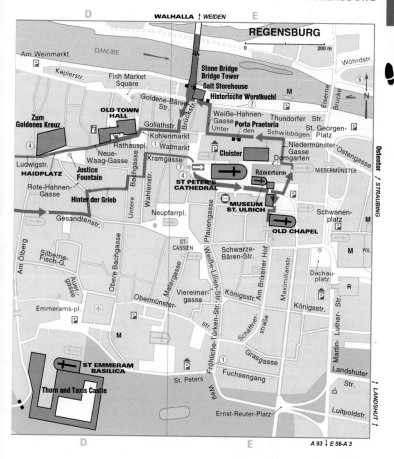

19C (Romantic period) to the late 20C. Artists represented include the Impressionist Lovis Corinth, German Expressionists and Secession artists Otto Dix and Oskar Kokoschka as well as Käthe Kollwitz, who is famous for her emotionally charged bronze sculptures.

AROUND ST. EMMERAM SQUARE
Basilika St. Emmeram

Emmeramsplatz 3. Open year-round Sun noon–6pm, Mon–Thu 10am–4pm, Fri 1pm–4pm. ✆ (0941) 510 30.

This edifice was once the abbey church of an 8C Benedictine monastery. A Gothic gateway on **Emmeramsplatz** leads to the huge Romanesque porch (12C) and the double doors at the church entrance, whose 11C sculptures depict Jesus Christ, St. Emmeram and St. Dionysius.

Schloss Thurn und Taxis (Thurn and Taxis Castle)

Emmeramsplatz 5. ✆ Guided tours (60min and 90min) daily 10.30am–4.30pm. Closed Dec 24 &25. ✆13.50€, child 10€. ✆ (0941) 504 81 33. www.thurnundtaxis.de.

The Thurn and Taxis princes held the German postal monopoly until the 19C. As compensation for losing the monopoly, they were given the St. Emmeram abbey buildings, which the family has occupied since 1816.

Tours take in the state apartments, lavishly decorated in Historicist style, as well as the cloister of the Basilica St. Emmeram.

Fürstliche Schatzkammer (Treasury)

Open Apr–early Nov Mon–Fri 11am–5pm, Sat–Sun 10am–5pm. ⊚4.50€. ✆(0941) 504 81 33.

The north wing of the Neoclassical former stables contains a branch of the Bavarian National museum. Displays include furniture, porcelain and weapons from leading workshops in Europe.

EXCURSIONS

Walhalla★

⏵ 11km/6.8mi east. Open Apr–Sept daily 9am–5.45pm; Oct daily 9am–4.45pm; Nov–Mar daily 10am–11.45am, 1pm–3.45pm. Closed Shrove Tue, Dec 24, 25 & 31. ⊚4€. ✆(09403) 96 16 80. www.walhalla-regensburg.de.

Built between 1830 and 1842 by Ludwig I of Bavaria, this Doric temple honours great German men and women. Inside are 127 marble busts and 64 commemorative plaques of famous soldiers, artists and scientists, politicians, musicians and other movers, shakers and thinkers.

Kloster Weltenburg★

⏵ 33km/20.5mi southwest, on the banks of the Danube. Open year-round, daily 8am–6pm. ♿✆(09441) 20 40. www.klosterschenke-weltenburg.de.

Right on a particularly scenic stretch of the Danube Gorge (Donaudurchbruch), Weltenburg Abbey was built by Cosmas Damian Asam in 1718. Its impressive church boasts an oval narthex and nave as well as a high altar dominated by a statue of St. George shown with the dead dragon at his feet. The dome bears a *trompe-l'œil* Asam composition on the theme of the Church Triumphant. The abbey operates the world's oldest monastic brewery (since 1050) and has an enchanting beer garden. The nicest way to get here is by boat (operates late Apr–Oct, 40min to abbey, 20min back; |9.70P round-trip) from Kelheim, a town on the Danube about 30km/18.5mi southwest of Regensburg.

ADDRESSES

🛏STAY

⊝**Am Peterstor** – *Fröhliche-Türken-Straße 12.* ✆*0941 545 45. www.hotel-am-peterstor.de. 36 rooms.* ⊒*5€.* Modernized in 2012, this basic, but comfortable hotel, located 5min from the centre, is one of the best budget accommodations in town.

⊝☺**Hotel Kaiserhof** – *Kramgasse 10.* ✆*(0941) 58 53 50. www.kaiserhof-am-dom.de. 30 rooms.* Welcoming guestrooms all offer views of the cathedral's twin towers. The breakfast room is set in a former 14C chapel with a high vaulted ceiling.

⊝☺☺**Hotel Goldenes Kreuz** – *Haidplatz 7.* ✆*0941 558 12. www.hotel-goldeneskreuz.de. 9 rooms. Café open*

Walhalla

© Pat Ivester/Michelin

daily 7am–7pm, Sun and hols 9am–7pm.
This has been the city's most famous
hotel since the 16C, when Emperor
Charles V stayed here. In contrast with
the beams, ancient stone and frescoes,
bedrooms are light and modern.

⚉/ EAT

⚉ **Wurstkuchl** – *Thundorferstraße 3.*
℘0941 466 210. www.wurstkuchl.de.
This 500-year-old tavern sits by the
Old Stone Bridge. Try the homemade
sausages cooked on the charcoal
grill, accompanied by sauerkraut and
Wurstkuchl mustard.

⚉⚉ **Haus Heuport** – *Domplatz 7*
℘(0941) 599 92 97. www.heuport.de.
This fine 13C mansion in the old town
(opposite the cathedral) has a cosy
restaurant and cocktail bar. Bavarian
classics and Mediterranean-inspired
cuisine is served in the dining room or
on the terrace.

⚉⚉⚉ **Silberne Gans** – *Werftstraße 3.*
℘0941 280 55 98. www.silbernegans.de.
This ultra-modern restaurant occupies
a renovated historic house on the
Danube, and has a summer terrace.

⚉⚉⚉⚉ **David** – *Watmarkt 5.*
℘(0941) 56 18 58. Closed carnival week,
2 weeks in Aug, Sun and Mon, www.
hotel-bischofshof.de. This restaurant in a
historic mansion serves Mediterranean
cuisine in a romantic setting as well as
outdoors in the beer garden.

TAKING A BREAK

Café Goldenes Kreuz – *Haidplatz 7.*
℘(0941) 5 72 32. This elegant café
occupies a historic building with
abundant Gothic design details. In
summer enjoy the people-watching
from the terrace facing Haidplatz.

Eichstätt★★

Eichstätt, a small Episcopal town
and seat of a Catholic university,
owes its Baroque character to its
reconstruction after the Thirty
Years' War; only the cathedral
survived the burning of the town
by the Swedish army. But Eichstätt
is also a centre of contemporary
architecture with dazzling buildings
designed by Karljosef Schattner,
Karl Frey and Günther Behnisch.

▶ **Population:** 13 200
▪ **Info:** Domplatz 8.
   ℘(08421) 600 14 00.
   www.eichstaett.info.
▶ **Location:** Eichstätt lies in
   the midst of the Altmühl
   Valley natural park.
▶ **Don't Miss:** The cathedral
   and the Residenzplatz.
▶ **Timing:** About half a
   day for highlights.

SIGHTS

Dom★ (Cathedral)

Like so many churches in Germany, the
14C cathedral is characterised by a mix
of architectural styles. The east tower
is Romanesque, the Gothic main portal
is decorated with Biblical figures and
scenes, while the west face was crafted
by Baroque masters Jakob Engel and
Gabriel de Gabrieli.
The Gothic **cloister★** was a 15C addition
to the cathedral.
As you enter, turn left towards the late
15C **Pappenheim Altar★★** in the north

transept. Carved from Jura limestone,
it rises almost 9m/29.5ft high. On the
other end, in the Gothic west choir, is
a famous 1514 statue by Loy Hering
depicting Eichstätt's first 8C bishop **St.
Willibald**.
Willibald's relics are housed in the
elaborate canopied Baroque altar by
Matthias Seynold behind the statue.
Leaving the cathedral via the eastern
exit takes you to the **Mortuarium★**,
a late-Gothic funerary chapel paved
with elaborate **tombstones**. The four

stained-glass windows on the east wall depicting the Last Judgement are by Hans Holbein the Elder (c. 1500). The **Diözesanmuseum** (cathedral treasury; open Apr–Oct Wed–Fri 10.30am–5pm, Sat–Sun 10am–5pm; ⊗3€, Sun 1€; www.dioezesanmuseum-eichstaett. de 08421 502 66) is located in historical rooms above the cloister that were turned into a modern exhibition space by Karljosef Schattner. Its 12 rooms are filled with outstanding examples of ecclesiastical art. Highlights include a gold and jewel-encrusted finger reliquary of St. Jacob (12C), intricately woven Baroque tapestries and late medieval sculpture.

Residenzplatz★

Next to the cathedral, Residenzplatz is framed by lavish Rococo townhouses, including the bishop's palace, that are the legacy of master builders Gabriel de Gabrieli and Maurizio Pedetti. An 18m/59ft-high column of the Virgin Mary rises from a cherub-festooned fountain in front of the bishop's palace.

Willibaldsburg (Willibald Castle)

Burgstraße 19.

This 14C hilltop castle is largely the work of Augsburg Renaissance architect Elias Holl. Within are two museums, a garden with fantastic **views★★** of the river and town and a hand-carved **well** *(Tiefer Brunnen)* that is an astonishing 76m/249.3ft deep.

The **Jura-Museum★** (open Apr–Sept Tue–Sun 9am–6pm; Oct–Mar Tue–Sun 10am–4pm; closed Jan 1, Shrove Tue, Dec 24, 25 & 31; ⊗4.50€; & 08421 29 56; www.jura-museum.de) has a fabulous collection of locally found fossils. Pride of place goes to an extremely rare fossilised skeleton of an archeopteryx, the creature that constitutes the evolutionary link between reptiles and birds. Upstairs, the **Museum of Pre-History and Early History** (see Jura-Museum; ⊗4€; 09141 894 50) chronicles regional history from the Stone Age to the early Middle Ages and counts a mammoth skeleton, Celtic weapons

and Roman measuring devices among its possessions.

EXCURSION

Schloss Ellingen

▶ 29km/18mi northwest of Eichstätt.

Guided tours hourly Apr–Sept Tue–Sun 9am–6pm (last tour at 5pm); Oct–Mar Tue–Sun 10am–4pm. Closed Jan 1, Shrove Tue, Dec 24, 25 & 31. ⊗4.50€. (09141) 974 790. www.ellingen-tourismus.de.

Ellingen served as the regional seat of the Teutonic Knights from the 13C until Napoleon's dissolution of the order in 1806. The **palace** *(Schloss)* was designed by Franz Keller (1718–25) and is largely Baroque infused with Neoclassical elements. The chapel has frescoes by Cosmas Damian Asam and stuccowork by Franz Roth. The huge twin-flight **main staircase★** is worth seeing, as is the small museum on the history of the Teutonic Order.

ADDRESSES

STAY

⊜**Hotel Zum Hirschen** – *Brückenstraße 9, 85072 Eichstätt-Wasserzell.* (08421) 96 80. www.hirschenwirt.de. Closed Jan–mid-Feb. 40 rooms. Restaurant⊜⊜. The family-owned Hirschen is a good base for Altmühltal explorations. Rooms are timeless and functional with country-style décor. Enjoy robust regional dishes in the restaurant with winter garden.

⊜⊜**Hotel Adler** – *Marktplatz 22.* (08421) 67 67. www.adler-eichstaett.de. Closed Dec 18–Jan 10, Feb 1–7, Oct 30–Nov 5. 28 rooms. This restored Baroque building has good-size contemporary rooms with cherrywood furnishings. No smoking throughout.

EAT

⊜⊜**Gasthof Krone** – *Domplatz 3.* (08421) 44 06. www.krone-eichstaett.de. Closed Wed. In the heart of the old town, this pleasant brewery-owned tavern is great for winding down and enjoying fresh, rib-sticking Bavarian food.

Burghausen★★

Situated right on the border with Austria, Burghausen has a lovely, well-preserved old town crowned by the longest hilltop fortress in Germany. The dukes of Bavaria, who became rulers of Burghausen in the 12C, converted its medieval castle into this formidable defence system that stretches for an impressive 1 043m/3 420ft atop a narrow, rocky spur.

▶ **Population:** 18 500

🏢 **Info:** Stadtplatz 112.
   ✆(08677) 88 71 40.
   www.tourismus.
   burghausen.de.

◔ **Location:** Burghausen
   lies within a curve of
   the River Salzach, which
   forms the border between
   Germany and Austria.

☺ **Don't Miss:** The Burg
   from which Burghausen
   takes its name.

🕐 **Timing:** Allow two to
   three hours to visit the
   Burg and its museums.

SIGHTS
Burg★★ (Castle)

Leave your car in the Stadtplatz and walk along the circular cliff road. Beneath the Wöhrenseeturm and beyond the lake, a steep path leads to the outer fortifications. From here, the ramparts are visible, stepped up the Eggenberg hill. The Georgstor, or **St. George's Gate**, is set in the innermost ring of battlements, which protect the last small medieval courtyard at the castle's centre. Inside are two museums worth visiting.

Staatsgalerie in der Burg
(Bavarian Picture Gallery)

Open Apr–Sept daily 9am–6pm; Oct–Mar daily 10am–4pm. ⌖4€.
✆(08677) 46 59. www.pinakothek.de.
Ongoing renovations may close parts of the museum through 2017.

The former ducal apartments in the main castle building house this small branch of the Munich Pinakothek art museum. The focus is on 15C and 16C paintings, sculpture and tapestries made in Austria and Bavaria.

From the observation **platform** *(62 steps, access from the second floor)*, enjoy splendid panoramic **views★** of Burghausen, the Salzach and the surrounding hills. The Gothic **chapel** *(in the same wing)* has elegant star vaulting.

Stadtmuseum
(Municipal Museum)

Open mid-Mar–Apr & Oct daily 10am–4pm; May–Sept daily 9am–6pm. ⌖2€.
✆(08677) 651 98.
www.burghausen.de.

The duchess' former private quarters *(main castle, last door on the right)* now tell the history of Burghausen through an eclectic collection of tools, weapons, folk art, furniture, town models, paintings and sculpture spread over four floors.

EXCURSIONS
Raitenhaslach

◑ 6km/3.7mi south.

Red marble tombstones commemorating 15C–18C abbots are a key feature of this 12C Cistercian church, modified in the Baroque style in the late 17C. The life of St. Bernard of Clairvaux is illustrated in the fine **ceiling frescoes** (1739) by Johannes Zick of Lachen.

Tittmoning

◑ 16km/10mi south.

On the west bank of the Salzach, Tittmoning preserves the remains of its medieval fortifications and a castle, a former residence of the Prince-Bishops of Salzburg. Two fortified gateways give access to the broad **Stadtplatz**. Brightly painted façades, some decorated with gilded figures, wrought iron signs, oriel windows and emblazoned fountains make this town a charming place to stop.

Altötting

▶ 21km/13mi northwest.

Each year a million pilgrims come to see the black Madonna statue renowned for miracles. It is housed in the tiny, octagonal 8C **Gnadenkapelle**★ (Chapel of Grace). The treasury of the **Gothic Collegiate Church** (*Stiftskirche*) holds the 15C **Goldenes Rössl**★★ (golden horse), an exquisitely-detailed portable gold altar given to Charles VI of France by his wife, Isabella of Bavaria.

Marktl am Inn

▶ 10km/6.2mi north.

in 2005 village son Joseph Ratzinger (b. 1927) became Pope Benedikt XVI.The former pontiff's **Birth House** (Marktplatz 11) is now a small museum.

Passau★★

Passau enjoys an enchanting setting at the confluence of the Inn, the Danube (Donau) and the Ilz rivers. The old town, with its Baroque churches and patrician houses, crowds onto the narrow tongue of land separating the Inn and the Danube. The Oberhaus fortress looms above town on a wooded bluff on the northern bank of the Danube. Situated right on the border with Austria and close to the Czech Republic, Passau also makes a good base for explorations of Bohemia and Upper Austria.

A BIT OF HISTORY

The Passau bishopric was founded in the 8C by English-born St. Boniface. By the late 10C it had become extraordinarily powerful and until the 15C, encompassed the entire Danube Valley, including Vienna. From the Middle Ages on, river trade (especially of salt, also called the "white gold") played an important role in Burghausen's prosperity. Today, it is a popular river cruise stop en route to Vienna and Budapest.

ADDRESSES

🛏 STAY

🍽🛏 **Hotel Post** – *Stadtplatz 39.* ℰ*(08677) 96 50. www.hotelpost.de. 30 rooms. Restaurant* 🍽🛏. This central inn has rooms that range from rustic to elegant and a restaurant serving modernised Bavarian home-cooking.

🍽🛏 **Bayerische Alm** – *Robert-Koch-Straße 211.* ℰ*(08677) 98 20. www.bayerischealm.de. 23 rooms. Restaurant* 🍽🛏🍸. Enjoy views of the Burg from your private balcony at this family-run inn on the town outskirts. The bi-level restaurant and beer garden serve fresh, light and healthy fare.

▶ **Population:** 50 500

ℹ **Info:** Rathausplatz 3, 94032 Passau. ℰ(0851) 95 59 80. www.passau.de.

▶ **Location:** Passau is in eastern Bavaria, right on the border with Austria, and consists of three quarters: Ilzstadt to the north, Innstadt to the south and the peninsula of Altstadt.

🅿 **Parking:** Find parking on the Domplatz and south of the Schanzlbrücke.

😊 **Don't Miss:** Views from the Veste Oberhaus, Dom St. Stephan, the Three Rivers Point.

🕐 **Timing:** Allow a day to enjoy Passau at leisure.

SIGHTS
OLD TOWN
Dom St. Stephan

Most of this late-Gothic **cathedral** was destroyed by fire in the 17C and rebuilt in the Baroque style.

The cavernous sanctuary is richly decorated with frescoes and stuccowork.

© Däniel Hermann/Dreamstime.com

Four **lateral chapels** feature paintings by the Austrian artist JM Rottmayr (1654–1730). From the Residenzplatz, visitors can admire the cathedral's **east end★★**, a remarkable late-Gothic work. The cathedral also houses the world's largest cathedral **organ★★**, with 17 774 pipes and 233 stops.

Residenzplatz

The square is bordered on the south by the early Neoclassical bishops' **New Palace**. The surrounding streets are still lined by arcaded houses with corbelling and concealed ridge roofs.

Rathausplatz

The 14C **Rathaus** (town hall) with its painted façade dominates this picturesque square. The tower dates to the late 18C.

Glasmuseum★★

Am Rathausplatz, in the Hotel "Wilder Mann". Open year-round daily 10am–5pm. ⊚7€. ℘(0851) 350 71. www.glasmuseum.de.

Glassware from Bohemia, Bavaria and Austria from 1700 to 1950 makes up the bulk of this precious collection of 30 000 pieces.

The most important display comes from **Bohemia** (*Biedermeier, Historicism, Jugendstil)*; note especially the Lobmeyr state goblet depicting the Marriage of

Neptune with Amphitrite, which is considered a key glasswork of the 19C.

Dreiflüsseeck★ (Three Rivers Point)

From St. Michaels-Kirche, go down to the Inn quayside.

The fast-flowing Inn River runs past the **Schaiblingsturm** (1481), once used to store salt. At the confluence of the three rivers, the greenish current of the Inn can be spotted running alongside the brown Danube waters and dark water of the Ilz before they mingle.

From the Danube bank, on the far side of the promontory, there is a fine viewpoint.

THE LEFT BANK OF THE DANUBE
Veste Oberhaus (Fortress)

This imposing citadel was built in 1219 as a refuge for the bishops against rebellious burghers. It is linked with the **Veste Niederhaus** by a fortified road. From the belvedere marked *Zur Aussicht*, near the parking lot, and from atop the tower *(142 steps)*, there are magnificent **views★★** over the Inn, the Danube and Passau itself.

The town's history, art and religious roots, including some paintings from the Danube School, are traced in the small **Oberhausmuseum**.

EXCURSION
Bayerischer Wald★
(Bavarian Forest)

The Bavarian Forest includes low, rounded mountains, wild rock bastions and isolated river valleys, and a protected national park area. The natural woodland draws a wide variety of animal species. Together with the Bohemian Forest on the Czech side, it forms the largest contiguous forest in Europe. The area is known for its glass industry with many studios, factories and shops.

🚗 DRIVING TOURS

SOUTHERN MOUNTAINS: FROM FREYUNG TO ZWIESEL★

Freyung to Zwiesel. 70 km/43.5mi. Allow 2hrs.

▷ To get to Freyung from Passau, take the B 12. Continue north to Mauth, then turn left towards Weidhütte.

👥 Hans-Eisenmann Haus

Neuschönau. ℰ08 558 96 150. www.nationalpark-bayerischer-wald.de. Open daily 9am–5pm. Closed mid-Nov–Christmas. Treetop Walk 8€, child 6€. This Bavarian Forest National Park Information Centre is the place to organise your exploration of the region. There are exhibit rooms (in German only) and a waymarked footpath *(7km/4mi, 3hrs)* into the large Tierfreigelände (Wildlife Enclosure), with lynx, bison, wolves, brown bears, wild cats and deer; there are aviaries too. You can also drive here. At the world's longest **tree-top walk** (1 300m/1 422yd), you can observe the woods from a height of 8m/26ft to 25m/82ft off the forest floor.

▷ Go back to Spiegelau to continue on to Frauenau.

Glasmuseum★

Am Museumpark 1, Frauenau. ℰ09 926 941 020. www.glasmuseum-frauenau.de. Open Mon–Fri 9am–5pm, Sat–Sun and holidays 10am–4pm. Closed mid-Nov to around Dec 20. ⊗5€.

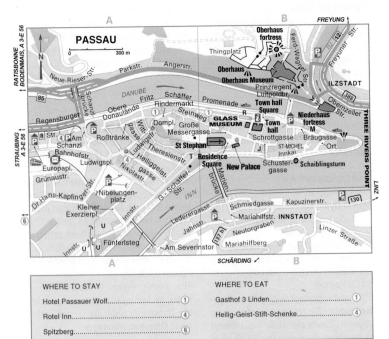

WHERE TO STAY		WHERE TO EAT	
Hotel Passauer Wolf	①	Gasthof 3 Linden	①
Rotel Inn	④	Heilig-Geist-Stift-Schenke	④
Spitzberg	⑥		

This museum traces man's 3 000-year love affair with glass and its link between art and industry. On display are works by American and German 20C artists. Look for the Pop Art exhibits.

NORTHERN MOUNTAINS: AROUND THE GROßER ARBER★

This circular, 65km/40m tour departs from Bodenmais (70km/43.5mi north of Passau). Allow 3hrs.

▶ To get to Bodenmais from Passau, take the B85 (Bayerische Ostmarkstraße) to Regen, then turn right.

Bodenmais★
This town with a healing climate lies in a pastureland at the southern foot of the forest's highest mountain, the Großer Arber (1 456m/4 775ft).

Lam
This charming winter-sports resort is located at the bottom of a broad valley. The valley rises gradually, to meadows and woods, and to the Lamer Winkel, which marks the start of the valley. A scenic road runs along the mountainside, with views of the Großer Arber, and rises to the pass known as the Brenner Sattel at 1 030m/3 379ft.

Hindenburg-Kanzel★
A **look-out point★** offers a fine view of the Lamer Winkel and the Arber.

Großer Arber★★
From the lower cable-car terminal, 1hr round-trip, including 20min walk. May–first snow daily 9am–4.30pm; first snow–mid-Jan 8.30am–4pm; late Jan–Apr 8.30am–4.30pm. 12€ round-trip in summer, 16€ per hour in winter. ℘(09925) 941 40. www.arber.de. From the upper terminal, a path leads to two rocky crags, one overlooking the **Schwarzer Regen depression★★**, and another (surmounted by a cross) with views of the Lamer Winkel and the forest to the north. The **Großer Arbersee★** lake sits to the right as the road

winds down through the forest. On the way are **views★** of the Zwiesel basin, the Falkenstein and the Großer Rachel.

ADDRESSES

🏠STAY

🛏️ **Rotel Inn** – *Donauufer, 50m/55yd from the main train station (Hauptbahnhof). ℘(0851) 951 60. www.rotel-inn.de. Closed Oct–Apr. 93 rooms 🛏️ 6€.* This modern hotel on the bank of the Danube has single and double rooms, but bathrooms are down the hall.

🛏️🍽️ **Hotel Passauer Wolf** – *Rinder-markt 6. www.hotel-passauer-wolf.de. ℘(0851) 931 510. 39 rooms. Restaurant🍽️.* This traditional establishment is mid-way between the Danube and the *Altstadt*'s pedestrian zone. Each room is furnished uniquely; the restaurant delivers rustic meals with river views on the side.

🛏️🍽️💰 **Spitzberg** – *Neuburger Straße 29. ℘(0851) 95 54 80. www.hotel-spitzberg.de. 35 rooms.* This striking, modern hotel is close to the old town and has attractive bedrooms.

🍴 EAT

🍽️ **Gasthof 3 Linden** – *Steinweg 6. ℘(9890) 11. www.gasthof-3linden.de.* Traditional cuisine is served in a trendy setting in this beautiful ancient stone *gasthof*. House specialities include *Krustenschweinbraten* (baked pork).

🍽️🍴 **Heilig-Geist-Stift-Schenke** – *Heiliggeistgasse 4. www.stiftskeller-passau.de ℘(0851) 26 07. Closed Jan 6–31 and Wed.* This establishment built in 1358 has a cosy, rustic atmosphere. Expect beautiful, vaulted ceilings, open fires and a charming vine-covered garden.

NIGHTLIFE

Café Duftleben – *Theresienstraße 22. ℘(9890) 94 30. www.cafe-duftleben.de.* In a former stable, this café features a terrace on the pedestrian zone. Snacks and cakes are available for munching on while listening to musical acts from gypsy jazz and blues to swing.

Northern Bavaria

Northern Bavaria

Don't expect lads in lederhosen or raucous oompah bands: the charms of northern Bavaria go far beyond the tourist brochure clichés. This is a region whose cultural landscape was shaped by some of the world's finest artists, Albrecht Dürer, Tilman Riemenschneider and Balthasar Neumann among them. Germany's most popular holiday route, the fabled Romantic Road, links enchanting villages and proud castles with spirit-lifting scenery. The region's biggest city is Nuremberg, which played special roles during both the Holy Roman Empire and the Third Reich, and today is especially famous for its Christmas market. Nearby Bamberg, also steeped in history, suffered hardly any wartime damage.

Highlights

Driving the Romantic Road

A trip along the Romantic Road is a wonderfully rewarding experience. Leaving Würzburg with its vineyard-ribboned hills and show-stopping Residence, the road carves through the idyllic Tauber Valley where you should stop at the palace of the Teutonic Order in Weikersheim and at the Riemenschneider altar in Creglingen before losing yourself in the tangle of medieval alleyways of Rothenburg ob der Tauber. Further on, Dinkelsbühl is almost as evocative but gets smaller crowds, while Nördlingen has a unique location inside a meteorite crater. Both are still encircled by their ancient town walls. *(For destinations further south ⟳ see MUNICH AND SOUTHERN BAVARIA.)*

Triumph and Trauma

South of Rothenburg, the A6 runs east to Nuremberg, a city that has certainly seen its historical ups and downs. It soared to political prominence in 1356 with the passage of the Golden Bull, reached its artistic zenith in the Renaissance under Albrecht Dürer and launched Germany's first railway in 1835. Alas, such glory was tainted in the 20C when the Nazi brass passed the anti-Semitic Nuremberg Laws in 1935 and held its mass party rallies here.

In 1945–46, the Allies chose the city to hold the Nazi war crime trials. Reminders of all these histories remain scattered throughout the town.

Canoeing, Wiesent Valley, Franconian Switzerland

© Alexander Rochau/Fotolia.com

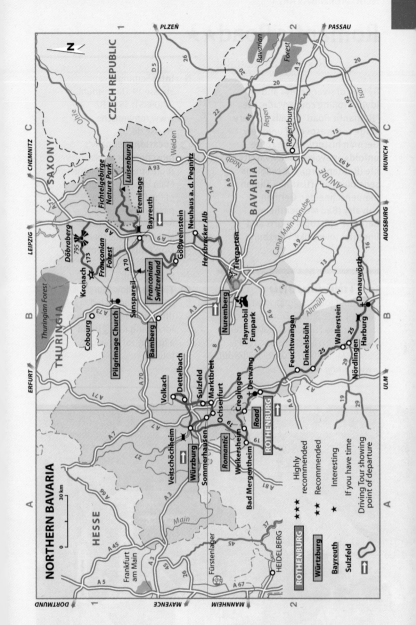

Off the Beaten Track

North of Nuremberg, tourist crowds get thinner despite some key destinations. Bamberg is famous for its beer and its neatly preserved ensemble of architectural gems, which garnered it UNESCO World Heritage listing. Bayreuth is usually mentioned in one breath with Richard Wagner, although it owes its most beautiful palaces to a woman, the Margravine Wilhelmine. Outdoor types, meanwhile, should steer to Franconian Switzerland, a fabulous playground of narrow valleys carved by sprightly streams and rock formations pockmarked with hundreds of caves. Canoeing, hiking, biking, caving and rock-climbing are all popular recreational activities here.

Romantic Road★★

Romantische Straße

By way of river valleys and an idyllic, rolling countryside, the "Romantic Road" recalls at every stage some aspect of uniquely German history. As the route unfolds, it evokes medieval city life (Rothenburg), the religious sensibility of artists like Tilman Riemenschneider, German chivalry (Bad Mergentheim), Baroque episcopal courts and Imperial towns like Würzburg.

Info: Segringer Strasse 19, Dinkelsbühl. ℰ(09851) 55 13 87. www.romantische strasse.de.

▶ **Location:** Germany's most popular tourist route stretches from the Main Valley to the foot of the Bavarian Alps, passing river valleys, fields, forests, orchards and pretty little towns.

Don't Miss: Rothenburg ob der Tauber, Dinkelsbühl.

Timing: Allow four hours for suggested driving tour ①; five hours for driving tour ②; and a full day for driving tour ③.

GETTING AROUND

The entire route is signposted Romantische Straße. From April to October, the Europabus travels the route in both directions once a day. Deutsche Touring (ℰ069196) 2078 501; www.touring.de).

Deutschordens Museum, Bad Mergentheim

© F1 Online/Tips Images

DRIVING TOURS

FROM WÜRZBURG TO ROTHENBURG

100km/62mi. Allow 4hrs.

▶ Leaving Würzburg★★

(👉see WÜRZBURG), the B27 descends towards the Tauber River Valley.

Bad Mergentheim★

Marktplatz 1. ✆(07931) 57 48 15. www.bad-mergentheim.de.
Bad Mergentheim was chosen as head-quarters for the Knights of the Teutonic Order in the 16. Set among the forested hills of the charming Tauber valley, it is a popular stop on the Romantic Road. It is celebrated for its historic old town, its castle and grounds and the healing qualities of its mineral springs.

Deutschordens Museum (German Teutonic Order Museum)

Schloss 16. Open Apr–Oct Tue–Sun 10.30am–5pm; Nov–Mar Tue–Sat 2pm–5pm, Sun 10.30am–5pm. Closed Dec 24, 25 & 31. ⊚6€. ⅋✆(07931) 522 12. www.deutschordensmuseum.de.
This 12C castle was extended in the mid-16C to become the residence of the Teutonic Order and its Grand Master. The museum occupies three floors and has an eclectic collection that ranges from historic dollhouses to medieval sculpture and panel paintings, faïences, and alabaster and marble reliefs from the Renaissance and Baroque periods, as well as ivory carvings.
On the second floor, the **New State Rooms** afford visitors a look at the audience chamber, the "State Bedroom" and the assembly hall (Kapitelsaal). Exhibits on the third floor trace the history of the Teutonic Order.

Weikersheim

🍴Guided tours (1hr) Apr–Oct daily 9am–6pm; Nov–Mar daily 10am–noon and 1pm–5pm. Closed Dec 24 & 31. ⊚6€. ⅋.✆(07934) 99 29 50. www.schloss-weikersheim.de.
Once the seat of the counts of Hohenlohe, this town features a castle (1580–1680) on the banks of the Tauber. Its magnificent **Rittersaal★★** (Knights' Hall) is typical of the transition between the Renaissance and Baroque styles. **Formal gardens** (1710), accented with grotesque statues in the Franconian style, end in a charming orangery.

▶ The narrow Tauber Valley begins above the town of Bieberehren. The road rises and falls over slopes covered alternately by woodland, orchards and willow-fringed riverbanks of the Tauber.

Teutonic Order

The Teutonic Order was founded as a Germanic Hospitaller community in the Holy Land; it became a religious order in 1198 when the knights returned home after the fall of Jerusalem. They became princes of sizable territories and estates, either by conquering them or by accepting them as gifts.
In 1525 the Grand Master of the order, Albrecht von Brandenburg-Ansbach, adopted Luther's teaching and suppressed the order's religious role. The community's territory of Prussia also became secular.
Dispossessed of its seat, the Teutonic Order elected as its new headquarters Schloss Mergentheim, which the order had controlled since 1219. The castle remained the Teutonic residence for three centuries. In 1809 Napoleon abolished the order.
Today it has reconstituted itself as a religious and charitable body and has its headquarters in Vienna.

Creglingen★

The isolated Herrgottskirche (open Apr–
Oct daily 9.15am–6pm, until to 6:30pm mid-
late Aug; Nov–Dec & Feb–Mar Tue–Sun
1pm–4pm; ∞2€; www.herrgottskirche.
de), 1.5km/1mi on the road to Blau-
felden, contains the **Altarpiece of
the Virgin Mary★★** carved by Tilman
Riemenschneider. Note how this artist
channelled his own sensibilities into the
exquisite expression of the Madonna at
the Assumption.

Opposite the church is the **Fingerhut-
museum** (thimble museum) – the only
one of its kind in Germany.

Detwang

In the church at Detwang another
Riemenschneider altarpiece★ depicts
the Crucifixion.

Rothenburg ob der Tauber★★★
See ROTHENBURG OB DER TAUBER.

FROM ROTHENBURG
TO DONAUWÖRTH

105km/64mi. Allow 5hrs.

Feuchtwangen

Once a Free Imperial City, this town was
also the birthplace of medieval minstrel
Walther von der Vogelweide. An attractive market square sits surrounded by
pretty houses and overlooked by a
parish church with an altarpiece of the
Virgin by Michael Wolgemut.

Installed in a 17C burgher's house is
the **Fränkisches Museum** (Museum
of Franconian Folklore), which displays
a collection of furniture and regional
pottery and costumes.

Dinkelsbühl★

Ramparts and watchtowers still surround
this idyllic medieval town, which, every
July, hosts a colourful festival (Kinderzeche) commemorating the town's protection from destruction in the Thirty
Years' War (*see Festivals and Events*).
The **Georgskirche★** retains its Romanesque tower. Other highlights include
the **Deutsches Haus★** *(Am Weinmarkt)*
and the Hezelhof *(Segringer Straße 7)*.

Wallerstein

From atop a promontory in the heart of
town *(Wallersteiner Felsen, access via the
Fürstlicher Keller)*, you can enjoy the vast
panorama of the Ries.

Nördlingen★

🛈 Marktplatz 2. *℘*090 81 84 116.
www.noerdlingen.de.

The former Free Imperial City of Nördlingen lies in the middle of the Ries basin
created by a giant meteorite about
15 million years ago. First recorded
in 898, it is only one of three German
towns still surrounded by a medieval
town wall.

St. Georgskirche★
(St. George's Church)

This late-15C hall-church is surmounted
by a majestic 90m/295ft-high,
copper-domed bell-tower, dubbed
affectionately **"Daniel"** (open Jan–
Feb & Nov daily 10am–4pm; Mar–Apr
& Oct 10am–5pm; May–Jun & Sept
9am–6pm; Jul–Aug 9am–7pm; Dec
9am–5pm; ∞3€). It is worth braving
the 350 steps to the top to fully appreciate Nördlingen's near-circular shape
and the crater within which it was built.
A watchman still lives up here and calls
out every half hour between 10am and
midnight. Originally, this action was
intended to make contact with the
guards on watch on the town gates.

The church **interior** is canopied by fan
vaulting. The pulpit (1499) is reached
via a corbelled staircase with only
three steps. Note the **organ** on the
finely worked baldaquin *(on the right
side)*. The main altar is Baroque in style,
but incorporates five statues created in
Gothic times. They depict Jesus on the
cross, St. Mary, St. John and two angels
and were created by Niclaus Gerhaert
von Leyden.

Stadtmauer★ (Town Walls)

The Nördlingen town walls are completely preserved and fully accessible.
The ramparts, which for the most part
are covered, extend over a length of
2 632m/2 878yd and are punctuated
by 5 gates and 14 towers.

One of the most attractive sections is along the battlements from the Berger Gate via the Alte Bastei, or old bastion, to the Reimlinger Gate.

To learn more about the fortifications and their role in the history of Nördlingen, stop by the small but excellent **Stadtmauermuseum** (open mid-Mar–Oct daily 10am–4.30pm; ⊛2€; ℘09081 91 80) in the Löpsinger gate tower. Exhibits include cannon and uniforms from the Thirty Years' War.

Stadtmuseum★ (City Museum)

Vordere Gerberstraße 1. Open mid-Mar–Oct Tue–Sun 1.30pm–4.30pm. Closed Nov–mid-Mar & Good Friday. ⊛4€. ℘(09081) 84 810. www.stadtmuseum-noerdlingen.de.

Housed in a former hospital, this engaging museum has four floors of displays covering the pre- and early history of the Ries basin, along with the political and economic influence Nördlingen exerted as a Free Imperial City. Art fans will be drawn to the collection of 19C painting and altar panels by Old German masters. A highlight here is the altar wings from the St. Georgskirche painted by Friedrich Herlin in 1462. Children, especially, will find of interest the huge model featuring around 6 000 tin figures in a re-creation of a famous Thirty Years' War battle that took place outside the town walls.

▲▲ Rieskrater-Museum★

Eugene-Shoemaker-Platz 1. Next to Stadtmuseum. Open May–Oct Tue–Sun 10am–4.30pm; Nov–Apr Tue–Sun 10am–noon, 1.30pm–4.30pm. Closed Jan 1, Shrove Tue, Good Friday, Dec 24–26. ⊛4€. ℘(09081) 847 10. www.rieskrater-museum.de.

The Ries meteorite crater was formed approximately 15 million years ago. Just imagine it: a giant stone sphere, 1km/0.6mi in diameter, hits the earth at a speed of c. 70 000kph/43 496mph, penetrating up to 1km/0.6mi into the rock. The energy of 250 000 nuclear atom bombs (such as that used in Hiroshima in Japan 1945) is released, and a wave of pressure and heat extinguishes all life within a range of 100km/62mi. A crater 14km/9mi in diameter forms, which eventually extends to 25km/16mi because of all the rock that subsequently caves in.

The crater, which was originally 4km/2.5mi deep, was gradually filled in over the course of millions of years, but was later partially excavated and opened up again.

The Rieskrater-Museum, which is housed in a carefully restored barn (1503), does a fine job of giving visitors an understanding of this mindboggling phenomenon.

Abtei Neresheim (Abbey)★

◗ 19km/12mi southwest on the B466. ❧Guided tours Easter–Oct Mon–Sat 11am and 3pm, Sun 11.15am and 3.15pm. ⊛By donation; 30€ for English-language tour. ℘(07326) 85 01. www.abtei-neresheim.de.

Built between 1745 and 1792, the abbey church was the last major commission designed by **Balthasar Neumann**. Inside, the seemingly weightless ceiling decoration is the work of Martin Knoller and was painted between 1771 and 1775.

Schloss Harburg

❧Guided tours (1hr) mid-Mar–Oct Tue–Sun 10am–5pm. ⊛5€. ℘(09080) 968 60. www.burg-harburg.de.

This large fortified castle looks down on a picturesque village along the banks of the Wörnitz. Tours take in the church, the watertower, the prison tower, the private quarters, the well and the festival hall.

◗ Leave via Mündlingerstraße, to the left, and take the Romantic Road to Mündling for Kaisheim.

Kaisheim

The former Cistercian abbey church was built at the end of the 14C in the full flower of the Gothic era. (The abbey itself is now a penal institution). Around the chancel is a 12-sided **ambulatory★** (to visit, apply at the presbytery). The 18C emperor's room in the Imperial foundation is open to the public *(on request)*.

Donauwörth

This Free Imperial City is proud of its historic pastel buildings along the Reichsstraße; the most impressive are the town hall and the *Fuggerhaus* (1543). The 18C Baroque pilgrimage church of Heilig Kreuz boasts Wessobrunn stuccowork. The Gothic Liebfrauenmünster has beautiful 15C murals. Parts of the town's fortifications still stand.

ADDRESSES

🛏 STAY

DINKELSBÜHL

⊜⊜ **Zum Goldenen Anker** – *Untere Schmiedgasse 22. ℰ(09851) 578 00. www.goldener-anker-dkb.de. 18 rooms. ⌕. Restaurant ⊜⊜.* This old inn has spacious country-style rooms and offers traditional cooking.

⊜⊜ **Hotel Kunst-Stuben** – *Segringer Straße 52, 91550 Dinkelsbühl. ℰ(09851) 67 50. www.kunst-stuben.de. ⌕. 14 rooms.* This small, welcoming property is managed by an artist couple happy to offer tours of their studio. Each room is individually furnished and immaculate.

WEIKERSHEIM

⊜⊜ **Laurentius** – *Marktplatz 5. ℰ(07934) 910 80. www.hotel-laurentius.de. 13 rooms. ⌕. Restaurant ⊜⊜, closed Mon–Tue.* Behind the cheerful yellow façade await spotless rooms with Italian furnishings. The restaurant is housed in a beautiful vaulted cellar.

FEUCHTWANGEN

⊜⊜⊜ **Romantik Hotel Greifen-Post** – *Marktplatz 8. ℰ(09852) 68 00. www. greifen.de. 35 rooms. Closed 1–7 Jan. ⌕. Restaurant ⊜⊜⊜, closed Sun dinner, Mon.* This 600-year-old establishment knows the true meaning of hospitality. Rooms are elegantly furnished in Renaissance, Romantic, 19C or country-house style. The dining room drips with historic charm. Indoor pool and sauna.

NÖRDLINGEN

⊜⊜ **Hotel Sonne** – *Marktplatz 3. ℰ(090 81) 50 67. www.kaiserhof-hotel-sonne.de. Closed 2 weeks in Nov. 37 rooms. ⌕. Restaurant ⊜⊜.* This traditional hotel in the heart of town dates from 1477. It has comfortable rooms and a country-style dining room with a vaulted ceiling.

🍴 EAT

BAD MERGENTHEIM

⊜⊜ **Bundschu** – *Milchlingstraße 24. ℰ(07931) 93 30. www.hotel-bundschu.de. Closed Mon.* This Mediterranean-style restaurant with a garden terrace serves regional cuisine and also has a few attractive modern rooms.

⊜⊜⊜⊜ **Zirbelstube** – *Poststraße 2-4. ℰ(07931) 59 30. www.victoria-badmergentheim.de. Closed Sun–Mon & 2 weeks in Aug.* The pine-coated walls and lovely paintings form an elegant backdrop for the richly nuanced classical fare created with regional ingredients whenever possible.

NÖRDLINGEN

⊜⊜⊜ **Meyer's Keller** – *Marienhöhe 8. ℰ(09081) 44 93. www.meyerskeller.de. Closed Mon–Tue.* This pleasant brasserie serves tasty regional dishes in a dining room accented by modern artworks and contemporary décor. In fine weather, sit under the canopy of shady old trees.

Würzburg★★

Würzburg lies at the northern terminus of the Romantic Road. Although much of the city centre was destroyed by bombs in just 22 minutes on 16 March 1945, the main sights have been meticulously rebuilt, including the splendid Prince-Bishops' Residence, which has been a UNESCO World Heritage Site since 1981. It was in Würzburg that Wilhelm Conrad Röntgen discovered X-rays in 1895.

A BIT OF HISTORY

The master of Würzburg – Flamboyant Gothic sculptor and woodcarver **Tilman Riemenschneider** (c. 1460–1531) was born in Heiligenstadt im Eichsfeld, Thüringia. He worked in Würzburg from 1483 and became town mayor in 1520–21. His work was always more than purely decorative and centred largely on expressing human emotions.

🐾 WALKING TOUR

OLD TOWN AND MARIENBURG FORTRESS
Residenz★★

♿ 🖋 (0931) 35 51 70. www.residenz-wuerzburg.de.
The residence of the rich and powerful Prince-Bishops, this 18C Baroque palace is one of the largest in Germany and was built under the direction of the architectural genius of **Balthasar Neumann**.

Schloss★★ (Palace)
Open Apr–Oct daily 9am–6pm; Nov–Mar 10am–4.30pm; ticket office closes 30min before closing. 🐾Some sections by guided tour only, throughout the day (11am and 3pm in English, also 4.30pm Apr–Oct). Closed Jan 1, Shrove Tue, Dec 24,25 & 31. 7.50€.
The monumental **Treppenhaus★★** (Grand Staircase) occupies the whole northern part of the vestibule and is one of Neumann's masterpieces. The huge **fresco★★** decorating the vaulted

- **Population:** 132 700
- **Info:** Am Congress Centrum and Marktplatz, 97070 Würzburg. 🖋(0931) 37 23 35. www.wuerzburg.de.
- **Location:** Former capital of the Duchy of Franconia, Würzburg lies on the banks of the Main, at the northwest border of Bavaria.
- **Parking:** You'll find parking garages throughout Würzburg. Visit http://wap.parkinfo.com for fees and locations.
- **Don't Miss:** The Residenz.
- **Timing:** Allow a couple of hours for the Residenz and its gardens and a full day for the suggested driving tour.

ceiling is by the Venetian **Giovanni Tiepolo** (1753) and illustrates the four then-known continents. In the **Weißer Saal** (White Room), between the Grand Staircase and the Imperial Hall, the **stucco ornamentation** is the work of Italian artist Antonio Bossi.

Old Main Bridge and Marienberg Fortress

© M. Hertlein/MICHELIN

NORTHERN BAVARIA

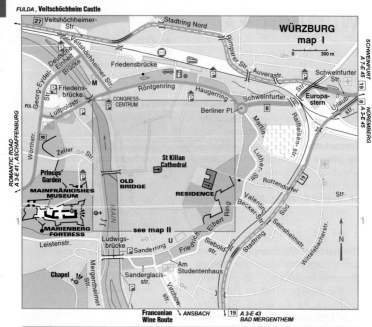

FULDA , Veitschöchheim Castle

WÜRZBURG map I

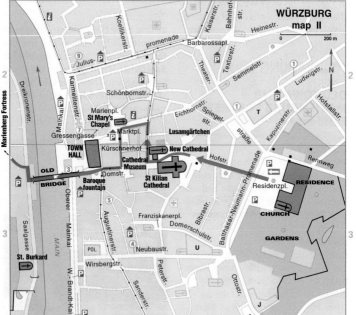

WÜRZBURG map II

WHERE TO STAY		WHERE TO EAT	
Hotel Amberger	①	Alte Mainmühle	③
Hotel Rebstock	④	Backöfele	⑤
Strauss	⑨	Bürgerspital	①
		Weinhaus zum Stachel	⑦

The oval **Kaisersaal★★** (Imperial Hall) on the first floor is splendidly adorned with **frescoes by Tiepolo**.

The **Paradezimmer** (Imperial Apartments) are a suite of restored rooms with Rococo stuccowork, tapestries and German furniture. The residence also houses a picture gallery with some fine **17C and 18C Italian paintings**, among them works by Bellucci, Canaletto and the Veronese school.

Hofkirche★ (Court Church)

The Residenz church is another work of Balthasar Neumann. Marble, gilding and ceiling frescoes by court painter Rudolf Byss all combine to form an exuberant composition. Two more **Tiepolo** paintings hang above the side altars: *The Assumption* and *The Fall of the Angels*.

Hofgarten★ (Court Gardens)

Astute use of old, stepped bastions has produced a layout of terraced gardens. From the eastern side, the whole 167m/545ft of the palace façade, with its elegant central block, is visible. The stucco is the work of Johann Peter Wagner.

Martin von Wagner Museum★

South wing. Picture Gallery: open year-round Tue–Sat 10am–1.30pm; Collection of Antiquities: Tue–Sat 1.30pm–5pm; Graphics Collection: by appointment. Closed Jan 1, Good Friday, Easter, May 1, Whit Mon, Oct 3, Nov 1, Dec 24 & 31. ℘(0931) 31 22 88. www.museum.uni-wuerzburg.de.

The university-affiliated museum boasts two grand collections as well as graphic works. On the second floor the **Gemäldegalerie★** (Picture Gallery) houses 14C–20C German and European works. Highlights are altar paintings by the masters of Würzburg (14C–16C) alongside Franconian sculpture, especially that of Riemenschneider. Dutch and Italian painters from the 16C to the 18C are well represented too (Tiepolo). The **Antikensammlung★** (Collection of Antiquities) on the third floor presents works from around the Mediterranean

dating as far back as the third millennium BC. Pride of place goes to an internationally renowned collection of **Greek vases★★** (6C–4C BC), but objects from Etruscan, Roman and Egyptian civilisations are also on display.

▷ From April to October, a bus shuttles between the Residenz and Marienberg fortress. To continue this tour, take either bus 9 from Residenzplatz or walk down Hofstraße to the cathedral.

Dom St. Kilian (Cathedral of St. Kilian)

Open Mon–Sat 10am–5pm, Sun 1pm–6pm. This columned basilica anchored by four towers was rebuilt after 1945 but has retained its original 11C–13C silhouette. The modern **Altar of the Apostles** holds three 16C **sculptures★** by Riemenschneider. The 18C **Schönborn Chapel** by Balthasar Neumann off the left transept contains the tombs of the Prince-Bishops from the Schönborn dynasty.

Museum am Dom (Cathedral Museum)

Open Apr–Oct Tue–Sun 10am–6pm; Nov–Mar to 5pm. ◉3.50€. ℘(0931) 38 66 56 00. www.museum-am-dom.de. This museum presents religious art from the 11C to the 21C, including a fantastic Crucifixion by Riemenschneider. Following a modern curatorial concept, it is organised by such themes as "Hoping", "Admonishing" and "Testifying" in order to encourage reflection and interaction on the visitors' part.

Neumünster (New Cathedral)

The imposing Baroque **west façade** of this church (1710–16) is attributed to Johann Dientzenhofer. In niches below the cupola you will discover a Riemenschneider *Virgin and Child* and a Christ figure in an unusual pose with arms folded below the chest (14C).

In the west crypt lies the **tomb of St. Kilian**, the missionary who was martyred in Würzburg in 689 and has since become the patron of the Franconians. The exit to the left of the chancel leads to the idyllic **Lusamgärtlein**, a small garden where the 13C troubadour-poet Walther von der Vogelweide was buried.

◐ Go north on Kürschnerstraße, then left on Eichhornstraße to arrive at Marktplatz.

Marienkapelle
(St. Mary's Chapel)

This fine Gothic chapel was financed by the town burghers in the 14C and 15C and boasts an attractive Annunciation on the tympanum of the north door-way. Inside the western front is the 1502 tombstone of Konrad von Schaumberg, carved by Riemenschneider and, on the north side, a **silver Madonna** made by the Master of Augsburg, J Kilian, in 1680.

◐ Cross Marktplatz and head down Schustergasse. At the end, turn right on Domstraße.

Rathaus (Town Hall)

The 13C town hall boasts a painted façade from the 16C and a charming interior courtyard. The western part, the **Roter Bau** (red building), is in late Renaissance style, while the Baroque **Vierröhrenbrunnen** (fountain) in front dates from 1765.

◐ Continue straight to the bridge.

Alte Mainbrücke★
(Old Main Bridge)

Built between 1473 and 1543, the bridge was embellished with a dozen monumental **stone statues** of saints in 1730. From the bridge, you can see the Alter Kranen (old crane) on the bank of the Main River, used to move goods from riverboats to land. A town landmark, it was built by the son of Balthasar Neumann, Franz Ignaz, around 1770. The old Customs House now contains the House of Franconian Wine (Haus des Frankenweins), where you can sample the local vintages.

◐ The most direct way to Marienburg fortress is signposted from the end of the bridge. A more scenic route goes through the vineyards (Weinwanderweg) hugging the slopes below the fortress. This pleasant walk (30min) offers lovely view, especially of St. Mary's Chapel.

Festung Marienberg★
(Marienberg Fortress)

Guided tours Apr–Oct Tue–Sun 11am, 2pm, 3pm and 4pm, Sat–Sun also 10am and 1pm (3pm tour in English). ⌗3.50€, combination ticket with Fürstenbaumuseum 6€. ♿ ☎(0931) 35 51 750. www.schloesser.bayern.de. From 1253 to 1719, this stronghold was the home of the Prince-Bishops of Würzburg. Built above the west bank of the Main, the original 13C castle was enlarged in the late Middle Ages and fortified after being stormed in 1631 by Swedish troops during the Thirty Years' War. The first-floor Prince-Bishops' apartments now house the **Fürstenbaumuseum** (Princes' Building Museum; open mid-Mar–Oct Tue–Sun 9am–6pm; ⌗4.50€), richly furnished and hung with paintings and tapestries, including one from 1564 depicting the family of Prince-Bishop Julius Echter of Mespelbrunn.

Mainfränkisches Museum★★
(Regional History Museum)

Second floor of Festung Marienberg, enter on the right in the first courtyard. Open Apr–Oct, Tue–Sun 10am–5pm, Nov–Mar to 4pm. Closed Shrove Tue, Dec 24, 25 & 31. ⌗4€, combination ticket with Fürstenbaumuseum 6€. ☎(0931) 20 59 40. www.mainfraenkisches-museum.de. This collection of Franconian arts and crafts is housed in the former arsenal; its most important section is the around 80 **sculptures by Tilman Riemensch-neider** (first floor), including Adam and Eve, Virgin Mary and Child and The Apostles. The vaulted galleries of the **Echterbastei** form a backdrop for statues, gold and silver religious plate, Gothic paintings and Franconian folk art. Also step down into the old cellar to admire the historic winepresses.

A Masterpiece in 210 Days

Disappointment with other painters led Prince-Bishop Carl Philipp von Greiffenclau to commission the best fresco artist of the day, Giovanni Battista Tiepolo, to embellish the palace. The painter arrived with his two sons on 12 December 1750. Tiepolo wanted for nothing; he was served eight courses at lunch and seven in the evening. In addition, he received three times the pay he earned in Venice.

Tiepolo had a reputation for painting with great speed, but the artist surpassed all estimates during his short three years in Würzburg. He created frescoes in the Imperial Hall and Residenz staircase, two altars for the Würzburg court church and one for Schwarzach Abbey (now in Munich's Alte Pinakothek) while also completing private commissions for local families.

Unable to paint during the winter, Tiepolo worked day and night for the rest of the year. It took him only 210 days to complete the vast and hugely intricate staircase fresco in the Residenz.

Käppele (Chapel)

Open Apr–Oct daily 8.30am–6pm; Nov–Mar daily 8.30am–4pm.

A monumental Way of the Cross leads to this Baroque pilgrimage church built by Balthasar Neumann in 1748. The adjoining chapel of mercy is connected via a "miracle passage". A **view**★★ unfolds from the chapel terrace, with the fortress of Marienberg rising above the vineyards.

EXCURSION
Schloss Veitshöchheim★

◐ 7km/4.3mi northwest. Echterstraße 10. Open Apr–mid-Oct Tue–Sun 9am–6pm. ⊛4.50€. ☎(0931) 915 82. www.schloesser.bayern.de.

The 17C summer residence of the Prince-Bishops was enlarged in 1753 by Balthasar Neumann. Rooms brim with shiny Rococo and Empire furniture and are festooned with stucco ornamentation by Antonio Bossi. The lavish **park**★ is a maze of shaded walks and arbours dotted with over 200 statues.

FRANCONIAN WINE ROUTE★
(Bocksbeutelstraße)

87km/55mi. Allow 1 day.

◐ Leave Würzburg on the B13 in the direction of Ansbach or Ochsenfurt.

Medieval monks introduced viticulture to Franconia, which enjoys a mild climate and hot, dry summers. The main varietals are dry white **Müller-Thurgau** and slightly fruitier **Silvaner**.

Ochsenfurt

Encircled by ancient **ramparts**★, Ochsenfurt's centre is a hodgepodge of half-timbered houses adorned with wrought-iron signs.

A mechanical clock in the lantern turret strikes the hours at the 15C **Neues Rathaus**. The **Stadtpfarrkirche St. Andreas**, built between the 13C and the 15C, has a fanciful interior.

◐ Turn left off the B13 and drive alongside the Main River.

Marktbreit

The town hall and city gate form a fine Renaissance ensemble (1579), complemented by two Baroque houses festooned with corner bay windows.

Sulzfeld

A highlight of this pretty wine-growing village is the Renaissance **town hall** with its scrolled gables.

◐ Pass through Kitzingen and Mainstockheim (on the east bank of the Main) and head for Dettelbach.

Dettelbach★

Clinging to the northern slopes of the Main Valley, Dettelbach sports a late-Gothic (c. 1500) town hall and 15C parish church, whose principal tower is linked by a wooden bridge to a smaller one. Northeast of the upper town is the 17C **pilgrimage church "Maria im Sand"**.

▶ Between Dettelbach and Neuses am Berg, the road runs through a plateau of vineyards, then drops back down into the Main Valley and crosses the river.

Volkach★

This delightful wine-growing town lies on the eastern side of a wide oxbow in the Main. Of the original medieval enclave only two gates bookend the main street: the **Gaibacher Tor** and the **Sommeracher Tor**. The 16C Renaissance **town hall** on the Marktplatz (with the tourist office) is fronted by a 15C fountain topped by a Virgin statue. Slightly further south is the **Bartholomäuskirche** (Church of St. Bartholomew), a late-Gothic building with Baroque and Rococo flourishes. At the northwestern edge of town (about 1km/0.6mi in the direction of Fahr), the 15C **pilgrimage church "Maria im Weingarten"** enjoys an idyllic vineyard setting. Inside is the famous limewood **Rosenkranzmadonna★** (Virgin with Rosary), a late Riemenschneider work (1512–24).

▶ Return to Würzburg via Schwarzach, turning right onto the B22. If continuing to Nuremberg via the B8, make a stop in Iphofen.

Iphofen

Half-timbered Iphofen is a popular stop for well-informed gourmets. The refined cuisine of Zehntkeller (℘09323 84 40; www.zehntkeller.de) and the creative fare made with locally sourced ingredients at Deutscher Hof (℘09323 33 48; www.deutscher-hof-iphofen.de; closed Wed–Thu) are both stand-outs.

ADDRESSES

🛏 STAY

⊜😋 **Hotel Amberger** – *Ludwigstraße 17–19. ℘0931 35 100. www.hotel-amberger.de. 70 rooms.* 🚗. This centrally located hotel features spacious modern rooms and a fine breakfast buffet.

⊜😋 **Hotel Rebstock** – *Neubaustraße 7. ℘(0931) 309 30. www.rebstock.com. 70 rooms. Restaurant* ⊜😋😋😋, *closed lunch, Sun & Mon and Aug.* Behind the Rococo façade of 1737, a range of rooms from elegant and modern to rustic and traditional awaits. The charming restaurant and bistro-style winter garden deliver continental cuisine.

⊜😋 **Strauss** – *Juliuspromenade 5. ℘0931 305 70. www.hotel-strauss.de. 77 rooms.* 🚗10€. *Restaurant*⊜😋, *closed Tue.* Close to the Old Town station, the Strauss has guest rooms that are modern and functional.

🍴 EAT

⊜😋 **Alte Mainmühle** – *Mainkai 1. ℘0931 167 77. www.alte-mainmuehle.de.* Situated next to the Alte Mainbrücke, this charming rustic restaurant serves regional and international dishes.

⊜😋 **Backöfele** – *Ursulinergasse 2. ℘0931 590 59. www.backoefele.de. Closed Dec 24–26 & Jan 1–2.* A city institution, this historic house is famous for its cosy rustic atmosphere.

⊜😋 **Bürgerspital** – *Theaterstraße 19. ℘(0931) 35 28 80. www.buergerspital-weinstuben.com.* The mood-lit tavern with its cross-vaulted ceiling is operated by Bürgerspital wine estate. Franconian specialities, including fish, accompany the excellent variety of local wines.

⊜😋 **Weinhaus zum Stachel** – *Gressengasse 1 (near Marktplatz). ℘(0931) 527 70. www.weinhaus-stachel.de. Closed Mon.* This traditional *Weinstube* with an idyllic courtyard dates to the 15C. Excellent Franconian wines and regional cuisine. In the evening, a small menu of refined dishes is available.

NIGHTLIFE
USEFUL TIPS
Try the bars along Juliuspromenade north of the city centre and Sanderstraße, south of the city centre.

Rothenburg ob der Tauber★★★

One of the oldest towns on the "Romantic Road", Rothenburg overlooks the winding course of the Tauber River from its rocky crag. Once behind the ramparts in the pedestrian-only medieval centre, visitors revel in the ancient houses, fountains and narrow, cobbled lanes evoking the 16C.

▸ **Population:** 11 000

🗎 **Info:** Marktplatz 2, 91541 Rothenburg. ✆(09861) 404 800.www.rothenburg.de.

◗ **Location:** The old town stands on a steep promontory overlooking the Tauber River.

🙢 **Don't Miss:** A stroll through the old town.

🕓 **Timing:** Allow 4hrs for the suggested walking tour.

👥 **Kids:** The mechanical clock on the Ratstrinkstube and a walk along the ramparts.

A BIT OF HISTORY

During the Thirty Years' War, Protestant Rothenburg was unable to withstand the Catholic siege by General Tilly's army. After 40 000 victorious mercenaries had pillaged the town for three months, Tilly decided to raze it unless, he declared, some local could empty a 3.4liter/6-pint tankard of wine in a single draught. A former town mayor, a man named Georg Nusch, volunteered and miraculously succeeded: Rothenburg was saved. Ever since, Rothenburgers have re-created the event at Pentecost. Rothenburg stagnated throughout the 17C and 18C, too poor to expand beyond its own walls.

In the 19C, however, the town's steep-roofed houses with their gables, staircase turrets and corner oriels were rediscovered by Romantic painters, and Rothenburg has since became a major tourist attraction.

🐾WALKING TOUR

OLD TOWN★★★

Starting at Marktplatz, follow the itinerary marked on the town map. Begin at the Town Hall. Allow half a day.

Herrngasse in Rothenburg

©Angela Jones/Bigstockphoto.com

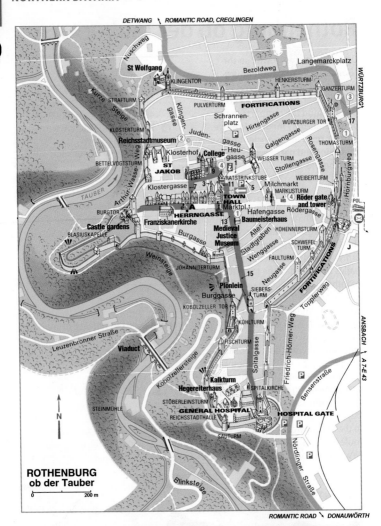

DETWANG / ROMANTIC ROAD, CREGLINGEN

ROTHENBURG
ob der Tauber

0 ————— 200 m

N

ROMANTIC ROAD \ DONAUWÖRTH

Rathaus★ (Town Hall)

This 14C structure has seen a number of architectural additions over the centuries. While there, visitors can inspect the **Historiengewölbe** (historic vaults), now a history museum, or climb the tower for a **view★** of the fortified town. North of Marktplatz is the gable of an ancient inn, the 1446 Ratstrinkstube (now the tourist office). The figures of its **mechanical clock**, dating from 1910, re-enact the famous legend of the *Meistertrunk* or Long Drink taken by the mayor to save the town (on the hour, 10am–10pm).

Baumeisterhaus

With its elaborate Renaissance façade and pretty courtyard, this former private house is one of the most beautiful buildings in Rothenburg. Statues on the first floor represent the seven virtues, those on the second the seven deadly sins.

Mittelalterliches Kriminalmuseum (Medieval Justice Museum)

Burggasse 3–5. Open May–Oct daily 10am–6pm; Nov & Jan–Feb 2pm–4pm; Mar & Dec 10am–4pm; Apr 11am–5pm. 5€. (09861) 53 59. www.kriminalmuseum.rothenburg.de. Punishment was swift and brutal, as you will learn at this museum which displays documents and instruments of public humiliation, torture and execution.

Plönlein

This picturesque corner of half-timbered houses is often photographed: one street is level, another ascending to the Siebers Tower, another descending. The fountain once supplied the fish stock used by Tauber fishermen.

Go past the Siebersturm (tower) and take Spitalgasse, named after the old hospital down the street, which is our next stop. Enter on your right.

Spital (General Hospital)

Most of the buildings of this hospital date back to the 16C and 17C. There are some fine art works in the Gothic chapel (Spitalkirche). The best viewpoint from which to appreciate the silhouette of the Hegereiterhaus, a pavilion with a pointed roof and turreted staircases topped by a lantern-shaped roof, is from the centre of the courtyard. In former times, the kitchens and servants' quarters were located here. The half-timbered old cellar and bakery are now a youth hostel. To the west, the former tithing barn has morphed into the Reichsstadthalle, a congress and event centre. Views from the top of the Kalkturm extend across the entire town. A walkway links the two towers, Stöberleinsturm au Sauturm.

Backtrack on Spitalgasse.

The southern entrance into the city is via the Spitaltor (Hospital Gate), a mighty 17C bastion wrapped around two oval inner courtyards. It has seven gates, a moat and a drawbridge and warrants thorough exploration inside and out.

Backtrack to Plönlein, turn left on Burggasse and leave the town centre via Kobolzeller Gate. Turn right and follow the trail below the ramparts. At the bottom of the valley, a double bridge (Doppelbrücke) straddles the Tauber River.

Burggarten (Castle Gardens)

All that remains of the double fortress erected on this promontory is a chapel, the Blasiuskapelle, which has been converted to a war memorial, and a fortified gateway, the Burgtor. The area is now a large public garden with magnificent views★.

Return to the town via the Burgtor; assailants unaware of the grimacing mask above the second gate risked being drenched in boiling oil here.

Herrngasse★

The mansions of medieval burghers line this busy commercial street. Inside the **Franziskanerkirche** (Franciscan church), note the 15C and 16C sculptures and the Creglingen Madonna (1400). Back on Herrngasse, peek at the hidden courtyards. Number 15 features a half-timbered gallery on embossed wooden pillars.

Turn left into Kirchgasse after the round fountain.

St. Jakobskirche★ (St. James Church)

Klostergasse 15. Open Apr–Oct daily 9am–5.15pm; Nov, Jan–Mar 10am–noon, 2pm–4pm; Dec 10am–4.45pm. 2€. (09861) 70 06 20. www.rothenburgtauber-evangelisch.de.

This 14C Gothic church shelters Tilman Riemenschneider's **Heiligblutaltar★★ (Altarpiece of the Holy Blood)** (1504). Note the tense expressions conveyed, as well as Jesus' compassion. The stained-glass windows in the east chancel are also worth closer inspection.

ADDITIONAL SIGHTS
Stadtmauer★ (Ramparts)
Constructed in the 13C and 14C, these ramparts, complete with gates and towers, are still perfectly preserved. Long stretches are open to the public.

St. Wolfgangskirche
Open Apr–Oct Wed–Mon 11am–1pm, 2pm–5pm (Oct until 4pm). ➹1.50€. ℘(09861) 404 92. www.rothenburgtauber-evangelisch.de. North of the Klingentor, this curious 15C Gothic church, fortified and incorporated into the barbican, doubled the defences of the gateway.

Reichsstadtmuseum (Imperial City Museum)
Open Apr–Oct daily 9.30am–5.30pm; Nov–Mar daily 1pm–4pm. Closed Shrove Tue, Dec 24 & 31. ➹4.50€. ℘(09861) 93 90 43. www.reichsstadtmuseum. rothenburg.de.
A Dominican monastery from 1258 to 1554, this building is now a local museum showcasing, among other collections, the Rothenburg Stations of the Cross (1494).
Also on view is the tankard reportedly drained by Mayor Nusch in front of General Tilly. Crafted in 1616, the tankard bears a design depicting the Emperor and the seven Electors.

ADDRESSES

🛏STAY
😊😊 **Hornburg** – *Hornburgweg 28, 91541. ℘(09861) 84 80. www.hotel-hornburg.de. Closed 2 weeks mid-Aug, 1 week late Oct–Nov & Dec 24–26. 10 rooms.* ⊑. This small hotel, decorated in Art Nouveau style, has loads of charm as well as a lovely garden.

😊😊 **Hotel Spitzweg** – *Paradeisgasse 2. ℘(09861) 942 90. www.hotel-spitzweg.de. 9 rooms.* ⊑. This 16C hotel has comfortable, rustic rooms and plenty of memorabilia of Romantic painter Carl Spitzweg, a Rothenburger.

😊😊 **Mittermeier** – *Vorm Würzburger Tor 9. ℘(09861) 945 40. www.villa mittermeier.de. 27 rooms.* ⊑10€. *Restaurant* 😊😊😊, *closed lunch, Sun & 1 week in Sept.* Friendly and dedicated staff as well as individually decorated themed rooms (e.g. "Africa" or "Spain") give this pretty sandstone villa an edge. The restaurant serves an upscale menu with a youthful, fresh style.

🍽 EAT
😊😊 **Altfränkische Weinstube** – *Klosterhof 7. ℘(09861) 64 04. www. altfraenkische-weinstube-rothenburg.de. Dinner only. Closed Tue.* Enjoy hearty traditional cooking in this cosy, atmospheric 650-year old inn.

😊😊 **Baumeisterhaus** – *Obere Schmiedgasse 3. ℘(09861) 947 00. www.baumeisterhaus.name.* This 1596 Renaissance gem opposite the town hall serves hearty Bavarian cuisine on two floors adorned with beautiful paintings. The courtyard is surrounded by half-timbered galleries.

😊😊 **Reichs-Küchenmeister** – *Kirchplatz 8. ℘(09 861) 9 700. www. reichskuechenmeister.com. Closed Jan–Mar & Mon–Tue.* This beautiful historic house includes a wine bar, a lovely garden restaurant and main dining room, off which are two, more cosy, small areas. The menu combines international and local specialities.

😊😊😊 **Die Blaue Sau** – *Vorm Würzburger Tor 7. ℘(09861) 94 54 30. www.blauesau.eu. Dinner only. Closed Sun and 1 week in Sept.* Delicious Italian cuisine is served in a vaulted cellar in this atmospheric *enoteca*.

TAKING A BREAK
USEFUL TIPS
Many cafés sell the locally famous *Schneeballen* (snowballs), which are cakes made with shortbread pastry and traditionally covered with icing or cinnamon.

Nuremberg★★

Nürnberg

Thanks to its location at the crossroads of two major trade routes, Nuremberg prospered in the Middle Ages and also enjoyed political standing as the frequent host city of the Imperial diets. In the 15C and 16C, it experienced a cultural flourishing nourished by some of the finest artists of the day, including Albrecht Dürer. The Nazi leadership regarded Nuremberg as so quintessentially "Germanic" that they chose to stage their huge party rallies here. Although badly bombed in World War II, the city still preserves a medieval aura, best experienced during the world's most famous Christmas market held here every December.

▶ **Population:** 493 000

▤ **Info:** Hauptmarkt 1, Königstraße 93, 90403 Nürnberg. ℘(0911) 233 60. www.tourismus. nuernberg.de.

◖ **Location:** The second-largest city in Bavaria after Munich, Nuremberg is served by the A9 and A3 autobahns.

🅿 **Parking:** Garages are located throughout the city. Visit http://wap.parkinfo.com for fees and locations.

◉ **Don't Miss:** The German National Museum and the old town.

◷ **Timing:** Allow a day for the German National Museum and for taking in all the sights.

👥 **Kids:** A walk along the city's medieval ramparts.

A BIT OF HISTORY

Nuremberg reached its political and economic heyday in the 15C and 16C. A crossroads of major trade routes and a mainstay for Franconian crafts-manship, the city once rivalled Augsburg in importance and wealth. The first German scientific university was founded in Nuremberg in 1526. Sculp-tors **Veit Stoß** (c. 1445–1533) and **Adam Krafft** (c. 1460–1508/09); bronze caster **Peter Vischer the Elder** (c. 1460–1529); **Michael Wolgemut** (1434–1519), painter of altarpieces, and his pupil **Albrecht Dürer** (1471–1528) were all based in this city and profoundly influ-

Pegnitz River and Heilig-Geist-Spital in old Nuremberg

© M. Hertlein/MICHELIN

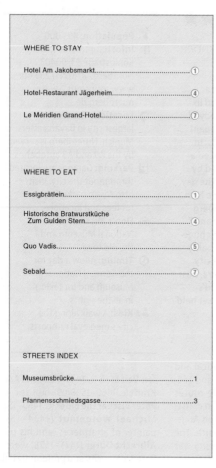

NUREMBERG

Playmobil Funpark, *ANSBACH* /

enced the artistic landscape in central Europe. From the 13C, **Hans Sachs** and the *Meistersänger* brought new life to a German poetic form and provided the inspiration for Richard Wagner's 1868 opera *Die Meistersänger von Nürnberg*. Here in Hitler's "ideological capital" of the Third Reich anti-Semitic laws were promulgated in 1935. It was no coincidence that the Allies chose Nuremberg to bring high-ranking Nazi officials before an international military tribunal to face charges of war crimes. The **Nuremberg trials (**November 1945 to October 1946) took place in the **Justizpalast** (Palace of Justice) on Fürther Straße, now a civil court. About two dozen of the accused were condemned to death by hanging.

GERMANISCHES NATIONALMUSEUM★★★ (GERMAN NATIONAL MUSEUM)

Kartäusergasse 1. Open year-round Tue–Sun 10am–6pm (Wed until 9pm). Closed Shrove Tue, Dec 24, 25 & 31. ⊙8€.
♿ ℘(0911) 133 10. www.gnm.de.
Founded in 1852, the museum possesses the largest collection of art and antiquities in Germany, although only 20 000 of its millions of items can be displayed at any given time.

⊘Since the museum is so vast, it is advisable to study the floorplan available upon entering and limit your time to the sections that interest you most. Allow 4hrs.

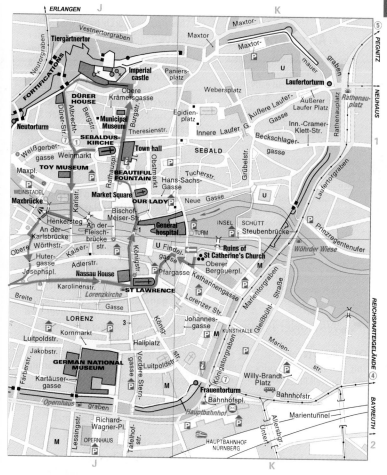

Upper Floors

The **picture gallery** (first floor, **Section B**) displays works by **Albrecht Dürer**, Hans Baldung Grien, Hans Holbein the Elder, Albrecht Altdorfer and Lucas Cranach the Elder. Later works include a *Self-portrait* by Rembrandt. Works by **Veit Stoß**, Tilman Riemenschneider and Ignaz Günther stand out within the sculpture collection.

The most noteworthy among the **scientific instruments (Section A)** is the so-called **Behaim terrestrial globe** (c. 1493), the oldest surviving depiction of the earth in globe form.

Also on view are medical instruments **(Section C)**, a collection of dolls and dollhouses (one from 1639) and in the folkloric galleries **(Section D)**, farm-house furnishings, clothing and religious art.

The second-floor galleries include 19C and 20C art and design **(Section E)**, notably Ernst Ludwig Kirchner's Expressionist *Self-portrait* (1914).

Ground Floor

The collection of medieval religious art **(Section C)** illustrates the work of craftsmen from the Carolingian period (9C) to the early Renaissance. Representative decorative arts include glass, ceramics, furniture and textiles. The gold- and silversmiths' work should not be missed. The section on ancient musical instruments **(Section D)** boasts the world's largest collection of historical pianos. The extensive prints and

Adam Krafft

Born in Nuremberg around 1460, Krafft left his mark on every church in the city. His early works (typical of the late-Gothic style) portrayed expressive figures with tumultuous draperies, and rich decorative reliefs. He then moved towards greater clarity and his later, more monumental, works assume more rounded and restrained poses (see the Stations of the Cross from St. John's Cemetery, dating from 1505, in the Germanisches Nationalmuseum).

drawings section and a numismatic collection (**Section F**) are worth viewing.

WALKING TOUR

OLD TOWN★★

This tour begins at a ruined church, a site that well illustrates the extent of destruction sustained during World War II. It also puts into perspective the enormous reconstruction effort undertaken by the town and its citizens.

Katharinenkirchenruine (Ruins of St. Catherine's Church)

Peter-Vischer-Straße.
Once part of a Dominican convent, St. Catherine's became the home of Nuremberg master singers from 1620 to 1778. It burned down in 1945 and was never reconstructed. Today, the partially roofed ruin hosts a popular summer concert series.

▶ Turn right on Oberer Bergauerplatz, then left on Pfarrgasse.

Lorenzkirche★ (St. Lawrence Church)

Lorenzer Platz 10. Open year-round Mon–Sat 9am–5pm, Sun 1pm–4pm. Closed Jan 1 & Dec 25. ☎(0911) 214 2500. www.lorenzkirche.de.

This pretty church has two Gothic choirs, one from the 13C, the other from the 15C. A magnificent rose window enlivens the west façade. Enter via the south door to admire Veit Stoß's 16C carved wooden masterpiece, **Annunciation★★**. Stoß also created the Crucifix above the high altar. The **tabernacle★★** (1493–96), crafted from limestone by Adam Krafft, stands left of the main altar. It features more than 100 figurines.

▶ As you head north on Königstraße, note Nassauer Haus (**Nassau House**) at the corner of Karolinenstraße. With its fortified tower, it is the oldest residential building in Nuremberg.

Heilig-Geist-Spital (Hospice of the Holy Spirit)

The **general hospital** is housed in a 14C–15C building, spread over two wide arches, spanning a branch of the Pegnitz. The covered part of the bridge, known as the **Crucifixion Courtyard** on account of Krafft's Crucifixion Group, used to be a home for the elderly.

▶ Continue walking straight after the bridge to reach the Hauptmarkt.

Frauenkirche★ (Our Lady's Church)

Hauptmarkt 14. Open year-round Mon & Thu 8am–6pm (Wed until 7pm), Tue & Fri 9am–6pm, Sat 9.30am–6.30pm, Sun 12.30pm–7pm. ☎(0911) 20 65 60. www.frauenkirche-nuernberg.de.
Dominating the Hauptmarkt, this Gothic church was built between 1355 and 1358 on the site of the synagogue destroyed in 1349. The main architect is believed to have been Peter Parler. The gable, with its pinnacles and niches, was designed by Adam Krafft (early 16C) and crowns the façade, one of the only original parts. The clock above the balcony, created in 1509 by Sebastian Lindenast and Georg Heuss, attracts visitors each day at noon for the *Männleinlaufen* (running of the little men). Colourful metal figurines representing the seven Electors are shown swearing allegiance to

Emperor Karl IV after the Golden Bull was issued in Nuremberg in 1356.
Inside, the **Tucher Altar** in the chancel is a masterpiece of the pre-Albrecht Dürer Nuremberg School of painting: the triptych (c. 1445–50) represents the Crucifixion, Annunciation and Resurrection. Note the depiction of Jesus on his way to school, in the chancel.

Schöner Brunnen★ (Beautiful Fountain)

The 14C Gothic four-tiered **fountain**, comprising 40 figures *(copies)* dominates the northwest corner of the central Hauptmarkt square.
At the top of the 19m/62ft-high pyramid, Moses is surrounded by the prophets; depicted around the base are the seven Electors and nine Old Testament and medieval heroes: three forefathers, three Jews and three Christians.
A seamless gold ring hangs from a railing *(on the upper part)*, where an apprentice locksmith is said to have placed it in the 17C. It has been polished by millions of hands that have touched it for good luck.
The hustle and bustle of the Hauptmarkt, particularly at the Christmas market, masks its grisly origins: the Jewish quarter stood there until 1349, when it was razed to the ground and its occupants murdered by the locals.

Stadtmuseum Fembohaus (Fembo Municipal Museum)

Burgstraße 15. Open year-round Tue–Fri 10am–5pm, Sat–Sun 10am–6pm. Closed Dec 24–25 & 31. 5€. ♿ ☎(0911) 231 25 95. www.fembohaus.de.
The museum occupies a 16C Renaissance mansion, the only patrician house to survive in its entirety. Exhibits cover the history of Nuremberg in traditional fashion and through a multimedia journey "narrated" by Albrecht Dürer and Hans Sachs *(4€)*.

Kaiserburg (Imperial Castle)

Open Apr–Sept daily 9am–6pm; Oct–Mar daily 10am–4pm. Closed Jan 1, Shrove Tue, Dec 24, 25 & 31. 7€. ☎(0911) 24 46 590. www.kaiserburg-nuernberg.de.
This city landmark perches on a sandstone outcrop in the northern part of the old town. Between 1050 and 1571, all Holy Roman Emperors spent at least some time in residence here.
Accessible by guided tour only, the **Palas** (main palace) is appointed with richly furnished rooms, and encompasses the Romanesque double chapel, the Deep Well and an extensive collection of tools and weapons.

Kaiserburg

©Milan Brunclik/istockphoto.com

👥 Stadtbefestigung★ (Fortifications)

Completed in the mid-15C, Nuremberg's fortifications have survived remarkably well. They consist of an inner and an outer ring (Zwingermauer), the ramparts of the former being topped by a covered parapet walk. A wide, dry moat (in which modern roads now run) was outside the latter. No fewer than 67 defensive towers still exist, including the four 16C **Great Towers:** Frauentor, Spittlertor, Neutor and Laufertor.

The most interesting section extends between the Kaiserburg and the Spittlertor and is easily explored on a 30min walk starting in the castle garden (Burggarten, below the Kaiserburg). From the ramparts walk to the watch-path, which can be followed as far as the Neutorzwinger. Continue inside the ramparts, then cross the suspension footbridge over the Pegnitz River before concluding the stroll.

Tiergärtnerplatz

The half-timbered houses around the picturesque square by the **Tiergärtnertor** (gate) suffered the least damage during World War II.

Albrecht-Dürer-Haus★ (Dürer House)

Albrecht-Dürer-Straße 39. Open year-round Tue–Fri 10am–5pm, Thu 8pm, Sat–Sun 6pm; Jul–Sept and during Christmas markets also Mon 10am–5pm). Closed Dec 24, 25 & 31. 👁5€. ℰ(0911) 231 25 68. www.museen.nuernberg.de.

The house where **Dürer** lived with his family from 1509 until his death in 1528 now houses a memorial exhibit shedding light on the life and times of this Renaissance giant. Watch a multimedia show to learn more about his work, then peruse original graphics and visit the re-created workshop where live printing demonstrations are held. Audio tours "narrated" by Agnes Dürer are peppered with personal anecdotes and provide insight into the family's daily life.

Sebalduskirche★

Albrecht-Dürer-Platz 1. Open Jun–early Sept daily 9.30am–8pm; Jan–Mar 9.30am–4pm; Apr–May & mid-Sept–Dec 9.30am–6pm. ♿ ℰ(0911) 214 25 00. www.sebalduskirche.de.

Nuremberg's oldest parish church was built around 1215 as a three-nave Late Romanesque basilica with two chancels, but was Gothicised shortly thereafter. To the right of the entrance, at the far end of the first chancel, the **St. Peter Altarpiece** (1485) takes pride of place, painted on a gold background in Michael Wolgemut's studio. In the centre, the richly decorated **baptismal font★** (c. 1430) is the oldest bronze religious work in Nuremberg. In the nave, on the inner side of the great left pillar, is the painted statue of St. Sebald (1390) and on the next column, the **Virgin Mary in Glory★** made of pear wood. The magnificent **reliquary shrine of St. Sebald★★** dominates the west chancel. The Gothic tomb was cast in bronze by Peter Vischer (1519) and his sons and is supported by dolphins and snails and adorned with a host of statuettes.

👥 Spielzeugmuseum★ (Toy Museum)

Karlstraße 13–15. Open year-round Tue–Fri 10am–5pm, Sat–Sun 10am–6pm, & Mon during Christmas markets 10am–5pm. Closed Dec 24–25, 31 & Jan 1. 👁5€, child 3€. ℰ(0911) 231 31 64. www.museen.nuernberg.de.

Nuremberg has been famous for making toys since the Middle Ages, and both old and new playthings are on display. There is a special play area for children.

▶ Follow Karlstraße; turn right onto Henkersteg (Executioner's Bridge), which makes a fine sight alongside the half-timbered Weinstade (wine store), one of Nuremberg's most beautiful buildings. Hutergasse (opposite) will take you to Ludwigsplatz. Turn right and continue to the foot of the Weisserturm (White Tower).

The bizarre Ehekarrussel (**Marriage Carousel**) **fountain**, completed in 1984 by sculptor Jürgen Weber, illustrates the poem by Hans Sachs: "Bittersweet married life".

⬭ Return via Breite Gasse or Karolinenstraße, two shopping streets.

The Mauthalle (Tollhouse) was built between 1498 and 1502 as an Imperial corn and salt store. Since 1572 it has served as a customs house and a local brewery.

ADDITIONAL SIGHT
Reichsparteigelände ★★ (Former Site of the Nazi Party Congress)

Bayernstraße 110 (at Luitpoldhain), exit Nuremberg on the B4 in the direction of Fischbach. Open year-round, Mon–Fri 9am–6pm, weekends 10am–6pm. Closed Dec 24–25, 31 & Jan 1. ⬭5€, audioguide included. Allow 2–3hrs. ✆(0911) 231 56 66. www.museums.nuremberg.de.

Few German cities were confronted with the face of National Socialism as directly as Nuremberg. The city was promoted by Hitler as the ideological capital of the Third Reich, and it was here that the Allies chose to establish the international military tribunal that would judge and condemn leading Nazis. The buildings that stand on the site where the Nazi Party rallies were held bear witness to the megalomania of the regime.

Opened in 2001, its Dokumentationszentrum (Documentation Centre) uses diverse modern educational media to help visitors understand the foundations of the Nazi party and its development, as well as the history of the Congress site and the Nazi era in the city.

EXCURSIONS
♣♦ Playmobil Funpark

⬭ 16km/10mi west of Nuremberg. Leave the city heading towards Ansbach. Open May–early Sept daily 9am–7pm; mid-Sept–Oct daily 9am–6pm. ⬭6€–11€

according to the season. ✆(0911) 96 66 17 00. www.playmobil-funpark.de.

Opened by the Playmobil company next to its headquarters at Zirndorf, this theme park is popular with families.

♣♦ Zoo (Tiergarten)

Am Tiergarten 30. Leave town via Bahnhofstraße, go as far as the station, then take Kressengartenstraße and Ostendstraße. Open year-round daily 8am–7.30pm. ⬭13.50€, child 6.50€. ✆(0911) 54 546. www.tiergarten.nuernberg.de.

Covering 63 ha/156 acres, this zoo, one of the largest in Europe, is home to the only dolphinarium in southern Germany. Ride the *Adler*, a scale model replica of Germany's first ever train (*Easter–Oct*). Stroll in the Hesperides Gardens, landscaped in the 17C and 18C on top of medieval peasant gardens.

🚗 DRIVING TOUR

HERSBRUCKER ALB

109km/67.7mi round trip. Allow half a day.

⬭ Follow Sulzbacher Straße, then take the A9 towards Bayreuth.

Neuhaus an der Pegnitz★

This charming locality, dominated by the tower of Burg Veldenstein, comes into view after a bend in the road.

⬭ Continue following the Pegnitz River towards Hersbruck.

Hersbruck

An attractive small town, Hersbruck has stately burghers' houses and the remains of medieval fortifications. The **Deutsche Hirtenmuseum** (*German Shepherds' Museum, Eishüttlein 7*) contains a folk art collection.

⬭ Continue towards Happurg over the Pegnitz bridge, from which, looking back, there is a fine view of the Wassertor.

ADDRESSES

🏨STAY

🛏️🍴 Hotel Am Jakobsmarkt –
Schottengasse 5. ☎(0911) 200 70.
www.hotel-am-jakobsmarkt.de. 72 rooms.
⌐10€. Rooms here are either modern
and functional or rustic and traditional.
They are spread over the main building
and a half-timbered annex reached via
an inner courtyard.

🛏️🍴 Hotel-Restaurant Jägerheim –
Valznerweiherstraße 75, 90480 Nürnberg-
Zerzabelshof. ☎(0911) 94 08 50.
www.hotel-jaegerheim.de. 33 rooms. ⌐.
Restaurant 🛏️🍴, closed Sun–Mon. This
quiet hotel near the exhibition grounds
is well served by public transport. It
has smart rooms with pale wooden
furniture, and a traditional restaurant.

🛏️🍴🍴🍴 Le Méridien Grand-Hotel –
Bahnhofstraße 1-3. ☎(0911) 232 20.
www.lemeridiennuernberg.com. 192
rooms. ⌐24€. Restaurant 🛏️🍴🍴.
This palatial hotel has welcomed guests
since 1896. Located next to the central
train station, it has luxurious rooms,
the nicest of which have Art Nouveau
furnishings. The restaurant exudes
refinement with marble floors and
slender pillars.

🍴EAT

USEFUL TIPS

The city's culinary speciality, *Nürnberger*
Rostbratwürste, is often offered as *Drei*
im Weckla (three sausages in a roll) at
stalls and in traditional restaurants.

🍴 Historische Bratwurstküche
Zum Gulden Stern –
Zirkelschmiedsgasse 26. ☎(0911) 205
92 88. www.bratwurstkueche.de.
The oldest sausage kitchen in town
occupies a historic house of 1419, with
woodsy, country-style wood décor.
Nuremberg sausage straight from the
beech-wood grill is the specialty.

🍴 Quo Vadis – *Elbinger Straße 28.*
☎(0911) 51 55 53. www.ristorante-
quovadis.de. Closed Mon. Delicious
Italian dishes are served up in a rustic
Mediterranean atmosphere.

🍴🍴🍴 Sebald – *Weinmarkt 14. ☎(0911)*
38 13 03. www.restaurant-sebald.de.
This charming house in the old town
harbours a modern restaurant and
bistro with a relaxed ambience. Sun-
yellow walls and warm colours give it a
Tuscan flair.

🍴🍴🍴🍴 Essigbrätlein – *Weinmarkt 3.*
Closed Dec 24–Jan 1, 2 weeks in Aug and
Sun–Mon. ☎(0911) 22 51 31. Here you'll
find innovative, modern cooking in
the elegant Old-World style of a 16C
inn at this top-rated restaurant near
Hauptmarkt.

NIGHTLIFE

Hausbrauerei Altstadthof –
Bergstraße 19–21. ☎(0911) 244 98 59.
www. hausbrauerei-altstadthof.de. This
old-style micro-brewery near the castle
is a nice spot to kick back at the end
of the day. Sit in the small bar or in the
beer garden.

CULTURE
USEFUL TIPS

Events are listed in the monthly
magazines *Plärrer* and *Prinz*, available
at bookshops and newspaper kiosks.
The free monthly listings magazine
Doppelpunkt can be picked up in bars,
restaurants and shops.

Online resources: www.kubiss.de,
www.events-nuernberg.de,
www. nuernberg-convention.de.

SHOPPING
USEFUL TIPS

Karolinenstraße, Breite Gasse and
Königsstraße are the city's busiest
shopping streets, with department
stores and a variety of specialty shops.
If you're looking for small gifts,
Lebkuchen are ideal. Traditionally made
during Advent, these spicy gingerbread
cookies are now available year-round
and often come in attractive
metal boxes.

Bamberg★★

Established in the Middle Ages, transformed in the 17C and 18C and spared wartime bomb-raids, Bamberg is one of Germany's most delightful towns with 2 300 well-preserved buildings in styles ranging from the Romanesque to the Baroque. UNESCO honoured Bamberg's old town by giving it World Heritage status in 1993. Foodies should try such local gastronomic delights as traditionally prepared carp *(Karpfen)*, and smoked beer *(Rauchbier)*, which tastes like bacon.

KAISERDOM★★ (IMPERIAL CATHEDRAL)

Open Apr–Oct daily 9am–6pm; Nov–Mar daily 9am–5pm. (0951) 502330. www.bamberger-dom.de.

Its four towers dominating Bamberg's skyline, the Cathedral of St. Peter and St. George was completed in 1237 in a transitional style bridging the Romanesque and the Gothic. The older of its two apses, the eastern Georgenchor, stands upon a raised terrace, while the western Peterschor is entirely Gothic. The finest of the cathedral entrances is the **Fürstenportal** (Princes' Gate) facing the Domplatz. It comprises 10 receding arches supported by fluted, ribbed columns decorated with apostles and

- ▶ **Population:** 70 000
- **Info:** Geyerswörthstraße 3. ℰ(0951) 2976 200. www.bamberg.info.
- **Location:** Bamberg was built on seven hills. The River Regnitz and the Rhine-Main-Danube Canal bisect the town; the historic centre is in the upper part of town.
- P **Parking:** Garages are in the old town, at Geyerswörthstraße 5; on the south side at Schützenstraße 2; and on the north side at Am Georgendamm and Hornthalstraße.
- **Don't Miss:** The Old Town, especially the Kaiserdom and the Rathaus.
- **Timing:** Plan on spending a full day to properly sample Bamberg's treasures (and beers).

prophets with Christ propped up in the tympanon. The **Adamspforte** (Adam's Door) features diamond and dog-tooth carving.

The interior brims with artistic masterpieces, including the celebrated 13C statue of an equestrian knight known

Kaiserdom

© Frank/Fotolia.com

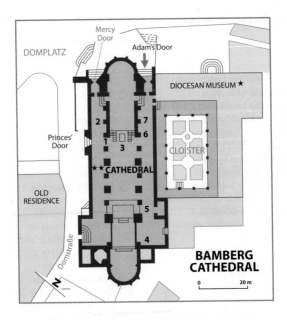

only as the **Bamberg Rider★★★ (1)** *(Bamberger Reiter)*, and the statuary group, **The Visitation (2)**. At the nave's centre is the **tomb★★★ (3)** of Emperor Henry II and his wife Kunigunde. It took native son Tilman Riemenschneider 14 years to complete the tomb. Note the 1523 **Christmas Altar★ (4)** by Veit Stoß depicting the Nativity, the funerary statue **(5)**, the statue representing the Christian church **(6)**, and another symbolising the Jewish Faith in the form of a blindfolded woman **(7)**.

The **Diözesanmuseum★ (Diocesan Museum)** displays medieval paraments, most importantly the 11C Star Cloak (a gift to Henry II, who founded the Diocese); Gothic liturgical artifacts; and devotional folk art. A lapidarium contains the originals of the statues that flank the cathedral's Adam's Gate.

☙WALKING TOUR

OLD TOWN
Allow 4hrs.

▶ Leave from the Obere Brücke bridge, which links the old town with the modern city centre.

Altes Rathaus★ (Old Town Hall)

Standing alone on an islet in the river, Bamberg's unusual medieval town hall is Gothic at its core but underwent a Baroque makeover in the 18C. Its charms include vividly painted *trompe l'œil* façades, a bridge tower and a small half-timbered annex, known as the Rottmeisterhaus.

▶ Climb Karolinenstraße to Domplatz square. Detour through adjoining streets, especially Judenstraße, to admire beautiful façades (e.g. Böttingerhaus Palace at no 14). Note the statues of the Virgin affixed to the corners of the buildings.

Alte Hofhaltung (Old Residence)

Open May–Oct Tue–Sun 9am–5pm; for special exhibits only Nov–Apr. ☞3.50€. ℘(0951) 87 11 42. www.schloesser.bayern.de.

Near the cathedral stands the 16C episcopal palace whose ornate doorway, called the **Schöne Pforte** (beautiful gate), leads to an inner **courtyard★★** *(Innenhof)* framed by half-timbered Gothic buildings. Inside, the moderately interesting Historical Museum chronicles Bamberg's cultural history.

▶ Cross the square.

Neue Residenz
(New Residence)

Domplatz 8. ☏ Guided tours (45min), Apr–Sept daily 9am–6pm; Oct–Mar daily 10am–4pm. Closed Jan 1, Shrove Tue, Dec 24, 25 & 31. ⊚4.50€. ♿ ✆(0951) 51 93 90. www.schloesser.bayern.de.

This palace, the largest building in Bamberg, includes two early 17C Renaissance wings *(on Obere Karolinenstraße)*; and two late-17C Baroque wings *(on the Domplatz)*, by local architect Leonard Dientzenhofer. On the first floor you can peruse paintings by Lucas Cranach the Elder and other Old German Masters, while on the second floor the Imperial apartments hold intricate parquet floors, Baroque furniture and authentic Gobelins tapestries. The **Emperors' Hall** *(Kaisersaal)* has outstanding portraits and allegorical frescoes.

▶ Turn right on Obere Karolinenstraße.

Kloster St-Michael
(St. Michael's Abbey)

Michelsberg 10f. ☛Closed indefinitely for repairs.

This historic Benedictine abbey on the Michaelsberg hill was commissioned in 1015 by Henry II and rebuilt in neo-Gothic style after a fire in 1610. It was remodelled again under the direction of the brothers Dientzenhofer in the 18C. Inside, ceiling frescoes depict the "Heavenly Garden" with 578 flowers and herbs.

Fränkisches Brauereimuseum
(Franconian Brewery Museum)

Michelsberg 10f. Open Apr–Oct Wed–Fri 1pm–5pm, Sat–Sun 11am–5pm. ⊚3.50€. ✆(0951) 530 16. www.brauereimuseum.de.

With its nine breweries, Bamberg is the beer capital of Franconia. This museum in the vaulted cellars of the former Benedictine abbey displays some 1 300

Christmas Crèche Tour

During Christmas-time, Bamberg is deluged by visitors eager to follow the city's enchanting Crèche Trail *(Bamberger Krippenweg)*. Dozens of churches, museums and squares are decorated with splendid, handcrafted Nativity scenes. The route kicks off in the cathedral with Veit Stoß's famous 1523 Nativity altar as well as a modern crèche that tells the famous story in eight enchanting scenes. Other tour highlights include multiple crèches in the peaceful *Maternkapelle* and an exhibit in the *Obere Pfarre* featuring more than 200 individual movable figures averaging 45cm/1.5ft in height. But each of the 33 stations is an artwork in itself, from the enormous manger in Schönleinsplatz with life-size figures in traditional local garb to the tiny crib in the church of St. Gandolf, seen through a special viewer.

objects that engagingly explain the process of beer making.

▶ Head back down into town through the terraced gardens. At the foot of the New Residence, pick up Dominikanerstraß to arrive at Untere Brücke bridge.

From the **Untere Brücke**, a fine view of the half-timbered houses of the old fishermen's quarter along the Regnitz River unfolds. It was nicknamed "Little Venice" (Klein Venedig) by Bavarian King Maximilian II. With their balconies and small gardens, sometimes with boats moored alongside, these medieval houses present a romantic and much-photographed setting. Every August, it forms the picturesque backdrop for the "Sandkerwa", a festival revolving around fishermen's jousting

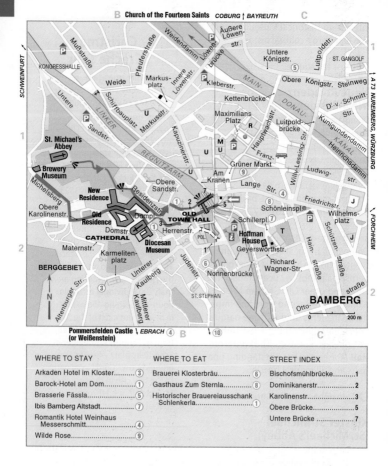

WHERE TO STAY	WHERE TO EAT	STREET INDEX
Arkaden Hotel im Kloster..........③	Brauerei Klosterbräu...............⑥	Bischofsmühlbrücke...........1
Barock-Hotel am Dom..............①	Gasthaus Zum Sternla.............⑧	Dominikanerstr..................2
Brasserie Fässla.....................⑤	Historischer Brauereiausschank	Karolinenstr......................3
Ibis Bamberg Altstadt................⑦	Schlenkerla.........................①	Obere Brücke.....................5
Romantik Hotel Weinhaus		Untere Brücke 7
Messerschmitt.....................④		
Wilde Rose..............................⑨		

competitions (*Fischerstechen*) and an Italian night.

E.T.A. Hoffmann House

Schillerplatz 26. Open May–Oct Tue–Fri 3pm–5pm, Sat–Sun 10am–noon. ⊘2€. www.etahg.de.

Ernst Amadeus Theodor Hoffmann (1775–1822) was one of the pre-eminent writers of the Romantic Age. His stories and novels had a profound influence on other European writers, French authors in particular. The house where Hoffmann lived between 1809 and 1813 still has some of the original furnishings as well as an exhibit on the man and his accomplishments.

EXCURSIONS

Schloss Weissenstein★

◖ 21km/12mi south in Pommersfelden.
Guided tours (1hr) Apr–Oct daily 10am–5pm (last tour 4pm). ⊘7€.
℘(09548) 981 80. www.schoenborn.de/weissenstein.html.

This palace, designed by Dientzenhofer and Hildebrandt in the 18C, is one of Germany's finest Baroque palaces. It features a stunning **double staircase★**. On the ground floor, an artificial grotto opens onto the garden, while the marble hall on the first floor showcases frescoes by Rottmayr. You'll also get to peek at the Elector's apartments, a gallery with paintings by Rubens, Titian and Cranach, and a dizzying hall of mirrors.

Wallfahrtskirche (Pilgrimage Church) Vierzehnheiligen★★

▶ 30km/18.6mi northeast in Bad Staffelstein. Open Mar–Oct daily 6.30am–8pm; Nov–Feb 7.30am–5pm, closed Thu 9am–4pm. ✆(09571) 950 80. www.vierzehnheiligen.de.

On an open hillside overlooking the Upper Main Valley, this pilgrimage church dedicated to the 14 Auxiliary Saints is a marvel of Baroque architecture created by the era's master builder Balthasar Neumann.

The Pilgrimage – In 1445 and 1446, a shepherd on this hillside reported repeated visions of the infant Jesus accompanied by the "14 Holy Helpers". The worship of this group of saints, actively encouraged by German Dominicans and Cistercians, occurred in the early 15C, when Mysticism prevailed. Visions and voices were commonplace (those heard by Joan of Arc, born in 1412, were of St. Catherine and St. Margaret, themselves members of the Auxiliary Saints). Devotion to the Holy Helpers remained alive for many years, attracting crowds of pilgrims to a chapel that was superseded, in the 18C, by this sumptuous Rococo church.

Exterior – The ochre sandstone basilica was built between 1743 and 1772 following designs by Balthasar Neumann. The west façade is framed by domed towers, while the ornately decorated gables are adorned with a statue of Christ flanked by allegorical figures of Faith and Charity.

Interior – The interior is laid out as a succession of three oval bays framed by colonnades and covered by low inner domes. The Rococo decoration features outstanding colour combinations inside the domes, delicate stuccowork, rich gold outlines defining the woodwork of the galleries, and graceful cherubs.

Nothelfer-Altar★★ (Altar to the "Auxiliary Saints")

The true heart of the church is the bay containing the altar to the Auxiliary Saints. A Rococo pyramid with a pierced baldaquin, this remarkable work was designed by Johann Michel Küchel, a student of Balthasar Neumann, and executed by Johann Michael Feuchtmayr and his fellow stucco-workers from the prestigious Wessobrunn School in 1764. It was placed in the physical centre of the church, right where the shepherd's visions were believed to have occurred. Artistic representations include:

♦ **Balustrade: 1)** St. Denys **2)** St. Blaise **3)** St. Erasmus **4)** St. Cyriacus (delivery from the devil at the final hour).

♦ **Altar niches: 5)** St. Catherine, patron saint of the learned, of students and girls wishing to marry (signifying the model of Christian wisdom) **6)** St. Barbara, patron saint of miners, artillerymen and prisoners (signifying the grace of a noble death).

♦ **Buttresses: 7)** St. Acacius (the agonies of death) **8)** St. Giles, the only intercessor not to suffer martyrdom **9)** St. Eustace (converted by the vision of

The Noble Dynasty of Saxe-Coburg

In a history of intrigue and diplomacy spanning centuries, the noble dynasty of Saxe-Coburg was related either directly or through marriage to nearly every royal family of Europe: Belgian, Portuguese, Russian, Swiss and Bulgarian. The marriage between Edward, the Duke of Kent, and the Coburg Princess Victoire produced Queen Victoria; she, in turn, married a cousin: Prince Albert of Saxe-Coburg.

a stag with a Cross between its antlers) **10)** St. Christopher (patron saint of travellers).

♦ **Atop the baldaquin: 11)** St. Vitus **12)** St. Margaret (intercession for the forgiveness of sins) **13)** St. George, patron saint of peasants and their possessions **14)** St. Pantaleon.

After exploring the abbey, trek up the slopes above the church for inspiring views of the edifice itself, the nearby fortress-like yellow sandstone abbey of Banz across the Main River, and the surrounding countryside.

Coburg★

◗ 46km/29mi north.

Dominated by a mighty fortress, Coburg was once the capital of the dukes of Saxe-Coburg. It has beautiful façades, especially around the Marktplatz.

Veste Coburg (Fortress)★★

Open Apr–Oct, daily 9.30am–5pm, Nov–late Mar, Tue–Sun 1pm–4pm. Closed Shrove Tue. ⊛6€. ℘(095 61) 87 90. www.kunstsammlungen-coburg.de. This well-preserved fortress, dating back to the 11C, is guarded by a triple ring of fortified walls. In 1530 Martin Luther famously sought refuge here while defending his faith at the Diet of Augsburg; the rooms in which he stayed are now a museum. The precious **art collections★** include paintings by Dürer and Cranach and the largest Venetian glassware collection in Europe.

Schloss Ehrenburg

•••Guided tours (50min), Apr–Sept Tue–Sun 9am–5pm; Oct–Mar 10am–3pm. Closed Jan 1, Shrove Tue, Nov 1, Dec 24, 25 & 31. ⊛4.50€. ℘(095 61) 80 88 32. www.sgvcoburg.de. This castle was the residence of the Dukes of Coburg from 1547 to 1918. Today the Renaissance palace features a Baroque interior with an early 19C English neo-Gothic façade. Castle rooms house sumptuous Empire and *Biedermeier* furniture. An art gallery contains works by German and Dutch masters.

ADDRESSES

🛏️STAY

⊖ Brasserie Fässla – *Obere Königstraße 19-21. ℘(0951) 26516. www.faessla.de. 26 rooms.* 🚇. These simple rooms above the brewhouse are ideal for sleeping off a beer or two!

⊖⊖ Arkaden Hotel im Kloster – *Karmelitenplatz (entrance on the road behind the church). ℘(0951) 509 8410. www.arkadenhotel-im-kloster.de. 37 rooms.* 🚇8.50€. This gorgeous, peaceful hotel close to the historic centre offers excellent value for money.

⊖⊖ Barock-Hotel am Dom – *Vorderer Bach 4. ℘(0951) 540 31. www.barockhotel.de. 19 rooms.* 🚇. Next to the cathedral, this hotel occupies a building with an elegant 18C Baroque façade.

⊖⊖ Ibis Bamberg Altstadt – *Theatergassen 10. ℘(0951) 980 480. www.accorhotels.com. 50 rooms.* 🚇10€. This chain hotel is located in the historic centre, a distinct advantage.

⊖⊖ Wilde Rose – *Kesselerstraße 7 (in the pedestrianised zone). ℘(0951) 98 18 20. www.hotel-wilde-rose.de. 29 rooms.* 🚇. Located in the heart of the city.

⊖⊖⊖ Romantik Hotel Weinhaus Messerschmitt – *Lange Straße 41. ℘(0951) 29 78 00. www.hotel-messerschmitt.de. 67 rooms.* 🚇. *Restaurant* ⊖⊖⊖⊖. This ancestral home of aviation pioneer Willy Messerschmitt has a modern annex and terrace restaurant.

🍴EAT

⊖ Brauerei Klosterbräu – *Oberer Mühmbrücke 1–3. ℘(0951) 522 65. www.klosterbraeu.de.* This brasserie serves local Franconian specialities. In summer dine on the terrace beside the Regnitz.

⊖ Gasthaus Zum Sternla – *Lange Straße 46. ℘(0951) 28750. www.sternla.de.* In the heart of town, Bamberg's oldest inn has a small garden and serves local Franconian specialities.

⊖ Historischer Brauereiausschank Schlenkerla – *Dominikanerstraße 6. ℘(0951) 560 60. www.schlenkerla.de.* This half-timbered establishment serves local specialities and smoked beer brewed on-site.

Bayreuth★

Bayreuth is the Holy Grail to Wagner fans who flock to town in August for the prestigious Bayreuth Festival. But Wagner was not the only one to leave his mark on the town. In fact, it was one of the most cultivated women of the 18C, the Margravine Wilhelmina, who transformed the town into the cultural centre it remains to this day.

A BIT OF HISTORY

Princess Wilhelmina, sister of Prussian King Frederick the Great, had the great misfortune to be paired with a rather dull husband: Margrave Friedrich of Brandenburg-Bayreuth. Herself a gifted artist, writer, composer and patroness, she turned her energy towards transforming Bayreuth into an artistic and cultural hub and surrounding herself with clever personages of the age. Some of Bayreuth's finest buildings date back to her lifetime (1709–1758).

Richard Wagner moved to Bayreuth in 1872 along with his wife, Cosima, the daughter of the Hungarian composer **Franz Liszt**. Wagner's music was stimulated by admiration for his father-in-law, who is said to be indirectly responsible for many of Wagner's masterworks. The writer and composer of *Parzival* and *Tannhäuser*, Richard Wagner searched far and wide for the ideal music venue. With the support of King Ludwig II of Bavaria, he designed his own Festival Hall *(Festspielhaus)*, revolutionary in its day for its generous audience space

- ▶ **Population:** 74 400
- **Info:** Opernstraße 22, 95444 Bayreuth. ℘(0921) 885 88. www.bayreuth.de.
- ◖ **Location:** The town sits between the wooded heights of the Fichtelgebirge and the desolate landscape of Swiss Franconia; A9 autobahn linking Munich and Berlin runs nearby.
- **P Parking:** There are plenty of parking garages.
- **Don't Miss:** The Bayreuth Festival if you're an opera fan.
- ⏱ **Timing:** Allow half a day.
- **Kids:** Cave explorations in tours 1 and 3.

as well as its outstanding acoustics. The first festival took place in 1876. After his death in 1883, the tradition continued under his daughter, Cosima and, subsequently, his son Siegfried, then his grandsons Wieland (d. 1966) and Wolfgang, who retired in 2008, passing on the torch to his daughters Eva Wagner-Pasquier and Katharina Wagner.

SIGHTS

Markgräfliches Opernhaus (Margrave Opera House)★

Opernstraße 14. Closed for renovation until at least 2016; the Information Center in the foyer remains open to visitors. ℘(0921) 759 69 22. www.bayreuth-wilhelmine.de.

Bayreuth Festival

From 25 July until 28 August, Bayreuth reverberates to the sound of Wagner. But don't think you can just show up and buy a ticket: you have to apply for one. Each year, more than half a million opera fans vie for the 60 000 tickets, which are allocated by lottery. Wait times of seven years or more are not uncommon. Applications can only be made in writing and need to be sent no later than mid-September for the next year's festival to: **Bayreuther Festspiele – Kartenbüro – Postfach 100262, 95402 Bayreuth, Germany**. Returned ticket are sometimes available on performance day, but you need to get up early: people start queuing around 6am. For details, see www.bayreuther-festspiele.de.

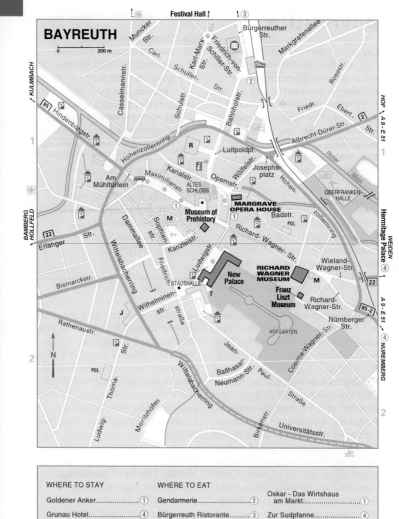

BAYREUTH

Margravine Wilhelmina commissioned this gorgeous Baroque theatre in 1748 as a venue for the opera and ballet. The austere façade gives no clue to the exuberance of the **interior decoration★** by Giuseppe Galli Bibiena of Bologna. The reds, greens and browns harmonise perfectly with the gilded stuccowork on the columns; the interior is constructed entirely of wood. Visitors are treated to a 45-minute sound and light show about the theatre and its patroness.

Neues Schloss (New Palace)

Open Apr–Sept daily 9am–6pm; Oct–Mar daily 10am–4pm. Closed Jan 1, Shrove Tue, Dec 24, 25 & 31. ⌨5.50€. ♿ ✆(0921) 759 690.

After a fire destroyed their old residence, Wilhelmina directed the construction of this palace and even designed some its most memorable features, including the **Broken Mirrors Cabinet★** *(Spiegelscherbenkabinett)*. Elsewhere the lavish **decorations★** reflect the masterful Rococo flourishes of stucco artist Jean

Baptiste Pedrozzi. Wilhelmina's private quarters were on the first floor of the north wing. On the ground floor are a small exhibition about this remarkable woman and a collection of Bayreuth porcelain. Elsewhere you can admire 18C Dutch and German paintings, including the *Four Seasons* cycle by Jan Brueghel the Elder.

Richard Wagner Museum★

Richard-Wagner-Straße 48.
⊶Closed for renovation until mid-2015. Infopoint bau.schau.stelle (Richard-Wagner-Straße 45) is open Apr–Sept daily 10am–4pm; Oct–Mar Thu–Sat 11am–3pm. ℘(0921) 75 72 816. www.wagnermuseum.de.
Haus Wahnfried, Wagner's private mansion built with funds from Ludwig II, is a key stop on any Wagnerian pilgrimage, even though the only remaining original feature of the house is the façade. Displays evoke the maestro's life and work as well as the history of the Bayreuth Festival. The composer and his wife are buried in the garden.

Franz Liszt Museum

Wahnfriedstraße 9. Open Jul–Aug daily 10am–5pm, Sept–Jun daily 10am–noon & 2pm–5pm. Closed Dec 24–25. ⌀2€. ℘(0921) 516 64 88. www.bayreuth.de.
The house where the piano virtuoso spent his final years is now a museum dedicated to his life and his work. Portraits, letters, his piano and other objects are engagingly presented. Liszt is buried in the town cemetery *(Stadtfriedhof – entrance on Erlanger Straße)*.

Festspielhaus (Festival Hall)

Festspielhügel 1–2 (enter via Karl-Marx-Straße). ⌀Guided tours Sept–Oct daily 10am, 11am, 2pm, 3pm; Nov–Apr Sat 2pm. ⌀7€. ℘(0921) 885 88. www.bayreuther-festspiele.de.
The Festival Hall on the Grüner Hügel (green hill) was inaugurated in 1876 with a performance of the *Ring of the Nibelungen* cycle. It ranks among the world's most important opera stages (although it does not have a resident ensemble). It is used only for the Wagner Festival.

Famous for its exceptional acoustics, the opera house incorporates many design elements that were revolutionary for the time. The orchestra, for instance, was hidden below the stage so that the audience could focus entirely on the performance. The amphitheatre layout provides excellent sight lines. The wooden seats, however, are infamous for their lack of comfort.

Urwelt-Museum Oberfranken (Museum of Prehistory)

Kanzleistraße 1. Open year-round, Tue–Sun 10am–5pm. Closed Dec 24–25. ⌀3.50€. ℘(0921) 51 12 11. www.urwelt-museum.de.
This museum presents the natural history of Upper Franconia over the last 500 million years.

EXCURSION

Schloss Eremitage (Hermitage Palace)★

◗ 4km/2.5mi east via Wieland-Wagner-Straße. Open Apr–Sept daily 9am–6pm; Oct 1–15 daily 10am–4pm. ⌀4.50€. ℘(0921) 759 69 37. www.schloesser.bayern.de.
This summer palace was a gift to Wilhelmina from her husband. She also built the **New Palace** *(Neues Schloss)* and created the English-garden-style **Schloßpark★** with its pavilions, follies and fountains, most famously the **Lower Grotto**, a basin with sculpture fountains whose jets blend with water from the surrounding arcade.

🚗 DRIVING TOURS

① FRANCONIAN SWITZERLAND★★ (Fränkische Schweiz)

Round-trip tour of 105km/65mi. Allow one day.

Tüchersfeld

This charming village is dramatically framed by jagged rocks.

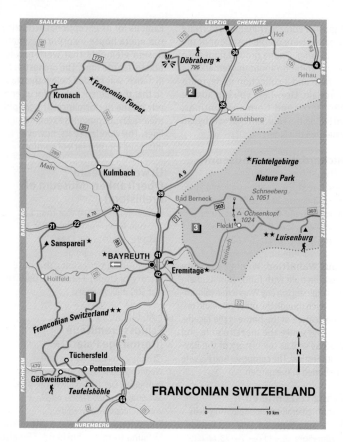

FRANCONIAN SWITZERLAND

Pottenstein

The castle, a former residence of the Prince-Bishops of Bamberg, overlooks the town. Natural wonders, like gorges and caves, dot the local countryside.

♣♣ Teufelshöhle (Devil's Cave)

🔦 Guided tours (45min) Apr–Oct daily 9am–5pm (last tour at 4.30pm); Nov–Mar Sun 11am–3pm; Dec 26–Jan 6 daily 11am–3pm (last tour at 3pm). Closed Dec 24 & 25. ⊚4.50€. ℘(09243) 208. www.teufelshoehle.de.

These are Germany's largest caverns. The Barbarossadom (Cathedral of Barbarossa) is especially impressive.

Gößweinstein★

This tiny village is dominated by a huge and richly decorated basilica designed between 1730 and 1739 by Balthasar Neumann. A 45min loop trail starting at

the castle above town leads to several fine **vistas★★** over the Wiesent valley.

Sanspareil★

After completion of Bayreuth's Eremitage, Margravine Wilhelmina and Margrave Friedrich converted an old hunting estate into an impressive **rock garden★** named Sanspareil ("without equal" in French).

Burg Zwernitz

Open Apr–Sept Tue–Sun 9am–6pm; Oct 1–15 Tue–Sun 10am–4pm. ⊚3.50€. ♿ ℘(0974) 80 89 09 11. www.schloesser.bayern.de

Before falling to Bavaria in 1810, this 12C fortress was the property of the Hohenzollern margraves from 1338. Re-opened in 2011, the fortress contains furnishings and a selection of 16C–18C weapons. The keep offers good **views**.

2 FRANCONIAN FOREST★ (Frankenwald)

Round-trip of 125km/78mi. Allow 5hrs.

Döbraberg★

🏃 45min round-trip walk. Climb to the look-out tower (795m/2 608ft). The majestic **panorama★** extends as far as the Thuringian Mountains in the north and Fichtelgebirge in the south.

Kronach

Festung Rosenberg (16C–18C), one of the largest medieval fortresses in Germany, towers over the small town of Kronach and the wooded heights of the Frankenwald. Inside, the Franconian Gallery displays works by medieval and Renaissance artists, including sculptor Tilman Riemenschneider and paintings by Kronach-born **Lucas Cranach the Elder** (👁see INTRODUCTION: Art).

Kulmbach

Once the seat of the Hohenzollern margraves, Kulmbach is famous today for its strong beers (Kapuziner, Mönchshof). The **Plassenburg★** (open Apr–Oct daily 9am–6pm; Nov–Mar daily 10am–4pm; closed Jan 1, Shrove Tue, Dec 24, 25 & 31; 👛4.50€; ♿ 🕿(09221) 822 00; www.schloesser.bayern.de), another well-preserved medieval fortress, melds a strong, defensive exterior with an elegant **Renaissance courtyard★★**. Displays include 300 000 **tin soldiers★** from the Deutsches Zinn-figurenmuseum (German Tin Figure Museum).

3 FICHTELGEBIRGE NATURE PARK★

Loop trip of 92km/57mi. Allow 5hrs.

The **panoramic route★** follows the Steinach Valley into the granite massif of the Fichtelgebirge. Above Fleckl, a cable-car climbs the **Ochsenkopf** (alt.1 024m/3 360ft).

Luisenburg★★

This labyrinth of enormous granite boulders makes for a pleasant hike along a pine-shaded, hilly path (blue arrows indicate the way up, red the way down). Several look-out points along the way afford views of the Fichtelgebirge.

ADDRESSES

◉ 🍽🍽 **Goldener Anker** – Opernstraße 6. 🕿(0921) 787 77 40. www.anker-bayreuth.de. Closed Dec 24–mid-Jan. 35 rooms. 🍽. Restaurant🍽🍽🍽. Owned by the same family since the 15C, each room at this venerable hotel has its own style, but all are spacious. The intimate restaurant serves upscale French cuisine.

◉🍽🍽 **Grunau Hotel** – Kemnather Straße 27 (east of Wieland-Wagner-Straße and Königsallee). 🕿(0921) 798 00. www.grunau-hotel.de. 60 rooms. 🍽. Situated on the top floors of a shopping centre, this modern hotel has spacious and quiet rooms. Guests get discounted access to a fitness centre.

🍽EAT

◉ **Oskar – Das Wirtshaus am Markt** – Maximilianstraße 33. 🕿(0921) 516 05 53. www.oskar-bayreuth.de. This restaurant in the former town hall has a pretty winter garden and a terrace. Bavarian specialities (great dumplings) make up the bulk of the earthy menu.

◉🍽🍽 **Bürgerreuth Ristorante** – An der Bürgerreuth 20. 🕿0921 784 00. www.buergerreuth.de. This restaurant serves excellent classic and home-style Italian cuisine.

◉🍽🍽 **Gendarmerie** – Bahnhostraße 14. 🕿0921 786 00. www.gendarmerie.de. Closed Sun lunch and dinner, Jun 9–15, Aug 30–Sept 7, Dec 22–Jan 10. This stylish French bistro is located near the station.

◉🍽🍽 **Zur Sudpfanne** – Oberkonnersreuther Straße 6, 95448 Bayreuth-Oberkonnersreuth (southeast along Nürnberger Straße) 🕿(0921) 528 83. www.sudpfanne.de. This popular restaurant housed in a former brewery building is well known for its creative international cuisine infused with local touches. Enjoy the leafy beer garden.

Central Germany

Central Germany

After travelling around Germany's heartland, it is easy to understand why the country is often called the "land of poets and thinkers". Martin Luther studied in Erfurt, posted his "95 Theses" in Wittenberg, and translated the Bible from Greek into German at Eisenach's Wartburg Castle. Nearby Weimar drew an entire cast of intellectual and creative giants, from Cranach to Bach, Goethe to Schiller, Herder to Liszt. The Bauhaus movement was born here, later peaking in Dessau. Architectural gems abound, from medieval cathedrals to Neoclassical palaces and fantastical Hundertwasser buildings. Those looking for nature should head for the trails of the Thuringian Forest or take a leisurely stroll around the richly landscaped gardens at Wörlitz.

Highlights

Touring Central Germany

A tour could begin in Marburg, a bustling university town about 100km/60mi north of Frankfurt. Its landmark church is dedicated to St. Elizabeth (1207–32), who was buried here after her short life of caring for the sick and poor while living at Wartburg in nearby Eisenach (incidentally the birthplace of Johann Sebastian Bach). From this hilltop castle, take in the verdant expanse of the Thuringian Forest, which is bisected by the 168km/104mi-long Rennsteig, Germany's oldest (since the 14C) and most popular long-distance hiking trail. It skirts postcard-pretty villages, including Goethe's old haunt, Ilmenau.

The town most closely associated with Germany's literary giant, though, is Weimar, where Goethe lived for 57 years. His authentically preserved home is now a place of pilgrimage, as is the one of his friend and colleague Friedrich Schiller. Along with a dozen other sites, the buildings were UNESCO-listed in 1999. Meanwhile, north of Weimar, you can connect with the darkest chapter in German history at chilling Buchenwald concentration camp memorial. Travelling east for 24km/15mi takes you to Erfurt, capital of the state of Thuringia and a university town since 1392. Its medieval centre is one of the best-preserved any-

Dom St. Marien and Severikirche, Erfurt

© Wasisevenr/Dreamstime.com

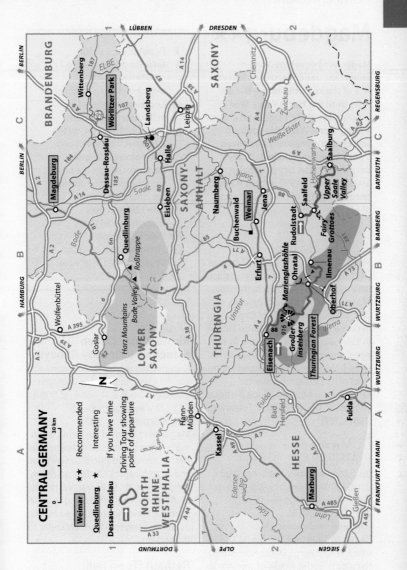

where in Germany with plenty of lovingly restored buildings and the unique Merchants' Bridge (Krämerbrücke). The cathedral is another showstopper. And don't miss a stroll around the tangled old town.

Like Weimar, Jena too was an intellectual centre during the Enlightenment but since the 19C it is primarily known as a city of science and optics. A tour of the Optical Museum is a must. If you have the kids in tow, make a quick detour down the scenic Saale Valley to the Feengrotten (Fairy Grottoes) in Saalfeld. Alternatively, steer north

and pay your respects to Georg Friedrich Händel in his birth town of Halle and to Martin Luther, a native of Eisleben. Wittenberg, where Luther posted his "95 Theses" against Church corruption, is further north, near the Bauhaus city of Dessau and the fabulous Wörlitz gardens. Finally, follow the Elbe up to Magdeburg where a key stop is the early-13C Dom, Germany's oldest Gothic cathedral and the burial site of Otto I, who was crowned first Holy Roman Emperor in 962.

Magdeburg★★

Magdeburg developed on an important trade crossroads and was one of the key cities in the Middle Ages until the Thirty Years' War brought the glory years to an end. During World War II, Magdeburg was almost completely destroyed by fire-bombing and in GDR days became a model city of socialist architecture. In 1990, it beat Halle to become capital of the federal state of Sachsen-Anhalt.

▶ **Population:** 230 500
🖩 **Info:** Ernst-Reuter-Allee 12. 𝒫(0391) 8380 402. www.magdeburg-tourist.de.
▶ **Location:** Magdeburg is in the heart of Sachsen-Anhalt and is served by the A2 (Berlin–Hannover) and A14 motoways (Leipzig).
🅿 **Parking:** Garages are near the Johanniskirche and on the Elbuferpromenade.
🚫 **Don't Miss:** A walk through the old town.
👥 **Kids:** Elbauenpark.
🕐 **Timing:** Magdeburg can be appreciated in one day.

A BIT OF HISTORY

Magdeburg was founded by Emperor Otto I, who built his favourite palace here and raised the town to the status of archbishopric in 968. The early success of this commercial centre, which declared its support for Martin Luther in 1524, was brought to an end in 1631 when imperial troops laid siege to the town before destroying it and killing most of its 20 000 inhabitants.

Famous local figures include Baroque composer Georg Philipp Telemann (1681–1767).

DOM★★★ (CATHEDRAL)

Open May–Sept daily 10am–6pm; Apr & Oct daily 10am–5pm; Nov–Mar Mon–Sat 10am–4pm, Sun 11.30am–4pm. ♿𝒫(0391) 541 04 36. www.magdeburgerdom.de.

Begun in 1209 and the burial site of Otto I, Magdeburg's Dom is considered the oldest Gothic house of worship in Germany and, at 120m/393.7ft long, is also one of the largest. The towers, though, were not completed until 1520. The light-flooded, if rather austere, interior is an artistic treasure trove.

The most precious works are the famous early-Gothic sandstone sculptures of the **Five Wise and Five Foolish Virgins** (1250). Also of note are the intricately carved choir stalls (1363) and the emotional war memorial by 20C artist Ernst Barlach.

OLD TOWN

Kloster Unser Lieben Frauen★★ (Our Lady Abbey)

Regierungsstraße 4-6. Open year-round Tue–Fri 10am-5pm, Sat–Sun until 6pm. Closed Dec 24–25 & 31. ⊚4€. 𝒫(0391) 56 50 20. www.kunstmuseum-magdeburg.de.

Magdeburg's oldest surviving building is a harmonious 12C Romanesque design converted into a concert hall and an art museum. On display are contemporary works by Giovanni Anselmo, Mario Merz, Siegfried Anzinger, Leiko Ikemura, Enrico Castellani and others, as well as sculpture from antiquity to the present.

Rathaus (Town Hall)

On Markt, outside the Italian Renaissance-style town hall, stands a gilded replica of the famous equestrian statue of the Magdeburg Knight (1240). The original is in the Kulturhistorisches Museum (Cultural History Museum).

Grüne Zitadelle★ (Green Citadel)

Breiter Weg 9. 🔊Guided tours (1hr) year-round Mon–Fri 11am & 3pm, Sat–Sun 11am, 3pm & 5pm (Apr–Oct also Mon–Fri 5pm, Sat–Sun hourly 11–5pm).

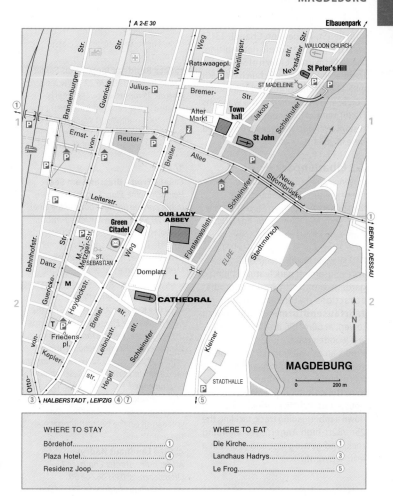

MAGDEBURG

Tours leave from the Citadel Infopoint. 6€. (0391) 620 86 55. www.gruene-zitadelle.de.

Close to the Dom, this whimsical pink building was the final work of Austrian cult artist and architect Friedensreich Hundertwasser (1928–2000). Completed in 2005, it perfectly reflects his design philosophy of wanting to create "a natural oasis for humanity within a sea of functional spaces". Construction of this unusual building in the heart of town engendered considerable controversy. It contains flats, offices, shops and a hotel as well as a permanent exhibition showcasing Hundertwasser's work and vision.

Johanniskirche (Church of St. John)

Open Mar–Oct Tue–Sun 10am–6pm; Nov–Feb Tue–Sun 10am–5pm. No visits on event days. (0391) 593 450. www.mvgm-online.de.

Magdeburg's oldest parish church (941), in which Martin Luther preached (see the memorial in front of the church), was all but destroyed during World War II. It is now used as an events and exhibition venue.

Petriberg (St. Peter's Hill)

North of the town hall, on the banks of the Elbe, three churches crown St. Peter's hill. The small Magdalenenkapelle (St. Madeleine Chapel, 1315) with its intricate Gothic net vaulting; the St. Petrikirche (Church of St. Peter), a three-aisled Gothic hall-church (14–15C) with a handsome Gothic red-brick south porch; and the Church of the Walloons (1285), named for a community of protestant Walloon refugees who settled here in 1694.

🚻 Elbauenpark★

Tessenowstraße 5a. Access from the city centre via Schleinufer and Markgrafenstraße. Open May–Sept daily 9am–8pm; Mar 10am–6pm, Apr & Oct 9am–6pm, Nov–Feb 10am–4pm. ⊜3€ (Nov–Apr ⊜1€) ♿ ℘(0391) 59 34 293. www.mvgm-online.de.
This amusement park features themed gardens, a butterfly house and other attractions that include the conical **Jahrtausendturm★★** (millennium tower), at 60m/196.8ft the world's tallest wooden tower.
Inside, an exhibit traces 6 000 years of science and technology and includes lots of hands-on experiments. Kids also love the colourful **Spielhaus** (playhouse) and such diversions as scooting down a tobogganing track, tackling the 25m/82ft-high Angerfelsen climbing rock, and getting lost and found in a leafy labyrinth.

ADDRESSES

🛏 STAY

⊜🍴 **Hotel Bördehof** – *Magdeburger Straße 42, 39179 Magdeburg-Ebendorf.* ℘(039203) 515 10. www.boerdehof.de. *60 rooms.* Near the autobahn, this converted farmhouse has cheerful, modern rooms. Cap off a day on the tourist track with a relaxing sauna or by watching the pretty birds fluttering around the on-site aviary.

⊜🍴 **Plaza Hotel** – *Halberstädter Straße 146–150.* ℘(0391) 605 10. www.12plaza.de. *104 rooms.* ⊑13€. *Restaurant* ⊜🍴. This hotel is on the outskirts of town and well served by public transport. Behind its modern, white façade await comfortable rooms

tastefully decorated in English country style. The restaurant serves classic German food.

⊜🍴🍴 **Residenz Joop** – *Jean-Burger-Straße 16.* ℘(0391) 626 20. www.residenz joop.de. *25 rooms.* This villa hotel is located in a quiet residential district. From 1903 until World War II it was the Swedish consulate. Rooms are spacious, comfortable and tastefully furnished.

🍽 EAT

⊜🍴 **Le Frog** – *Brasserie am See* – *Heinrich-Heine-Platz 1 (in the Rotehorn public park on the right bank of the Elbe).* ℘(0391) 531 35 56. www.lefrog-md.de. This glass pavilion occupies a pretty lakeside spot in the sprawling Rotehorn park. Whether it's coffee and cake, a Mediterranean meal or a late-night cocktail, there's something for everyone here. Pleasant *Biergarten*.

⊜🍴 **Die Kirche** – *Alt Prester 86 (on the right bank of the Elbe: cross the two arms of the river and follow Cracauer Straße, Genthiner Straße and Pechauer Straße south).* ℘0391 535 33 52. www.restaurant-die-kirche.de. Closed Mon. Reservation recommended. This fine-dining place enjoys an exceptional location in an ancient neo-Gothic church. In summer, you can sit on the beautiful terrace at the water's edge.

⊜🍴🍴 **Landhaus Hadrys** – *An der Halberstädter Chaussee 1, Ottersleben.* ℘0391 662 66 80. www.landhaus-hadrys.de. Closed Sun & Mon. This bright, modern restaurant is set in a lovely old villa with a nice lounge and a pleasant terrace.

NIGHTLIFE

Alex – *Ulrichplatz 2 (southeast of the roundabout between Ernst-Reuter-Allee and Otto-von-Guericke-Straße).* ℘(0391) 59 74 90. www.alexgastro.de. This hotspot for the young and young-at-heart bustles all day long. In the morning, crowds come for the big breakfast buffet, at night for cocktails. A good place to watch the sun set over the Ulrichplatz fountain.

Wörlitzer Park★★

Wörlitzer Park is the oldest landscaped park on the European mainland and part of the Garden Realm created by Prince Leopold III around Dessau between 1764 and 1800. Retaining all its original magic, the park has enchanting canalside trails, voluptuous hedges and lakes with small islands reached by ferry or gondola. In 2000, the gardens' special appeal was recognised by UNESCO, which placed Wörlitz on its list of World Heritage Sites.

🗓 **Info:** Förstergasse 26, 06786 Wörlitz. ℘(034905) 310 09. www.woerlitz-information.de.

◐ **Location:** Wörlitzer Park is 17km/10.5mi west of Dessau. From the A9 (Leipzig–Berlin), take exit 10 and follow the B185 to Orienbaum, then the B107 to Wörlitz.

⊘ **Don't Miss:** The gardens.

◷ **Timing:** Allow at least half a day to see the grounds and buildings.

⁂ **Kids:** Exploring the lake and small islands by boat.

A BIT OF HISTORY

Prince Leopold III Friedrich Franz von Anhalt-Dessau (1740–1817), known as "Father Franz" to his subjects, was an enlightened ruler to whom the welfare of his small state was paramount (⚑*see DESSAU)*. His endeavours extended far beyond material matters; he sought to link the beautiful with the practical, promoting literature, music, architecture and garden design.

A number of trips to England provided him with food for progressive thought and paved the way for his planned reforms. It was also in England that he saw his first landscaped parks and was inspired to create such a park environ ment of his own. Master builder **Friedrich Wilhelm von Erdmannsdorff,** who had accompanied him on his trips, acted as his assistant and like-minded adviser. The gardens were completed around 1800.

VISIT

Schloss★ (Palace)

⚓Guided tours (1hr) May–Sept Tue–Sun 10am-6pm, Apr & Oct 10am–5pm. ⊛6€. ℘(034905) 40 90. www.gartenreich.com.

Built by Erdmannsdorf between 1769 and 1773, this is the earliest Neoclassical palace outside of England; it replaced an earlier Baroque hunting lodge.

Admiring the scenery on board a gondola

©World Pictures/Photoshot

The dignified two-storey yellow-and-white building stands against a backdrop of mature trees. Erdmannsdorff made ingenious use of the many technical innovations of the day, including water pipes, lifts, cast-iron stoves, folding beds and cupboards, all of which vastly improved the living standard of the ruling family.

The original interior has survived virtually intact and sports ceiling frescoes and murals inspired by antiquity. Most sculpture and carpentry work was undertaken by local people.

The elegant **Speisesaal** (dining room) with its elaborate stucco decoration and slim Corinthian pillars, and the great **Großer Festsaal** (banqueting hall) are striking. The **library** is richly hung with paintings (Snyders, Van Ruysdael, Antoine Pesne) and fitted with furniture, the highlight of which is the suite of Roentgen pieces.

Gotisches Haus★ (Gothic House)

🥄 Guided tours (1hr) Apr & Oct Sat & Sun 11am & 4pm; May–Sept Tue–Fri 11am & 4pm, Sat–Sun 11am, noon, 3pm & 4pm. ⬤6€. 𝒫(034905) 40 90. www.gartenreich.com.

One of the earliest neo-Gothic buildings in Germany, the Gothic House was erected between 1773 and 1813. The canal-facing main façade was inspired by the Church of Maria dell' Orto in Venice. While the palace served official purposes, this structure was the prince's private refuge. Through Swiss scholar Johann Caspar Lavater, he acquired an outstanding **Swiss stained-glass★** collection from the 15C to the 17C, which has intact. All rooms feature 16C–18C paintings by Dutch, German and Italian masters, including Tintoretto and Lucas Cranach the Elder.

Wörlitzer Park by Gondola★

Boats depart from the pier (Gondolastation) Apr–Oct daily 11am–4pm; May–Sept daily 10am–6pm. 45min. ⬤8€. www.woerlitz-information.de or www.gartenreich.

com. Phone ahead to book gondola tours for groups 𝒫(034905) 2 02 05.

An enchanting way to experience the charms of this extensive garden landscape is being poled around in a romantic gondola. Tours travel across Lake Wörlitz, glide through a canal and pass the Gothic House. Each boat seats up to 15 people comfortably.

EXCURSION
Lutherstadt Wittenberg

▶ 23km/14mi east of Wörlitz.
🏛 Schlossplatz 2. 𝒫(03491) 49 86 10. www. lutherstadt-wittenberg.de.

Wittenberg enjoys a pleasant location between the wooded hills of Fläming and the Elbe. The town was the centre of Martin Luther's work. Summoned by the Elector Friedrich the Wise (1502) to teach philosophy at his newly founded university, **Martin Luther** was at the same time appointed the town preacher. On October 31, 1517, he posted his famous "95 Theses" against Church corruption. This act was a key step towards the Reformation and a new era in the religious and political history of the Western world. In 1547, a year after Luther's death, **Emperor Charles V** seized Wittenberg and reputedly meditated over the tomb of the great Reformer. The "Lutherstadt" prefix was added to Wittenberg in 1938.

Sites related to Luther and his fellow reformer Philipp Melanchton were inscribed on UNESCO's list of World Heritage Sites in 1996.

A historic university town, Wittenberg also attracted many other talented people, including the master painter Lucas Cranach the Elder.

Schlosskirche★ (Castle Church)

Am Schlossplatz. ⚬ Closed for renovation until 2017. 𝒫(03491) 40 25 81. www.schlosskirche-wittenberg.de.

The original castle church burnt down in 1760, destroying the original doors on which Luther pinned his famous "95 Theses" condemning the abuses of the Church. The text, though, is engraved in the new bronze door from 1858.

Twin towers of Stadtkirche St. Marien over the houses of Markt

©Thomas Röske/Fotolia.com

Luther's tomb lies below the pulpit; next to his is that of his dear friend and supporter, Philipp Melanchthon. Also note Peter Vischer's bronze epitaph of Friedrich the Wise to the left of the main altar.

Markt★ (Market Square)

Wittenberg's central square is bordered by gabled houses, including the birthplace of Lucas Cranach the Elder at no 4 who lived and worked at Schlossstraße 1 from 1513–50. In front of the late-Gothic (1440) town hall stand 19C statues of Luther and Melanchthon.

Stadtkirche St. Marien (Parish Church of St. Mary)

On Kirchplatz, east of the market square. Open Easter–Oct Mon–Sat 10am–6pm; (Nov–Easter until 4pm), Sun year-round from 11.30am. ℘(03491) 404 415. www.stadtkirchengemeinde-wittenberg.de.

Luther himself preached and was married to Katharina von Bora in this triple-aisle Gothic (14C–15C) church that got a neo-Gothic makeover in the 18C. The key piece of artistry is Lucas Cranach's 1547 **Reformation Altar★★**. Cranach also crafted the elaborate epitaphs in the chancel. Older still is the **baptismal font★** created by Hermann Vischer of Nuremberg in 1457.

Lutherhaus★

Collegienstraße 54. Open Apr–Oct daily 9am–6pm; Nov–Mar Tue–Sun 10am–5pm. ✆6€. ℘(03491) 4203 118. www.martinluther.de.

Luther's former home (1508–46), a converted monastery, presents a comprehensive and engaging exhibit about the man, his life and the impact of his teachings on the world. Aside from instructive explanatory panels, there are top-notch paintings (including Lucas Cranach's *Ten Commandments*), period artefacts (Bibles, garments, coins) and a room furnished by Luther himself in 1535.

Melanchthonhaus

Collegienstraße 60. Open Apr–Oct daily 10am–6pm; Nov–Mar Tue–Sun 10am–5pm. ✆4€. ℘(03491) 420 31 10. www.martinluther.de.

Luther's companion, Philipp Melanchthon, lived and died in this elegant gabled Renaissance home. The author of the *Confession of Augsburg* was a moderate man who dedicated himself to reconciling the different factions of the Reformation. His study and documents relating to his work can be seen in this house.

Dessau-Rosslau

Dessau-Rosslau is indelibly associated with the Bauhaus School, which was based here from 1925 to 1932. Having the greatest concentration of Bauhaus structures garnered Dessau-Rosslau UNESCO World Heritage Site status in 1996. Although the town was heavily war-damaged and rebuilt in socialist style, it is not devoid of charm. Along with the Bauhaus buildings, Prince Leopold III's landscaped gardens are most scenic.

▶ **Population:** 78 500

Info: Zerbster Straße 2c, 06844 Dessau. ℘(0340) 204 14 42. www.dessau-tourismus.de.

◖ **Location:** Flanked by the Elbe and the Mulde rivers, Dessau is just off the A9 autobahn linking Berlin and Munich.

Don't Miss: The Bauhaus buildings that put the city on the cultural map. Note: A 24hr pass for all Bauhaus buildings is 22€.

◷ **Timing:** Allow three hours to explore the Bauhaus sites.

BAUHAUS SITES

Bauhausgebäude★ (Bauhaus Building)

Gropiusallee 38. Open year-round daily 10am–5pm. Closed Dec 24 & 31. Guided tours (1hr) daily 11am and 2pm, also noon and 4pm Sat–Sun. 7€, combined ticket including tour 16€. ℘(0340) 650 82 50. www.bauhaus-dessau.de.

The "Design Academy", built according to plans by Walter Gropius, opened in 1926 and displays key features of the Bauhaus style: cubic blocks, lack of visible supports and glazed façades. Gropius and Mies van der Rohe served as its successive directors. You are free to walk around, but in order to see Gropius' office, the auditorium and other rooms not generally open to the public you need to join a guided tour. Some rooms are once again used as a school.

Meisterhäuser★ (Master Houses)

Ebertallee 69–71. Open Apr–Sept daily 10am–5pm; Oct–Mar, Tue–Sun 11am–5pm. 7.50€. ℘(0340) 650 81 16. www.meisterhaeuser.de.

Walter Gropius masterplanned this row of houses for himself and his Bauhaus professors (built 1925–26). Destroyed in the war, three of them have been rebuilt and are open to the public: the **Kandinsky-Klee-Haus**, the **Muche-Schlemmer-Haus** and the **Feiningerhaus**. The latter houses a centre dedicated to the Dessau-born composer Kurt Weill.

Törtensiedlung

The Bauhaus-designed Törten housing estate south of the centre was built between 1926 and 1928 to relieve a housing shortage and to give workers an opportunity to own their own homes. Although few of the 314 terraced houses have remained unchanged, the unmistakable Bauhaus style is still clearly in evidence.

© Martin Brück, 2005, Bauhaus Dessau Foundation

Bauhausgebäude

The Bauhaus Movement

One of the seminal aesthetic movements of the 20C, the Bauhaus School was founded by architect Walter Gropius in Weimar in 1919. He was joined by Paul Klee, Ludwig Mies van der Rohe, Wassily Kandinsky and other top talents of the day who taught architecture, design, painting and sculpture in an interdisciplinary approach.

As the political climate in Weimar turned conservative, the school moved to Dessau in 1925 where they moulded a new style of living in Bauhaus workshops. In 1932, they moved again, this time to Berlin, only to be closed down for good by the Nazis in 1933. Their design concepts, however, survived, and in fact it is hard to imagine 20C and 21C architecture without the Bauhaus.

ADDITIONAL SIGHT
Georgium

⊶ Closed for renovation until at least 2016. ℘(0340) 61 38 74. www.georgium.de.

Surrounded by the richly landscaped English-style Georgengarten park, this 18C Neoclassical palace houses a prized art collection of Old Masters (Cranach, Grien), 18C Frankfurt paintings and Dutch artists from the 16C and 17C.

ADDRESSES

🏠 STAY

⊖ **City-Pension** – *Ackerstraße 3a. ℘(0340) 882 30 76. www.city-pension-dessau.de. 24 rooms.* This central hotel has functionally furnished, light and airy rooms. The generous breakfast buffet is great for starting the day.

🍴 EAT

⊖⊖ **Das Pächterhaus** – *Kirchstraße 1, 06846 Dessau-Ziebigk. ℘(0340) 650 14 47. www.paechterhaus-dessau.de. Closed Mon.* This nicely restored 1743 half-timbered house delivers seasonal dishes and excellent wines in its cosy rooms or the lovely garden at the back.

Halle★

Halle must balance its heritage as an old university town and birthplace of Georg Friedrich Händel with its legacy as the centre of the chemical industry in GDR days. Since 1990, the town has progressed and cleaned up in leaps and bounds and is again ready for a close-up look– and not only during the biannual Händel Festival.

SIGHTS
Marktplatz★

This huge square is dominated by the belfries of the Marktkirche and by the **Roter Turm** (red tower), built in the 15C and almost 80m/262.4ft high. An 1859 statue of Händel surveys the square.

▶ **Population:** 240 000

🛈 **Info:** Marktplatz 13, 06108 Halle. ℘(0345) 122 99 84. www.stadtmarketing-halle.de. Contact or visit the tourist office for a Halle Welcome Card.

◖ **Location:** Halle is on the Saale River, some 30km/18.6mi northwest of Leipzig.

🅿 **Parking:** Händelhauskarree garage on Hallorenring.

🕑 **Don't Miss:** Moritzburg Art Gallery, Händel-Haus.

🕐 **Timing:** Allow about half a day for Halle, plus another half a day for the excursions.

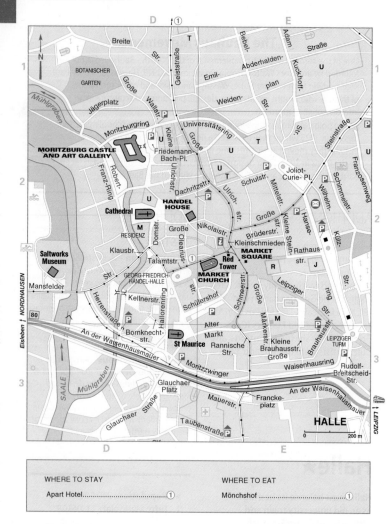

Marktkirche (Market Church)★

Open Jan & Feb Mon–Sat 11.30am–4pm, Sun 3pm–4pm; Mar–Dec Mon–Sat 10am–5pm, Sun 3pm–5pm. ℘(0345) 517 08 94. www.marktkirche-halle.de.

This three-aisled 16C Gothic hall-church was wedged between two existing towers belonging to different Romanesque churches whose naves had been torn down. The **reredos★** of the high altar carries a Virgin and Child painted by a pupil of the Cranach School. The most important exhibit, though, is Luther's death mask on display in its own room in the northwest tower (⊜2€).

The tower can be climbed (Mon–Sat 3pm & 4pm, Sun noon & 1pm; ⊜6€, including guided church tour).

Kunstmuseum Moritzburg★★ (Moritzburg Art Gallery)

Friedemann-Bach-Platz 5. Open daily 10am–6pm (Thu until 8pm). Closed Dec 24 & 31. ⊜6€, 4€ after 5pm, after 6pm Thu). ℘(0345) 21 25 90. www.stiftung-moritzburg.de.

Moritzburg castle was built in the 15C as a residence of the archbishops of Magdeburg and partly converted into a museum in the early 20C. It now houses a significant collection of 19C and 20C **German art**, presenting a sweeping survey of various periods, including Romanticism, Impressionism and Expressionism. Sections of the palace ruined since the Thirty Years' War were recently covered, nearly doubling the exhibit space.

Händel-Haus★

Grosse Nikolaistraße 5. Open Apr–Oct Tue–Sun 10am–6pm; Nov–Mar 10am–5pm. Closed Dec 24–25 & 31. ⌕4€. ♿ ✆(0345) 50 09 00. www.haendel-in-halle.de.

One of the world's most famous composers, **Georg Friedrich Händel** (1685–1759) was born in this big half-timbered house in 1685. Exhibits trace major stations in his life and career as well as regional music history. An adjacent building presents two floors of precious historical musical instruments.

Moritzkirche (St. Maurice)

Hallorenring.

This three-nave church, built between 1388 and 1511, has reticulated and star-vaulted ceilings typical of the Flamboyant Gothic style. Inside are naively expressive sculptures by Conrad Einbeck, most notably the *Man of Sorrows*, the statue of St. Maurice (1411) and a Pietà (1416).

Dom (Cathedral)

Domplatz 3. Open Jun–Oct Mon–Sat 2pm–4pm and by arrangement. ✆(0345) 202 13 79. www.dom-halle.de.

This three-aisled Gothic abbey church (14C) was transformed by Cardinal Albert of Brandenburg in 1520. The statues of Christ, the apostles and saints that decorate the pillars were created around 1520 in the workshop of the gifted sculptor Peter Schroh and foreshadow the Renaissance stylistically.

♟ Technisches Halloren-und Salinemuseum (Salt Museum)

Mansfelder Strasse 52. Open Tue–Sun 10am–5pm. Closed Jan 1, Dec 24–25 & 31. ⌕3.80€. ✆(0345) 209 32 30. www.salinemuseum.de.

The Saltworks Museum has displays on the history of salt mining in the region.

EXCURSIONS

Doppelkapelle Landsberg (Double Chapel)

▶ In Landsberg, 19km/12mi east. ✆Guided tours (1hr) May–Oct Sat 3pm, Sun 11am and 3pm or by appointment. ⌕2€. ✆(0346 02) 206 90.

The Romanesque double chapel of **St. Crucis** sits atop a rocky spur and is one of only 30 chapels in Germany where common people celebrated Mass in the lower chapel while the nobility sat upstairs. The **capitals★** on the columns are richly adorned. From the balcony, there is a superb **view★**.

Eisleben

▶ 34km/21mi west of Halle.

Memories of **Martin Luther** are evoked in this small mining town at his **birthplace** (*Luther-Geburtshaus, Seminarstraße 16*) and the house where he died (**Luther-Sterbehaus**, *Andreaskirchplatz 7*), both now museums on UNESCO's list of World Heritage Sites. He was baptised at the Church of St. Peter and St. Paul, and gave his last sermon at St. Andreas Church. An 1883 Luther statue anchors Marktplatz.

ADDRESSES

🛏 STAY

⊖⊜**Apart Hotel** – *Kohlschütterstraße 5.* ✆*0345 525 90. www.apart-halle.de. 49 rooms.* ⌑. Formerly a privately owned grand villa with high ceilings and stucco decoration, this hotel has rooms and a bar that sport a 1920s theme. There's also a sauna.

♟/EAT

⊖**Mönchshof** – *Talamtstraße 6.* ✆*0345 202 17 26. www.moenchshof-halle.de. Closed Sun dinner.* You'll find reliable regional fare next to the cathedral, amid traditional dark wood-panelling.

Quedlinburg★

Lorded over by a rock pinnacle crowned by a castle and an abbey church, half-timbered Quedlinburg is one of the picture-perfect towns in the Harz region. More than 700 houses in the historic centre are classified as historical monuments, a fact that elevated the town to UNESCO's World Heritage List in 1994.

▶ **Population:** 23 200

Info: Markt 4. ℘(03946) 90 56 24. www.quedlinburg.de.

Location: Quedlinburg is near the A14 autobahn (Leipzig–Magdeburg), and an ideal base for exploring the Harz Mountains.

Don't Miss: The Schlossberg.

Timing: Allow half a day for a leisurely tour of the old town and the Schlossberg.

OLD TOWN★
Markt★ (Market Place)

The early 17C Renaissance **Rathaus** (town hall) borders the northern side of the market place. On the left of the façade stands a statue of Roland (c. 1440). Houses built in the 17C and 18C frame the other three sides of the square.

Historic Streets★

Circle St. Benediktkirche via Markt-straße and Kornmarkt to explore the cobbled lanes behind the **Rathaus**, then return to the Markt along Breit-straße, where several picturesque alleyways open off it. On the far side of the square, stroll towards the castle by way of Wordgasse, Hohe Straße and Blasiistraße. On one side of the charm-ing **Schlossbergplatz★**, at no 12, stands the late 16C **Klopstockhaus** (open Apr–Oct Wed–Sun 10am–5pm; ⊜3.50€; ℘(03946) 2610) in which the poet Friedrich Gottlieb Klopstock was born in 1724. Today it contains exhibits chronicling his life and work.

Lyonel-Feininger-Galerie★

Behind the Klopstock Museum, Finkenherd 5A. Open Apr–Oct daily 10am–6pm; Nov–Mar daily10am–5pm. Closed Dec 24 . ⊜6€. ♿℘(03946) 689 5930. www.feininger-galerie.de.

Schlossberg

© 3quarks/Dreamstime.com

This gallery houses works by Expressionist painter Lyonel Feininger (&see infobox). Born in New York City, Feininger trained in France and Germany, where he exhibited with the *Blaue Reiter* group in 1913. After World War I he joined the Bauhaus.

SCHLOSSBERG★
Stiftskirche St. Servatius★★ (Collegiate Church)

On the site of the original 9C church, the present basilica was begun in 1070 and ranks as one of the most important Romanesque houses of worship in Germany. Beneath the chancel, the **crypt★★** is divided into three aisles with diagonal rib-vaulting decorated by **frescoes★** depicting scenes from the Bible. The **Domschatz★★** (treasury) holds manuscripts and a 10C Gospel. Above all, the **Quedlinburg Knotted Carpet★** is kept in the sacristy.

Enjoy a beautiful **view★** over the city from the large terrace near the church.

Schloss (Palace)

The 16C–17C palace formed part of the abbey, and took on its irregular floor plan due to the rocky base on which the castle was built.

The **Schlossmuseum★** (open Apr–Oct Tue–Sun 10am–6pm; Nov–Mar Tue–Sun 10am–4pm; closed Jan 1, Dec 24–25; ⊜4.50€; ℘(03946) 90 56 81) presents the history of Quedlinburg.

The Abbess' Reception Room, the Throne Room and the Princes' Hall (mid-18C) can be visited.

EXCURSION
Gernrode

● 7km/4.3mi south.

The collegiate church of **St. Cyriacus★**, first documented in 961, is another fine example of Ottonian-period Romanesque architecture with a typical three-aisle nave, flat ceiling and upper galleries. The hall crypt is among the earliest of its type in Germany. Upstairs is the **Holy Sepulchre group★**, a rare example of Romanesque sculpture.

Lyonel Feininger (1871–1956)

Born in New York City to musicians, Feininger was fascinated from a young age by the visual universe of the American metropolis. At the age of 16, he was sent to Germany to study music, but quickly became interested in sculpture and started a career drawing picture books.

Over time, Feininger became a painter known for melding Expressionism and Cubism, and focusing on apparently banal subjects (factories, boats, ports and buildings). In 1919 Walter Gropius invited Feininger to join the Bauhaus, where he taught until the closure of the school by the Nazis.

ADDRESSES

⌂ STAY

⊜⊜⊜ **Ringhotel Theophano** – *Markt 14. ℘(03946) 963 00. www.hotel theophano.de. 26 rooms. ⌐. Restaurant⊜⊜⊜.* The rooms in this hotel are particularly charming, with tasteful pastel tones; some have four-poster beds. The restaurant is housed in the vaulted wine-cellar of this half-timbered building.

⊜⊜⊜⊜ **Schlosshotel Zum Markgrafen** – *Weingarten 30. ℘(03946) 811 40. www.schlosshotel-zum-markgrafen.de. 12 rooms. ⌐.* This beautiful 1898 villa was completely renovated in the 1990s after stints as a Soviet military command post and a textile factory. Surrounded by a small park, it has elegant rooms with stucco ornamentation, coffered ceilings and murals.

Erfurt★

Erfurt, the state capital of Thuringia, is a peaceful, captivating university town with an enchanting silhouette of steeples and bell-towers. The cobbled lanes of its lively old town are lined with carefully restored, centuries-old buildings. It is the main city closest to the geographical centre of reunified Germany.

▶ **Population:** 200 800

🛈 **Info:** Benediktsplatz 1, 99084 Erfurt. ℘(0361) 664 00. www.erfurt-tourismus.de.

◖ **Location:** Erfurt lies off the A4 autobahn, between Gotha and Weimar.

🅿 **Parking:** Garages near the Dom, the main train station and throughout town.

👁 **Don't Miss:** Mariendom, Severikirche.

🕐 **Timing:** Spend about one day seeing the main sights.

A BIT OF HISTORY

A trading town – Erfurt was founded as a bishopric by the English missionary St. Boniface in 742. Its strategic location along the important trade route linking the Rhineland with Russia – the Via Regia – greatly contributed to the town's prosperity in the Middle Ages. So did the production of a much sought-after blue pigment derived from the woad plant. In the 15C, Erfurt joined the Hanseatic League.

Spirituality and Humanism – Nicknamed "Thuringian Rome" because of its roughly 90 churches and chapels, Erfurt has long attracted religious thinkers. The influential Christian mystic **Master Eckhart** was born in nearby Gotha, and in 1298 became prior of Erfurt's Dominican convent and vicar-provincial of Thuringia.

Two centuries later **Martin Luther** shook the religious world with his "95 Theses" protesting Church corruption posted on the church door in Wittenberg. Luther studied at Erfurt university between 1501 and 1505, entered the Augustinian monastery and was ordained as a priest before setting off for Wittenberg in 1511.

AROUND THE DOMPLATZ

The Domplatz is dominated by two imposing houses of worship: the Mariendom (St. Mary's Cathedral) and the Severikirche (Church of St. Severus). In the square's centre, an obelisk commemorates a visit in 1777 by the Archbishop of Mainz.

Dom St. Marien★★ (St. Mary's Cathedral)

Erfurt's most prominent landmark, the cathedral was completed in the 14C and stands on top of several predecessors dating back to the 8C. Its richly ornamented **triangular portals★★** at the north entrance consist of two doors set obliquely and supporting elegant statuary groups depicting the Apostles and the Wise and Foolish Virgins.

The church's **interior** boasts several important artworks: the Romanesque altar of the Virgin (1160); the **bronze candelabrum★** shaped like a man and known as "Wolfram" (1160); the melodious Gloriosa bell (1497); and the intricately worked choir stalls (14C). The stained-glass **windows★** above the choir (c. 1370–1420) depict episodes from the Old and New Testaments as well as from the lives of various saints. Luther was ordained as a priest here in 1507 and held his first lectures in the *Auditorium Coelicum* below the church.

Severikirche★ (Church of St. Severus)

Linked to the cathedral by a sprawling, 70-step open staircase, St. Severi is a five-nave early-Gothic hall church that also harbours its share of treasures. The saint's remains were brought to Erfurt from Ravenna, where, in 836, he served as a bishop; they have been enshrined since the 14C in an elaborate sarcophagus★. Also note the stone Madonna (1345) and the 15m/45ft-high baptismal font (1467)

AROUND THE FISCHMARKT
Fischmarkt (Fish Market)
Inside the imposing neo-Gothic **Rathaus** (town hall; open year-round Mon, Tue, Thu 8am–6pm, Wed until 4pm, Fri until 2pm, Sat–Sun 10am–5pm) are some **frescoes★** illustrating the lives of Luther, Faust and Tannhäuser. The square is framed by magnificent town houses that reflect the wealth of the one-time woad traders. Standouts include the buildings known as "Zum Breiten Herd" and "Zum Roten Ochsen".

Krämerbrücke★ (Merchants' Bridge)
This bridge across the little Gera River, built in 1325, is the only one north of the Alps with houses built on it. Most are narrow, half-timbered structures dating from the 16C to the 19C. The bridge is 18m/59ft wide and 120m/393.7ft long.

Angermuseum★
Anger 18. Open year-round Tue–Sun 10am–6pm. ᴓ6€. ℘(0361) 655 5660. www.angermuseum.de.
This museum presents medieval art from Thuringia in a Baroque building from 1706. Among its highlights are 14C and 15C **altarpieces★★**; a **Pietà★★** by the Master of St. Severinus; and sarcophagi and paintings by Hans Baldung Grien. The focus of the picture gallery is 18C–19C German landscape painting.

Augustinerkloster (Augustinian Monastery)
Guided tours hourly Apr–Oct Mon–Sat 9.30am–5pm, Sun 11am and noon; NovMar Mon–Fri 3.30pm, Sat 9.30am–2pm Sun 11am. ᴓ6€, or 7.5€ with Luther cell. ℘(0361) 576 600. www.augustinerkloster.de.
This austere monastery is an important stop for Martin Luther pilgrims. The Reformer stayed here as an Augustinian monk from 1505–11. Tours take in the room where Luther lived and exhibits about his life and accomplishments.

ᴓ Admission to the church, where he held his first mass, is free.

Zitadelle Petersberg (Petersberg Citadel)
Guided tours offered by the Erfurt tourism bureau (ᴓ5.50-7.50€; ℘0361 66 40 120; www.erfurt-tourismus.de) or by Friends of the Petersberg Citadel (by appointment; ℘(0361) 417 1402; www.petersberg.info).
One of the best-preserved Baroque fortifications in central Europe, this citadel was built between 1665 and 1707 atop the foundations of a Benedictine monastery. It contains a **museum** on military history (open daily 10am–6pm), but to explore the subterranean defensive tunnels you must join a guided tour.

EXCURSION
Gotha★
▶ 25km/15.5mi west via the B7.
One of the oldest settlements in Thuringia (775), Gotha prospered as an important trade-route stop in the Middle Ages. After the Thirty Years' War, the local dukes built the first and largest Baroque palace in Thuringia: the U-shaped **Schloss Friedenstein** (open Tue–Sun 10am–5pm; Nov–Apr until 4pm; ᴓ10€; ℘03621 82 34 0; www.stiftungfriedenstein.de), now home to several museums.
If you have limited time, focus on the **Schlossmuseum**, whose extravagant rooms are a perfect backdrop for an eclectic collection of coins, sculpture, antiques, etchings and even objects from Ancient Egypt. Walls are graced with paintings by such masters as Cranach the Elder and Rubens, although top billing actually goes to the famous *Gotha Lovers* by an anonymous artist. The **Kunstkammer** (art chamber) boasts such exotic items as engraved ostrich eggs, carved ivory and decorated coconut shells.
The other museums deal with local folk art and nature, but more interesting is the Baroque **Ekhof-Theater**.

Weimar★★

Many non-Germans associate Weimar with the ill-fated Weimar Republic, which existed uneasily between World War I and the Hitler years. But in fact, the town's claim to fame in European history rests unerringly on the extraordinary flowering of intellectual and artistic talent here, attracting Luther, Cranach, Bach, Wieland, Schiller, Liszt and, perhaps most importantly, Germany's greatest classical poet, Johann Wolfgang von Goethe.

A BIT OF HISTORY

Intellectual and cultural hotbed – Weimar's heyday coincided with the succession, in 1758, of Duchess Anna Amalia. It was during her reign that the town's intellectual reputation grew, largely because of **Goethe** (1749–1832). He was appointed minister of the small, provincial capital and produced the majority of his life's work here, including his dramatic masterpiece, *Faust*.
Goethe's success went hand-in-hand with that of **Friedrich von Schiller**, who moved permanently to Weimar in 1799. The work produced by these two close friends, along with the writings of the theologian **Johann Gottfried Herder** (1744–1803), a disciple of Kant, raised Weimar's literary reputation to that of "home of German Classicism".

▸ **Population:** 64 400

🛈 **Info:** Markt 10. 📞(03643) 74 50. www.weimar.de.

◖ **Location:** Set on the banks of the Ilm, Weimar is in the heart of Thuringia, around 20km/12.4mi from the state capital Erfurt. The A4 autobahn links the town with Dresden to the east and Frankfurt to the southwest (via the A5).

🅿 **Parking:** Convenient central parking is in a garage near the Goethe House.

✦ **Don't Miss:** The suggested walking tour, Buchenwald.

🕐 **Timing:** Allocate a full day to truly sample Weimar's legacy, especially if visiting Buchenwald.

A couple of centuries earlier, from 1552 until his death a year later, **Lucas Cranach the Elder** had worked in Weimar on his final masterpiece: the altarpiece triptych for the Parish Church of St. Peter and St. Paul. **Johann Sebastian Bach** was organist and choirmaster here from 1708 to 1717. In 1848 **Franz Liszt** took the position, and became the driving force behind Weimar's School of Music, which still bears his name today. In 1860, Grand Duke Alexander founded the **Weimarer Malerschule** (Fine Arts

Statues of Goethe and Schiller

Academy), where a numerous late-19C artists studied, including Hans Arp, Max Liebermann and Christian Rohlfs.

It was under the influence of such celebrated graduates as **Arnold Böcklin** (1827–1901) that painters spearheading the contemporary avant-garde movement developed the "Weimar School". Under Walter Gropius, the institution spawned the Bauhaus, the influential college of architecture and design.

The Weimar Republic (1919–33) – The constitution of the Weimar Republic was drafted and adopted in 1919 by the German National Assembly as delegates convened at the Deutsches Nationaltheater (German National Theatre). The government itself, however, was never based in Weimar as members returned to Berlin just one week after adopting the text. The humanist tradition of Goethe's town had merely provided the budding democracy with a welcome counterpoint to the politically oppressive atmosphere of postwar Berlin.

✒.WALKING TOUR

HISTORIC CENTRE★★

Weimar's chief highlights – mostly related to heroes of the German Renaissance or Enlightenment – cluster within a compact area in the bustling pedestrian city centre. The main squares are Theaterplatz, with the National Theatre and Bauhaus Museum, and the neighbouring Marktplatz.

Goethes Nationalmuseum und Wohnhaus★★ (Goethe National Museum and Private Residence)

Frauenplan 1. Open Apr–Sept Tue–Sun 9.30am–6pm; Oct–Mar Tue–Sun until 4pm. Closed Dec 24. ☜12€. ✆(03643) 54 54 00. www.klassik-stiftung.de.

Germany's greatest man of letters lived in this 1709 Baroque mansion for 50 years, first as a tenant then, after 1792, as owner until his death in 1832. The interior is largely the way he left it. The living room, study, library and bedroom are all furnished with paintings and sculptures from Goethe's times.

Tickets also give access to a permanent exhibition next door that is concerned less with the man himself than with the period of the Enlightenment and all the great minds that shaped it, including Wieland, Herder, Schiller, Anna Amalia and her son, Duke Carl August.

▶ Exit the museum and follow Ackerwand to Frau von Stein House.

Haus der Frau von Stein

Ackerwand 25.

Charlotte von Stein, lady-in-waiting to Anna Amalia and Goethe's longtime muse, lived in this house for 50 years until her death in 1827. For now, the building is still home to the Goethe Institute language school and cultural centre. However, in 2008 the city sold the building to a Spanish art collector who has financed its badly needed restoration, initiated in June 2014 and expected to take one year; plans for the house include a Dalí exhibition centre with café and restaurant, as well as a 14-room inn.

▶ Continue to the end of Ackerwand, which leads to Platz der Demokratie.

Platz der Demokratie

The equestrian statue of Grand Duke Carl August dominates this square. On the south side, the former palace (1757–74) is occupied by the **Franz Liszt Hochschule für Musik**. The 16C–18C **Grünes Schloss** (Green Palace) houses the **Duchess Anna Amalia Library** (open year-round Tue–Sun 9.30am–2.30pm; ☜7.50€; ✆03643 54 54 01; www.klassik-stiftung.de) with medieval manuscripts, early printed works, rare 16C–17C documents and 18C volumes. The library re-opened in late 2007 after being partially destroyed in a devastating fire three years earlier.

▶ Leave Platz der Demokratie, and head for the Markt and Cranach-Haus.

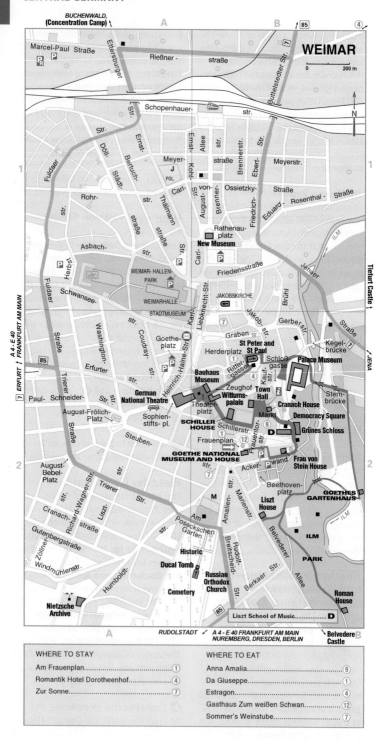

WEIMAR

0 | 200 m

BUCHENWALD, (Concentration Camp)

Marcel-Paul Straße

Rießner- straße

Schopenhauer-

A 4 - E 40 FRANKFURT AM MAIN

ERFURT / FRANKFURT AM MAIN

Tiefurt Castle

JENA

New Museum

WEIMAR-HALLEN-PARK

WEIMARHALLE

STADTMUSEUM

JAKOBSKIRCHE

Goethe-platz

Herderplatz

St Peter and St Paul

Palace Museum

Bauhaus Museum

German National Theatre

Theater-platz

Wittums-palais

Town Hall

Cranach House

Democracy Square

Grünes Schloss

SCHILLER HOUSE

GOETHE NATIONAL MUSEUM AND HOUSE

Frau von Stein House

GOETHES GARTENHAUS

Liszt House

ILM PARK

Historic Ducal Tomb

Russian Orthodox Church

Cemetery

Nietzsche Archive

Roman House

Liszt School of Music.............................. D

RUDOLSTADT

A 4 - E 40 FRANKFURT AM MAIN NUREMBERG, DRESDEN, BERLIN

Belvedere Castle

WHERE TO STAY	
Am Frauenplan	①
Romantik Hotel Dorotheenhof	④
Zur Sonne	⑦

WHERE TO EAT	
Anna Amalia	⑨
Da Giuseppe	①
Estragon	④
Gasthaus Zum weißen Schwan	⑫
Sommer's Weinstube	⑦

Cranach-Haus

The famous painter spent the last years of his life in this Renaissance house (1547–49) at Markt 12, adorned with scrolled gables. His studio was on the third floor.

The **Rathaus** (town hall), opposite, was built c. 1500 but was heavily remodelled in the mid-19C.

▶ Take Schillerstraße in the direction of Theaterplatz.

Schillers Wohnhaus★ (Schiller's Private House)

Schillerstraße 12. Open Apr–Oct Tue–Sun 9.30am–6pm; Nov–Mar Tue–Sun 9.30am–4pm. Closed Dec 24. ✆7.50€. ☏(03643) 54 54 00. www.klassik-stiftung.de.

Schiller moved here in 1802 to be near his great friend Goethe, and in this house he wrote *William Tell* and *The Bride of Messina*. The museum examines his life and work.

▶ Continue to Theaterplatz.

Deutsches Nationaltheater (German National Theatre)

Theaterplatz 2. www.nationaltheater-weimar.de.

The present 1907 structure was built on the site of a 1779 Baroque building. It was in this previous theatre that Schiller's great plays were staged and directed by Goethe, and it was here, in 1850, that Richard Wagner's *Lohengrin* was first performed. In 1919 the German National Assembly adopted the constitution of the Weimar Republic here. In front of the present building stand the **statues★★** of Goethe and Schiller, sculpted in 1857 by Ernst Rietschel.

Bauhaus-Museum

Theaterplatz. Open year-round daily 10am–6pm. ✆4.50€. ☏(03643) 545 400. www.klassik-stiftung.de.

The Bauhaus School was founded in 1919 Weimar by Walter Gropius and cohorts and occupied this building until the group was forced to move to Dessau in 1925. The small permanent collection introduces the major players, their innovative approach to architecture and design and their impact on the modern aesthetic. Exhibits also pay homage to the School of Applied Arts founded in Weimar in 1908 by Henry Van de Velde.

Wittumspalais

Theaterplatz. Open Apr–Oct Tue–Sun 10am–6pm; Nov–Mar Tue–Sun 10am–4pm. Closed 24 Dec. ✆6€. ☏(03643) 54 54 00. www.klassik-stiftung.de.

After her husband's death, Anna Amalia moved to this Baroque palace where she held her illustrious salons with Goethe, Schiller, Herder and Wieland in attendance. Rooms are representative of the late 18C for a person of her standing. Note the Neoclassical ballroom and the late Baroque ceiling frescoes.

▶ Go to Herderplatz via Zeughof, then Rittergasse.

Stadtkirche St. Peter und Paul (or Herderkirche)

Am Herderplatz.

This triple-nave Gothic hall-church was built between 1498–1500 but turned Baroque-style in the 18C. It is also known as the Herderkirche, in memory of the sermons preached here between 1776 and 1803 by the philosopher Johann Gottfried Herder, who is buried here.

The famous **Cranach Triptych★★**, begun by Lucas Cranach the Elder and finished by his son in 1555, represents the Crucifixion on its central panel and is surrounded by scenes from the Old and New Testaments. Luther and Cranach the Elder are depicted on the right.

▶ Follow Schloßgasse to the square.

Schlossmuseum (Palace Museum)

Open Apr–Oct Tue–Sun 9.30am–6pm; Nov–Mar 9.30am–4pm. ✆7.50€. ☏(03643) 54 54 00. www.klassikstiftung.de.

Built under Duke Carl August, the early 19C city palace (*Stadtschloss*) features some of Germany's finest Neoclassicist apartments and important Weimar artworks. Highlights include a **Cranach collection★★**; Flemish and Italian paintings; and work by Hans Baldung Grien, Albrecht Dürer and Bartholomäus Bruyn the Elder. The Weimar School and German Impressionists and Expressionists (Max Beckmann, Max Liebermann) are also represented.

Ilm Park★★

"Weimar is in fact a park in which they happened to build a town," wrote Adolf Stahr in 1851. Expansive green spaces continue to shape modern Weimar. This magnificent riverside park parallels both banks of the Ilm River from the palace of Tiefurt to the Belvedere, yet is steps from the town centre.

Goethes Gartenhaus★★

Open Apr–Oct Tue–Sun 10am–6pm; Nov–Mar 10am–4pm. ⊛6€. ℘(03643) 54 54 00. www.klassik-stiftung.de.
Duke Carl August gave this summer residence as a gift to Goethe, and the great man liked it so much that he frequently used it a retreat until the end of his life. *Wilhelm Meister's Theatrical Mission*, major parts of *Iphigenia*, and early drafts of *Egmont* and *Torquato Tasso* were written in this humble cottage.

▶ Cross the park in the direction of the Belvederer Allee.

Liszt-Haus

Marienstraße 17. Open Apr–Oct Tue–Sun 10am–6pm; Nov–Mar Tue–Sun 10am–4pm. ⊛4€. ℘(03643) 54 54 00. www.klassik-stiftung.de.
The great composer lived and taught in this converted garden house between 1869 and 1886. The period rooms are preserved so neatly it feels as though Liszt could be returning at any moment. His study, living, dining and bedrooms are filled with personal items; note the Bechstein grand piano.

ADDITIONAL SIGHTS

Neues Museum

Rathenauplatz. Open Apr–mid-Nov Wed–Mon 10am–6pm; late Nov–Mar 10am–4pm. ⊛4€. ♿℘(03643)54 54 00. www.klassik-stiftung.de.
This 19C neo-Renaissance building presents art by the international avant-garde since 1960, with emphasis on German art, Italian *Arte Povera*, and American Minimal and Conceptual Art. During the Third Reich it was the headquarters of Thuringia's Nazi administration.

Fürstengruft (Ducal Tomb)

Historischer Friedhof.
Johann Wolfgang von Goethe is buried alongside Grand Duke Carl August and Weimar's other ducal rulers in a **mausoleum** (open Apr–Oct Wed–Mon 10am–6pm; Nov–Mar 10am–4pm ⊛4€; ℘03643 54 54 00; www.klassik-stiftung.de) in the 19C **Historischer Friedhof** (historical cemetery). A 2006 investigation found that other remains, believed to have been those of Schiller, were not.
The **Russian Orthodox Church** nearby was built in the 19C for Maria Pavlova, Grand Duchess and daughter-in-law of Carl August. Goethe's muse, Frau von Stein, is also buried in this cemetery.

Nietzsche-Archiv (Nietzsche Archive)

Humboldtstraße 36. Open Apr–Oct Tue–Sun 11am–5pm. ⊛3€. ℘(03643) 54 5 400. www.klassik-stiftung.de.
The philosopher **Friedrich Nietzsche** (1844–1900) spent the last three years of his life in this house. Suffering from mental illness, he was nursed by his sister, Elisabeth. After his death, in her role as self-appointed caretaker of her brother's intellectual property, she moved the Nietzsche Archive, which she had founded in 1894, to this building, and hired Henry Van de Velde to turn the ground floor into an exhibit space. The most beautiful part of the archive is the **library★**. Notice the bust of Nietzsche by Max Klinger. Documents chronicle the life and works of the author of *Also sprach Zarathustra*.

EXCURSION
Buchenwald Museum and Memorial

▶ 8km/5mi northwest. Open Apr–Oct Tue–Sun 10am–6pm; Nov–Mar 10am–4pm. Grounds open until dusk. Closed Jan 1, Dec 24–26 & 31. ♿ ☏(03 643) 430 200. www.buchenwald.de.

Near Weimar, in the Ettersberg Forest, stood one of the largest Nazi concentration camps. Some 250 000 people were deported to Buchenwald; over 50 000 died there before the camp was liberated by Americans on 11 April 1945.

The **Gedenkstätte Buchenwald** (memorial centre) shows a film tracing the history of the camp. A tour of the camp starts at the gatehouse, still bearing the chilling slogan: *"Jedem das Seine"* ("You get what you deserve"). Each residential barrack is outlined on the ground; at the far end, a building used for storing the inmates' possessions is now a museum. Outside the camp, a road leads to the quarry where prisoners were worked to death.

From 1945 to 1950, the Soviet occupation force set up **Special Camp 2**, in which Nazi criminals, officials and political prisoners were interned. Over 7 000 are believed to have died here. From the entrance *(1km/0.6mi towards Weimar)* the Steles' Way leads to the **Avenue of Nations**, which links three mass graves. The last of these brings you to the **Buchenwald Memorial**. In 1943, some 20 000 prisoners were sent to Camp Dora, north of Nordhausen (☏ *see map p247)*, to convert underground shafts into a manufacturing plant for V-2 rockets. It too is a memorial today.

ADDRESSES

🏨 STAY

🛏 **Hotel Zur Sonne** – *Rollplatz 2.* ☏*(03643) 862 90. www.thueringen.info/ hotel-zur-sonne.html. 21 rooms.* ☕. *Restaurant*🍴. This neat brick house sits in the heart of the old town. Rooms are modern and attractively furnished, and the restaurant is a no-nonsense tavern-style.

🛏🛏 **Hotel Am Frauenplan** – *Brauhausgasse 10.* ☏*03643 494 40. www.hotel-am-frauenplan.de. 48 rooms.* ☕. Opposite Goethe's former home, this was once the palace of the Countess von Bernstoff. Bedrooms are comfortable and cosy. Breakfast is served in the courtyard when warm.

🛏🛏🛏 **Romantik Hotel Dorotheenhof** – *Dorotheenhof 1, 99427 Weimar–Schöndorf.* ☏*(03643) 45 90. www.dorotheenhof.com. 60 rooms.* ☕. *Restaurant* 🍴🍴🍴. This pretty hotel, in an idyllic park location above the town, used to belong to a 19C cavalry captain and now delights guests with cosy country-style rooms. The elegant restaurant is canopied by a charming vaulted ceiling.

🍴 EAT

🍴 **Estragon** – *Herderplatz 3.* ☏*03643 90 85 99. www.acc-cafe.de.* Opposite the Church of St. Peter and St. Paul, this eatery is a good little find; the menu is based on simple, flavoursome organic soups and salads.

🍴 **Sommer's Weinstube Restaurant** – *Humboldtstraße 2.* ☏*(03643) 40 06 91. www.wein-sommer.com. Closed Sun.* This family-run restaurant exudes an old-fashioned charm. The wine list complements Thuringian specialities.

🍴 **Trattoria Da Giuseppe** – *Eisenfeld.* ☏*03643 81 48 38. Closed all day Sun, and Mon and Tue evenings.* The locals come to Guiseppe's inviting trattoria for his pizzas, fresh tagliatelle and red wines, sourced direct from Italy.

🍴🍴🍴 **Gasthaus zum Weissen Schwan** – *Frauentorstraße 23.* ☏*(03643) 90 87 51. www.weisserschwan.de. Closed Sun–Mon.* This inn was a favourite with Goethe. Thuringian food is served.

🍴🍴🍴🍴 **Restaurant Anna Amalia** – *Markt 19, in Hotel Elephant.* ☏*(03643) 80 26 39. www.restaurant-anna-amalia. com. Closed Sun and Mon dinner.* This sophisticated restaurant is a perfect setting in which to enjoy Marcello Fabbri's classic Mediterranean-influenced cuisine.

Jena

Jena has developed steadily since the foundation of its university in 1548, drawing numerous scientists and intellectuals over the centuries, including Wilhelm von Humboldt, Schiller and Hegel. Goethe worked on his philosophical treatise while French and Prussian armies battled outside the gates in 1806. Jena is also famous for its optics, established in the mid-19C by Carl Zeiss and Ernst Abbe, inventors of the scientific microscope.

▶ **Population:** 102 500

🛈 **Info:** Markt 16, 07743 Jena. ℘(03641) 49 80 50. www.jenatourismus.de.

◗ **Location:** Jena is northeast of the Thuringian Forest, just off the A4 autobahn and about 23km/14.3mi east of Weimar.

⊘ **Don't Miss:** Zeiss Planetarium and Optical Museum.

🕐 **Timing:** Jena can be explored in a day.

👥 **Kids:** Zeiss Planetarium.

SIGHTS

Johannistor (St. John's Gate)
Along with the Pulverturm on the other side of the Marktplatz (market square), this gate is all that remains of the 14C fortifications.

Stadtmuseum and Kunstsammlung (City Museum and Art Collection)
Open year-round Tue, Wed & Fri 10am–5pm, Thu 3pm–10pm, Sat–Sun 11am–6pm. Closed Jan 1, Dec 24–25 & 31. ⊛4€. ℘(03641) 49 82 61. www.stadtmuseum.jena.de.

This museum presents regional art and milestones in Jena's history in a partially half-timbered building.

Stadtkirche St. Michaelis
This collegiate church of the Cistercians got a Gothic facelift in the 15C. Note the canopied porch on the south side.

Goethe-Gedenkstätte (Goethe Memorial)
Fürstengraben 26. Open Apr–Oct Mon–Sun 11am–3pm. Closed May 1, Ascension Day. ⊛1€. ℘(03641) 93 11 88. Exhibits in this former inspector's house at the Botanical Gardens, where Goethe stayed while in Jena, focus mostly on his accomplishments as a politician and natural scientist.

Schillers Gartenhaus (Schiller Museum)
Schillergässchen 2. Open Tue–Sun 11am–5pm (Nov–Mar Tue–Sat) . Closed public holidays. ⊛2.50€. ℘(03641) 93 11 88. www.uni-jena.de/gartenhaus.html. Schiller wrote several of his famous works (Wallenstein, Maria Stuart) while spending the summers of 1797 to 1799 in this garden house. Ground-floor exhibits track his life in Jena, while upstairs, the family's private quarters include his study and bedroom.

Stadtkirche St. Michaelis

© Volker Lissner/Fotolia.com

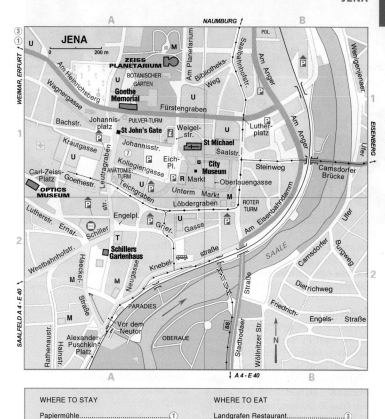

NAUMBURG
JENA
WEIMAR, ERFURT
EISENBERG
SAALFELD A 4 - E 40
A 4 - E 40

WHERE TO STAY		WHERE TO EAT	
Papiermühle	①	Landgrafen Restaurant	③
		Scala - Das Turm Restaurant	⑦

👤👤 Zeiss Planetarium★

Open year-round Tue–Sun, showtimes vary. ⌒8.50€–9.50€ (child 7€– 8€). ♿ ℘(036 41) 88 54 88. www. planetarium-jena.de.
This state-of-the-art planetarium presents celestial shows geared towards both adults and children.

Optisches Museum★ (Optics Museum)

Carl-Zeiss-Platz 12. Open year-round Tue–Fri 10am–4.30pm, Sat 11am–5pm. Closed public holidays. ⌒5€. ♿ ℘(03641) 44 31 65.
www.optischesmuseum.de.
The museum retraces 500 years of the history of optics with a collection of spectacles, telescopes and photographic equipment. You can also visit a workshop from 1866.

🚗 DRIVING TOUR

UPPER SAALE VALLEY★

From Rudolstadt to Saalburg. 61km/38mi. Allow 4hrs.

The winding Saale River forms a natural link between towns like Jena and Halle, masterpieces of sacred architecture like Merseburg and Naumburg, and numerous riverside castles.

Rudolstadt

Once the seat of the princes of Schwarzburg-Rudolstadt, this town is dominated by the fine silhouette of 18C **Schloss Heidecksburg★** (open Tue– Sun 10am–6pm, Nov–Mar until 5pm); ⌒7€; ℘03672 429 00; www.heidecks-burg.de). Several magnificent Rococo

Feengrotten

© bfh/Fotolia.com

rooms★★ are open to the public, and there's also a regional history museum. **Views★** from up here are particularly delightful.

Saalfeld

The façade of the Renaissance **Rathaus** (town hall) in Marktplatz (market square) centres on a stepped tower with two oriel windows. The historic rooms of a Franciscan abbey house the **Stadtmuseum Saalfeld** (open year-round Tue–Sun 10am–5pm; closed Dec 24 & 31; ✆5€; ♿; ℘03671 59 84 71; www.museumimkloster.de), with collections on local history and folklore.

👤👥 Feengrotten★ (Fairy Grottoes)

⏵ 1km/0.6mi southeast of Saalfeld on the B281. 🔁Guided tours (45min) May–Oct daily 9.30am–5pm; Nov–Apr 10.30am–3.30pm (Jan Sat and Sun only); ✆15.50€ (child 10€). ℘(03671) 550 40. www.feengrotten.de.

The subterranean grottoes of this abandoned slate mine are a whimsical wonderland with stalactite and stalagmite formations sparkling in a myriad of fantastic colours.

⏵ Leave Saalfeld on the B85. Cross the Saale at the Hohenwarte Dam and drive along the Hohenwarte reservoir (Talsperre) for 10km/6.2mi via Drognitz and Remptendorf to the Bleiloch reservoir.

Saalburg

Now a lakeside town, Saalburg lost its outskirts when the valley was flooded. Note the remains of the 16C fortifications.

ADDRESSES

🛏️STAY

☞ **Hotel Papiermühle** – *Erfurter Straße 102. ℘03 641 45 98 98. www.papiermuehle-jena.de. 24 rooms. ☐.* Two pretty brick houses make up this family-run hotel and inn dating to 1737. Bedrooms are decorated with dark-wood furnishings.

🍴/EAT

☞☞ **Landgrafen** – *Landgrafenstieg 25. ℘03 641 50 70 71. closed Mon and Tue, except public holidays. www.landgrafen.com.* Known as "The Balcony of Jena" because of its breathtaking views over the city, this restaurant immediately beneath the town's landmark tower offers homemade Thüringer cuisine.

☞☞☞ **SCALA – Das Turm Restaurant** – *Leutragraben 1. ℘03 641 35 66 66. www.scala-jena.de.* Patrons enjoy international fine dining with panoramic views through floor-to-ceiling windows at this restaurant.

Naumburg★

Pretty Naumburg lies on the edge of the Thuringian basin, surrounded by terraced vineyards and wooded hillsides topped by castles. Lordly town houses, sturdy fortifications and above all, the exceptional cathedral still reflect the town's heritage as a wealthy medieval trading centre. The philosopher Friedrich Nietzsche spent a lot of time in the town at various stages of his life.

▶ **Population:** 30 000

🔲 **Info:** Markt 6, 06618 Naumburg. ℘(03445) 27 31 20. www.naumburg-tourismus.de.

◖ **Location:** Naumburg is in the heart of the Saale-Unstrut wine-growing region, about 50km/31mi south of Halle.

◈ **Don't Miss:** Cathedral St. Peter and St. Paul.

🕐 **Timing:** Allow half a day to see Naumburg.

A BIT OF HISTORY

The seat of a bishopric since 1028, Naumburg started developing as a civic entity in the 12C, becoming an important trading centre in the late Middle Ages. The "Peter-Pauls-Messe" held here was a serious rival to the trade fair in Leipzig. Largely spared damage during World War II, in 1991 Naumburg was one of five cities in the former East Germany to be selected as a model for restoring historic city centres.

SIGHTS

Dom Sts. Peter und Paul★★ (Cathedral of Saints Peter and Paul)

Domplatz 16/17. Open Mar–Oct daily 9am–6pm (Sun from 11am); Nov–Feb 10am–4pm (Sun from noon). ₰6.50€. ℘(03445) 23 01 10. www.naumburger-dom.de.

This double-chancel cathedral is a perfect example of the stylistic evolution from late Romanesque to early Gothic. The Romanesque nave was built in the early 13C; by the late 13C the western section was completed with early-Gothic features.

The eastern chancel is separated from the central nave by the only remaining hall-church rood screen in Germany. The western chancel is bathed in ethereal light thanks to extraordinarily luminous stained-glass windows. It features another magnificent **rood screen★★**. This one is by the artist known only as the Master of Naumburg and depicts poignant, lifelike scenes of the Passion. The splendid central portal shows a Crucifixion group, surmounted by the Majesty of God as a fresco in a quatrefoil. The same master also created the famous **statues★★★** of the cathedral's benefactors, Uta and Ekkehard.

Marktplatz (Market Square)

The large market square is framed by 16C–17C houses as well as the **Town Hall**. A late-Gothic building, it has a beautiful portal from 1612 and boasts six transverse gables with tracery decoration. The same façade design is repeated on the Schlösschen (1543), behind which towers the church of St. Wencelas. The Hohe Lilie (municipal museum), with its late-Gothic corbie gable and traced transom, stands at the entrance to Herrenstraße.

St. Wenzel-Kirche★ (Church of St. Wenceslas)

A church on this site was first recorded in 1228. The present building was constructed in the 15C as a late-Gothic hall-church. Features added during the Renaissance include five tribunes built between 1610 and 1618.

In the 18C, though, the interior got its Baroque makeover resulting in a mirror-vaulted ceiling, and a magnificent carved altar and pulpit. The organ is one of the largest surviving ones built by **Zacharias Hildebrand** and was put through its paces by none other than

Organ, St. Wenzel-Kirche

©Milan Systemtechnik/istockphoto.com

the famous composer Johann Sebastian Bach himself. Inside the church are also two fine paintings by **Lucas Cranach the Elder**: *The Adoration of the Magi* (1522) and *The Blessing of the Children* (1529).

Joys of the Grape

Two lovely rivers give Germany's northernmost wine-growing region its name: the Saale and the Unstrut. Only 665ha/1 643 acres in size, this area has a viticultural heritage going back 1 000 years and considers Freyburg as its unofficial capital. Some 30 grape varieties grow in these limestone and red sandstone soils, on vineyards clinging to steep riverside terraces that are drenched by up to 1 600 hours of sunshine a year. Most varietals are dry, fresh and white, with Müller-Thurgau as the leader, followed by Weissburgunder (pinot blanc), Silvaner and Riesling.
Only a quarter is dedicated to red wines, mostly Dornfelder and red Burgundy.

Town Houses

In Jakobstraße note the **Alte Post** (1574) with its three-storey oriel. Houses in **Marienstraße** sport ornate portals that reflect the burghers' one-time prosperity. **Herrenstraße** features some fine oriels, including the town's oldest house at no 1. The Lorbeerapotheke, an old pharmacy next door, has a splendid oriel, as does the house at no 8 (1525).

Marientor (St. Mary's Gate)

This is the only one of the five original town gates to have survived. It is a rare example of a double gate with gatehouses, a curved courtyard to trap intruders, and a watchpath. It is 14C at its core but was extended in the 15C.

Nietzsche-Haus

Weingarten 18. Open year round Tue–Fri 2pm–5pm, Sat–Sun 10am–5pm. 3€. ℘(03445) 20 16 38. www.mv-naumburg.de.
From 1890 until 1897, during his mental and physical decline, Nietzsche was cared for in this house by his mother. Photos and documents evoke the intellectual life and body of work created by this controversial philosopher.

Eisenach★★

The history of Eisenach is closely linked with the reformer Martin Luther, who went to school here and later translated the New Testament into German while in hiding at Wartburg castle. Eisenach is also the birthplace of the composer Johann Sebastian Bach and a gateway to the Thuringian Forest.

▶ **Population:** 44 100
▌ **Info:** Markt 24, 99817 Eisenach. ℘(03691) 792 30. www.eisenach.de.
◖ **Location:** Eisenach is on the northwestern edge of the Thuringian Forest, just off the A4 autobahn.
⊛ **Don't Miss:** The Wartburg.
◷ **Timing:** Allow at least three hours for the Wartburg.

A BIT OF HISTORY

At the heart of Germany – At the beginning of the 13C, the *Minnesänger* (℘ *see INTRODUCTION: Music*) held legendary singing contests in the Wartburg, a custom that inspired Wagner's opera *Tannhäuser.*

Martin Luther attended school in Eisenach and sought refuge at the Wartburg in 1521–22 while under papal ban. He translated the New Testament from the Greek into the German vernacular here (℘ *see INTRODUCTION: History*). Eisenach is also the 1685 birthplace of composer **Johann Sebastian Bach**.

WARTBURG★★

Allow 2hrs. Park in the pay car park below the castle and walk about 15min or take bus 10 from the train station or Karlsplatz. ☞Guided tours (1hr) Apr–

Oct daily 8.30am–5pm, gates close at 8pm; Nov–Mar daily 9am–3.30pm, gates close at 5pm; (English tour year-round at 1.30pm); ☞9€. ℘(036 91) 25 00. www.wartburg-eisenach.de.

Built between 1155 and 1180, Wartburg castle is one of the best-preserved and most imposing Romanesque structures, despite later alterations in other architectural styles. It has been on UNESCO's list of World Heritage Sites since 2000. Perched on a rocky spur, the castle welcomes visitors through a 12C entrance leading into a 15C–16C **outer courtyard** *(Erster Burghof)* framed by half-timbered buildings. Inside the fortified complex is the **Palas★**, where the landgraves resided. Enjoy sweeping **views★** of Eisenach, the Thuringian Forest and the Rhön foothills from the ramparts and south tower.

Wartburg

© Eisenach-Wartburgregion Touristik GmbH

Martin Luther in the Wartburg

After refusing to renounce his reformist views at the Diet of Worms on 18 April 1521, Martin Luther (*see INTRODUCTION: History*) was excommunicated, declared an outlaw and placed under papal ban. To prevent his arrest, his protector Frederick III, the Elector of Saxony, spirited Luther to the Wartburg where he spent the next 10 months living as an anonymous knight named Junker Jörg. He spent his days translating the New Testament from Greek into German, a major linguistic achievement that helped unify the many German dialects into a common language. More profoundly, though, it made the Bible more accessible to ordinary people, which contributed greatly to the success of the Reformation movement.

Tours take in the **Hall of the Troubadours** (Sängersaal), where Moritz von Schwind's monumental fresco illustrates the *Minnesänger* contest. Tours end in the **museum** and the **Lutherstube**, the austerely furnished room where Martin Luther stayed while working on his translation.

ADDITIONAL SIGHTS
Markt
The market place is bordered by administrative buildings and town houses surrounding a fountain with a statue of Eisenach's patron saint, St. George.

Schloss (Castle)
Markt 24. Open year-round Wed–Sun 11am–5pm. ⌾4€. ℘(036 91) 67 04 50.
The former residence of the local dukes houses the **Thüringer Museum**, a collection of porcelain, paintings and folk art from the 18C–20C.

Rathaus (Town Hall)
Eisenach's three-storey 16C town hall was built on the site of an old tavern and blends Baroque and Renaissance elements. It was remodelled after a fire in 1636. Note that the tower is slightly tilted.

Georgenkirche
Markt. Open Apr–Oct daily 10am –12.30pm, 2pm–5pm; Nov–Mar daily 10am–noon and 2pm–4pm.
℘(03691) 21 31 26.
This triple-aisled 16C church contains the tombs of several landgraves of Thuringia. Luther preached here in 1521 despite his being officially banned from the Holy Roman Empire. Johann Sebastian Bach was baptised here in 1685.

Predigerkirche
The late 13C early-Gothic church houses the **wooden sculpture collection★** formerly in the Thuringian Museum. Carvings date from the 12C–16C.

Lutherhaus
Lutherplatz 8. Closed for renovation until at least mid-2015; exhibit relocated to Creutznacher Haus (across the street at Markt 9) open Apr–Oct daily 10am–5pm (closed Mon Nov–Mar). Closed Dec 24–Jan 1 ⌾6€. ℘(03691) 298 30. www.lutherhaus-eisenach.de.
Martin Luther lived in this half-timbered house between 1498 and 1501 while studying at the Latin School. A modern exhibition uses paintings, documents and multimedia terminals to tell the story of his life and accomplishments.

Bachhaus (Bach Museum)
Frauenplan 21. Open year-round daily 10am–6pm. ⌾8.50€. ♿℘(03691) 793 40. www.bachhaus.de.
The actual house where Johann Sebastian Bach first saw the light of day no longer exists, but it looked very much like the 600-year-old half-timbered structure that now holds a museum dedicated to the composer.
Recently expanded and modernised, it traces his life and accomplishments

through manuscripts, scores and portraits of the prolific Bach family. Visits include a live concert played on period instruments. A new annex has listening stations.

Automobile Welt Eisenach

Friedrich-Naumann-Straße 10. Open year-round Tue–Sun 11am–5pm. ⍟5€. ♿ ✆(03691) 772 12. www.awe-stiftung.de. Vehicle manufacturing has been part of Eisenach's history since 1896 and car buffs and nostalgic types should make a beeline to this automobile museum housed in the original 1935 plant. Boxy GDR-era vehicles, a 1907 Wartburg Dixi, cool sports cars and eccentric prototypes are among the collections.

🚗 DRIVING TOUR

THURINGIAN FOREST★★

Eisenach to Ilmenau. 110km/68mi
Allow 1 day.

The Thuringian Forest is one of the most beautiful natural regions in Germany and is hugely popular with hikers, cross-country skiers and outdoor types. The mid-level massif is littered with charming villages where traditional skills and craftsmanship are kept alive.

The delightful forest road mainly parallels the **Rennsteig**, a 168km/104mi-long 🚶 hiking trail that keeps to the forest's higher elevations, crossing the Großer Inselsberg (916m/3 005ft) and Großer Beerberg (983m/3 225ft) peaks.

▶ Leave Eisenach in the direction of Gotha.

Großer Inselsberg

🚶1hr round-trip walk.
The **views★★** from the summit take in much of the forest.

👥 Marienglashöhle★

🔦Guided tours (45min) Apr–Oct daily 9am–5pm; Nov–Mar daily 9am–4pm. ⍟6€. ✆(03623) 31 16 67. www.tropfsteinhoehlen.de.

Rennsteig trail signpost, Thuringian Forest

This natural **mine** produces crystalline gypsum, a mineral used in the decoration of church altars and the protection of pictures of the Virgin Mary. This watery gypsum was named *Marienglas* (Mary's glass) in the Middle Ages.

▶ The road cuts across the Rennsteig and twists between the Regenberg and the Spießberg. Consider a hike through the Ebertswiese, a marsh- and meadowland. Steinbach is overlooked by the Hallenburg ruins. The road continues towards Oberhof via the grasslands of the Kanzlergrund.

Oberhof★

At 800m/2 625ft, Oberhof is the forest's most important winter sports centre and the host of annual biathlon and nordic combined (cross-country skiing and ski-jumping) world cups. More than 4 000 plant species grow In the **Rennsteiggarten** botanical park. Follow the B247 to the car park lot of the **Ohratalsperre** reservoir, which supplies water to Weimar, Jena, Gotha and Erfurt.

▶ Leave Oberhof towards Schmücke.

WHERE TO STAY

Auf der Wartburg.................... ①

Göbel's Sophien Hotel.................. ⑥

Kaiserhof.................... ⑨

Villa Anna.................... ④

WHERE TO EAT

Turmschänke.................... ②

Villa Antik.................... ⑤

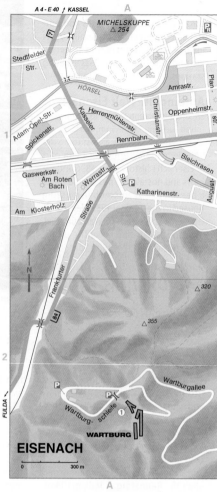

EISENACH

Ilmenau

On the forest's northern fringe, Ilmenau has always been associated with Goethe, said to have been particularly fond of its natural beauty. A plaque in his memory adorns the wall of the *Amtshaus* in Marktplatz, which now features a small Goethe museum.

🚶 The **Goethewanderweg** (hiking trail) links sites associated with the great writer.

ADDRESSES

🏨 STAY

Göbel's Sophien Hotel – *Sophienstraße 41. ☎03 691 25 10. www. sophienhotel.de. 66 rooms. ☕ 14€.* This family-owned international-style establishment, in the centre of town, offers quality rooms, a spa and sauna.

Kaiserhof – *Wartburgallee 2. ☎03 691 888 90. www.kaiserhof-eisenach.de. 49 rooms. ☕.* Spacious comfortable rooms are the hallmark of this traditional old hotel in the heart of town. Dining room with vaulted ceiling.

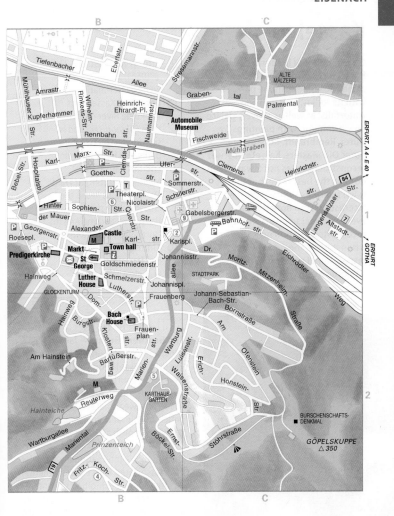

⊜⊜ **Villa Anna** – *Fritz-Koch-Straße 12.* *℘03691 239 50. www.hotel-villa-anna.de. 15 rooms.* ⊒. This hotel offers a winning combination of historic atmosphere and modern elegance.

⊜⊜⊜⊜ **Auf der Wartburg** – *In the Wartburg fortress, limousine shuttle available from the station if requested. ℘03 691 79 70. wartburghotel.arcona.de. Closed Jan 6–Feb 6. 37 rooms.* ⊒. This restored, atmospheric medieval hotel is perched on a mountaintop, surrounded by forest. Its restaurant enjoys an equally impressive setting.

♟ EAT

⊜⊜ **Villa Antik** – *Wartburgallee 55. ℘03 691 72 09 91. www.villa-antik.de. Closed Mon–Tue.* This charming 19C villa near the city centre is home to an elegant restaurant with stucco decoration and antique furniture; it serves regional cuisine.

⊜⊜⊜ **Weinrestuarant Turmschänke** – *Karlsplatz 28. Closed Sun. ℘03 691 21 35 33. www. turmschaenke-eisenach.de.* The rustic setting of the medieval Nicolaiturm is an ideal spot for the inspired regional cuisine of Ulrich Rösch.

Kassel★

Once the seat of landgraves, Kassel is renowned for the romantic Wilhelmshöhe park, with its follies, grottoes and waterfalls, as well as a lovely palace now brimming with paintings by Dürer, Rembrandt, Rubens and other Old Masters. Kassel's postwar reconstruction has not always been done in the best taste, but the town's various sights make it an interesting stop nonetheless. Every five years, the art world focuses its attention on Kassel when it hosts the renowned international contemporary art exhibition called Documenta.

▶ **Population:** 194 000

▣ **Info:** Wilhelmsstraße 23. ℘(0561) 70 77 07. www.kassel-marketing.de.

◗ **Location:** Kassel hugs the Fulda River *(boat tours from Fuldabrücke)* and is surrounded by two nature parks, the Habichtswald and the Naturpark Meißner-Kaufungen Wald. The town also lies at the crossroads of the A7 (Fulda–Hannover) and the A44 (to Dortmund) autobahns.

◷ **Timing:** Allow half a day for a visit of the Wilhelmshöhe park.

Jakob and Wilhelm Grimm

© World Pictures/Photoshot

A BIT OF HISTORY

The Brothers Grimm – Jakob (1785–1863) and Wilhelm Grimm (1786–1859) lived in Kassel from 1805 to 1830, working as court librarians. Fascinated by legends and folklore, the brothers collected a wealth of stories published under the title *Kinder und Hausmärchen*, known in English as *Grimms' Fairy Tales*.

Documenta – Internationally, Kassel is often associated with the Documenta, an international exhibition of contemporary art held for 100 days every five years since 1955. The next one is in 2017.

WILHELMSHÖHE★★
Park★★

This sprawling Baroque park boasts nearly 800 tree species, and in the late 18C, was transformed into an English style garden. **Löwenburg**, a mock medieval castle built around 1800, is a fine example of the era's Romanticism. The park is lorded over by the 72m/236ft-tall **Hercules★** *(Herkules)*, emblem of Kassel and highlight of the park. **Views★★** from up here are predictably fine. Below, a **water staircase** *(Kaskadentreppe)* shoots an enormous **cascade★** of water into the Neptune and Fountain pools.

Schloss Wilhelmshöhe (Palace)

Open year-round Tue–Sun 10am–5pm (Wed until 8pm); Jan 1 noon–5pm. Closed Dec 24-25 & 31. 6€. (0561) 31 68 01 23. www.museum-kassel.de.

Completed in 1803, the palace now houses a prized **Antikensammlung★** (collection of antiquities) from Greece and Rome. There are Greek vases, the 2C **Kassel Apollo**, a series of busts, a sarcophagus, urns and other precious objects on view.

If time is limited, head straight to the outstanding **Gemäldegalerie Alter Meister★★★** (Old Masters picture Gallery). Important works by German painters include Altdorfer's *Crucifixion*, a triptych *(Reisealtar)* by Cranach the Elder, Dürer's *Portrait of Elizabeth Tucher* and *Hercules at Antioch* by Hans Baldung Grien. The Dutch and Flemish Schools are represented by Rembrandt's *Portrait of Saskia van Uylenburgh*, Rubens' *Crowning of a Hero* and Jordaens' *The Painter's Betrothal*. Also on display here are landscapes by Jan Brueghel, Jacob van Ruisdael and Jan Steen. Works by Italians (Tintoretto, Titian, Bassano), Spanish (Ribera, Murillo) and French (Poussin) artists complete the collection.

ADDITIONAL SIGHTS
Karlsaue Park★

The most popular sections of this 18C riverside park are the gardens below the Schöne Aussicht terrace, and the Siebenbergen Fulda island. The Baroque orangery is home to the **Astronomisch-Physikalisches Kabinet** (open year-round Tue–Sun 10am–5pm, Thu until 8pm; Jan 1 noon–5pm; closed Dec 24, 25 & 31; 3€; 0561 31 68 01 23), with a rich collection of astronomical instruments and clocks as well as an attached planetarium. Models demonstrate observable scientific phenomena and there area displays explaining the evolution of technology since antiquity.

Hessisches Landesmuseum★ (Hessian State Museum)

Brüder-Grimm-Platz 5. (0561) 31 68 01 23. www.museum-kassel.de. Closed for renovation.

This sprawling museum displays artefacts and objects related to the cultural history of the Hesse region dating from prehistory to the present. Its extensive collections range from Stone Age tools and medieval sculpture and precious 17C porcelain to centuries' worth of decorative objects. Pride of place goes to a major collection of coloured Bohemian crystal and locally forged silverware. There are also hundreds of items tracking the evolution of wall coverings from the 18C to the 20C (Deutsches Tapetenmuseum).

EXCURSION
Göttingen

▶ 47km/29.2mi north on the A7.

Along with Heidelberg, Tübingen and Marburg, Göttingen is a town defined by its university, which was founded in 1734. Some 44 Nobel Prize winners have either studied, taught or conducted research here.

The charming old town bustles with students on bicycles and is filled with Gothic churches and Neoclassical university buildings.

The 13C–15C **Altes Rathaus** (old town hall) harbours the tourist office. It is perhaps best known for what lies beneath it: the **Ratskeller** (wine cellar), a rustic tavern that is probably the liveliest spot in Göttingen. At the front is the **Gänselieselbrunnen** (goose girl fountain), the city's emblem. Newly anointed PhDs must give her a kiss.

One of the city's most impressive views is the **Vierkirchenblick**, with a church on each point of the compass if seen from the southeast corner of the market: east, St. Albanikirche; south, St. Michaelskirche; west, St. Johannis; and north, St. Jakobi with the tallest tower in town.

The eastern part of the old town is dotted with **half-timbered houses**.

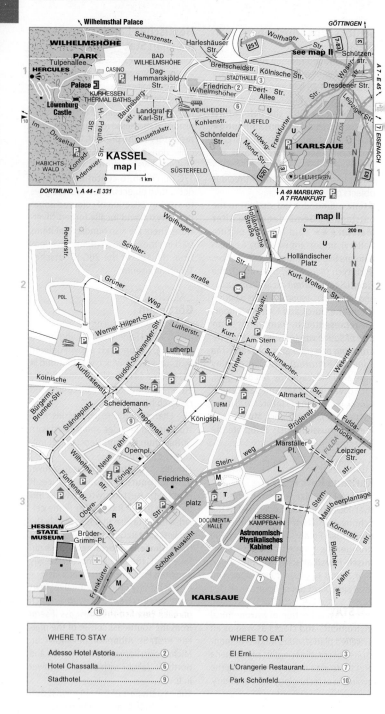

WHERE TO STAY

Adesso Hotel Astoria....................②

Hotel Chassalla...........................⑥

Stadthotel..................................⑨

WHERE TO EAT

El Erni..③

L'Orangerie Restaurant...............⑦

Park Schönfeld............................⑩

Town centre, Göttingen

One beauty is the **Junkernschänke★** *(Barfüßerstraße 5)*, a 16C Renaissance inn with a stunning multicoloured façade. Finally, a visit to Göttingen should include a stop at the **Städtisches Museum** (municipal museum; Ritterplan 7/8; open year-round Tue–Fri 10am–5pm, Sat–Sun 11am–5pm; closed major public holidays; ⚷ partially closed for renovation; ⬡ entry is free during renovation; ℘0551 400 28 43; www.museum.goettingen.de), housed in a well-preserved half-timbered Renaissance building. It contains comprehensive exhibits on Göttingen's historical and cultural development. Art fans are drawn to the rooms housing religious works, paintings by regional artists and contemporary glass art. Children cherish the collection of old toys from as far back as the 19C, and can participate in a wide variety of activities, including interactive guided tours.

ADDRESSES

🛌 STAY

⊜⊜ **Adesso Hotel Astoria** – *Friedrich-Ebert Straße 135. ℘(0561) 728 30. www.adessohotel.com. 40 rooms. ⬡5€.* This turn-of-the-19C house near the town hall offers quiet, contemporary bedrooms.

⊜⊜ **Hotel Chassalla** – *Wilhelmshöher Allee 99. ℘(0561) 927 90. www.hotel-chassalla.de. 44 rooms. ⬡5€.* This friendly family-owned hotel in the town centre offers simple but comfortable rooms.

⊜⊜ **Stadthotel** – *Wolfsschlucht 21. ℘(0561) 78 88 80. www.stadthotel kassel.de. 42 rooms. ⬡6€.* This plain but modern hotel is conveniently situated between the Hauptbahnhof and the theatre, opposite the main shopping area. Rooms are spacious.

🍽 EAT

⊜⊜ **El Erni** – *Parkstraße 42. ℘(0561) 71 00 18. www.el-erni.de.* New Spanish cuisine is the order of the day at this elegant modern yet rustic restaurant.

⊜⊜ **L'Orangerie** – *An der Karlsaue 20. ℘(0561) 286 103 18. www.orangerie-kassel.de. Closed Mon–Tue Oct–Mar.* Set in a very elegant early-18C Baroque building, the Orangery restaurant has a magnificent terrace equally suited to a candlelit dinner or just a drink.

⊜⊜⊜ **Park Schönfeld** – *Bosestraße 13. ℘(0561) 7397 6744. www.parkschoenfeld.com. Closed Sun.* Residing in a parkland setting, this restaurant is housed in part of an 18C manor house.

Fulda

Fulda is closely linked with Christian history in Germany. Its Baroque core, with the cathedral, palace and mansions of the nobility, recall a time when Prince-Bishops guarded the tomb of English missionary St. Boniface.

▶ **Population:** 63 500
▮ **Info:** Bonifatiusplatz 1. ℘(0661) 102 18 14. www.tourismus-fulda.de.
◖ **Location:** Fulda is the economic and cultural centre of eastern Hessen and is close to Thuringia and Bavaria.

SIGHTS
Dom (Cathedral)
Fulda's cathedral got its Baroque looks in 1704 under Johann Dientzenhofer. St. Boniface is buried in the crypt below the high altar. The alabaster bas-relief at the base of the 18C **funerary monument★** represents the saint. His reliquaries are at the **Dommuseum** (open Apr–Oct Tue–Sat 10am–5.30pm, Sun 12.30pm–5.30pm; Nov–Mar Tue–Sat 10am–12.30pm, 1.30pm–4pm, Sun 12.30pm–4pm; closed mid-Jan–mid-Feb; ∞2.10€; &; ℘0661 872 07; www.bistum-fulda.de).

Michaelskirche★
Built around an eight-columned 9C rotunda with a stout, square tower, this church overlooks the cathedral forecourt. The vaulted crypt is Carolingian.

EXCURSIONS
The Rhön
◗ 104km/65mi southeast of Fulda.

The remnants of an enormous extinct volcano, the Rhön's craggy peaks rise up to 1 000m/3 280ft above bleak moorlands. Strong winds make the area popular with gliders.

Gersfeld
◗ 31.5km/19.5mi southeast of Fulda.
The most central resort in the Rhön, Gersfeld has a Protestant **church** (1785) where the placement of organ, altar and pulpit liturgically symbolises the Lutheran reform.

The Kreuzberg★
At the end of a steep climb awaits a splendid **view★** from the second-highest peak in the Rhön (Calvary; 928m/3 045ft). The highest, the Wasserkuppe, can be seen to the north (950m/3 117ft). The **panorama★★** extends as far as Fulda and the Vogelsberg.

Marburg★★

Marburg is distinguished by a great castle and an imposing Gothic church. The latter is dedicated to St. Elizabeth, the Hungarian princess who retired here to care for the sick and poor. For centuries, her relics made Marburg a major pilgrimage centre, but after the Reformation it became a hub of Protestant scholarship and theology, largely due to its prestigious 16C university. Today, Marburg is still a busy student

▶ **Population:** 78 000
▮ **Info:** Pilgrimstein 26, 35037 Marburg. ℘(06421) 991 20. www.marburg.de.
◖ **Location:** Marburg sits on a rocky outcrop above the Lahn River and at the centre of a triangle formed by Frankfurt, Kassel and Cologne.
⌖ **Don't Miss:** St. Elizabeth's Church.
◷ **Timing:** Allow 2–3 hours.

town and has some of the liveliest nightlife in the region.

A BIT OF HISTORY

St. Elizabeth (1207–31) – Princess Elizabeth, daughter of the King of Hungary and intended bride of Landgrave Ludwig of Thuringia, was brought under the care of the Thuringian court to Wartburg castle near Eisenach *(see EISENACH)* at the age of four. Early in her life she became known for her kindness towards the sick and unfortunate. She married Ludwig in 1221, but after he died of the plague in 1227, Elizabeth was heartbroken and withdrew to Marburg. Here she dedicated her life to helping the sick and the poor. She died, most likely of exhaustion or a disease, at the age of 24.

A place of pilgrimage – Elizabeth was canonised only four years after her death (1235). Her remains were exhumed the following year to be immortalised in the superb Gothic church built in her honour. A steady stream of pilgrims flocked here to pay her respects, making Marburg one of the largest centres of pilgrimage in Western Christianity.

Seat of the Reformation – In 1529 Elizabeth's descendant, **Philip the Magnanimous**, abolished the cult of relics and re-buried Elizabeth's remains in a local cemetery. Philip later invited reformers Martin Luther and Hyldrych Zwingli to the famous "Marburg Religious Discussion" (1529).

ELISABETHKIRCHE★★ (ST. ELIZABETH CHURCH)

Open Apr–Sept daily 9am–5pm; Oct–Mar 10am–4pm. (Sun 11am year-round). Shrine: 2.50€. ♿; ✆(06421) 655 73. www.elisabethkirche.de.
The first truly Gothic church in Germany was built between 1235 and 1283. It is also considered the country's first hall-church and is filled with important art treasures. As you amble around, pay special attention to the following: **(1)** a statue of St. Elizabeth (c. 1470) wearing an elegant court gown, in the nave; **(2)** an openwork Gothic rood as well as

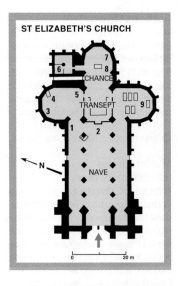

ST ELIZABETH'S CHURCH

a modern Crucifix by Ernst Barlach; **(3)** an altarpiece of the Pietà (1360); **(4)** the tomb of St. Elizabeth (after 1250); **(5)** the remains of 14C–15C frescoes in the niches; and **(6) St. Elizabeth's Shrine★★** *(Elisabethschrein)* in the old sacristy. This masterpiece in gold was completed by craftsmen from the Rhineland c. 1250. Other highlights: **(7)** St. Elizabeth's Window assembled from 13C medallions; **(8)** a 1510 statue of St. Elizabeth personifying Charity, by Ludwig Juppe; **(9)** *The Landgraves' Chancel*, the necropolis of the descendants of St. Elizabeth.

ADDITIONAL SIGHTS

❯ Leaving the church, climb up to the old town by way of the Steinweg – an unusual ramp with three levels. It continues as the Neustadt and then the Westergasse. Turn right into Marktgasse.

Marktplatz★ (Market Square)

The upper market *(Obermarkt)* is still framed by historic buildings. Particularly outstanding examples include nos 14 and 21, from 1560; no 23; and no 18, a stone house of 1323, the oldest preserved house still inhabited. The fountain, dedicated to St. George, is a popular meeting spot.

Rathaus (Town Hall)

Marburg's town hall is a 16C Gothic building much beloved for its mechanical cockerel that crows reliably on the hour every hour. It sits in a lofty perch atop the Renaissance tower, which was added in 1581 because the original building was considered too modest.

▶ Take Nikolaistraße to Marienkirche.

Marienkirche
(Church of St. Mary's)

This late-13C church sits adjacent to a Gothic former ossuary. From the terrace, there is a fine view over the roofs of the old town to the valley beyond. Past the church, you can glimpse the castle above. At the end of the esplanade, a passage leads down to the late-15C **Kugelkirche** (open year-round Mon–Fri 8am–6pm, Sat–Sun 10am–6pm; www. st-johannes-marburg.de), a fine, small church in the late-Gothic style.

▶ Climb some more steps, this time to the top of the Kugelgasse. Before the Kalbstor fortified gate, turn right on Ritterstraße.

The house at Ritterstraße 15 once belonged to legal historian Friedrich Karl von Savigny (1779–1861), one of the founders of the "Historical School" of the study of law. He was also a key member of the "Marburg Romantics" group that also included Clemens von Brentano, Achim and Bettina von Arnim and Jakob and Wilhelm Grimm.

Schloss★ (Palace)

From the 13C to the 17C, the landgraves of Hessen resided in this hilltop castle, which treats you to sweeping **views** of the Lahn Valley from the terrace. Surviving buildings (13C–15C) include the Gothic Princes' Hall with its double nave; the west hall, which reveals excavations of the previous fortress (9C and 11C); the south hall, with its memorials of the founding of the university (1527) and of the religious debates that took place in Marburg in 1529; and the castle chapel with its medieval ceramic floor.

Museum für Kulturgeschichte★ (Museum of Cultural History)

Open Apr–Oct Tue–Sun 10am–6pm; Nov–Mar Tue–Sun 10am–4pm. Closed Jan 1, Dec 25-26 & 31. ◉4€. ℘(06421) 282 23 55. www.uni-marburg.de/uni-museum.

After touring the historical palace rooms, proceed to the 15C Wilhelmsbau wing, which houses this sprawling museum. It has five floors of exhibits spanning the period from the Bronze Age to the present day.

Of particular note are findings from a 5C Merovingian warriors' grave, Celtic coins, Romanesque crucifixes, fragments of stained glass from the St. Elisabethkirche, a 15C tapestry depicting the story of the Prodigal Son, and a collection of medieval shields and armour. On the two top floors, the spotlight is on daily life in the 18C and 19C. Assembled are a hodgepodge of glass, porcelain, dollhouses and costumes as well as fully decked-out *Biedermeier* and *Jugendstil* period rooms.

Museum für Bildende Kunst (Fine Arts Museum)

Ernst-von-Hülsen-Haus, Blegenstraße 11 (next to the Stadthalle performance hall). ⊶Closed for renovation until at least late 2015. ℘(06421) 282 23 55. www.uni-marburg.de/uni-museum.

Four centuries of paintings, graphics and sculpture grace the rooms of this museum in a 1927 building that blends Neoclassical and Art Deco elements. Key canvases include *Adam and Eve* by Flemish painter Louis Finson (1610) and Carl Spitzweg's *Der Briefbote im Rosenthal* (*The Letter Carrier in Rosenthal*, ca. 1858). There are fine examples of Expressionism (Lovis Corinth's *Bacchanal*, 1921) and New Objectivity (Carlo Mense's *Mother with Children*, 1925). The arc of art spans all the way to more contemporary works, such as examples of new figurative painting (Bernard Schultze, Dieter Krieg, Hans-Hendrik Grimmling) and installations by such practitioners as Hannsjörg Voth.

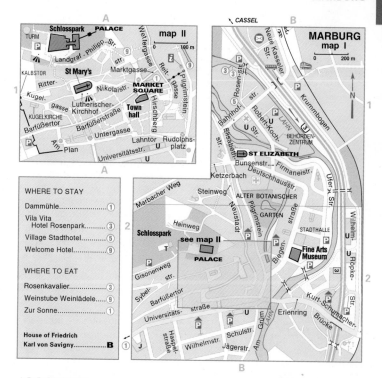

ADDRESSES

🛏 STAY

🍴🛏 **Dammühle** – *Dammühlenstraße 1, 35041 Marburg-Wehrshausen-Dammühle (6km/3.7mi west along Barfüßertor).* ℘*(06421) 935 60. www.hotel-dammuehle. de. 26 rooms. ⬛. Restaurant*🍴🛏. This small half-timbered 14C mill has prettily decorated, comfortable rooms, some very modern and spacious. There's country-style dining and a large *Biergarten*, and for children, crazy golf and a playground.

🍴🛏 **Village Stadthotel** – *Bahnhofstraße 14. ℘(06421) 68 58 80. www.village-stadthotel.de. 20 rooms.* ⬛. This small, well-run hotel in the city centre has modern, stylish, comfortably furnished rooms.

🍴🛏 **Welcome Hotel** – *Pilgrimstein 29. ℘(06421) 91 80. www.welcome-hotel-marburg.de. 150 rooms.* ⬛. Set at the foot of the Schlossberg, this property features simple but stylish rooms and apartments, plus a restaurant with a terrace and a pleasant bar.

🍴🛏🍴🛏 **Vila Vita Hotel Rosenpark** – *Anneliese Pohl Allee 7-17. www.rosenpark. de. ℘(06421) 600 50. 178 rooms. ⬛. Restaurant*🍴🛏🍴🛏. This luxurious hotel located beside the Lahn is known for its wellness and spa facilities, including an indoor pool. International cuisine is served in the restaurant.

🍴 EAT

🍴 **Weinstube Weinlädele** – *Schlosstreppe 1. ℘(06421) 142 44. www.weinlaedele.com.* This historic inn puts a contemporary twist on favourite regional dishes. *Flammkuchen* are a speciality.

🍴🛏 **Zur Sonne** – *Markt 14. ℘(06421) 171 90. www.zur-sonne-marburg.de.* Cosy dining rooms spread across several floors of this 16C half-timbered gem serving classic German cuisine, pasta dishes and inspired specials.

🍴🛏🍴🛏 **Rosenkavalier** – *Anneliese Pohl Allee 7-17. www.rosenpark.de. ℘(06421) 600 50.* This elegant restaurant serves international fare, and in summer, barbecue dinners on the terrace.

The East

The East

This chapter covers Saxony, which has been for centuries one of the country's most prosperous and culturally sophisticated states. Two cities of very different character dominate: no-nonsense Leipzig with its traditions as a trading town and centre of music and the arts; and playful Dresden, nicknamed "Florence on the Elbe" for its Baroque appearance and extraordinary art collections. Dresden is also the gateway to Saxon Switzerland, the region's most dramatically beautiful area, in which nature has moulded sandstone into bizarre columns, battered cliffs, tabletop mountains, and deep valleys and gorges. Upriver from Dresden, Meissen is the birthplace of European porcelain and home to one of the world's most famous china brands.

Highlights

1 Historical and New Green Vault Collections in **Dresden** (p585)

2 Views from the Bastei in **Saxon Switzerland** (p588)

3 A leisurely **boat ride** on the Elbe River (p592)

4 A tour of **Meissen**'s porcelain factory (p599)

5 A concert in the Neues Gewandhaus in **Leipzig** (p605)

A State of the Arts

A journey through Saxony is an encounter with a rich musical and artistic legacy. In Leipzig you can walk in the footsteps of Johann Sebastian Bach, who worked as cantor of the St. Thomas Church, whose famous boys' choir (Thomanerchor) has delighted music-lovers since 1212. Felix Mendelssohn-Bartholdy founded Germany's first conservatory in Leipzig in 1843, where Robert Schumann signed up as a professor. Two years later, Mendelssohn became music director of the prestigious Gewandhaus Orchestra. All of these institutions still exist to this day, but of late Leipzig has also made its mark in the contemporary fine arts.

In fact, the New Leipzig School is the most important artistic movement to come out of Germany since reunification, and paintings by many of its leading practitioners, especially Neo Rauch, are sought after by collectors world-wide.

Although not as trendsetting as Leipzig, Dresden also has a strong artistic heritage, measured more by the size, depth and quality of its art collections, as well as by the inspiration it provided to such famous painters as Canaletto and Caspar David Friedrich. How many of the artworks have survived is all the more astonishing given Dresden's near total devastation in World War II. Since then, the city has risen phoenix-like from the ashes.

Making an intricate teapot, Museum of Meissen Art

MEISSEN/A&C Media Community e.K.

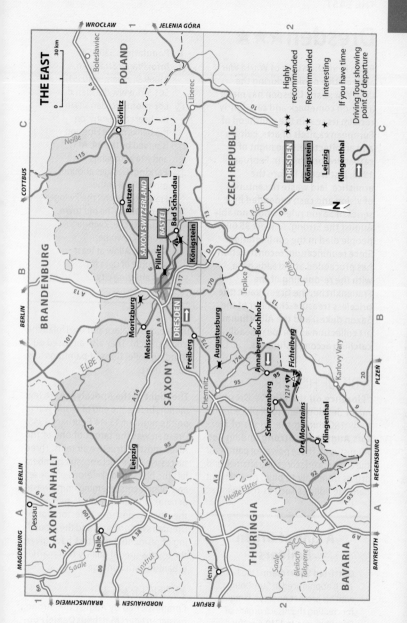

THE EAST

Highly recommended ★★★
Recommended ★★
Interesting ★

Driving Tour showing point of departure

DRESDEN ★★★
Königstein ★★
Leipzig ★
Klingenthal

Unique Souvenirs

Shopping in Saxony means one can buy unique handmade gifts. A popular souvenir from Dresden is the original *Stollen*, a fruit-filled cake enjoyed at Christmastime. Gorgeous Christmas ornaments and decorations are still produced in the Ore Mountains in the southern part of the state. In Meissen, you can buy the famous hand-painted porcelain straight from the factory.

The town is also the hub of the Saxon Wine Region, one of the northernmost in Europe. Although the vineyards may be relatively few in number, wine has been cultivated here for nearly 850 years thanks to more than 1 500 hours of sunshine in an average year.

Dresden★★★

Risen from the ashes of World War II and relative neglect during the Cold War years, Dresden has made a full-on comeback and can rightly reclaim its seat in the pantheon of European capitals of arts, culture and architecture. One night of carpet fire-bombing in February 1945, just weeks before the armistice, laid waste to centuries of vision and cash expended by a series of Saxon rulers, most notably August the Strong. At least 35 000 people died in the conflagration. Since reunification, reconstruction has proceeded at a steady pace, with the re-opening of the Frauenkirche, the Green Vault (the priceless treasure-chamber of the Saxon dukes) and the Albertinum art collection as the most headline-catching accomplishments.

▶ **Population:** 530 754
▪ **Info:** Prager Straße 2b, 01069 Dresden. ☎(0351) 501 501 www.dresden.de.
▶ **Location:** Dresden sits in the heart of Saxony, on the banks of the Elbe and is served by the A4, A13 and A14 autobahns.
🅿 **Parking:** Garages abound, especially near the Frauenkirche and the Zwinger.
◉ **Don't Miss:** The old town, Frauenkirche, Zwinger, Grünes Gewölbe.
🕓 **Timing:** Allow at least a couple of days for this amazing city.

A BIT OF HISTORY

"Florence on the Elbe" – Dresden's major development took place in the early 18C during the reigns of Electors **August the Strong** and his son Augustus III. These powerful patrons of the arts enticed scores of craftsmen and artists from Italy to build magnificent Baroque edifices such as the Zwinger, the Japanese Palace and the Hofkirche (court church). They also amassed outstanding collections of paintings and objets d'art.

The Night of the Apocalypse – A few months before the end of World War II, on the night of 13–14 February 1945, Dresden was the target of one of the Allies' most destructive air raids. Three successive waves of Lancaster bombers left the blackened skeletons of houses and monuments emerging from a waste of smoking ruins. In all, 75 percent of the city was destroyed. Restoration of Dresden's historic sites and the rebuilding of residential quarters have given the town a special quality that marries urbanism with heritage.

ZWINGER★★★

Commissioned by August the Strong, master architect **Matthäus Daniel Pöppelmann** (1682–1737) designed and realised this stunning Baroque palace between 1711 and 1728. Sculpture was provided by Balthasar Perlmoser. Painstakingly reconstructed, the complex now houses several museums (most famously the Old Masters Picture Gallery), and is one of Dresden's key attractions.

A Line of Organ Builders

Gottfried Silbermann (1683–1753) apprenticed in Strasbourg with his brother Andreas, famous for creating the Alsace organs of Ebersmunster. In 1710, Gottfried settled in Freiberg, designing instruments with remarkable tone. Of the 51 organs attributed to him, those in Freiberg are the best. Gottfried's nephew Johann Andreas followed suit, and designed 54 organs in the Upper Rhine region.

PRACTICAL INFORMATION

TELEPHONE AREA CODE: *035*

TOURIST INFORMATION

Tourist Offices – Dresden Information also has two offices: one across from the Hauptbahnhof (main train station) at Wiener Platz 4, *daily 8am–8pm*; the other near the Frauenkirche at Neumarkt 2, *Mon–Fri 10am–7pm, Sat 10am–6pm, Sun 10am–3pm (reduced hours Jan–Mar)*. For **ticket reservations**, call Dresden Information at *(0351) 501 501. Mon–Sat 9am–4pm*. Or visit www. dresden.de.

City Magazines – SAX (www.cybersax. de), the freebies BLITZ! (www.blitz-stadt magazin.com) and Frizz (www.dresden-frizz.de) provide complete listings information. *SAX* is sold at newspaper kiosks and bookshops, while the other two are found in bars, boutiques and tourist offices, as is the monthly *Dresdner Kulturmagazin (www.dresdner.nu)*.

Daily papers – *Sächsische Zeitung; Dresdner Neueste Nachrichten*.

Tourist Cards – Available at tourist offices and DVB service centres, the **Dresden-City-Card** (29.90€ valid 48hrs) lets adults use all buses, trams and Elbe ferries, plus free entry to 12 State Art Collections and discounts for other museums.

The **Dresden-Regio-Card** (79.90€ valid 4 days) includes free rides on the S-Bahn trains along the Elbe to e.g. Meissen, Pirna and Königstein, discounts for rides on various narrow-gauge trains, and discounts at the region's main museums.

Post Offices with Late Hours – **Altmarkt-Galerie** (Webergasse 1, inside the shopping centre; Mon–Sat 9am–9pm) and **Königsbrücker Straße 21–29** (Mon–Fri 9am–7pm, Sat 10am–1pm).

INTERNET

www.dresden-tourist.de; www. dresden-online.de; www.dresden.de.

GETTING THERE AND AROUND

AIRPORT

Drivers coming from Leipzig should take the A14 east to the A4 *(114km/70mi)*; from Berlin, follow the A113 south to the A13 *(190km/118mi)*.

Dresden Airport *(DRS; (0351) 881 33 60; www.dresden-airport.de)* is less than 10km/6.2mi north of the city centre. S-Bahn trains (S2) run into town from the airport throughout the day.

RAIL

Direct **Deutsche Bahn** train service to and from Leipzig, Berlin, Meissen, Frankfurt and other cities. Dresden has two railway stations: *Dresden-Hauptbahnhof* south of the old town and *Dresden-Neustadt* (Schlesischer Platz 1). Most trains stop at both.

PUBLIC TRANSPORT

Dresden's largely pedestrianised historic centre contains most sights and museums and is compact enough for walking. The city is served by a network of trams and buses operated by Dresdner Verkehrsbetriebe *(DVB; (0351) 857 10 11; www.dvb.de)*. There are service centres at the Hauptbahnhof, *Mon–Fri 8am–7pm, Sat 8am–6pm, Sun 9am–6pm*; Postplatz and Prager Straße, *Mon–Fri 9am–7pm, Sat 9am–6pm (Postplatz also Sun 10am–6pm)*; Pirnaischer Platz *Mon–Sat 9am–5pm* and Albertplatz *Mon–Fri 9am–6pm, Sat 9am–4pm*. Tickets are available at station vending machines, aboard and at service centres. The basic fare is 2.20€. One-day passes *(Tageskarte)* cost 6€ and are worthwhile if you plan on multiple trips. One-day family/group tickets *(Familientageskarte)* start at 8.50€. The DVB is integrated into the Verkehrsverbund Oberelbe *(VVO; 0351 852 65 55, Mon–Fri 9am–6pm, Sat 9am–4pm; www.vvo-online.de)*, which also covers "Swiss Saxony" *(Sächsische Schweiz)*, the eastern Erzgebirge Mountains and parts of the Oberlausitz area.

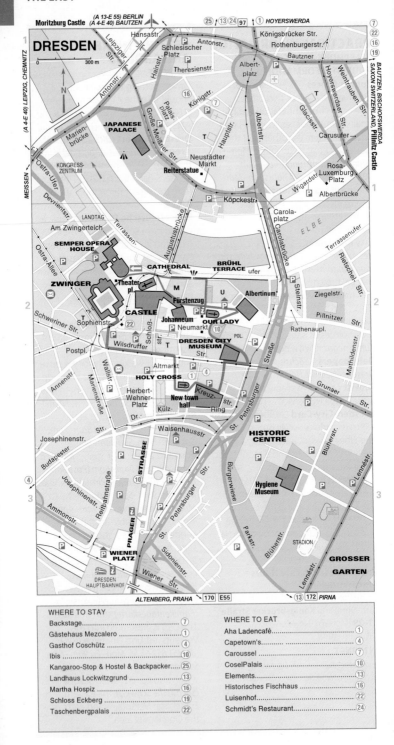

DRESDEN

300 m

WHERE TO STAY

Backstage	⑦
Gästehaus Mezcalero	①
Gasthof Coschütz	④
Ibis	⑩
Kangaroo-Stop & Hostel & Backpacker	㉕
Landhaus Lockwitzgrund	⑬
Martha Hospiz	⑯
Schloss Eckberg	⑲
Taschenbergpalais	㉒

WHERE TO EAT

Aha Ladencafé	①
Capetown's	④
Caroussel	⑦
CoselPalais	⑩
Elements	⑬
Historisches Fischhaus	⑯
Luisenhof	㉒
Schmidt's Restaurant	㉔

👁 *The best view of the complex is from the entrance through the Carillon Pavilion.*

The huge rectangular courtyard is bookended by the **Wallpavillon★★** (Rampart Pavilion) to the north and the **Glockenspielpavillon** (Carillon Pavilion) on the opposite end. It is in the former that the Zwinger's harmonious marriage of sculpture and architecture best expresses itself. Crowning the pavilion is a statue of August the Strong's idol **Hercules** carrying the world on his back.

The Wallpavillon leads to a terrace and the **Nymphenbad★★** (Bath of the Nymphs). The southwest side of the complex, the **Zwinger Gallery**, is best seen from the outside passing beneath the gorgeous **Kronentor** (Crown Gate). Opposite, the **Semperbau** (Semper Building) is a 1847 work of Gottfried Semper with sculpture by Ernst Rietschel.

Gemäldegalerie Alte Meister★★★ (Gallery of Old Masters)

In the Semperbau. Open year-round Tue–Sun 10am–6pm. Closed Dec 24. 📷10€. 📞(0351) 49 14 20 00. www.skd.museum.
*The admission ticket price also includes access to the **Armory** and the **Porcelain Collection**.*
Established by Augustus the Strong and Augustus III, the Gallery of Old Masters

is one of the largest and most prestigious of its kind. The most important masters from the Italian Renaissance and the Baroque period are represented, as are Dutch and Flemish painters from the 17C.

Italian paintings are hung on a red background, Dutch and Flemish paintings on a green background and Spanish and French paintings on a blue background.

Ground Floor
Galleries 1–4 contain tapestries after sketches by Raphael and numerous townscapes by Bernardo Bellotto, otherwise known as Canaletto, who painted Dresden and Pirna with such extraordinary precision that many paintings were used as blueprints during the postwar reconstruction.
Galleries 5–6 house paintings by Dresden masters.

1st Floor
Galleries 101–102: Works by Silvestre and Canaletto.
Galleries 104–106 and 108–111: Flemish and Dutch painting from the 16C–17C. Rembrandt's *Self-portrait with Saskia* **(Gallery 106)**, Rubens' *Bathsheba* and Vermeer's *Girl Reading a Letter by the Window* **(Gallery 108)**.
Gallery 107: Paintings by the early Netherlandish (Jan van Eyck) and early

Gemäldegalerie Alte Meister

© SKD / Juergen Loesel

German (masterpieces by Holbein, Cranach the Elder and Dürer) schools.

Gallery 112: 17C French painting (Claude Lorrain, Nicolas Poussin).

Galleries 113–121: 16C Italian painting. Works by Veronese, Tintoretto, Giorgione *(Sleeping Venus)*, Titian, in **galleries 117–119**. A highlight is Raphael's portrayal of the Virgin and Child, the *Sistine Madonna,* in **gallery 117**.

Gallery 116: Paintings by Botticelli, Mantegna and Pintoricchio *(Portrait of a Boy).*

2nd Floor

Gallery 201: Pastel painting. Jean-Étienne Liotard's *Chocolate Girl*, world's largest collection of works by Rosalba Carriera (75 pastels).

Gallery 202: 18C French painting.

Galleries 203–207: 18C Italian painting with works by Tiepolo and Crespi.

Galleries 208–210: Spanish painting (El Greco, Murillo, Zurbarán, Velázquez).

Galleries 211–216: 17C and 18C German painting.

Porzellansammlung★★ (Porcelain Collection)

Open year-round Tue–Sun 10am–6pm. Closed Dec 24. ⌾6€. ♿ ℘(0351) 49 14 20 00. www.skd.museum.

This gallery displays porcelain from the famous factory at **Meissen**, as well as rare and precious imports from Japan and China. Do not miss the "dragoon vases" for which the Elector paid with 600 dragoon soldiers in 1717, or the life-size porcelain figures from Meissen (early 18C). For background, visit the exhibit devoted to Johann Friedrich Böttger (1682–1719), credited with inventing European porcelain in 1708.

Mathematisch-Physikalischer Salon★★ (Salon of Mathematics and Physics)

Open year-round Tue–Sun 10am–6pm. Closed Dec 24. ⌾6€. ℘(0351) 49 14 20 00. www.skd.museum.

The inventive genius of scientists is documented in 16C-19C clocks and instruments, including sun, sand, oil, artistic and automatic timepieces.

NEUSTADT★ (NEW TOWN)

Reached via Augustusbrücke, Dresden's Neustadt spreads across a medieval city quarter destroyed by fire in 1685 and subsequently rebuilt in stone. It was spared from total devastation in 1945. Just beyond the bridge, Neustädter Markt is dominated by the gilded **equestrian statue★** of Augustus the Strong.

Stroll along the pedestrianised **Hauptstraße** to reach Albertplatz square, which is graced by two fountains.

Königstraße, which radiates southeast from Albertplatz, is one of Dresden's most elegant streets and is lined with beautifully restored Baroque, Neoclassical and Gründerzeit town houses.

From Albertplatz, follow Alaunstraße north into the lively student quarter teeming with bars, cafés, pubs, clubs and restaurants and accented by the **Kunsthofpassage**.

🐾 WALKING TOUR

The Elbe River divides Dresden into two distinct parts. South of the river, the old town *(Altstadt)* is dominated by the Zwinger, Semperoper and Frauenkirche; in the north, the new town *(Neustadt)* is anchored by Albertplatz.

HISTORIC CENTRE★★★ (ALTSTADT)

Start your tour on Theaterplatz, which is flanked by the Zwinger, the Semper Opera House and the Hofkirche cathedral.

Semperoper★★ (Semper Opera House)

Theaterplatz 2. 🐾 Guided tours daily. ⌾10€. Tours in English 3pm, but check with the box office, as times can change. Tours are available only on rehearsal- and performance-free days.

℘(0351) 320 73 60. www.semperoper-erleben.de, www.semperoper.de.

Altstadt by the Elbe – Hofkirche on the right

Numerous operas premiered at this famous venue, including *Der Rosenkavalier* by Richard Strauss. Designed by Gottfried Semper in Italian Renaissance style, it first opened in 1841 but had to be rebuilt a mere three decades later after being devastated by a fire.

Six sculptures surviving from the original structure were incorporated into this modern replica, open since 1985. They represent Schiller and Goethe *(above the entrance)*, Shakespeare and Sophocles *(on the left)* and Molière and Euripides *(on the right)*.

▶ Cross Theaterplatz and head to the Hofkirche.

Ehemalige Katholische Hofkirche★★★ (Former Court Cathedral)

Open year-round Mon–Tue 9am–6pm, Wed–Thu 9am–5pm, Fri 1pm–5pm, Sat 10am–5pm, Sun noon–4pm. ✆(0351) 484 47 12.

This enormous 18C basilica is the largest church in Saxony and was strongly influenced by the Italian Baroque. It is dominated by an 86m/282ft bell-tower and decorated with statues of the saints and apostles. Above the high altar, a painting (1765) by Anton Raphael Mengs depicts the Ascension.

The Baroque pulpit was executed by Balthasar Permoser in 1722, while the organ was the last work (1750–55) of the master craftsman **Gottfried Silbermann**. Several kings and princes of Saxony are buried in the crypt, as is the heart of August the Strong, whose body lies in Kraków's cathedral.

Residenzschloss (Castle)

Open year-round Wed–Mon 10am–6pm. Closed Dec 24. ∞12€. ♿. ✆(0351) 49 14 20 00. www.skd.museum.

After a top-to-bottom makeover, Dresden's Renaissance palace now houses the dazzling Historical Green Vault and the New Green Vault – both brimming with hand-crafted *objets d'art* assembled by Augustus the Strong – as well as the Armoury.

▶ Follow Sophienstraße around the palace.

Historisches Grünes Gewölbe★★★ (Historical Green Vault Collections)

Enter via Sophienstraße.

The re-created Historical Green Vault is a veritable walk-in treasure chest consisting of nine rooms sheathed in mirrors, ivory, amber, marble, gold and silver. They are a perfect setting for the unique items, displayed without pro-

Dresden-Hellerau: Germany's First Garden City

Ebenezer Howard's late-19C "Garden City Movement" inspired German entrepreneur Karl Camillo Schmidt to found a similarly progressive community in Hellerau in 1909 (www.dresden-hellerau.de). Top architects Heinrich Tessenow, Hermann Muthesius and Curt Frick collaborated on what would become Germany's first Garden City. The community and its annual festival attracted artists and visionaries from throughout Europe. Under the National Socialists and in the postwar years it served military purposes, but now it is slowly being returned to its former glory.

tective glass just as they would have been during the times of Augustus the Strong. Cut-stone vessels, rhinoceros-horn goblets and astronomical table clocks are among the more noteworthy treasures.

Neues Grünes Gewölbe★★★
(New Green Vault Collections)
Enter via Sophienstraße.
In a modern setting on the palace upper floor, the New Green Vault features some of the collection's most stunning objects. Highlights include a cherry pit engraved with 185 faces (16C), a boat fashioned entirely from ivory (1620), a sculpture of a moor carrying a plate of emeralds by Balthasar Perlmoser (1724) and a hat clasp with a 41-carat green diamond (1769).
Tickets for the Residenzschloss are also good for the **Türckische Cammer** (Turkish Chamber) in the same building. On view again for the first time in 70 years, it is one of the oldest and most important collections of Ottoman art anywhere in the world outside Turkey.

Rüstkammer★★ (Armoury)
Even dedicated pacifists should be able to appreciate the artistry of this precious collection of hand-crafted ceremonial weapons. The inventory includes 1 300 objects from the 15C to 19C hailing from places throughout Europe and the Middle East. There is also a collection of child armour, worn during tournaments held in the court of Saxony.

▷ Backtrack to the Hofkirche, continue to Schlossplatz and turn right onto Augustusstraße.

Fürstenzug★
(Procession of the Princes)
Augustusstraße is parallelled by a detailed 102m/335ft-long ceramic **mural** hand-painted onto 24 000 Meissen porcelain tiles. It depicts Saxon rulers from 1123 to 1904.

▷ Follow Augustusstraße to Neumarkt.

Frauenkirche★
(Church of Our Lady)
Open year-round Mon–Fri 10am–noon, 1pm–6pm, limited hours at weekends.
&. ℘(0351) 6560 6100.
www.frauenkirche-dresden.de.
Designed by Georg Bähr and first consecrated in 1726, this landmark lingered as a postwar ruin for decades but after reunification, funds poured in from around the world to finance its resurrection. An exact replica opened in 2005, topped again by the striking 95m/312ft-high dome that characterises the town silhouette. **Views★★** from the top are stupendous (open Mar–Oct Mon–Sat 10am–6pm, Sun 12.30pm–6pm; Nov–Feb Mon–Sat 10am–4pm, Sun 12.30pm–4pm).

Verkehrsmuseum (Transport Museum) at Johanneum
Augustusstraße 1, enter from Neumarkt.
Open year-round Tue–Sun 10am–6pm.
Closed Jan 1, Dec 24, 25 & 31.
⊚7€. ℘(0351) 864 40.
www.verkehrsmuseum-dresden.de.

The Renaissance-era **Johanneum** once housed the royal stables and is now a transport museum with a big collection of vintage cars, model trains and original planes.

▷ Take Brühlsche Gasse off Neumarkt and walk towards the river.

Brühlsche Terrasse (Brühl Terrace)

The so-called "Balcony of Europe", this riverside promenade was built onto the ancient fortifications; it offers fantastic **views★** of the Elbe and the Neustadt.

▷ Follow the Brühlsche Terrasse east to the Albertinum.

Albertinum★★

Enter from Brühlsche Terrasse or Georg-Treu-Platz. Open year-round Tue–Sun 10am–6pm. ⊚10€. ♿ ℘(0351) 49 14 20 00. www.skdmuseum.

This stunning art collection presents paintings and sculpture from the Romantic period to the present. In 2010 it re-opened after extensive renovation due to 2002 flood damage.

▷ Head south on Schiessgasse to Wilsdruffer Straße via Landhausstraße.

Stadtmuseum (City Museum)

Wilsdruffer Straße 2. Open year-round, Tue–Sun 10am–6pm (Fri 7pm). ⊚5€. ♿ ℘(0351) 488 73 01. www.stmd.de.

Built between 1770 and 1775 for the Saxon government, this Baroque building has exhibits detailing Dresden's history from its founding in the 13C. Special emphasis is placed on the 19C and 20C.

▷ Follow Gewandhausgasse to Kreuzstraße.

Neues Rathaus (New Town Hall)

This early 20C neo-Renaissance building is surmounted by a golden statue of Hercules. Trips up the 100m/328ft **tower** *(partly by lift)* are available (⚷ closed for renovation until 2015).

Kreuzkirche (Holy Cross)★

Open Mon–Fri & Sun 10am–6pm, Sat 10am–3pm. Tower ⊚3€. ℘(0351) 439 39 20. www.kreuzkirche-dresden.de.

Just west of the town hall, Dresden's oldest church has origins in the early 13C and has been home to the famous Kreuzchor boys' choir for nearly as long. The current structure is a neo-Baroque beauty from 1900 with more than 3 600 seats, making it one of the largest Protestant churches in Germany.

ADDITIONAL SIGHTS

🧑👤 Deutsches Hygiene-Museum (German Hygiene Museum)

Lingnerplatz 1. Open year-round Tue–Sun 10am–6pm. Closed Jan 1, Dec 24–25. ⊚7€. ♿ ℘(0351) 484 64 00. www.dhmd.de.

The name may be odd, but the exhibits are intriguing. Using glass and wax figures, anatomical models and interactive stations, this museum looks at human existence from a biological, social and cultural perspective.

Asisi Panometer

Gasanstalstraße 8b. Open year-round Tue–Fri 10am–5pm, Sat–Sun 10am–6pm. ⊚11.50€. ℘(0351) 860 39 40. www.asisi.de.

This space uses a 360-degree panorama and advanced technology to take you on a virtual journey back to Dresden's 18C Baroque heyday during the reign of Augustus the Strong.

EXCURSIONS

Schloss Moritzburg★ (Moritzburg Palace)

▷ 14km/8.7mi northwest, via Hansastraße. Open Apr–Nov 2 daily 10am–5.30pm; Nov 15–Jan 4 Sat–Sun 10am–4.30pm. Closed Jan 5–Mar. ⊚7€. ℘(035207) 87 30. www.schloss-moritzburg.de.

Built in the 16C by Duke Moritz of Saxony, this hunting lodge has an idyllic island location. It was turned into a Baroque pleasure palace under Augustus the Strong in the 18C.

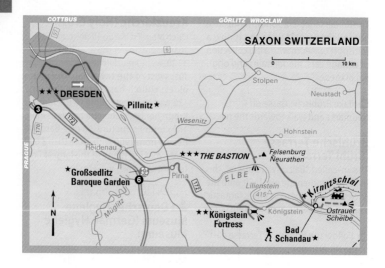

Schloss and Park Pillnitz★ (Pillnitz Palace and Park)

◐ 15km/9.3mi southeast via Bautzener Straße. Open May–Oct Tue–Sun 10am–6pm; Nov–Apr visit by guided tour only on weekends. Closed Dec 24 & 25. ✆8€. ℘(0351) 261 32 60; www.schlosspillnitz.de.

This Baroque riverside summer palace has Chinese flourishes. It is surrounded by vine-covered slopes and a lush garden. A popular day trip from Dresden, it is easily reached by boat or bike.

Aside from strolling and picnicking, you can learn about court life in the museum in the Neues Palais (New Palace). Decorative arts and Augustus the Strong's throne are displayed in the Bergpalais and Wasserpalais outbuildings (open May–Oct Tue–Sun 10am–6pm; ✆4€).

Freiberg★

◐ 37km/23mi south.

Lying at the foot of the Erzgebirge mountain range, Freiberg once pegged its wealth to an abundance of silver, copper and various minerals.

The key sight is the 15C **Cathedral★★** (➥ 45min guided tour May–Jun, Sept– Oct & Dec Mon–Sat 11am, 2pm & 3pm, Sun 11.30am, 2pm & 3pm; Jul–Aug & Nov Mon–Sat 11am & 2pm, Sun 11.30am & 2pm; ✆3-4€; ♿; ℘03731 30 09 66. www.freiberger-dom.de). It is filled with

important religious artworks, including the **tulip pulpit★★**, a masterpiece by sculptor Hans Witten (c. 1505); the Gottfried Silbermann **organ★★**; and the Romanesque golden **portal★★** from 1230 at the entrance.

Schloss Augustusburg★

◐ 75km/46.5mi southwest. ℘(037291) 38 00. www.die-sehenswerten-drei.de. Elector Augustus I built this castle as a hunting lodge in 1570 atop the Schellenberg hill (515m/1 690ft). The chapel has an altar painting by Lucas Cranach the Younger (1571) that shows the elector surrounded by his 14 children. The castle houses several exhibitions, most importantly a comprehensive motor-cycle museum.

🚗 DRIVING TOUR

SAXON SWITZERLAND★★★

78km/49mi. Allow one day.

Saxon Switzerland is one of Germany's most striking natural wonders, an area of craggy sandstone cliffs, rock outcrops, whimsical pinnacles and deep gorges carved by the Elbe River. The valley can be explored by road following the itinerary below, or by river on one of the "Weiße Flotte" boats linking Dresden and Bad Schandau.

▶ Leave Dresden to the east via Pillnitzer Landstraße.

Schloss Pillnitz★
See DRESDEN: Excursions.

Bastei★★★
To avoid the biggest crowds, arrive early or late in the day. Sunset is especially nice. Perched on a rocky outcrop, the Bastei was the site of a 13C wooden castle. Today it is most famous for its sweeping **views★★** across the Elbe and the almost otherworldly rock formations that form the heart of the Saxon Switzerland National Park. Only a few foundations survive from the original castle, which is reached via the photogenic 76m/249.3ft-long stone **Basteibrücke** *(bridge)*. From here, a series of narrow footbridges *(not suitable for the vertigo-prone)* take you through the ruined fortress and to ever more spectacular views.

▶ Follow the S165 (Basteistraße) east, then turn right onto the S163 to Bad Schandau via Waltersdorf.

Bad Schandau★
This spa town renowned for its iron-rich waters is the region's main tourist centre.
The **Nationalparkzentrum** (Dresdner Straße 2b; open Feb 1–Feb 16 Tue–Sun 9am–5pm; Feb 17–Feb 28 daily 9am–5pm; Mar 1–Mar 31 Tue–Sun 9am–5pm; Apr–Oct daily 9am–6pm; closed Jan; 2€; 035022 502 40; www.lanu.de) has interpretive and interactive exhibits about the national park's flora, fauna and history and makes for a good introduction to the region and its unusual natural charms.
At the town exit, towards Schmilka, the **Personenaufzug** *(lift; open Apr & Oct daily 9am–6pm; May–Sept daily 8am–7pm; Nov–Mar daily 9am–5pm; 2.80€)* whisks you up a 50m/164ft-high tower for great views of the surrounding countryside. From here a trail

leads to another viewpoint over the Schrammsteine rock massif in about one hour.
These formations are especially popular with rock climbers. If you want less exertion, board the nostalgic **Kirnitzschtalbahn★** railway, which trundles through a canyon alongside a creek and eventually arrives at a waterfall.

▶ Cross the Elbe at Bad Schandau and turn right along the B172 to Königstein.

Festung Königstein★★ (Königstein Fortress)
Open Apr–Oct daily 9am–6pm; Nov–Mar daily 9am–5pm. 7€.
(035021) 646 07.
www.festung-koenigstein.de.
A great sweep of the Elbe arrives at the tabletop mountain called **Königstein** (360m/1 181ft), which is crowned by a formidable fortress. Built between the 13C and the 16C, it served at one time as a prison whose list of famous inmates included porcelain inventor JF Böttger *(see MEISSEN)*; August Bebel, co-founder of the Social Democrat party; and Fritz Heckert, co-founder of the Spartacists and a prominent German Communist.
From the rampart walk, you will have far-reaching **views★★** of the Liliental tabletop mountain across the Elbe and as far as Bohemia.

▶ Continue along the B172 as far as Pirna, then turn left towards the Barockgarten.

Barockgarten Großsedlitz★
Open Apr–Aug daily 8am–8pm; Sept–Mar daily 8am–sunset. 4€.
(03529) 563 90.
www.barockgarten-grosssedlitz.de.
This French-style garden was commissioned in 1719 by Count Wackerbarth and is considered a prime example of Baroque landscape gardening.

ADDRESSES

⌂ STAY

Gästehaus Mezcalero – *Königsbrücker Straße 64.* ℘*(0351) 81 07 70. www.mezcalero.de. 25 rooms.* ⌷*6.50€.* Artistically decorated with a Mexican–Aztec theme, this upscale hostel-hotel puts you equally close to nightlife and the sights. The cheapest beds are in dorms, and some rooms share baths.

Ibis Hotels – *Prager Straße.* ℘*0351 48 56 48 56. www.ibis-dresden.de. 918 rooms (in three buildings).* ⌷*10€.* Occupying three huge Soviet-era buildings along Prager Straße, this chain hotel wins few marks for aesthetics, but its rooms offer standard international-style comforts and are steps away from the town's historic monuments.

Kangaroo-stop Hostel & Backpacker – *Erna-Berger Straße. 8–10 (300m/330yd from Neustadt station).* ℘*0351 314 34 55. www.kangaroo-stop.de. 24 rooms.* ⌷*5€.* The main advantage of this basic, friendly hostel is its price and central location. BBQs and campfires are organised on the outside terrace.

Landhaus Lockwitzgrund – *Lockwitzgrund 100.* ℘*(0351) 271 00 10. www.landhaus-lockwitzgrund.de. 11 rooms.* ⌷. *Restaurant*⌷⌷. The former stables of a noodle factory have been ingeniously converted into a romantic country estate. Rooms pair modern conveniences with historic features, and the upscale restaurant enjoys a fine reputation with guests and locals alike.

Backstage – *Prießnitzstraße. 12.* ℘*0351 888 77 77. www.backstage-hotel.de. 12 rooms.* ⌷*10€.* This trendy, affordable hotel is set in an old dairy, just a few minutes' walk from the centre of town. Rooms are large, light and comfortable, decorated by young local artists and craftspeople.

Gasthof Coschütz – *Kleinnaundorfer Straße 1.* ℘*(0351) 401 03 58. www.gasthof-coschuetz.de. 11 rooms.* ⌷. *Restaurant* ⌷⌷. Four generations have run this well-furnished, comfortable hotel on the city outskirts. The restaurant features

regional cuisine, select wines and seating on two terraces in summer.

Hotel Martha – *Nieritzstraße 11.* ℘*(0351) 817 60. www.hotel-martha-dresden.de. Closed Dec 22–27. 50 rooms.* ⌷. *Restaurant*⌷⌷. Affiliated with a non-profit Christian organisation, this hotel has a superb central location, nice rooms with classic furniture, some in *Biedermeier style*, and a cosy restaurant specialising in potato-based dishes in the vaulted cellars.

Schloss Eckberg – *Bautzner Straße 134.* ℘*(0351) 809 90. www.schloss-eckberg.de. 84 rooms.* ⌷*16.50€. Restaurant*⌷⌷. A dreamy riverside park filled with artworks surrounds this unique estate. Choose from antique-filled rooms in a neo-Gothic palace or modern ones in the Kavaliershaus, which also has three saunas. Guests enjoy breakfast at the palace, which also has a superb restaurant with views of the city skyline across the river.

Hotel Taschenbergpalais Kempinski– *Taschenberg.* ℘*0351 419 20. www.kempinski.com/en/dresden. 214 rooms.* ⌷*31€.* This imposing Baroque palace, linked to the castle by a passage, was built in 1705 by Augustus the Strong for his mistress, the Countess of Cosel. Largely destroyed in World War II, it has been splendidly rebuilt by Kempinski hotels in a "modern-with-Baroque-nuances" style to reflect its former glory. Rooms and suites have been refurbished with wooden inlay, marble and period touches.

⍩ EAT

Historisches Fischhaus – *Fischhausstraße 14 (5km/3mi northeast of city centre via Bautzner Straße.)* ℘*(0351) 89 91 00. www. historisches- fischhaus.de.* In business since 1573, this atmospheric restaurant in a leafy setting on the city outskirts specialises in the fresh catch of the day. It is also a great place to try the local beer and wine.

Aha Ladencafé – *Kreuzstraße 7.* ℘*0351 496 06 73. www.ladencafe.de.* ⍝. The arty New World-style café serves soups, salads and vegetarian dishes at reasonable prices. The building also features exhibitions and a craft shop.

⊜⊜ **Capetown's** – *Weisse Gasse 1.* ℘*0351 497 62 80. www.capetowns.de.* Set on a pleasant pedestrianised street, very close to Notre Dame, this is a good place to try South African cooking, or simply to relax with a beer or cocktail.

⊜⊜ **CoselPalais** – *An der Frauenkirche 12.* ℘*0351 496 24 44. www.coselpalais-dresden.de.* Next to the Frauenkirche, the 18C baroque palace of Count Cosel, bodyguard of Frederick Augustus, is now home to a courtyard restaurant and café; the latter serves pastries on Meissen plates, the former serves light Franco-German cuisine and excellent wines from Saxony.

⊜⊜ **Luisenhof** – *Bergbahnstraße 8.* ℘*(0351) 214 99 60. www.luisenhof-dresden.de.* Set in a historic 19C building, this restaurant is called "Dresden's balcony" for its sweeping town views. Only fresh, seasonal ingredients are used and the cakes are homemade and delicious.

⊜⊜⊜ **Schmidt's Restaurant** – *Moritzburger Weg 67.* ℘*(0351) 804 48 83. www.koenig-albert.de. Closed Sun; dinner only Sat.* At this sleek modern restaurant off the beaten path in Hellerau, it's all about the food. The menu, featuring creative approaches to European classics, changes weekly. You can order a 5-course or an 8-course tasting menu.

⊜⊜⊜⊜ **Caroussel** – *Königstraße 14.* ℘*(0351) 800 30. www.buelow-palais.de/ caroussel. Closed Sun–Mon. Reservation recommended.* Meals are celebrations in this elegant dining room. The contemporary culinary concoctions use the best the region has to offer, from venison to lamb to mushrooms and fruit. In fine weather, enjoy your meal alfresco in the glass-covered inner courtyard.

⊜⊜⊜⊜ **Elements** – *Königsbrückerstraße 96.* ℘*(0351) 27 21 696. www.restaurant-elements.de. Closed Sun.* A newcomer on the Dresden restaurant scene, Elements is earning kudos for its delicious international cuisine and warm, welcoming atmosphere.

TAKING A BREAK

Café Schinkelwache – *Theaterplatz 2.* ℘*(0351) 490 39 09. www.restaurant-dresden.de.* A stately old guardhouse designed by Karl Friedrich Schinkel has been reborn as a classic café where you can relax from sightseeing over fresh pastries or a light meal.

Café Toscana – *Schillerplatz 7 (5km/3mi east of old town on the Elbe).* ℘*(0351) 310 07 44. www.cafe-eisold.de.* This popular coffeehouse with winter garden and terrace boasts views of the *Blaues Wunder* bridge and a 12m/39ft-long cake buffet.

Dresdner Molkerei Gebrüder Pfund – *Bautzner Straße 79.* ℘*(0351) 810 59 48. www.pfunds.de.* Possibly the world's most famous dairy shop, Pfunds is decorated with a kaleidoscope of hand-painted tiles and equiped with a café and restaurant specialising in cheese-based dishes. It is hugely popular with coach tourists.

ENTERTAINMENT

Cafés, bistros and restaurants abound in the old town around the **Frauenkirche** and on **Weisse Gasse** near Altmarkt. In the **Neustadt**, upscale places concentrate on **Königstraße**, while a lively, more youthful scene dominates north of **Albertplatz**, especially on **Alaunstraße** and **Louisenstraße**.

Ballhaus Watzke – *Kötzschenbroder Straße 1 (corner of Leipziger Straße).* ℘*(0351) 85 29 20. www.watzke.de.* This brew-pub is set in a former dancehall with picture-perfect views of the old town from the riverside beer garden. Enjoy them while quaffing a glass of cold, unfiltered house lager and tucking into a plate of hearty *Haxe* (roasted pork knuckle).

Brauhaus am Waldschlösschen – *Am Brauhaus 8b (2km/1.2mi east of Albertplatz; follow Bautzner Straße).* ℘*(0351) 652 39 00. www.waldschloesschen.de.* At this attractive brew-pub you can enjoy a delicious *Dunkel* or a refreshing *Hefeweizen* along with cocktails and traditional dishes. There's live music Mon–Sat and splendid views across the Elbe from the beer garden anchored by a seven-tiered bronze fountain.

Italienisches Dörfchen –
Theaterplatz 3. ☏(0351) 498 160. www.italienisches-doerfchen.de. This gastro complex includes a fine Italian restaurant, a café, a beer garden and a riverside terrace. Some rooms have magnificent exposed beams, stuccowork and ceiling frescoes.

Winzerstube Zum Rebstock –
Hauptstraße 17. ☏(0351) 5 63 35 44. www.winzerstube-zum-rebstock.de. This sweet little wine tavern overlooks a quiet courtyard accented with a fountain and herb garden. Glasses of wine from Saxony and the Nahe region can be paired with nibbles or a full meal.

Fährgarten Johannstadt – *Käthe-Kollwitz-Ufer 23b. ☏(0351) 459 62 62. www.faehrgarten.de. Closed Nov–Mar.* Kick back in this leafy beer garden and watch the Elbe steamers pass by, preferably at sunset. If the aroma of wood-fired steaks doesn't tempt you, perhaps the delicious beers and wines will. There's a playground for children.

Semperoper – *Theaterplatz. ☏(0351) 491 17 05. www.semperoper.de.* An evening at this illustrious opera house will not be soon forgotten. The busy performance schedule includes full-length operas as well as ballet, jazz, classical concerts and contemporary dance. Book early or hope for last-minute cancellations.

SHOPPING

Dresden's main shopping streets are **Prager Straße** (department stores) and **Wilsdruffer Straße**. The best and most central all-purpose shopping centre is the **Altmarkt-Galerie**. In the new town, steer towards **Königstraße** (elegant boutiques), **Hauptstraße** (chains) and **Alaunstraße** (funky boutiques).

Kunsthofpassage – *Enter from Alaunstraße 70 or Görlitzer Straße 23. www.kunsthof-dresden.de.* This series of five courtyards, each designed by a different local artist, brims with independent boutiques selling everything from ceramics to jewellery, fashion to home accessories.

Neustädter Markthalle –
Metzer Straße 1. ☏(0351) 810 54 45. www.markthalle-dresden.de. This restored 1899 market hall has been reborn as a gourmet shopper's nirvana. Pick up fresh produce and local specialities along with toys and teas, flowers and Freiberg porcelain on the ground floor and in the basement, or fashions on the upper floor.

Markets – *Altmarkt. Mon–Sat from 9.30am.* The Spring Market *(Frühlingsmarkt)* is held here in Apr–May, the Autumn Market *(Herbstmarkt)* in Sept–Oct and the *Striezelmarkt* in Nov–Dec.

SIGHTSEEING
CITY TOURS BY COACH

Stadtrundfahrt Dresden – *☏(0351) 899 56 50, www.stadtrundfahrt.com,* 2hr tours. From Apr–Oct tours run 9:30am–10pm every 15-30 min; from Nov–Mar 9:30am–8pm every 30min. Day tickets cost ⊜20€ and are valid for unlimited stops, basic tours around the Zwinger, Frauenkirche, Pfunds Molkerei and the Fürstenzug, an evening city tour, and admission to Schloss Pillnitz. Departure Augustusbrücke/Schlossplatz and 21 other stops such as Königstraße, Dr. Külz-Straße and the Frauenkirche.

WALKING TOURS

Themed walking tours are organised by igeltours ☏(0351) 804 45 57; www.igeltour-dresden.de.

BOAT TOURS

Sächsische Dampfschiffahrt, *☏(0351) 86 60 90, www.saechsische-dampfschiffahrt.de,* offers 90min Elbe cruises in faux paddle-wheel steamers for ⊜14€-16€. Trips daily (11am, 1pm, 3pm; May–Sept also 5pm) from the Terrassenufer. Other options include Schloss Pillnitz, Meissen and "Swiss Saxony".

TRABI SAFARI

☏(0351) 89 90 01 10, www.trabi-safari.de, from 34€. Climb behind the wheel of an authentic GDR Trabant car and follow your guide, who narrates the tour while driving a separate vehicle.

Bautzen★

Crowning a rocky outcrop skirted by the Spree River, Bautzen has managed to retain its old-fashioned charm despite wars and the deprivations under the East German regime. It has been the cultural and political capital of the Sorbs, Germany's only ethnic minority, for more than 100 years. Sorbs descended from a Slavic people and speak a language related to Czech and Polish. Signs are bilingual and women still wear folkloric headdresses during traditional festivals such as the symbolic *Hexenbrennen* (witches' burning) on 30 April.

WALKING TOUR

OLD TOWN
Hauptmarkt
(Main Market Square)

The old market square is surrounded by nicely restored Baroque houses and a three-story 18C town hall built by Johann Christoph Naumann.

Reichenstraße leads east from the market square to the **Reichenturm** (Tower of the Rich; open Apr–Oct daily 10am–5pm; ⊕2€; ℘03591 46 04 31; www.bautzen.de), a 56m/179ft severely leaning tower that offers an excellent view of the city.

▶ **Population:** 39 607

🄸 **Info:** Hauptmarkt 1, 02625 Bautzen. ℘(035 91) 420 16. www.bautzen.de.

◖ **Location:** Bautzen is on the A4 autobahn linking Dresden and Görlitz.

🄯 **Timing:** Allow at least four hours to see the cathedral and Ortenburg Castle and to wander along the ramparts.

Dom St. Peter★

This hall-church (1213–1497) is shared by Roman Catholics and Protestants *(Catholic Masses in the chancel; Protestant services in the main nave).* Construction began early in the 13C, with the southern section enlarged in the 15C.

The 85m/279ft tower was crowned with a Baroque cupola in 1664. Inside the cathedral, note the large **Crucifix** (1714) by Balthazar Permoser; the **Baroque high altar** (1722–24) by G Fossati in the chancel; an **altar painting** by GA Pellegrini; and the Princes' Loggia (1674) in the Protestant section.

◖ Follow the road that runs past the cathedral as far as the monastery.

Remnants of the **monastery** date back to 1683, while the southern façade with its imposing portal is from 1755.

Bautzen with Alte Wasserkunst on the left

▶ Now follow Schloßstraße.

This charming street with restored Baroque houses leads to Ortenburg castle.

Schloss Ortenburg

Where Ortenburg stands today was once a fortified complex completed c. AD 600 and expanded in 958 by Heinrich I. Two 15C fires destroyed the original, but in the late 15C, when the region fell under Hungarian rule, Hungarian king Matthias Corvinus had it rebuilt in late-Gothic style. A relief portrait of the king graces the tower of the north wing. The Thirty Years' War left profound scars, removed by renovations after 1648. In 1698, three Renaissance gables were added.

Sorbisches Museum/ Serbski Muzej

Open Apr–Oct Tue–Fri 10am–5pm, Sat–Sun 10am–6pm; Nov–Mar Tue–Fri 10am–4pm, Sat–Sun 10am–5pm. Closed Dec 24–25 & 31. ☜5€. &. ℘(03591) 270 87 00. www.museum.sorben.com.

In the former Salt House, an annex added to Ortenburg palace in 1782, the **Sorbian Museum** illustrates the history, culture and way of life of the Sorbs from the 6C to the present.

Town Ramparts★

The 17 surviving medieval fortification towers give Bautzen its distinctive silhouette. A walk along the ramparts is like travelling back centuries in time. En route, you'll pass the enchanting ruins of the **Nikolaikirche** and its historic cemetery with ornate headstones that are veritable works of art.

Alte Wasserkunst★

Open daily Apr–Oct 10am–5pm; Feb, Mar, Nov & Dec until 4pm; Jan Sat–Sun 10am–4pm. ☜2.50€. ℘(03591) 415 88. www.altewasserkunstbautzen.de.

This formidable defensive and watertower has been standing since 1558 and supplied the town's water until 1965. Recently restored, it houses a fascinating technological exhibition. Sprawling views over the town and surroundings are obtained from the top.

ADDRESSES

🛏 STAY

⊖⊜ **Villa Antonia** – Lessingstraße 1. ℘(03591) 50 10 20. www.hotel-villa-antonia.de. 13 rooms. ☐. Restaurant ⊖⊜. This charming little hotel in a late 19C villa has bright and timelessly furnished rooms. The restaurant specialises in Austrian cuisine.

⊖⊜ **Dom Eck** – Breitengasse 2. ℘(03591) 50 13 30. www.wjelbik.de. 12 rooms. ☐. Over-shadowed by the cathedral, this artist-decorated and family-owned hotel delivers Sorbian hospitality in modern and comfortable rooms.

⊖⊜⊜ **Goldener Adler** – Hauptmarkt 4. ℘(03591) 486 60. www.goldeneradler.de. 30 rooms. ☐. Restaurant ⊖⊜. Situated right in the heart of the historic centre, this upscale hotel occupies a lovingly restored 16C building. Rooms lack no mod-cons, while the restaurant sports a romantic cross-vaulted ceiling.

🍴 EAT

⊖ **Mönchshof** – Burglehn 1. ℘(03591) 49 01 41. www.moenchshof.de. Time-travel back to the Middle Ages at this congenial inn, where you'll be eating without utensils amid historical vaults or on the terrace with sweeping views.

⊖⊜ **Wjelbik** – Kornstraße 7. ℘(03591) 420 60. www.wjelbik.de. Closed Mon. Sample Sorb culinary specialities such as elderberry soup or braised beef with horseradish at this historic restaurant. Dishes often use locally sourced ingredients.

⊖⊜ **L'Ambiente** – Hauensteingasse 1. ℘(03591) 270 757. www.l-ambiente.de. Closed Sun. If you are in the mood for Mediterranean dishes, steer the compass to this restaurant. It serves gourmet-level creations (including fresh lobster) alongside inspired pizza and pasta.

Görlitz★

Germany's easternmost city rose to prosperity during the 15C and 16C through textile manufacture and trade in woad (blue dye). World War II miraculously spared the town's more than 4 000 historic houses and today it is a veritable 3D textbook of architecture with fine examples of Renaissance, Baroque, Neoclassical and Art Nouveau buildings. Görlitz sits right on the border with Poland, from which it is separated by the Neisse River. The town opposite is called Zgorzelec.

▶ **Population:** 54 042

▯ **Info:** Obermarkt 32, 02826 Görlitz. ℘(03581) 475 70. www.goerlitz.de.

▶ **Location:** Görlitz stretches along the west bank of the Neiße River, which has formed the border with Poland since 1945.

◉ **Don't Miss:** The old town.

◕ **Timing:** Görlitz can be seen in a day.

▲▲ **Kids:** Outdoor recreation in the Zittauer Gebirge (👆see Excursions).

OLD TOWN★

Most of Görlitz's sights are concentrated in the historic town, which is anchored by two central squares, the Obermarkt and the Untermarkt.

Obermarkt

Fine Baroque houses line up along the north side of Görlitz' largest square, while its western flank is punctuated by the **Reichenbacher Turm** (open late Apr–Oct Tue–Sun 10am–5pm; ⊛3€; ℘03581 67 13 55; www.museum-goerlitz.de), a fortified 52m/170.6ft-high tower first mentioned in 1376. Some 165 steps lead to a viewing platform for fine **views★**. The nearby **Kaisertrutz** (℘03581 67 13 55; www.museum-goerlitz.de) is a massive late-Gothic keep (1490) that was once part of the medieval town fortifications. It houses exhibits on regional history.

Dreifaltigkeitskirche (Holy Trinity Church)

Open Apr–Dec Mon–Sat 10am–6pm, Sun 11.30am–6pm; Jan–Mar by appointment . ♿℘(03581) 428 70 00. Dating from the 13C, this church boasts exquisite **choir stalls★** (1484) and two valuable altars: the Baroque high altar (1713) by Caspar Gottlob von Rodewitz, a student of Permoser, and the late-Gothic winged **Golden Maria altar★** in the Barbara chapel. Its skinny bell-tower is nicknamed "Mönch" (monk).

Barockhaus (Baroque House)

Neißstraße 30. Open year-round Tue–Sun 10am–5pm. Closed Dec 24 & 31. ⊛5€. ℘(03581) 67 13 55. www.museum-goerlitz.de.
Southeast of the square, this imposing Baroque mansion (1727–1729) houses the city's fine art collection as well as decorative objects from the 16C–19C, beautiful Renaissance and Baroque furniture and precious glass. Also note the elaborately painted 18C **armoires★** on the second floor and the engravings section with works from the 16C–20C.

Untermarkt★

This historic square is framed by buildings attesting to Görlitz's one-time wealth: the 14C *Rathaus* (town hall); the Baroque Alte Börse (old stock exchange; 1706–14), now a hotel; and the 1706 Alte Waage (weigh-house).

"Silesian Heaven"

"He who doesn't know 'heaven' hasn't lived," goes a Silesian saying. Perhaps that is why their national dish is the *Schlesisches Himmelreich*. Prepared from pickled pork and dried fruit, it is served with a light lemon sauce and white bread dumplings.

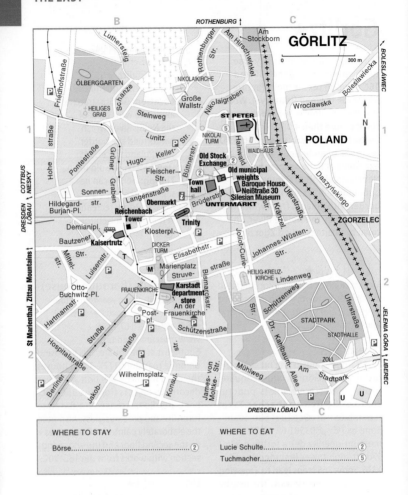

WHERE TO STAY		WHERE TO EAT	
Börse	(2)	Lucie Schulte	(2)
		Tuchmacher	(5)

Schlesisches Museum (Silesian Museum)

Brüderstraße 8. Open year-round Tue–Sun 10am–5pm. ⊕5€. ♿ 𝒫 (03581) 879 10. www.schlesisches-museum.de. The imposing Renaissance-era Schön-hof mansion is home to this modern museum detailing the cultural and political history of the region of Silesia. The emphasis is on arts and crafts of the 17C–19C. Important items include geographical views of Silesia, objects from tourism and art from the local mountains. Industrial culture, town life and the art of the classical modern movement are also included.

St. Peterskirche★

Open Apr–Dec Mon–Sat 10am–6pm, Sun 11:30am–6pm; Jan–Mar by appointment. ♿ 𝒫 (035 81) 428 70 00. A city landmark, this twin-towered church resides on a hilltop high above the Neiße. Completed in the late 15C, it contains a magnificent 17C **pulpit** with gilded acanthus leaves and a **great organ** by Eugenio Casparini (1703).

Karstadt-Warenhaus

An der Frauenkirche 5–7. Fairly plain on the outside, this steel-framed department store (1912–13) is an Art Nouveau jewel beyond its heavy doors. The most eye-popping feature is its kaleidoscopic glass ceiling.

ADDRESSES

🏠STAY

🍴🍴 **Börse** – *Untermarkt 16.* ☎*03581 764 20. www.boerse-goerlitz.de. 27 rooms.* 🛏. This ancient exchange hall, right in the city centre, has a splendid Baroque façade (1714) and has been expertly converted into a luxury hotel. Bedrooms are large, stately, comfortable and tastefully furnished with beautiful, out-of-the-ordinary antiques.

🍴 EAT

🍴🍴 **Lucie Schulte** – *Untermarkt 22.* ☎*03581 41 02 60. www.lucieschulte.de.* This pretty, stylish restaurant is tucked away in a narrow alleyway by the market. International and regional cuisine is served in an attractive vaulted dining room.

🍴🍴🍴 **Tuchmacher** – *Peterstraße 8.* ☎*03581 473 10. www.tuchmacher.de. Closed Mon lunch.* Set in an inviting Renaissance bourgeois town house (now a hotel), Tuchmacher serves fine local and regional cuisine and has a pleasant courtyard.

Annaberg-Buchholz★

After the discovery of silver and tin ore in 1491 and 1496, Annaberg and Buchholz experienced an economic boom; at its peak, 600 mines enriched the people in the capital of the Erzgebirge (Ore) Mountains. In the 16C, as the silver petered out, lace production became Annaberg's most important industry. Today the town's principal attraction is its Gothic cathedral.

🛈 **Info:** Adam-Ries-Straße 16, 09456 Annaberg-Buchholz. ☎(03733) 18 80 00. www.erzgebirge-tourismus.de.

🢒 **Location:** The mountains follow the border of Germany and the Czech Republic for about 150km/93mi.

🕐 **Timing:** Allow at least three hours for the suggested driving tour.

SIGHTS

St. Annen-Kirche★★

Open Apr–Dec Mon–Sat 10am–5pm, Sun noon–5pm; Jan–Mar Mon–Sat 11am–4pm, Sun noon–4pm. ☎(03733) 231 90. www.annenkirche.de.

Built between 1499 and 1525, St. Anna's is one of the most important late-Gothic hall-churches in Germany. Twelve slender pillars support the vaulted ceiling, each yoke covered by a "blossom baldaquin". The gallery parapets feature scenes from the Old and New Testaments. Especially noteworthy is the **Schöne Tür★★** (beautiful door), a multi-coloured portal designed in 1512 by Hans Witten, one of this region's most accomplished wood carvers of the late-Gothic period. He also created the church's Madonna sculpture and the delicate baptismal font. References to Annaberg's mining past are evident in the **pulpit★★** (1516), which is decorated with the relief figure of a miner. Also note the painted panels behind the **Miners' Altar★** (Bergmannsaltar, c. 1520), depicting various stages of mine work in that period. The tower, which is still inhabited by the keeper, can be climbed from May to September.

Erzgebirgsmuseum mit Besucherbergwerk

Große Kirchgasse 16. 🢒🢒Guided tours (1hr) year-round daily 10am–5pm. Closed Dec 24 & 31. 🎫5.50€ (museum and mine). ☎(037 33) 234 97. www.annaberg-buchholz.de.

This museum retraces local history with an emphasis on mining. It has some endearing examples of local folk art. Annexed to the museum is the **Im Gößner** mine, which opened at the height of Annaberg's prosperity c. 1498. *The entrance shaft is in the museum courtyard.*

Technisches MuseumFrohnauer Hammer (Frohnau Forge Technical Museum)

Sehmatalstraße 3. ✎ Guided tours (1hr) year-round daily 9am–noon, 1pm–4.30pm. Closed Jan 1, Dec 25. ⊛3€. ✆(037 33) 220 00. www.annaberg-buchholz.de/hammer. This 15C mill complex south of the old town started out as a flower mill, then housed a coin mint. In the 17C it was converted into an iron forge. On tours you get to see close-ups of the historic hydraulic bellows and the power-hammers, some of them massive in size. Upstairs is a wide array of objects produced at the forge, while the gallery opposite presents artistic woodcarvings. Visits wrap up in the former miller's mansion, where you can observe a lace-maker at work.

🚗 DRIVING TOUR

THE ORE MOUNTAINS★

81km/50.3mi (93km/57.7mi via Schwarzenberg).

▶ Follow the B95 from Annaberg-Buchholz to Oberwiesenthal.

For centuries, the Ore Mountains yielded silver, tin, cobalt, nickel and iron in sumptuous amounts, bringing great prosperity to this remote region of Saxony. When the mines petered out, locals turned to craftmaking as a source of income. Many of Germany's finest Christmas ornaments and decorations are still produced here, often by hand, to this day.

Fichtelberg

The highest peak of the Erzgebirge, the Fichtelberg soars 1 214m/3 983ft above the ski resort of Oberwiesenthal. Ride the chair-lift to the top for a sweeping **panorama★**.

▶ A pretty forest road winds from Oberwiesenthal to Ehrenzipfel. Optional detour to Schwarzenberg.

Schwarzenberg

Resting on a crag, this historic town boasts a 12C fortress that became the Elector's hunting lodge in 1555-58. The adjacent Baroque **St. Georgenkirche★** dates to 1690-99.

▶ The road reaches the Sosa Talsperre, a pretty reservoir and a nice spot for taking a break. The route then climbs along the winding valley of the Zwickauer Mulde to Klingenthal.

Klingenthal

This former mining community is best known for the musical instruments made here since the mid-17C. The Baroque church **Zum Friedenfürsten**, which features an unusual octagonal floor-plan, makes a pleasant stop for stretching your legs.

ADDRESSES

🛏 STAY

⊜⊜ **Wilder Mann** – *Markt 13.* ✆03733 14 40. www.hotel-wildermann.de. 71 rooms. ⊒. *Restaurant*⊜⊜. This fine hotel occupies a Gothic Flamboyant-style building dating from 1509, one of the oldest houses in the city, complete with vaulted entrance hall. Bedrooms are modern and there is a sauna. Its Silberbaum restaurant occupies the atmospheric, vaulted Kartoffelkeller (potato cellar), which specialises in potato-based dishes, of course.

🍴 EAT

⊜⊜ **Zum Hammer** – *Tannenberg, 6km/4mi north of Annaberg-Buchholz. Untere Dorfstraße 21.* ✆03733 529 51. www.zumhammer.de. Open lunch and dinner weekends; dinner only Mon–Fri. Dark wooden beams, tiled floors and rustic furniture give this restaurant a rustic atmosphere.

Meissen★

Meissen is famous for its porcelain, distinguished by its logo showing a pair of crossed swords in blue. At the heart of Germany's second-most northerly wine growing region, it also produces pleasantly fruity dry white wines. Meissen's historic centre, which is remarkably well preserved, is dominated by the flamboyant Albrechtsburg and the cathedral.

▶ **Population:** 27 135
- **Info:** Markt 3, 01662 Meissen. ℘(03521) 419 40. www.touristinfo-meissen.de.
- **Location:** Meissen lies in the picturesque Elbe Valley, near Dresden.
- **Don't Miss:** The Burgberg and Museum of Meissen Art.
- **Timing:** It takes about half a day to explore Meissen.

A BIT OF HISTORY

It was in 1708, in the reign of Augustus the Strong, that **Johann Friedrich Böttger** (1682–1719) discovered the formula for creating the white hard-paste porcelain until then made only in China. In 1710 Augustus the Strong founded the Royal Saxon Porcelain Factory.

OLD MEISSEN

The old town has plenty of Gothic and Renaissance charm. **Marktplatz** is dominated by the late-Gothic **Rathaus** (town hall, 1470–86), the late-15C Bennohaus, the Renaissance **Marktapotheke** (pharmacy; 1555–60), and the Hirschhaus with a 1642 doorway.

Frauenkirche (Church of Our Lady)

Currently undergoing renovation.
This late-Gothic hall-church with its fine star-vaulting cuts a commanding presence on the Marktplatz. Its carillon bells are made of Meissen porcelain. For fine views of the town and the river, climb the **tower** (open daily 10am–4pm; ⚅2€; www/freunkirche-meissen.de).

BURGBERG★★

On a hilltop above the old town, the castle **Albrechtsburg★** (open Mar–Oct daily 10am–6pm; Nov–Feb daily 10am–5pm; closed Dec 24–25; ⚅8€; ℘03521 470 70; www.albrechtsburg-meissen.de) is one of the finest civic examples of the late-Gothic (1521–24) style. An exhibit on the ground floor illuminates the historical and technical aspects of por-

celain making, while the second floor boasts a stunning collection of medieval sculpture. Two rooms tell the story of the castle as the site of Europe's first porcelain factory. Next door, the **Dom★** (Cathedral) is a Gothic hall-church built from 1250 atop a Romanesque sanctuary and completed in the late 15C. Note the **funerary plaques★** in the **Fürstenkapelle** (Dukes' Chapel) and the **lay brothers' altar★** *(Laienaltar)* in front of the rood screen, which can be traced to Lucas Cranach the Elder. The **Stifterfiguren★★** (benefactors' statues) in the chancel represent Emperor Otto I and his second wife, Empress Adelaide.

Museum of Meissen Art★

Talstraße 9. Open May–Oct daily 9am–6pm; Nov–Apr daily 9am–5pm. Closed Dec 24–26. ⚅9€. ℘(03521) 46 82 08. www.meissen.com.
In 1865, the studios and workshops of the Meissen factory were transferred from the Albrechtsburg castle, where they had been for 150 years, to this site about 1km/0.6mi southwest of the town centre.
Start your visit by joining a guided tour of four **demonstration workshops★★**, where the processes of manufacturing, decorating and firing porcelain can be observed *(expect long queues)*. This portion of the tour is followed by a spin around the **Schauhalle** (exhibition room), which displays the world's largest collection of Meissen porcelain from 1910 to today.

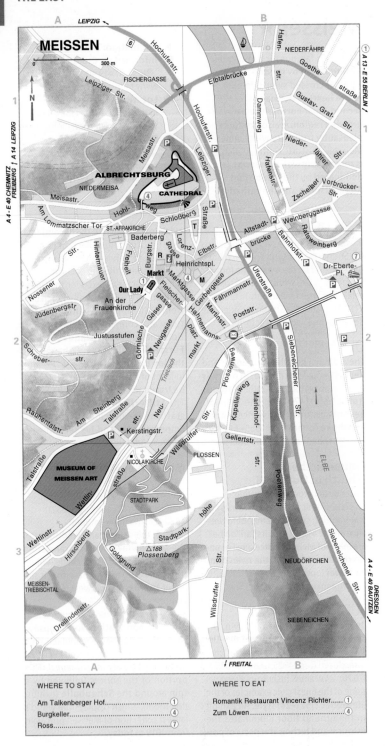

MEISSEN

0 — 300 m

WHERE TO STAY

Am Talkenberger Hof	①
Burgkeller	④
Ross	⑦

WHERE TO EAT

Romantik Restaurant Vincenz Richter	①
Zum Löwen	④

ADDRESSES

🖘STAY

Hotel Am Talkenberger Hof –
*Am Talkenberger Hof 15, 01640 Coswig,
near Meissen.* ✆*(03523) 743 17. www.
talkenberger-hof.de.* 🛏 *9 rooms.* A warm
atmosphere reigns at this charming
inn draped in vine leaves and flowers.
It's right on the Saxon Wine Road and
has clean, well cared-for rooms with
country-style furnishings. From the
terrace you can enjoy superb views
over the Elbe Valley.

Ross – *Großenhainer Straße 9.
✆03521 75 10. www.hotelrossmeissen.de.*
🛏 *39 rooms.* This centuries-old
coaching inn, opposite the station, has
been converted into a modern hotel by
the Eichholz family.

Burgkeller – *Domplatz 11.
✆03521 414 00. www.hotel-burgkeller-
meissen.de. 10 rooms.* 🛏 *Restaurants*
🛏. The elegant bedrooms of this
alluring small hotel, established in 1881,
overlook the cathedral.

🍽 EAT

**Romantik Restaurant Vincenz
Richter** – *An der Frauenkirche 12.
✆03 521 45 32 85. www.vincenz-richter.de
Closed last 3 weeks Jan and Mon.*
This charming picture-book, historic
property began life as a draper's
business in 1523. It now serves regional
cooking. In summer, patrons dine in the
delightful inner courtyard.

Zum Löwen – *Heinrichplatz 6.
✆03 521 411 10. www.welcome-hotels.
com/hotel-goldener-loewe-meissen/
gastronomie.* The main restaurant serves
creative regional and international
cuisine in an elegant setting. The
Weinstube offers regional dishes of
excellent value.

Leipzig★

Leipzig has been renowned as a
place of commerce since the Middle
Ages, but the city also has a proud
musical heritage. Bach, Wagner
and Mendelssohn-Bartholdy all
lived here, and its orchestras and
musical institutions still enjoy a
fine reputation throughout Europe.
In the late 1980s, Leipzig was a
leading centre of the peaceful
protests that led to the downfall of
the German Democratic Republic,
paving the way for the reunification
of the two Germanies in 1990 (*see
INTRODUCTION: History*).

▶ **Population:** 531 582
ℹ **Info:** Katharinenstraße 8,
04109 Leipzig. ✆(0341) 710
42 60. www.lts-leipzig.de.
◐ **Location:** Leipzig lies in the
far west of Saxony, at the
confluence of the Weiße
Elster and Pleiße rivers.
🅿 **Parking:** Garages are
plentiful, especially near
the main train station.
◈ **Don't Miss:** Bach Museum,
St. Thomas Church and the
Musical Instrument Museum;
a concert at the Gewandhaus.
◑ **Timing:** Allow a full day to
explore Leipzig's musical
and political heritage.

A BIT OF HISTORY

The Leipzig Fairs – The first mention
of Leipzig was in the chronicle of Bishop
Thietmar of Merseburg (975–1018),
who noted the death of the Bishop of
Meissen in "Urbs Lipzi". The township
of "Lipzk" was granted a city charter
around 1165, roughly the year when
it held its first **trade fair**. It is still held
today, making the fair the oldest in the
world.

One of the world's earliest books,
the *Glossa Super Apocalipsim*, was
printed in Leipzig in 1481. These days,
Leipzig sustains its literary heritage

Gewandhausorchester Leipzig

Many orchestras were founded as court orchestras, but not the Leipzig Gewandhaus Orchestra, which got its start in 1843 thanks to donations from wealthy burghers. The orchestra got its unusual name ("cloth-hall orchestra") because its first performance space in 1781 was in the converted Clothworkers' Guildhall.

Famous composers and performers appeared here over the centuries, and Beethoven's *Triple Concerto*, Schubert's *Symphony in C major*, Mendelssohn's *"Scottish" Symphony* and Brahms' *Violin Concerto in D major* all premiered here.

In 1884, the orchestra finally got its own purpose-built concert hall. Bombed in 1944, it was rebuilt in modern fashion in 1981. Famous Gewandhaus directors have included Felix Mendelssohn-Bartholdy, Arthur Nikisch and Kurt Masur. Since 2005 it has been helmed by Riccardo Chailly.

with an annual **book fair**, Germany's second-largest after Frankfurt's. Leipzig also enjoys a fine reputation musically, thanks to the Choir of St. Thomas (Thomanerchor), the Gewandhaus Orchestra and the Felix Mendelssohn-Bartholdy University of Music and Theatre.

A prosperous city – The discovery in the 16C of silver in the Erzgebirge Mountains ensured Leipzig's prosperity. Today the city is still an important economic centre with corporate investors that include Porsche and BMW.

OLD TOWN★

The historic centre of Leipzig, south of the impressive central station *(Hauptbahnhof)* with its huge shopping centre, is encircled by a ring road tracing the town's medieval fortifications.

Altes Rathaus★
(Old Town Hall)

Anchoring the Markt, this long, low building with its decorated façade and dwarf gables is a typical example of German Renaissance architecture. It was completed in 1556 after plans by Hieronymus Lotter. The tower features a balcony for town pipers or heralds. Today the building houses the local history museum, the **Stadtgeschichtliches Museum** *(open year-round Tue–Sun 10am–6pm; closed Dec 24, 25 & 31; ∞6€; ⚒; ℘0341 965 13 20; www.stadtgeschichtliches-museum-leipzig.de).*

Zeitgeschichtliches Forum★
(Forum of Contemporary History)

Grimmaische Straße 6. Open year-round Tue–Fri 9am–6pm, Sat–Sun 10am–6pm. ℘(0341) 222 00. www.hdg.de.
This modern and engaging museum chronicles the history of the German Democratic Republic, the daily lives of its citizens, and the peaceful movement that led to the GDR's downfall.

Alte Börse★
(Old Exchange)

On the Naschmarkt.
This former commodities market (built 1678–87) was Leipzig's first Baroque edifice. Today it is a splendid venue for receptions, concerts and other events. The statue outside (by Carl Seffner, 1903) shows Goethe as a student.

Katharinenstraße

North of the Alte Börse.
Of the Baroque houses on the west side of Katharinenstraße the finest is the **Romanushaus** *(at the Brühl)*, built in 1701 by Johann Gregor Fuchs. The neighbouring houses *(nos 21 and 19)* were built in the mid-18C. Also designed by Fuchs, the Fregehaus *(no 11)* belonged to the wealthy banker Christian Gottlob Frege, whose trade emporium stretched across Europe and extended to America.

Museum der Bildenden Künste★★
(Fine Arts Museum)

Katharinenstraße 10. Open year-round Tue, Thu–Sun 10am–6pm, Wed noon–8pm. ⊚5€. ♿ ✆(0341) 21 69 90. www.mdbk.de.

A striking 34m/111.5ft-high glass cube is the modern home of a fantastic art collection with works from the late Middle Ages to the present. Highlights include rooms dedicated to native sons Max Beckmann and New Leipzig School representative Neo Rauch.

Notable **German Old Masters** include works by Master Francke, Lucas Cranach the Elder and Hans Baldung Grien. **Flemish Old Masters** are represented by disciples of van Eyck and Rembrandt, van der Weyden, Frans Hals and van Ruisdael. **Italian Masters** include Conegliano, Francia and Tintoretto. **German 19C painters** receive ample space, with works by Anton Graff, Tischbein, CD Friedrich, Spitzweg, Böcklin, Liebermann, Klinger and Leibl.

The Sculpture Department displays works by, among others, Permoser, Thorvaldsen, Rodin and Klinger. The collection of prints and drawings offers a virtually unbroken survey of graphic art from medieval times to the present.

Nikolaikirche★
(Church of St. Nicholas)

Nikolaistraße. Open year-round Mon–Sat 10am–6pm. ✆(0341) 124 53 80. www.nikolaikirche-leipzig.de.

This 12C church played a key role in the peaceful revolution of 1989. From 1982 a **prayer group** of Christians and non-Christians met at the church every Monday at 5pm to pray for peace. In 1989 tensions rose as troops attacked unarmed citizens. On Monday, 9 October, 1 000 socialist unity party members were summoned to the church. As the prayer group left the church, a crowd of 10 000 was waiting, all holding candles. Dedicated to St. Nicholas, the patron saint of merchants, the edifice was originally Romanesque in style but under-

Mädlerpassage

© Mauritius/Photononstop

Arcades

Leipzig's glass-roofed arcades are remarkably well restored and now make an attractive setting for a great variety of shops, cafés and bars.

Mädlerpassage – *Opposite Naschmarkt.* This is the grandest and best known of the arcades, home to Auerbachs Keller, where Goethe set scenes in *Faust.*

Specks Hof – *Schuhmachergäßchen.* The restoration of this 1911 trade hall preserved its best old features while modernising the whole.

Strohsack – This modern arcade links Nikolaistraße with Ritterstraße. Check the time on the glass-covered clock in the floor.

Steibs Hof – *Between Brühlstraße and Nikolaistraße.* This 1907 trade fair house appeals with its blue-and-white tiled courtyards.

Jägerhofpassage – *Between Hainstraße and Grosse Fleischergasse.* This 1914 *Jugendstil* arcade with ivory-tiled walls now houses a cinema.

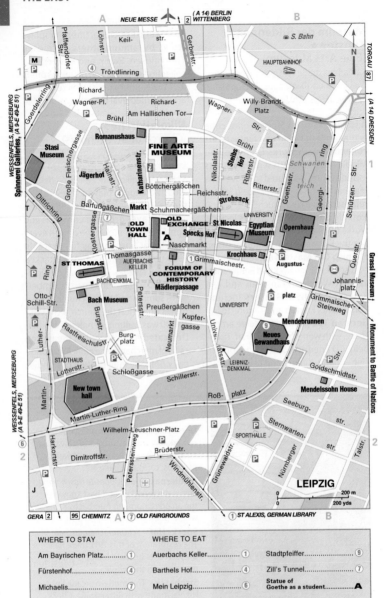

NEUE MESSE · (A 14) BERLIN WITTENBERG · (A 14) DRESDEN · TORGAU 87

HAUPTBAHNHOF

S. Bahn

WEISSENFELS, MERSEBURG, Spinnerei Galleries, (A 9-E 49-E 51)

Pfaffendorfer Str. · Keil-str. · Löhrstr. · Gerberstr. · Tröndlinring · Richard-Wagner-Pl. · Richard-Am Hallischen Tor · Wagner- · Willy-Brandt-Platz · Str. · Brühl · Goerdelerring · Große Fleischergasse · Hainstr.

Romanushaus · FINE ARTS MUSEUM · Katharinenstr. · Nikolaistr. · Steibs Hof · Ritterstr. · Goethestr. · Georgi-ring · Schützen- Str. · Schwanen-teich

Stasi Museum · Jägerhof · Barfußgässchen · Böttchergäßchen · Reichsstr. · Schuhmachergäßchen · Strohsack · UNIVERSITY

Dittrichring · Klostergasse · Markt · OLD TOWN HALL · OLD EXCHANGE · Specks Hof · St Nicolas · Egyptian Museum · Opernhaus

Ring · Thomasgasse · AUERBACHS KELLER · Naschmarkt · Krochhaus · Augustus- · Grassi Museum · Monument to Battle of Nations

ST THOMAS · BACHDENKMAL · FORUM OF CONTEMPORARY HISTORY · Mädlerpassage · Grimmaischestr. · platz · Grimmaischer Steinweg · Johannis-platz

Otto-Schill-Str. · Bach Museum · Petersstr. · Preußergäßchen · Kupfer-gasse · UNIVERSITY · Mendebrunnen

Rastfreischulstr. · Burgstr. · Burgplatz · Neumarkt · Universitätsstr. · Neues Gewandhaus · Goldschmidtstr. · Str.

Luther- · STADTHAUS · Lotterstr. · Schloßgasse · Schillerstr. · LEIBNIZ-DENKMAL · Mendelssohn House

WEISSENFELS, MERSEBURG, (A 9-E 49-E 51)

Martin- · New town hall · Martin-Luther-Ring · Roß-platz · Seeburg-str. · Sternwarten-str.

Harkortstr. · Wilhelm-Leuschner-Platz · Brüderstr. · SPORTHALLE · Nürnberger Str. · Talstr.

Dimitroffstr. · POL. · Petersteinweg · Windmühlenstr. · Grünewaldstr. · LEIPZIG

GERA 2 · 95 CHEMNITZ · OLD FAIRGROUNDS · ST ALEXIS, GERMAN LIBRARY

200 m / 200 yds

went Gothic modifications, including the 14C chancel and west towers and the 16C triple nave and central tower. Its impressive Neoclassical **interior★**, by Carl Dauthe, dates back to the late 18C. Pale, fluted pillars end in light green palm leaves, while the vaulting is coffered in rose with stucco flowers. In the narthex and chancel hang 30 paintings.

Thomaskirche★ (Church of St. Thomas)

Thomaskirchhof. Open year-round daily 9am–6pm. ℘(0341) 22 22 40. www.thomaskirche.org.

First documented in 1212, this late-Gothic triple-aisle church took on its present appearance in the late 15C. **Johann Sebastian Bach** was cantor here for 27 years and is buried opposite the altar. The church is also renowned for the **St. Thomas Boys' Choir** (Thomanerchor), once directed by Bach, which occasionally performs during concerts and church services.

Bachmuseum

Thomaskirchhof 15-16. Open year-round Tue–Sun 10am–6pm. Closed Dec 24, 25 & 31. ⊚8€. ♿ ℘(0341) 913 72 02. www.bachmuseum-leipzig.de.

The Bach Museum occupies the 16C home of the Bose merchant family, who were good friends with the Bachs. Revamped and expanded, it introduces visitors in interactive fashion to the great composer, his family and his times. Aside from perusing documents and instruments, you get to customise the instrumentation of a chorale and learn how to date a Bach manuscript.

Ägyptisches Museum★ (Egyptian Museum)

Goethestraße 2. Open year-round Tue–Fri 1pm–5pm, Sat–Sun 10am–5pm. Closed Jan 1, May 1, Dec 24 & 31. ⊚5€. ♿ ℘(0341) 973 70 15. www.uni-leipzig. de/~egypt/.

The 9 000 exhibits in this museum range from antiquity to the Christian era.

THE RING ROAD AND AREA
Augustusplatz

This vast square is encircled by some of Leipzig's most important cultural institutions. The entire north side is taken up by the monumental **Opernhaus** (opera house), dating from the 1960s. Behind it is a pleasant park with a duck pond and a statue of Richard Wagner. On the square's west end looms Leipzig's first skyscraper, the **Krochhaus** (1928–29), which in 1970 was bested by the MDR Hochhaus next to the Neues Gewandhaus concert hall. Leipzig University is here as well.

Neues Gewandhaus

Inaugurated in 1981, this famous concert hall is home to the famous Gewandhausorchester. The massive auditorium has seats for up to 1 900 music fans. The

Musicians in Leipzig

Johann Sebastian Bach composed and worked in Leipzig from 1723–1750 as cantor of St. Thomas and as music director for all the town's churches. Bach had faded into obscurity when **Felix Mendelssohn-Bartholdy** became director of the Gewandhaus orchestra in 1835. He turned Leipzig into a city of musical renown, established Germany's first musical conservatory and composed numerous original musical works. **Clara Wieck** and **Robert Schumann** lived in a Neoclassical house at Inselstraße 16, which now contains a memorial exhibit. The *Spring Symphony* was composed here.

bust of Beethoven (1902) in the foyer is a work by Leipzig-born Max Klinger. The neo-Baroque **Mendebrunnen** Fountain (1886) outside the Gewandhaus is anchored by an 18m/ 59ft granite obelisk ringed by figures from Greek mythology symbolising the importance of water for humankind.

Mendelssohn-Haus (Mendelssohn House)

Goldschmidtstraße 12. Open year-round daily 10am–6pm. ⊚7.50€. ℘(0341) 127 02 94. www.mendelssohn-stiftung.de.

This house was the last residence (1845–47) of the famous composer **Felix Mendelssohn-Bartholdy**, who moved to Leipzig in 1835 to head the prestigious Gewandhaus orchestra. The museum in his first-floor apartment uses letters, compositions, original furniture, watercolours that he painted himself and other memorabilia to illustrate his life, times and accomplishments. *Concerts (⊚15€) are held in the Musik Salon every Saturday at 11am.*

Neues Rathaus
(New Town Hall)

The 19C town hall was built on the foundations of Pleißenburg Castle, best known as the scene of a famous argument between Luther and Eck in 1519.

ADDITIONAL MUSEUMS
Museen im Grassi ★
(Grassi Museum)

Johannisplatz 5–11. ⬭Combination ticket to two Grassi museums is 12€, to all three, 15€. www.grassimuseum.de.
The Grassi museums complex was built between 1925 and 1929 in the Expressionist style, with echoes of Art Deco, by Carl William Zweck and Hans Voigt. It comprises three museums organised around four inner courtyards.

Museum für Angewandte Kunst★
(Museum of Applied Arts)

Open year-round Tue–Sun 10am–6pm. Closed Dec 24 & 31. ⬭5€. ♿℘(0341) 222 91 00. www.grassimuseum.de.
This collection covers European arts and crafts from the Middle Ages to the early 20C. Exhibits include furniture (e.g. Nuremberg hall cabinet, 16C), porcelain (Meissen), glassware (Venetian, Bohemian) and valuable *Jugendstil* pieces (Gallé, Lalique).

Museum für Völkerkunde★
(Museum of Ethnography)

Open year-round Tue–Sun 10am–6pm. Closed Dec 24 & 31. ⬭8€. ♿℘(0341) 973 19 00. www.mvl-grassimuseum.de.
One of the oldest and most important ethnographic museums in Europe, this institution explores the history and culture of the peoples of Asia, Africa, America and Oceania.

Museum für Musikinstrumente★
(Museum of Musical Instruments)

Open year-round Tue–Sun 10am–6pm. Closed Dec 24 & 31. ⬭6€. ℘(0341) 973 07 50. http://mfm.uni-leipzig.de.
One of Europe's finest of its kind, this museum displays 5 000 instruments from five centuries and from around the world, as well as an interactive sound laboratory.

Museum in der Runden Ecke
(Stasi Museum)

Dittrichring 24. Open year-round daily 10am–6pm. Closed Jan 1, Dec 23–26 & 31. ℘(0341) 961 24 43. www.runde-ecke-leipzig.de.
In the former *Stasi* headquarters, this exhibition provides a look at the machinations and methods used by the infamous East German Ministry for State Security to spy on its own people.

Spinnerei Museum/Galleries

Spinnereistr. 7. Open year-round Tue–Sat 11am–6pm. Closed Jan 1, Dec 25 & 31. ℘(0341) 498 02 22. www.spinnerei.de.
For fans of contemporary art, this gallery complex is a must-see. Housed in a former cotton factory repurposed as art galleries, the Spinnerei has become the heart of the vibrant Leipzig art scene.

ADDRESSES

⬭STAY

⬭⬭**Hotel Am Bayrischen Platz** – *Paul-List-Straße 5. ℘(0341) 14 08 60. www.hotel-bayrischer-platz.de. 32 rooms.* ⬭. Karl Marx slept here in 1874, and you can stay in the same room. Other rooms at this villa-style hotel are smaller and less fancy but still tastefully furnished.

⬭⬭⬭**Hotel Michaelis** – *Paul-Gruner-Straße 44. ℘(0341) 267 80. www.michaelis-leipzig.de. 62 rooms.* ⬭. *Restaurant* ⬭⬭⬭, *closed Sun.* Built in 1907 and now a listed building, this hotel has been renovated with an eye for detail. Rooms are harmonious, elegant and individually styled, while the restaurant is modern and tastefully decorated.

⬭⬭⬭⬭**Hotel Fürstenhof** – *Tröndlinring 8. ℘(0341) 14 00. www. hotelfuerstenhofleipzig.com. 92 rooms.* ⬭25€. *Restaurant* ⬭⬭⬭⬭, *closed Sun.* Behind the façade of this classic mansion (1770) awaits a luxuriously elegant interior. Service is impeccable and the Mediterranean-style spa complex is an oasis of relaxation. The restaurant has a refined setting.

♈/EAT

Barthels Hof – *Hainstraße 1.* *℘(0341) 14 13 10. www.barthels-hof.de.* At this carefully restored 18C restaurant, choose one of three dining rooms: the elegant white-linen Webers Speisestube, the cross-vaulted Barthels wine tavern and the historical cellars. Two courtyards beckon in good weather. It's a fine establishment to sample classic Saxon cuisine.

Mein Leipzig – *Käthe-Kollwitz-Straße 71. ℘(0341) 21 55 944. www. restaurant-meinleipzig.de.* Taking its name from a quote by Goethe, this classic restaurant offers an elegant yet relaxed setting in which to enjoy German and Mediterranean dishes. There's a cosy bar in the cellar.

"Zill's Tunnel" Restaurant – *Barfußgässchen 9. ℘(0341) 960 20 78. www.zillstunnel.de.* This restaurant-cum-tavern has been doling out German and Saxon dishes since 1841.

Auerbachs Keller – Historische Weinstuben – *Grimmaische Straße 2 (Mädler-Passage). ℘(0341) 21 61 00. www.auerbachs-keller-leipzig.de.* A Leipzig institution, this wine tavern and restaurant has been in business since 1525. It was a favourite hangout of Goethe and reportedly provided inspiration for a scene from *Faust*. The cuisine is classic and traditional.

Stadtpfeiffer – *Augustusplatz 8. ℘0341 217 89 20. www.stadtpfeiffer.de. Dinner only. Closed Sun–Mon and Jul–Aug.* Petra and Detlef Schlegel go to great lengths to welcome their guests and serve faultless seasonal cuisine. There is a tasting menu (6 courses 118€, 5 courses 108€, 4 courses 98€) plus à la carte dishes.

TAKING A BREAK
USEFUL TIPS
Leipziger Lerchen ("Leipzig larks") are a local speciality found in all cake shops. The actual bird once contributed to the town's culinary reputation, but when the king of Saxony banned lark hunting in 1876, bakers transferred the name to a new pastry, made of shortbread and almond paste.

NIGHTLIFE
USEFUL TIPS
Lively bars cluster in the city centre between the Brühl and the Neues Rathaus. The most animated lane is the Barfußgässchen in the pedestrian zone, which is chock-a-block with bars, restaurants and cafés. West of here, Gottschedstraße draws scores of night owls and students. For alternative flair, head south to Karl-Liebknecht-Straße, locally known as "Karli". In the west, fans of contemporary art like Karl-Heine-Straße, which leads to the Spinnerei gallery complex.

PUBLICATIONS
The monthly calendar of events, *Leipzig im…* is available at the tourist office for 0.50€, while the listings magazine *Prinz* can be found online at prinz.de/leipzig.

SHOPPING
USEFUL TIPS
Leipzig is a great place to shop. Many of the finest stores are in such glass-roofed arcades as the Mädlerpassage, Specks Hof, Strohsack, Steibs Hof and Jägerhofpassage. The biggest shopping centre is housed in the main train station.

INDEX

INDEX

INDEX

INDEX

INDEX

INDEX

🛏 STAY

🍴 EAT

Thematic Maps

Maps and Plans

	Sight	Seaside Resort	Winter Sports Resort	Spa
Highly recommended	★★★	≜≜≜	✳✳✳	‡‡‡
Recommended	★★	≜≜	✳✳	‡‡
Interesting	★	≜	✳	‡

Tourism

◉⟹	Sightseeing route with departure point indicated	AZ B	Map co-ordinates locating sights
🏛🕆🏛🕆	Ecclesiastical building	🛈	Tourist information
🕎 ☪	Synagogue – Mosque	⤨ ⁙	Historic house, castle – Ruins
🏠	Building (with main entrance)	⌣ ✿	Dam – Factory or power station
■	Statue, small building	✩ ⌒	Fort – Cave
✝	Wayside cross	⊓	Prehistoric site
◎	Fountain	▼ ₩	Viewing table – View
—•—►►	Fortified walls – Tower – Gate	▲	Miscellaneous sight

Recreation

🏇	Racecourse	🚶	Waymarked footpath
⛸	Skating rink	◆	Outdoor leisure park/centre
≋ ▦	Outdoor, indoor swimming pool	👿	Theme/Amusement park
⚓	Marina, moorings	🐾	Wildlife/Safari park, zoo
⌂	Mountain refuge hut	❀	Gardens, park, arboretum
□–■–■–□	Overhead cable-car	🐦	Aviary, bird sanctuary
🚂	Tourist or steam railway		

Additional symbols

═══ ═══	Motorway (unclassified)	✉ ☎	Post office – Telephone centre
❶ ❶	Junction: complete, limited	✉	Covered market
▭▬ ▬	Pedestrian street	•✕•	Barracks
I = = = = I	Unsuitable for traffic, street subject to restrictions	△	Swing bridge
▭▭ - - - -	Steps – Footpath	⛏ ✕	Quarry – Mine
🚈 🚌	Railway – Coach station	Ⓑ Ⓕ	Ferry (river and lake crossings)
□+++++□	Funicular – Rack-railway	🚢	Ferry services: Passengers and cars
—•— 🚇	Tram – Metro, underground	⇌	Foot passengers only
Bert (R.)...	Main shopping street	③	Access route number common to MICHELIN maps and town plans

Abbreviations and special symbols

Ⓒ	Capital of a "Canton" (Kantonshauptort)	P	Offices of cantonal authorities (Kantonale Verwaltung)
G	Local police station (Kantonspolizei)	POL.	Police (Stadtpolizei)
H	Town hall (Rathaus)	T	Theatre (Theater)
J	Law courts (Justizpalast)	U	University (Universität)
M	Museum (Museum)	🅿	Park and Ride

Useful Words and Phrases

COMMON WORDS AND PHRASES

	Translation
ja, nein	yes, no
danke	thank you
bitte	please
Hallo (informal)	Hello
Tschüss (informal)	Bye
Guten Tag (formal)	Good day
Auf Wiedersehen (formal)	Goodbye
eins, zwei, drei	one, two, three
vier, fünf, sechs	four, five, six
sieben, acht	seven, eight
neun, zehn	nine, ten
links, rechts	left, right
Wie geht es Ihnen?	How are you?
Sprechen Sie Englisch?	Do you speak English?
Ich spreche kein Deutsch.	I don't speak German.
Was kostet das?	How much is it?
Das ist zu teuer	That's too expensive.
Wo ist...?	Where is...?
Ich heisse...	My name is...
Wieviel Uhr ist es?	What time is it?
Ist der Tisch frei?	Is that table taken?
Die Rechnung, bitte.	The bill, please.
Haben Sie ein Zimmer frei?	Are there any rooms available?
Wo ist die Toilette?	Where is the loo?
Hilfe!	Help!
Entschuldigung	Sorry
Montag	Monday
Dienstag	Tuesday
Mittwoch	Wednesday
Donnerstag	Thursday
Freitag	Friday
Samstag	Saturday
Sonntag	Sunday
Ein Bier, bitte	A beer, please.
Frühstück	Breakfast
Mittagessen	Lunch
Abendessen	Dinner
Imbiss	Snack
Polizei	Police
Krankenhaus	Hospital
Rufen Sie einen Arzt!	Call a doctor!
Es ist ein Notfall!	Emergency!
gut	good
schlecht	bad
Ich habe mich verirrt.	I'm lost.
Wie weit ist es...?	How far is it?

Nürnberger Rostbratwürste

© Karl-Friedrich Hohl/iStockphoto.com

REGIONAL SPECIALITIES

BAVARIA AND FRANCONIA

Leberknödel: Dumplings of liver, bread and onion, sometimes in broth.
Leberkäs: Minced beef and pork (no liver), cooked in the form of a loaf.
Knödel: Dumplings of potato or soaked bread.
Steckerlfisch: Skewered grilled mackerel, often served at festivals such as Oktoberfest.
Rostbratwürste: Small sausages grilled over beechwood charcoal.

BADEN-WÜRTTEMBERG

Schneckensuppe: Soup with snails.
Spätzle: Egg-based handmade pasta in long strips.
Maultaschen: Pasta stuffed with a mixture of veal and spinach.
Geschnetzeltes: Thinly sliced veal in a cream sauce.

RHINELAND-PALATINATE

Sauerbraten: Beef marinated in wine vinegar, served with potato dumplings.
Reibekuchen: Potato pancakes served with apple or blueberry sauce.
Saumagen: Stuffed pork belly with pickled cabbage.
Schweinepfeffer: Highly seasoned pork ragout, thickened with blood.
Federweißer: Partially fermented new wine accompanied by an onion tart.

HESSEN AND WESTPHALIA

Töttchen: Ragout of brains and calf's head, cooked with herbs.
Pfefferpothast: Stew cooked with pepper, lemon and capers.

THURINGIA

Linsensuppe mit Thüringer Rotwurst: Lentil soup with Thuringian sausages.

SAXONY

Leipziger Allerlei: Vegetable medley e.g. of peas, carrots and asparagus.
Dresdener Stollen: Dense butter cake with dried fruits.

LOWER SAXONY AND SCHLESWIG-HOLSTEIN

Aalsuppe: Sweet-and-sour eel soup with prunes, pears, vegetables and bacon.
Labskaus: Traditional sailor's dish: beef, pork and salted herrings with potatoes and beetroot, served with gherkins and fried egg.
Grünkohl mit Pinkel: Minced kale cooked with smoked sausage and onion.

YOU ALREADY KNOW THE GREEN GUIDE,
NOW FIND OUT ABOUT THE MICHELIN GROUP

The Michelin Adventure

It all started with rubber balls! This was the product made by a small company based in Clermont-Ferrand that André and Edouard Michelin inherited, back in 1880. The brothers quickly saw the potential for a new means of transport and their first success was the invention of detachable pneumatic tires for bicycles. However, the automobile was to provide the greatest scope for their creative talents. Throughout the 20th century, Michelin never ceased developing and creating ever more reliable and high-performance tires, not only for vehicles ranging from trucks to F1 but also for underground transit systems and airplanes.

From early on, Michelin provided its customers with tools and services to facilitate mobility and make traveling a more pleasurable and more frequent experience. As early as 1900, the Michelin Guide supplied motorists with a host of useful information related to vehicle maintenance, accommodation and restaurants, and was to become a benchmark for good food. At the same time, the Travel Information Bureau offered travelers personalised tips and itineraries.

The publication of the first collection of roadmaps, in 1910, was an instant hit! In 1926, the first regional guide to France was published, devoted to the principal sites of Brittany, and before long each region of France had its own Green Guide. The collection was later extended to more far-flung destinations, including New York in 1968 and Taiwan in 2011.

In the 21st century, with the growth of digital technology, the challenge for Michelin maps and guides is to continue to develop alongside the company's tire activities. Now, as before, Michelin is committed to improving the mobility of travelers.

MICHELIN TODAY

WORLD NUMBER ONE TIRE MANUFACTURER

- 70 production sites in 18 countries
- 111,000 employees from all cultures and on every continent
- 6,000 people employed in research and development

Moving
for a world

Moving forward means developing tires with better road grip and shorter braking distances, whatever the state of the road.

CORRECT TIRE PRESSURE

RIGHT PRESSURE

- Safety
- Longevity
- Optimum fuel consumption

-0,5 bar

- Durability reduced by 20% (- 8,000 km)

-1 bar

- Risk of blowouts
- Increased fuel consumption
- Longer braking distances on wet surfaces

forward together
where mobility is safer

It also involves helping motorists take care of their safety and their tires. To do so, Michelin organises "Fill Up With Air" campaigns all over the world to remind us that correct tire pressure is vital.

WEAR

DETECTING TIRE WEAR

The legal minimum depth of tire tread is 1.6mm.
Tire manufacturers equip their tires with tread wear indicators, which are small blocks of rubber moulded into the base of the main grooves at a depth of 1.6mm.

Tires are the only point of contact between the vehicle and road.

The photo below shows the actual contact zone.

If the tread depth is less than 1.6mm, tires are considered to be worn and dangerous on wet surfaces.

NEW TIRE

WORN TIRE
(1,6 mm tread)

Moving forward
means sustainable mobility

INNOVATION AND THE ENVIRONMENT

By 2050, Michelin aims to cut the quantity of raw materials used in its tire manufacturing process by half and to have developed renewable energy in its facilities. The design of MICHELIN tires has already saved billions of litres of fuel and, by extension, billions of tons of CO_2.

Similarly, Michelin prints its maps and guides on paper produced from sustainably managed forests and is diversifying its publishing media by offering digital solutions to make traveling easier, more fuel efficient and more enjoyable!

The group's whole-hearted commitment to eco-design on a daily basis is demonstrated by ISO 14001 certification.

Like you, Michelin is committed to preserving our planet.

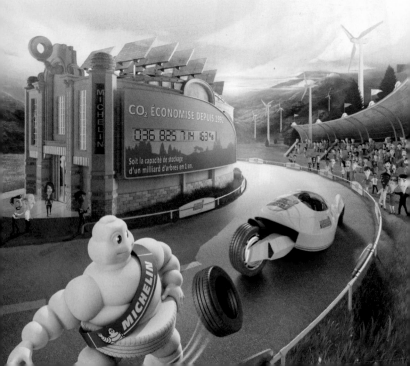

Chat with Bibendum

Go to
www.michelin.com/corporate/en
Find out more about
Michelin's history and the
latest news.

QUIZ

Michelin develops tires for all types of vehicles.
See if you can match the right tire with the right vehicle…

France
- Alsace Lorraine Champagne
- Auvergne Rhône Valley
- Bordeaux, Aquitaine & the Basque Country
- Brittany
- Burgundy Jura
- Châteaux of the Loire
- Dordogne Berry Limousin
- France
- French Alps
- French Riviera
- Languedoc Tarn Gorges
- Normandy
- Northern France and the Paris Region
- Paris
- Poitou-Charentes, La Rochelle & Cognac
- Provence
- Pyrenees Roussillon
- Wine Regions of France

Rest of Europe
- Austria
- Germany
- Greece
- Italy
- Poland
- Portugal Madeira The Azores
- Rome
- Sicily
- Spain
- Switzerland
- Tuscany
- Venice and the Veneto
- Wine Trails of Italy

British Isles
- Great Britain
- Ireland
- London
- Scotland

Asia
- Chennai and Tamil Nadu
- Delhi, Agra & Jaipur
- Japan
- Singapore
- South Korea
- Taiwan
- Thailand

North America
- California
- Canada
- Chicago
- Florida
- Mexico Guatemala Belize
- New England
- New York City
- Quebec
- San Francisco
- USA East
- USA West
- Washington, DC

South America
- Argentina
- Colombia
- Rio de Janeiro

Visit your preferred bookseller for Michelin's comprehensive range of maps and famous red-cover Hotel and Restaurant guides.

THEGREENGUIDE **GERMANY**

Editorial Director	Cynthia Clayton Ochterbeck
Editor	Gwen Cannon
Contributing Writers	Kristen de Joseph, Donna Stonecipher, Eric Lucas
Production Manager	Natasha G. George
Cartography	Peter Wrenn
Photo Research	Nicole D. Jordan
Interior Design	Natasha G. George, Jonathan P. Gilbert
Cover Design	Chris Bell, Christelle Le Déan
Layout	Natasha G. George, Nicole D. Jordan
Cover Layout	Michelin Travel Partner, Natasha G. George

Contact Us
Michelin Travel and Lifestyle North America
One Parkway South
Greenville, SC 29615
USA
travel.lifestyle@us.michelin.com
www.michelintravel.com

Michelin Travel Partner
Hannay House
39 Clarendon Road
Watford, Herts WD17 1JA
UK
℘01923 205240
travelpubsales@uk.michelin.com
www.ViaMichelin.com

Special Sales
For information regarding bulk sales,
customized editions and premium sales,
please contact us at:
travel.lifestyle@us.michelin.com
www.michelintravel.com

Note to the reader Addresses, phone numbers, opening hours and prices published in this guide are accurate at the time of press. We welcome corrections and suggestions that may assist us in preparing the next edition. While every effort is made to ensure that all information printed in this guide is correct and up-to-date, Michelin Travel Partner accepts no liability for any direct, indirect or consequential losses howsoever caused so far as such can be excluded by law.